THE
MYTHICAL WEST

THE MYTHICAL WEST

AN ENCYCLOPEDIA OF
Legend, Lore, and Popular Culture

RICHARD W. SLATTA

A B C ☙ C L I O

Santa Barbara, California   ∩   Denver, Colorado   ∩   Oxford, England

Copyright © 2001 by Richard W. Slatta

All rights reserved. No part of this publication may be reproduced, stored in a retrieval system, or transmitted, in any form or by any means, electronic, mechanical, photocopying, recording, or otherwise, except for the inclusion of brief quotations in a review, without prior permission in writing from the publishers.

Library of Congress Cataloging-in-Publication Data
Slatta, Richard W., 1947–
   The mythical West : an encyclopedia of legend, lore, and
popular culture / Richard W. Slatta.
      p. cm.
   Includes bibliographical references and index.
   ISBN 1-57607-151-0; ISBN 1-57607-588-5 (e-book)
   1. Folklore—West (U.S.)—Encyclopedias.   2. Popular
culture—West (U.S.)—Encyclopedias.   3. Legends—West
(U.S.)—Encyclopedias.   I. Title.
GR109.S53   2001
398′0978′03—dc21

                         2001002784

06 05 04 03 02 01   10 9 8 7 6 5 4 3 2 1

This book is also available on the World Wide Web as an e-book. Visit abc-clio.com for details.

ABC-CLIO, Inc.
130 Cremona Drive, P.O. Box 1911
Santa Barbara, California 93116-1911

This book is printed on acid-free paper.
Manufactured in the United States of America

☛ Design by Jane Raese. Title page photo: Castle Valley, Utah (© Jane Raese)
All photos courtesy of the author unless otherwise noted.

With love, to my mother, *Amy Irene (Solberg) Slatta,*
now in her ninth decade of loving, caring, and sharing

CONTENTS

ENTRIES

A

Action Figures
Action Shooting
Adams, Ansel
Alamo
Appleseed, Johnny
Area 51
Autry, Gene
Aztlán

B

Baca, Elfego
Barbecue
Bass, Sam
Battles or Massacres
Bean, Judge Roy
Beckwourth, Jim
Bemis, Polly
Bicycle Corps
Bigfoot or Sasquatch
Billy the Kid
Bingham, George Caleb
Bonanza
Bridger, Jim
Brown, Molly
Buffalo Soldiers

Bulette, Julia
Buntline, Ned
Butch Cassidy and the Sundance Kid

C

Calamity Jane
Camel Corps
Carson, Kit
Cattle Kate
Cattle Mutilations
Cavalry Trilogy
Chisholm, Jesse, and Chisum, John
Clark, Charles "Badger," Jr.
Cody, William Frederick "Buffalo Bill"
Colter, John
Comparative Frontier Mythology
Cooper, D. B.
Copland, Aaron
Cortez Lira, Gregorio
Cortina, Juan Nepomuceno
Cowboy Poetry

D

Dallas
Dart, Isom
Dead Man's Hand

INTRODUCTION

"This is the West, sir. When the legend becomes fact, we print the legend." A newspaper editor delivers this famous line to Senator Ransom Stoddard (played by James Stewart) in the 1962 classic film *The Man Who Shot Liberty Valance*. Stoddard, of course, did not actually kill the notorious gunman, but in the film the facts of history become less important than the legend that gives rise to his celebrity and political career. *The Mythical West* takes the contrary view, insisting that we should, as best we can, disentangle and distinguish between western fact and myth. Why? Because everyone from national politicians and lobby groups to corporate advertisers invokes western myth and imagery. Western images serve as shorthand symbols of patriotism, democracy, rugged individualism, and a host of other virtues. Thus broadly held but faulty assumptions about the nation's historical past shape real events and lead to real consequences. Myth can even influence public policy, just as legend shaped the career of the fictional Ransom Stoddard. The overarching goal of this book is to identify, describe, and analyze many myths of the Old West and

the New so that readers can distinguish them from historical fact.

The deaths of Roy Rogers and Gene Autry in 1998 made front-page news and saddened millions of fans around the world. The grief over the passing of these singing cowboy heroes reminds us forcefully that the West has been America's most potent source of myth and legend since the days of the forty-niners, George Armstrong Custer, and Buffalo Bill Cody. Furthermore, thanks to film, television, and other electronic mass media, including the Internet, western myths and legends now reach a worldwide audience.

Myth is more powerful, pervasive, and alluring than history. Recognizing this reality, this encyclopedia focuses not on historical events but rather on the plethora of legendary, mythical images, events, people, and places associated with the Old West and the New. This book traces myths through folk legends, art, literature, and popular culture. For example, the discussion of Billy the Kid only briefly sketches the "facts" of his life as we know them. Rather, it concentrates on the many myths and depictions that come down to us through novels and films.

What is included in this encyclopedia? A few definitions from *Merriam-Webster's Collegiate Dictionary* (on-line at *http://www.m-w.com*) help to illustrate the criteria for inclusion. This source tells us that myth, from the Greek *mythos,* is a "traditional story of ostensibly historical events that serves to unfold part of the world view of a people or explain a practice, belief, or natural phenomenon." *The Mythical West* includes many such tales, such as the story explaining the significance of the white buffalo and the story of Aztlán, mythical southwestern homeland of the Aztecs. A myth may also be "a popular belief or tradition that has grown up around something or someone; *especially:* one embodying the ideals and institutions of a society or segment of society." The West is rife with such myths, most notably those relating to putative frontier virtues, such as rugged individualism, democracy, and opportunity. Finally, a myth might be "a person or thing having only an imaginary or unverifiable existence." The subjects of many of the entries in *The Mythical West,* like Pecos Bill and Bigfoot, fit this last category.

The subjects of other entries are "mythical" (a word dating in English from 1669) because they are "based on or described in a myth especially as contrasted with history" (*Merriam-Webster's Collegiate Dictionary,* on-line). In some cases, such as that of Jeremiah "Liver-Eating" Johnson, an actual historical figure—the mountain man John Johnson—becomes mythologized. Thus Liver-Eating Johnson is included in *The Mythical West.* Usually, "mythical" means "existing only in the imagination: fictitious,

imaginary." Hence, you will find imaginary animals, such as the famed jackalopes of Douglas, Wyoming. But "mythical" can also mean "having qualities suitable to myth: legendary," so we examine the lives of real people, from Cody to Autry, flesh-and-blood humans, whose careers catapulted them into the realm of the legendary.

"Lore," a term dating from before the twelfth century, consists of "traditional knowledge or belief." "Legend," a word dating from the fourteenth century, can be (1) "a story coming down from the past; *especially:* one popularly regarded as historical although not verifiable"; (2) "a body of such stories"; (3) "a popular myth of recent origin"; or (4) "a person or thing that inspires legends" (*Merriam-Webster's Collegiate Dictionary,* on-line). This encyclopedia covers many mythmakers and purveyors of legend and lore in the popular media, from pulp fiction to movies to television.

I tried to include many mythical subjects that most readers would not have encountered before. To paraphrase an old automobile ad, "This is not your father's encyclopedia." I also tried to extend coverage in all directions to include the wondrous diversity that is the American West. Thus, you'll find figures important to Latino/Chicano, Mormon, and women's history. (See also Rafaela G. Castro's *Dictionary of Chicano Folklore* [Denver, CO: ABC-CLIO, 2000]). You will learn about Johnny Kaw, a personage probably not well known outside Kansas. You'll meet Glenn Stone, Arizona's "muffler man," and you'll learn why fewer swallows now return to the famous California mission of San Juan Capistrano.

As a final criterion for inclusion, I used the Internet. This ubiquitous network encompasses an amazing range of subjects. In deciding whether to include a topic, I checked to see how many Internet sites treated the subject and how profoundly they treated it. This seemed to me to be a good indicator of whether the topic had worked its way into American or even world popular culture. For example, I included Poker Alice Ivers, who is commemorated by a restaurant, an inn, and two musical groups—one in South Dakota and another in Switzerland. Likewise Cattle Kate has evolved from an intriguing historical figure into a major clothing company. However, I dropped the mythical Cerro de Oro mine because no major Web sites treat that topic. I am fully prepared to defend the Internet as a useful, if imperfect, measure of cultural salience. (See *History of the Internet* [Denver, CO: ABC-CLIO, 1999].)

The geographical part of the title, "The West," refers to the trans-Mississippi American West (but not Alaska and Hawaii). This includes the Great Plains, Rocky Mountains, Texas, Southwest, Great Basin, California, and Pacific Northwest. (Sorry, Minnesota and Paul Bunyan, you didn't make the cut.) The Canadian West has generated a wealth of fascinating frontier mythology, but limitations of time and space do not permit me to cover our neighbor to the north. On Canada's mythical and historical West, I recommend *The Wild West* by Bruce Patterson and Mary McGuire (Banff, Alberta, Canada: Altitude Publishing, 1993).

ABC-CLIO has a very strong existing list on Native American topics, so I have not duplicated that coverage here. For information on Indian history, legend, and lore, see these excellent books: *Native Americans: An Encyclopedia of History, Culture, and People* (1998); *Encyclopedia of Native American Shamanism: Sacred Ceremonies of North America* (1998); *Native American Literatures: An Encyclopedia of Works, Characters, Authors, and Themes* (1999); *Legend and Lore of the Americas before 1492* (1993); *Encyclopedia of Creation Myths* (1994); *Dictionary of Native American Mythology* (1992); *Encyclopedia of American Indian Costume* (1994); *Encyclopedia of American Indian Wars, 1492–1890* (1997); *Encyclopedia of Native American Healing* (1996); *The Native American Rights Movement* (1996); and *Reference Encyclopedia of the American Indian,* 7th ed. (1995).

The Mythical West treats images and legendary figures popularized in the media, but it does not cover media history or folklore per se. These topics are capably handled in other ABC-CLIO volumes: *The Media in America* (1995); *Folklore: An Encyclopedia of Beliefs, Customs, Tales, Music, and Art* (1997); and *Encyclopedia of Folklore and Literature* (1998). In keeping my focus clearly on the West, I have also avoided overlap with Jan Harold Brunvand's *Encyclopedia of Urban Legends* (2001).

In sum, through this book you will enter a dreamland, a fantasyland, a land of great promise and hope, a land of broken and fulfilled dreams, bigger-than-life heroes, and ghost towns. Unlike most "bloodless" factoid encyclopedias that lack interpretation, verve, and nuance, this one strives to convey vividly the sense of wonder, power, and magic associated with the legendary West. No single book can pretend to be comprehensive, but I have tried to be as inclusive as space permits, within the limits noted above. Did I omit a topic that you strongly believe should have been included? Make your case! E-mail a subject summary and source information to me at Slatta@ncsu.edu.

ACKNOWLEDGMENTS

A Note on Sources

Traditionally, historians glean most of their data from manuscript and printed documents, such as diaries, letters, speeches, and myriad government publications. In the pursuit of myth, I turned to rural and urban folklore, poems, literature, oral traditions, and popular media. Besides combing sources from folklore and popular culture, I made extensive use of the Internet to analyze the diffusion of American western images around the world. Internet sources provide information that is up-to-date, broad-ranging, and often humorous. By using both historical sources of the past and today's Internet, this book demonstrates the strong links between past myth and present popular culture. *The Mythical West* is alive, well, changing, and growing.

Electronic Sources

Of the many on-line sources used, the most important are *Encyclopedia Britannica Online, Ingenta* (a bibliographical research tool), *The Electric Library, EBSCOhost, Academic Universe,* and *America: History and Life* (published by ABC-CLIO). CD-ROM software provided very basic but helpful factual background. I used *World Book* and *Compton's Electronic Encyclopedia,* Dan L. Thrapp's *Encyclopedia of Frontier Biography* (Lincoln: University of Nebraska Press, 1995), and Robert J. Nash's wonderful *Encyclopedia of Western Lawmen & Outlaws* (Dallas: Zane Publishing, 1995). For topics on the Lone Star state, the *Handbook of Texas Online (http://www.tsha.utexas.edu/hand book/)* is comprehensive and invaluable. For western literary currents, visit two Web sites: *http://www.Readwest.com* and *http://www.ReadtheWest.com.* I also used a variety of search engines, including Inktomi, Snap, Google, and Britannica.

Print Sources

Readers interested in further historical background on entries relating to cowboys and ranch life should consult my previous ABC-CLIO publication, *The Cowboy Encyclopedia* (1994; paperback, New York: W. W. Norton, 1996), which won the 1995 American Library Association award as an "Outstanding Reference" and the 1994 *Library Journal* award as "Best Reference Source." Also useful on the history of the West is *The New Encyclopedia of the American West,* edited by Howard R. Lamar (New Haven,

CT: Yale University Press, 1998). I have taken pains to complement, not overlap, existing reference works on the American West.

Pardners on the Range
I extend thanks to Todd Hallman at ABC-CLIO, who helped to shape the concept and coverage of this book and to push it to fruition. I had excellent research and writing assistance from many talented students at North Carolina State University: Julie J. Anders, P. S. Crane, Thomas Edward Davis, Daniel Cornelius Gunter III, Ellen J. Oettinger, Kaleb J. Redden, Michael L. Sileno, Jane Veronica Charles Smith, Michael Thomas Smith, Andrew Mebane Southerland, and William F. Zweigart. Other contributors include Dan Buck and Anne Meadows, Michael Crawford, Patti Dickinson, Castle McLaughlin, and Z. Ervin. Entries written by these contributors carry their bylines.

The irrepressible Joe Blyth, friend and ex-student, provided constant reminders of the enduring links between western history and myth. Writer Jeff Morey generously provided important materials on the Earps. Barbara S. Duffy and Lewis Dibble provided key local history documents on Owen Wister's visits to Winthrop and the Methow Valley of Washington State. A special thanks to Guy Louis Rocha, certified archivist, and to the Nevada State Library and Archives for permission to reprint five delightful articles from their on-line feature "Historical Myth a Month" *(http://dmla.clan.lib.nv.us/docs/nsla/archives/myth/).* I also offer a heartfelt *gracias* to Danelle Crowley, fellow Peace Corps alum and genuine Texan, for taking me to two of the Lone Star State's most mythical and wonderful spots: Luckenbach (population about 25) and Big Earl's Barbecue in Kerrville.

Finally, I thank the many dedicated students of the American West, especially members of the Western History Association, the Western Writers of America, and the H-West on-line discussion list. Without the many fruits of their research labors, I would not have had the pleasure of writing this book.

Richard W. Slatta (Slatta@ncsu.edu)
Proprietor, Lazy S Ranch, Cary, NC
Ride on over to the Lazy S at
http://social.chass.ncsu.edu/slatta
July 2001

The magnificent western landscape of the United States has awed and transfixed all who have journeyed there. The great rivers of the West, like the Columbia, well served Native Americans, providing food and transportation, long before the arrival of Europeans.

The towering mountain ranges of the West served as barriers to travel and settlement.

But the mountains also provided habitat for beaver and other animals, giving rise to famous mountain men, like John Colter and Jim Beckwourth, of the nineteenth century.

European exploration and settlement of the Southwest began with the Spanish in the sixteenth century. Architecture, food, language, and culture in the West still exhibit a strong Spanish flavor.

Immense herds of buffalo provided sustenance and shaped the way of life for
Native American plains cultures.

However, by the 1870s and 1880s, cowboys and longhorn cattle had replaced
the vast bison herds throughout the West.
Only the foresight of a few westerners saved the species from extinction.

Cattle ranchers built great empires and fortunes, and these cattle barons built accordingly, as evidenced by the Littlefield House in Austin, Texas.

The cowboy culture gave rise to many icons of the West, including blue jeans, chaps, boots, and the famed Stetson hat. Donning such garments allows anyone to participate in the magic of the mythical West.

STETSON

Economic booms, spurred by ranching, railroads, logging, mining, and farming, gave way to busts, leaving ghost towns and deserted ranches throughout the region.

During the twentieth century, nostalgia for the Old West revealed itself in novels, films, radio, and television. B-western cowboy stars, such as Lash Larue, shown here in a 1981 photo, thrilled audiences as they galloped across the silver screen.

Much has changed in the West, but not the enchanting grandeur of its natural beauty.
People continue to marvel at its rugged, foreboding deserts and mountains;

Its rushing waterfalls;

Its sparkling, crystal-clear mountain lakes.

And, like the pioneers of old, people continue to explore its vast wilderness areas. The mythical West lives on!

THE
MYTHICAL WEST

ABBEY, EDWARD

1927–1989, writer. *See* Monkey Wrench Gang

ACES AND EIGHTS

See Dead Man's Hand

ACTION FIGURES

Introduction

In 1964 Hasbro coined the term "action figure" to describe its new line of military figures, G.I. Joe. Hasbro knew that to market what was essentially a doll to boys (and their parents), it needed a fresh angle. "Action figure" implied a toy that little boys could use in active ways, something far more manly than simply dressing up a doll. The line was a huge hit, and it didn't take long for America's love for the Old West to show up in this new format.

The early 1960s also featured a strong lineup of **television** Westerns. With *Gunsmoke, The Rifleman, Maverick,* **Bonanza,** and other shows being viewed by millions of boys, toy companies realized the vast market potential of western-themed action figures. Although action figures have changed drastically in format, form, and style over the decades, one thing has remained: the popularity of the western theme.

The translation of the western mythos into playthings corresponded nicely with children's play habits. Most important to children are the "white hats," or good guys. These characters will (hopefully) be the ones children relate to; through them children can place themselves in the action.

Next, children need "black hats," or bad guys. Villains provide the conflict, the evil that must be overcome and defeated. Finally come the secondary characters: henchmen on the side of evil or (often comic) sidekicks on the side of good. Just as in the western movies and TV shows that children watch, these secondary characters can be injured, kidnapped, and rescued and can serve as bit actors in the stories they play out.

White Hats in the Sandbox

From the very beginning, toy companies knew the qualities required of their good guys in any action-figure line: bravery, integrity, courage, strength, humility, and other laudable traits. During the 1960s, the heroes of television westerns, like Matt Dillon, Lucas McCain, Rowdy Yates, and the Cartwrights, exuded these qualities. But the age of licensing well-known characters from shows was still years off. Instead, toy companies, like Marx, developed western action-figure lines based predominately on fictional characters they themselves created.

However, one real-life character appeared in Marx's first line and has been in very many action-figure lines since: Gen. George Armstrong Custer starred as a white hat in the very first western-themed line of figures, Marx's Best of the West series. Only two other real-life characters—Daniel Boone and Geronimo—joined Custer in the series of more than 20 figures. Custer has since been produced dozens of times, by many different companies in many different styles, but one thing has remained the same: he's always a good guy.

Today, of course, we realize that Custer wasn't as pure and innocent as we were led to believe by our grade school history teachers. But the mythos of General Custer as the ultimate military hero—

giving his life to defend the West from the "heathen" Indian—stuck with his action figure over the decades.

Why did Custer remain such a popular choice? Certainly there were plenty of other names well known to the average child. A few figures did occasionally get made of these characters. But none has the distinction of being represented as a plastic icon so many times. Custer even showed up when he made little sense in context, for example, in the Legends of the Lone Ranger line of the early 1980s.

Custer's powerful mythos and martyrdom, combined with his easily recognized appearance, make him an ideal choice for an action-figure white hat. His mythos represents everything heroic about the western frontier, and dying a hero's death added extra spice and appeal. His long, flowing blond hair, distinct facial hair, and military uniform allowed manufacturers to produce a figure that children would know on sight as

General Custer. He stood out as a marketer's dream, a widely recognizable figure with all the right qualities, and no one left to collect royalties.

Other famous real-life western heroes did make it into plastic. Wild Bill Hickok, Buffalo Bill **Cody, Calamity Jane,** Belle **Starr,** Annie **Oakley,** Wyatt Earp, Doc Holliday, Davy Crockett, Daniel Boone, Jim Bowie, and others have all been made into toys for children. All were portrayed as the white hats.

By the late 1970s, licensing characters from movies and television shows became the de facto standard. Toys from TV shows and movies like *The Legend of the Lone Ranger, Butch and Sundance: The Early Years, Wild Wild West, Grizzly Adams, How the West Was Won,* and **Zorro** became the norm, while lines based on generic characters slowly disappeared. Still, even today the most resilient of the famous western heroes show up occasionally in the toy aisles. Their myth is still strong enough to lure

children and companies alike back to the tales of their heroics.

Evil in the Toy Box: The Black Hats

Toy companies faced a tougher task in creating the black hats. Sure, they found some straightforward candidates–**Billy the Kid** and Jesse **James,** the most common. The villain of the **Alamo,** Santa Anna, was even produced once. In general, however, the evil characters were either licensed characters from a movie or show, such as Butch Cavendish from *The Lone Ranger,* or a generic "baddie" developed from an accepted concept of a true western villain.

What may be surprising for many is that Native Americans only rarely appeared as evil characters. Even during the 1960s, Native characters, like Tonto, were marketed as friends of the cowboys. When they did appear as villains, they were usually portrayed as misunderstood, not bad. Of course, this subtlety did not necessarily translate into play style. I recall many kids who used Native characters as their main enemy force.

Companies strongly relied on the color black to create their villains. Even when using a well-known character, such as Jesse James, the toy manufacturer carefully dressed him predominately in black. Sam Cobra, for example, the only character in the large Best of the West set who was marketed as purely bad, was dressed, quite nattily, all in black, complete with all-black accessories.

In marketing, these bad boys' dishonesty, cowardice, and untrustworthiness were their key selling points. No one was portrayed as a murderer, not even an actual felon such as Billy the Kid. Rather, they were often thieves, and gambling was one of their usual pastimes. The prevailing mythos represented the western bad guy as a stagecoach, train, or bank robber or as a cowardly, dishonest poker player. Probably for fear of offending parents, the manufacturers downplayed the idea that these men were real killers.

Sam Cobra, from Marx's Best of the West line, personified this type of character. A no-good, cheating gambler, he came with many deceitful accessories. A special knife could be hidden in his sleeve, a derringer could be hidden in his belt buckle, and another could be cached in a cue ball. No ideal western villain would be complete without his bundle of dynamite to blow up the bank's safe. Cobra was an oddity, though, being marketed very clearly as a bad guy. Most others, even Jesse James and Billy the Kid, were simply sold as one more player in little Bobby's dugout of characters, allowing the child to decide the role they would play.

Once licensing characters from major shows became the norm, those charac-

ters that were evil on the show were naturally evil in toy form as well. Butch Cavendish, the nemesis of the Lone Ranger, is possibly the best example. Dressed predominately in black and riding a black horse, he was the antithesis of the Masked Man. Specific play sets developed with Butch Cavendish in mind almost always involved robbery as the crime. These figures represented a less-violent evil. The description of El Lobo, another villain in the Lone Ranger's West, is a perfect example: "El Lobo, the Mexican Outlaw, scheming enemy of the Lone Ranger." Deceitfulness, either in stealing or while playing cards, was the predominate trait of the western bad guy action figure.

The Portrayal of Western Minorities

The American West had many minority members, many of them not as much in the minority as traditional depictions would have us think. Native Americans, African Americans, Hispanics, Asians, and women of all nationalities played major roles in the story of the American West. Surprisingly, all have been represented in the toy box as well, and not just as villains.

As noted earlier, although "Indians" were present in almost every western line produced, only rarely did they appear as bad. In general, they served as sidekicks, buddies, compadres. Any negative elements in their personas were usually presented as the result of a misunderstanding, as in the case of Red Sleeves, part of the Lone Ranger series, billed as "the noble foe, the fierce Apache." The packaging explained, "Few who lived in the Old West were more

feared and less understood than Red Sleeves, the Indian who rode alone. Driven from his tribal land by Butch Cavendish's outlaw band, Red Sleeves mistakenly blamed all men for the evils of a few." Even during the 1960s and '70s, toy companies largely avoided stereotyping minorities.

Although African Americans played a major role in the real Old West, they played a far smaller one in the plastic version. During the last 40 years, there have only been a handful of black western figures available, mostly fictional. The only real-life example is Nat Love, one of the most famous African-American cowboys and perhaps the model for **Deadwood Dick.**

Female figures enjoyed a more prominent role in the toy box because manufacturers hoped to lure little girls as customers. Real-life characters, such as Calamity Jane, Belle Starr, and Annie Oakley, served as action figures, and companies created many other fictional characters as well. Even if girls had little interest in them (Barbie provided fierce competition), the female figures provided "damsels in distress" for little boys to rescue. The companies should be

given some credit, however, for outfitting these females not just with compacts and lipstick but with .45s and Winchesters. Native American female figures, in stark contrast to their Caucasian counterparts, did not appear as armed warriors.

It may seem surprising at first to see such diversity in toys, particularly when it was clearly not intended to broaden the market audience. Toy companies knew that although children were their market, parents held the purse strings. If little Johnny pointed out an action figure that did not appear different enough from others in the same line, a parent might tell him, "You don't need that; you already have one." A sale would be lost. Distinctly different clothes, hairstyles, and skin colors helped toy manufacturers convince parents that little Johnny really did need just one more figure.

The best representation of such marketing diversity was a line called The Ready Gang, produced by Marx in the late 1970s. The three characters included the Sundown Kid (the blond Caucasian), Ringo (Mexican), and Trooper Gibson (the black ex-soldier). This line is today very sought-after by collectors, not only because of its quality but also because of its diversity.

Conclusions

The mythos of the American West lends itself perfectly to the fantasy world of action figures. In every line, good guys and bad guys are necessary for childhood role playing. With the well-known myths of characters such as General Custer, Billy the Kid, and Geronimo, some real-life western people fit the archetypal roles perfectly. The ambiguity of the real

West, where the lines between good guy and bad guy could be extremely blurred, has at times made it difficult to place people in clear-cut roles. Manufacturers didn't try to pigeon-hole their characters; they simply produced a variety and let the kids sort it out.

It is in the characterization of these action figures that we see the bare mythos of the American West. Good guys are honest, brave, and trustworthy. Bad guys are liars, gamblers, cheats, and thieves. We may recognize the historical inaccuracy, but this mythos is so ingrained in our society that we accept it as a given even in the toys we buy our children. Western toys produced by foreign companies in foreign lands carry these same ideals. The American West has been marketed and sold to the entire world in this fashion through TV, movies, books, and even our own history classes. For some, these deeply rooted stereotypes may seem outdated or even dangerous, but for most little kids and big kids alike, it's just about playing "cowboys and Indians."

—Michael Crawford

See also Butch Cassidy and the Sundance Kid; Earp Brothers; Lone Ranger

References

Western Action Figure Archive: *http://www. atomgroup.org/WAFA1.htm.*

ACTION SHOOTING

Each year, a host of reenactors dress up in period costumes to re-create historical eras, battles, and other events. Reenactors play the parts of mountain men, soldiers, dance hall girls (and prostitutes), and gunfighters, thereby vicariously enjoying life in the Old West. Among the more colorful, noisy, and action-filled recreations are action-shooting contests held at various locations around the country. Mike Venturino describes one such event:

In a blur of movement, the cowboy jumps up, draws his gun and starts spraying hot lead around the saloon. As he hammers away, the bad guys begin to fall. The first six-gun empties, and the cowboy pulls out a second. But even when that one is spent, he's not out of danger. He grabs a shotgun off a nearby table and blasts his way toward the exit, firing so rapidly that the gun's side-by-side barrels sound nearly as one. When he finally clears the room and kicks open the double swinging doors, there's more trouble outside: Another band of outlaws lines the street. To make matters worse, he's out of ammo. Amid a jangle of spurs and a swish of chaps leather, he runs to his horse, where his trusty Winchester rifle waits. Whisking it clear of the scabbard, he levers in the first round and lets fly, swinging the gun from side to side with incredible speed and accuracy. At last, he squeezes off his final shot. Breathing hard, he waits for the dust to settle. His heart sinks. One of the bad guys is still standing. (Venturino 1988)

Action shooters generally dress the part, wearing period cowboy costumes, handlebar mustaches, and other sartorial touches. They might be firing authentic, historical weapons or recent-vintage reproductions. But most importantly, they are firing at targets, not at other human beings. The Single Action Shooting Society (SASS, 15,000 members) and the National Congress of Old West Shootists (NCOWS) serve as organizing bodies for groups in some 40 states and many foreign countries. An estimated 50,000 people, probably more than 75 percent of them men, participate in these contests worldwide. Even countries without a history of Wild West violence enjoy the action. For example, the Western Action Shooting Society bills itself as "New Zealand's premier cowboy action shooting group."

The governing organizations specify the types of firearms permitted. Cowboy action shooters must fire single-action revolvers that require cocking the hammer manually before each shot. The design of rifles and carbines must predate 1899. Arms manufacturers Winchester and Black Hills produce ammunition designed specially for cowboy shooters.

Colt's famous single-action Army Revolver, "The Peacemaker," is the handgun of choice. The gun has undergone only minor changes since its 1873 introduction for the U.S. Cavalry. Today's models, priced at about $1,200, are produced only in .45 Colt and .44–.40 calibers, the most popular rounds with action shooters.

Contest design shows great creativity and challenges competitors with the novel and unexpected. Contestants might have to shoot from fake horses that roll on tracks. They might take aim from atop stagecoaches, around obstacles, or running or rolling. Both speed and accuracy count, as in an authentic Old West shoot-out.

Many action shooters assume that their play re-creates historical reality. A few shooters, however, are more savvy. Floyd D. P. Oydegaard offers wonderfully detailed and informative Internet instruction on "How to Be a Pistolero: A Guide to Old West Historical Reenacting." He details dress, mannerisms, weapons, aliases, and other critical parts of re-creating the persona of an Old West gunslinger. However, he also reminds practitioners that for virtually every Old West gunslinger, "The Legend was much worse than the real man. That was what the public wanted to believe. . . . the truth was never so interesting."

Indeed, western films are rife with references to the gunplay and mayhem that characterized the mythical West. (Peggy Thompson and Saeko Usukawa have gathered more than 100 pages of great western film quotes into *Tall in the Saddle: Great Lines from Classic Westerns*.) Jerry Valance (played by John Ireland) in *Red River* (1948) expresses the usual worshipful attitude toward guns expressed in westerns: "You know, there are only two things more beautiful than a good gun: a Swiss watch or a woman from anywhere." In the 1939 film *Dodge City*, trail boss Wade Hatton (Errol Flynn) asks the town's barber, "Well, what's the news in Dodge?" "Well, just about the same as always," replies the barber. "Gambling and drinking and killing. Mostly killing."

In *El Dorado* (1967), gunslinger Nels McCloud (Christopher George) delivers a bit of pop philosophy to his gang: "Faith can move mountains. But it can't beat a faster draw." As a counterpoint, feisty bar owner Vienna (Joan Crawford) warns in *Johnny Guitar* (1954) that "boys who play with guns have be ready to die like men."

An exchange in *The Last of the Fast Guns* (1958) injects another healthy dose of realism to movie fiction: "You wanted to see me?" asks gunfighter Brad Ellison (Jock Mahoney). "I wanted to see the winner," replies John Forbes (Carl Benton Reid). "Nobody wins in a gunfight," replies Ellison.

The most famous parody of action shooting and Old West role playing came in the campy 1973 science fiction film *Westworld,* which provides a delightful, dark, bizarre story of action shooting gone bad. Michael Crichton wrote and directed the film, set in a high-tech theme park of the future. Vacationers, for $1,000 per day, interact with lifelike robotic cowboys, prostitutes, and more in an Old West setting. However, owing to unexplained malfunctions, the usually obliging robots begin killing the visitors. In a brilliant casting touch, actor Yul Brynner reprises his persona from **The Magnificent Seven** as one of the gunslinger robots programmed to always lose the shoot-out.

What is fascinating about the new action-shooting pastime is that it has very little to do with the realities of the Old West. Blazing gunfights rarely happened. Aware of the danger posed by guns, frontier towns passed and enforced strict **gun control** laws. The famous duels, with gunslingers facing each other down on Main Street, are much more a product of filmmakers than of history. The notorious inaccuracy of side arms left most men loath to trust their lives to them. If someone needed killing, ambush or back shooting, rather than face-to-fact combat, generally prevailed. In this sense, Jack McCall's murder of Wild Bill Hickok with a cowardly shot from behind is more representative of the Old West than is the stereotypical glint-eyed, "mano-a-mano" gunfight.

A panel of experts on violence in the Old West discussed the issue at the 1999 Western History Association meeting in Portland, Oregon. Ex–Secretary of the Interior Stewart L. Udall moderated the discussion. Quoting the late Arizona historian Bert Fireman, Udall reaffirmed that "the West was not won by guns. It was won by shovels and sweat" ("How the West Got Wild" 2000). Historian Robert R. Dykstra agreed that "the uniquely savage and homicide-ravaged Old West is a construct as phony as America's favorite 'invented tradition'—the quick-draw street duel reenacted every day in a score of tourist venues."

In the same panel, Michael A. Bellesiles quoted Robert Warshow's observation in his 1954 analysis of western film: "The two most successful creations of American movies are the gangster and the Westerner: men with guns." Bellesiles pointed to Owen Wister's novel *The Virginian,* which "popularized the gunfight, the standard of any western. The fact that such gunfights were incredibly rare hardly mattered when compared with the enormous romantic power of such a man-to-man face-off." Historical reality notwithstanding, legions of action shooters continue to replicate movie fiction, while imagining that they are partaking of western fact.

The mythology and fictive nature of action shooting, however, does not blunt the enthusiasm, as shooters expend an estimated 24 million rounds of ammunition per year. Recreational, pretend gunplay, however, is not without its critics. In the wake of the horrific Littleton, Colorado, student massacre and similar school tragedies, many people have asked whether gunplay should be presented as a lighthearted pastime and a tourist attraction. Parents, in particular, feared that children might become enamored of the glorification of quick-draw violence and perhaps act on those impulses.

See also Wister, Owen, and Winthrop, Washington

References
"How the West Got Wild: American Media and Frontier Violence." Roundtable discussion. *Western Historical Quarterly 31,* no. 3 (Autumn 2000): 277–296.
Oydegaard, Floyd D. P. "How to Be a Pistolero: A Guide to Old West Historical Reenacting": *http://www.sptddog.com/sotp/persona. html.*
Thompson, Peggy, and Saeko Usukawa. *Tall in the Saddle: Great Lines from Classic Westerns.* San Francisco: Chronicle Books, 1998.
Venturino, Mike. "Slingin' Lead." *Popular Mechanics* 175, no. 4 (April 1998): 76–80.

Sources of Further Information
The Gunfighter Zone: *http://www.gunfighter. com.*
The Single Action Shooting Society: *http:// www.sassnet.com/.*
Western Action Shooting Society, New Zealand: *http://www.wass.org.nz/.*

ADAMS, ANSEL
1902–1984

San Francisco–born Adams spent his life taking pictures. He labored as a commercial photographer for 30 years, but his visually stunning, mostly black-and-white photographs of western landscapes brought him fame.

An only child, Adams was perhaps more than a little spoiled; his formal schooling ended in his early teens as he chafed under the regimentation of school. His parents employed private tutors to complete his studies. He enjoyed the piano and considered music as a career. In 1916 he visited Yosemite Valley and took his first landscape photographs. The grandeur of Yosemite lit a fire in him, and he determined to capture and share its stunning beauty on film. He studied photography, returning to Yosemite each summer.

Like John Muir and other early conservationists, Adams realized that the natural wonders of the West could easily be lost. He joined the Sierra Club in 1920 and served on its board of directors from 1934 until 1971.

Parmelian Prints of the High Sierras, his first portfolio, appeared in 1927. The work of Paul Strand would exert a strong influence on Adams's photographic vision. The following year he married Virginia Best and began working as an official photographer for the Sierra Club. By the early 1930s, his work enjoyed considerable exposure and success. He joined with Edward Weston, Imogen Cunningham, and others to found Group f/64. They devoted themselves to excellence at all elements of photography, from composition and lighting to careful exposure and exquisite printmaking. He also codified his meticulous approach to exposure, processing, and printing into what he called "the zone system." In 1933 the Ansel Adams Gallery opened in San Francisco.

Adams extended his range from California across the West. On his first trip to the Southwest, in 1928, he wrote from Santa Fe, New Mexico, to his wife that "the photographic material is simply immense—beyond any imagination. I would not be in the least surprised were our destiny to establish us here" (Adams with Alinder 1996). He published not only portfolios of his work but also instructional guides to photography. He also taught courses and helped establish one of the first departments of photography at the California School of Fine Arts (later the San Francisco Art Institute).

In 1941 Secretary of the Interior Harold Ickes commissioned Adams to take photographs for murals to grace the Interior Department's new building. He traveled throughout the West, shooting, among other things, his most famous picture, "Moonrise, Hernandez, New Mexico." His environmental ethic grew even stronger. "Photography," he wrote in 1945 for the *Sierra Club Bulletin,* "more than any other visual medium, effectively reveals not only the aspects of the natural world, but also the tragic results of its violation."

Thanks to a Guggenheim Fellowship in 1948, Adams spent the year taking memorable photographs in national parks and monuments. A portfolio of those prints appeared in 1950. Although he is best known for his landscapes, in 1953 he collaborated with skilled "people photographer" Dorothea Lange for a *Life* magazine study of Mormons in Utah.

The tonality, saturation, range, and richness of an Adams print are immediately recognizable. His works, gracing countless posters, calendars, note cards, and other media, carried his consciousness of the need for conservation around the world. In later years, he gave up the rigors of traipsing through the wilderness he so loved and settled in Carmel, California. In 1980 he received the Presidential Medal of Freedom from Jimmy Carter, on the recommendation of Gerald Ford. The citation reads:

At one with the power of the American landscape, and renowned for the patient skill and timeless beauty of his work, photographer Ansel Adams has been visionary in his efforts to preserve this country's wild and scenic areas, both on film and on Earth. Drawn to the beauty of nature's monuments, he is regarded by environmentalists as a monument himself, and by photographers as a national institution. It is through his foresight and fortitude that so much of America has been saved for future Americans.

In July 1983 Adams tried to encourage Carter's successor, Ronald Reagan, to show some concern for the environment. He recorded his disappointment and very negative impressions in a letter to fellow photographer David Hume Kennerly:

The meeting with RR was not funny; it was very discouraging. He is very gracious and persuading, but it was like confronting a stone wall. . . . I was told I had "15 or 20 minutes" but I ended up with 50! He talked for a time at first and I was scrambling for my priorities. I said most of what I had to say. I think it is a marvelous country when a citizen can talk with the President and tell him he (the citizen) thinks he is seriously misinformed. I felt with a sinking feeling that this country is in very poor hands. The

The Alamo, San Antonio, Texas

subsequent interview might do some good; it has been published all over the world. WAKE UP, AMERICA (AND KENNERLY!!) We are facing disaster! ALL BEST, as ever! Ansel (Kennerly Web Site)

The master photographer and activist died on 22 April 1984 of heart failure aggravated by cancer. However, his vast corpus of beautiful prints remains among the most important and stunning visual records of the great American West.

References

Adams, Ansel, with Mary Street Alinder. *Ansel Adams: An Autobiography.* Boston: Little, Brown, 1985, 1996.

Alinder, Mary Street. *Ansel Adams: A Biography.* New York: Henry Holt, 1996.

Kennerly, David Hume. "Ansel Adams: An American Icon": *http://www.enn.com/features/1999/11/110299/ansel_5302.asp.*

Sources of Further Information

Masters of Photography Biography: *http://www.masters-of-photography.com/A/adams/adams.html.*

AFRICAN AMERICANS

See Beckwourth, Jim; Bicycle Corps; Buffalo Soldiers; Dart, Isom; Deadwood Dick; Exodusters; McJunkin, George; Pickett, Willie M. "Bill"

ALAMO

Along with the battle at the **Little Big Horn,** the defense of the Alamo ranks as one of the two most storied battles in western history. Since 1905 the Daughters of the Texas Republic have safeguarded this state and national treasure located in downtown San Antonio. More than 2.5 million people visit the 4.2-acre complex each year. Plays, pageants, films, and a plethora of books continue to commemorate and, in some cases, hotly debate what transpired at the Alamo on 6 March 1836. Men remove their hats in respect when entering, and interior photographs are only permitted once a year, on 6 March.

The priests and mission Indians who inhabited the Alamo, first called Mission San Antonio de Valero, could never have foreseen the importance the humble mission would take on. The mission was originally established at another location in 1718. Construction at the present site began in 1724, and workers laid the cornerstone of the church on 8 May 1744. In 1793, after some 70 years of operation marred by frequent Apache and Comanche attacks, Spanish officials secularized the Alamo and San Antonio's four other missions. In the early 1800s the site's purpose changed from religious to military as Spain stationed a cavalry unit there. Soldiers began calling the old mission "the Alamo" in honor of their hometown, Alamo de Parras, Coahuila, Mexico. The Alamo continued to have military significance and use through Mexico's war for independence from Spain and after.

Even the site's popular name is colored by legend. Many insist that the name "Alamo," Spanish for "cottonwood," came from the rows of trees planted along the Alameda, a prominent nearby San Antonio street. However, the term appears well before the stately cottonwoods were planted. A cause cannot come after its supposed effect.

The Texan uprising against Mexico's central government brought renewed fighting to the Alamo. In December 1835 Ben Milam led Texan and Tejano volunteers against Mexican troops in San Antonio. After several days of close fighting, they defeated the Mexican forces, occupied the Alamo, and strengthened its defenses. On 23 February 1836 Gen. Antonio López de Santa Anna and his army of several thousand arrived outside San Antonio, nearly taking the force at the Alamo by complete surprise.

Why Santa Anna concentrated his considerable force on a strategically unimportant target stirred conjecture and legend. Hidden treasure, perhaps? Based on thin evidence, in 1992 Frank Buschbacher concluded that Jim Bowie must have succeeded in his quest to find a large cache of silver from the fabled **San Saba Mine** and that he had carried the fortune to the Alamo and hid it in the fortress well. At Buschbacher's urging, archaeologists from St. Mary's University in San Antonio excavated the Alamo's well in early 1995. Alas, only a few shards and other fragments appeared; not the San Saba treasure.

The Alamo's 182 defenders, under the command of Col. William B. Travis, held out for 13 days. Travis sent out a plea for reinforcements, signed "Victory or Death." Only a band of 32 volunteers from Gonzales arrived, on the eighth day of the siege. They "swelled" the ranks of the defenders to nearly 200 fighters. Texas declared its independence from Mexico during the siege on 2 March.

Travis offered his men three options: rush the enemy outside the fortress, surrender, or remain inside and defend the Alamo to the death. The men chose the third option. According to legend and film, as hope faded, Travis drew a line on the ground and asked any man willing to stay and fight to step over. All except one complied, agreeing to fight to the death. In the early morning of 6 March, Mexican soldiers overran the compound, killing or capturing all the combatants. The exact facts concerning those final hours remain vigorously disputed.

Santa Anna did not savor his victory long. Spurred by cries of "Remember the Alamo," Texan forces dealt his army a swift, devastating blow at San Jacinto on 21 April, capturing the general in the process. Mexico held San Antonio until May, then demolished much of the Alamo and its outer walls before withdrawing. Capt. Juan N. Seguín reoccupied the town on 4 June 1836.

Among the heroes of the Alamo, several have ties to other western legends. One of Gene **Autry**'s ancestors, 42-year-old Micajah Autry, died there. North Carolina–born, he left his family and ventured to Texas, arriving in December 1835. "I go whole hog in the cause of Texas," he wrote his family, as he became part of the Texan army (Alamo Official Web Site). He fell in love with Texas and its opportunities, relishing the 5,000 acres of land that military service would net him and his family. In a letter to his wife, Martha, he noted in a postscript that "Col. Crockett has joined our company" (Alamo Official Web Site).

David "Davy" Crockett had already become a living legend before his death at the Alamo. The consummate frontiersman, hunter, teller of tall tales, and congressman from Tennessee had already made his way into literary legend. James Kirke Paulding used Crockett as the model for his hero Nimrod Wildfire in *The Lion of the West.* The play opened in New York City on 25 April 1831. Books supposedly based on Crockett's life and exploits began appearing soon thereafter.

Disenchanted with political life, Crockett headed west with several other men on 1 November 1835. He planned "to explore the Texes [*sic*] well before I return" (Lofaro). In his last letter, written to his family on 9 January 1836, he called Texas "the garden spot of the world." He closed his letter with the admonition, "Do not be uneasy about me, I am among friends."

It is the manner of Crockett's death at the Alamo, not his life, that has inspired long-standing controversy. Susanna Dickinson, wife of army officer Almaron Dickinson, said that Crockett died outside the Alamo, one of the first to fall in the fighting. This seems unlikely, however, because Travis had written that during the first bombardment Crockett had ranged widely in the Alamo, "animating the men to do their duty." Later reports laud Crockett's deadly gunfire, including a near miss on Santa Anna. Colonel Travis's slave Joe, the only male Texan to survive the battle, reported seeing Crockett lying dead, surrounded by slain Mexicans. According to Joe, only one man, named Warner, surrendered to the Mexicans, only to be promptly shot. Other wild tales of the 1830s had Crockett clubbing Mexicans with his empty rifle or even surviving as a slave working in a Mexican salt mine.

In 1975 the translation and publication of a diary kept by Mexican Lt. Col. Jesús Enrique de la Peña (1807–1841) added another version of Crockett's death. The translation included several

Monument to the fallen at the Alamo, San Antonio, Texas

errors, indicative of the dangers of relying on a translation rather than an original document. According to de la Peña's eyewitness account and corroborating documents, Mexican forces captured Crockett and about six other Alamo defenders at six o'clock that morning. Santa Anna, furious that his order to take no prisoners had been violated, quickly ordered the men executed. According to de la Peña, they were bayoneted and then shot. The Mexican soldiers "thrust themselves forward, in order to flatter their commander, and with swords in hand, fell upon these unfortunate, defenseless men just as a tiger leaps upon his prey. Though tortured before they were killed, these unfortunates died without complaining and without humiliating themselves before their torturers" (de la Peña 1997). Interestingly, although rife with errors, lies, and plagiarism, an 1836 book by Richard Penn Smith, *Col. Crockett's Exploits and Adventures in Texas . . . Written by Himself,* gave what may be a reasonably accurate account of Crockett's capture and execution.

According to Crockett hero worshippers, such as New York firefighter/arson investigator turned amateur historian Bill Groneman, the Mexican officer's diary was a forgery, not to mention a smear on Crockett's heroism. In his 1994 book *Defense of a Legend,* Groneman leveled the forgery charge, based on very flimsy evidence and no expert forensic examination. He has since backed off somewhat from his assault on the diary. Joseph Musso, a Los Angeles–based historic illustrator, likewise has questioned the diary's authenticity. "It doesn't have 110 years of human records behind it" (CNN News Report 19 November 1998), he charged, pointing out that it appeared mysteriously in the hands of a Mexican coin dealer in 1955.

Intrigued by Groneman's assertions and concerned by his lack of evidence, James E. Crisp, a Texas native and associate professor of history at North Carolina State University, delved into the question of the diary's authenticity. Through painstaking research throughout the country, Crisp unraveled the diary's many mysteries and effectively shredded Groneman's arguments against its authenticity. The central points of Crisp's rebuttal can be found in his introduction to a new edition of the diary, *With Santa Anna in Texas: A Personal Narrative of the Revolution,* which reprints the 1975 translation by Carmen Perry.

Others weighed in against the Mexican officer's account as well, including CBS News anchorman Dan Rather, a native Texan who grew up in Houston. In a letter to the *New York Times* (30 March 1997), he criticized those who would take the word of a Mexican officer, someone who "would have had the most to gain by discrediting the defenders of the Alamo." In response, historian Garry Wills shot back that Rather illustrated the fact that "Texans are rarely sane on the subject of the Alamo" (Wills 1997). Wills pointed out that de la Peña, certainly no apologist for Santa Anna, deplored Crockett's execution and admired his "stoic conduct" in the face of death.

Texas poet, critic, and *Harper's Magazine* contributing editor Michael Lind also waded into the fray. Among other things, Lind disputes some of the documents that corroborate de la Peña's account, notably a letter written 19 July 1836 by George M. Dolson, a Texan army officer and translator. Once more, Crisp points up errors and oversights in Lind's explanation and offers effective rebuttal to the poet's points. Roger Borroel has translated and analyzed a number of de la Peña's writings, adding further credence to his reports.

The diary that gave rise to such controversy had resided quietly at the John Peace Library at the University of Texas at San Antonio for nearly 25 years. Then John Peace III, son of the man for whom the library was named, decided to put the 700-page manuscript on the market. In November 1998 the original manuscript sold at auction for $388,000. Charles Tate and Tom Hicks, two alumni of the University of Texas at Austin, purchased the famous document and donated it to their alma mater.

The Butterfield and Butterfield auction house had the document tested scientifically. According to the auction house's Gregory Shaw, the memoir's paper is of high rag content, typical of papers of the early nineteenth century. "We were able to determine, unequivocally, that the paper was manufactured between 1825 and 1832 and, perhaps more importantly, that the ink when applied to the paper was fresh and the paper has not been treated or tampered with in any way" (CNN News Report 19 November 1998). "I have no doubt that they are authentic," added Crisp. "They have passed every test" (CNN News Report 19 November 1998).

Rice University filmmaker Brian Huberman even created a documentary about the controversy. His film, *Davy Crockett and the Peña Diary,* premiered on 29 April 2000 in Austin. It traces the many controversies and fascinating characters involved in the famous diary's past and present. And to add to the confusion, Stephen Harrigan, a writer for *Texas Monthly,* published yet another novelized version of the famous story titled *The Gates of the Alamo.* Harrigan has expressed skepticism about the diary's authenticity.

Hollywood, of course, has also taken a hand in creating and spreading Alamo myths. A Houston attorney, Donald Burger, assembled an on-line list of major recent films and **television** shows about the Alamo. Both film and television treatments appeared in 1955. Frank Lloyd directed the movie version, *The Last Command,* which featured Sterling Hayden, Anna Maria Alberghetti, Richard Carlson, and Ernest Borgnine. In one of the most famous portrayals, Fess Parker and Buddy Ebsen starred in Disney's *Davy Crockett, King of the Wild Frontier.* Originally shown as three segments of the television series *The Wonderful World of Disney,* it spawned a very popular, separate TV series. *The Alamo: Thirteen Days to Glory* (1986) starred James Arness (of *Gunsmoke* fame), Brian Keith, Alec Baldwin, and Raul Julia.

Without question, however, the most famous treatment came in 1960 at the hands of John Wayne, who directed and starred as Davy Crockett in *The Alamo.* The film also featured Richard Widmark, Richard Boone, and newcomer Frankie Avalon. Stock western character actors Ken Curtis, Denver Pyle, Chill Wills, and Wayne's son Patrick also appeared. British actor Laurence Harvey played Colonel Travis. The original cut of 199 minutes ran nearly as long as the epic battle itself. Wayne had to cut some 38 minutes for the version shown in movie theaters.

Production problems plagued the venture. According to critic Brian Garfield, "Wayne spent nearly thirteen million 1960 dollars to make this interminable epic which is by turns adolescent, lusty, glutinous, ribald, simpering and flabbily actionful." Garfield terms it "a good example of Hollywood at its worst: nearly a classic for students of awful movies" (Garfield 1982). Its strongest feature turned out to be its music, written by Dimitri Tiomkin and Paul Webster. Their hit song, "The Green Leaves of Summer," received an Oscar nomination. The film also received nominations for Best Picture, Best Supporting Actor (Chill Wills), Best Cinematography (Color), Best Score (Drama or Comedy), and Best Editing. However, it only won in the category of Best Sound, and certainly would have won no prizes for historical accuracy.

As the Web site The Nitpickers Site has pointed out, Wayne took considerable liberties with Alamo history. The entire assault took place before dawn, so the Mexican Army could not have paraded down the streets of San Antonio in daylight beforehand. In Wayne's version, Bowie is wounded and carried to a cot in the chapel. Crockett has to force Jim Bowie back to his hospital bed. Actually, Bowie was confined to a cot before the battle with either pneumonia or tuberculosis and a broken leg. These ills, not Crockett, kept him on his cot.

Crockett arrived at the Alamo with 13 men, not 23 as depicted in the film. Likewise, Juan Seguín did not arrive at the Alamo with the Gonzales volunteers, nor did he die at the Alamo. Rather, he left with messages and did not return until well after the battle. In Wayne's dramatic version of Crockett's death, he swings his long rifle Betsy at his attackers until a Mexican lancer stabs him. He gamely staggers through the chapel door and torches several kegs of gunpowder, which blow out the chapel walls.

This last dramatic touch may not have strayed as far from the historical record as other creative touches. According to writer Lon Tinkle, the Texans planned to create such an explosion when their numbers dwindled to the last man. At the end of the battle, Maj. Robert Evans dashed for the powder cache in the chapel, torch in hand. Mexican gunfire cut him down before he could reach the powder. (However, it's worth recalling that in his 1958 book *Thirteen Days to Glory,* Tinkle also mangled the diarist's name, altering it to "Gonzalez Pena.")

Thus, battles about the Alamo, its events, and its legacy continue to rage. Even though de la Peña's manuscript is authentic, we can still ask, Is it accurate? Do other key pieces of historical evidence exist, awaiting the diligent researcher? Don Carleton, director of the Center for American History at the University of Texas, put the problem succinctly: "Many Texans like to hold on to their historical myths."

Novelist Stephen Harrigan recognized the same social phenomenon:

> The Alamo is a very well cultivated myth, and as such it speaks to our deepest hopes that we are capable of heroism and selflessness. Simply put, we remember the Alamo with such fervor because it continually inspires us to believe that there is something worth dying for, and if the time ever came for us to "cross the line" we might be able to find the courage to do so. Of course, that is the myth. The reality of the Alamo is far more complex—and ultimately, I think, far more interesting.

Like so much of western history, much of the turf remains controlled by buffs, amateurs, and ideologues. So too, with the Alamo, ideology, hero worship, and myth emerge far stronger and more vibrant than historical reality.

References

Alamo Official Web Site: *http://www.the alamo.org.*

CNN News Report 19 November 1998: *http://www.cnn.com/US/9811/19/alamo.auction /#4.*

de la Peña, Jesús Enrique. *With Santa Anna in Texas: A Personal Narrative of the Revolution* (1975). Trans. Carmen Perry, with an introduction by James E. Crisp. College Station: Texas A & M University Press, 1997.

Edmondson, J. R. *The Alamo Story: From Early History to Current Conflicts.* Plano: Republic of Texas Press, 2000.

Garfield, Brian. *Western Films: A Complete Guide.* New York: Da Capo, 1982.

Lofaro, Michael A. "Crockett, David." Handbook of Texas Online: *http://www.tsha.utexas.edu/handbook/online/articles/view/CC/fcr24.html.*

Wills, Garry. "Texas Pride." *Outrider,* 20 June 1997.

Sources of Further Information

Daughters of the Republic of Texas Library at the Alamo, select bibliography: *http://www.drtl.org/alamorev.html.*

Donald Burger's List of Films and TV Shows about the Alamo: *http://www.burger.com/alafilms.htm.*

Lind, Michael. "The Death of David Crockett." *Wilson Quarterly,* Winter 1998: *http://*

wwics.si.edu/organiza/affil/WWICS/OUT REACH/WQ/WQSELECT/CROCK.HTM.

The Nitpickers Site: *http://www.nitpickers.com/ movies/titles/1219.html.*

Texas Military Forces Museum Web Site, maintained by Gary Butler: *http://www. kwanah.com/txmilmus/tnghist3.htm.*

APPLESEED, JOHNNY

1774–1845

John Chapman became famous in American myth as Johnny Appleseed. He roamed the frontier, planting apple trees to nourish future pioneers and settlers. Chapman believed that the apple tree would help alleviate hunger and starvation as the West became more populated.

Born to Nathaniel and Mary Chapman in Massachusetts in 1774, Chapman received an unexceptional education and lived a relatively uneventful life until he converted to the Swedenborgian religion. He became one of only 400 members in America at the time. He swore off all "evils," including women and alcohol, and began his task of planting orchards in frontier regions. He planted his first apple orchard in western Pennsylvania around 1796. From there, he continued to Ohio, Kentucky, Indiana, and Illinois. Johnny Appleseed covered nearly 100,000 square miles of land in apple trees. Although he worked east of the Mississippi River, Chapman became strongly identified with the American frontier, and thus, the West. His biographer, Newell D. Hillis, described the pioneer as having "the sweetest smile, the most wondrous face, and the greatest soul" (Hillis 1917). Chapman lived simply, carrying only a bag of seeds and a shovel. He used neither gun nor knife and never chopped down trees or killed animals. Indians and settlers alike welcomed and respected him.

At age 70, John Chapman died of pneumonia at his friend William Worth's home in Indiana. His estate revealed that, far from being poor, he had owned and leased vast amounts of land, which he had already covered in apple trees. His grave is located near Fort Wayne, Indiana. The epitaph reads, "He lived for others."

A welter of myths surrounds Johnny Appleseed. One portrays him as wearing a pot for a hat and walking barefoot through the snow. He is also depicted in rags, sometimes dressed in a potato sack with holes cut for arms and legs. Johnny Appleseed is characterized as the toughest yet gentlest frontiersman to ever grace the West. Johnny supposedly sang the same song repeatedly: "Oh, the Lord's been good to me, / And so I thank the Lord, / For giving me the things I need, / The sun and the rain and the appleseed." This verse became a popular song and prayer, used by Girl Scout and Boy Scout programs, among others. Disney immortalized his story in a 1948 cartoon. Johnny's tradition of singing continues with the Johnny Appleseed District Barbershop Competition and a string of festivals across the United States.

Several government and commercial entities have honored Johnny Appleseed and capitalized on his name and reputation, as well. The U.S. Postal Service produced commemorative five-cent **stamps,** and the federal government made 11

March official Johnny Appleseed Day. The Johnny Appleseed Trail in north central Massachusetts promotes itself as the path that he followed, even though he never planted orchards in that state. The Johnny Appleseed all-hemp catalog sells all-natural products.

The apple lies at the center of many of the myths. Supposedly, Johnny Appleseed's deep love for the fruit stemmed from an apple blossom that he first saw upon his birth. By some accounts, Johnny gave a bag of seeds to the young Abe Lincoln. His fame even extended beyond the earth. According to legend, when he died God called him to heaven to plant apple orchards there. Today his namesake apple, the Jonathan, remains among the top-ten sellers in the United States.

–Julie J. Anders

References

Hillis, Newell Dwight. *The Quest of John Chapman: The Story of a Forgotten Hero.* London: Macmillan, 1917.

Nissenson, Hugh. *The Tree of Life.* New York: Harper and Row, 1985.

AREA 51

The top-secret U.S. Air Force base at Groom Lake, Nevada, has long fascinated UFO and conspiracy buffs. Books, articles, and Web sites have proposed various theories about what really goes on at "Area 51," also sometimes known as "Dreamland" or "the Ranch." The most prevalent theory is that Area 51 houses the wreckage of a spacecraft that purportedly crashed at **Roswell, New Mexico,** in 1947, as well as the diminutive bodies of the alien pilots. Air Force scientists have supposedly used these artifacts to "reverse engineer" (that is, to develop based on the evidence of the wreckage) flying saucer–like aircraft for the U.S. military.

Many details about aliens and UFOs at Area 51 emanate from the stories of Robert Lazar. In 1989 Lazar claimed to have worked for the federal government on secret alien technology deep in the Nevada desert. He reported that the government housed nine different types of flying saucers there, the result of a long-standing collaboration with mysterious, otherworldly visitors. Fearful that his former employers intended either to erase his memory through drugs or hypnosis or to simply kill him, he decided to go public with his claims.

Lazar's credibility has come under question. The self-proclaimed MIT-educated physicist actually graduated from a California community college. His long-standing efforts to encourage a film version of his story suggest financial gain as a motive for his actions. His 1990 conviction for pandering (he set up a computer system for a Las Vegas brothel) further embarrassed him. Supporters, however, see his legal problems and the lack of documentation to support his story as further evidence of a government conspiracy to discredit him. He remains an important, controversial figure in the development of the legend of Area 51.

The Dreamland myth entered the public arena largely through **television** and films. The television program *The X-Files* located parts of two humorous 1998 episodes at Dreamland. The TV program derives much of its popularity from the clever use of interrelated story lines about alien visitors and government conspiracies. This interplay fits well with the supposed activities at Area 51. The hugely successful motion picture *Independence Day* similarly played with the mystery of Area 51. In that film, the military kept the existence of the base and the alien technology stored there secret even from the president, who expressed outrage when he learned of the deception.

The intense public interest in Area 51 is understandable; the unknown fascinates and inspires us. Most of the world's cultures have created myths about strange, alien beings with extraordinary knowledge and powers, beings who descend from the heavens. The idea that those in power would cover up such matters for their own benefit is hardly new. Conspiracy theories are as old as the Bible. Previous generations have blamed sinister events on a variety of scapegoats, including Freemasons, Rosicrucians, Jesuits, and Jews. In the modern world, many people see the federal government as the likely villain. The many scandals that have plagued national leaders in recent decades further stimulate such suspicions.

Area 51's documented history is nearly as fantastic as any theory. The CIA and the U.S. Air Force first created a small base on the remote Nevada site in 1955 to test the experimental U-2 spy plane, which soon began surveillance flights over Soviet-controlled areas. Subsequent land acquisitions allowed Dreamland to grow to its present large size. The success of the U-2 (which came in under budget and ahead of schedule) led to a number of other secret Air Force projects at the base. Scientists there developed both the SR-71 Blackbird and the F-117A Stealth fighter. During the 1980s the government probably conducted tests of advanced antiballistic missile technology at Groom Lake as part of the Strategic Defense Initiative program (the so-called Star Wars program).

Recent sightings of bizarre objects flying over the base's restricted airspace probably indicate the development of even-more-advanced aircraft. The very secrecy that necessarily attends such research, however, will undoubtedly continue to fuel speculation about extraterrestrial links to Area 51. Perhaps government counterintelligence agents, as some conspiracy theorists propose, encourage such speculation in order to deflect attention from the real technology used there. Regardless of its origins, the myth of Area 51 shows no signs of disappearing.

–Michael Thomas Smith

References

Darlington, David. *Area 51: The Dreamland Chronicles.* New York: Henry Holt, 1997.

Good, Timothy. *Alien Liaison: The Ultimate Secret.* London: Random Century, 1991.

Patton, Phil. *Dreamland: Travels inside the Secret World of Roswell and Area 51.* New York: Random House, 1998.

ARGENTINA

See Comparative Frontier Mythology

AUSTRALIA

See Comparative Frontier Mythology

AUTRY, GENE

1907–1998

In many ways, Orvon Gene Autry, born in Tioga, Texas, lived the rags-to-riches dream that many people still associate with the American West. Even his family background reflects links to western popular culture. His father, Delbert, worked as a tenant farmer, cattle dealer, and horse trader, a storied profession of the Old West. The family moved to Achille, Oklahoma, and later to Ravia, Oklahoma, about 20 miles east of the present town of Gene Autry. (Autry was to purchase 1,200 acres on the west side of Berwyn, Oklahoma, to graze his livestock. Acknowledging his celebrity, in 1941 the town changed its name to Gene Autry, Oklahoma.)

Music entered Autry's life early, thanks to his mother, Elnora, and his paternal grandfather, William. The latter, a Baptist minister, prompted young Gene to sing in the church choir and bought the 12-year-old his first guitar. Gene worked as a telegraph operator and traveled with a medicine show, another staple of Old West popular culture. He met living legend Will Rogers one night in Chelsea, Oklahoma, when the comedian dropped by to send out a few messages. Rogers offered encouraging words when he heard the youngster singing and strumming his guitar. Autry's early singing style reflected the influence of the father of modern country music, Jimmie Rodgers, "the Singing Brakeman."

No overnight success, Autry got off to a faltering start in New York City show business. In 1927 he returned to Tulsa, Oklahoma, to sing on radio station KVOO. In 1931 he recorded his first hit song, "That Silver-Haired Daddy of Mine" (written with Jimmy Long). He moved to a bigger radio market with WLS in Chicago, performing as "Oklahoma's Singing Cowboy." There he met Smiley Burnette, the talented, rotund comedian who would become Autry's sidekick in a long string of radio and film performances.

Autry and Burnette first sang in a Mascot film that also starred the screen's first singing cowboy, Ken Maynard. *In Old Santa Fe* (1934) marked the beginning of Autry's long cinema singing career. The film also boosted the career of another soon-to-be-famous sidekick, George "Gabby" Hayes. Autry appeared in *Mystery Mountain,* another Maynard film that appeared later the same year. In 1935 he rode across the silver screen in a sci-fi/western serial titled *The Phantom Empire.* Autry then moved to Republic Pictures, where he shot 58 pictures, from *Tumbling Tumbleweeds* in 1935 to *Robin Hood of Texas* in 1947. By 1940 Autry had risen to become one of the nation's most popular movie stars, a network radio star, and a top-selling recording artist. He would star in 91 westerns produced by Republic and Columbia from 1935 through 1953. Only Mickey Rooney, Clark Gable, and Spencer Tracy outranked him as a career box office attraction.

Autry also played a leading role in shaping another huge area of western popular culture, the American rodeo industry. He became involved in rodeo as a performer and producer through his Flying A Rodeo. As a rodeo producer during the 1940s, he changed the nature of modern rodeo away from sports competition and toward popular theater. He marginalized the contestants in general and women in particular. Autry helped reduce women, who once starred and competed against men, to secondary roles as barrel racers and rodeo queens. He also spiced rodeos with his own singing performances. The introduction of singers and other entertainers shifted the focus away from contestants and toward celebrity performers.

Autry often played himself in his films, which helped increase the audience's identification with him. He understood the charm of the B-western and how to deliver it to an audience. Autry listed his recipe for success in his autobiography *Back in the Saddle:* a good story and good music, a dash of comedy and romance, and fights and chases played out under vast western skies. He added his own special touches: lots of singing, his wonder horse, Champion, a good dose of humor, and touches of modernity, with telephones, automobiles, and other twentieth-century gadgetry.

Autry used his popularity to preach rock-solid values, mandated, he says, by Herb Yates at Republic Studios. The Ten Commandments of the Cowboy, aimed at admiring youth, well summed up the values that Autry and other cowboy heroes represented. The hero never takes unfair advantage; never betrays a trust; tells the truth; is kind to children, the elderly, and animals; is tolerant; helps those in distress; works hard; respects women, his parents, and the law; is clean in his thought, speech, and habits; and is patriotic.

Autry showed his patriotism by enlisting in the Army Air Corps in 1942. "Every movie cowboy ought to devote time to the army winning or to helping win until the war is done—the same as any other American citizen," he said (McDonald 1987). Autry made a sincere patriotic sacrifice. His annual salary of $600,000 in 1941 fell to little more than $100 per month in the army. In his absence, a singing newcomer named Roy **Rogers** laid claim to the title King of the Cowboys.

The war years and changes in the movie industry set Autry to thinking more seriously about his financial future. He invested skillfully and displayed the good economic horse sense that would make him a multimillionaire. From the late 1940s through 1953, he made 32 more movies with his own Gene Autry Productions. His half-hour **television** program, *The Gene Autry Show,* ran weekly on CBS from 23 July 1950 until 7 August 1956. His credits eventually included his popular *Melody Ranch* radio program, more than 90 films, an equal number of television episodes, and hundreds of recorded songs.

In 1960 he put Champion out to graze and hung up his spurs. His business interests in the electronic media, the California Angels baseball team, hotels, and ranches kept him busy. The Country Music Hall of Fame inducted Autry as a member in 1969. He still had time for old friends, however. He continued to give money to a destitute, alcoholic Ken Maynard until the actor's death in 1973.

Autry's longtime first wife, Ina Mae Spivey, died in 1980. In 1982 he married his second wife, Jackie Elam, and he quit drinking.

Autry's fame and fortune never went to his head. Cowboy singer Michael Martin Murphey tells the following story: In 1936 Autry

got together with John Wayne at a movie opening, and they got drunk together. John Wayne, a little bit tipsy, said, "You know, Gene, had I been able to sing, your career woulda' been history. You would never have made it." And apparently Gene's retort to that was, "Hey, it's not my singing, it's my extra-fine acting that has carried me through." Gene never considered himself a very good actor and never considered himself a very good singer either. He was very humble about that.

Autry remained vigorous and active throughout his life. In 1993 his theme song, "Back in the Saddle Again," enjoyed a popular revival on the sound track for the film *Sleepless in Seattle*. The sound track stayed on *Billboard Magazine*'s charts for more than a dozen weeks, selling more than 2 million copies. Autry coauthored the song with Ray Whitley and first recorded it in 1939.

Autryville, in Sampson County, North Carolina, commemorates the singer's name and memory. Located just east of Fayetteville, the tiny town is populated by about 79 families, totaling 166 people. More prominently, two museums also feature the story of Autry's life and legacy. The Autry Museum of Western Heritage in Los Angeles near Griffith Park opened in November 1988. It per-

petuates the mythical and movie West that he helped to shape. A superb facility, the museum also offers an engaging look at western history and culture and includes excellent research materials. As the museum's Web site notes,

The galleries also present the story of the West by contrasting the historical with the mythological. Art, film, and advertising have shaped perceptions of the region, and The Autry explores contemporary culture, as well as historical realities. Whether it is the art of Albert Bierstadt, Frederic **Remington**, or N. C. Wyeth; the tools, clothing, and firearms of people who inhabited the West; or the costumes, scripts, and props of western film and television, The Autry offers an enjoyable and engaging opportunity to discover the legacy of the West.

On Autry's eighty-fifth birthday on 29 September 1992, 100 schoolchildren gathered at the museum to serenade him with "Happy Birthday." A cowboy riding a galloping steed topped his birthday cake, big enough to feed far more than 100 hungry children. As Autry observed, "Kids have always supported me. I've always had a great following of kids." Outfitted with his usual white cowboy hat, Autry expressed a special birthday wish: "My wish is that everybody's dream would come true."

The Gene Autry Oklahoma Museum of Local History is located in the old Gene Autry School building in the town bearing his name. Each September, the museum, funded solely by donations, sponsors a film and music festival that attracts many B-western film stars and fans. In 1997 Rhino Records honored the singer with *Gene Autry: Sing, Cowboy, Sing,* a three-CD box collection that includes an informative booklet.

Autry died, after a prolonged illness, in Studio City, California, on 2 October 1998. His passing, just three months after that of Roy Rogers, saddened fans around the world. His second wife, Jackie, and his sister Veda survive him. The only entertainer to earn five stars on the Hollywood Walk of Fame, he is remembered fondly for his films, musical recordings (635), television episodes, radio (16 seasons of *Melody Ranch*), and live performances.

It's fitting that a modern-day cowboy legend like Gene Autry should also be tied to older western legends, such as the Alamo. One of Gene's ancestors, North Carolina–born Micajah Autry, fought and died at the most famous battle in Texas history, the **Alamo,** on 6 March 1836. His name is prominently inscribed on the tall granite monument that towers in front of the old San Antonio mission/fortress.

However, a living link also connects Autry and the Alamo. Joseph Blyth III, a retired automotive industry consultant, is also related to Micajah and Gene Autry. Furthermore, Blyth acted as an extra in a number of B-western and other films. Thus, myth connects with myth, but so do flesh-and-blood human beings, like the Autrys and Blyth.

References

Autry, Gene, with Mickey Herskowitz. *Back in the Saddle.* Garden City, NY: Doubleday, 1978.
Autry Museum of Western Heritage Web Site: *http://www.autry-museum.org/.*
LeCompte, Mary Lou. *Cowgirls of the Rodeo: Pioneer Professional Athletes.* Bloomington: Indiana University Press, 1993.
McDonald, Archie P., ed. *Shooting Stars: Heroes and Heroines of Western Film.* Bloomington: Indiana University Press, 1987.

Source of Further Information

Gene Autry Oklahoma Museum of Local History: *http://www.cow-boy.com/museum.htm.*

AVERILL, JIM

Ca. 1855–1889 (also Averell), accused rustler. *See* Cattle Kate

AZTLÁN

Aztlán is the legendary first city of the Aztecs, apparently located in what is now the American Southwest. No physical location has even been found, and much of the Aztec oral traditions have been lost. Like the **Seven Cities of Gold,** Aztlán has acquired a magical reputation. According to Aztec tradition, the Aztecs left Aztlán in 1111 C.E. and journeyed southward for some two centuries. Once in a permanent and secure location in the central valley of Mexico, they destroyed their written records and rewrote them in a manner favorable to the tribe. The Aztecs created a rich body of myth and legend, illustrated with much symbolism. They reported no defeats or weaknesses and portrayed themselves as a messianic people chosen by the Gods.

The name *Aztlán* may be broken down into two words in Nahuatl, *aztatl,* "heron," and *tlan (tli)* "place of." *Tlantli* literally means "tooth" and denotes being rooted in place. This word is often used to indicate a settlement or home. Words in Nahuatl have three meanings: literal, syncretic, and connotative. The connotative meaning of *Aztlán* is "place of whiteness." Several theories surround this meaning. These include the idea of a city built in a land of white-skinned giants or in a snow-covered land. The myths also contain repeated images of the number seven. The Aztecs believed they crawled from the center of the earth to arrive at the city. It is often called Aztlán of the Seven Caves. Or it may be depicted as having seven temples: one central large step-pyramid surrounded by six lesser sanctuaries. After the arrival of the Spaniards in Mexico, a parallel myth emerges of the Seven Cities of Gold.

Like the Aztec capital of Tenochtitlan, Aztlán was supposedly built on an island. It has even been suggested that Aztlán was the legendary Atlantis. It may be assumed that Aztlán was located in northwestern Mexico or southwestern America near the coast or an estuary. One historian has posited the exact site to be San Felipe Aztlán in the state of Nayarit, Mexico.

Aztlán symbolized the beginning of the Aztec civilization and Mexican heritage. It signifies acceptance and cultural pride for all Mexican Americans (Chicanos). To many Mexicans and Mexican Americans, Aztlán presents a venerable, dignified heritage. Since the mid-1970s,

the University of California at Los Angeles has published a well-known journal named *Aztlán,* which focuses on Chicano issues, lifestyles, and history. LUChA (La Union Chicana por Aztlán) provides a popular focal point for Chicano student pride at many universities. The club uses Aztlán as a symbol both of its members origin and of their future goals of cultural identity and acceptance as Mexican Americans.

Several groups and companies capitalize on the automatic recognition and identification of Aztlán with people of Mexican heritage. This symbolism has been used in several political campaigns over the years as well. Representing lost Mexican lands and identity, Aztlán remains a potent political symbol. Companies in the American Southwest, such as Aztlán Archaeology, Aztlán Graphics, and Aztlán Productions, take advantage of the name's broad recognition. Even the arts make the most of the name. The Ballet Folklórico Aztlán travels with productions of historical representations of ceremonies and tribal dances believed to have begun in Aztlán and continued throughout the Aztec culture.

—Julie J. Anders

References

Azteca Web Page: *http://www.azteca.net/aztec/index.html.*

Meyer, Michael C., and William L. Sherman. *The Course of Mexican History.* New York: Oxford University Press, 1999.

Sitchin, Zecharia. *The Lost Realms.* New York: Avon Books, 1990.

BACA, ELFEGO

1865–1945

Elfego Baca is among the most colorful and controversial figures in New Mexico's history. A true Renaissance man of the American Southwest, during his long life he worked as a frontier gunfighter and ruffian (in his youth), a lawyer, sheriff, district attorney, school superintendent, mayor, and perennial candidate for state and national office. Born during the last days of the Civil War and dying at the end of World War II, Baca's action-filled life is interesting enough. However, this did not stop friends, authors, journalists, and even Walt Disney from embellishing and mythologizing his life.

Myths about his life even surround Baca's birth. According to one account, his 19-year-old mother gave birth to him while playing baseball. Unknowingly pregnant, she jumped to catch a ball and out popped little Elfego with a thud. Another story claimed that a hostile southwest Indian war party had kidnapped

him as a baby. Living up to his portentous childhood, Baca matured to be a true prodigy of frontier skills, especially with firearms.

One memorable event supposedly occurred in October 1884, when Baca served as a deputy sheriff in Socorro County. Only 19 years of age, he had already earned a reputation as one of the best gunmen in New Mexico. In the small town of Frisco, about 125 miles southwest of the town of Socorro, a gang of cowboys from the Slaughter Ranch got drunk and began terrorizing the Mexican townspeople. When the deputy sheriff of Frisco sent for help, the young lawman went to the rescue.

Baca persuaded the justice of the peace to deputize him, and he immediately arrested and jailed one of the cowboys. The next day, a gang of 80 bloodthirsty men fired on the jail. Backed into a log *jacal* (simple hut), Elfego single-handedly held off the siege for 36 hours, killing four and wounding six of the attackers. During the barrage, the cool-headed Baca even took time to cook breakfast. Some of the cowboys later pressed charges against Baca for the killings, but the judge acquitted him after he presented the door to the *jacal* as evidence. It contained more than 400 bullet holes.

The standoff against 80 cowboys followed Baca for the rest of his days and earned him a reputation for bravely upholding the law. Many accounts of his early life, however, reveal a more ruffian side. New Mexican judges tried him for murder three times; each time he was acquitted. Baca claimed to have been acquainted with **Billy the Kid** and Pancho Villa. The latter supposedly once put a $30,000 reward on Baca's head for stealing one of his guns.

According to contemporaries, despite his shortcomings Baca earnestly desired to be the best lawman in the Southwest. As sheriff of Socorro County, instead of chasing indicted criminals, he would write them a letter. He warned that if they did not turn themselves in, he would "understand that they were resisting arrest and would feel justified in shooting them on the spot."

Baca went on to study law, and the New Mexico Bar admitted him in 1894. A tenacious campaigner for justice, he excelled in the courtroom and soon earned an appointment as district attorney and was elected mayor. Once a friend being tried for murder in El Paso enlisted his help. A local journal quoted Baca as replying, "I'm on my way with three eyewitnesses." This quote stuck with Baca throughout his life, although he admitted to a newspaper in 1939 that he had never said it.

In his later years, Baca's stories and folklore became so popular with local residents that he ran for several district offices, and even for the U.S. House of Representatives (unsuccessfully). During one of his campaigns, he printed up a pamphlet highlighting his gunfighter days. It became so popular that he began selling them for ten cents apiece.

In 1928 Kyle Crichton, a local advertising executive, wrote a book titled *Law and Order, Ltd.: The Rousing Life of Elfego Baca.* He based the work on personal interviews and Baca's pamphlet but added further embellishments to the already outlandishly mythologized stories.

Elfego Baca died in 1945 at the age of 80. In 1958 *True West* magazine published yet another brief biography of Baca. According to the article, he had been run over by a fire engine, stabbed with an ice pick, and wounded critically in a knife fight, and he had survived an automobile accident and some 50 gunfights. Thirteen years after the gunfighter's death, Walt Disney produced a television series titled *The Nine Lives of Elfego Baca.* The series, starring Robert Loggia, did for Baca's life what Disney did for many people and events of the western frontier: delivered yet another bigger-than-life mythical being to American popular culture. The mythical Baca can still be seen today on weekly reruns on the Disney Channel.

In 1959 Disney released another film, *Elfego Baca–Six Gun Law.* It featured a promising young actress named Annette Funicello in her big-screen debut. Recently, the History Channel produced a more factual account of Baca's life, attempting to demythologize him. In 1994 Howard Bryan wrote *Incredible Elfego Baca: Good Man, Bad Man of the Old*

West, which portrayed both the good and bad aspects of his character. The following year Bryan's book won the coveted Spur Award from the **Western Writers of America, Inc.,** for Best Western Nonfiction.

—*Andrew Mebane Southerland*

See also Disney Frontierland

References

Bryan, Howard. *Incredible Elfego Baca: Good Man, Bad Man of the Old West.* Santa Fe, NM: Clear Light Publishers, 1993.

Crichton, Kyle. *Law and Order, Ltd.: The Rousing Life of Elfego Baca.* 1928. Reprint, New York: Arno Press, 1974.

BARBECUE

Barbecue is one of the American West's favorite foods and pastimes. There are as many different ways to cook it as there are myths about its origin. Barbecue may have originated with Cro-Magnon man somewhere in France around 30,000 B.C.E. He occasionally cooked his meat over an open flame. A more recent source is the Arawak culture that Columbus met upon his arrival in the Caribbean in 1492. These people cooked meat over a rack of wood and flavored it with available fruits and herbs. They built a large fire and put *barbacoa* (meat) over it, thus creating the modern-day barbecue.

Yet another source claims that barbecue came from a tribe of cannibals in South America. The term "barbecue" was commonly used from about 1660 forward in the Carolinas and Virginia. North Carolina proudly claims to be "the birthplace of (American) barbecue," owing to its long history of hog farming.

Another report of barbecue comes from Brazil more than 200 years ago. Gauchos on a ranch roasted a cow on a spit in celebration of the arrival of a popular priest. They completed the party with music and a large gathering of friends. The Portuguese and Spanish tradition slowly spread up and across the Western Hemisphere, finally reaching the American West. The practice is still embraced for the great flavor it imparts to meat and for its ease of cooking.

The Great American Barbecue Instruction Book defines barbecue as "meat cooked in the dry heat of wood coals at temperatures of about the boiling point of water" (Hale 1985). Herbal rubs, marinades, bastes, or sauces flavor the meat. The most popular type of western sauce begins with tomato catsup and brown sugar or molasses. The chef then inventively adds whatever additional flavorings he or she wishes.

Cooks in the West barbecue beef, game, fowl, goat, and even mutton, while southerners generally use pork. A 1995 Barbecue Industry Association survey claimed that nearly 85 percent of American families own a gas grill, which they use more than once a week on average to do what they call "barbecuing."

Barbecue has made its way into popular culture throughout the nation. Many restaurants all across the West specialize in this style of cooking. They range in theme from down-home, "sawdust on the floor" places to upscale, five-star dining establishments renowned for their chefs and cuisine. Some widely known barbecue eateries include The Pit in Duncanville, Texas, where diners can choose their meat before they cook it, and Elk Country Bar-B-Q in Pinedale, Wyoming, just outside Yellowstone National Park. The Texas Beef Council, the National Pork Producer's Council, and the American Poultry Association all produce pamphlets and have special Web sites addressing the many tasty ways to barbecue their products. The U.S. Department of Agriculture promotes barbecuing as a healthy and delicious method of cooking.

The influence of barbecue has even extended to the music industry. In the 1920s Barbecue Bob performed as a leading jazz and blues guitarist. One of his biggest hits was "Barbecue Blues." The Internet hosts many barbecue-related sites. Barbecuen.com is an excellent source of recipes and information on various brands of equipment, as is the BBQ.COM home page. One of the most enjoyable, comprehensive, and insightful books produced recently is *The Barbecue Bible* by Steven Raichlen. It examines the art and culture of barbecue in 25 countries around the world and also shares several recipes and techniques.

The art of barbecue has reached legendary status owing to its widespread popularity and excellent taste. Back in 1898, the news editor of the *Rushville Standard* lauded barbecued meat as "the finest we ever tasted." Since then, appreciation has continued to grow, making barbecue a staple of western culture and cuisine.

—Julie J. Anders

References

Barbecuen on the Internet: *www.barbecuen. com.*

BBQ.COM Home Page: *www.bbq.com.*

Hale, C. Clark "Smoky." *The Great American Barbecue Instruction Book.* McComb, MS: Abacus, 1985.

_____. *The Great American Barbecue and Grilling Manual.* McComb, MS: Abacus, 1999.

_____. "Origins of Barbecue." *Gourmet Connection Magazine: http://gourmetconnection .com/ezine/articles/697bbori.shtml.*

Origin of Barbecue: *http://www.barbacoa. com.br/ingles/churrasc.htm.*

Raichlen, Steven. *The Barbecue Bible.* New York: Workman, 1998.

BARKER, S. OMAR

1894–1985, poet. *See* Cowboy Poetry

BASS, SAM

1851–1878

Born in Mitchell, Indiana, Sam Bass left home at age 18 and headed for Texas. During his brief life, he worked as a teamster, farmer, cowboy, gambler, and robber. In 1874 he befriended Joel Collins, and two years later they trailed north on a cattle drive. They pushed the herd all the way to Deadwood, South Dakota, where they tried their luck with a saloon, casino, and mine. Failing at all of them, they decided that robbing stagecoaches and trains would yield riches more quickly. In September 1877 their gang of six stole $65,000 in gold coin and other valuables from a Union Pacific train in Big Springs, Nebraska.

Back in Texas, Bass and his new gang successfully robbed several trains. In July

1878, however, a gang member named Jim Murphy tipped off the **Texas Rangers.** The lawmen ambushed and wounded Bass as he tried to rob the bank in Round Rock. Ranger George Harrell is officially credited with firing the shot that eventually killed Bass. However, Dick Ware, credited with killing outlaw Seaborn Barnes, may have actually been the one to shoot Bass. Lawman A. W. Grimes also received mortal wounds during the fight. Bass, shot through the torso, managed to escape but could not ride far. He used strips of his shirt to bind up his wounds, but a posse found him resting under a tree the next morning. He died the next day, on 21 July, his twenty-seventh birthday. His dying words are recorded thus: "Yes, I am Sam Bass, the man that has been wanted so long. It is ag'in' my profession to blow on my pals. If a man knows anything, he ought to die with it in him" ("The Story of Sam Bass").

Like that of many outlaws, Bass's stature grew after his death, aided by a sense of injustice over his betrayal. A few years after his death, his sister had a tombstone erected engraved with this epitaph: "A brave man reposes in death here. Why was he not true?" Souvenir hunters chipped away the monument, which was later replaced with a granite tombstone erected by the Sam Bass Centennial Commission.

Texas and the nation still remember the fallen bank robber as "Texas's Beloved Bandit" or "Robin Hood on a Fast Horse." During the 1930s, a popular cowboy song, "The Ballad of Sam Bass," by John Benton, added to his heroic legend. According to the lyrics, "a kinderhearted fellow you'd seldom ever see." The ballad also made plain Jim Murphy's

reward for his treachery: "What a scorchin' Jim should get when Gabriel blows his horn."

Old West fans still visit Bass's grave site at the Round Rock Cemetery located in Old Town on Sam Bass Road. The town also hosts the Sam Bass Community Theatre, a nonprofit drama group, and the Sam Bass Youth Baseball League. Tiny Rosston, Texas, a supposed Bass hideout, celebrates Sam Bass Day on the third Saturday of July.

What happened to Bass's treasure? Stories abound. One legend locates his hidden gold in a cave in East Mountain at Mineral Wells. Another tale argues that Bass hid his gold in a cave west of Prairie Dell near Big Blue Spring. It is unlikely that Bass could have spent all of his gold, given the spare retail opportunities of Texas. Perhaps he did rob more for sport than for profit, which only adds to his celebrity.

References

Gard, Wayne. *Sam Bass.* Boston: Houghton Mifflin, 1936.

Miller, Rick. *Sam Bass and Gang.* Austin, TX: State House Press, 1999.

Reed, Paula, and Grover Ted Tate. *The Tenderfoot Bandits: Sam Bass and Joel Collins, Their Lives and Hard Times.* Tucson, AZ: Westernlore Press, 1988.

"The Story of Sam Bass": *http://www.ci.round rock.tx.us/planning/rrcollection/mainstreet/s ambass.*

BATTLES OR MASSACRES

At dawn on 29 November 1864, at Sand Creek, Colorado, Col. John M. Chivington ordered an attack by 700 volunteer soldiers. Their target: a village of about 500 peaceful Cheyenne and Arapaho Indians. Although village chief Black Kettle desperately waved a pole with both an American flag and a white peace flag attached in an attempt to deter them, the soldiers charged and fired, determined to wipe out the village. They very nearly succeeded. After their initial surprise, some Indians resisted rather than simply allowing themselves and their families to be killed. At the end of the day, about 150 Indians and nine soldiers lay dead. Women and children comprised some two-thirds of the dead Cheyenne and Arapaho; most had been savagely mutilated by the volunteers.

Chivington ordered his men to take no prisoners. This order was so commonplace in Indian warfare that Chivington apparently thought it required no explanation in his official report. The politically ambitious former Methodist minister commanded a regiment of untrained Denver citizens who had enlisted for only 100 days. He wasted no time in announcing that he had won a glorious victory over the "savages." Back in the mile-high city, the discharged volunteers triumphantly displayed souvenirs of the slaughter, including severed ears, fingers, scalps, and genitals.

Public sentiment in Colorado and much of the West firmly supported the actions of Chivington's men, but the rest of the country expressed disgust and horror. Chivington probably only escaped being court-martialed by resigning. The scandal and public outcry also forced Colorado's governor, John Evans, to resign. A congressional investigation detailed and condemned the atrocities carried out by the Colorado volunteers. To most historians and much of the pub-

lic, Sand Creek has come to be seen not as a battle but as a massacre.

It is not entirely clear why some clashes between white soldiers and Native Americans are remembered as battles and others as massacres. One reason may be that official reports by the officers involved sometimes succeeded in depicting the engagement as a "battle." Chivington's official report on Sand Creek, for example, stated that his soldiers "pressed forward rapidly" in their attack and that his subordinates "ably handled" their men. Chivington's second-in-command wrote proudly, "The historian will search in vain for braver deeds than were committed on that field of battle." Many such reports did succeed in mythologizing a massacre as a battle. However, in some cases other witnesses left key accounts that did not coincide with the official military record. At Sand Creek, most important among these truth seekers was Maj. Edward W. Wynkoop.

Wynkoop's report condemning Chivington and the barbarous conduct of his command succeeded in preventing Chivington's fabrication of events from entering the American cultural memory. Many massacres, however, were not exposed as such at the time. Officers who had won fame and honor for their services in the Civil War sometimes ordered and led massacres. The reputations of these "heroes" lent a veneer of respectability to their attacks on Indian camps and authority to their official stories.

On 27 November 1868 George Armstrong Custer's Seventh Cavalry regiment attacked a Cheyenne village in Oklahoma. Ranald S. Mackenzie led the Fourth Cavalry in an assault on a Kickapoo village in Mexico on 18 May 1873. John Gibbon's Seventh Infantry charged a Nez Percé camp in Montana on 28 July 1877. Highly respected former Civil War generals commanded in each of these encounters. Each resulted in substantial numbers of Native American fatalities, although estimates of the numbers vary. On each occasion, however, U.S. soldiers killed mostly women and children. These scenes of violence have generally been remembered as battles, not massacres. They are known to military historians as, respectively, the Battle of the Washita, the Battle of Remolino, and the Battle of Big Hole.

Like Sand Creek, all of these "battles" involved soldiers acting under the authority of the U.S. government. In each case Indians offered some armed resistance, generally after the soldiers' initial surprise attack. In reality, all four of these military actions were surprise attacks by U.S. soldiers on Indian villages in which most of those killed were noncombatant women and children. Why only the occasional protest at the time? Few Americans of the time questioned the need to pacify the "Indian frontier." Fewer still questioned the official reports that painted Indian-white conflict as heroic battles. However, in these four cases—and probably in many more—"massacre" is the proper, accurate term for the engagements. Military historians are only now examining a wider range of such mythical "battles," often incorporating Native American sources, to recover the real story of these events.

—*Michael Thomas Smith*

References

Brown, Dee. *Bury My Heart at Wounded Knee: An Indian History of the American West.* New York: Henry Holt, 1970.

Josephy, Alvin M. Jr. *The Civil War in the American West.* New York: Vintage Books, 1993.

Utley, Robert M. *Frontier Regulars: The United States Army and the Indian, 1866–1891.* New York: Macmillan, 1973.

Source of Further Information

Meyers, J. Jay. "The Notorious Fight at Sand Creek." *Wild West* 11, no. 4 (December 1998): *http://www.thehistorynet.com/Wild West/articles/1998/1298_cover.htm.*

BEALE, EDWARD F.

1822–1893, U.S. Army lieutenant. *See* Camel Corps

BEAN, JUDGE ROY

1825?–1903

Judge Roy Bean is most famous for his notorious antics and verdicts as "The Law West of the Pecos." Like many authorities of the West, Judge Bean was an amalgam of justice and banditry and far from strictly judicious. An early outlaw and occasional troublemaker, he both administered and faced the wrath of the law. He rendered his verdicts from the same room where he distributed liquor: in a courtroom, saloon, and billiard hall where he presided as judge, jury, and bartender. He had only three months of formal education and little knowledge of textbook law, but that did not prevent him from handing out flamboyant, inconsistent rulings. His colorful style of law generated countless legends and stories, many of which are still debated today.

Born in Kentucky around 1825, Roy Bean left home at age 16 to follow his two older brothers, Joshua and Sam, westward. He met up with his brother Sam in San Antonio, Texas. They organized a large trading expedition into Mexico in 1848 and then decided to stay in Chihuahua, where they opened a saloon and trading post. The venture lasted until Roy killed a Mexican outlaw who tried to rob the store. The threat of retaliation by the outlaw's mob and the local law forced Roy to flee for California.

In 1849 he joined up with his other brother, Joshua, in California. Joshua also owned a successful saloon and would later become the first mayor of San Diego. In February 1852, however, Roy landed in jail after dueling with a Frenchman jealous of his popularity with women. Lady friends smuggled him knives inside hot tamales; Roy used them to escape from jail in April. By this time, Joshua had opened another saloon and gladly accepted his escaped brother's help. Roy spent the greater part of his time working in the bar, but he also went on an occasional bandit chase with the California Rangers. About two years later, the third party of a love triangle murdered Joshua, leaving Roy in control of the saloon. In 1859, after a turbulent relationship with a local señorita, Roy left for New Mexico, where brother Sam served as sheriff.

In 1863 Roy moved back to San Antonio, where he married and fathered four or five children. He made a less-than-honest living with several shady practices, earning his San Antonio neighborhood the name "Beanville." He sold firewood, which he appropriated from land without the consent of the owner. He sold milk, which he watered down with river water. That scheme worked for some time, until a customer found a minnow in the milk. Roy exclaimed, "By Gobs, that's what I get for waterin' them cows down at the river." Before long, however, his marriage turned sour, and he left San Antonio.

Roy headed for Vinegaroon, Texas, where the railroad had brought hundreds of workers together in a tent city near the confluence of the Rio Grande and Pecos River. He set up a tent and began selling liquor and goods to the workers. Roy drank a lot of his own stock and was often disorderly, so he fit right in with the rough laborers. It is here that the legend of Roy as a judge begins. One story claims that he simply set himself up as the justice of the peace for the area without any authority. In truth, however, his role as a judge came about because of the isolated, rowdy frontier atmosphere of Vinegaroon. The nearest courtroom stood a week's ride away. Hoping to establish some form of justice, authorities appointed Bean justice of the peace for Precinct 6, Pecos County, Texas, on 2 August 1882. He moved to Langtry, a nearby settlement that he later claimed to have named for his favorite actress, Lillie Langtry. With the exception of a single term, the citizens continually reelected Roy from 1882 until 1902.

Langtry was little more than a tent city when Roy moved there. It did not take long, however, before Roy built the Jersey Lilly saloon, which he did name for Lillie Langtry. Declaring himself "The Law West of the Pecos," he began distributing his unorthodox brand of justice.

Judge Roy Bean's courthouse and saloon

The Jersey Lilly also housed a saloon and billiard hall.

The signs on the building boldly proclaimed THE JERSEY LILLY, JUDGE ROY BEAN, JUSTICE OF THE PEACE, LAW WEST OF THE PECOS, BILLIARD HALL, and WHISKEY AND BEER. Bean used the legal system to acquire the signs: When a sign painter came to town, Bean supplied him with drinks, arrested him for public drunkenness, and tied him up. The judge sentenced the painter to two days of hard labor, which translated into the signs he wanted.

The courtroom occupied the east end of the building; there were two poker tables in the middle and a bar on the west end. The court furnishings included a rough table, the judge's law book sitting on a beer keg, and three benches. Bean liked control and seldom used a jury, saying he would add an extra bench if he ever felt a jury was necessary. Banging his pistol like a gavel, he brought court to order with proclamations such as "Order, by Gobs! This honorable court is now in session; and any galoot that wants a snort before we start, let him step up to the bar and name his pizen" (Watson 1998). He kept his pet bear Bruno in court just for good measure; the animal was supposedly renowned as a beer drinker.

Bean used a single law book, *The Revised Statutes of Texas, 1879,* for all his rulings. The state of Texas sent him a new book every year, but he used them to start fires. Bean commonly justified his rulings in a very arbitrary manner. "It is the judgment of this court that you are hereby tried and convicted of illegally and unlawfully committing certain grave offenses against the peace and dignity of the State of Texas, particularly in my bailiwick. I fine you two dollars; get the hell out of here and never show yourself in this court again. That's my rulin'" (Watson 1998). A Bean sentence might range from hanging to buying drinks for all in attendance; it generally benefited the accused to buy drinks for everyone anyway.

Judge Bean kept no records of his cases and permitted no appeals. According to one story, a man from San Antonio once tried to appeal a fine. The judge listened to his speech, then laid his pistol on the bar and bluntly replied, "There is no appeal from this court, and that's my rulin'." An affluent lawyer once requested that Bean issue a writ of habeas corpus. Instead of complying, Bean threatened to hang the man for using foul language. He fined people for almost any offense and kept the money, explaining that the court had to be self-sufficient. When Bean got complaints from the capital about not turning in the proper portion of the fees, he sent a curt response to Texas's governor, Stephen Hogg: "Dear Governor, You run things in Austin and I'll run them down here. Yours Truly, Roy Bean."

One of Bean's favorite ploys to get money involved the train traffic through Langtry. Bean strategically positioned his saloon so that passengers, thirsty from the long ride, could come in and get a quick drink. He quickly served the customers but took his time in making change. When the train whistle sounded, people vociferously demanded their change. Bean immediately found them guilty of using foul language in his court and fined them the exact amount of change they were due.

People wanted cold drinks because of the heat, so Bean put up a sign that said ICE COLD BEER in order to attract them. He was always "jest out," or he would put a lump of glass in the tumbler to deceive his buyers.

Bean rendered one of his most famous verdicts against a corpse. A worker fell off a bridge and died. Bean was called to examine the dead body. He immediately confiscated the corpse's pistol "for the use of the court." He also fined the corpse the amount of money found on it, $40, for carrying a concealed weapon. Stories diverge on the outcome: Bean either kept the money or gave it to the dead man's friends to bury him.

Some historians labeled Bean "the Hanging Judge," but that title more appropriately belongs to Isaac Charles **Parker.** Other sources labeled Bean with the slogan "Hang 'em first, try 'em later." According to historian Jack Skiles, however, Bean's cases, with the exception of an occasional murder, generally dealt with minor misdemeanors. Although he sentenced a few people to hang, Bean secretly allowed even these to escape. Perhaps Bean's best-known claim to fame was his adoration of actress Lillie Langtry. The town of Langtry had already been named, for a railroad boss before Bean arrived. Nevertheless, the judge steadfastly insisted he had named the town in honor of Lillie. He did name his bar, the "Jersey Lilly," for her, and he named his home across the street "The Opera House" in anticipation that she would one day perform there. He hung a tattered picture of Lillie in the bar and reportedly offered many a toast to her. A man once dared to challenge Bean's assertion that Lillie was the prettiest woman in the world. The critic even added that he thought she looked "like a range heifer." The infuriated judge arrested the man for slander and fined him $20 for the incident. When a cow thief came before the court and mentioned that he had seen Miss Langtry perform, Bean pardoned him in exchange for describing the actress's performance.

Although he never met Lillie Langtry, Bean often bragged of their mythical relationship. He went to San Antonio once to see her perform and was supposed to meet the actress afterward. However, the terrified admirer could not bring himself to go backstage to meet her. He admired her from afar and even subscribed to theatrical publications so that he could get additional pictures and news. He wrote to her often and invited her to Langtry; some stories say she even wrote back. Supposedly, when Bean sent word that he had named the Jersey Lilly after her, Lillie was so touched that she offered to put up a drinking fountain in the town square. Bean wrote back that he thought it was a bad idea. Although he was appreciative, Bean said that "if there's anything these hombres of Langtry don't drink, it's water."

In early 1904 Miss Langtry finally decided to accept the judge's offer and visit the city he had supposedly named for her. When she stepped off the train, the townspeople of Langtry, dressed in their finest, greeted her and honored her with a reception. Unfortunately, Roy Bean had died ten months before. Lillie stayed in Langtry long enough to hear stories about the judge's antics and judicial style as well as about his fascination for her. When she left, the townspeople felt moved to offer her Roy's pistol and his pet bear. Although the bear escaped, Lillie cherished the pistol for the rest of her life. She later wrote how much she wished that Roy had been alive when she visited.

Roy's work to promote a world championship boxing match added to his legend. Peter Maher held the world title for prizefighting, though he had received the title without a fight. Bob Fitzsimmons challenged his claim, and promoter Dan Stuart arranged the fight in Arkansas. Arkansas prohibited the fight, so Stuart moved the fight to El Paso, Texas. However, the Texas governor had outlawed prizefighting in the state, and Congress followed suit by banning it in all federal territories.

The ever-resourceful Bean offered to hold the fight in Langtry. When the train arrived, packed with fans and unwanted lawmen, Bean served drinks at the Jersey Lilly and then led the crowd down to the Rio Grande. He had made a makeshift ring on a sandbar in the river, with a bridge made of beer kegs and scrap lumber leading to it. The fight took place 21 February 1896, outside of American jurisdiction and two days from the nearest Mexican soldier. The **Texas Rangers** could do little more than watch helplessly from a bluff as Fitzsimmons flattened Maher in 95 seconds. Afterward, everyone returned to the Jersey Lilly for beers at a dollar apiece, and reporters sent newspaper reports across the nation. Those present called the judge "the cleverest man in Texas," and he became known nationwide.

As Bean's fame grew, so did the myths surrounding him. Many newspaper articles and dime novels featured his antics. In the movie *Streets of Laredo* and in the Larry McMurtry novel of the same name, Bean meets his fate on the steps of his courthouse, dying by a Mexican outlaw's bullet. The story could not be further from the truth. In 1903 Bean went on a drinking binge in nearby Del Rio. His son

Sam and other friends found him the next day nearly in a coma. He died shortly after.

The legend of Roy Bean lives on, however, in films such as *The Ballad of Judge Roy Bean.* Walter Brennan won an Oscar playing Roy Bean in *The Westerner,* which costarred Gary Cooper. In the movie, Bean fights against injustice and is shot and killed backstage at the feet of Lillie Langtry. In 1956 Edgar Buchanan played Bean in a weekly television series. Paul Newman played the judge in a 1972 movie, *The Life and Times of Judge Roy Bean.* Newman shoots and hangs with abandon, and dies amid a barrage of bullets, shouting "For Texas, and Miss Lillie!" History buffs and tourists from across the world visit the Judge Roy Bean Visitor Center, marveling at his refinished courtroom, pool hall, and saloon; his cactus garden; and other exhibits. Imitation is a sincere form of flattery: Another Jersey Lilly Saloon can be found in Ignomar, Montana, selling **mountain oysters** and other western delicacies.

–*Kaleb J. Redden*

References

Benningfield, Damond. "The Boxing Championship That Wasn't." *American West* 23, no. 1 (1986): 63–65.

Robbins, Peggy. "Law West of the Pecos." *American History Illustrated* 8, no. 4 (1973): 12–22.

Watson, Bruce. "Hang 'Em Now, Try 'Em Later." *Smithsonian* 29, no. 3 (1998): 96–107.

Source of Further Information

"Judge Roy Bean": *http://www.judgeroybean. com/jrbhistory.html.*

BECKWOURTH, JIM

1798 OR 1800–1866 OR 1867

Born a slave in Virginia, Jim Beckwourth became one of the earliest legendary mountain men. A mulatto, he was the son of Sir Jennings Beckwith, a white slaveholder, and a mulatto slave woman. His father took him to Louisiana Territory in 1810 and then on to St. Louis. His father apparently manumitted him, for Jim Beckwourth appears in records thereafter as a "free Negro." However, according to another version, the youth fled west after striking a blacksmith to whom he was apprenticed.

In 1823 Beckwourth signed on with a fur-trading expedition. The following year, he worked, handling horses, for Gen. William Ashley's expedition to the Rocky Mountains. His penchant for exaggerating greatly inflated his importance in his later stories. He took up trapping, and over the next few years, he learned the skills of a mountain man. Perhaps because his facial features somewhat resembled those of a Native American, he felt at home in the frontier West. According to his own tale, the Crow captured him, then insisted he was the long-lost son of Chief Big Bowl. They adopted him into the tribe. Beginning in 1828, he lived for at least six years among the Crow Indians. He married a series of Indian women, possibly as many as ten. He served as an important cultural broker, and as a result, white traders got profitable furs and Indians got needed goods. He later related stories of his great strength and prowess, and no one could contradict his tales. He often said, "My faithful battle-axe was red with the blood of the enemy."

The mountain man returned to white society in 1833, presumably leaving behind his Indian wives and any children he may have fathered. He retained Indian dress and hair braids, which added to his exotic persona. He worked at various jobs, including as a muleteer, trader on the Santa Fe trail, and saloon keeper. In April 1850 he again showed his frontier skills by locating a pass through the Sierra Nevada near what is now the California-Nevada state line northwest of Reno. His wagon road opened a way for migrants to reach the California goldfields. Beckwourth maintained a ranch and way station on the trail summit at the mountain pass that now bears his name. A nearby peak, valley, and town also memorialize his contributions.

In 1854 a traveler named Thomas D. Bonner stopped by the inn. The man listened intently to Beckwourth's recollections and inventions of frontier life. Two years later, Harper and Row published the resulting book: *The Life and Adventures of James P. Beckwourth, Mountaineer, Scout, and Pioneer, and Chief of the Crow Nation of Indians.* (The University of Nebraska Press reissued the book in 1972.) Those stories marked the beginning of the Beckwourth legend. Bonner even changed the spelling of the hero's name from its original Beckwith.

Beckwourth fought briefly in the Mexican War and then returned to Missouri for a time. The lure of Colorado silver strikes in 1859 pulled him back west. Not striking it rich, he returned to the frontier skills of his youth. The U.S. Cavalry hired him during the Cheyenne War of 1864. He probably worked as a guide and interpreter. He accompanied Colorado troops during the infamous Sand Creek Massacre, although his exact role remains unclear. He then settled near Denver. Like much of his life, his death is also shrouded in mystery and myth. He may have died in 1866 while visiting Crow Indians. Some versions attribute his demise to a hunting accident. Others argue that death came from poison administered by a vengeful former wife or by Crow who believed he had earlier brought smallpox to their village. Another version suggests accidental food poisoning. Still other sources place his death the following year, near Denver.

Beckwourth's mixed ethnicity has probably contributed to his reputation as a liar. White "experts" could simply not cope with black heroes. Annotating his copy of Bonner's book, nineteenth-century historian Francis Parkman wrote "much of this narrative is probably false." He added, tellingly, "Beckwith is a fellow of bad character—a compound of white and black blood." Gen. William Tecumseh Sherman recorded a contradictory reaction to Beckwourth after meeting him in 1848. He termed the mountain man "one of the best chroniclers of events on the plains that I have encountered, though his reputation for veracity was not good."

According to historian Kenneth W. Porter, Beckwourth would "be regarded rather as a great liar than as a great 'mountain man.'" Thanks to a more recent, careful biographer, Elinor Wilson, Beckwourth's reputation has been somewhat improved. We learn from Wilson that some of Beckwourth's incredible tales appear to be true. A skilled western raconteur, he amplified his own role in events. Although he also sometimes added entertaining elements to amuse the listener, he mostly recounted actual events. Had Beckwourth been white, he would surely rank among the well-known heroes of the frontier West. As one of the first mountain men to have his experiences published, he contributed substantially to Rocky Mountain ethnography and frontier history. Marysville, California, celebrates Beckwourth Frontier Days the first weekend in October at Beckwourth Riverfront Park.

References

"James Pierson Beckwourth": *http://www.beckwourth.org.*

Wilson, Elinor. *Jim Beckwourth: Black Mountain Man and War Chief of the Crows.* Norman: University of Oklahoma Press, 1972.

BEMIS, POLLY

1852–1933

Polly Bemis's Chinese origins destined her to be ridiculed and discriminated against her entire life. Nevertheless, she conquered the racism of the American West, marrying and settling down on a homestead along the Salmon River in Idaho. Her neighbors described her as an independent, good-humored woman, well loved by her community. Her fellow pioneers appreciated her skill at nursing and healing the sick. She served as a role model for other women of her race as she farmed in Idaho as she had in China.

Born in 1852, Lalu Nathoy lived with her poor family on their farm in China. Some sources say a famine forced her fa-

ther to sell her to bandits for nothing more than a bag of seed. Lalu arrived in America in the early 1870s, where a Chinese man bought her for $2,500. Upon her arrival in Idaho, Lalu took the name Polly Bemis. In 1872 she began living as a slave and concubine to an old Chinese man. Labeling Polly a "prostitute," as some sources do, is inappropriate. In Chinese tradition, concubines were legal, recognized members of the family. Some owners of concubines profited by sharing their female slaves with other men, but we have no direct evidence that Polly's owner did so.

According to legend, a white man named Charlie Bemis won Polly in a poker game. Both Polly and her close friend J. A. Czizek, vehemently denied this rumor. In an alternate story line, the old Chinese man died, leaving her free. In any case, Polly lived with Charlie during the census of 1880, though they did not marry until 1894. She performed surgery on Charlie in September 1890, removing bullet shards he had acquired during a "gambling affray." She saved his life again by rescuing him from a burning cabin. Their homestead on the Salmon River became her beloved home. She wished to be buried where she could still hear the river's roaring water. Polly Bemis died in 1933 in Idaho, and she is buried near her river.

Ruthanne Lum McCunn used details of Polly Bemis's life for her 1981 historical novel, *Thousand Pieces of Gold*. In China, people refer to others' daughters as their "thousand pieces of gold." Lalu's father calls her his "thousand pieces of gold" to reassure her when she fears she will be sold. McCunn paints a picture of a girl in China whose community reduces her to a stereotype of her sex and of a woman in America whose community oppresses her as a stereotype of her heritage. Lalu's mother complains of her working on the farm instead of marrying and raising children. Men in America treat her as a slave and prostitute, ignoring her worth as a woman and a human being. By defying these views and becoming successful as a respected farming wife in Idaho, Lalu proves herself as a woman of fortitude, determination, and spirit.

Polly Bemis was childless, and in the novel, Charlie discusses with Polly her choice not to have children. McCunn's treatment of this issue is mere speculation, since records do not explain why she had no children. McCunn did add to Lalu's life, however. Several fictional characters embellish the novel, including two men with whom the fictional Polly has romantic relationships. One is the bandit Ding, who originally buys her from her father. The other is Jim, the man who buys her in America at the auction and whose heart Polly breaks. Polly's only historical recorded romance is with her husband, Charlie, although her role as a slave and concubine involved other relationships.

A movie adaptation of *Thousand Pieces of Gold* came out in 1991, telling Polly's story again for a much wider audience. Dennis Dunn plays Jim, the young Chinese man who purchased Polly, and Rosalind Chao plays Polly. The movie, directed by Nancy Kelly, also stars Michael Paul Chan as Hong King, an old Chinese saloon keeper, and Chris Cooper as the kind-hearted Charlie Bemis. Lalu is a fiercely independent and determined woman in the movie, creating a life for herself in the West. The real-life Polly Bemis is always described as a very kind and happy woman, full of vitality, but not as fiery as the movie implies. Her example as a determined woman remains true in both contexts, and this determination is the most important lesson to learn from her life, at first traumatic, but ultimately full of contentment.

Polly and Charlie Bemis's ranch on the Salmon River remains a popular attraction for tourists, and river tours include it on their stops. The site is now only accessible by jet ski or jet boat, thus limiting the number of visitors. Recently, Chinese history has been receiving more attention from the public, yielding more research and books. Chinese American history is becoming a popular field of study, and Polly Bemis occupies a special place in it. An illustrated children's book of her life is under way, as is a young-adult book describing her life.

Several stories, from Oregon and Hawaii, of other women mirror Polly's story. Like Polly, these women used their knowledge of Chinese herbs to establish themselves in their communities, not as slaves, but as valued women. Polly Bemis well exemplifies women's struggles in the pioneer West. She represents the strength associated with the rugged individuals who met the challenges of the western frontier. She was inducted into the Idaho Hall of Fame in August 1996.

—*Ellen J. Oettinger*

References

Cheung, King-Kok. "Self-fulfilling Visions in *The Woman Warrior* and *Thousand Pieces of Gold." Biography* 3, no. 2 (1990).

Ling, Huping. *Surviving on the Gold Mountain: A History of Chinese American Women and Their Lives.* Albany: State University of New York, 1998.

McCunn, Ruthanne Lum. *Thousand Pieces of Gold: A Biographical Novel.* San Francisco: Design Enterprises of San Francisco, 1981.

Wegars, Priscilla. "Polly Bemis": *http://www.u idaho.edu/LS/AACC/research.htm#Polly.*

BENTEEN, FREDERICK W.

1834–1898, soldier. *See* Little Big Horn

BENTON, JESSE ANN

1824–1902, wife of John Charles Frémont. *See* Frémont, John Charles

BICYCLE CORPS

In the 1890s, amid a national bicycle craze, the U.S. Army experimented with outfitting an infantry unit with bicycles. Black troops of the Twenty-Fifth Infantry Regiment in Missoula, Montana, rode bicycles over long distances. Although the tests succeeded, rapid advances in the development of the internal combustion engine meant that mechanized trucks and jeeps, not bicycles, would be the army's future.

Bicycles had two big boosters in the army at the time, Second Lt. James A. Moss, commander of the Twenty-Fifth, and Maj. Gen. Nelson A Miles. They convinced the army brass to mount 20 infantrymen on bicycles. In July 1896 the bicycle corps took its first long ride, ped-aling north 126 miles to Lake McDonald and back. During the three-day outing they encountered the full gamut of Montana weather—heavy rains and strong winds—as well as deep mud and steep grades. They suffered punctured tires, broken pedals, and loose rims and chains. The corps gained valuable experience for the following month's even more challenging test.

The next test came in August 1896 when the Twenty-Fifth bicycled from Fort Missoula to Fort Yellowstone in ten days and then back. Despite rough roads and difficult weather, they made the 800-mile round trip, managing to cover 72 miles on their best day. Old photographs show the troops riding around Old Faithful and other Yellowstone Park sites.

The famed artist Frederic **Remington** observed the bicycle corps on maneuvers. Writing in *Cosmopolitan* magazine (February 1897), he noted that "in the colored regiments their first sergeants are all old soldiers—thirty years and upward in the frontier service. What will be done to replace them when they expire is the question; or rather nothing will be done. Their like will never come again, because the arduous conditions which produced them can never re-occur, unless you let me be secretary of war and burn the barracks" (Remington 1897).

The bicycle corps's longer test came during June and July of the following year. They rode 1,900 miles over 41 days from Missoula to St. Louis, Missouri. Two white officers, a Montana journalist named Ed Boos, and 20 black troops made the epic trek. Pvt. John Findley ably made repairs to keep the bicycles functioning. They rode single-gear Spalding bikes, with no fenders but with sturdier metal rather than wooden rims. Each man strapped some 55 pounds of supplies on the bicycle and also carried a ten-pound rifle. Hail pummeled the troops as they entered Wyoming.

The odd spectacle of bicycling black troops attracted great curiosity in the mostly white western towns on their route. Occasionally, contingencies of the League of American Wheelmen rode out to greet them. Mud often clogged the wheels, so the men pushed or carried their bikes. Rain and snow pelted them in the mountains, and they often rode into stiff head winds.

The plains brought no relief. In western Nebraska, 110-degree weather, choking sand, and alkali desert greeted them. Even though sickened by alkali fumes, they still managed to ride 35 miles per day. Conscious of their importance as role models, these troops gamely met and surmounted hunger, illness, and horrendous conditions. In Crawford, Nebraska, they joined the town's celebratory Fourth of July parade.

At 6 P.M. on 24 July, they pedaled wearily into a suburb of St. Louis. Lieutenant Moss gave the welcome order "Rest your wheels." The men had averaged 55 miles per day, moving at half the cost and twice the speed of a walking infantry unit. A follow-up ride from Missoula to San Francisco planned for 1898 never occurred, for war broke out in Cuba.

The Twenty-Fifth fought against Spanish troops in the Cuban campaign, but they fought as conventional infantry, not as bicycle troops. They supported the attacks at El Caney and San Juan Hill that made Theodore Roosevelt and his Rough Riders national heroes. Regrettably, the Twenty-Fifth would have a second, more-unfortunate encounter with Roosevelt, now president, in 1906. Unfairly accused of some shootings in Brownsville, Texas, the Twenty-Fifth and some 100 other black troops were dishonorably discharged by the president.

The tale of the Twenty-Fifth has a happier ending. In 1973 the government reversed the dishonorable discharges against the black soldiers. The following year, a group of African Americans recreated their epic ride across the Great Plains.

References

Remington, Frederic. "Vagabonding with the Tenth Horse." *Cosmopolitan,* February 1897. Reprinted in Remington, Frederic. *The Collected Writings of Frederic Remington.* Edited by Peggy and Harold Samuels. N.p.: Castle, 1986.

Schmitzer, Jeanne Cannella. "Twenty-Fifth Infantry Bicycle Corps." American History Online: *http://www.exocet.com/yellowjackets/bikecorp.htm.*

BIGFOOT OR SASQUATCH

Since the early nineteenth century, scores of people in the Northwest have reported encounters with unusually large, bipedal beasts with hair covering nearly all of their bodies. Hundreds of reports generally agree that these creatures measure between 7 and 12 feet tall, weigh between 700 and 1,000 pounds, and have broad shoulders, flat faces and noses, sloped foreheads, pronounced eyebrow ridges, cone-shaped heads, humanlike limbs, glowing eyes of various colors, and fur color ranging from reddish-brown, black, and beige to white. Large statues in Benbow, California, and Vermillion Bay, Ontario, Canada, provide two artists' conceptions of the animal. These mysterious beasts, which we have come to know as Bigfoot or Sasquatch, have become a fixture in the folklore of the American West. Many folks, including eyewitnesses, investigators, and a handful of scientists, argue that Bigfoot is real, that he has been lurking about our national forests right under our noses. In fact, many Native American peoples wonder what took the rest of us so long to recognize Bigfoot's existence.

Native American legends have spun tales of giant, upright, forest-dwelling beasts for centuries. Algonkian Indians of the Midwest know Bigfoot as Witiko or Wendigo; they describe the animal as a cannibalistic giant with supernatural powers. The Huppa of the Klamath Mountains in northern California tell stories of the Omah, and the Skagit Indians of northern Washington believe in Kala'litabiqw, a spirit that has moss growing on its head and can cross the Cascade Mountains in a single stride. Other northwestern tribes tell tales of Steta'l, mountain giants that kidnap children. Even records of Spanish priests from the late eighteenth century reveal accounts of gargantuan, nocturnal, cannibalistic beasts covered with hair from head to toe.

But what about more recent sightings of this elusive animal? Descriptions of a large, wild, forest-dwelling creature first appeared in local newspapers in the late nineteenth century. Eyewitnesses in California reported a sighting of a five-foot-

tall reddish-brown creature that whistled and played with sticks from a hunter's fire. Another notable incident occurred in 1924 in Oregon, when four prospectors claimed that after they spied and shot at a seven-foot-tall apelike animal, a number of these creatures laid siege to their cabin, hurling rocks and beating on the walls throughout the night. Today this site is known as Ape Canyon. In 1958 Bigfoot became known nationally after a road crew in northern California discovered trails of 16-inch-long footprints. Investigators made plaster casts of the prints. When the Associated Press got wind of and printed the story, along with a photograph of the casts, the tale of the mysterious beast that reporters dubbed "Bigfoot" spread across the nation, and the mythical creature became an instant celebrity. The name stuck.

Many scientists immediately dismissed Bigfoot as either an elaborate hoax or a misidentified species. Nevertheless, once this enigmatic creature, also referred to as "America's abominable snowman," became the subject of widespread media attention, many folks began to sit up and take notice. Several curious investigators, such as Bigfoot authorities John Green and René Dahinden, began to interview witnesses, collect data, and write articles and books about their findings. The conundrum also caught the attention of a man named Roger Patterson. Patterson eagerly roamed the woods of the Pacific Northwest, camera in hand, hoping he could capture the now-famous creature on film in order to prove its existence. In 1967, while searching for Bigfoot in northern California, Patterson claimed to have gotten his wish. He shot 28 feet of film of a female Bigfoot from three different angles. Debate over the authenticity of the film swiftly followed and still rages today.

Scientists who dispute the authenticity of the Patterson film, such as John Napier, claim that in the film, Bigfoot's gait was suspiciously self-conscious and that the upper half of the body was abnormally rigid. For example, the creature did not turn its head when it moved to look at the camera; it had to pivot at the hips, as if its movements were restricted by a cheap, uncomfortable costume. Also, the length of the stride was inconsistent with the footprint size (footprints were later uncovered at the site). Moreover, the beast had a male body form but female breasts, an odd contradiction. Patterson himself was not sure of the speed on which his camera was set at the time of filming. This uncertainty poses a problem because the speed helps determine whether the creature's gait was like that of a human or not. Also, some investigators claim to see a metal fastener on the beast's chest in enlargements of the prints, although Bigfoot believers bitterly dispute this assertion, claiming the object in question is nothing more incriminating than light reflecting off a monster's fur.

Still, a number of scientists believe there is something to the Bigfoot phenomenon. Grover Krantz is an anthropologist at Washington State University who nearly lost his job over his investigations of Bigfoot. He believes that giant primates from the Old World migrated to North America thousands of years ago. Bigfoot represents their modern-day descendants. Investigators like Krantz find it difficult to ignore the hundreds of consistent reports of sightings and footprints, not to mention the large body of data gathered: casts, photographs, feces and hair near discovered tracks, audio tapes of Bigfoot vocalizations, and the Patterson film. Some have even attempted to describe the social organization, or lack thereof, of Bigfoot and to estimate the number of these creatures. Thousands may live in the wilds of North America. Bigfoot studies have received research grants, universities have sponsored Bigfoot conferences, researchers have published Bigfoot articles in scholarly journals, and there is even a research center devoted to the creatures, the Bigfoot Information Center in The Dalles, Oregon.

Many other sightings have occurred since the famous Patterson encounter. Most notably, in 1982 a U.S. Forest Service patrolman claimed to have spotted an approximately eight-foot-tall, 800-pound Bigfoot in the Umatilla National Forest, which extends across northeastern Oregon and southeastern Washington. Investigators made casts of the tracks left behind. Krantz studied the casts of the highly detailed footprints and deemed them credible. He believes that the prints are genuine and that they reveal the following: The animal is flat-footed and has no arch to its foot, which is consistent with the creature's enormous weight; the prints were pressed deeply into the ground, which supports the idea that a heavy animal made them; and the casts reflect complex skin patterns that suggest an animal that is neither ape nor human. Investigators found no human tracks near the site.

Those who contest the evidence claim the prints must be a hoax. They cite the following evidence: The stride never varied, the prints were not deep enough into the ground to coincide with the animal's estimated weight, and the prints looked as if someone had deliberately rocked the creature's foot from side to side. Skeptics also doubted the patrolman's credibility. During a subsequent interview, he admitted to having falsified the prints.

Despite substantial evidence to the contrary, true believers in Sasquatch persist. Many Web sites and books are devoted to Bigfoot. The existence of a number of organizations (such as the Western Bigfoot Society), documentary films (such as *Manbeast*), and newsletters (such as *Big Foot News,* with a circulation of about 10,000) attest to the continuing appeal of Bigfoot. Hollywood has cashed in on the legend, making movies like *Harry and the Hendersons* and *Legend of Boggy Creek.* In 1995 the movie *Bigfoot: The Unforgettable Encounter* presented a very sympathetic character. In the movie, Bigfoot, aided by a boy named Cody (the most popular western boy's name of the 1990s), eluded the bad guys and retired to a wildlife sanctuary.

Tabloids have published stories in which women tell of their torrid love affairs with the mysterious beasts. And beware if you are planning to slay a Bigfoot in Skamania County, Washington: There is a $10,000 fine for killing the elusive, hairy beast.

So is Bigfoot real? Is a reclusive colony of Bigfoot (or is that Bigfeet?) laughing at us somewhere in the wilderness? Or are we the butts of an elaborate hoax that has endured for centuries? One can only imagine how society would react if we do locate the creature someday. The primate would probably face the bleak prospect of either confinement in a zoo, endless testing in research facilities, or guest appearances on *The Jerry Springer Show.*

–*Jane Veronica Charles Smith*

References

Clark, Jerome, and Nancy Pear, eds. *Strange and Unexplained Phenomena.* New York: Visible Ink Press, 1997.

Gordon, David George. *Field Guide to the Sasquatch.* Seattle, WA: Sasquatch Books, 1992.

Shackley, Myra. *Wildmen: Yeti, Sasquatch, and the Neanderthal Enigma.* Chichester, Sussex: Thames and Hudson, 1983.

BILLY THE KID

1859?–1881

Of all the tales of the West, perhaps none so captures the minds of Americans and of people worldwide as the tale of Billy the Kid, the boy gunslinger. In terms of historical significance, Billy pales in comparison to many other western figures. As a result, most scholars spend little energy on the Kid, and some resent the public's fascination with him.

Nevertheless, well over a century after his death, public obsession with Billy the Kid as an icon of the West continues unabated. The reason is simple: What the Kid lacks historically, he makes up in legend. Indeed, his transformation into a notorious western myth stems largely from the lack of certain historical data about his life. Images of him range from a cold-blooded villain to the Robin Hood of the West. The Billy the Kid that most people "know" is imaginary.

Born Henry McCarty, he used many aliases, going by William "Billy" Bonney, William Antrim, Kid Antrim, and, of course, Billy the Kid. Myth surrounds his life right from his birth. He was probably born in New York, but other claimants include Missouri, Illinois, Indiana, Ohio, and Kansas. Some sources depict the Kid as a short, ugly, uneducated bandit. In fact, he was educated and literate. He wrote several letters asking for pardon to Lew Wallace, governor of New Mexico at the time (and author of *Ben Hur*). Billy spoke both Spanish and English, and according to some sources, he exhibited both intelligence and a good sense of humor. He stood about five feet, seven inches tall, average height for his time. Despite his crooked teeth, many women seemed to find him charming.

Billy's life of crime inspires even more discrepancies. At its grandest, the number of men he shot is said to reach as high as 27. By far the most common statistic of folklore holds that Billy killed 21 men, one for every year of his life. Historical records confirm only four deaths, and the Kid's defenders argue that he killed only in self-defense.

Legend says Billy claimed his first victim at 12 years of age in defense of his mother. The more likely story is that he killed his first man at age 17, when a bully sat on him and beat him up. Some sources indicate that Billy the Kid met Jesse **James** and turned down an offer to join his gang.

Records indicate that Sheriff Pat Garrett killed Billy in Fort Sumner, New Mexico, in 1881. However, some 20 men claimed to be the Kid later in life. Most famous among these was Brushy Bill Roberts, who claimed he had escaped Garrett's bullets and hidden and who

later rode in Buffalo Bill's Wild West Show. Although many researchers argue strongly against this case, the legends persist.

Billy the Kid became the subject of more than 40 movies, ranging from serious to ridiculous and even obscene. *Billy the Kid, aka The Highwayman, Rides* came out in 1930. Shot on location in Lincoln County, New Mexico, the movie had a romanticized plot that portrayed Billy as a rebel hero. Interestingly enough, actor John Mack Brown, who played Billy, supposedly used the outlaw's actual guns during filming.

Billy the Kid Returns, which appeared eight years later, put a new twist on the old legends. Filled with music and action, the film starred Roy **Rogers** as a Billy the Kid look-alike. The hero used his physical similarities to return law and order to Lincoln County after the real Billy the Kid had died.

Two more-recent incarnations include *Pat Garrett and Billy the Kid,* directed by Sam Peckinpah, and *The Left Handed Gun,* starring Paul Newman. Many critics consider the former to be the best and most accurate interpretation of Billy's story. The Kid, played by Kris Kristofferson, wanders aimlessly across the Southwest, while Pat Garrett serves the somewhat corrupted law. The movie ends with Garrett shooting Billy, then shooting his own reflection, indicating his sense of betrayal to self.

The Left Handed Gun marks the evolution of the Kid's character from one of either evil or romantic extremes to that of an illiterate victim of circumstance. It also served to reinforce the myth that Billy was left-handed, a claim that most research now indicates is false. Someone mistakenly printed an old photograph of

Billy with the negative reversed, giving rise to the error.

In 1988 Billy returned to the cinema in *Young Guns* and *Young Guns II*. The former reprises Roy Rogers's portrayal of Billy as a young hero. His gang plays a larger role than in earlier films. *Young Guns II* shifts emphasis back toward the interpretations taken by *The Left Handed Gun* and *Pat Garrett and Billy the Kid*. It even revives the legend that Pat Garrett did not kill Billy the Kid, as it opens with an old man claiming to be Billy, who then tells the story.

Billy the Kid versus Dracula, a bizarre treatment, came out in 1965 and acquired a cult following. In addition to this cross-cultural exchange of legendary figures, the Kid has also appeared on screen with Mickey Mouse. In *The Beard*, Billy had a fantasy fling with Jean Harlow that won an Obie award and generated an obscenity trial.

Billy the Kid also emerges as a character in both music and theater. In the country music industry, which often highlights the West, artist Billy Dean uses Billy the Kid to contrast modern life to the ways of the past. His song "Billy the Kid" reached number one on country music charts, with a chorus of "I miss Billy the Kid, the times that he had, the life that he led." Jon Bon Jovi sings on the soundtrack from *Young Guns II,* and Bob Dylan appears on the soundtrack from *Pat Garrett and Billy the Kid.* Billy the Kid is also the name of a band, and he is the subject of works by many amateur and professional songwriters around the world.

Aaron **Copland,** one of America's premier composers, wrote a ballet suite about Billy. Described as "quintessentially American," it remains one of Copland's best-known works. Copland composed the suite after America suffered through the Great Depression and World War II. With this theme from popular culture, he tried to reach out to a wider audience, to uplift people's spirits in times of trouble. In doing so, he introduced themes and myths of the West to the cultured world of symphony and ballet.

In New Mexico, the heart of Billy the Kid country, interest in him remains high. The Billy the Kid Outlaw Gang, a nonprofit organization, strives to "preserve, protect and promote Billy the Kid/Pat Garrett history in New Mexico." The gang formed in 1987 in response to a museum built in Hico, Texas, that claimed that Brushy Bill Roberts, who died there, was the real Billy the Kid. Today, the gang has more than 400 members, hailing from 43 states and seven countries. They work with state agencies to put up historical markers related to Billy the Kid and to distribute brochures promoting these sites. The New Mexico area is also home to the Billy the Kid scenic byway, featuring many guided tours.

Besides these more-direct influences, the Kid's mythology extends into popular culture and sport. The press will christen almost any successful, young competitor named Billy "Billy the Kid." We find Billy "the Kid" Irwin in boxing; baseball and football players also use the name. In the rising sport of NASCAR, fans call young talent Jeff Gordon "The Kid."

In observations on the tragic shootings at Columbine (Colorado) High School in 1999, some commentators recalled the Kid to shed light on the situation. Some critics asserted that violence among youth stems from satanic music, Nazi worship, or access to bomb-making Web sites. Others, however, countered that the Kid had shot others at a tender age, and he had never heard of Marilyn Manson, Nazis, or the Internet.

Further testimony to Billy's continued presence in the minds of Americans came during a national gun auction held in 1999. A gun collector from Charlotte, North Carolina, paid $46,000 for an 1876 Colt single-action Army Revolver used by Billy the Kid. The gun, which Billy supposedly used to escape from the Lincoln County jail, would have been worth a mere $1,200 if the Kid had not used it. Such a dramatic increase in value reflects Billy the Kid's continuing hold on the American imagination.

—*Kaleb J. Redden*

See also Copland, Aaron; Lincoln County War

References

Kadlec, Robert F., ed. *They "Knew" Billy the Kid: Interviews with Old-Time New Mexicans.* Santa Fe, NM: Ancient City Press, 1987.

Tatum, Steven. *Inventing Billy the Kid: Visions of the Outlaw in America, 1881–1981.* Albuquerque: University of New Mexico Press, 1982.

BINGHAM, GEORGE CALEB

1811–1879

George Caleb Bingham, "the Missouri Artist," is best known for his prosaic, naturalistic portrayal of scenes from the American West. In his nostalgic genre paintings of the midnineteenth century, Bingham depicted a distinct subculture: the hardy, adventuresome boatmen, fur traders, and trappers who braved the Missouri and Mississippi Rivers. By portraying these men engaged in their everyday activities, Bingham effectively captured the spirit of early frontier life in nineteenth-century America. He drew upon his boyhood memories when Missouri was the frontier West, a land yet untamed. Thanks to Bingham, we have a corpus of powerful, romantic images of the rowdy world of "Mike Fink" river men, a vital colorful piece of western legend and lore. (Fink, ca. 1770–1823, became the stereotypical frontier boatman, boastful, hard-drinking, hard-fighting.)

Bingham's family moved from Virginia to Franklin, Missouri, in 1819 when he was only eight years old. He developed a passion for drawing and sketching early on and first earned money by painting portraits in the 1830s. He traveled to Philadelphia to attend the Academy of Fine Arts in 1837 and then moved on to Washington, D.C., for more portrait painting in 1840. He returned to Missouri, where, in 1845, he created his first genre painting in his studio, the *Fur Traders Descending the Missouri*. For this painting Bingham reached back in his memory to the days before the steamboat took over the river and large corporations took over the fur trade. In the painting, a French fur trapper and his "half-breed" son serenely stare straight ahead as they quietly paddle their canoe along the Missouri River. The figures stand out in sharp contrast to the hazy, atmospheric background, which focuses the viewer's attention directly on the trapper and his son. Bingham used muted colors (greens, browns, and yellows) and an almost impressionistic landscape and pensive figures to create a tranquil mood.

Through his series of paintings of flatboatmen, Bingham not only gained recognition as a painter of the western genre but also earned his reputation as "the Missouri Artist." In *The Jolly Flatboatmen* (1846) and *Jolly Flatboatmen in Port* (1857), he portrayed the river men "whooping it up": dancing, fiddling, smoking, drinking, lounging, laughing, and having an all-around good time. Again, muted, muddy coloring; a hazy, atmospheric sky; and sharply etched figures characterize the works. Bingham created a pyramidal composition to focus attention on the high-stepping, happy-go-lucky river man in the center, surrounded by his joyful comrades.

Bingham's river paintings tell a story of what life was like for the early pioneers who roughed it, seeking adventure in the land of the unknown. They portray a romanticized world inhabited by riverboat ruffians who ruled the western waters at the beginning of the nineteenth century. Yet that life had largely disappeared even by the mid-1840s, when Bingham began his riverboat series. Like his contemporary Alfred Jacob **Miller,** Bingham ably captured images that came to symbolize the spirit of the frontier West, before fences, towns, and railroads.

Other paintings in Bingham's repertoire also represent western legend and symbolize the early frontier. One of these is his 1845 painting *The Concealed Enemy.* An Osage Indian, rifle in hand, perches high upon a rocky bluff. He looks as though he is waiting to attack something or someone in the distance.

Although Bingham created only a few works with Indian themes, this painting is important because it depicts a member of an Indian group that frontiersmen forced out of Missouri in the 1830s. *The Concealed Enemy,* then, represents the mythic view of the Indian as an enemy to be cut down. The work both memorializes and glorifies the disappearance of "savages" from the Missouri Territory.

Bingham's *Shooting for the Beef,* painted in 1850, tells the story of what Missouri frontiersmen did for amusement in the early nineteenth century. Men are lining up to take shots at a target attached to a tree. The prize, a fattened steer, is tethered to a cabin marked "grocery/Postoffice" in the background. The best shot got to choose the best portion of the steer (the fifth quarter) to eat after the match. Much whooping and hollering accompanied such events, which Bingham probably recalled from his youth. This painting is important for its evocation of a traditional frontier pastime, once a weekly occurrence, that had begun to fade away by the midnineteenth century. Through his pictorial record of the event, set against the backdrop of a barren frontier land, Bingham was already beginning to establish the nostalgic western tradition of mythmaking.

A final painting worth noting is Bingham's *Daniel Boone Escorting Settlers through the Cumberland Gap,* or *The Emigration of Daniel Boone* (1851). Boone represented the spirit of western exploration and migration, the spirit of the true pioneer. In this historical genre painting, Bingham wished to capture a moment in time out west. Boone calmly yet forcefully leads his family through a dark, threatening wilderness into the unknown territory of Kentucky. The man to Boone's left, toting the ever-present protective rifle, sports a coonskin cap, the well-known symbol of the rugged western adventurer. The painting demonstrates how pioneers sought a new and promising way of life in the West, as well as how they accomplished that feat: by venturing out into the unknown. Bingham's representation of Daniel Boone's exodus reminds us of early western exploration, settlement, and expansion and presents Boone as a noble, courageous hero.

Bingham stopped portraying the western scene in the late 1850s after the Art-Union, an organization that financed his work, became defunct. He returned to his roots as a portrait painter and became heavily involved in both local and state politics. Yet his early work celebrating raw frontier life remains his most important legacy.

Bingham's paintings hang in many galleries and museums throughout the United States. To see *Fur Traders Descending the Missouri,* one only needs to venture to the Metropolitan Museum of Art. *Jolly Flatboatmen in Port* hangs at the St. Louis Art Museum; *The Trapper's Return* is at the Detroit Institute of Arts; and *Daniel Boone Escorting Settlers through the Cumberland Gap* is on display at the Washington University Gallery of Art in St. Louis. However, if a trip to either New York or Missouri is not on the agenda, one can always view the paintings at these museums' Web sites.

—*Jane Veronica Charles Smith*

References

Bloch, E. Maurice. *George Caleb Bingham: The Evolution of an Artist.* Berkeley and Los Angeles: University of California Press, 1967.

Rash, Nancy. *The Painting and Politics of George Caleb Bingham.* New Haven, CT: Yale University Press, 1991.

Rogers, Meyric R., James B. Musick, and Arthur Pope. *Four American Painters: Bingham, Homer, Ryder, and Eakins.* Reprint, New York: Arno Press, 1969.

Sources of Further Information

Detroit Institute of Arts Web Site: *www.dia.org.*

Metropolitan Museum of Art Web Site: *www.metmuseum.org.*

St. Louis Art Museum Web Site: *www.slam.org.*

Washington University Gallery of Art Web Site: *http://www.wustl.edu/galleryofart/.*

BLACK COWBOYS

See Dart, Isom; Deadwood Dick; McJunkin, George; Pickett, Willie M. "Bill"

BONANZA

> With a horse and a saddle, and a range full
>   of cattle,
> How rich can a fellow be?
> On this land we put our brand,
> Cartwright is the name,
> Fortune smiled, the day we filed the Ponderosa claim. (Television theme song)

NBC's *Bonanza* hit the **television** airwaves on 12 September 1959. During 10 of its 14 years on television, it ruled Sunday nights. From 1964 to 1967, more Americans watched this western than any other program. It entertained a worldwide audience of 280 million people. Producer David Dortort consciously tried to create a program that would stand out sharply from run-of-the-mill sitcoms and formula westerns of the time. His creativity did not immediately charm audiences, but the new phenomenon of color programming helped keep the show afloat. Scenic shots along the northern shores of Lake Tahoe, Nevada, helped push more consumers toward purchasing a new color set, a major goal of NBC's parent company, television manufacturer RCA.

Dortort also had a social agenda with his unusual cast lineup: First, he created strong, male heroes, hoping to counter the image of the bumbling, inept sitcom male, still a staple of Hollywood. Harkening back to Owen Wister's novel *The Virginian,* he presented his cowboys as latter-day Knights of the Round Table. Their collective stand for right would help civilize the Wild West.

The bass-voiced patriarch Ben Cartwright most closely matched the powerful, steely-eyed western hero. The three sons, however, displayed very different, sometimes comic traits, somewhat akin to the characters in *The Three Mesquiteers* serials, B-western heroes of an earlier age. Adam, the brooding, aloof eldest son, relied on brains more than brawn. In sharp contrast, Hoss, the gentle, lovable giant with a heart of gold, exhibited great strength and compassion and not-so-great wit. Handsome, flirtatious Little Joe, impulsive and romantic, often got into trouble, giving the others the opportunity to rescue him.

The vast Ponderosa ranch, a true western ranching, mining, and timber empire, provided a huge, inviting stage for the Cartwrights. Dortort also chose then relatively unknown actors who would not overshadow their characters with celebrity. The cast members (Lorne Greene, Pernell Roberts, Dan Blocker, and Michael Landon) became some of the best known television personalities in the world.

By the early 1970s, the scripts had become rather predictable. Changing tastes demanded that women appear other than as victims to be rescued. However, Dan Blocker's sudden death in 1972 devastated both the show's fans and its cast. Fiddling with the cast did not fill the gap, and NBC abruptly canceled the series, airing the last episode on 16 January 1973.

Along with *Gunsmoke, Bonanza* ranks as one of the great television westerns. Three decades after the show's demise, countless fan clubs, collectors, and Web sites memorialize the popular western. Episode summaries, cast career histories, tidbits about the Ponderosa—all remain alive and well. Can't remember the names of the cast's horses? You'll find the names on-line: Ben's, Dunny Waggoner and Big Buck; Adam's, Sport and Beauty; Hoss's, Ginger, Paiute, and Chubb; Little Joe's, Paint and Cochise.

In 1994 the TV movie *Bonanza: The Return* aired. It had familiar themes with a new cast. The hit film *City Slickers* (1991) paid homage as its stars sang the *Bonanza* theme song as they galloped across the plains. Fans still hungering for a taste of their favorite TV ranch can visit Bonanza and Ponderosa restaurants. According to their ads, "both of these family-friendly restaurants specialize in tasty flame-grilled steaks accompanied by a vast buffet of flavorful foods."

Fans can also visit the actual Ponderosa Ranch, complete with ranch house and a chapel for that memorable western wedding. The sprawling ranch occupies 600 acres at Incline Village off Highway 28 on the north shore of Lake Tahoe. The set is complete with working blacksmiths, a saloon, antiques, a shooting gallery, and even live gunfights!

See also Wister, Owen, and Winthrop, Washington

References

Bonanza History: *http://bonanza1.com/history/*.
Classic TV: *http://classictv.about.com/tvradio/classictv/msub27.htm*.
Ponderosa Ranch: *http://www.ponderosaranch.com/*.

BONNEY, WILLIAM H.

1859?–1881, outlaw. *See* Billy the Kid

BOWIE MINE

See San Saba Mine

BRAND, MAX (FREDERICK SCHILLER FAUST)

1892–1944, writer. *See* Pulp Novelists

BRAZIL

See Comparative Frontier Mythology

BRIDGER, JIM

1804–1881

Nineteenth-century mountain men often come down to us as little more than crude, barbaric rogues and recluses who cared only about financial gain. Does this stereotype accurately portray the legendary Americans who initially tramped through the Rocky Mountains? Clearly not. The true mountain man not only trapped beaver and shot game but also discovered, explored, and lived upon lands that no white person had seen before. These mountain men paved the way for the later western expansion that changed the face of the country. One of the formidable mountain men who helped shape the American West, James "Jim" Bridger, represents the quintessential mountain man.

Born in Richmond, Virginia, in 1804, Bridger moved with his parents and two siblings to St. Louis, Missouri, at the age of 12. In 1816 both his mother and brother died. Jim's father died the following year, leaving 13-year-old Jim to care for his little sister. The teenager signed on as a blacksmith's apprentice. His restless nature, however, demanded more challenge and novelty. Five years later, the youth responded to an advertisement that St. Louis businessman William H. Ashley posted in the *Missouri Gazette*. The ad called for enterprising young men to join Maj. Andrew Henry's party to hunt and trap along the Missouri River. Bridger fell in love with the untamed wilderness, where he would spend his adult life.

Around 1824 Bridger joined Capt. John

H. Weber's party destined for South Pass through the Rocky Mountains. The group camped along Bear Lake, which stretches over the border of present-day Utah and Idaho. Some men of the party bet on Jim's chances of finding the source of Bear Lake. According to Indian legend, the lake's source had foul-tasting water. Eager to establish himself as a man of courage and prowess, Bridger set out alone to find the source of the lake. When he finally reached a large lake that fit descriptions in Indian lore, he tasted its water. He confirmed the water's bad taste and determined why: It was salty. Although some authorities question whether Bridger was indeed the first white man to encounter the Great Salt Lake, his "discovery" surely represents one of his greatest achievements. This big, thick-necked, muscular, shaggy-haired, tanned man would cast a large shadow across the western frontier.

Shortly afterward, Bridger left Weber's party. He moved about for nearly a year with other trapping groups. In 1827 he successfully navigated the notorious Bad Pass, a 20-mile river located at the bottom of Big Horn Canyon near the border of Montana and Wyoming. Bridger not only mastered crossing the treacherous river, with its numerous rapids and small falls, but he did so on a tiny driftwood raft, thereby gaining him the respect of fellow trappers and Indians alike. In 1829 Bridger led a brigade of fellow trappers that invaded the Blackfoot Nation, a group of Indians that Bridger despised because they had ambushed so many of his comrades.

Bridger continued trapping and exploring the American West, encountering modern-day Yellowstone Park along the way. In fact, Bridger ranks with John **Colter** as one of the first Anglos to experience and recount the unusual natural phenomena of Yellowstone. He even climbed the western social ladder, moving from trapping for a fur company to becoming partner in one (the Rocky Mountain Fur Company, 1830 to 1834). While hunting, making trails, and learning the geography of the West, Bridger attended many **rendezvous** (annual meetings where trappers sold their wares).

In 1843 the explorer opened Fort Bridger in Wyoming, a collection of crude log buildings that included a supply store, a blacksmith shop, and living quarters inside a wooden stockade for protection. Bridger's partner Louis Vàzquez operated the fort, which they envisioned as a way station for emigrants. Bridger followed his urge to venture out into the wilderness. He guided Capt. Howard Stansbury's group into the frontier in 1850. He also led Sir George Gore, an Irish nobleman and sport hunter, on a big-game safari around 1855. Sir Gore befriended Bridger while they traveled together. The nobleman often read Shakespeare and Sir Walter Scott's account of the battle of Waterloo to the mountain man after dinner while the exhausted hunters reclined around the campfire. Although the fighting prowess of the British impressed Bridger, he scoffed at the florid language of the bard, finding it "too highfalutin."

Many travelers passed through the fort, including California forty-niners and Mormons. In fact, in 1847 Bridger met Brigham Young at his fort, where they discussed the prospect of the Mormon pioneers settling near the Great Salt

Lake. The two men would eventually come to distrust and despise one another. Within a few years, however, Fort Bridger closed its doors for good. In 1853 Young, now governor of Utah, sent a posse to Fort Bridger to arrest Bridger for supposedly inciting Indian attacks on the Mormons in Utah. The mountain man fled his fort unscathed but never returned. He and Vàzquez sold the fort to the Mormons in 1855.

That same year, Bridger purchased a farm just south of Kansas City, Missouri, but again spent little time on his property. Between 1857 and 1858, he aided Col. Albert Sydney Johnston and the U.S. Army against the Mormons. Bridger also guided an army expedition that explored the headwaters of the Missouri and Yellowstone Rivers and the surrounding mountains between 1859 and 1864. He guided Capt. William F. Raynolds and Capt. William O. Collins and earned the respect of both men. The U.S. Army also employed Bridger between 1865 and 1868 to help fight the Sioux. Bridger then returned to his farm in Missouri, where his son Felix joined him in 1871 after serving in the Civil War.

During his lifetime, Bridger married three Native American women and sired five children. Five different Indian nations celebrated Bridger as friend and chief. Although illiterate, he was a polyglot who spoke English, Spanish, French, and a number of Native American languages. Groups gave him various names. His Crow friends called him "Casapy," which means the Blanket Chief, because of the elaborate dress he wore on special occasions. Others referred to the authoritative Bridger as "Old Gabe," since in the Bible, the angel Gabriel revealed Jehovah's will to peo-

ple. Bridger knew Mike Fink and Kit **Carson**, fellow legendary mountain men. He befriended Presbyterian missionary Dr. Marcus Whitman. In 1835 Whitman removed an arrowhead from Bridger's back; the mountaineer had been shot during a skirmish with Blackfeet at Pierre's Hole a few years prior. The famed western artist Alfred Jacob **Miller** sketched Bridger traipsing about on horseback and wearing a plumed helmet and steel cuirass that Sir William Drummond Stewart, a Scottish nobleman and sport hunter, had given him at an 1837 rendezvous.

Bridger frequently asserted that he had gone without eating a piece of bread for 17 years, that instead, he had lived off the land. This teller of tall tales did more than just trap and hunt. He worked as an "Indian fighter," fur trapper and trader, guide, storekeeper, scout, explorer, and discoverer. He located trails and passes through the Rocky Mountains that opened the region to emigrants. In fact, he led more wagon trains into the West than any other scout. Bridger also helped fill in the map of the expanding nation, with his keen sense of geography and nearly photographic memory. He marked the path that the overland mail, the Union Pacific Railroad, and Interstate 80 would follow. Bridger also served as an interpreter and mediator at a number of peace conferences between Native Americans and the U.S. government.

Ned **Buntline** (Edward Zane Carroll Judson) wrote several dime novels that mythologized Bridger's career. In 1935 residents of Bridger, Montana, initiated its annual Jim Bridger Days celebration, which included flower shows, footraces, and boxing matches. They dedicated the Jim Bridger Memorial, a large structure made up of rock and ore samples from landforms and trails that Bridger explored, including Yellowstone Park. People of the Clarks Fork Valley continue the celebration each July. The Museum of the Mountain Man in Pinedale, Wyoming, houses Bridger's .40-caliber rifle, engraved "J. Bridger 1853."

One of the few blemishes on Bridger's record occurred when, as a teenager, he deserted badly injured fellow mountain man Hugh **Glass.** After Bridger's death in 1881 at the age of 77, his family buried him near his farm. In 1904 Maj. Gen. Grenville Dodge, who had once consulted Bridger about the selection of a route for the Union Pacific Railroad through the mountains, ordered the remains removed. Dodge had Old Gabe buried in Mount Washington Cemetery in Kansas City, Missouri, where an elaborate monument commemorates his many feats.

Today Bridger's memory lives on. One senses Bridger's presence when traveling in the western states. Many landmarks are named after Bridger, such as Bridger National Forest and Fort Bridger, now a state park in Wyoming. The explorer traveled as far south as Mesa Verde and as far north as the Yukon. A mountain chain, peak, range, creek, butte, flats, and a road also bear his name.

—*Jane Veronica Charles Smith*

References

Alter, F. Cecil. *Jim Bridger*. Norman: University of Oklahoma Press, 1962.

Caesar, Gene. *King of the Mountain Men: The Life of Jim Bridger*. New York: E. P. Dutton, 1961.

Utley, Robert M. *A Life Wild and Perilous: Mountain Men and the Paths to the Pacific*. New York: Henry Holt, 1997.

Source of Further Information

Jim Bridger: *http://www.wtp.net/bridger/trappers.html.*

BROWN, DEE

1908–   , writer. *See* Gentle Tamers

BROWN, MOLLY

1867–1932

Born in 1867 in Hannibal, Missouri, Margaret "Maggie" Brown (she was never known as Molly in real life) became one of the most famous survivors of the tragic 1912 sinking of the ocean liner *Titanic.* Each retelling of the tale has given this famous westerner a prominent role. From *The Unsinkable Molly Brown* (play 1960, film 1964) to *Titanic* (1997), she has represented the irreverent, democratic, indomitable spirit of the West.

Born to the family of John Tobin, a poor Irish immigrant, young Margaret had only the rudiments of a grammar school education. The family's poverty forced her into the workforce, as a waitress, at age 13. One tall tale about her childhood claims she was nearly drowned when a cyclone hit her raft as she floated down the Mississippi. None other than Mark Twain, Hannibal's most famous resident, came to her rescue and then advised her to go west. She would later report that the famous author and her father had been fast friends. About 1884 she actually did follow her brother westward to the mining boomtown of Leadville, Colorado. There she met and charmed silvermine manager James Joseph "J. J." Brown. J. J. and Maggie married in 1886. They quickly had two children, Larry and Ellen (known as Helen).

Maggie's fellow worker Thomas F. Cahill described her in glowing terms: "She was exceptionally bright, a most interesting conversationalist, had a charming personality and this coupled with her beauty made her a very attractive woman. It is easy to understand that at about this time the handsome young Jim Brown fell in love with her" (Molly Brown House Museum Web Site). Photographs show a rather less glamorous woman.

Legends about her arose immediately. One popular fiction asserts that the Browns lost a $300,000 mining payroll when it accidentally burned in a potbelly stove. The legend is based on a real happening: Some $75 in coins were scorched. "You know that story isn't true," Maggie's cousin Dolly Brown charged about the potbelly stove tale; "why do you let them keep telling it?" "It's a damn good story," Maggie replied. "And I don't care what the newspapers say about me, just so they say something" (Molly Brown House Museum Web Site).

In 1894 Brown hit a solid vein of gold, a real find in this famous silver country. The couple left their rustic two-bedroom log cabin outside Leadville for the charm and society of Denver. Alas for the young and ambitious woman, Denver high society initially rebuffed her nouveau riche attempts at social climbing. Her extravagant Parisian opera garb and considerable jewelry attracted much notice, not usually favorable. She made some inroads among fashionable charities, but she never attained status among the "Sacred 36," Denver's social elite. She also

faced discrimination for being Irish and Roman Catholic. As a further blow, she and J. J. separated, although he continued to provide generous financial support until his death.

The publicity-seeking Maggie began making her way into society from New York to Newport to Europe. She regaled high society with tall tales of the West. Her fateful 1912 cruise aboard the *Titanic* ended at 2:30 A.M., 15 April, when the vessel sank. As she recalled, "Suddenly [there was] a rift in the water, the sea opened up and the surface foamed like giant arms spread around the ship, and the vessel disappeared from sight, and not a sound was heard." Of the approximately 2,300 people aboard, 70 percent perished.

Maggie reportedly performed with bravery and strength aboard lifeboat number six. She apparently took effective command from the unnerved quartermaster Robert Hichens. She and other women helped row the boat to safety and later nursed injured passengers on the rescue ship *Carpathia*. Her ability to speak several foreign languages served her well as she aided survivors of many nationalities.

The American press found the exploits of "the Unsinkable Mrs. Brown" irresistible. When the *Carpathia* docked in New York, reporters asked her about her survival. "Typical Brown luck," she asserted. "We're unsinkable." In Denver, J. J. Brown reportedly commented, "She's too mean to sink."

Her exploits brought her the celebrity and respect she had always craved. Even Denver society honored her with a fine luncheon, hosted by Mrs. Crawford Hill. Maggie became increasingly political, running unsuccessfully for the U.S. Senate in 1914. She remained highly visible and outspoken, sometimes inviting lawsuits with her plainspoken views.

The Brown family fortune had diminished considerably over the years. J. J.'s death in 1922 tempered Maggie's high-society life. She had become increasingly eccentric and estranged from her family, but she never lost her taste for publicity. She died in modest surroundings, at New York's Barbizon-Club Hotel. She is buried at Holy Rood Cemetery in Westbury on Long Island.

In addition to her media fame, various historical sites memorialize the heroine. Her childhood home in Hannibal stands just a few blocks away from the Mississippi River. The small frame house, at the corner of Denkler Alley and Butler Street, has been restored by the Marion County Historical Society. It consists of only a single bedroom, a kitchen, a front room, and a basement room dug into the side of a hill.

Her Denver home, now the Molly Brown House Museum, located at 1340 Pennsylvania Street, remains a popular tourist attraction as "The Home of the Heroine of the Titanic." J. J. had purchased the house in 1894 for $30,000. He transferred the title to Maggie four years later, perhaps owing to his declining health. She owned the house until her death, but neither she nor her family lived there. Her celebrity, however, continues to draw some 40,000 curious, admiring visitors annually. Historic Denver, Inc., collects funds and oversees the house's restoration and maintenance.

Maggie became known as Molly thanks to Meredith Wilson's 1960 stage play. In two very different versions, Deb-bie Reynolds played Molly in the 1964 film, and Kathy Bates starred in the 1997 blockbuster *Titanic.* Despite the exaggerations of play and film, Maggie's real-life optimism, brashness, and courage elevated her to the pantheon of genuine western heroes.

References

Iversen, Kristen. *Molly Brown: Unraveling the Myth.* Boulder, CO: Johnson Books, 1999.

Molly Brown House Museum: Telephone: 303-832-4092; Web Site: *http://www.molly brown.org.*

Titanic's Molly Brown Birthplace and Museum Web Site: *http://www.mollybrown museum.com.*

Whitacre, Christine. *Molly Brown, Denver's Unsinkable Lady.* Denver, CO: Historic Denver, 1984.

BRYAN, WILLIAM JENNINGS

1860–1925, politician. *See Wizard of Oz, The Wonderful*

BUFFALO BILL

1846–1917. *See* Cody, William Frederick "Buffalo Bill"

BUFFALO SOLDIERS

In July 1866 Congress passed legislation to establish four African-American regiments, the Ninth and Tenth Cavalries and the Twenty-Fourth and Twenty-Fifth Infantries, for the post–Civil War U.S. Army. Cheyenne and Comanche tribes called men in these enlisted units "Buffalo Soldiers." Today the term "Buffalo Soldiers" has come to represent African-American participation in western military service and the honorable and illustrious achievements of those wearing the uniform.

Despite blatant racial discrimination and hardships, blacks served in the Union Army during the Civil War. More than 180,000 enlisted, and more than 33,000 gave their lives to a country that had yet to realize them as individuals. Their service prompted the legislative decision to create the Ninth and Tenth Cavalries 16 months after the war had ended. Section 3 of an act of Congress entitled "An Act to Increase and Fix the Military Peace Establishment of the United States" called for the two regiments, which were formed in Greenville, Louisiana, and Fort Leavenworth, Kansas. For more than two decades, these troops assumed responsibility for the less-desirable duties on the outskirts of the frontier. The soldiers conducted campaigns against Native Americans from Montana to Texas, and they subdued Mexican revolutionaries, outlaws, comancheros, all with little or no recognition. They provided a strong front against Apaches, Arapahos, Cheyenne, Comanches, and Kiowas.

The Indians may have called the black cavalrymen "Buffalo Soldiers" because their dark hair and skin reminded them of the curly mane of the buffalo. Another possibility is that the Indians may have compared the Buffalo Soldiers' fighting with that of a wounded or cornered buffalo, which fights ferociously, showing great courage under dire circumstances. Black soldiers served at posts in the most rugged and difficult areas of the American West. They have recently been given credit for exploring and mapping vast areas of the Southwest. They built and repaired frontier outposts, strung hundreds of miles of telegraph lines, protected stagecoach and mail routes, and provided key protection for railroad crews working among Indians and outlaws. The Twenty-Fifth Infantry Regiment in Montana experimented with using bicycles for troop movement. This **bicycle corps** proved effective, but motorized transit rendered the concept obsolete.

Conditions for Buffalo Soldiers were rough but generally comparable to those for white regiments. Instead of U.S. Army–issued weapons, however, the African-American regiments used weapons left over from the Civil War. Typical Ninth and Tenth Cavalry issue included .69-caliber rifles with bayonets, .44-caliber Colt Army revolvers, and .36-caliber Colt Navy revolvers. If these were unavailable, they used old sabers or daggers. Enlisted men worked seven days a week, resting only on Christmas and the Fourth of July. Small creeks provided the only bathing facilities; disease posed a serious problem. Rations typically included bacon, potatoes, or vegetables from nearby gardens. In addition to food, clothing, and shelter, soldiers received less than 50 cents a day (about $13 a month). Most enlisted for five years.

Young artist Frederic **Remington** rode with the Buffalo Soldiers and described the rigors for *Century* magazine in April 1889: "The great clouds of dust choke you and settle over horse, soldier, and accouterments until all local color is lost and black man and white man wear a common hue. The 'chug, chug, chug' of your tired horse as he marches along becomes infinitely tiresome, and cavalry soldiers never ease themselves in the saddle."

Because of the small number of active soldiers in the U.S. military in 1898 (only 28,000), President William McKinley called for state volunteers. Four regiments of black soldiers serving in the West, mostly former slaves who had served during the Civil War, went south for training. These fighting men, in addition to having to deal with extreme racism, had to cope with limited supplies. The Buffalo Soldiers fought throughout the campaign in Cuba. Their most important contribution came in the battle for the village of El Caney, in which soldiers from the Twenty-Fifth Infantry forced the Spanish forces to surrender. The exploits of these men have been immortalized in a song, "Buffalo Soldier," by the late, great reggae artist, Bob Marley. Other groups, such as America's Buffalo Soldiers Re-Enactors Association (ABSRA) and several motorcycle groups named after the famous soldiers, keep their memory alive today.

Despite their achievements, few Buffalo Soldiers were recognized during or after their duty of service. Between 1865 and 1899, 417 men received the Medal of Honor for their service in the Indian Wars. Only 18 were black. Desertion during the war became the biggest problem, at one point reaching as high as 25 percent. White regiments had desertion rates some three times those of black regiments. Black cavalry and infantry units also had lower rates of alcoholism than did white troops. Their history survived through scarce formal recognition and recollections of veterans and descendants.

Though Buffalo Soldiers were never fully recognized before their service ended, many refused to forget. A recent resurgence of black-history awareness prompted efforts by modern military and social leaders to revive and recount African-American military efforts of the past. In 1981 Gen. Colin Powell noted that Americans had failed to award Buffalo Soldiers due credit for their eight decades of service. He developed the Buffalo Soldier Educational and Historical Committee to record and disseminate their history. Ten years later, a monument recognizing Buffalo Soldiers and their achievements was erected in Fort Leavenworth, Kansas, home of the original Tenth Cavalry. On 28 July 1992, a national resolution recognized Buffalo Soldier Day (reflecting the founding date, 28 July 1866, of the original four African-American regiments). In April 1995 the U.S. Postal Service issued **stamps** honoring the Buffalo Soldiers.

Many organizations exist independently across America, fondly remembering a heroic past that escaped notoriety and widespread public acceptance. The Buffalo Soldiers Law Enforcement Motorcycle Club of Vallejo, California, for example, promotes its cause through local charities and service events, slowly spreading a history that refuses to die. Actor Danny Glover starred in the movie *Buffalo Soldiers* (1997), one of many films focusing on military prejudice. Popular culture has accepted the story of their struggle, but important parts of their role in U.S. history remain to be told.

—William F. Zweigart

References

Fowler, Arlen L. *The Black Infantry in the West, 1869–1891.* 1971. Reprint, Norman: University of Oklahoma Press, 1996.

Leckie, William H. *The Buffalo Soldiers: A Narrative of the Negro Cavalry in the West.* Norman: University of Oklahoma Press, 1967.

BULETTE, JULIA

?–1867

One of the most conspicuous women in Nevada's history is the Comstock prostitute Julia Bulette. In her brief lifetime, the "soiled dove" was a colorful minor figure in Virginia City's early heyday. However, with her brutal murder in 1867 and the hanging of the alleged killer the following year, Julia became a bigger-than-life legend. The mythmaking and "fakelore" continues today in spite of the facts.

Author Marla Kiley, in her article "The Immoral Queens of the Red Light District," wrote in the July 1997 issue of *True West* magazine of the accumulated fiction and fable associated with Julia Bulette. "Almost instantly," Kiley writes, "Julia was wearing silk, velvet, and sable furs. Shortly after her arrival on the scene she was making $1,000 a night and also accepted payment in the form of bars of bullion, diamonds, or rubies" (Kiley 1997). Absolute nonsense and pure poppycock!! Although it is true that Bulette had seen better days, she died in debt: According to estate records, her bills exceeded her assets. Kiley then describes Julia as "a beautiful and willowy woman who seemed to float as she walked"; in fact, she was neither beautiful nor willowy, and it is unlikely that this rather heavyset woman would seem to float when she walked.

Kiley's imagination runs wild in painting an exaggerated, glamorized portrait of Julia Bulette's life. We know that in the approximately four years that Julia lived on the Comstock, she was a well-known prostitute and had worked in the best brothels; however, she was certainly no rich, gorgeous courtesan. Earlier writers even elevated her to the position of madam and "the 'queen' of Virginia City's sporting row."

Kiley claims Bulette's two-room crib near the corner of D and Union Streets in Virginia City was a small parlor house "referred to as Julia's Palace." Then, in a flight of fancy, she tells us that Julia rode "around town in a lacquered brougham with side panels emblazoned with a crest of four aces, crowned by a lion couchant" and attended events "at the Opera House cloaked in a floor length purple velvet cape lined with sable." Nothing could be further from the truth!

So who was this woman who looms larger than life 130 years after her untimely demise? As with most prostitutes, both now and then, there is much mystery to Julia Bulette's life. Some versions of her life story present her as an Englishwoman who immigrated to Louisiana, where she married, then left her husband and entered prostitution; others claim she came to New Orleans from France, where she had been recruited as a prostitute. Recent research indicates she was actually born near Natchez, Mississippi, and worked as a prostitute in New Orleans. Julia would travel to northern California to ply her trade before arriving on the Comstock by 1863.

We do know she quickly became a favorite among Virginia City's Fire Engine Company No. 1. The firemen elected her an honorary member in exchange for her favors and gifts. Other accounts in the *Territorial Enterprise* noted Bulette's enthusiastic support of the fire department and her presence at fires, where she worked the brakes of the handcart engines. Fire Engine Company No. 1 participated in Julia's funeral procession through the streets of Virginia City in January 1867.

Clearly, Julia was more than a run-of-the-mill prostitute before she died in her early 30s. Journalist Alfred Doten of the *Gold Hill News* attended a ball hosted by "Jule" in June 1866. The *Territorial Enterprise* bemoaned her tragic death, claiming "few of her class had more friends," although the "good" women of the community were generally relieved to see her leave the scene. Law enforcement officials diligently pursued the person who had robbed and killed her, ultimately hanging one John Millian after the convicted murderer had exhausted all his appeals. On 24 April 1868, more than 4,000 spectators, including Mark Twain, who was touring the country following a trip to Europe and the Middle East, witnessed the execution.

Susan James, in her excellent *Nevada Magazine* article, the "Queen of Tarts," traced the romance and mythmaking, if not downright lying, linked to Bulette back to a few twentieth-century writers of Nevada history: George Lyman, Lucius Beebe and Charles Clegg, and Effie Mona Mack. Marla Kiley, who borrowed liberally from Lyman's potboiler *The Saga of*

the Comstock Lode (1934), is the most recent, but will probably not be the last, to play tricks on the living and the dead in recounting Julia Bulette's colorful and controversial career as a prostitute. The fakelore will never die, but those of us who do our homework know better than to believe it. Hopefully, one day we may learn much more about the facts of Julia's short life. We have certainly had more than our fair share of fiction and fable.

−Guy Louis Rocha

References

James, Susan. "Queen of Tarts." *Nevada Magazine,* September/October 1984.
Kiley, Marla. "The Immoral Queens of the Red Light District." *True West,* July 1997.

BULLS

See Rodeo Bulls

BUNTLINE, NED

1823–1886

This prolific **pulp novelist** led an exciting, vagabond life. At age 13, he ran away from home to work as a cabin boy. He left behind a solid, respectable, middle-class family. Details of his life are difficult to verify because he applied what became his literary trademark, exaggeration, to his own life as well as to his novels. His birth in Stamford, New York, is well documented, but he gave three different birth dates. His naval service continued until the early 1840s. He also married the first of at least five wives at this time.

In May 1844 the world first heard the name by which Judson would become famous. In Philadelphia, he published two issues of *Ned Buntline's Magazine*. During the next 25 years, he wrote, started several short-lived magazines, earned extra money as a bounty hunter, incited a riot in New York, and narrowly escaped hanging by a mob. His decades of labor over a seemingly endless string of dime novels finally paid off, earning him a comfortable income, reputedly $20,000 per year.

In 1869 Buntline met young army scout William F. **Cody** at Fort McPherson, Nebraska. The 46-year-old writer transformed the 23-year-old Cody into the hero of four dime novels and a play. Eager, thrill-seeking readers snapped up *Buffalo Bill, the King of the Bordermen; Buffalo Bill's Best Shot, or The Heart of Spotted Tail; Buffalo Bill's Last Victory, or Dove Eye, the Lodge Queen;* and *Hazel Eye, the Girl Trapper.* Ever indifferent to truth, Buntline presented Cody as, among other things, a temperance crusader. The real-life Buffalo Bill thoroughly enjoyed prodigious drinking binges.

Buntline's play *The Scouts of the Prairie, or Red Deviltry As It Is,* hastily written with Cody, opened in Chicago on 18 December 1872. The never-modest Buntline even wrote himself into the action: He had himself delivering a temperance lecture. With Chicago street people appearing as Pawnee chiefs and Italian dancer Giuseppina Morlacchi appearing as the Indian maiden Dove Eye, the production reflected Buntline's trademark mythmaking and utter lack of realism.

Critics and the public enjoyed this mythical, preposterous play. The *Richmond Enquirer* noted approvingly that "Ned Buntline and his two confreres, Cody and Omohundro, better known as 'Buffalo Bill' and 'Texas Jack' with their 'Live Indians,' drew another good house.... The way the Scouts handle their navy revolvers is the main secret of their success.... the handsome appearance made by these two gentlemen ... represent[s] in a measure, real scenes of which they have been the actual heroes" (*Richmond Enquirer,* 15 May 1873).

Even a terrible script and production could not dull Cody's star luster. Crowds loved him, and a western hero was born. Buntline also enlisted Virginia-born John Burwell Omohundro Jr. to play Texas Jack. Omohundro had experience as a cowboy and scout and showed his skill with the lasso onstage.

Countless other pulp writers picked up on the topic and made Cody a living legend to fans of the "penny dreadfuls" (pulp novels). As Cody's fame grew, Buntline enjoyed even greater success by having his name linked to that of the great plainsman. An attractive rogue, he became the leading western pulp writer of his day. His mixed character and checkered past prompted Jay Monaghan to title his biography of Buntline *The Great Rascal.*

See also Pulp Novelists

References

Milton, John R. *The Novel of the American West.* Lincoln: University of Nebraska Press, 1980.

Monaghan, Jay. *The Great Rascal: The Exploits of the Amazing Ned Buntline.* Boston: Little, Brown, 1951.

Tuska, Jon, and Vicki Piekarski. *The Frontier Experience: A Reader's Guide to the Life and Literature of the American West.* Jefferson, NC: McFarland, 1984, 1990.

_____, eds. *Encyclopedia of Frontier and Western Fiction.* New York: McGraw-Hill, 1983.

BUNYAN, PAUL

See Johnny Kaw; Pecos Bill; Stone, Glenn

BURIED WORKERS

See Hoover Dam

BUSH, GEORGE W.

1946–   , politician. *See* Politicians and Western Myth

BUTCH CASSIDY AND THE SUNDANCE KID

Butch Cassidy was born Robert LeRoy Parker, the eldest of 13 children in a Mormon family, on 13 April 1866 in Beaver, Utah. As a teenager, he fell under the influence of a young rustler named Mike Cassidy and later borrowed his surname for an alias. He acquired the nickname "Butch" working at a butcher shop in the early 1890s, and it was as George "Butch" Cassidy that he served time in a Wyoming prison for stealing a horse. (This led the Pinkerton Detective Agency and others to think his given name was George, rather than Robert.)

The Sundance Kid was born Harry Alonzo Longabaugh, the youngest of five children in a Baptist family, in the spring of 1867 in Mont Clare, Pennsylvania. He headed west at the age of 15, for a while ranched with cousins in Colorado, and then worked as a drover and bronco buster in Wyoming, Montana, and Alberta. He earned his nickname while jailed in Sundance, Wyoming, for horse theft.

Exactly when Butch and Sundance first met is unknown, but both belonged to a loose-knit outlaw gang that operated in the Rocky Mountain West in the late 1800s and early 1900s. Today, the group is usually called "the Wild Bunch," but the newspapers of the era preferred fancier tags like the Hole in the Wall Gang, the Robbers' Roost Gang, the Powder Springs Gang, the Notorious Johnson County Gang, or the Train Robber's Syndicate. The earliest recorded reference to the gang as the Wild Bunch—slang for a group of cowboys on a spree, a herd of unbroken horses, or a band of outlaws—came in a November 1902 memorandum from the Pinkerton Detective Agency to the American Bankers Association. By then, ironically, the gang had all but ceased to exist.

Butch, Sundance, and their comrades-in-arms may have been wild, but they were never much of a bunch. Although perhaps as many as 30 outlaws participated in crimes attributed to the gang, hardly any of them committed more than a couple of holdups with each other. Furthermore, it is unclear how many crimes they actually perpetrated, inasmuch as famous outlaws are often blamed for others' deeds. The gang's first verifiable heist was the 1889 robbery of a bank in Telluride, Colorado, by Butch Cassidy, Matt Warner, and Tom McCarty; the last was Ben Kilpatrick's ill-fated assault on a train in Texas in 1912. The majority of the gang's crimes, however, took place between 1896 and 1901. During that period, those in which both Butch and Sundance actively participated included no more than two train robberies and one bank job.

By the time the Pinkertons began calling the gang the Wild Bunch, many of its core members had been arrested or killed. Matt Warner had gone straight in 1900, after several years in prison. Ben Kilpatrick, William Ellsworth "Elzy" Lay, and Harvey Logan were still in jail (although Logan would escape and then commit suicide after a botched train robbery in 1904). Will Carver, George Currie, Sam Ketchum, Lonnie Logan, Bill and Fred McCarty, and Joe Walker were already dead and buried.

Meanwhile, Butch and Sundance had fled to South America, accompanied by the mystery woman known as Etta Place. The Pinkertons called her Etta on their WANTED posters, but she signed hotel registers as Ethel. She acquired the surname "Place" by traveling as the wife of Sundance, who was now using the alias Harry A. Place (Place being his mother's maiden name). Although no record of the marriage has been found, Sundance introduced her to family and friends as his wife. In a letter to a Wyoming pal, he said they had met in Texas. She has been described as a prostitute, a teacher, or both, but no one knows her true origin or fate.

In any case, the couple met up with Butch—who now called himself James Ryan—in New York City early in 1901 and they all steamed south to Argentina. (Why they picked Argentina is unknown, but the newspapers of the day touted homesteading opportunities there.) After arriving in Buenos Aires, they sought the advice of the U.S. vice-consul, George Newbery, who suggested they head for Patagonia, as southern Argentina is known. He owned an *estancia* (ranch) there and wanted to recruit other North Americans to colonize a large tract of government land just north of the Cholila Valley in the Chubut Territory.

The trio took his advice and journeyed to Cholila, where they settled on 625 hectares of government land in June 1901 and began raising cattle, sheep, and horses. They registered their brands with territorial authorities and joined neighbors in petitioning the government for more land. By all accounts, the bandits stayed out of trouble in Cholila, except for one instance in which Butch was questioned about having facilitated the escape of his friend Robert Evans, who had been arrested on suspicion of having stolen money from an *estancia* manager. Evans, who may have been from Montana, made himself scarce, and Butch was never charged in the case. (Evans and a Texan named William Wilson later committed several crimes that were mistakenly blamed on Butch and Sundance, who had long since left Argentina. Evans and Wilson died in a shoot-out with police in 1911.)

While Butch and Sundance ranched, the Pinkertons sleuthed. Through postal informants (who opened mail addressed to the outlaws' families), they learned that the fugitives were in Argentina. After veteran operative Frank Dimaio finished a case in Brazil, he went to Buenos

Aires to see what he could learn. Dimaio located their banker and visited Vice-Consul Newbery, who told him the trio was living in Cholila.

The Pinkertons sought funds from clients to send a posse after Butch and Sundance, but the banks and railroads declined to chip in. The agency had to be satisfied with arranging for WANTED posters in Spanish and warning the Buenos Aires police chief, in characteristically ominous rhetoric, that "it is our firm belief that it is only a question of time until these men commit some desperate robbery in the Argentine Republic. They are all thorough plainsmen and horsemen, riding from 600 to 1,000 miles after committing a robbery. If there are reported to you any bank or train hold up robberies or any other similar crimes, you will find that they were undoubtedly committed by these men" (Meadows 1996).

Sure enough, in February 1905 two "Yankees" held up a bank in Río Gallegos, 700 miles south of Cholila. Although the descriptions of the robbers didn't fit Butch and Sundance very well, and although evidence indicated that they had been in Cholila at the time of the robbery, the police jumped to the obvious conclusion. Tipped off by a friend about orders to detain them for questioning, the bandits sold most of their holdings and fled to Chile in May 1905.

Later that year, all three briefly returned to Argentina, and with an unidentified accomplice, they robbed a bank in Villa Mercedes de San Luis. The robbers galloped west, pursued by several armed posses, and escaped over the Chilean border. Very little is known about Butch and Sundance's activities in Chile, but they spent some time in the northern port of Antofagasta in 1905 and

1906. From another postal informant, the Pinkertons learned that Sundance—using the alias Frank Boyd—had run into an unnamed difficulty with Chilean authorities but that he had settled the matter with the help of Frank Aller, the U.S. vice-consul in Antofagasta.

Shortly after the Villa Mercedes holdup, Ethel sailed back to the United States for good. The last known report of her whereabouts put her in San Francisco in March 1906, perhaps using the name Ethel Matthews. Later that year, Butch (under the alias James "Santiago" Maxwell) and Sundance (under the alias H. A. Brown) made their way up into Bolivia and found work at the Concordia Tin Mine as muleteers and payroll guards. Mine manager Percy Seibert knew they had been outlaws, but he "never had the slightest trouble getting along with" either of them, and they often dined at his home (Meadows 1996).

In late 1907 the bandits made an excursion to Santa Cruz, a frontier town in Bolivia's eastern savanna. In a letter to friends at Concordia, Butch said he had found just the place he had been looking for and predicted, "If I don't fall down I will be living here before long." Sometime in 1908 he and Sundance quit their jobs at Concordia. In August they turned up in Tupiza, a town in southern Bolivia. Butch was now calling himself James "Santiago" Lowe (an alias from his New Mexico days), and Sundance was using the name Frank Smith or H. A. Brown (accounts vary). Lying low while planning the holdup apparently intended to finance their Santa Cruz venture, they camped intermittently with English engineer A. G. Francis, who was running a gold dredge on the nearby Río San Juan del Oro.

The bandits initially intended to rob a bank in Tupiza, but the arrival of a contingent of cavalry soldiers led them to shift their focus to the Aramayo, Francke mining company, which sent unguarded payrolls overland from Tupiza to its headquarters in Quechisla. When Aramayo manager Carlos Peró picked up the weekly payroll on the morning of 3 November 1908 and headed north, Butch and Sundance were not far behind. Peró stayed overnight in Salo and set off again shortly after dawn. The bandits, now ahead of him on Huaca Huañusca (Dead Cow Hill), relieved him of the payroll and a company mule at about 9:30 in the morning.

Released unharmed, Peró sent word to Aramayo officials, and posses were soon looking for two armed gringos with a dark-brown mule bearing the company's distinctive Q brand. Meanwhile, Butch and Sundance had made their way south to Francis's camp. In the morning, they conscripted him to guide them on a looping escape route that put a mountain range between them and most of the posses. The next day, the bandits let Francis go and rode on alone. They were heading north, probably toward Oruro, site of Sundance's last known address.

At sundown on 6 November, they rode into the mining town of San Vicente and sought lodging for themselves and forage for their mules. The *corregidor* (local justice) arranged for them to stay in a spare room off the walled patio of a villager's adobe house. The *corregidor* then alerted a four-man posse (an army captain, two soldiers, and a policeman) that had arrived that afternoon in search of the Aramayo bandits. The captain was sleeping or otherwise indisposed, but the two soldiers and the policeman went to investigate at once. As they entered the patio and approached the bandits' room, Butch appeared in the doorway and shot the leading soldier. The Bolivian responded with a rifle shot before retreating to a nearby house, where he died within minutes. The other soldier and the policeman also fired and retreated, then stationed themselves outside the patio door and began firing into the bandits' room. The captain appeared and asked the *corregidor* to gather villagers to surround the house and prevent the bandits from escaping. As the *corregidor* hastened to comply, he heard three desperate screams from within the room. By the time the house was surrounded, the firing had ceased.

The next morning, Butch's body was found stretched out on the floor, with one bullet wound in the temple and another in the arm. Sundance's corpse was on an adobe bench behind the door. He had been shot once in the forehead and several times in the arm. The witnesses concluded that Butch had put Sundance out of his misery and then turned the gun on himself. Later reports claimed they had left their rifles outside and were down to their last bullets when they committed suicide. In reality, Sundance's rifle lay beside his body, and both men had plenty of ammunition. Also among the bandits' effects were the Aramayo payroll and a map of Bolivia with penciled annotations coinciding with their known movements in Bolivia. Peró later identified the corpses as those of the men who had robbed him. An inquest was held, but the officials never identified the bandits by name.

Word soon spread among Butch and

Sundance's friends in Bolivia that they had died in San Vicente. The last report of their whereabouts in that country was an item in a Tupiza biweekly, *El Chorolque,* which listed Santiago Lowe as a guest at the Hotel Términus at the beginning of November. This lends credence to a report by writer James D. Horan that a Reverend Wenberg had run into Butch in a Tupiza hotel and greeted him as Mr. Maxwell—the name Butch had been using when Wenberg met him during his Concordia days. "I'm fine," Butch coldly replied, "but my name is Lowe" (Meadows 1996).

In 1909 mail sent to Sundance went unanswered, and rumors of his death reached Chile. His erstwhile benefactor Frank Aller wrote the American legation in La Paz for "confirmation and a certificate of death" (Meadows 1996) for two Americans—one known as Frank Boyd or H. A. Brown and the other as Maxwell—who had reportedly been "killed at San Vicente near Tupiza by natives and police and buried as *'desconocidos'* [unknowns]" (Meadows 1996). Aller said he needed proof of Boyd/Brown's death to settle his estate in Chile. The legation forwarded the request to the Bolivian foreign ministry, which eventually sent a summary of the inquest report and "death certificates for the two men, whose names are unknown" (Meadows 1996).

The bandits' South American friends may have learned of their fate early on, but their North American friends had to wait. Although the Bolivian newspapers carried several articles on the Aramayo holdup and its aftermath, they never identified the slain bandits. A wire-service story in a Buenos Aires daily was the first to link the crime with Butch and Sundance: "There are opinions that these are the ones who held up the *Banco de la Nación* in Villa Mercedes" (Meadows 1996). Within a few years, varying accounts of the shoot-out began appearing in English. The first came from Hiram Bingham, who had traveled through Tupiza two weeks after the event and mentioned it in his travelogue *Across South America* (1911).

In 1913 *Wide World Magazine* published "The End of an Outlaw," in which A. G. Francis related his encounters with the two bandits, whom he identified as Kid Curry and Butch Cassidy. (He knew the pair only by their Tupiza aliases and apparently mixed up the Sundance Kid with Kid Curry when he wrote his article.) Although much of Francis's account was accurate, the Pinkertons dismissed it as a fake, written to make a buck.

In his 1922 book *Six Years in Bolivia,* English miner A. V. L. Guise reported the death of two gringo bandits in a shoot-out with Bolivian soldiers in Cochabamba, a city in central Bolivia, far from San Vicente. In *Tales of the Old-Timer* (1924), Western writer Frederick R. Bechdolt had Butch and Sundance dying at their Argentine ranch in a 1906 shoot-out "with more than 100 soldiers." Because Bechdolt interviewed people who had known the bandits in the West, it seems clear that the fact of their death in a South American shoot-out was known in the United States by then, even if the details were murky.

Arthur Chapman (best known for his treacly poem "Out Where the West Begins") interviewed the bandits' friend Percy Seibert for the article "'Butch' Cassidy," which appeared in *The Elks Magazine* in April 1930 and has been quoted by historians ever since. Chapman described Butch as the "coolest, cleverest, and most dangerous outlaw of his age," while Seibert jumbled places and dates and credited Butch and Sundance with crimes they couldn't possibly have committed. As for the shoot-out, which he correctly placed in San Vicente, Seibert inflated the tiny patrol to a "company of Bolivian cavalry" who charged the outlaws' house: "Revolvers blazed from door and window, and men began to stagger and fall in the courtyard." Seibert also introduced the anecdote of Sundance's desperate run across the courtyard to fetch the rifles and ammunition.

Charles Kelly incorporated the Seibert-Chapman version of the San Vicente shoot-out into *Outlaw Trail* (1938), the first book-length history of the Wild Bunch. James D. Horan, who wrote several books about the bandits, also depended heavily on Seibert. When William Goldman wrote the screenplay for the 1969 hit movie *Butch Cassidy and the Sundance Kid,* he relied on Kelly's and Horan's work.

By the time the film appeared, Butch and Sundance's adventures had long since been hopelessly exaggerated and romanticized. A 1930 *Denver Post* article, for example, blamed them for "raids on banks, mining offices, and trains in Argentina, Peru, Brazil, Chile, and Bolivia," and the *New York Mirror* in 1937 lionized them for "a series of daring holdups" in Argentina, adding that the "gauchos loved being robbed by the dashing 'gringos'–because they stole in the grand manner." In reality, they apparently committed only two holdups during their eight years in South America.

Inspired by the popularity of the movie, writers took up the story again in the 1970s, this time with a dramatically revisionist view: The outlaws had not died in Bolivia but had returned to the United States and lived out their remaining years in relative obscurity. Many reports fueled this new view, including testimony from old-timers, apparently reliable sources, and friends of friends. A plethora of reports had one or both of the men living or dying in Europe (in France or Ireland), Latin America (in Argentina, Bolivia, Brazil, Chile, Ecuador, Honduras, Mexico, Peru, Uruguay, or Venezuela), or the United States (in Alaska, Arizona, California, Colorado, Georgia, Idaho, Montana, Nevada, New Mexico, Oregon, Tennessee, Utah, Washington, or Wyoming). Butch dominated the sightings and death legends, perhaps because at least one impostor was making the rounds in the West claiming to be him.

The return theories gained credence because of the lack of hard evidence about the shoot-out; historians had never documented the fact that such a shoot-out had taken place, let alone who had died in it. No one had done any research in Bolivia or even looked at the available collections of early-1900s South American newspapers in the States. Indeed, the Southern Hemisphere continues to be terra incognita to Western historians. Howard Lamar's much-acclaimed *New Encyclopedia of the American West* (1998), for example, has Butch and Sundance roosting "quietly in the backcountry of Brazil near the Chilean border" (Lamar 1988), though they never lived in Brazil–which, in any event, has no border with Chile.

Another factor that may have contributed to the revisionist view is the romantic notion of "the return of the bandit," who cannot die because he represents hope. "Men can live without justice, and generally must," according to historian and bandit expert Eric Hobsbawm, "but they cannot live without hope" (1981). There was also the conceit that intelligent outlaws like Butch and Sundance could not have been outwitted by a posse in a Third World country like Bolivia. In fact, however, the Bolivians captured most payroll bandits—invariably foreigners—who operated during the early 1900s.

The first and most significant revisionist was Lula Parker Betenson, Butch's youngest sister, who was a baby when he left home. In *Butch Cassidy, My Brother* (1975), a memoir of the Parker clan's life in frontier Utah and her sibling's career, Betenson wrote that he had visited the family in 1925. She said he had died in Spokane in 1937 but was not the Cassidy impostor who had died near Spokane that same year. She refused to say what name her brother was using when he died, and she never provided any proof of his return. Researchers who met Betenson surmised that she didn't know much about her brother's life. She implied to a couple of them that she was just having fun with her stories, and one of her sons said point-blank that Butch's alleged 1925 visit had never happened. Moreover, Butch's father said he had never seen his son again after he went to South America, and a niece said Butch's brothers had looked for him for years without learning what had become of him.

Butch as the "good bandit" was another of Betenson's themes. "He was known as Robin Hood in North and South America," she wrote, "robbing the rich and often giving to the poor." His friend Josie Bassett agreed: "Butch took care of more people than FDR, and with no red tape." It is true that Butch and Sundance were well liked and respected, but they were hardly philanthropists. The best that can be said of them is that they stole company money rather than personal belongings and that they usually shot only at people who were shooting at them.

Western writer Larry Pointer's 1977 book *In Search of Butch Cassidy* combined a history of the Wild Bunch with an attempt to prove that William T. Phillips, a Michigan native who owned a machine shop in Spokane, Washington, was the returned Butch Cassidy. Pointer based much of his case on Phillips's unpublished manuscript, "The Bandit Invincible," an account of his supposed life as Cassidy. Some of the manuscript's details conform with what is known of the outlaw's life in Wyoming, where Phillips had worked as a young man, but aspects of Butch's life elsewhere in the United States were wrong, and the South American portion of the manuscript was ludicrous. Phillips located the bandits' ranch in the wrong part of Argentina and had them holding up railroads not yet built when they were in the area. He proffered an extensive (and improbable, considering the era) round of plastic surgery in Paris as the deus ex machina to account for the differences in his and Butch's appearances.

In 1983 outlaw buff Ed Kirby published *The Rise and Fall of the Sundance Kid,* another book at war with itself. The first half is a straightforward narrative of Sundance's life until his apparent death in Bolivia. The second half is an incongruous effort to prove that the handsome, nearly six-foot-tall Sundance Kid had returned to the United States as the five-foot-three Hiram BeBee, a homely drunk who died in the Utah State Penitentiary in 1955 while serving a life sentence for murdering a sheriff. Kirby suggested that osteoporosis might explain how the 30-something Sundance could have shrunk into the elderly BeBee. A 1919 mug shot of a much younger BeBee, however, showed him to have always been gnomish in height and appearance.

In the 1980s and 1990s Butch and Sundance went under the loupe all over again. The tales of their return got a skeptical reevaluation, and researchers finally combed judicial, police, and newspaper archives in Argentina, Chile, and Bolivia. The resulting research produced a slew of articles in outlaw and Western history journals and several new books. Two key judicial reports were found. One contained some 1,000 pages addressing outlawry in Patagonia during and after Butch and Sundance's residency there. The other was the long-lost file from the Bolivian judicial inquest into the circumstances surrounding the deaths of the two gringo bandits in San Vicente. Much of this material can be found in Anne Meadows's *Digging Up Butch and Sundance* (1996).

In *Sundance, My Uncle* (1992), Donna Ernst provided a wealth of new information about her outlaw in-law's childhood and experiences as a young cowboy. With *Butch Cassidy: A Biography* (1998), Richard Patterson contributed the first thoroughly documented look at the icon's career. Butch and Sundance have also begun to intrigue historians in Argentina, including Marcelo Gavirati, Os-

valdo Topcic, and Ricardo Vallmitjana. Gavirati's *Buscados en la Patagonia: Butch, Sundance, Ethel, Evans y Wilson* (1999), for example, surveys their stay in Patagonia and their connection to other outlaws there.

The legend of Butch and Sundance is certain to live on. "Some folks say [Butch] never died in South America," Paul Turner told a Salt Lake City *Deseret News* columnist in 1999. "Myself, I like to think the old boy's still alive out there, whoopin' it up." Turner, who operates the Butch Cassidy Museum in Richfield, Utah, added that "anybody who'd like to hear a Butch Cassidy legend or two, give me a call. . . . What I don't know I'll make up."

—Anne Meadows and Daniel Buck

References

Ernst, Donna. *Sundance, My Uncle*. College Station, TX: Early West, 1992.

Gavirati, Marcelo. *Buscados en la Patagonia: Butch, Sundance, Ethel, Evans y Wilson*. Buenos Aires: La Bitácora, 1999.

Hobsbawm, Eric J. *Bandits*. Rev. ed. New York: Pantheon, Delacorte, 1969, 1981.

Kelly, Charles. *The Outlaw Trail*. 1938, 1959. Reprint, Lincoln, NE: Bison Books, 1996.

Kirby, Ed. *The Rise and Fall of the Sundance Kid*. Iola, WI: Western Publications, 1983.

Lamar, Howard R., ed. *The New Encyclopedia of the American West*. New Haven, CT: Yale University Press, 1998.

Meadows, Anne. *Digging Up Butch and Sundance*. Rev. ed. New York: St. Martin's Press, 1994; Lincoln, NE: Bison Books, 1996.

Patterson, Richard. *Butch Cassidy: A Biography*. Lincoln, NE: Bison Books, 1998.

Pointer, Larry. *In Search of Butch Cassidy*. Norman: University of Oklahoma Press, 1977.

CALAMITY JANE

1852 OR 1856–1903

In a region filled with tall tales, perhaps no one worked as hard or as successfully at building her own legend than Calamity Jane. She holds the reputation of a hard-drinking, wild-shooting, tough-talking woman of the Wild West. She wore men's buckskins instead of dresses, risked her life to save innocent citizens, and brought "calamity" wherever she traveled. Her rough, cowgirl image has been transformed in popular culture, but her name brings with it visions of dust, gun smoke, and defiance.

Martha Jane Cannary (also called Martha Jane Cannary Burke) may have been born near Princeton, Missouri, on 1 May 1856. Most of our knowledge of her youth comes from her not very reliable memoir: *Life and Adventures of Calamity Jane by Herself* (1896, available on-line at several locations). According to legend, her parents died on a west-bound wagon train, leaving her orphaned at an early age. She traveled the West, doing odd jobs to survive. She quickly became enamored of the wild, open West.

She drifted to Wyoming and up to South Dakota, finding work with Gen. George Crook's expedition against Native American tribes. Perhaps because employers often overlooked Jane on account of her sex, she dressed and acted as the cowboys did, often passing as a man. She also worked in a dance hall in Deadwood, South Dakota, where she wore women's clothing and played a more feminine role. Usually, however, she roamed about in a buckskin suit, enjoying hunting, gambling, gunfighting, cussing, and drinking with men. "It was a bit awkward at first," she reported, "but soon I got to be perfectly at home in men's clothes" (Canary 1896).

Jane's relationship with Wild Bill Hickok remains mythical and undocumented. According to a diary alleged to be by Jane but probably forged, they married secretly while in Kansas on 1

September 1870, and Jane gave birth to their daughter, Jean (or Janey) Hickok McCormick, on 25 September 1873. The same diary indicates that the two divorced in 1876. Jane supposedly gave the child up for adoption. Larry McMurtry, in his novel *Buffalo Girls* (1990, film version 1995), played upon this myth and has Jane writing a series of letters to her daughter. However, at the end of the book, Jane reveals that "I wanted you so much that I made you up. . . . You are the child I would have chose, Janey, had I been normal—why can't I at least have you in my head . . . ? I guess you rose out of my hopes, Janey—I had thought I put them out of my heart long ago, when all the doctors told me I couldn't bear a child" (McMurtry 1990). Several sources, including her own autobiography, report her marriage to Clinton Burke in 1885 and the birth of their baby girl in 1887.

Jane bragged in her autobiography of working as a scout for General Custer during his military raids, of saving many endangered citizens, and of other daring feats. Her stories usually stretched the truth; many are total fabrications. Oddly, although Jane boasted of many courageous and daring accomplishments, she did not mention true acts of kindness, such as nursing smallpox victims.

Canary died in 1903, a poor woman plagued by alcohol abuse and loneliness. She reportedly requested to be buried next to Wild Bill Hickok in Deadwood, and her grave remains there today.

Both Martha Jane and Buffalo Bill **Cody** report that she received her nickname from the same event. She found a Captain Egan surrounded by Indians, facing certain death, in South Dakota.

According to both accounts, she boldly rode into the middle of the Indians, rescued the wounded captain, and carried him on her horseback to camp. On the way, he named her "Calamity Jane."

Other stories claim she acquired her name at the various hotels or houses where she worked as a prostitute before her service to the military. Her propensity for action and danger followed her everywhere, and "Calamity" may indicate the constant trouble she found.

Martha Jane is also credited with saving a stagecoach of six passengers from a large band of Indians. According to her own account, she quietly and deftly took over the stagecoach and returned it to safety. In Buffalo Bill's story, she, "by a daring feat," saved everyone's lives, including that of the driver, Jack McCall. Jane later claimed she had helped capture McCall for killing her alleged lover, Wild Bill Hickok.

Jane also claimed to have ridden for the Pony Express and as a scout for General Custer. "I was considered a remarkably good shot and a fearless rider for a girl of my age," she reported (Canary 1896). She wrote so convincingly that countless subsequent writers accepted her tall tales as fact. In *Burs under the Saddle,* a book pointing up historical errors in the works of others, Ramon F. Adams refutes many Calamity Jane myths.

Calamity Jane's ties to Wild Bill Hickok are probably a fabrication. According to some historians, she knew him only a little more than six weeks. However, several descriptions of her profound grief at the news of his death suggest a deeper connection. In her autobiography, she called him her friend and described the actions she took to hunt down Jack Mc-Call. Jane does not mention her wailing over Wild Bill's death, but others reported her intense mourning. Her emotional reaction sparked newspaper stories of their supposed romantic relationship, and eventually she began discussing their romantic encounters. The facts have never been sorted out, but the rumors increased in the years after her death. Her supposed final request to be buried next to him has been interpreted as a wish to be reunited in the other world—and as a desire for more fame.

Pulp novelists of the time seized upon and increased her notoriety. A magazine called *Deadwood Dick* began publication in 1899. This weekly dime novel for boys included accounts of the fictional **Deadwood Dick**'s adventures in the Wild West. *Deadwood Dick's Doom, or Calamity Jane's Last Adventure* describes the misadventures of the two characters. The pulp describes Jane as a "graceful, pretty girl-in-breeches" with a "stern expression of her sad eyes."

The twentieth-century media perpetuated the myth of the supposed love between Calamity Jane and Wild Bill. Countless books and many movies describe their romance and gloss over their hard lives on the frontier. *The Plainsman* (1936), starring Jean Arthur and Gary Cooper, and *Calamity Jane,* a 1984 CBS television movie, both present the two as partners in crime fighting and in life. In *The Plainsman,* Wild Bill does not outwardly show his love for Calamity, but he carries her picture with him everywhere. Jane loses his affection after she exposes a military troop's route to the Indians.

Larry McMurtry's *Buffalo Girls* depicts Martha Jane differently. In the novel, Calamity is a confused and lonely woman who creates an imaginary daughter for herself to write to and dream about. McMurtry adds a further twist, intimating that she was a hermaphrodite. After her death, her best friend Bartle Bone tells one of his companions that he "thought he might just see what the man knew about something he had been curious about for a long time—namely, whether Calamity had been a woman or a man" (McMurtry 1990).

The film version shows her closely linked to Wild Bill and bearing a baby girl, whom she gives up after his death. She has close friends who support and aid her. Her choice of men's clothing is only noticeable on her trip to England, where she is contrasted with Annie **Oakley,** a prim, feminine straight-shooter. In this portrayal, Martha Jane is a balanced and happy individual, who often loses her fiery temper but who is down-to-earth and dependable.

In her autobiography, Jane said she had a daughter by her husband Clinton Burke. After he deserted her and fled charges of tax evasion, the child lived at a boarding school and remained separated from her mother for the remainder of her life. Certainly, the story of a short, passionate romance with another Wild West legend is more entertaining than the story of life with a cowardly tax-evader.

Like her mother, Calamity's supposed daughter became the object of myth and legend. In 1941 a woman named Jean Hickok McCormick declared herself to be the daughter of Wild Bill and Jane. She presented her mother's diaries and letters as "proof." The diaries record

Jane's short marriage to Wild Bill, their divorce, and the placement of their child in foster care. The man who checked most thoroughly into the documents, Clarence S. Paine, found many disturbing contradictions. It is also very likely that Jane could neither read nor write, making the production of a diary problematic. James D. McLaird's 1995 article in *Montana* magazine thoroughly debunks McCormick's claims.

Regardless of the facts of her life, Calamity Jane captured the imagination of magazine and pulp fiction writers, who began her transformation from woman to myth. Edward Wheeler, for example, linked Jane to his creation **Deadwood Dick.** She appeared as Dick's wife or, more often, sweetheart in several Wheeler books, including *Deadwood Dick on Deck, or Calamity Jane, the Heroine of Whoop-Up: A Story of Dakota.*

Television also took up Jane's story. *The Legend of Calamity Jane,* a 1990s cartoon, shows main characters and settings inspired by her many myths. The program tells of Martha Jane's background in the West, loosely using her lack of parents as a backdrop, and shows Wild Bill Hickok as a teammate and love interest. Her band of crime fighters travels the Old West crushing outlaws and bandits. This portrayal of Calamity Jane, although very modern and glamorized, shows that her heroic aura is timeless.

Theaters still produce a musical called *Calamity Jane,* adapted from the screenplay by James O'Hanlon. Doris Day, a beautiful and very feminine actress, plays Calamity Jane in the movie version. Featuring songs such as "The Black Hills of Dakota" and "Secret Love," the musical shows Jane as a lovelorn cowgirl. Her rough image as a rider and gunfighter remain present, but her actions are driven by emotion.

Reenactors have repopulated the West with heroes and villains. Since the late 1980s, Coloradan Glenda Bell has played Calamity Jane as the "Western Woman Wildcat" who "shares the humorous ups and downs of her life as she keeps body and soul together." It is unlikely that we will ever uncover the facts of Calamity Jane's life, but that does not keep her legend from exerting a powerful, enduring hold on American popular culture.

Entertainers continue to profit from the allure of Calamity Jane's name. She has been made a member of the Vestal Virgins Cosmic Baseball Team, along with actress Marilyn Monroe and poets Emily Dickinson and Sylvia Plath. The teams have virtual baseball games and have been "playing" since 1995. Also in an athletic vein, a successful women's Ultimate Frisbee team from Indiana University call themselves "Calamity Jane." Seven women of a barbershop-type choir of the same name hold their own in a male-dominated genre, maintaining a strong bass sound as the foundation for their music instead of high, delicate harmonies.

Calamity Jane's bragging character and tough disposition created a figure that will forever remain the embodiment of a rough-and-tumble western cowgirl. She remains a symbol of strength and of the defiance of social norms. Her celebrity also reflects an ongoing need for heroes and for enthralling if unlikely stories. Her name will forever be associated with the Wild West and its values of individualism, boldness, and courage.

—Ellen J. Oettinger and Richard W. Slatta

References

Adams, Ramon Frederick. *Burs under the Saddle: A Second Look at Books and Histories of the West.* Norman: University of Oklahoma Press, 1964, 1989.

Canary, Martha Jane. *Life and Adventures of Calamity Jane by Herself* (1896). Available on-line at several locations.

Fielder, Mildred. *Wild Bill and Deadwood.* Seattle, WA: Superior Publishing Company, 1965.

Knowles, Thomas W., and Joe R. Lansdale, eds. *The West That Was.* New York: Wings Books, 1993.

McLaird, James D. "Calamity Jane's Diary and Letters: Story of a Fraud." *Montana: The Magazine of Western History* 45, no. 4 (Autumn 1995): 20–35.

McMurtry, Larry. *Buffalo Girls.* New York: Pocket Books, 1990.

Sollid, Roberta Beed. *Calamity Jane: A Study in Historical Criticism.* 1958. Reprint, Helena: Montana Historical Society Press, 1995.

CAMEL CORPS

In 1836 Maj. George H. Crosman urged the U.S. War Department to utilize camels in the campaigns being waged against Indians in Florida. He argued that the ability of camels to operate with a minimum of food and water made them superior to other pack and riding animals. As a U.S. senator and later secretary of war under President Franklin Pierce, Jefferson Davis supported the idea. He firmly believed that military operations in the deserts of the West would require a desert animal, the camel.

In 1855 Davis insistently proposed a camel corps to Congress and received a $30,000 appropriation for "the purchase of camels and the importation of dromedaries, to be employed for military purposes" (Jacobs). In May Maj. Henry Wayne traveled to Tunis and purchased 33 animals for about $12,000. Once loaded onto the deck of the specially modified naval storeship *Supply,* the camels began their odyssey to south Texas. Forty-four more camels arrived in a later shipment.

The first batch of camels landed at Indianola, Texas, on 29 April 1856, but bad weather and shallow water prevented unloading for two weeks. On 4 June Wayne pointed his camel caravan westward to Victoria. There, Mary A. Shirkey clipped camel wool from the animals, spun it, and knit a pair of camel-pile socks for the president of the United States.

From Camp Verde, Texas, the camels worked successfully in operations against Indians and in transporting supplies. According to Major Wayne, they could carry 600 pounds without difficulty, several times what a mule could manage. They traveled long distances without water and would eat virtually any plant. One trek took the camel corps into the wild, unexplored Big Bend region along the Rio Grande in west Texas.

Several camel drivers, including a Syrian named Hadji Ali, accompanied the beasts from North Africa. American soldiers soon corrupted his name to "Hi Jolly." In reality, he may not have been Middle Eastern at all but a Greek named Philip Tedro.

Lt. Edward Fitzgerald Beale undertook another experiment in June 1857. The army planned to set up a route from Texas through the desert Southwest to convey mail and supplies. They surveyed a wagon route along the thirty-fifth parallel from Texas to the Pacific Ocean. The Beale Road, which ran from Fort Defiance, New Mexico, to the Colorado River, became a popular route for prospectors. With Hi Jolly as chief driver, their caravan of camels traveled 25 to 30 miles a day, with loads of 600 to 800 pounds each. The corps successfully reached California.

Beale deemed the effort a great success:

> The harder the test they [the camels] are put to, the more fully they seem to justify all that can be said of them. They pack water for days under a hot sun and never get a drop; they pack heavy burdens of corn and oats for months and never get a grain; and on the bitter greasewood and other worthless shrubs, not only subsist, but keep fat. I look forward to the day when every mail route across the continent will be conducted and worked altogether with this economical and noble brute. (Jacobs)

Davis's successor as secretary of war, John Floyd, shared Beale's enthusiasm. He reported to Congress in 1858 that "the entire adaptation of camels to military operations on the Plains may now be taken as demonstrated" (Jacobs). He unsuccessfully asked for funds to purchase 1,000 more camels.

Politics, not inherent deficiencies, doomed the army's use of camels. The outbreak of the Civil War redirected military attention elsewhere. Nonetheless, during the war 80 camels and two Egyptian drivers passed into Confederate hands. However, other problems arose during the camel experiments. The rocky soils of the Southwest had proven un-

kind to the camels' feet. And mules and horses, essential to the army, panicked at the sight and smell of these odd, foreign creatures.

Hollywood would take notice of this odd chapter in southwestern history. In 1954 the film *Southwest Passage* re-created the camel corps story, with Rod Cameron playing Lt. Edward Beale. John Ireland and Joanne Dru costarred. Although *Southwest Passage* took a shot at historical accuracy, a much later effort by Disney turned the project into a travesty. The Disney film, *Hawmps!* (1976), provided a decidedly humorous, indeed, ridiculous retelling of the story. The film starred several veteran western actors, including Slim Pickens, Denver Pyle, and Jack Elam.

The army auctioned off some of the camels, but others escaped into the desert, only to be shot as pests by prospectors and hunters. Two private efforts at raising camels followed the pioneering government experiments. Both failed, in one case leaving 89 hapless animals abandoned and wandering the sand dunes near Galveston.

After the army abandoned the camel experiment, Hi Jolly lived the remainder of his life in Arizona. He operated a freighting business between Colorado River ports and mining camps until it failed. He released his last camel in the desert near Gila Bend and later married a Tucson woman and fathered two children. For a time he mined in Quartzsite, Arizona, where he died in 1902 at age 73. A colorful pyramid-shaped tomb marks his grave in the Quartzsite cemetery.

Camels also showed up elsewhere in the West. A mining company in British Columbia used and then released some

Bactrian camels. The animals drifted south into Nevada and Idaho. Other Arabian camels roamed the deserts of Texas, California, and Arizona. The last authenticated sightings came in the early twentieth century, but local residents claim that some of the hardy beasts still survive in remote areas.

One legendary camel became known as the "Red Ghost." In 1883 a large beast trampled a woman. Clumps of reddish fur clung to a nearby thorn bush, and huge hoofprints appeared in the mud. A few days later, a large, unidentified animal tromped through a tent where two miners lay sleeping. Again large hoofprints, twice the size of those left by horses, and pieces of red fur marked the site. A rancher reported that the animal, now known to be a camel, carried a rider who did not appear to be alive. Later prospectors saw something fall from the camel's back. They retrieved the object, which turned out to be a human skull.

The so-called Red Ghost and its headless rider continued to frighten people for the next decade until an Arizona farmer finally shot it in 1893. The animal had at last shaken off the remnants of its dead rider, though it still carried leather straps where the corpse had been attached. No one ever identified the ghoulish phantom rider.

References

Boyd, Eva Jolene. *Noble Brutes: Camels on the American Frontier.* Plano: Republic of Texas Press, 1995.

Faulk, Odie B. *The U.S. Camel Corps: An Army Experiment.* New York: Oxford University Press, 1976.

Jacobs, Ellen. The Camel Corps Page: *http://artemis.simmons.edu/~jacobs/camel.html.*

Woodbury, Chuck. "U.S. Camel Corps Remembered in Quartzsite, Arizona." *Out West* 18 (April 1992): *http://www.outwest-newspaper.com/camels.html.*

CANADA

See Comparative Frontier Mythology

CANNARY, MARTHA JANE

1852 or 1856–1903. *See* Calamity Jane

CANNIBALISM

See Donner Party; Packer, Alfred

CARSON, KIT
1809–1868

At five-feet, six inches tall, Christopher Houston Carson stood as one of the giants of Western exploration. The first of the mountain men to gain a national reputation, he would go on to become a scout and guide, Indian agent, and army officer. A century after his death, his life would become mythologized in several admiring television and film depictions.

Born on Christmas Eve, 1809, in Madison County, South Carolina, young Kit entered the world as the ninth of 14 children. His family moved to the area of Boone's Lick, Missouri, and Old Franklin,

Howard County, Missouri, where he became a crack shot with a rifle. His father died when Kit was but nine years old, so the need to work kept him from learning to read or write. He became apprenticed to a saddle maker five years later.

In 1826 the youngster headed west, reaching Santa Fe, New Mexico. He worked at odd jobs until he met moccasinned and buckskin-clad mountain men. In 1829 he hired on with Ewing Young on a trapping expedition bound for California. He further improved his frontier survival skills and returned to Taos two years later. During the next several years, he used the town as a base for fur-trapping expeditions throughout the Rocky Mountains.

Like many mountain men, Kit married an Indian woman, an Arapaho. They had one daughter, named Adaline. After the death of his first wife, he married a Cheyenne woman. His character attracted favorable commentary. "Clean as a hound's tooth," recalled one friend. A man whose "word was as sure as the sun comin' up." In the early 1840s, he worked as a hunter supplying meat to the Colorado fort of William Bent.

In 1842, while returning to Missouri to visit his family, Carson happened to meet John C. **Frémont,** who soon hired him as a guide. Over the next several years, Carson helped guide Frémont to Oregon and California and through much of the central Rocky Mountains and the Great Basin. His service with Frémont, celebrated in Frémont's widely read expedition reports, quickly made Kit Carson a national hero. He appeared in popular fiction as a rugged, courageous mountain man who performed superhuman feats.

After completing the journey, Carson returned to Taos and in 1843 married another woman, María Josefa Jaramillo. He then rejoined Frémont's second expedition and led the party on a difficult crossing over the Sierra Nevadas. Two years later, Carson and Frémont teamed up again at Bent's Fort. They arrived in California at the outbreak of the war with Mexico in 1846. The pair assisted the Bear-Flag rebellion of American colonists fighting against the Spanish. Carson led the forces of U.S. Gen. Stephen Kearney from New Mexico into California when a Californio band led by Andrés Pico challenged American occupation of Los Angeles later that year.

Gen. William Tecumseh Sherman met Carson in California and described the man whom legend presented as so much larger than life: "I cannot express my surprise at beholding a small, stoop-shouldered man, with reddish hair, freckled face, soft blue eyes, and nothing to indicate extraordinary courage or daring. He spoke but little, and answered questions in monosyllables" (Guild and Carter 1988). At the end of the war, Carson returned to New Mexico and took up ranching. By 1853 he and his partner were able to drive a large flock of sheep to California, where gold rush prices paid them a handsome profit.

During this time, Carson made several remarkable trips across the entire continent, carrying dispatches between Washington, D.C., and California. His heroic deeds, already famous in the West, now stirred the imagination of easterners. Political infighting in Washington soured him on politics and military life, so he returned to Taos and his wife. They would eventually raise seven children. In 1854 he received an appointment as Indian agent at Taos. He served his Indian constituency well, continuing to display the same honesty and integrity that characterized his life.

The coming of the Civil War brought him back into uniform. His First New Mexican Volunteer Infantry Regiment fought not against the Confederacy but against Apaches, Navajos, Kiowas, and Comanches. Carson played a prominent and memorable role in the Civil War in New Mexico. He helped organize the New Mexico Volunteer Infantry, which saw action at Valverde in 1862. Most of his military actions, however, concentrated on moving the Navajos to a distant reservation.

In 1863 Carson initiated a brutal economic war against the Navajos. His troops destroyed crops, orchards, and livestock in an attempt to force the Navajos to comply with government orders. The devastation left the Navajos open to attack by their traditional enemies, Utes, Pueblos, Hopis, and Zunis. In 1864 most of the Navajos surrendered. Carson led some 8,000 Navajo men, women, and children on a 300-mile forced march, the "Long Walk," from their Arizona homeland to Fort Sumner, New Mexico. The captives remained confined in the disease-ridden camp for four years.

Ill health forced Colonel Carson to retire in 1867. The following year, he and his large family moved to Boggsville, Colorado, near present-day La Junta. Despite his failing health, he aided Ute Indians in pleading their grievances in Washington. The end was near. His wife died on 23 April 1868, one month before the old scout. The bold, fearless trailblazer died at Fort Lyons, Colorado, on 23 May 1868, soon after eating a buffalo steak prepared by his friend Aloys Scheurich.

Carson provided an irresistible and bona fide hero, ready-made for the popular media. Silent film star Fred Thomson played the scout in a 1928 film. B-western hero Johnny Mack Brown starred in the 1933 film *Fighting with Kit Carson*. Later film incarnations included *The Painted Stallion* (with Sammy McKim, 1938) and *Overland with Kit Carson* (with Wild Bill Elliott, 1939). These popular-culture portraits focused on his early trailblazing, not on his unfortunate service against southwestern Indians during the Civil War.

Television also returned to the irresistible life of the old scout. During the 1950s, actor Bill Williams starred in the popular television series *The Adventures of Kit Carson*. Williams and his sidekick Don "El Toro" Diamond shot more than 100 episodes from 1951 until 1954. (Williams died at age 77 of complications from a brain tumor on 21 September 1992.) Rip Torn played Carson in a 1986 TV miniseries that featured Richard Chamberlain as John C. Frémont.

The Kit Carson Home and Museum in Taos, New Mexico, commemorates his life. The scout also has a town named for him, a small rural community (population about 300) located on the eastern plains of Colorado. His admiring biographers Thelma S. Guild and Harvey L. Carter suggest correctly that "Americans do well to remember Kit Carson as one of their heroes, for Fortune has seldom smiled upon a more deserving character" (Guild and Carter 1988).

References

Guild, Thelma S., and Harvey L. Carter. *Kit*

Carson: A Pattern for Heroes. Lincoln: University of Nebraska Press, 1984, 1988.

Thrapp, Dan L., ed. *Encyclopedia of Frontier Biography.* 4 vols. Lincoln: University of Nebraska Press, 1988; CD-ROM ed., 1994.

Source of Further Information

Kit Carson Home and Museum: Telephone: 505-758-0505; Web Site: *http://taoswebb. com/TAOS/MAT/kit.html.*

CASSIDY, BUTCH

1866–1911, outlaw. *See* Butch Cassidy and the Sundance Kid

CATTLE KATE

1862?–1889

Ellen Liddy "Ella" Watson, aka Cattle Kate, has the dubious honor of being the only woman hanged in the state of Wyoming. Accused of cattle rustling, she and her husband Jim Averill swung from ropes along Wyoming's Sweetwater River on 20 July 1889. Whether she did indeed steal and sell cattle or whether land-hungry ranchers trumped up the charges against her remains hotly debated.

Born in Ontario, Canada, Ella's family moved to Lebanon, Kansas, to homestead. The tall, restless young woman married Bill Pickle at age 18. Her husband drank too much and abused her. She finally secured a divorce and headed west, first to Denver, then to Wyoming. Her first marriage, like many thereafter, proved very short-lived. Strong-willed and attractive,

Watson worked as a cook in several frontier towns, including Cheyenne and Rawlins. Her detractors argue that she supported herself as a prostitute.

She met Jim Averill (or Averell), a Johnson County rancher with lands along the Sweetwater River near Independence Rock. Accounts vary as to whether they actually married or not, but she did take out a marriage license. By some accounts, they operated not as spouses but as business partners. According to this latter view, she worked out of Averill's store as a prostitute. From her homestead near Steamboat Rock, she also assisted in rustling cattle.

Defenders of Averill and Watson point out that neighboring ranchers were land hungry. One version of their hanging points to the Hesse family, who used threats and intimidation to acquire neighboring ranches. Averill and Watson refused to yield, so the Hesses supposedly hung the pair in Spring Creek Canyon without trial or fanfare. Twelve hours after the hangings, deputies arrived from Casper and arrested members of the Hesse family. A trial failed to convict any of the Hesses. One witness, a young boy, died mysteriously shortly before he was to testify. Three other witnesses disappeared without testifying.

Yet another version of their hanging focuses on the cattle barons of the Wyoming Stock Growers Association, especially Albert J. Bothwell. Averill had written letters critical of Bothwell to the press. Modern researcher George W. Hufsmith charges that Bothwell trumped up charges against Averill and Cattle Kate in order to take their land. They represented the kind of small ranchers that larger outfits widely believed to be nothing more than rustlers. In this version of their deaths, a mob of 20 or so hanged the unfortunate pair. The lynching touched off the so-called Powder River (or Johnson County) War, which pitted large ranchers against their smaller neighbors.

Regardless of the facts of her life and death, Cattle Kate remains a fixture of western popular culture. Tourists can enjoy a stay at Cattle Kate's Lodge in Greer, Arizona. Kathy Bressler's Cattle Kate, Inc., offers "Contemporary Clothing with the Look and Feel of the Old West." Although her character remains in dispute, her name serves these two businesses well.

Sources of Further Information

Cattle Kate, Inc.: *http://www.cattlekate.com/ introduction.html.*

Cattle Kate Page: *http://w3.trib.com/~leebo/ kate.htm.*

Cattle Kate's Lodge: *http://www.wmonline.com /cattlekates/.*

CATTLE MUTILATIONS

Over the past three decades, farmers and ranchers in the West (as well as throughout the nation) have reported hundreds of unusual livestock deaths. These ranchers have found their livestock, mostly cattle, dead, without a clear cause: no bullet or knife wounds and no traces at the scene. What's more, the animals bear highly unusual and consistent mutilations. Someone or something has been deliberately removing certain organs (patches of skin, tongues, lips, ears, eyes, genitalia, rectums, and tails) and has frequently drained the animals of blood. Most people refer to these bizarre killings as "cattle mutilations" or, more colloquially, "cat mutes."

The first recorded cattle mutilation occurred in 1967 at the King Ranch in the San Luis Valley of southern Colorado. Rancher Harry King found his three-year-old Appaloosa horse, Lady, lying on her side, dead, two days after she had disappeared. The owner found the animal's corpse shocking and unsightly: Lady had no flesh from the neck up, and the exposed skeleton appeared as though the sun had decayed the body for a considerable time. Even more bizarre, Lady's tracks stopped nearly 100 feet away from her remains. Forty feet away from the body stood a broken bush and a small, circular configuration of eight holes about four inches deep.

Strange reports soon began to circulate in other western states, including North Dakota, South Dakota, and Nebraska. By the mid-1970s, ranchers in every western state had reported baffling animal mutilations. A rash of puzzling cattle deaths broke out in Montana in 1975. That same year, people in Council, Idaho, discovered six dead cattle with missing tongues, sexual organs, and udders. Residents of New Mexico repeatedly found the bodies of cattle with sex organs and rectums removed.

Baffled and frightened westerners soon sought explanations for the inexplicable chain of events. Many observers attributed the grotesque killings to satanic cults. Police agencies in Idaho and Montana successfully linked a few cattle mutilation cases with local Satanist groups. Yet investigators have generally found little evidence linking the widespread killings to cults. Others have argued that ravenous scavengers have selectively consumed certain organs of the animals, which had simply dropped dead from natural causes. Opponents of this view, however, argue that wild predators lack the ability to make such clean, precise rips and tears. Other people have reported seeing a large, "hairy beast" in their backyards during the same time frame in which many animal killings have occurred. Could the culprit be **Bigfoot**?

Conspiracy buffs speculate that members of the U.S. government are secretly involved in the mutilations. These theorists argue that the government is conducting covert chemical warfare experiments on western ranchers' livestock. Proponents of this theory point to the sightings of mysterious, unidentified black helicopters flying at unusually low altitudes prior to the discovery of several mutilations. These fears reflect the longstanding distrust that many westerners feel for the federal government, which owns vast amounts of western land. The U.S. government, however, is both resourceful and powerful enough to gather cattle for research without pilfering them from hapless ranchers.

One of the most popular theories to account for cattle mutilations suggests that humankind is not alone in the universe. Several witnesses—including ranchers, police officers, and "mutologists"—have linked the puzzling events to extraterrestrials, who beam the animals up into their ships and conduct biological experiments on them. Evidence cited includes the absence of tracks around the carcasses; eyewitness sightings of strange balls of bright, fast-moving lights in the sky; the unexplained nature of the killings; and the widespread occurrence

of mutilations near **Roswell, New Mexico**, and **Area 51**, Nevada. Some mutologists have speculated that aliens have repeatedly visited earth over the past several years to harvest bovine DNA to create biological clones. Whether the motivations of these visitors are insidious or benign varies with the theorist.

Fed up with the uproar, in 1975 Governor Richard D. Lamm of Colorado ordered a statewide investigation of the strange livestock deaths, calling the phenomenon "one of the great outrages in the history of the western cattle industry" (*Washington Post,* 1 January 1986). The Colorado Bureau of Investigation (CBI) thoroughly examined more than 200 reported incidents. They concluded that scavenging animals had caused most of the strange mutilations and blamed human copycats for the remaining cases, which showed evidence of knife incisions.

The CBI probe did not mitigate public concern. Congress ultimately stepped in and funded a federal investigation in 1979. Kenneth Rommel, a former FBI agent who specialized in counterintelligence, directed the year-long investigation, called "Operation Animal Mutilation," which focused on cases in New Mexico. Rommel personally inspected the corpses of 25 supposed "mutes," perused several reports, and interviewed specialists, including veterinarians, reporters, forensic pathologists, livestock association officials, and paranormal investigators. His heavily documented and convincing report blamed Mother Nature for almost every case. Rommel concluded that predatory animals had created many of the wounds. He also asserted that the mass media played a key role in perpetuating myths surrounding the deaths, thereby compounding the problem and creating hysteria.

Conspiracy buffs, especially those who believe that aliens visit the earth to abduct helpless bovines, deny Rommel's conclusions. Emmy award–winning documentary filmmaker Linda Moulton Howe produced a popular documentary—*A Strange Harvest,* which aired on HBO in 1980—supporting the alien thesis. She also wrote a book by the same name, published in 1989. Skeptics and believers alike have produced numerous Web sites on the subject. Scoffers have also created tongue-in-cheek cartoons about the phenomenon. The FBI agent Fox Mulder of the popular television show *The X-Files* has referred to the infamous cattle mutilations. In 1982 Alan Rudolph directed a movie called *Endangered Species* about a New York police officer investigating cattle mutilations in the West. The myth surrounding the causes of cattle mutilations lives on in popular culture. The fascination with the mystery itself remains, with all the varied explanations retaining their champions.

—*Jane Veronica Charles Smith*

References

Howe, Linda Moulton. *A Strange Harvest.* Cheyenne, WY: Pioneer Printing, 1989.

Rommel, Kenneth M., Jr. *Operation Animal Mutilation: Report of the District Attorney First Judicial District State of New Mexico.* Santa Fe, NM: Criminal Justice Department, 1980.

CAVALRY TRILOGY

At the climax of director John Ford's classic 1939 film *Stagecoach,* when John Wayne and his companions are on the verge of being massacred by Apaches, a welcome bugle call heralds their rescue. The cavalry arrives to save the day, as it so often did in western films. Nine years later, however, the great director examined these legendary guardians of the frontier much more closely. In three films released between 1948 and 1950—his "cavalry trilogy"—Ford scrutinized and mythologized the lonely, violent, duty-driven world of the horse soldiers.

Fort Apache, the film that began the trilogy, featured lead performances by two of Ford's favorite actors, John Wayne and Henry Fonda. Fonda, surprisingly and effectively cast as a humorless tyrant, arrives from the East in the movie's opening to take command of Arizona's remote Fort Apache. He quickly loses the respect of his troops as a result of his arrogance and carelessness. Even worse, he treacherously breaks his subordinate Wayne's word of honor to Cochise that the cavalry would not attack the Apaches. Foolishly dividing his inferior forces, Fonda manages to get nearly his entire command wiped out. At the film's memorable conclusion, set years later, Wayne praises Fonda's bravery and sacrifice of his men. Realizing that the country needs heroes, Wayne conveniently forgets the futility and wastefulness of the slaughter.

Fort Apache beautifully evokes the humdrum, regimented routine of a remote western army post. Ford also demonstrates with power and subtlety the heartbreak and loss that inevitably accompany warfare. With regard to historical accuracy, *Fort Apache* does not bear close scrutiny, nor was it intended to do so.

Real-life troops based at Fort Apache

never fought a comparable action, nor did Cochise ever win such a large-scale, decisive battle. Ford actually based Fonda's character on George Armstrong Custer, and he modeled the final battle on Custer's defeat at the **Little Big Horn.** He simply moved the action from Montana to Arizona and changed the tribe from Sioux to Apache. Adding an extra layer of unreality, the film's "Apaches" are actually Navajos. Furthermore, shooting took place in Ford's beloved Monument Valley, New Mexico, hundreds of miles from the Arizona locations purportedly depicted. *Fort Apache* may be bad history, but it represents fabulous movie mythmaking.

Ford's sequel, *She Wore a Yellow Ribbon,* tells a less epic tale. Cavalry commander John Wayne, nearing retirement, leads his men on a patrol, trying to preserve the peace after Custer's defeat. The film consists of a series of small vignettes, many quite memorable. Wayne's troops find dead soldiers and citizens on several occasions and have to bury these unfortunates. The troops had recently sighted the war party responsible for the murders but could not pursue them because of preexisting orders. A former Confederate general serving as a Seventh Cavalry private dies, and his comrades bury him with full honors. A young sergeant, alone and pursued by Indians, escapes by jumping a ravine on his horse. A peace parley with an elderly chief fails, as he acknowledges that he cannot prevent his young men from fighting the encroaching whites, even though he realizes this will lead to certain disaster for the Indians. Surprisingly, though, these events do not lead to a violent conclusion. Instead, Wayne cleverly drives off the Indian horses, bringing about a peaceful resolution to the conflict.

She Wore a Yellow Ribbon features one of John Wayne's best performances. Ford discovered Wayne and gave him the role in *Stagecoach* that, along with his role in *Red River,* made him a star. The director, however, had long viewed his friend and protégé as something of an oaf, albeit one with great screen presence. As a result, Ford resisted giving Wayne complex roles or large amounts of dialogue. However, impressed by Wayne's acting in the previous year's *Red River* (directed by Wayne's friend Howard Hawks), Ford decided he could trust his star with a more fully developed character. The results confirmed his assessment. *She Wore a Yellow Ribbon* features many haunting folk songs, terse exchanges of dialogue, and gorgeously shot but desolate scenery, memorably evoking the harsh, lonely lives of soldiers. Ford succeeds in commemorating their sacrifices with his mythic image of the gallant, honorable men who protected the West and brought peace to the frontier.

Ford's fictionalized version of the events following Custer's defeat bears little relation to actuality. Troops poured onto the western plains after the Seventh Cavalry's embarrassing defeat by the Sioux, but they did not pursue the same restrained tactics used by Wayne in this film. The government and army high command, headed by President Ulysses S. Grant and Gen. William Tecumseh Sherman, determined to break forever the power of the plains Indians. Troops attacked and burned Indian villages, often not sparing women and children. Army forces arrested Crazy Horse, leader of the victorious forces at the Little Big

Horn, then killed him while he was in captivity. Ford tells a more enjoyable, but less accurate, version of these events.

After *She Wore a Yellow Ribbon,* Ford initially intended to turn to other subjects. Republic Pictures, however, informed him that it would only finance his personal project *The Quiet Man* (filmed in 1952) if he first cranked out another western. He obliged by filming *Rio Grande,* the last and least remembered film in the trilogy. The stars of *The Quiet Man* also appear in *Rio Grande:* John Wayne, Maureen O'Hara, and Victor McLaglen. In *Rio Grande,* Wayne's cavalry troops mostly concern themselves with rescuing children captured by the Apaches, which they accomplish by a stealthy, illegal raid into Mexico. Meanwhile, in *The Quiet Man,* in a fairly conventional romantic subplot, Wayne's estranged wife O'Hara rails against his insensitivity but finally yields to his manly charm.

The cavalry excursion into Mexico portrayed in *Rio Grande* closely resembles an actual event: an 1873 raid across the border led by Col. Ranald Mackenzie. Unlike in the film, the forces involved in the real event belonged to the Fourth Cavalry, not the more famous Seventh Cavalry. Also unlike in the film, Mackenzie's forces killed mostly women and children on their raid, which they carried out in order to take, not rescue, hostages. By this tactic they hoped to convince Indians in Mexico to halt their own raids into Texas.

Wayne's fictionalized character takes great liberties with the historic figure that Ford modeled it on. *Rio Grande* accurately portrays the officer as a veteran of the Civil War's Shenandoah campaign and as a trusted friend and subordinate of Gen. Philip Sheridan. The real Mackenzie, however, never married. He suffered throughout the remainder of his life from lingering pain from severe injuries sustained during the Civil War and in campaigns against the Indians. He eventually fell victim to mental illness, which caused his removal from command and hastened his untimely death. It is difficult to imagine him involved in Hollywood-style romantic tribulations with Maureen O'Hara, as presented in the film. Mackenzie is one of the frontier army's most legendary figures but hardly one of its most romantic.

Despite flaws and inaccuracies, Ford's cavalry trilogy has stood the test of time. Although perhaps not on the same level as his great, resonant western masterpieces *The Searchers* and *My Darling Clementine,* very few films do compare to those classics. By presenting his films' soldiers as heroic, devoted, capable, and yet human figures, Ford succeeded in creating an indelible image of the cavalry in the West. We may read in books about the actual characters and events that inspired these films, but the power of the stories and images that he created will continue to overshadow that reality in our minds, for better or for worse.

—Michael Thomas Smith

References

Carnes, Mark C., ed. *Past Imperfect: History according to the Movies.* New York: Henry Holt, 1995.

Gallagher, Tag. *John Ford: The Man and His Films.* Berkeley and Los Angeles: University of California Press, 1986.

Robinson, Charles M., III. *Bad Hand: A Biography of General Ranald S. Mackenzie.* Austin, TX: State House Press, 1993.

Sinclair, Andrew. *John Ford*. New York: Dial Press, 1979.

CHAPMAN, JOHN

1774–1845, pioneer. *See* Appleseed, Johnny

CHINESE

See Bemis, Polly

CHISHOLM, JESSE, AND CHISUM, JOHN

Two prominent westerners of the nineteenth century have often been confused in the public mind, owing to somewhat similar names and a number of other similarities: Jesse Chisholm (1805–1868), a trader and trailblazer but never cattleman nor cowboy, created what would become the Chisholm Trail. John Simpson Chisum (1824–1884) became a prominent cattleman in west Texas and New Mexico. Both men were born in Tennessee and later came West. Chisum's father had originally spelled the name "Chisholm," and the names are pronounced the same. The two men, however, were not related.

In addition to his work as a trader, Jesse Chisholm served as an interpreter and peace negotiator for the U.S. Army in their dealings with various Indian tribes. He supposedly could converse in 14 Native dialects. He also guided expeditions of travelers. Unlike some of his contemporary frontier traders, Chisholm earned a reputation for honesty, fairness, hospitality, and morality—never selling liquor to Indians, for example. He operated trading posts at several Oklahoma locations, including ones near present-day Asher, Oklahoma, a few miles west of Oklahoma City, and near Purcell. He also traveled among Indian villages, selling merchandise from his wagon.

John Chisum's family moved to Texas in 1837. There, he worked at various jobs, including that of clerk for Lamar County. He began ranching in 1854, and 12 years later, following the Civil War, he moved his herds into New Mexico. He settled at Bosque Redondo, about 30 miles north of present-day **Roswell**, New Mexico. During the 1870s, his spread burgeoned outward from South Spring to include some 60,000–100,000 cattle, grazing along 150 miles of the Pecos River in the Staked Plains.

Whereas Chisum had to fight off raiding Indians, Jesse Chisholm generally enjoyed amicable relations with Native Americans. In 1861, for example, Chisholm guided the Shawnee and other Indians to a place of safety on the Arkansas River at the present location of Wichita. Four years later, he laid out a trail from Wichita to the Wichita-Caddo Agency, where the city of Anadarko now is located. Such trailblazing would earn him his place in history. The great Chisholm Trail began with his treks between Wichita, Kansas, and the Cimarron River crossing just south of the present town of Dover, Oklahoma, a total distance of about 150 miles. Eventually extended to some 800 miles, this wagon route became the Chisholm Trail, the path of hundreds of thousands of longhorns driven north from Texas through "Indian Territory" (Oklahoma) and on to Kansas cattle towns.

John Chisum earned his place in New Mexico history. He marked his cattle with a long ear slit, called a "jinglebob." The term also became the nickname for his vast ranch. Although he was a powerful figure in the economy and politics of frontier New Mexico, Chisum does not appear to have been actively involved in the infamous **Lincoln County War.** Two of the principals of the conflict, Alexander McSween and John Tunstall, numbered among his friends. During the local conflict, **Billy the Kid** apparently stayed on Chisum's ranch for a time. The cattleman supported Pat Garrett's election as Lincoln County sheriff in 1880.

Chisholm died within hours after he was stricken gravely ill near Greary, Oklahoma. He was buried in an old Indian burying ground. A simple granite marker attests to his life of frontier hospitality: "No one left his home cold or hungry." The Chisholm Trail Museum near Waurika, Oklahoma, memorializes his life. John Chisum, who never married, died in Eureka Springs, Arkansas, in 1884, and is buried in Paris, Texas. Although he estimated that rustlers and conflict had made off with 10,000 cattle, he still left an estate valued at half a million dollars. Both men left significant marks on the history and legends of the West.

References

Lamar, Howard R., ed. *The New Encyclopedia of the American West.* New Haven, CT: Yale University Press, 1998.

Thrapp, Dan L., ed. *Encyclopedia of Frontier Biography.* 4 vols. Lincoln: University of Nebraska Press, 1988; CD-ROM ed., 1994.

CLANTON BROTHERS

See Earp Brothers

CLARK, CHARLES "BADGER," JR.

1883–1957

The original cowboy poet "lariat," Badger Clark is the most revered name in the genre. Like Curley Fletcher and Bruce Kiskaddon (*see* **Cowboy Poetry**), he helped create a corpus of authentic poetry based on western range life. Born in Iowa, he grew up in South Dakota, son of a preacher. During his youth, he spent a few years as part of a failed agricultural colony in Cuba. Conflicts with Spanish families there led to some jail time.

After his return to South Dakota, he wrote for the *Lead Daily Call.* Like so many others, Clark migrated to the Southwest for health reasons following a bout of tuberculosis. He cowboyed at the Cross I Quarter Circle Ranch near Tombstone, Arizona. He expressed his joy of the cowboy life in verse, sending his poems to his family in letters. Clark learned he could sell and perform his poetry when he received ten dollars for one of his "letter poems," which his stepmother had sent to a magazine. As he explained, "Boys, I knowed then I'd found my life's work—no boss, no regular hours and no responsibility—I was a poet."

He successfully traded the saddle for the pen. He published his first book, *Sun and Saddle Leather,* in 1915 and his only novel, *Spike,* a decade later. In later life, he returned to South Dakota, a state that named him its poet laureate in 1937. Near Custer, the state of South Dakota preserves his bachelor log cabin, the Badger Hole. The town of Hot Springs hosts an annual Badger Clark Hometown Cowboy Poetry Gathering. Cowboy poets of today speak his name with reverence and continue to recite many of his works, most notably "A Cowboy's Prayer":

Oh Lord, I've never lived where churches
    grow.
I love creation better as it stood
That day You finished it so long ago
And looked upon Your work and called it
    good.
I know that others find You in the light
That's sifted down through tinted window
    panes,
And yet I seem to feel You near tonight
In this dim, quiet starlight on the plains.
I thank You, Lord, that I am placed so well,
That You have made my freedom so
    complete;
That I'm no slave of whistle, clock or bell,
Nor weak-eyed prisoner of wall and street.
Just let me live my life as I've begun
And give me work that's open to the sky;
Make me a pardner of the wind and sun.
And I won't ask a life that's soft or high.
Let me be easy on the man that's down;
Let me be square and generous with all.
I'm careless sometimes, Lord, when I'm in
    town,
But never let 'em say I'm mean or small!
Make me as big and open as the plains,

As honest as the hoss between my knees,
Clean as the wind that blows behind the
    rains,
Free as the hawk that circles down the
    breeze!
Forgive me, Lord, if sometimes I forget.
You know about the reasons that are hid.
You understand the things that gall and
    fret;
You know me better than my mother did.
Just keep an eye on all that's done and said,
And right me, sometimes, when I turn
    aside,
And guide me on the long, dim trail ahead
That stretches upward toward the Great
    Divide.

References

Lamar, Howard R., ed. *The New Encyclopedia of the American West.* New Haven, CT: Yale University Press, 1998.

Thrapp, Dan L., ed. *Encyclopedia of Frontier Biography.* 4 vols. Lincoln: University of Nebraska Press, 1988; CD-ROM ed., 1994.

CLOVIS MAN

See McJunkin, George

CODY, WILLIAM FREDERICK "BUFFALO BILL"

1846–1917

Scout and buffalo hunter, William Frederick "Buffalo Bill" Cody lived the reality of frontier life in the American West. As the first great Wild West showman, however, he shaped the mythology of the frontier more strongly than any other single person. The town of Cody, Wyoming, with its magnificent museum complex dedicated to Cody, provides a fitting tribute to this extraordinary man. During his more than 30 years in show business, he presented his vision of the real "Wild West" to crowds across the United States and Europe. The wild action of Indian attacks; galloping horses, cattle, and bison; trick shooting; and equestrian feats provided a thrilling distillation of Cody's western adventures. Viewers left convinced they had witnessed the drama and excitement of the Old West as it really was.

Cody was born on 26 February 1846 in the town of Le Claire in Scott County, Iowa Territory. Eight years later, his family moved west and settled near Leavenworth, Kansas. His father died in 1857, leaving young William as the family provider. At age 14, he rode as a mounted messenger for the Majors and Russell company and later for the Pony Express. Once, in an emergency, he reputedly made an epic 322-mile journey, riding a total of 21 horses. He served in the Civil War with irregular militia units and with the Seventh Kansas Volunteer Cavalry. His wartime duties included scouting, spying, and possibly stealing horses for the Union cause.

Cody met Louisa "Lulu" Frederici while serving in the military and married her in 1866. Theirs would be a stormy marriage that included both a divorce and a reconciliation. They briefly ran an inn in Kansas after the war, but Cody could not abide a sedentary life. He rode further west, hiring on as a scout and guide. In 1867 and 1868 he earned his nickname, Buffalo Bill, by shooting thousands of the animals as food for railroad workers. With characteristic flair, he even gave his government-issue gun a name, the Lucretia Borgia.

Cody also worked on the Indian frontier. Gen. Philip Sheridan named him chief of scouts for the Fifth U.S. Cavalry. Cody impressed him with a 60-hour, 350-mile ride to deliver dispatches. His decade of cavalry service began in 1868. He fought in several campaigns against the Indians. He killed a Sioux chief named Tall Bull and later bestowed that name on a prize horse. His most famous Indian encounter occurred on 17 July 1876 while scouting for Gen. Wesley Merritt. He killed and scalped a Cheyenne Indian chief named Yellow Hand (or Yellow Hair). Cody would later reenact this dramatic episode countless times in his Wild West Show.

The dime novelist Ned **Buntline** played a major role in transforming Cody from frontier scout and buffalo hunter to western hero. The two met in 1869. A popular and prolific writer, Buntline authored about 400 dime novels. Buntline drew upon many sources, including his own colorful background, for inspiration. He made Cody the hero of four novels, the first titled *Buffalo Bill, the King of the Bordermen.*

By the early 1870s, Cody's fame as a bold, brave frontiersman had grown considerably. The year 1872 proved especially eventful. He guided a highly publicized buffalo hunting expedition for Grand Duke Alexis of Russia. Nebraskans elected Cody to the state legislature, but he soon resigned. He also got into theater. On 16 December he appeared as himself at the Chicago opening of Buntline's play *Scouts of the Prairie*. What the farcical play lacked in artistry, Cody made up for with charisma and energy. The excitement of screaming Indians and blasting six-guns thrilled audiences. Cody broke with Buntline after a year but never lost his zest for performing.

Buffalo Bill became very popular among the seemingly insatiable eastern readers of the "penny dreadfuls" (pulp novels). In addition to Buntline's four novels about Cody, the prolific Prentiss Ingraham wrote another 121. All told, more than 1,000 pulp publications made Cody their hero.

Cody used his new notoriety to begin a theatrical career. He toured for 11 years, acting in various melodramas depicting life and death on the frontier. In 1879 Cody took a personal hand in creating his own mythology. He worked with Frank E. Bliss to publish his first autobiography, *The Life of Hon. William F. Cody, Known as Buffalo Bill*. His flair for showmanship and organization came to the fore three years later when he organized a Fourth of July celebration for his hometown, North Platte, Nebraska. The showman and promoter convinced town leaders to sponsor an "Old Glory Blowout." The events, including a rodeo competition and fancy horseback feats, provided the germ for his world-famous show.

The following summer, Cody began touring with his Wild West Show, an exhibition of Indian fights, roundups, stage robberies, and buffalo hunts. It opened at the Omaha fairgrounds on 19 May 1883. Gordon "Pawnee Bill" Lillie worked for Cody as an interpreter. The show's stars included Johnny Baker, the Cowboy Kid, and Buck Taylor, King of the Cowboys. Taylor, like Cody, became immortalized in pulp literature. Prentiss Ingraham's 1887 potboiler about Taylor began his rise as a literary legend of the West.

Annie Oakley (Phoebe Anne Moses), called "Little Sure Shot," joined the show for the 1884–1885 season and became a leading attraction. This diminutive woman's unerring marksmanship transfixed audiences everywhere. Cody's partner, Nate Salsbury, deserves much credit for keeping the big show running. Cody sometimes incapacitated himself with drink. Salsbury contributed a steadying influence, logistical skills, and shrewd business sense.

In 1887 Cody and Salsbury packed up their cast of 200 actors and 300 head of livestock and sailed to England. They performed for Queen Victoria's Golden Jubilee; the fascinated queen requested an encore performance. The troupe performed at Earl's Court for 30,000–40,000 people each day from May through October. They returned for a multiyear tour of the Continent in 1889. An estimated 6 million people saw Cody's appearances at the 1893 Chicago World's Fair. Promoters of Wyoming's Cheyenne Frontier Days, first held in 1897, invited Cody's troupe to perform there the following year.

Cody considered his show an educational endeavor (and he avoided the term "show"). He desired to give audiences an authentic look at real frontier events as he had lived them. He promised audiences "the grandest, most realistic and overwhelmingly thrilling war-spectacle ever seen." Granted, he took considerable theatrical license in embellishing things, but crowds loved it. He did recruit authentic, old-time cowboys, bona fide Indians, mostly Lakota, and an international cast. He broadened his show's ethnic makeup by hiring two Hispanic cowboys from San Antonio, Texas. "Champion Vaquero Rider" Antonio Esquivel performed off and on from 1883 to 1905. Another vaquero, José "Mexican Joe" Berrara, amazed audiences with his rope tricks. He also included Argentine gauchos and Russian Cossacks. He renamed the expanded operation "Buffalo Bill's Wild West and Congress of Rough Riders of the World."

Cody spent his money lavishly, foolishly, and generously. Much of his wealth went into his 4,000-acre Scout's Rest Ranch in western Nebraska. His Wyoming investments included 400,000 acres in the Big Horn basin and the founding of Cody, complete with the Irma Hotel (named for his beloved daughter). He also founded a newspaper, *The Cody Enterprise.* Cody's considerable talents did not include shrewd investing. He lost half a million dollars in a mining scam. His marriage to Louisa, always conflict-ridden, ended in divorce. Cody claimed that she had tried to poison him at Christmas in 1900 and sued for divorce. The stormy, sensational proceedings came to a head in 1905. Cody lost his suit and had to pay Lulu's $318 in court costs. The two reconciled five years later.

Beset by financial woes, Cody briefly—from 1911 to 1913—joined his show with that of a rival. Maj. Gordon W. "Pawnee Bill" Lillie had organized his Far East show in 1888. He recognized the appeal of exotic costumes, such as that worn by Mexican *charros* (richly attired horsemen). He also emphasized the special

Irma Hotel, Cody, Wyoming, named for Cody's daughter

skills of foreign riders, skills that made them great hits with North American audiences. Like Cody, Lillie toured widely throughout the United States and Europe.

Eventually, production, labor, and travel costs for such shows became too great. The Cody show alone included more than 200 performers and even more animals. In 1913 both Wild West show promoters faced bankruptcy. At 70 years old, Cody gamely appeared with the 101 Ranch Wild West show in a rather unsuccessful 1916 season. His health declined

Statue of Cody in front of the Buffalo Bill Historical Center, Cody, Wyoming

along with his finances, and he died in Denver on 10 January 1917.

Like his life, Cody's burial became a matter of flamboyance and controversy. He had often expressed the wish for burial in Cody, Wyoming, the town that he had created. According to his wife, however, he changed his mind shortly before dying. She said that he now favored Lookout Mountain, west of Denver. The fact that Harry Tammen and the *Denver Post* agreed to pay funeral and other expenses probably played a role in the change of venue.

Cody's cultural significance has continued to grow. Cowboy singer Michael Martin Murphey counts Cody among his personal heroes. Murphey often performs in a long buckskin coat reminis-cent of Cody's dress. Some original film of Cody survives, and countless B-westerns have perpetuated his mythology.

Cody's life and legend are commemorated at several locations. The most impressive memorial is a vast museum complex, the Buffalo Bill Historical Center, in Cody, Wyoming. Exhibits of posters, paintings, photographs, and artifacts document Cody's life as well as his Wild West Show. The center also includes the Cody Firearms Museum, Plains Indian Museum, Whitney Gallery of Western Art, and the McCracken Library. The Buffalo Bill Memorial Museum sits adjacent to his grave on Lookout Mountain in Colorado. His Scout's Rest Ranch, near North Platte, Nebraska, also draws visits from Cody's many fans. "Cody" as a first name remains popular among western families, whose little boys proudly carry a cultural link to one of the Old West's genuine heroes and legends.

See also Pulp Novelists

References

Rosa, Joseph G., and Robin May. *Buffalo Bill and His Wild West: A Pictorial Biography.* Lawrence: University Press of Kansas, 1989.

Russell, Don. *The Lives and Legends of Buffalo Bill.* Norman: University of Oklahoma Press, 1960.

Thrapp, Dan L., ed. *Encyclopedia of Frontier Biography.* 4 vols. Lincoln: University of Nebraska Press, 1988; CD-ROM ed., 1994.

Source of Further Information

Buffalo Bill Memorial Museum Web Site: *http://www.buffalobill.org.*

COLTER, JOHN

1775?–1813

In the early 1800s, John Colter (also spelled Coulter) became the first white man in Wyoming and explored much of eastern Idaho and southwestern Montana. He was the first white man to see the upper valley of the Bighorn, the Teton Range, Jackson's Hole, Pierre's Hole, the headwaters of the Colorado and Snake Rivers, and Union Pass. Colter also saw the thermal springs in the Yellowstone territory that are now named Colter's Hell. His treks as a fur trapper added to the **Lewis and Clark expedition**'s maps of this unknown region, and his rash adventures in the mountain wilderness created many legends. The story of Colter's Run, his miraculous escape from a band of more than 500 Blackfoot Indians, remains famous in the history of mountain men.

Colter was born in Virginia around 1775, although William Clark recorded him as being a young man from Kentucky. Thomas James (*Three Years among the Indians and Mexicans,* 1846), a member of the Missouri Fur Company in 1807, described his character: "His veracity was never questioned among us and his character was that of a true American backwoodsman. He was about thirty-five years of age, five feet ten inches in height and wore an open, ingenious, and pleasing countenance of the Daniel Boone stamp. Nature had formed him, like Boone, for hardy endurance of fatigue, privations, and perils" (James 1846).

Colter was not always as wise and levelheaded as James described him. While in the army in 1803 and 1804, his drinking earned him the reputation of being a troublemaker. His lack of discipline made him a poor soldier but also a creative, ingenious explorer and trapper. His daring nature, rash decision making, and adventurous mind-set served him well on the frontier.

Colter joined Lewis and Clark's expedition in 1804. He traveled extensively with them and eventually left to join two fur trappers named Dixon and Handcock. He soon left them and teamed with George Drouillard; they became members of Manuel Lisa's fur-trapping encampments. They traveled with Lisa's St. Louis Missouri Fur Company to the Rockies and constructed Fort Raymond. The trappers settled in the mountain wilderness among tribes of Indians, including the Shoshone, Flathead, Crow, Blackfeet, and Sioux. Colter and Drouillard spread the news of the trapping fort to these tribes around the area.

In the winter of 1807/1808, Colter traveled alone through the snowy mountain wilderness to the distant tribes, informing them of the new business in the area. He explored uncharted areas of the American West, becoming the first white man to see the thermal springs supposedly on the rim of Yosemite Lake. However, many historians claim that he actually discovered the "Stinking Water" Shoshone River near present-day Cody, Wyoming. No one believed his stories of this strange, beautiful place. His compatriots ridiculed him for his tall tales, dubbing the part of Yellowstone Park that he described "Colter's Hell."

Skeptics did not believe Colter's fantastic descriptions of Yellowstone Park. Old Faithful

Blackfoot Indians attacked often and came to know Colter as a killer of their braves. Colter became friends with the Crow Indians, and like many other mountain men after him, he wore Indian garb and practiced many Indian ways. He left the area in the fall of 1808 after his legendary escape from the Blackfeet, but he returned with Maj. Andrew Henry to Fort Raymond in 1809. In 1810, while Colter traveled to Three Forks on the Jefferson River, the Blackfoot Indians again attacked him and his party. He vowed that if God saved him, he would never return to the mountains. He survived and settled as a yeoman farmer on the Missouri frontier, a neighbor of Daniel Boone's. He lived with a woman named Sally in a cabin that he constructed.

Other versions of his life tell of a short marriage to Nancy Hooker instead, but all agree that he did have a son.

Colter died of jaundice in his home in 1813, before he turned 40. He died too poor to afford a proper funeral or burial. According to some sources, his wife covered his body and set out on her own, leaving him in their cabin. Much in the spirit of John Colter, she headed for unknown places, alone and with little more than a few belongings.

By far the most famous of all of the trapper's adventures was Colter's Run. In 1808 the Blackfoot Indians attacked Colter and his partner John Potts as they paddled the Jefferson River near Three Forks. Colter, assuming the Indians would only rob them, turned the canoe to shore. An arrow pierced Potts's hip; rather than risking capture and torture, Potts chose to shoot an Indian. Arrows soon riddled his body.

The Indians dismembered his corpse and threw his entrails at Colter's face, who was now stripped of his weapons and clothing. After readying himself for certain torture and death, Colter realized that the Indians were giving him a very slim chance for survival. Asked about his foot speed, he answered that he was a very slow runner. In fact, Colter had always won footraces, and he proved himself very swift and smart that afternoon. The chief put Colter in a field a few hundred yards from the tribe of more than 500 Blackfoot Indians and told him to run. Colter sprinted six miles to the nearest river, his nose streaming blood and his feet full of prickly pear spikes. A glance over his shoulder showed him only one remaining pursuer; Colter shocked him with an abrupt stop and about-face.

The ill-fated Indian fell, broke his spear, and died by Colter's hand. The trapper hid in a beaver dam and watched the Indians search for him for the remainder of the day. He could see them walking over the dam and feared they would set it on fire. They did not, and after their departure, he swam downstream. He still had to cover hundreds of miles through snow to return to Lisa's fort. He subsisted on roots and berries and arrived naked and nearly unrecognizable in the snow, with no weapons or food. Several of his acquaintances recorded his story firsthand. John Bradbury reported that Colter made the trip to the fort in seven days, covering the distance quickly, considering his ordeal. According to Thomas James, he traveled the 300 miles to the fort in 11 days. "The whole affair is a fine example of the quick and ready thoughtfulness and presence of mind in a desperate situation, and the power of endurance." James also described Colter's scaling an "almost perpendicular mountain" during his return to the fort, a "feat probably never performed before by a mortal man" (James 1846). Several of the reports from his contemporaries describe his incredible adventure; most are too amazing to be true. The reported distance of his journey after escaping the Indians ranged from 100 to 1,000 miles, and the elapsed time of his walk from 5 to 11 days. Regardless of the specifics, his escape and journey remain remarkable feats.

In 1997 Lillian Ruth Colter-Frick published a book titled *Courageous Colter and Companions* about the mountain men of the early nineteenth century. The book focuses on John Colter's life but includes information about the other people with whom he had contact. The author, a descendant of Colter, wished to further his legend as a great explorer. Many authors of children's books and articles have used the story of Colter's Run. Examples include Mary Blount Christian's children's book *Who'd Believe John Colter?* Linda Roberts published an article in 1991 titled "The Adventures of John Colter" in *Cobblestone* magazine. The story made such an impression that the magazine's young readers voted John Colter Person of the Year.

Because of his daring sense of adventure and his dauntless explorations, John Colter is universally appealing to and admired by audiences of all kinds, except probably the Blackfoot Indians. Today, the land that he explored and described to William Clark remains some of the most wildly beautiful in the United States. Much of the area is protected as national and state parks. Tales of his encounters still circulate today, perpetuating the spirit of the mountain man and fur trapper.

—*Ellen J. Oettinger*

References

Gibson, Elizabeth. "John Colter, Mountain Man." *The Old West,* 9 June 1999.

James, Thomas. *Three Years among the Indians and Mexicans.* 1846. Reprint, Lincoln: University of Nebraska Press, 1984.

Utley, Robert M. *A Life Wild and Perilous: Mountain Men and the Paths to the Pacific.* New York: Henry Holt, 1997.

COMPARATIVE FRONTIER MYTHOLOGY

By examining frontiers elsewhere in the world, we help illuminate the unique and transcendental elements of myths of the American West. Myths are not only remnants of a remote past; they also exert a powerful influence over contemporary events. John Clayton, of **Gallatin Writers, Inc.,** recently examined "Montana's Weirdo Fringe: Dangerous Frontier Myths" (*Seattle Times,* 31 July 1996). "As Wallace Stegner noted, the West in general was built not by 'rugged individualists,' but people acting in groups, in the sorts of community activities exemplified by a barn-raising," writes Clayton. "Of course community activities eventually become institutionalized, and that often means government. Which brings us to the Freemen. Many people have pointed out that these hypocrites denounced government despite being on the dole. But they've failed to point out, as historian Patricia Nelson Limerick documented, that it's a time-honored Western tradition."

Richard White took up the same issues in his 1996 presidential address to the Western History Association. He also pointed to "the Unabomber and the Freemen; we had militias in Arizona, Montana, and Washington. There have been bombings in Oklahoma City and Nevada. We have the county independence movement, the Aryan Nations, and the more extreme fringes of Wise Use." He illustrated that what he called "the weirdness of the West" is built upon widely held myths shared by right-wing westerners. Mythical values and assumptions about the past continue to shape human actions.

Themes

Four broad areas of myth have developed out of frontiers in North and South America and Australia:

1. The Golden Frontier of Treasure, Abundance, and Opportunity
2. The Desert Frontier of Barbarism and Emptiness
3. Frontier as Past
4. Frontier as Future

Golden Frontier of Treasure, Abundance, and Opportunity

Alluring tales of treasure greeted the earliest Spanish and Portuguese explorers in this hemisphere. Beginning with Álvar Núñez Cabeza de Vaca, explorers brought back tales of a land "abounding in gold and silver, with [seven] great cities whose houses were many stories high, whose streets were lined with silversmiths' shops, and whose doors were inlaid with turquoise" (quotation from Hammond 1940).

Francisco Vásquez de Coronado, after traveling for months in the wilderness, reached the so-called **Seven Cities of Gold** in the land he named Cibola. Real, as opposed to imaginary, gold strikes would lure immigrants westward for centuries. As Joseph A. Rodríguez has pointed out, early Spanish conquistadors may not have found gold, but they won the battle of history. From the swallows of San Juan Capistrano to the novel ***Ramona,*** Old Spanish California took on a romantic atmosphere. Not until the 1960s did Chicano activists begin challenging the myth of Spanish triumphalism in California and the American Southwest.

In South America, the wealth of the Chibchas or Muiscas in the Andes created a vision of El Dorado, "the gilded one." The mass of golden artifacts at the Gold Museum in Bogotá, Colombia, illustrates that this myth of great golden riches has some very tangible roots. Indeed, by 1600, New Granada had exported more than 4 million ounces of gold. Output eventually totaled some 30 million ounces.

In contrast, Portuguese explorers would search in vain for the precious metal for nearly two centuries. Finally, *bandeirantes* (frontier slave hunters and explorers) discovered riches in Minas Gerais in 1695, and Brazil's first gold rush was on.

Charles Dana Wilber is credited with building the myth of the trans-Mississippi West as a lush garden. He used "scientific" evidence to argue that "rain follows the plow." Unusually high rainfall levels during the 1870s and early 1880s strengthened the garden myth. But then low rainfall levels returned. Many families departed, with signs on their wagons reading "In God we trusted, in Kansas we busted."

Canada experienced "the last best West" in the early twentieth century. Under the faulty frontier belief that "rain follows the plow," tens of thousands of farmers besieged Alberta and Saskatchewan. To their sorrow, they learned firsthand about the true aridity of much of the western plains. Only later would irrigation make sustainable agriculture possible in the region.

Europeans of the nineteenth century plunged into the Australian outback, certain they would discover a massive inland waterway. Indeed, they did discover a massive lake, but alas, they were a million years too late. What had once been a large freshwater lake had become a vast salt pan. Perhaps the name of a body of water in Western Australia says it best: Lake Disappointment.

Many groups in the United States, of course, followed Horace Greeley's advice to "Go west." Pioneers gamely walked westward along the Oregon Trail. Mormons and their handcarts left persecution in the Midwest for freedom in Utah. After the Civil War, ex-slaves, so-called **Exodusters,** fled the South, and "Texodusters" deserted Texas for dreams of land and freedom in Kansas. Thousands of white "Confederados" also left the South, hoping to create a New South on the Brazilian frontier. Later, "Okies" and "Arkies" (Oklahomans and Arkansans) left the twin disasters of the Great Depression and the Dust Bowl for California, the Promised Land.

As Richard Francaviglia has argued recently, the **Disney Frontierland** represents and perpetuates many fundamental and widely shared myths about the American West. Walt Disney put it well: "In Frontierland, we meet the America of the past, out of whose strength and inspiration came the good things of life we enjoy today" (in Francaviglia 1999).

Desert Frontier of Barbarism and Emptiness

Oddly, along with the myths of gold, garden, and riches there arose parallel negative myths. Stephen H. Long, who surveyed a portion of the Louisiana Purchase in 1819, labeled these western territories the "Great American Desert." Walter Prescott Webb created an uproar in the 1850s by reaffirming this view that much of the inland West was desert.

To the north in Canada, the so-called Palliser's Triangle in southwestern Saskatchewan stood as a forbidding desert barrier to settlement. John Palliser's expedition reconnoitered western Canada during the late 1850s. His report, submitted to the Royal Geographical Society, concluded pessimistically that to establish communications entirely within British territory from the east to the Red River would be very difficult and costly because of the semiarid and thus uninhabitable country in southern Saskatchewan and southern Alberta. In short, the Great American Desert did not stop at the U.S. border.

In South America, Brazil's Amazon region and Argentina's Patagonia remained largely uninhabited by Europeans until the twentieth century. And in Australia, with two-thirds of its land area technically desert, no Horace Greeley urges people to the frontier. Instead, we have dreadful warnings of children lost forever in the outback.

Australia: Beyond the Fatal Shore, a PBS program that aired in early September 2000, treats the hard memory of European Australia's grim beginnings as a penal colony. The vast, wide-open spaces of the outback created a powerfully agoraphobic vision of the Australian interior. Today, 99 percent of all Australians live in the cities and suburbs, mostly clinging to the coastline.

Whereas in the Americas, great open spaces set people free and promised new opportunities, in Australia, open space was a restrictive prison. Any attempt to

A powerful western myth is that of the "Great American Desert"

escape into the outback's forbidding terrain invited hardship, starvation, and death. Nonetheless, over the past 200 years, the white urge to conquer this harsh landscape has laid the foundation for Australia's nation building. It also set in motion an inevitable clash with the continent's Aborigines, who were spiritually bonded with and well adapted to the vast inland deserts.

Like the landscape, the inhabitants of these frontiers generated mostly negative imagery. Viewed as savages and barbarians, the colored native populations generated fear and loathing. Even after whites penetrated the wild lands, frontier inhabitants remained fearful specters, uncivilized, dangerous. Gauchos of Argentina and *llaneros* of Venezuela and

Colombia—mixed-blood cowboys—were viewed as little better than the Natives. Argentina's Domingo F. Sarmiento provided the best-known paradigm of these dangerous frontiersman in his 1845 book *Civilization and Barbarism.* "Indian country," or in Australia, "Aborigine country," did not invite anything other than conquest.

Frontier as Past

During the late 1980s, revisionist historians of the American West expended lots of time and energy trying to bury Frederick Jackson Turner (the American historian who emphasized the role of the frontier in the development of U.S. national character) and expunge "frontier" (the so-called F-word). The motivation was sound: to introduce post-Turnerian themes, to explore greater cultural and ethnic diversity, to examine important continuities and changes. However, as Patricia Nelson Limerick's work well illustrates, this was a case of throwing out the baby with the bathwater. In 1987 Limerick pronounced "frontier" to be "an unsubtle concept in a subtle world" (Limerick 1987). Seven years after publishing *The Legacy of Conquest,* she recognized, somewhat to her chagrin, that

> as a mental artifact, the frontier has demonstrated an astonishing stickiness and persistence. It is virtually the flypaper of our mental world; it attaches itself to everything—healthful diets, space shuttles, civil rights campaigns, heart transplants, industrial product development, musical innovations. . . . Whether or not it suits my preference, the concept works as a cultural glue—a mental and emotional fastener that, in some very curious and unexpected ways, works to hold us together. (Limerick 1994)

Yes, despite flaws in the Turner formulation, the frontier as a historical process, an ideological force, and a cultural artifact is simply too powerful and important to dismiss.

Frontier as Future

As Limerick acknowledged, the contradictions and hollowness of past frontier myths have not dulled the attraction of frontier metaphor as *the* place of future opportunity. Brazil's push to the west took physical form in the 1960s with the creation of the new national capital of Brasília on the edge of the Amazonian wilderness. Today *garimpeiros* (gold miners), most working illegally, have created a new Amazonian gold rush.

Hoping to emulate Brasília's success, Argentina briefly renamed its currency the *austral* to point national energy south toward its vast, still sparsely settled Patagonian frontier. In similar fashion, Venezuela pins its hopes on its remote, inland Orinoco River basin. In each case, the frontier is seen as a land of unlimited opportunity and resources, the key to future national greatness.

And of course, space and undersea exploration remain framed in frontier terminology and concepts. How could it be otherwise, after years of watching Jean-Luc Picard inviting us on voyages through *Space: The Final Frontier?*

The Smithsonian Institution developed a special exhibition of more than 200 items from the *Star Wars* films—costumes, props, models, and paintings; the mythic underpinnings of the story. Called The Magic of Myth, the exhibit began in 1999 and will continue to several venues, ending up in Sydney, Australia, in 2002. In the George Lucas films, Chewbacca wears bandoliers, like a good, old-time Mexican revolutionary. Han Solo, with his trusty blaster strapped to his leg, is the very model of the Old West gunslinger. Lucas used these accessories to create links to a romantic, frontier America.

Cyberspace is also conjuring images of the frontier. As one writer has already pointed out, many professionals already "telecommute from town to town practicing their craft for a variety of clients. . . . Some have described this trend as a return to the myth of the American frontier. People are out there with their laptops and cellular telephones, riding the range, prospecting, being cowboys and cowgirls again" (Greinacher 1998). Others will undoubtedly join the ranks of those riding the cyber range.

Conclusion

Interest in comparative frontier analysis remains strong. The June 1999 issue of the *American Historical Review* carried "From Borderlands to Borders," by Jeremy Adelman and Stephen Aron, and published replies and follow-ups in the October issue. Although he confines his remarks to the United States, Paul F. Starrs utilizes a comparative regional perspective in *Let the Cowboy Ride: Cattle Ranching in the American West* (1998). Collections of essays edited by David Weber and Jane Rausch (*Where Cultures Meet,* 1994) and by Donna Guy and Tom Sheridan (*Contested Ground,* 1998) bring comparative analysis to Western Hemisphere frontiers, as does Richard W.

Slatta, *Comparing Cowboys and Frontiers* (1997). As metaphor, as myth, and as historical category, place, and process, the frontier shows little real signs of passing, either in the United States or abroad.

[I presented an earlier version of this essay at the Western History Association conference in San Antonio, Texas, 13 October 2000.]

References

Francaviglia, Richard. "Walt Disney's Frontierland as an Allegorical Map of the American West." *Western Historical Quarterly* 30, no. 2 (Summer 1999): 155–182.

Greinacher, Udo. "Living Like the Jetsons" (1998): *http://www.daap.uc.edu/udo/rpt_web/research/jetsons/jetsons.HTM.*

Hammond, George P. *Coronado's Seven Cities.* Albuquerque, NM: U.S. Coronado Exposition Commission, 1940.

Limerick, Patricia Nelson. *The Legacy of Conquest: The Unbroken Past of the American West.* New York: W. W. Norton and Company, 1987.

———. "The Adventures of the Frontier in the Twentieth Century." In *The Frontier in American Culture,* ed. James R. Grossman. Berkeley and Los Angeles: University of California Press, 1994.

Slatta, Richard W. *Comparing Cowboys and Frontiers.* Norman: University of Oklahoma Press, 1997.

Sources of Further Information

Australia: Beyond the Fatal Shore: *http://www.pbs.org/wnet/australia/episode1and2.html.*

Comparative Frontiers Bibliography: *http://courses.ncsu.edu/classes/hi300001/comparebib.htm.*

The Magic of Myth: *http://www.starwars.com/smithsonian/.*

COOPER, D. B.

On a cold, stormy night in Portland, Oregon, on 24 November 1971, a nondescript middle-aged man, dressed in a plain suit and dark glasses, with briefcase in hand, boarded Northwest Airlines Flight 305 bound for Seattle, Washington. After the plane had reached its cruising altitude, the man, who identified himself as Dan Cooper, passed a note to a nearby stewardess. The note carried a startling message: Cooper had a bomb in his briefcase. He was hijacking Flight 305.

Cooper briefly cracked open his briefcase to allow the stewardess to see the red cylinders and heap of wires inside. She informed the captain of the passenger's demand. After concluding that Cooper did indeed mean to blow up the plane if his demands were not met, the captain radioed Seattle-Tacoma Airport. He informed authorities of the threat and of what Cooper wanted in exchange for the safe return of his 36 fellow passengers. Airline officials and FBI authorities scrambled to meet the skyjacker's demands: four parachutes and $200,000. Upon touchdown in Seattle one hour later, authorities were ready to make the exchange.

The FBI gave Cooper the parachutes and 10,000 $20 bills, photocopied so they could be identified later. Cooper then released all passengers and two of the three stewardesses, keeping the pilots and one stewardess. Cooper ordered them to remain in the crew compartment and to fly the plane toward Mexico. He stipulated an altitude of no higher than 10,000 feet, wing flaps at 15 degrees, and landing gear down. This would cause the plane to travel no faster than 200 miles per hour, barely enough to remain airborne. When the plane landed in Reno to refuel, Cooper, the money, and two parachutes were nowhere to be found.

Cooper had literally disappeared into thin air. FBI agents searched the plane for clues. Agents surmised that Cooper used cords from two of the parachutes to wrap the moneybag around his waist. He then jumped with his loot from the slow-moving plane. During the next two weeks, a few hundred soldiers searched for Dan Cooper in the forested woods of southwestern Washington. Thanks to media error, the mystery skyjacker became known as "D. B." Cooper. Despite intensive efforts, searchers found nothing.

Nothing, that is, until an eight-year-old boy dug up $5,800 of Cooper's loot from a sandbar along the bank of the Columbia River near Vancouver, Washington, on 10 February 1980. Officials could read the serial numbers on the badly damaged bills. They confirmed that the money came from the ransom paid to Cooper on that stormy Thanksgiving eve. This led some to conclude that Cooper must have landed in or near the Columbia River and escaped. However, others, like Ralph Himmelsbach, the FBI agent who led the investigation of the case until his retirement in 1980, believe that Cooper probably perished upon impact or shortly thereafter.

Because Cooper jumped out of the plane from a mere 10,000 feet in the air, Himmelsbach contended that Cooper would have had too little time to open his parachute. Even had he opened it in time, he still would have sustained at least minor injuries. Since he would have landed in rugged wilderness, he would have been ill prepared to wade through a cold river and dense thickets to get to civilization. Some parachute and survival experts claimed that Cooper could have made it, although his chances were slim. Many experts concurred with Himmelsbach that Cooper's remains probably ended up at the bottom of the Columbia River.

Who was Cooper? Himmelsbach thinks he was probably a career criminal, an asocial loner with nothing to lose. According to journalist Max Gunther, Cooper was bitter over his dead-end, boring career and recent divorce. He commandeered Flight 305 because of an unusually severe midlife crisis.

Former FBI agent Bernie Rhodes and probation and parole officer Russell Calame contend that Cooper was a Mormon Sunday school teacher and ex–Green Beret whose real name was Richard McCoy. In 1972 McCoy hijacked United Airlines Flight 855. His crime closely resembled Cooper's caper of the previous year. This time, however, authorities quickly caught, convicted, and sentenced the hijacker to 45 years in prison. Although McCoy escaped two years later, in August 1974, authorities located him within two months and killed him in a shoot-out.

Rhodes and Calame believe McCoy and Cooper were the same person because their looks and methods were far too similar to be coincidental. Also, information on McCoy's whereabouts in November 1971 is sketchy. What's more, authorities found newspaper clippings detailing Cooper's crime in McCoy's vehicle and in his home. These clippings, however, may only prove that McCoy was obsessed with emulating the mysterious perpetrator of the 1971 hijacking, making him a copycat hijacker, not Cooper. Moreover, given the harsh weather and poor jumping conditions that Cooper encountered in 1971, it is highly unlikely that he lived to re-create his moment of glory. The real Cooper probably lies decomposing somewhere in the Pacific Northwest wilderness.

Little more than a thief and extortionist to authorities, Cooper achieved cult status through his daring and memorable act. Americans immortalized Cooper in song ("The Ballad of D. B. Cooper"), film (*The Pursuit of D. B. Cooper*), and books (such as *Skyjacker's Guide, or Please Hold This Bomb While I Go to the Bathroom*). People in the Pacific Northwest buy and sell D. B. Cooper T-shirts and bumper stickers and hold D. B. Cooper bowling tournaments. The town of Ariel, Washington, where authorities once believed Cooper had landed, sponsors an annual D. B. Cooper celebration called Cooper Caper or Cooper Day. In Salt Lake City, Utah, a restaurant called D. B. Cooper's hosts a Jump Night party. The restaurant gives away either a round-trip ticket to Seattle or parachuting lessons. In 1984 members of the U.S. Air Force squadron that pursued Cooper on the day of his notorious feat held the D. B. Cooper Debacle Dining-In, a formal dinner at McChord Air Force Base. Several Web sites are devoted to the infamous skyjacker.

Cooper's caper had more serious consequences as well. As a result of the skyjacking, authorities required all airports to install screening devices that can detect explosives. Also, because Cooper opened the back stairway in midair—a dangerous maneuver—engineers developed and installed a latching device called a "Cooper's Vane" to prevent such actions.

Many wonder why Cooper achieved such legendary and mythical status. Some attribute his celebrity to the fact that he was the first person to hijack a plane for nonpolitical reasons: He simply wanted money. Cooper was also the first hijacker to parachute from the hijacked plane. What's more, Cooper's caper remains the only unresolved hijacking in U.S. history. After all, everyone loves a good mystery.

Why do people romanticize what Cooper did? According to those who annually celebrate his notorious deed, Cooper symbolizes the ordinary, lone, working-class guy who broke out, beat the system, and may have gotten away with it. He represents the rebellion of the common man, a folk hero bold enough to take extreme chances, regardless of the consequences. Cooper had guts. What more could one ask of a western hero?

Is D. B. Cooper still out there? Is he living the good life with what remains of his $194,200? Or was he in fact Richard McCoy, the escaped convict who died in 1974? Or did he perish somewhere along the Columbia River in Washington before he was able to enjoy even a bit of his booty? As with many legendary figures of the West, we may never know for certain. The answer to the mystery of what became of D. B. Cooper has probably died, or, more exciting yet, will die, with him.

—Jane Veronica Charles Smith

References

Gunther, Max. *D. B. Cooper: What Really Happened.* Chicago: Contemporary Books, 1985.

Rhodes, Bernie. *D. B. Cooper: The Real McCoy.* Salt Lake City: University of Utah Press, 1991.

Wallechinsky, David. *The People's Almanac Presents the Twentieth Century.* Boston: Little, Brown, 1995.

COPLAND, AARON

1900–1990

Born in Brooklyn, New York, to immigrant Jewish parents from Poland and Lithuania, Aaron Copland rose to become America's foremost composer. He studied with Nadia Boulanger in Paris but built his reputation on imaginative handling of solidly American folk themes.

In 1938 Copland wrote the music for a new American Ballet Theater (ABT) production on a western theme. With a libretto by Lincoln Kirstein and choreography by Eugene Loring, the ballet became a musical story about the legendary outlaw **Billy the Kid.** Drawing upon one of the most powerful and best known of western figures, Copland made the most of his material.

The world premiere of *Billy the Kid* was held at the Civic Opera House in Chicago, Illinois, on 16 October 1938. Eugene Loring (as Billy), Marie Jeanne (as Mother/Sweetheart), Todd Bolender (as Alias), and Lew Christensen (as Pat Garrett) performed in the premiere. The ABT premiere came some two months later, starring Loring, Alicia Alonso, David

Nillo, and Richard Reed in the roles, respectively.

Copland followed up the great success of *Billy the Kid* by returning to another western theme four years later. For its 1942/1943 season, the Ballet Russe de Monte Carlo commissioned Agnes de Mille to choreograph and Aaron Copland to compose music for a new ballet on a western theme. The collaboration resulted in *Rodeo, or The Courting at Burnt Ranch.* Drawing upon western folk melodies for inspiration, Copland titled his suites "Buckaroo Holiday," "Corral Nocturne," "Saturday Night Waltz," and "Hoedown."

The Ballet Russe premiere was held at New York's Metropolitan Opera House on 16 October 1942. The original cast starred Agnes de Mille, Frederic Franklin, Casimir Kokitch, Milada Mladova, Eleanora Marra, Dorothy Etheridge, and Ruth Riekman. The ABT premiere occurred eight years later in Wiesbaden, Germany. That performance featured Allyn McLerie (as Cowgirl), John Kriza (as Champion Roper), James Mitchell (as Head Wrangler), and Charlyne Baker (as Ranch Owner's Daughter).

This lighthearted story depicts the battle of the sexes, something of a *Taming of the Shrew* goes West. A young cowgirl, a tomboy, rides with the cowhands and even competes against them (unsuccessfully) as a rodeo bronco buster. She also fails in romance: She is unable to attract the head wrangler, who only has eyes for the rancher's daughter.

Scene two takes viewers to a Saturday night dance after the rodeo. The melodic material in the second suite comes largely from western American folk songs. The cowgirl languishes unnoticed, although the chivalrous champion roper dances with her to cheer her up. She rushes off stage and returns wearing a very feminine, attractive dress. Now the wrangler and the roper compete for her attention, thus giving the ballet a fairy-tale happy ending.

In "Buckaroo Holiday," the cowboys of Burnt Ranch celebrate their day off with dancing and singing. The music is based on the tunes of "If He'd Be a Buckaroo by Trade" and "Sis Joe." In "Corral Nocturne," the mood becomes quiet, in marked contrast to the preceding vigor and action. The principal theme of "Saturday Night Waltz" builds on elements of the traditional cowboy song "Old Paint." Heady action returns with "Hoedown," a lively southwestern barn dance.

Copland's western ballets had much the same cultural impact as did Owen Wister's novel *The Virginian*. They dignified western themes and made them acceptable to American high culture. Performed during the heyday of B-western movies, the ballets showed that western artistic themes could soar above the level of mass culture. Both ballets remain important in the repertoires of many ballet companies worldwide. Historical recordings of the music continue to sell well, and new performances appear frequently. Only someone of Copland's prodigious talent, sterling reputation, and cultural sensitivity could have taken "low-brow" western themes and elevated them to the ballet stage.

See also Wister, Owen, and Winthrop, Washington

References

Copland, Aaron, and Vivian Perlis. *Copland:*

1900 through 1942. New York: St. Martin's Press, 1999.

Pollack, Howard. *Aaron Copland: The Life and Work of an Uncommon Man.* Urbana: University of Illinois Press, 2000.

COPPER HILL, ARIZONA

See Ghost Towns

CORTEZ LIRA, GREGORIO

1875–1916

Gregorio Cortez Lira has been commemorated in a famous *corrido* (border song) and more recently in a popular film. Cortez killed a Texas sheriff, probably as a result of a Spanish-English misunderstanding. His success in evading several posses and the **Texas Rangers** raised him to folk hero status as a Tejano who resisted white oppression.

Born in Mexico on 22 June 1875, near Matamoros, Tamaulipas, Cortez grew up near Manor, outside of Austin. During the 1890s, he and his brothers Romaldo and Tomás labored as vaqueros and farmhands throughout neighboring counties. Gregorio thus gained an excellent knowledge of terrain that served him well during his flight. His brothers may have been involved in various horse thefts as well. On 20 February 1890, he married Leonor Díaz. They had four children. Charging abuse, Leonor received a divorce on 12 March 1903. In late 1904, while in jail, Cortez married Estéfana Garza of Manor. He married for a last time shortly before his death in 1916, possibly to Ester Martínez.

Cortez's fateful journey into myth and folklore began 12 June 1901. Sheriff T. T. "Brack" Morris of Karnes County, along with deputies John Trimmell and Boone Choate, showed up at the Cortez home ten miles west of Kenedy, Texas, looking for a horse thief described only vaguely as "a medium-sized Mexican with a big red broad-brimmed Mexican hat." Divisions of language and culture probably precipitated the fatal conflict. Choate served as translator, but he was not very skilled and questions in English became accusations in Spanish. Some of the misunderstanding involved a mare that Cortez had recently acquired legally. Misunderstanding bloomed quickly into suspicion, and Morris shot and wounded Romaldo and narrowly missed hitting Gregorio. The latter returned fire, killing the sheriff. The deputies quickly retreated to the town of Kenedy.

Realizing the deputies would return with a posse, Gregorio moved his feverish brother into the brush. After dark, the two made their way to Kenedy, where Gregorio left his wounded brother with their family. He then walked north toward the Gonzales-Austin vicinity, some 80 miles away. His name graced the front page of every major Texas newspaper. The *San Antonio Express* reported, "The trail of the Mexican leads toward the Río Grande," so the posse headed south.

Cortez hid with friends on a ranch near Belmont, where Sheriff Robert M. Glover of Gonzales County and his posse found him. During the shoot-out, Glover and a posse member named Henry Schnabel were killed. (The latter may have been shot accidentally by a drunken deputy rather than by Cortez.) The wanted man escaped again and walked south nearly 100 miles to the home of another friend, Ceferino Flores. There he obtained a pistol, a sturdy mare, and a saddle, and he pressed on toward Laredo. Three days of hard riding over some 300 miles killed the mare. Cortez secured another horse for the final leg of his flight.

Having killed two sheriffs, his reputation in the press grew mightily. To the *Seguin Enterprise* he became an "arch fiend." According to the *San Antonio Express,* Cortez headed "a well organized band of thieves and cutthroats." As the paper saw it, the law needed "to fill up the whole country with men and search every nook and corner and guard every avenue of escape." Governor Joseph D. Sayers and citizens of Karnes County posted a $1,000 reward for Cortez's capture. Huge posses, special trains, and tracking dogs kept up the pursuit.

The contest divided the people of south Texas. Some Tejanos, Sheriff Ortiz of Webb County, and Assistant City Marshal Gómez of Laredo hunted Cortez. Other Tejanos, however, cheered the fugitive's ability to evade the hated *rinches,* as they termed Texas Rangers. During the hunt, at least nine persons of Mexican descent had been killed, three wounded, and seven arrested. Even the *San Antonio Express* recognized his "remarkable powers of endurance and skill in eluding pursuit."

Meanwhile, Cortez boldly walked into the town of Cotulla in broad daylight. He then followed the railroad tracks to the outskirts of Twohig. The exhausted man lay down by a water tank and slept all night, all day, and all the next night as well. About noon on 22 June 1901 (his twenty-sixth birthday), Cortez walked into a sheep camp where Jesús "El Teco" González recognized him. Probably motivated by the sizable reward, González led a posse to Cortez. Ten eventful days had passed since the shoot-out between Cortez and Sheriff Morris.

Jailed in San Antonio, Cortez saw his network of popular support increase. Some Tejanos considered González a traitor to his people and ostracized him. Supporters among mutual aid and worker societies created a legal-defense fund. The first of Cortez's several trials opened in Gonzales on 24 July 1901. At this trial, all the jurors except A. L. Sanders found Cortez guilty of murdering Henry Schnabel. The court sentenced him to 50 years in prison for second-degree murder.

An outraged mob of 300 men tried to lynch Cortez. Shortly thereafter, Gregorio's wounded brother Romaldo died in the Karnes County jail. In early 1902, the Texas Court of Criminal Appeals reversed the verdicts against Cortez. In April 1904 Cortez faced his last trial, this time in Corpus Christi. A jury of Anglo-American farmers found Cortez not guilty in the death of Sheriff Morris. They accepted the defense's contention that Morris had attempted an unauthorized arrest. Gregorio had shot the sheriff to defend himself and his brother. Tejanos rightly greeted the verdict as a great victory for all Mexican Americans.

However, a Gonzales County jury had found Cortez guilty of the murder of Sheriff Robert M. Glover. The trial, held in Columbus, resulted in a life sentence for Cortez. He was something of a celebrity to his jailers. They gave him the entire upper story of the jail as a "honeymoon suite" when he married Estéfana Garza. He entered the Huntsville Penitentiary on 1 January 1905.

In July 1913, Governor O. B. Colquitt granted Cortez a conditional pardon. Two months later, he jumped into the great revolution engulfing Mexico. Oddly, he rode with the conservative forces of Victoriano Huerta. Wounded, he returned to Manor and later to Anson, Texas. He married for the last time in early 1916 and died of pneumonia soon thereafter, age 41, on 28 February. He lies buried in a small cemetery eight miles outside of Anson.

Borderland Tejanos quickly recorded Cortez's exploits in their *corridos*. "El Corrido de Gregorio Cortez" appeared as early as 1901. A recording of the song made by Pedro Rocha and Lupe Martínez in San Antonio in October 1929 still exists. In cantinas, in country stores, and on ranches, Mexicans and Mexican Americans still sing his ballad and recall his heroic struggle. Folklorist Américo Paredes brought the Cortez story and song to a wider audience in his 1958 book *"With His Pistol in His Hand": A Border Ballad and Its Hero*. Although the book initially attracted only limited attention, one angry Texas Ranger threatened to shoot the author.

In recent decades, the rise of Chicano politics and growing Hispanic consciousness brought Cortez and the Paredes book greater attention. In 1982 the film *The Ballad of Gregorio Cortez,* directed by Robert M. Young, brought the tale to a much wider audience. The movie starred Edward James Olmos as Cortez. Like many other controversial western figures, Cortez is remembered as both hero and outlaw.

References

Orozco, Cynthia E. "Cortez Lira, Gregorio." Handbook of Texas Online: *http://www. tsha.utexas.edu/handbook/online/articles/ view/CC/fco94.html.*

Paredes, Américo. *"With His Pistol in His Hand": A Border Ballad and Its Hero.* Austin: University of Texas Press, 1958.

Sonnichsen, Philip. "More about the Corrido Gregorio Cortez": *http://www.sp.utexas.edu/ jrn/gcortez3.html.*

CORTINA, JUAN NEPOMUCENO

1824–1892

Along with **Gregorio Cortez Lira,** Juan Nepomuceno "Cheno" Cortina stands as a symbol of Tejano resistance to Anglo-American encroachment and racism. His greatest feat came in 1859 when he captured the town of Brownsville, Texas. Born in Camargo, Tamaulipas, Mexico, Cortina grew up just south of the Rio Grande in a wealthy ranching family. In the 1840s he moved north into territory claimed by both Texas and Mexico to manage lands owned by his mother. His family would lose some of these lands, but by the 1850s Cortina had become a powerful rancher and political boss for the South Texas Democratic Party.

Cortina's turn to the outlaw life began on 13 July 1859 in Brownsville, where he witnessed an Anglo city marshal pistol-whipping one of his former employees.

Cortina demanded the marshal stop striking the man. The marshal refused, so Cortina shot him in the shoulder and fled with the beaten man to safety. With this classic blow struck for social justice, Cortina's career as a legend and social bandit had begun.

Two months later, on 28 September, Cortina led an armed force back into Brownsville to mete out some popular justice. He released several Mexicans whom he felt had been unfairly imprisoned and executed four Anglos who had killed Mexicans but had gone unpunished. Some of his followers urged "Death to the gringos!" But Cortina did not go on a rampage. Instead, he withdrew to a nearby ranch and issued a proclamation establishing the Republic of the Rio Grande and explaining his actions on behalf of persecuted Tejanos:

> To defend ourselves, and making use of the sacred right of self-preservation, we have assembled in a popular meeting with a view of discussing a means by which to put an end to our misfortunes.
>
> These, as we have said, form, with a multitude of lawyers, a secret conclave, with all its ramifications, for the sole purpose of despoiling the Mexicans of the lands and usurp them afterwards. This is clearly proven by the conduct of one Adolph Glavecke, who, invested with the character of deputy sheriff, and in collusion with the said lawyers, has spread terror among the unwary, making them believe that he will hang the Mexicans and burn their ranches, &c., that by this means he might compel them to abandon the country, and thus accomplish their object. . . . Our families have returned as strangers to their old coun-

try to beg for an asylum. (PBS, "Documents")

The next six months became known as Cortina's War. **Texas Rangers** struck back furiously, often indiscriminately punishing any Hispanic in the south Rio Grande Valley. Cortina, who soon had 500 or 600 armed men under his command, resumed his raids after Texas Rangers executed one of his lieutenants in Brownsville. The Mexican government, fearing that Cortina's actions would embroil them in another war with the United States, sent a joint Mexican-Anglo force against Cortina, but he quickly defeated it.

Many Tejanos supported Cortina and his cause, aiding his troops and refusing to help U.S. officials. On 23 November 1859, he issued another proclamation to rally his supporters:

> Compatriots: A sentiment of profound indignation, the love and esteem which I profess for you, the desire which you have for that tranquillity and those guarantees which are denied you, thus violating the most sacred laws, is that which moves me to address you these words, hoping that they may prove some consolation in the midst of your adversity.
>
> Many of you have been robbed of your property, incarcerated, chased, murdered, and hunted like wild beasts, because your labor was fruitful, and because your industry excited the vile avarice which led them. A voice infernal said, from the bottom of their soul, "kill them; the greater will be our gain!"
>
> Mexicans! Is there no remedy for you? Inviolable laws, yet useless, serve, it is true, certain judges and hypocritical au-

thorities, cemented in evil and injustice, to do whatever suits them, and to satisfy their vile avarice at the cost of your patience and suffering; rising in their frenzy, even to the taking of life, through the treacherous hands of their bailiffs. The wicked way in which many of you have been often-times involved in persecution, accompanied by circumstances making it the more bitter, is now well known; these crimes being hid from society under the shadow of a horrid night, those implacable people, with the haughty spirit which suggests impunity for a life of criminality, have pronounced, doubt ye not, your sentence, which is, with accustomed insensibility, as you have seen, on the point of execution.

Mexicans! Peace be with you! Good inhabitants of the State of Texas, look on them as brothers, and keep in mind that which the Holy Spirit saith: "Thou shalt not be the friend of the passionate man; nor join thyself to the madman, lest thou learn his mode of work and scandalize thy soul." (PBS, "Documents")

Despite his broad, popular support, Cortina's force could not withstand the U.S. Army, which defeated the Tejanos in Rio Grande City on 27 December 1859. Nevertheless, sporadic raids and attacks continued for several months along the 100-mile stretch of border from Brownsville to Rio Grande City.

Forced to retreat to Mexico, Cortina found a new cause. He joined the patriot army of Benito Juarez battling the French forces that occupied Mexico in 1862. In 1863 he rose to the rank of general in the Mexican Army, and he later served as acting governor of Tamaulipas. He also supported Union partisans in Texas dur-ing the U.S. Civil War. However, Mexican politics turned against Cortina and other liberals. In 1876 the dictator Porfirio Díaz imprisoned Cortina in Mexico City, where he languished for 14 years. He died in Tamaulipas in 1892.

Cortina generated conflicting legacies. In Anglo and Texas Ranger history, he is little more than a common criminal, an outlaw who ignored the judicial system. Tejano folklore, in contrast, links him to broader issues of resistance to Anglo oppression and encroachment.

Unlike other Latino folk heroes, Gregorio Cortez Lira and Joaquin Murieta, Cortina has not had a major motion picture made about his life. Cortina does appear, however, as a supporting figure in the 1997 film *One Man's Hero* (Orion Pictures), directed by Lance Hool. The film highlights a love triangle between Irish-American soldier John Riley (Tom Berenger), Cortina (Joaquim de Almeida), and Cortina's girlfriend (Marta Romo). Cortina is a bandit-turned-soldier. Riley is one of the "San Patricios," Irish soldiers who switched sides to fight for Mexico during the Mexican-American War. Riley's platoon is brutally punished for crossing the Mexican-American border to attend Catholic services. This injustice leads them to change sides. Thus, like Cortina, the San Patricios are fighting for cultural integrity and justice against Anglo-American abuses. Despite the lack of popular-culture exposure, Cortina, "the Robin Hood of the Rio Grande," remains a folk hero for many Latinos.

References

PBS, "Documents of the Brownsville Uprising of Juan Cortina": *http://www.pbs.org/weta/thewest/resources/archives/four/cortinas.htm.*

PBS. *The West: www.pbs.org/weta/thewest/ wpages/wpgs000/w010_001.htm.*

COWBOY POETRY

ALSO COWGIRL POETRY

Westerners, often living in near or complete isolation, invented myriad ways to entertain themselves. Homemade fun, including music and poetry, provided important forms of recreation. Generally performed only among family and friends, original songs and poems remained largely anonymous and in oral tradition until the late nineteenth century.

By the early 1880s, poems had begun to appear in print, mostly in local newspapers. The *Trinidad Weekly News* (Colorado) published a poem written by "P. R. W." in its edition of 28 September 1882. Titled "The Cow Boy," it paints a rip-roaring picture of the cowboy, not unlike the cowboy presented in the pulp fiction of the time. The poem asks, "Who 'packs' a pair of Colt's Frontiers, / And sets the town upon its ears, / And man nor devil neither fears? / The Cow Boy." Another version appeared in the *Las Vegas Daily Optic* (New Mexico) on 12 November 1884: "Who is it paints the town so red, / And in the morning has a head / Upon him like a feather-bed? / The cowboy."

Gradually, more authors' names began appearing with their creations. Harry Ellard published a few poems in 1899, including a brief one titled "The Poet Lariat of the Ranches." His works appeared in a Colorado Springs, Colorado, newspaper named *Facts.* Some cowboy poetry got set to music, and Jack Thorp and others collected and published it. Most poetry, however, remained unknown outside of intimate circles of friends and family. Some poets contributed original verse to stockmen's publications, such as the *Stock Grower's Journal.* This weekly, published in Miles City, Montana, reprinted poems in the 1890s. D. J. O'Malley (1867–1943) contributed several, including "When the Work Is Done Next Fall" (first called "After the Roundup"). Cowboy singer Michael Martin Murphey has pronounced this poem, later turned into a song, his all-time favorite.

During the twentieth century, poems by more cowboy poets found their way into print. Bruce Kiskaddon (1878–1950) worked as a cowboy throughout the Southwest and Australia. Encouraged by a rancher named G. T. "Tap" Duncan, he published a small collection of poems in 1924 titled *Rhymes of the Ranges.* He later gave up cowboy life, married, and settled in Los Angeles. He continued to write, selling many poems to Nelson Crow, who published *Western Livestock* magazine. Crow published another collection of Kiskaddon works as *Western Poems* in 1935. In 1987 Gibbs M. Smith published *Rhymes of the Ranges,* an excellent collection of his works in a book edited and introduced by Hal Cannon.

Charles "Badger" Clark Jr. (1883–1957), a minister's son, wrote one of the most famous cowboy poems, "A Cowboy's Prayer." Texas poet laureate **Red Steagall** (1938–   ) delivered the poem at a White House prayer breakfast. "The Glory Trail" is another of Clark's often-recited works.

Carmen William "Curley" Fletcher (1892–1954) worked as a cowhand and rode in some of the nation's earliest rodeos. He often wrote poems and sent them to loved ones. He wrote his most famous piece, "The Strawberry Roan," after participating in the Cheyenne, Wyoming, rodeo (Frontier Days) in 1914. Originally titled "The Outlaw Broncho," the poem inspired songs and films, and it remains one of the most beloved poems of the West. Western magazines, newspapers, and ranch trade journals began to carry Fletcher's work. Real, working cowboys memorized and recited his poems. *Songs of the Sage* (1986), a new edition of Fletcher's work edited by Hal Cannon and published by Gibbs M. Smith, brought his artistry to a new generation of readers.

Squire Omar Barker (1894–1985) was born in a log cabin in Sapello Canyon near New Mexico's Sangre de Cristo Mountains. The youngest of 11 children, he grew up hunting, riding horses, and working cattle on the family's homestead, loving the rugged mountain country. Like the later western nature writer Edward Abbey (1927–1989), he worked as a U.S. forest ranger, in this case in the Carson National Forest. He served in World War I and in 1924 graduated from New Mexico Normal University (now New Mexico Highlands) in Las Vegas, New Mexico, where he continued to teach English.

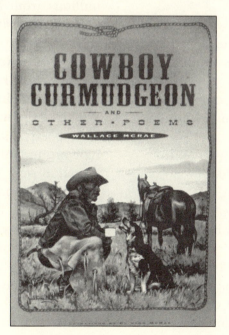

Barker also wrote prolifically and became known as the "Sage of Sapello" and the "Poet Lariat of New Mexico." In his busy writing life, he authored some 2,500 poems, 1,200 articles, and 1,500 stories and novelettes. Some of his works show his vibrant sense of humor. He laughed at the quirk of naming that made his initials "S. O. B." and once raised cattle under the Lazy SOB brand. "A Cowboy's Christmas Prayer" is his most famous poem. For 25 years, Leanin' Tree greeting cards of Boulder, Colorado, has published Christmas cards incorporating the famous poem.

Ranch poetry waned in popularity for a few decades from the 1940s through the early 1980s. However, the genre burst back on the national stage with the western revival of the mid-1980s. Thanks to the efforts of Jim Griffin, Hal Cannon, and other folklorists, cowboy and cowgirl poetry became hugely popular. Inspired by the success of cowboy poetry gatherings in Elko, Nevada (first held in January 1985), countless towns throughout the West now hold such events. Today, for the first time in history, a handful of poets can earn a living through their art. The Western Folklife Center of Salt Lake City and Elko remains a vital force in recovering and preserving the works of old poets and encouraging new ones.

Wallace D. "Wally" McRae (1936–   ) is one of today's foremost cowboy poets. He comes from a family of ranchers. His Scottish grandfather, John B. McRae, bought 160 acres in Montana in the early 1880s to start the McRae Ranch. Today, McRae runs the Rocker Six Cattle Company, a 30,000-acre ranch in Rosebud County, Montana.

McRae skillfully and powerfully records impressions of Montana ranch life. But he is also a poetic conscience for people who care about the West, the land, and the people. "I think the cowboy tradition has things of value inherent in it," says McRae, "and poetry lets me share that. I also think there's a search for roots, a more simple life and maybe personal freedom and my poems speak to that." In "Things of Intrinsic Worth," he captures the bitterness of losing the beauty and majesty of western lands for quick profit:

> Great God, how we're doin'! We're rollin' in
>   dough,
> As they tear and they ravage The Earth.
> And nobody knows . . . or nobody cares . . .
> About things of intrinsic worth.

McRae is equally eloquent about the human cost of economic "progress" in the West:

> "Sold to the highest bidder!"
> The gavel crashes down.
> Another rural family
> Goes shamblin' into town.

McRae wrote the cowboy's favorite humorous poem, "Reincarnation." The poem goes far beyond cheap laughs by mixing cowboy common sense and dialect with abstract philosophical issues. "Reincarnation" humorously reduces the issue of immortality and the afterlife to a pile of horse manure. I had the great pleasure and honor of hearing McRae re-cite "Reincarnation" at the 1991 Elko Cowboy Poetry Gathering. With typical modesty, he insists, "It's a superficial poem; I don't know what the attraction is." His humor is often self-deprecating. In one poem, he chronicles the misadventures of his son Clint but concludes by admitting: "I wasn't like him, growing up. I was a whole lot worse."

Nevada native Waddie Mitchell quit high school at age 16 to follow in his father's cowboy bootsteps. Along with cowboying, young Mitchell enjoyed collecting and reciting old cowboy poems and helped organize the first poetry gathering at Elko. Inspired by the warm reception, he gradually moved away from ranching to writing and performing poetry. His trademark handlebar mustache and ready grin became familiar to millions from appearances on Johnny Carson's *Tonight Show* and elsewhere.

Like Will Rogers long ago, Baxter Black is the dean of today's cowboy humorists. He can shoe a horse, string a fence, diagnose horse illnesses, bang out a Bob Wills classic on his flat-top guitar, and write poetry. He jokes that he has more hair around his lip than on his head. Raised in New Mexico, he spent his first career in the mountain West "tormenting cows." Now he lives in Arizona and travels the country dispensing cowboy wisdom and humor.

Since 1982 Black has rhymed his way into the national spotlight, and he now stands as the best-selling cowboy poet. He's written more than a dozen books (including a rodeo novel), recorded a basketful of audio and video tapes, and achieved notoriety as a syndicated columnist and radio commentator. His varied venues have ranged from *The

Photo taken at WestFest of cowboy poet Baxter Black (right)
with his father-in-law, Guy Logsdon, musicologist

Tonight Show and PBS to NPR (National Public Radio) and the National Finals Rodeo (NFR). His books are prominently displayed in big-city libraries and small-town feed stores.

Cowgirls have also raised their poetic voices. Cowgirl poet Hilma (Volcano) Volk, entertainer, rhyming storyteller, humorist, ventriloquist, and harmonica player, worked with the U.S. Fish and Wildlife Service for more than eight years. She has also trained horses and helped her neighbors with haying and herding. She now lives near Coeur d'Alene, Idaho, and performs widely at poetry gatherings. Her theme poem and book title reflect her whimsical humor and appeal: "Manure Happens."

Georgie Sicking is known as "a cowboy who just happens to be a woman." After working more than 100,000 miles in the saddle, the Fallon, Nevada, rancher qualifies as an authentic cowgirl. An admitted tomboy, she became a cowhand at 16, a pretty wisp of a girl in a male-dominated profession. She worked hard to secure the cowboy's highest accolade, being referred to as a "top hand," a person who can do any job on the ranch and do it well.

Whether she recognizes it or not, Sicking has served as a pioneering western feminist. Her poems record her life and experiences "in a country where they didn't ride mares and they didn't hire women." With two self-published books (*Just Thinkin', More Thinkin'*), she even attracted the attention of radio maven Paul Harvey in February 1998 and won a spot in the Cowgirl Hall of Fame. One of her poems, "Be Yourself," illustrates her philosophy of living and advice for wanna-be cowgirls:

When I was young and foolish
    the women said to me
take off those spurs and comb your hair
    if a lady you will be
forget about those cowboy ways,
    come and sit awhile
we will try to clue you in on women's ways
    and wiles.

Beloved singing cowboy and cowboy poet Buck Ramsey (1939–1998) died at the age of 59. Admired for his talent and grit, Ramsey spent more than half his life confined to a wheelchair. In 1961, while working for the Coldwater Cattle Company, a shank bit broke on his horse's bridle. He fell beneath his horse, and his injuries left him wheelchair-bound. The accident did not dull his wit and talent, and he remained a popular performer at major western cultural gatherings. He won several awards for his prose, poetry, and music, among them the Golden Spur Award from the National Cowboy Hall of Fame.

Hundreds of poetry gatherings and publications (notably *American Cowboy Poet* magazine, published by Rudy Gonzales, and *Cowboy Magazine*) provide outlets for cowboy/cowgirl poetic creativity. On-line publications, including ReadWest.com and ReadtheWest.com, also publish works by contemporary poets. One can only conclude that, yes, real cowboys are poets at heart.

References

Logsdon, Guy. "Cowboy Poets." In *Hoein' the Short Rows,* ed. Francis Edward Abernethy. Fort Worth, TX: South Methodist University Press, 1988.

Stanley, David, and Elaine Thatcher, eds. *Cowboy Poets and Cowboy Poetry.* Urbana: University of Illinois Press, 2000.

White, John I. "A Montana Cowboy Poet." *Journal of American Folklore* 80 (July 1967): 113–129.

"A COWBOY'S CHRISTMAS PRAYER"

See Cowboy Poetry

"A COWBOY'S PRAYER"

See Clark, Charles "Badger," Jr.

CROCKETT, DAVID "DAVY"

1786–1836, frontiersman, hunter, teller of tall tales, and congressman from Tennessee. *See* Alamo

CUSTER, GEORGE ARMSTRONG

1839–1876, American army officer. *See* Little Bighorn

DALLAS

Along with the Ponderosa of **Bonanza** fame, Southfork Ranch of the prime-time soap opera *Dallas* is the best-known ranch in the world. Just as the Cartwrights and their sprawling Nevada ranch came to symbolize nineteenth-century ranch life, so the Ewings and their vast north Texas spread became identified with the twentieth.

Airing from 1978 through 1991 in almost 100 countries, *Dallas* created a story line and characters very different from those of *Bonanza.* Instead of an honorable patriarch and his likable sons, *Dallas* featured a cast of devious, bickering, ambitious back-stabbers. Foremost among the bad guys stood John Ross "J. R." Ewing Jr. (played by Larry Hagman, who gained international star status from the series). Other characters included Eleanor "Miss Ellie" Southworth Ewing Farlow (Barbara Bel Geddes), Bobby James Ewing (Patrick Duffy), Sue Ellen Shepard Ewing Lockwood (Linda

Gray), Pamela Jean Barnes Haynes Ewing (Victoria Principal), and a host of others. Family patriarch John Ross "Jock" Ewing Sr. presided until actor Jim Davis died in 1981.

The cast played out their schemes at Southfork Ranch, complete with a large, white ranch house, located some 40 minutes north of downtown Dallas. According to the show's mythical history, Enoch Southworth founded the ranch on the "south fork" of its water source in the midnineteenth century. He ran the spread, building a cattle empire, until 1901. Then son Aaron took over, honoring his father's wish that oil not be drilled for on the precious land. Following Aaron's death in 1953, the ranch passed to Eleanor "Ellie" Southworth Ewing, wife of Jock.

Dallas opened immediately with family conflict in its premier season. J. R. jockeyed constantly to maintain and increase his power. In good old B-western fashion, this cowboy soap opera presented stereotypical characters and exaggerated plot lines. Fans loved to hate the bad guys and cheer for those who suffered at their hands. The "Who Shot J. R.?" episode became one of the most hyped television events of all time. The first prime-time soap opera, *Dallas* also inspired a popular spin-off series, *Knots Landing.*

The ranch, expanded beyond the original site, has been open to the public since 1985. In addition to being a popular tourist site, the ranch includes a 63,000-square-foot conference and event center, a rodeo arena, dining facilities, and a gift shop. Through worldwide syndication and Web sites, a new generation of fans can continue the fascination with Southfork and its inhabitants.

References:

Classic TV: *http://classictv.about.com/.*
Dallas: http://www.dallas.ndirect.co.uk/.
Southfork Ranch: *http://www.southforkranch. com.*

DART, ISOM

1855–1900

Isom Dart, an African-American cowboy, is famous mostly because of his death. In the winter of 1900, hired gun Tom Horn apparently shot and killed Dart, whom he suspected of rustling. Horn, in turn, met a violent end, accused of murder and hanged in Wyoming.

As is true of many black cowboys, little is known about Isom Dart's life. A Texas-born cowboy, Dart and his friend Matt Rash drove herds north from Texas and finally settled in extreme northwestern Colorado at Brown's Park in Routt County. Their cabin lay along a widely known outlaw trail frequented by Butch Cassidy's Hole in the Wall Gang, among others.

William Loren Katz, in *The Black West,* argues that Dart had a long history of riding outside the law. None of his many arrests for cattle rustling resulted in a conviction. According to one story, a Wyoming deputy sheriff arrested Dart and placed him on a buckboard bound for jail. The buckboard ran off the road, injuring the deputy. Instead of leaving, however, Dart administered first aid, drove the deputy to Rock Springs for treatment, and turned himself in at the jail.

According to a more positive interpretation of Dart's activities, Dart was a skillful rider who slowly built a cattle herd not by rustling but by purchasing stock with wages earned by breaking wild horses. Residents in the Cold Spring Mountain area reported getting along well with the black cowboy-turned-rancher. In July 1900 a threatening, mysterious note appeared demanding that certain ranchers leave the area. Although Dart's name appeared on the list, he was determined to stay.

Unfortunately for both Rash and Dart, the hired killer Tom Horn had been brought in to enforce the threat. Horn tracked Rash to his cabin near Cold Spring Mountain. The killer pretended to be a prospector named James Hicks. Rash invited him to dinner, and Horn dined with him on the night of 8 July 1900. After eating, Horn excused himself, went outside, and hid behind a tree. When Rash stepped outside, Horn shot him three times; he then quickly rode to Denver to create an alibi. Rash lived long enough to try to write the name of his killer with his own blood. However, he wrote Horn's alias, "Hicks," so the real killer could not be immediately identified.

Horn believed that Dart and a gang of five other black cowboys had been rustling cattle. Some three months later, on a crisp October morning, Horn hid behind a large rock outside Dart's mountain cabin. Dart and his companions ate breakfast, and then Dart and George Bassett stepped out into the cool fall air to inspect the cattle pens that held their supposedly rustled cattle. Horn reportedly fired either one or two shots from a .30-.30 rifle, striking Dart's head and killing him instantly. His five companions raced back to the cabin to hide, while Horn mounted up and made a getaway. Friends buried Dart in an isolated grave near his old cabin in Brown's Park.

Whether Rash, Dart, and their friends actually rustled cattle remains unclear. Perhaps the pervasive racism of the time, not rustling, caused their murders.

References

Henry, Will. *One More River to Cross: The Life and Legend of Isom Dart.* New York: Random House, 1967.

Katz, William Loren. *The Black West: A Documentary and Pictorial History of the African American Role in the Westward Expansion of the United States.* New York: Touchstone, 1996.

Old West Gravesites: Isom Dart: *http://www. dimensional.com/~sgrimm/idart.htm.*

DEAD MAN'S HAND

On 2 August 1876, Jack McCall gunned down James Butler "Wild Bill" Hickok while he played poker at the Number Ten Saloon in Deadwood, Dakota Territory. At the moment of his death, Hickok held two pairs, aces and eights, a combination known thereafter as Dead Man's Hand. Hickok and his fateful hand of cards passed immediately into the annals of American mythology.

Wild Bill Hickok started his career serving as a marshal in Kansas cow towns, such as Hays City and Abilene. During the Civil War, he performed a number of tasks for the Union, including espionage. He served as a scout for Gen. George Armstrong Custer in the Black Hills of South Dakota. He also drove stagecoaches, served as sheriff in a number of midwestern towns, and even rode in Buffalo Bill Cody's Wild West Show. He also carried a reputation as a shrewd and successful gambler. Wild Bill earned his greatest reputation from the trail of dead bodies he supposedly left along the way.

In June 1876 Hickok, possibly with friends **Calamity Jane** and Colorado Charlie Utter, joined the gold rush in the Black Hills of the Dakota Territory. Hickok, however, realized that true opportunity lay not in the mines but in the pockets of naive prospectors at local poker tables. On 2 August, only a few weeks after arriving in Deadwood, he strolled into the Number Ten Saloon to take his daily drink with bartender Harry Young and to check out the action. Hickok combined good marksmanship with several basic rules for survival: He always poured his drinks with his left hand to keep his gun hand ready. He never sat with his back to the door. But as fate would have it, on the day he entered the saloon, the only seat open at the poker table faced away from the front swinging door. Reluctantly, Wild Bill succumbed to temptation and took the open seat.

To Hickok's left at the table sat an old riverboat engineer, Captain Massie, who still wore his riverboat cap. Across the table sat a cowboy named Con Stapleton, and to Hickok's right sat the owner of the bar, Carl Mann. Myth shrouds much about the afternoon's events. Wild Bill twice asked to switch seats before he entered the game. Stapleton protested that seats shouldn't change in the middle of the game and reassured him that he would watch his back. Massie joked that no one would shoot Wild Bill in the back.

Hickok had lost a few hands when "Crooked Nose" Jack McCall entered the saloon at 4:10 P.M. and sat down at the bar. The ante went all the way around to Hickok, who supposedly said, "I'll bet a dollar on general principle." Captain Massie quickly replied, "You must be a man of high principle; I'm out." Stapleton and Mann both met the bet and then called Wild Bill's hand. At that moment, McCall arose from his bar stool and walked up behind the card players. He fired one fatal shot from a .45-caliber pistol. The shot tore through Hickok's skull before the other men at the table could shout a warning. Ironically, all the remaining cartridges in McCall's pistol proved to be defective.

As McCall quickly fled the bar, Hickok's lifeless body fell to the floor of the saloon. As Stapleton leaned over the fallen man, the bartender announced that nothing could be done to help. Stapleton supposedly retorted, "Forget helping him; I want to see his hand." Wild Bill's cards revealed two black aces, two black eights, and the jack of diamonds. Stapleton declared it a "dead man's hand" and insisted the ante should be his. Captain Massie and Mann refused the re-

quest and allowed Wild Bill to posthumously win the hand. According to legend, they gave the winnings to Calamity Jane.

Jack McCall avoided sentencing by representing himself as the brother of a man whom Wild Bill had killed. However, after bragging recklessly about killing one of the West's greatest gunfighters, McCall received a second sentencing. He was tried and hung in Yankton, capital of Dakota Territory, on 1 March 1877. He lies buried in an unmarked grave. His motive for the murder remains in dispute: perhaps to avenge a gambling loss to Hickok, perhaps to collect a bounty on the famous gunman's head. Why a cowardly shot from the back? "I didn't want to commit suicide," he said.

Hickok's Dead Man's Hand took on a life of its own. Every summer, tourists pour into the historic Old Towne Hall of Deadwood, South Dakota, to witness reenactments of Wild Bill's death and the capture and trial of Jack McCall. Number Ten Saloon is still furnished with Wild Bill's chair, set with its back to the door. The saloon claims it is the only museum in the world with a bar.

The myth has been preserved in a wide range of media. We have a screenplay, "Dead Man's Hand," by Ronald Ecker; a Bob Dylan song, "Gambling Willie"; and a T. S. Eliot poem, *The Hollow Men*. There is even a country music band bearing the name "Aces and Eights." In 1979 Hickok was nominated as a charter member of the Poker Hall of Fame at Binion's Horseshoe Casino in Las Vegas. Bad luck dogged a fellow Hall of Famer, Tom Abdo, who died of a heart attack while playing a poker game in

1982. It is not known whether any of his fellow players checked the cards in his hand.

—*Andrew Mebane Southerland*

References

Fielder, Mildred. *Wild Bill and Deadwood*. Seattle, WA: Superior Publishing Company, 1965.

Rosa, Joseph G. *Wild Bill Hickok: The Man and His Myth*. Lawrence: University Press of Kansas, 1996.

DEADWOOD DICK

The literary character Deadwood Dick is yet another example of art influencing life. Edward L. Wheeler introduced the character in his first pulp novel, published in 1877. Wheeler wrote many more novels before his death in 1885; indeed, the Deadwood Dick series alone ran to 64 books. The hero, an easterner gone west, often dons a black costume and mask as he fights against "purse-proud aristocrats" and other enemies. As far as western heroes go, he is something of a social bandit, battling the rich and powerful who threaten the well-being of the common folk. After Wheeler's death, a number of men seeking notoriety and wealth claimed to be the real person who had inspired the character. With the author safely dead, no one could conclusively disprove the claims.

One would-be Deadwood Dick was Robert Dickey. According to his story, he fought in the Civil War with the Pennsylvania Cavalry, then headed west to fight Indians under Gen. George Crook and Gen. Alfred Terry. He had less success in pushing his claim to be Deadwood Dick. Unlike Nat Love, he penned no book to boost his claim. He ended his life in Denver as a drifter. Arrested for vagrancy, he died in a hospital there in February 1912.

Dick Cole had a stronger logical claim to the title because he actually drove a Deadwood stagecoach. More often called Little Dick, he may have been the first to claim the famous moniker. Alas for Little Dick, the more heroic nickname did not stick. Another South Dakota man, Richard Bullock, also staked his claim and failed. A respected shotgun messenger, he worked in Lead, South Dakota, and died in Glendale, California. Likewise, Richard F. Palmer, who died in Cripple Creek, Colorado, failed to convince a wide audience that he was the real old-time hero.

Richard Clark (or Clarke), born in either Ireland or England, played the role of Deadwood Dick more fully than many of his rivals. Having emigrated to the United States as a youth, Clark joined the Black Hills gold rush in 1876. He labored at nondescript jobs in Crook City, Whitehead, and Lead, South Dakota. Beginning in 1924, the city of Deadwood began hosting its Days of '76 parade. Clark joined others who dressed up as Deadwood celebrities and rode in the parade. He decked himself out in a long-haired wig, ample hat, twin pistols, high leather boots, and pseudo-buckskin outfit, probably props from a local theatrical supply house.

In 1927 the city fathers sent Clark, dressed as Deadwood Dick, to Washington, D.C., where he invited President Calvin Coolidge to vacation in the Black Hills. Inspired by his own publicity, Clark began to create stories about his mythical past to fit his newfound persona. The enterprising Deadwood Chamber of Commerce, with a nose for publicity and tourist dollars, built Clark a summer cabin in Pine Crest Park near Deadwood. There, he genially greeted visitors. Deadwood old-timers knew he was a fraud, but a huge crowd gathered for his funeral. His grave site remains a popular tourist spot, notwithstanding the fact that Deadwood Dick, a figment of a **pulp novelist**'s imagination, never existed at all.

The most successful pretender was an African American named Nat Love. Born a slave in Tennessee or possibly Ohio, Love sought a better life out West, where he worked as a cowhand from Texas to South Dakota. He published his memoirs in 1907: *The Life and Adventures of Nat Love, Better Known in the Cattle Country as "Deadwood Dick."* (The University of Nebraska Press reissued the book in 1995 with an introduction by Brackette F. Williams.)

Love relates his supposed adventures in typical western tall-tale fashion. His life story reads much like a pulp novel, with brave, heroic deeds at every turn. He claimed to have acquired his nickname by winning a roping contest in 1876 in Deadwood, South Dakota. He also claimed to have won a shooting contest in that famed Old West boomtown. Exactly where fact left off and fancy took over can never be known. As Ramon Adams observed, Love "either has a bad memory or a good imagination" (Adams 1989). But the black cowboy certainly became one of the more successful self-promoters of his day.

The Deadwood Dick character has resurfaced time and time again. He reemerged in a 15-episode B-western serial. In this incarnation, starring Don Douglas, Dick is a masked hero who valiantly battles "The Skull," known as the worst outlaw in the West. (The serial is still available on videotape.) In his very influential book *Virgin Land: The American West as Symbol and Myth* (1950), Henry Nash Smith devotes several pages (99–102) to a discussion of Deadwood Dick as a distinctive type of western hero.

The name lives on today in a number of ways. One can still stop for a drink at Deadwood Dick's Bar and Grill in Deadwood, South Dakota. One can also purchase an R-rated T-shirt commemorating the long-vanished hero. The Adams Museum in Deadwood houses historical artifacts linked to Deadwood Dick. In 1997 Steven C. Levi resurrected Nat Love in yet another literary incarnation in *Deadwood Dick: A Biographical Novel* (published by Holloway House). In November 1997 the drama department of the Bishop Noll Institute in Hammond, Indiana, presented six performances of *Deadwood Dick, or The Game of Gold,* directed by Elizabeth Conley. Like many western heroes of fact and fiction, Deadwood Dick seems immortal.

References

Adams, Ramon Frederick. *Burs under the Saddle: A Second Look at Books and Histories of the West.* Norman: University of Oklahoma Press, 1964, 1989.

Durham, Philip, and Everett L. Jones. *The Negro Cowboys.* Lincoln: University of Nebraska Press, 1965, 1983.

Katz, William Loren. *Black People Who Made the Old West.* New York: Crowell, 1977.

Thrapp, Dan L., ed. *Encyclopedia of Frontier Biography.* 4 vols. Lincoln: University of Nebraska Press, 1988; CD-ROM ed., 1994.

DEATH VALLEY

"Death Valley is a place of myth, history and stark beauty," writes photographer Michael H. Reichmann. "For the landscape photographer there are few places in the American Southwest that offer so much variety and contrast in such a relatively small area" (Reichman). A three-hour drive from Las Vegas, the valley features but two small towns: Stove Pipe Wells and Furnace Creek. A national historic site since 1933 and national park since 1994, the location has long fascinated and frightened outsiders.

Death Valley is hot and dry, receiving less than two inches of rain a year. Daytime temperatures routinely exceed 100 degrees Fahrenheit. Spring can be very windy, but if winter wetness cooperates, flowers may bloom in February and March. At more than 280 feet below sea level, Badwater, a small salt pond, is the lowest point in the Western Hemisphere. Startling views are available at many points, including rolling sand dunes, stark cliffs, and the famous Zabriskie Point.

Death Valley National Park includes some 3.4 million acres of spectacular desert scenery, rare wildlife, complex geology, wilderness, and historical sites. The park is bounded on the west by 11,049-foot Telescope Peak and on the east by 5,475-foot Dante's View. California Highway 190 traverses the park east/west. South of the park, Interstate 15 passes through Baker, California, on its way from Los Angeles to Las Vegas.

A landscape as bizarre and forbidding as Death Valley is bound to generate myths. According to Richard F. Boland, chief spokesperson of the Timbisha Shoshone tribe, white society and the National Park Service created a very damaging myth about Death Valley: As evidenced in the name, white society has blithely assumed that no one could survive in the region. However, according to Boland, "The lands are replete with historical encampments, hunting trails, burial grounds, hidden springs and archeological sites that have powerful traditional and spiritual significance. Instead of the Valley just perpetrating 'death' as the National Park Service would have visitors believe today, the arid land and natural resources have sustained a resilient and creative desert people and a rich Native American culture for thousands of years" ("Despair in Death Valley").

After creating the national park in 1933, the federal government confined the park's Native American population to a tiny 40-acre camp. As Boland points out,

Until the tribe was cut off from its land in 1933, [Native Americans] had been an integral part of the ecological equation– cultivating mesquite, pine nuts and other indigenous plant life for food, developing and preserving springs for their own use and to protect and enhance the wildlife, and selectively burning underbrush to prevent forest fires in the mountains. The Timbisha Shoshone tribe holds the secret to surviving in one of the most awesome deserts in the world and the public most assuredly would love to learn the knowledge and wisdom directly from the people who possess it. Until now the National Park Service has kept all this a closely guarded secret lest the truth of its land theft also has to be revealed. ("Despair in Death Valley")

The stark, forbiddingly beautiful landscape has been a magnet drawing filmmakers to Death Valley. *The Rider of Death Valley* (Universal, 1932) brought Tom Mix, Lois Wilson, Francis Ford, and Iron Eyes Cody to the valley. The last would later become famous in more films and in TV public service announcements on behalf of protecting the environment. Monogram filmed *Where Trails Divide* (1937), directed by Robert N. Bradbury. In 1940 came *Twenty Mule Team* (Metro-Goldwyn-Mayer), with Wallace Beery, Leo Carrillo, and Anne Baxter. Many producers, aware of the valley's magic, highlighted the location in their films' titles: *Riders of Death Valley* (1941), *Death Valley* (1946), *Death Valley Gunfighter* (1949), and most famous, the television series *Death Valley Days.*

Although mostly B-western directors shot films at Death Valley, many bigger names also worked there. In 1948 John Ford directed *The Three Godfathers* (Metro-Goldwyn-Mayer [MGM]), starring John Wayne, Pedro Armendariz, Harry Carey Jr., Ward Bond, Mildred Natwick, Jane Darwell, Ben Johnson, and Francis Ford. Two years later came another MGM film, *King Solomon's Mines,* with Deborah Kerr and Stewart Granger. In 1953 William Holden, Eleanor Parker, and John Forsythe appeared in *Escape from Fort Bravo,* directed by John Sturges. In 1961 Marlon Brando directed and starred in *One-Eyed Jacks* (Paramount). Taking advantage of the otherworldly scenery, Paramount filmed *Robinson Crusoe on Mars.* Equally strange was the 1970 film *Zabriskie Point,* featuring Rod Taylor and Harrison Ford. Sam Shepard did some of the script writing in this critique of aggressive, materialistic Ameri-can culture. The 1982 film *Death Valley* presented the dilemma of a city boy visiting Tucson, Arizona, only to find himself the target of a psychotic criminal.

The valley has also influenced music. In November 1996 the Walkabouts released a CD titled *Death Valley Days: Lost Songs and Rarities, 1985 to 1995* (Glitterhouse). More than a million tourists each year continue to explore the region. More than 50 years ago, young **Jerry Van Meter** nearly lost his life crossing the difficult terrain on horseback. Despite modern technology, Death Valley will remain a place where people only survive if they respect and understand the powerful natural forces that operate there.

References

"Despair in Death Valley." 1996: *http://www. nativenet.uthscsa.edu/archive/nl/9603/0149. html.*

Historical Myth a Month: *http://dmla.clan.lib. nv.us/docs/nsla/archives/myth/.*

Geology of Death Valley: *http://geology.wr. usgs.gov/docs/usgsnps/deva/deva1.html.*

Movie Making Exterior Locations: *http:// www.oxy.edu/~jerry/homeloc.htm.*

Reichman, Michael H. The Luminous Landscape Web Site: *http://www.luminous-land scape.com/death_valley.htm.*

DENVER, JOHN

1943–1997

John Denver set the spirit of the Rocky Mountain West to music. His song "Rocky Mountain High" became an anthem for people who shared his awe and enthusiasm for the West's mountain grandeur.

But the Colorado Rocky Mountain high
I've seen it rainin' fire in the sky
The shadow from the starlight
is softer than a lullaby
Rocky Mountain high, Colorado

Denver embraced the beauty and splendor of the Rocky Mountain West with childlike glee. His love for Colorado even dictated his stage name: Henry John Deutschendorf Jr. became John Denver. He unabashedly celebrated the region in song and in the way he lived his life. He also worked strenuously to save the West from the ravages of overdevelopment and pollution. Millions of people around the world, sublimely indifferent to the cultural dictates of the sophisticated East, joined with Denver, through his music, in celebrating life, love, and the wonder of the West.

Denver was born in storied **Roswell, New Mexico,** on 31 December 1943, the son of a U.S. Air Force pilot. By age 11 he strummed the guitar and dreamed of being a performer. After a brief stint studying architecture at Texas Tech University, he began his commercial singing career in Los Angeles. As a performer, he adopted the name of the famous Rocky Mountain city. Colorado would become his home and would inspire many of his hit songs. His big break came when he earned a spot with the Chad Mitchell Trio. He sang lead with the trio for two years, honing his song-writing abilities at the same time. His poignant composition "Leaving on a Jet Plane" became a number-one hit for Peter, Paul, and Mary and brought him even greater recognition.

In the early 1970s, he quickly climbed to the top of the popular music charts with memorable, melodic ballads and country-inspired tunes such as "Take Me Home, Country Roads"; "Rocky Mountain High"; "Sunshine on My Shoulders"; "Back Home Again"; "Thank God, I'm a Country Boy"; and "Poems, Prayers, and Promises." He often wrote, as in "Annie's Song," of love and nature:

You fill up my senses like a night in the
   forest
like the mountains in springtime,
like a walk in the rain,
like a storm in the desert,
like a sleepy blue ocean
You fill up my senses,
come fill me again.

Despite critics who disdained his folksy, "hokey" music and manner, Denver's popular appeal remained strong, earning him 14 gold albums and 8 platinum albums in the United States alone. He is one of the top five recording artists in the sales history of the music industry.

His career in acting began in 1977 with the humorous hit *Oh God!,* in which he costarred with George Burns. He made many television specials, with costars ranging from Jessica Tandy to Itzhak Perlman to Kermit the Frog. He made his last film, *Walking Thunder,* in Utah in 1993. The following year, he published his autobiography, coauthored with Arthur Tobias: *Take Me Home.*

Denver used his music to support a wide range of environmental and humanitarian causes. Such message songs include "Amazon (Let This Be a Voice)," "I Want To Live," "It's about Time," "Let Us Begin (What Are We Making Weapons

For?)," and "Higher Ground." "My music and all my work stem from the conviction that people everywhere are intrinsically the same," Denver said.

> When I write a song, I want to take the personal experience or observation that inspired it and express it in as universal a way as possible. I'm a global citizen. I've created that for myself, and I don't want to step away from it. I want to work in whatever I do—my music, my writing, my performing, my commitments, my home and personal life—in a way that is directed towards a world in balance, a world that creates a better quality of life for all people. (John Denver.net)

He acted upon this global philosophy in the 1980s, defying Cold War emotions. He sang concerts in the Soviet Union in 1985 and 1987 and in the People's Republic of China in 1992.

Denver revered the beauty of the West and injected a strong environmental ethic into his music and his life. In 1976 Denver and Aikido master Tom Crum created the Windstar Foundation, which promotes a holistic approach to global issues and works toward a sustainable future for the world. He also supported many other environmental groups, including the Cousteau Society, for whom he wrote the soaring anthem "Calypso." Environmentalists as well as music fans mourned his death in 1997. Sierra Club president Adam Werbach spoke for many:

> John Denver lifted up so many with his music, and stood as a beacon of environmental hope. His commitment to the environment was heartfelt, and so many of us were fortunate to have been able to listen to his messages about beauty in nature and how important it is to cherish our natural world.
>
> John Denver was personally dedicated to the preservation and appreciation of our planet, and he selflessly gave his voice and talent to the causes of environmental protection. We will always remember him for this.

Denver's personal life had its ups and down, events that he often conveyed through his songs. He married and divorced twice, first Ann Martell (1967–1983) and then Cassandra Delany (1988–1992). John and Ann adopted two children, Zachary and Anna Kate. He and Cassandra had one daughter, Jesse Belle.

A man who lived life passionately, Denver reveled in the out-of-doors: backpacking, hiking, fishing, and golfing. He also enjoyed flying, a pursuit that brought him to his death on 22 December 1997, off the rocky California coastline. Following his death, Denver was cremated, and his ashes were sprinkled over the Rocky Mountains that he loved to roam.

Denver's sensibilities resonated with people around the world, but he spoke a very western idiom. Many westerners could identify with the lyrics of his song "Fly Away":

> Life in the city can make you crazy
> For sounds of the sand and the sea
> Life in a high-rise can make you hungry
> For things that you can't even see
> Fly away, fly away, fly away.

Fan clubs and Web sites around the world perpetuate his words and music. Emily Parris hosts an active on-line fan club and does much of the writing for the site. "Music does bring people together; it allows us to experience the same emotions," Denver said (Rocky Mountain High Fan Club). "People everywhere are the same in heart and spirit. No matter what language we speak, what color we are, the form of our politics or the expression of our love and our faith, music proves: We are the same" (John Denver.net).

References

CNN Interactive: *http://www.cnn.com/US/9710/13/denver.update/*.

John Denver.net: *http://www.johndenver.net/8.shtml*.

Rocky Mountain High Fan Club with Emily Parris: *http://www.sky.net/~emily/*.

DISNEY FRONTIERLAND

Amusement parks have become as integral a part of American pop culture as apple pie. Several such parks transport visitors to mythical lands, from outer space to fairyland castles. The crème de la crème of theme parks are undeniably the Disney properties. Four of these are located around the globe. Disneyland, in Anaheim, California, opened in 1955, and Disney World, outside Orlando, Florida, opened in 1971. Other parks now exist in Tokyo and 20 miles outside Paris, and a fifth may be built in Hong Kong.

These parks immerse visitors in Walt Disney's vision of the mythic West. Disney (1901–1966) invented the theme park, produced the first full-length animated movie *(Snow White and the Seven Dwarfs)*, and originated the modern mul-

timedia corporation. His own rags-to-riches life resonates well with the heroic mythology of opportunity and success in the American West. A *Time* magazine poll included Disney among its most influential people of the twentieth century, recognizing his tremendous cultural impact in a variety of media.

Each of the four parks is divided into different lands. Frontierland brings to life Disney's version of the Old West. Seven attractions await visitors to this land, in addition to western-oriented restaurants (including one named for **Pecos Bill**) and, of course, a welter of shops. This entry focuses primarily on Frontierland, in the original park, Disneyland in Anaheim, California. Tokyo Disneyland calls the equivalent land "Westernland," perhaps because the term would be clearer to the Japanese.

The cultural importance of Disney's famous theme parks extends well beyond the entertainment of children from all over the world. As Richard Francaviglia notes:

> Disney created more than a contrived *place*. In Frontierland, he presented a simplified image of the region that reaffirmed widespread popular beliefs about the historical geography of the West. It may be tempting to dismiss such popular conceptions, but we do so at our own peril: like the dime novels and Wild West shows originating in the nineteenth century, they sustain the region's past as a significant mythological element in American culture.

Big Thunder Mountain Railroad

This is the primary ride in Disneyland's Frontierland, and as such it is the one that guests visit the most. One on-line tour guide notes that "the line for this can stretch around the mountain and then wind around more in the enclosed area." This ride is a Wild West roller coaster. Riders board five-car trains and embark on a runaway mine train for a roughly four-minute journey. The passengers travel "through bat caves, by snakes, goats, turtles, and even experience an earthquake in an abandoned mine." The scenery is reminiscent of what one would expect to see on western **movie sets.** It is even rumored that "the 2 'Donkey Engines' that are by the queue are from the Disney movie *Hot Lead and Cold Feet.*" "The Mountain that houses Thunder Mountain Railroad is modeled after the granite outcroppings of rock that constitute the 'Rock Pile' on Broken Arrow Mountain in Squaw Valley, USA." Finally, many of the props from the gold rush era—buckets, carts, and mining equipment—actually came from western **ghost towns.** The park's diligent designers scoured the West to find authentic artifacts.

Fantasmic

Fantasmic, a summer and weekend pyrotechnic show, pits Mickey Mouse and his friends against villainous Disney characters. The battle occurs on the Rivers of America, the waterway in Frontierland housing the paddleboat and Tom Sawyer's Island. This new attraction has won only mixed reviews. One visitor commented that this was "useful as a shunt to draw people off the rides so that we could jump on them unmolested." One has to wonder why a presentation dealing with villainous, mystical characters is situated in the heart of Frontier-

land rather than in Fantasyland. Perhaps Disney designers wished to depict the raw, sometimes violent frontier. However, Disney often situated Mickey Mouse in Old West settings, so the Frontierland battlefield fits with earlier themes.

Frontierland Shooting Exposition

Most amusement parks have some form of shooting gallery, and Disneyland is no exception. Participants fire electronic rifles to activate different targets, including vultures, tombstones, saloon paraphernalia, and even Boot Hill. As in **action shooting,** visitors can vicariously take on and defeat the bad guys, with guns blazing, just like in the movies. These shootouts are associated with popular but erroneous perceptions of the Old West.

Golden Horseshoe Review

The Golden Horseshoe Review, a stage presentation based upon the stage shows found in Old West Towns, is housed in the Golden Horseshoe Saloon. This structure replicates the type of establishment frequented by old-time gamblers, gunfighters, and cowboys. The music being played, however, is not from the Old West. Rather, most songs come from the western culture created by films and **television** shows of the 1950s and '60s. Visitors hear theme songs from *Blazing Saddles,* **Bonanza,** *The Wild Wild West,* and **Pecos Bill.**

Tom Sawyer's Island

The centerpiece of Frontierland, surrounded by the Rivers of America, is Tom Sawyer's Island. Following the tradition of many of Mark Twain's tales, this attraction is aimed squarely at children.

In essence, it is a playground. One description suggests to parents that the island is "definitely a place to take them [children] in the later afternoon when they are becoming antsy from waiting in lines all day."

The island also re-creates life on the frontier rivers, notably Tom Sawyer's Mississippi. "In the early years of Disneyland, you could bring your own fishing rod and catch live catfish off the docks of Tom Sawyer Island. Unfortunately, most of the fish ended up in the trash bins, because it wasn't practical to carry them around all day, especially in the summer." Visitors travel around the island on rafts, just like Huckleberry Finn and Tom Sawyer.

Mark Twain and *Columbia*

Frontierland includes two more waterborne delights. The *Mark Twain* is a replica of a paddle-wheel steamer that once traveled up and down the Mississippi during Mark Twain's life. The vessel is appropriately named: Twain was the author who brought life on the Mississippi to life for many readers, and he also operated a paddle-wheel steamer.

The second ship on the Rivers of America, *Columbia,* is a replica of the first ship to sail around the world. Like its paddle-wheel counterpart, the vessel takes passengers on a brief excursion around the Rivers of America. However, in addition to its circumnavigation of the globe, the *Columbia* has an important link to the West: "It was the *Columbia* and her Captain Gray who first discovered the Columbia River, bordering Oregon/Washington." Therefore, the river was actually named after the ship, not vice versa.

Disney uses these two vessels to impart not only historical knowledge but also a sense of life in the Old West. Passengers in essence journey back into time to the trials their ancestors underwent. Disney undoubtedly had this in mind when designing Frontierland. As the Disney Web site notes of the *Mark Twain,* "like the paddle wheelers that used to travel up and down the Mississippi, this vessel will open your eyes to the wildlife, and the dangers, of frontier living a century ago." As Disney himself said, "I don't like formal gardens. I like wild nature. It's just the wilderness instinct in me, I guess."

Euro Disney's Wild West

The centerpiece of the French Disney experience is a re-creation of Buffalo Bill **Cody**'s Wild West Show held in a venue of 1,000 seats. Patrons enjoy authentic cowboy "chuck" (food), then sit transfixed as cowboys, Indians, **Pony Express** riders, the Deadwood stage, ten Canadian bison, and other Wild West icons charge into action. A reincarnated Annie **Oakley** practices her crack shooting. Owing to restrictive French laws concerning abuse of animals, no rodeo-style events can be performed. This re-creation in France is not as far-fetched as it might seem. Cody's famous original show toured Europe several times, to burgeoning crowds and rave reviews.

Disney and the West

The Disney Corporation and in particular its founder Walt Disney have always placed an emphasis on the West, as Disney did on other elements of traditional Americana. He recognized the power and popularity of western themes early in his career. During the 1920s, he and his brother Roy created comedy animated films based on the antics of Lewis Carroll's Alice. In March 1924 they filmed their fourth adventure, *Alice's Wild West Show.* Several Disney movies have dealt with the West as a central part of the plot. Even during the Mickey Mouse Club shows, one show per week would be set aside as western day. Mickey would appear decked out not in cowboy gear but in the furs worn by the traders and explores of the frontiers of the United States.

All of these uses and images of the West derive from Walt Disney's own experiences. He was born at the turn of the century, just at the closing of the western frontier. His first cartoon with Mickey Mouse, "Steamboat Willy," is set aboard a steamship like the ones that traversed the inland waterways, such as the Mississippi, of the Old West. Disney brought famous western and frontier characters, including Davy Crockett, **Elfego Baca, Daniel Boone,** Texas John Slaughter, and Zorro to television. Disney movies still include many western characters or themes. Two recent hits, *Toy Story* and *Toy Story 2,* both have as a central character a cowboy doll, Woody, whose voice is performed by Tom Hanks.

Disney's version of the Old West, as seen in Frontierland, meshes nicely with the mythology of rugged individualism on the American frontier. "It is ironic," writes Richard Francaviglia, "that Disney depicted the western frontier as a place of individual initiative when, in fact, its settlement resulted from large scale federal presence in the form of troops, infrastructural improvements (roads), and economic incentives such as land grants"

(Francaviglia 1999). Indeed, in the real Old West, collective, not individual action, spelled survival on the frontier, with wagon trains, roundups, barn raisings, community harvests, and quilting bees.

Visitors of all ages continue to bask in Disney's nostalgic, idealized vision of the Old West. And today, Disney's theme parks preserve and present that mythical vision to a worldwide audience at many different venues.

—*Thomas Edward Davis*

References
The Disney Source: Frontierland: *http://disney landsource.com/frontier/index.html.*

Doug's Disneyland Trivia: *http://www.pacific sites.com/~drhoades/trivia.htm.*

Francaviglia, Richard. "Walt Disney's Frontierland as an Allegorical Map of the American West." *Western Historical Quarterly* 30, no. 2 (Summer 1999): 155–182.

DONNER PARTY

The story of the Donner Party is one of the most gruesome and disturbing tales of the American West, a deformation of the American Dream. The journey of these 87 individuals across the mountains and plains of a new frontier yielded not happiness and freedom but bitter living conditions and near-starvation. A century and a half later, Americans remain transfixed and fascinated by this tragedy of cannibalism and survival.

In the mid-1840s, a new adventure emerged for many Americans. The thrill of traveling west challenged people rich and poor, of all ages, and from every social class. Promises of wealth and opportunity echoed through society, and tens of thousands began the long, arduous journey west. Most braved the trip in covered wagons containing all their possessions. Most followed the path that became known as the Oregon Trail. Suffering and hardships awaited, and many emigrants lost their lives to disease, starvation, and harsh weather conditions.

Before the Donner Party left Springfield, Illinois, on 16 April 1846, they carefully equipped themselves with nine covered wagons and plenty of food, ammunition, and oxen for the travels ahead. The Reed and Donner families traveled together, both leaving successful lives in Springfield for the promise of wealth and opportunity in California. Upon reaching Independence, Missouri, their journey took a disastrous turn. George Donner, the appointed leader of the group, decided to follow the suggestions of Lansford W. Hastings, a geographer and aspiring tour guide. His 1845 publication, *The Emigrant's Guide to Oregon and California,* mentioned a quicker route to California that could save weeks of travel time. Turning off the established path just beyond Fort Laramie, the group, now numbering 20 wagons, made steady progress. Several weeks into the journey, however, it became clear that the route was more a hypothesis than an actual trail. The Donner Party found themselves struggling through difficult terrain, their supplies running low.

On 26 September 1846, the party stumbled up the original trail along the Humboldt River. Their path had not only been difficult; it had taken them an extra 125 miles and several weeks out of their way. The group now faced a dangerous race against time. Fall would soon turn to winter, bringing harsh snowstorms. The party, too far along to turn back, decided to push ahead and try to reach California before winter's onset. Traveling in such a large group proved to be difficult. They could cover only 10 to 12 miles on a good day. Rations and group morale withered steadily, and cold weather threatened.

When they reached the Sierra Nevadas, the Donner Party had covered almost 2,000 miles on foot or in covered wagon. They remained determined to reach their destination. As rations diminished, hunger, illness, and anger increased. Eliza Donner wrote in her diary of their grim situation: "Anguish and dismay now filled all hearts. Husbands bowed their heads, appalled at the situation of their families. . . . We must proceed, regardless of the fearful outlook." The huge drifts of snow made traveling with wagons almost impossible, and after a few days a snowstorm forced them to halt. Huddled together in the fierce and bitter winds of winter, women and children cried from hunger, and men clasped their hands together in desperation, looking for an answer. Conditions took yet another turn for the worse.

Nearly six months later, on 25 April 1847, the 46 surviving members of the Donner Party emerged slowly from the wilderness, their faces stricken with delirium and disbelief. Almost a year to the day after their ill-fated journey began, they arrived in Bear Valley, California. Half of them had perished. Questions arose as to how the group, out of food and unable to hunt, had survived several months of harsh winter. Their answer both intrigued and disgusted the entire nation. Even before they arrived in California, tales of their situation and alleged cannibalism had spread quickly through newspapers and word of mouth. Their plight snowballed with journalistic exaggeration and sensationalism, and stories emerged of a group that had delighted themselves in the taste of human flesh, practicing ritualistic cannibalism in the Sierra Nevadas. Emigration to California suffered a temporary but sharp decline. The Donner Party became the hottest topic in the West, and the truth quickly disappeared among the hundreds of rumors and wild stories of "what really happened."

In 1849 Donner Pass became the source of the next gold blitz, and more than 100,000 opportunists flooded the area hoping to strike it rich. One year later, California became the thirty-first state, and the image of a cruel and rugged West slowly faded into the background. Donner Lake, the spot where many in the party were found face down in the snow, missing the flesh of their arms and legs, became a popular tourist attraction for historians and vacationers. PBS television released a documentary depicting the horrific journey, featuring journal entries and important information about the tragedy. Remnants and personal belongings quickly became high-priced souvenirs that fed the public's craving for information on the mysterious Donner Party.

Several concerns about the Donner Party keep its history alive, and each generation of historians asks new questions about the disaster. For example, accounts differ about the Reed family's original wagon. Virginia Reed described in her journal a lavishly equipped two-level wagon, featuring comfortable beds for each member of the family and modern conveniences, such as a mirror and a stove. She coined the term "Pioneer palace car," but no other documentation verifies that this wagon ever existed. Another discrepancy concerns the whereabouts of the body of Tamsen Donner, the wife and mother of the Donner family. Several accounts say she was the last to leave when searchers found the party the following spring, claiming she would not leave her dying husband. However, according to Patrick Breem, a "Mrs. Donner" was one of the dead buried at Donner Lake. Since the only other Donner female, Eliza, died at Alder Creek, some conclude that Tamsen never completed the journey after all.

A larger debate also arose over who was to blame. Early reports blamed the Donners for their stupidity in traveling during the winter and their callousness in eating the flesh of their dead companions. After the 1930s, historians named Lansford Hastings the culprit for his ill-conceived and perhaps imaginary "short-cut" through such unforgiving terrain.

Despite the unclear details of this now-historic journey, the Donner Party will forever be seen as a tragic flaw in a romanticized period, a curiously unforgettable group of people among the hundreds of thousands who made the trip west. Most observers fail to notice the underlying struggle that took place, the extreme test of human character that these men, women, and children underwent. The pressure of starvation brought out heroism and selflessness for many under the worst circumstances and forced others to make choices the average person will never have to make. Of the 41 people who died, more than half of them were grown men, those most capable of surviving. Women and children made up the majority of the original party, yet through the efforts of the group all but five women and 14 children survived.

Fascination for this tragedy refuses to die. A diary entry from Eliza Donner found later clearly describes their desperate situation and the desperate measures they took to survive. Stranded and weak in the bitter cold of the Sierra Nevadas, she wrote, "Even the wind seemed to hold its breath as the suggestion was made that were one to die, the rest might live. Then the suggestion was made that lots be cast and whoever drew the longest slip should be the sacrifice. The slips of paper were prepared and Patrick Dolan drew the slip." The gruesome acts these innocent people forced themselves to commit evoked in the American public a sense of awe and disgust. Along with the story of Colorado's putative cannibal, Alfred **Packer**, the story of the Donner Party reveals the dark, gruesome side of the heroic West.

—William F. Zweigart

References

McClashan, C. F. *History of the Donner Party.* Stanford, CA: Stanford University Press, 1940.

Stewart, George. *Ordeal by Hunger.* Lincoln: University of Nebraska Press, 1986.

DOUGLAS, WYOMING

See Jackalopes

EARP BROTHERS

The Earp brothers—half-brother Newton Jasper Earp (1937–1928), James Cooksley (1841–1926), and Virgil Walter (1843–1905), all born in Hartford, Kentucky; Wyatt Berry Stapp (1848–1929), born in Monmouth, Illinois; Morgan (1851–1882) and Warren Baxter (1855–1900), both born in Pella, Iowa—were peace officers, gamblers, prospectors, saloon owners, wanderers, and western legends.

At the end of the famous gunfight at the OK Corral, Wyatt Earp and John "Doc" Holliday stood without a scratch. Most of the other Earps did not fair as well. Virgil would be crippled, and Morgan and Warren murdered, by the dawn of the twentieth century. Wyatt would end his days an old man in Los Angeles, an unpaid consultant to movie studios interested in his perspective on the "real" Old West. Of this famous western family, only James and Newton managed to stay out of serious trouble their entire lives.

The sons of Nicholas Earp inherited his wanderlust; it has been said that the patriarch covered some 8,000 miles in his lifetime, pulling up stakes and relocating the family when the fancy struck him. In addition, the Earp boys also learned respect for the law. Although they may not have always been on the right side of the law, they respected it and generally acted in its spirit.

The Earp brothers traversed the West, sometimes alone and sometimes together, living in Kansas, Arkansas, Arizona, California, Colorado, Idaho, and Alaska, among other states. They followed the trails to opportunity and adventure. Alternately gamblers, buffalo hunters, saloon owners, miners, and farmers—but never cowboys—the most famous Earp brothers always came back to enforcing the law. They married, some of them several times, but remained an extremely close family throughout their lives. Brothers to the end, they fought, lived, and died for each other.

Legend surrounds the lives of the brothers, but most of it swirls around Wyatt. Virgil and Morgan are forever immortalized for their parts in the OK Corral shoot-out. Were it not for that, the two would probably not have been famous. All three devoted much of their lives to enforcing the law, most famously in Dodge City, Kansas, and Tombstone, Arizona.

Wyatt and another legendary lawman, Bartholomew "Bat" Masterson, earned reputations for cleaning up the wilder elements in the roaring cow town of Dodge City, Kansas. Later, Wyatt and his brothers quickly cleaned up Tombstone in only a few months, but during that short period, they became living legends.

The Earps' quarrel with the Clanton and McLaury families, which culminated in the famous showdown, was factual. It has been transformed into legend, however, told and retold for more than a century, re-created and reenacted in books, song, **television,** and movies. Stuart N. Lake's 1931 biography, *Wyatt Earp: Frontier Marshall,* is a firsthand account of Wyatt's life, told to Lake by Wyatt himself in the last years of his life. It consists of part truth and part legend, probably because by the end of his days the two had all been mixed together in Wyatt's mind. Walter Noble Burn's 1927 work, *Tombstone: An Iliad of the Southwest,* concentrates on the people and events surrounding the town of Tombstone.

Like these two books, two recent films also differ in emphasis and approach. *Tombstone* (1993), starring Kurt Russell and Val Kilmer as Wyatt and Doc, and *Wyatt Earp* (1994), starring Kevin Costner and Dennis Quaid, offer two differing views of the Earps. *Wyatt Earp,* more than three hours long, goes into great and faithful detail about Wyatt's entire life, from Illinois to Alaska. Earp is depicted at both his best and his worst.

Tombstone, on the other hand, is a more typical film, with legendary, larger-than-life heroes. It focuses on the Tombstone days and the Earps' confrontations with "the cowboys." Wyatt is an untouchable, unbendable heroic lawman. Both films accurately present the facts about Morgan's murder on a pool table and Virgil's words to his wife, Allie, after he was shot in the arm: "Don't worry, I've still got one good arm to hold you with" (which, according to Wyatt's third wife, Josephine, is just what Virgil said). Both films end with Wyatt embracing Josephine and preparing to embark on "a series of adventures." They searched for gold, journeying to Alaska, Nevada, Arizona, and eventually California.

Unfortunately, the reliability of Josephine Sarah Marcus Earp's memoir, *I Married Wyatt Earp,* has been called into question. Author Glenn G. Boyer admitted that he, not Earp's wife, was the source of the information. An unapologetic Boyer explained the deception by describing himself as a novelist, not a historian. As he flippantly explains, "I'm the literary artist that created the figure I chose to call Ten Eyck," a fictional Tombstone newspaperman ("Casey and Glenn Interview"). Regrettably, most of the publications about the Earps have come from writers, not professional historians. Many of these writers operate with indifference to or ignorance of the rigorous refereeing system that guides true scholarship. However, even the referee system of professional historiography sometimes fails.

Among the embarrassed parties is the University of Arizona Press, which published the Boyer fiction as fact. To the press's credit, it withdrew the book from publication after Boyer admitted the book was his creation. Jeff Moyer, Tony

Ortega, Gary L. Roberts, and Casey Tefertiller exposed Boyer's fiction. As the last observed, "I hope Western readers will recognize the importance of this problem and why it is a concern to us all. If we do not demand the truth about history in nonfiction books, there is no reason for studying history at all" (Tefertiller 1997).

Other "facts" about the Earp family have also come under scrutiny. Biographers have long maintained, marveling, that Wyatt Earp lived his dangerous, violent life without suffering a gunshot wound. As it turns out, his luck ran out in Nome, Alaska, at the end of June 1890. Earp and his partner Charles Hoxie owned and operated the Dexter Saloon. According to a press report, filed two weeks after the event, Earp had a quarrel with a customer. Earp reached for his pistol, which was lying behind the counter, but the customer quickly drew and shot him through the right arm, resulting in a substantial loss of blood. Oddly, none of Nome's newspapers reported the incident, although we do have a photograph showing Earp with his arm in a sling, standing between Ed Eiechstadt and John Clum.

For the most part, the Earp family has won the battle of history. They are generally viewed as upstanding lawmen on a dangerous frontier. Supporters point to their faithful service, family loyalty, courage, and skill in upholding the law. Their blemishes and errors remain minor footnotes in history.

—*P. S. Crane and Richard W. Slatta*

References

Barra, Allen. *Inventing Wyatt Earp: His Life and Many Legends.* New York: Carroll and Graf, 1998.

"Casey and Glenn Interview": *http://cooper65. freeyellow.com/page17.html.*

Lake, Stuart. *Wyatt Earp Frontier Marshall.* Boston: Houghton Mifflin, 1931.

Lamar, Howard R., ed. *The New Encyclopedia of the American West.* New Haven, CT: Yale University Press, 1998.

Tefertiller, Casey. *Wyatt Earp: The Life behind the Legend.* New York: John Wiley, 1997.

EASTWOOD, CLINT

1930–

Clint Eastwood has emerged as the most important figure in western film since John Ford. His eerie, violent, taciturn, sometimes supernatural heroes have added an entirely new dimension to the western film hero. From "the Man with No Name" in Sergio Leone's spaghetti westerns to the morally flawed gunman-turned-farmer-turned-bounty-hunter in *Unforgiven,* Eastwood gives us powerfully gripping figures who walk the fine line between hero and antihero. "People don't believe in heroes," he says. "I disagree with the Wayne concept. I do the stuff Wayne would never do. I play bigger than life characters, but I'd shoot the guy in the back."

Eastwood has labored in the **television** and film industry for more than 40 years. However, the industry did not recognize his contributions with an Oscar until 1992, when *Unforgiven* won for Best Film and Best Director. In 1994 the Cannes Film Festival also honored Eastwood by naming him head of its jury.

Like John Wayne and James Arness, Eastwood has a stature (six foot, four inches) and powerfully projected physical strength that helped him portray larger-than-life heroes. The CBS television series *Rawhide* (1959–1966) established his cowboy credentials as Rowdy Yates. In the 1960s, however, Italian director Sergio Leone and Eastwood worked together to make the dangerous, laconic "Man with No Name" an international success. Leone actually wanted James Coburn to star but hired Eastwood because it would cost less. However, the director came to greatly admire Eastwood's minimalist, indolent performances. *A Fistful of Dollars* (1964), *For a Few Dollars More* (1965), and *The Good, the Bad, and the Ugly* (1966) made Eastwood's cold-blooded yet sympathetic killer an international hero. "I'm very close to the Western," says Eastwood. "That's where my roots are."

Eastwood combined the manly brusqueness of John Wayne with a matter-of-factness about killing that resurfaced again and again in the movies he later directed. In *A Fistful of Dollars,* he instructs an undertaker to "get three coffins ready." He quickly shoots down four bad men because "my mule don't like people laughin.'" Catching his math error, Eastwood adds a measure of extra-dry, black humor: "My mistake. Four coffins."

Some of Eastwood's most powerful performances have come in films that he also directed: *High Plains Drifter* (1972), *The Outlaw Josey Wales* (1976), *Pale Rider* (1985), and *Unforgiven* (1992). He dedicated the last film to his mentors Leone and Don Siegal. In many films, his motives are hardly the noble ones of the traditional western hero. Greed and revenge, not lofty altruism, motivate his characters. As the mysterious mercenary in *High Plains Drifter,* Eastwood emerges as an earthy, avenging angel. The townspeople of Lago hire his fast gun to save them from outlaws, but they quickly learn they have struck a devil's bargain.

The drifter turns the social and political order upside down, literally painting the town red and renaming it "Hell." He rapes, drinks, bullies, and kills—all this before the bad guys get to town. The final shoot-out and great conflagration destroy the town. Eastwood is the antithesis of the traditional hero, whose efforts would save the town. The drifting stranger rides away in the glare of the flames, having revenged himself on evil men and on a cowardly, evil town.

As the *Pale Rider,* Eastwood adds more overtly religious elements to his avenging angel/devil character. This time, he is a mysterious preacher who defends a mining town with gunfire and dynamite against a gang of bad guys. Visual and dialogue conceits conjure images from Sergio Leone's *Once upon a Time in the West* and *Shane.* As in *High Plains Drifter,* it seems that Eastwood's avenger is the reincarnation of an earlier character who was brutally murdered. *Pale Rider* brought Eastwood his first critical acclaim, at the 1985 Cannes Film Festival. Today he markets Pale Rider Beer with the wry slogan, "You didn't expect Clint Eastwood to make a salad dressing, did you?"

Eastwood also shows how easily characters from the Old West make the transition to modernity. Dirty Harry Callahan, a San Francisco police detective, brought the same hero/antihero attributes to the modern big city. Wielding a Smith & Wesson Bluenose .44, today's equivalent of the cowboy's Colt .45, Callahan represented the same type of avenger, willing to break the law when he deems it necessary. Like his cowboy counterparts, Callahan spoke in brief, pithy phrases: "Make my day." "Do you feel lucky, punk?" Eastwood even tied these "urban westerns" to the more traditional type. For example, at the end of *Dirty Harry,* he flings off his detective's badge, much as Gary Cooper did in *High Noon.*

Eastwood's William Munny in *Unforgiven* provides a more complicated but still recognizable rendering of a hero with feet of clay. Bounty money and grief, not lofty ideals, motivate Munny, a retired gunman, to strap on his pistol again. In a touch of self-deprecating humor, Eastwood has the aging character fall off his horse a few times. As in many other Eastwood westerns, the hero makes a comeback: Munny, brutally beaten nearly to death, makes a slow recovery with the assistance of friends, and comes back in the film's climax to take bloody revenge.

Eastwood repeatedly reminds viewers that in the Old West or in the New, heroes and villains, black hats and white, are not easily distinguishable. Eastwood gives us not the simplicity and clarity of the old B-westerns but morality plays that are much darker, filled with primal energy, more complicated, more troubling, and more interesting. In the year 2000, the ever-creative Eastwood took his heroics into space, starring as an aging astronaut in *Space Cowboys.* A PBS documentary aired during September of the same year honoring Eastwood's life and work.

References

Johnstone, Iain. *Clint Eastwood: The Man with No Name.* New York: Quill/William Morrow, 1981, 1988.
Sennett, Ted. *Great Hollywood Westerns.* New York: Abradale Press, 1990, 1992.

ECO-GUERRILLAS

See Monkey Wrench Gang

ENVIRONMENTALISTS

See Adams, Ansel; Cowboy Poetry; Denver, John; Gallatin Writers, Inc.

EWING, J. R.

See Dallas

EXODUSTERS

The end of Reconstruction and the departure of federal troops from the South in 1877 ushered in a new wave of racial oppression against African Americans. Like many others before them, former slaves looked to the West for a new start, for new opportunities. Thousands of these so-called Exodusters deserted the South for the West in the 1870s, hoping to find their own promised land.

Parishioners in black churches across the South listened to hopeful letters from early Exodusters. "When I landed on the soil [of Kansas]," wrote John Solomon Lewis, "I looked on the ground and I says this is free ground. Then I looked on the heavens and I says them is free and beautiful heavens. Then I looked within my heart and I says to myself, I wonder why I was never free before?" (PBS, *The West* Web Site).

In the spring of 1879, a false rumor spread like wildfire that the federal government had set aside all of Kansas for former slaves. More than 15,000 African Americans poured into Kansas within the next year. By the peak year of the "Great Exodus," 1879, more than 50,000 African

Americans had migrated westward seeking better lives, mostly in Kansas but also in Missouri, Indiana, and Illinois.

White westerners did not greet the influx with open arms. The *Wyandotte (Kansas) Herald* described the 1879 exodus in this way:

> During the past ten days, a large number of colored immigrants from Louisiana, Alabama, Mississippi and Tennessee have landed in Kansas. Nearly all of them are penniless, many are sick, and all of them are objects of sympathy. A public hearing was held at the courtroom Tuesday afternoon to take steps for their relief and to provide against spreading contagious disease. (Kancrn Web Site)

Whites in Wyandotte County published a petition of concern:

> Within the last two weeks over a thousand Negroes, direct from the South, have landed at Wyandott. None of them have money to carry them further west, or to purchase the necessary wherewithal to supply their most urgent necessities of food and shelter. Large numbers have died, and at least 5% of the whole number are sick with pneumonia and kindred complaints. In a word, over a thousand paupers have within a very short period of time been thrown into a town of about five thousand people, who are unable to properly provide for their wants. (Kancrn Web Site)

More than any other single person, Benjamin "Pap" Singleton (1809–1892) motivated African Americans to go west. Born in Nashville, Tennessee, he worked as a slave for several masters but always managed to escape. He fled to Canada, then ran a boardinghouse in Detroit, Michigan, that frequently sheltered runaway slaves.

Following the Civil War, he returned to his home state. He initiated an effort to purchase farmland for blacks but failed because white landowners refused to sell at fair prices. Singleton then turned his sights westward to Kansas. Along with a partner named Columbus Johnson, he staked out a settlement in Cherokee County (which failed) and in a second location in Morris County. He used posters to publicize the settlements and helped hundreds of poor blacks from Tennessee to move to Kansas between 1877 and 1879. His strenuous efforts earned him the title "Father of the Exodus."

Some Exodusters lacked funds to continue their westward trek. Many stopped and erected tents on the old Exposition Grounds in Kansas City, Missouri. These pioneers began establishing the city's black presence in the area south of Truman Road between Charlotte Street and Virginia. Over time, African Americans established businesses in northeast Kansas, such as Arthur Bryant's Barbecue, located at Eighteenth and Prospect. Another restaurant, Gates Barbecue, opened at many locations in the area.

Segregation laws kept blacks and whites separate. In Kansas City, the African-American neighborhood of Belvidere Hollow centered on Troost near Independence Avenue. Another neighborhood, Hicks Hollow, extended east of Prospect from Independence Avenue northward to Saint John. By 1913 the city's African-American population numbered some 16,000.

Freedmen also deserted Texas for Kansas, lured by a homestead act promising free land. "Kansas fever" gripped as many as 12,000 of these "Texodusters," especially those from Washington, Burleson, Grimes. Nacogdoches, Walker, and

Waller Counties. Richard Allen urged a planned, gradual movement out of the state. At a convention held in Houston in 1879, delegates urged against hasty action and warned against swindlers at both ends of the journey. The out-migration created serious labor shortages for white farmers in many parts of Texas.

One of the most successful Exoduster settlements arose at Nicodemus in Graham County, Kansas. Colonists from Kentucky established the town in July 1877. Although lacking needed tools, seed, and money, they survived their first winter on the plains. Some sold buffalo bones; some traveled 35 miles to work for the Kansas Pacific Railroad at Ellis. By 1880, however, Nicodemus held a population of 400 determined settlers. Their descendants and buildings from the early pioneers remain there today.

Edward P. McCabe joined the colony in 1878. He became the first African American to hold a major state office in Kansas, serving two terms as auditor (1883–1887). Original settlers Z. T. Fletcher and his wife, Jenny Smith Fletcher, operated the town's first post office. The Fletchers first lived in a humble dugout on the northwest corner of the township. In addition to serving as secretary of the colony, in 1880, Z. T. built the town's first hotel, the St. Francis, as well as a livery stable. His wife, Jenny, daughter of town founder W. H. Smith, also taught school and helped establish the A. M. E. Church. Their hotel left the family for a time, but in the 1920s Fred Switzer, a great-nephew raised by the Fletchers, purchased it again. When he married Ora Wellington in 1921, they made the hotel their home.

By 1887 Nicodemus could boast several churches, stores, lodges, a school, and two newspapers. However, the town's bright future dimmed when a projected railroad failed to reach them. The town got a new life in 1999, however, when the play *Flyin' West,* written by Pearl Cleage, opened at the Topeka Civic Theatre. The play re-created the plight of the Exodusters who "flew" to Nicodemus, Kansas, in search of freedom. The town also makes up part of the Library of Congress's *American Memory* on-line exhibit. Like other pioneering westerners, the Exodusters overcame travails and their efforts stand as monuments to the courage and determination that built the West.

References

American Memory, Library of Congress. Nicodemus, Kansas: *http://www.loc.gov/exhibits/african/nico.html.*

Athearn, Robert G. *In Search of Canaan: Black Migration to Kansas, 1879–80.* Lawrence: Regents Press of Kansas, 1978.

Blankenship, Bill. "Exodusting Off History." Electric Café: *http://cjonline.com/stories/011599/ele_flyinwest.shtml.*

Digital History, Exodusters: *http://www.digitalhistory.com/schools/NortheastMiddleSchool/afram.htm.*

Govenar, Alan B. *African American Frontiers.* Boulder, CO: ABC-CLIO, 2000.

Kancrn Web Site: *http://KcK.Kancrn.org/immigration/cbackground.cfm.*

Lawrence, Dennis. "African-Americans Migration to Wyandotte County, 1860–1900": *http://KcK.Kancrn.org/immigration/dissertation97.htm.*

Painter, Nell Irvin. *Exodusters: Black Migration to Kansas after Reconstruction.* New York: Knopf, 1976.

PBS. *The West* Web Site: *http://www.pbs.org/weta/thewest/program/episodes/seven/theexodust.htm.*

FERRIS WHEEL

The story of George Washington Gale Ferris Jr. and his invention of the Ferris wheel is more a story of confusion than of myth. A recent article in the *Reno Gazette-Journal* about the former McKinley Park School in Reno credited architect George A. Ferris with inventing the Ferris wheel. Even Nevada's former first lady, Sandy Miller, at one time confused the two men. It happens all the time because they have the same first and last names. Yet by the time George A. Ferris had designed the "Spanish Quartet" (four Spanish mission–style schools) in Reno and the governor's mansion in Carson City, Nevada, in the early 1900s, George Washington Gale Ferris Jr., a civil engineer who had spent much of his childhood in Nevada, had long since died. Nor were the two Nevada families related!

Once again, let's set the record straight: George W. G. Ferris Jr. was five years old (born 14 February 1859) when his family moved from Galesburg, Illinois, to Carson Valley in the Nevada Territory in the summer of 1864. The story goes that his inspiration for the Ferris wheel came from his fascination with the operation of the large undershot water wheel at Cradlebaugh Bridge on the Carson River. Presumably, he imagined what it would be like to be riding around on one of its buckets. George W. G. Ferris Jr. and his family lived on a ranch about two miles north of present-day Gardnerville before moving to Carson City in 1868.

George W. G. Ferris Sr.'s residence was on the southeast corner of Third and Division Streets (the restored house is still there, at 311 W. Third), and George Sr. surrounded his house with trees imported by rail from Illinois. The legacy of this Ferris family included not only the Ferris wheel but much of the landscaping of Carson City in the 1870s, including the capitol grounds (the spruce pine that is now the state Christmas tree was planted by George Sr. in 1876). George Sr.

left the area in 1881 and moved to Riverside, California.

In 1875 George Jr. left the household to attend the California Military Academy in Oakland. In 1880 he graduated from Rensselaer Polytechnic School in Troy, New York, with a degree in civil engineering. George Jr. began his professional work in New York City and designed bridges, tunnels, and trestles throughout the industrial Northeast and Midwest. He headed a civil engineering firm in Pittsburgh, Pennsylvania, when he came up with the idea of the Ferris wheel for the World's Columbian Exposition in Chicago in 1893.

When the 250-foot-tall Ferris wheel finally opened on 21 June, it was an overwhelming success and the fair's primary attraction. During the 19 weeks it operated, the Ferris wheel carried 1,453,611 paying customers. Its gross take was $726,805.50. The wheel was duplicated for the 1900 Paris Exposition, and in 1904, the original wheel was moved to St. Louis for the Louisiana Purchase Exposition. On 11 May 1906, the wheel was dynamited and scrapped; a Chicago newspaper referred to it as "America's rival to the Eiffel Tower." However, George W. G. Ferris Jr. did not live to see what happened to his Ferris wheel. He died on 22 November 1896 in Pittsburgh at the age of 37.

So who was the George A. Ferris who sometimes gets credit for the Ferris wheel? This George was born in Philadelphia on 31 January 1859 (two weeks before George W. G. Ferris Jr.). He was educated in Quaker schools and at Swarthmore College, and he later moved to Colorado and northern California. In 1906 he opened an office in Reno,

Nevada, as an architect. George A. Ferris designed most of the schools in Reno after his arrival, as well as high schools in Las Vegas, Nevada; Eureka, California; and Austin, Texas. His design for the Nevada governor's mansion was accepted by Acting Governor Denver Dickerson in 1908. In the mid-1920s, Ferris and the prominent architect Frederic J. DeLongchamps jointly supervised the plans for the state building in downtown Reno, where Pioneer Auditorium stands today. George A. Ferris died at St. Mary's Hospital in Reno on 12 August 1948, leaving a son, Lehman A. "Monk" Ferris, to carry on the architectural firm. Lehman died in 1997 at the age of 103.

The moral of this story: Don't just assume, because two names are similar, that they name one and the same person. A little homework can go a long way in avoiding inadvertently playing tricks on the living and the dead.

—Guy Louis Rocha

Reference

Jones, Lois Stodieck. *The Ferris Wheel.* Carson City, NV: Grace Danberg Foundation, 1984.

FIELDS, "STAGE COACH" MARY

1832–1914

Born a slave in Hickman County, Tennessee, Mary Fields gained her freedom after the Civil War. At six feet tall and 200 pounds, she towered above most folks and had no fear of hard work. She first found shelter and work among Roman Catholic nuns as the maid and friend of Mother Amadeus, an Ursuline sister. The sisters left the convent in Toledo and went west to the new St. Peter's Convent near what is now Cascade, Montana. Mother Amadeus fell ill with pneumonia in 1885 and called for her beloved black friend. Mary quickly traveled to St. Peter's Convent and nursed the nun back to health.

"Black Mary," as she was called, neither looked nor acted like the average novice. She had little use for the Mass, but she loved to smoke cigars, had a thirst for liquor, and could shoot accurately. She generally toted a .38-caliber Smith & Wesson shotgun strapped under her apron. Despite her behavior and habits, the nuns loved and supported her.

Mary wore men's pants under her dress and apron to ward off the winter cold. According to local legend, she had shoot-outs with several men who angered her and ran several others out of town. Already past 50 years of age, she worked at the convent for ten years without compensation, hauling freight and doing heavy labor. One winter night, a pack of wolves spooked her horses. Her wagon, laden with food supplies, overturned. The ever-dependable Mary protected the vital shipment through the night. She also washed clothes and linens, tended a large flock of chickens, and cared for the gardens at the convent.

Finally, however, her wild antics, capped by a shoot-out with a mission handyman, exhausted Bishop Brondell's patience. He asked her to leave, but thanks to intervention by Mother Amadeus, Mary secured a government mail route. In 1895 she and her mule Moses went to work delivering mail in central Montana. Her imposing presence on top of the mail stage earned her the nickname "Stage Coach Mary."

After retiring from mail delivery at age 70, she took up yet other careers, first opening a restaurant and then taking in laundry at her home. She also fervently supported the town's baseball team, baby-sitting and spoiling the players' children. Townspeople loved Mary, even building her a new house after hers burned in 1912. She received special permission from Cascade's mayor to drink in the male-only saloons of the town. She achieved celebrity status, often enjoying free meals. Uncertain of her exact birth date, Mary celebrated the occasion at least twice each year. On those festive days, town officials closed school in her honor.

Mary touched the lives of other legendary westerners. Charles Marion **Russell,** Montana's famous cowboy artist, spent some time in Cascade. In his whimsical 1897 pen-and-ink drawing *A Quiet Day in Cascade,* he shows Mary spilling her basket of chicken eggs as a rampaging hog knocks her down.

A young Montana native named Gary Cooper also knew of the famous African-American woman. In 1959 he wrote a fond remembrance of her for *Ebony* magazine. She is buried in a small cemetery alongside the road between Cascade and the St. Peter's Convent, a route that she had traveled so often during her life.

References

Mary Fields: *http://www.lkwdpl.org/wihohio/fiel-mar.htm.*

Miller, Robert Henry. *The Story of Stagecoach Mary Fields.* Englewood Cliffs, NJ: Silver Burdette Press, 1995.

Time-Life Books. *African Americans/Voices of Triumph: Perseverance*. Alexandria, VA: Time-Life Books, 1993.

Westerners: *http://www.thehistorynet.com/ WildWest/articles/02963_text.htm*.

FILMS

See Cavalry Trilogy; Movie Sets

FLOYD, CHARLES ARTHUR "PRETTY BOY"

1904–1934, outlaw. *See* Pretty Boy Floyd

FOLSOM MAN

See McJunkin, George

FORD, JOHN

1894–1973, film director. *See* Cavalry Trilogy

FORT APACHE

See Cavalry Trilogy

FOX, VICENTE

1942–   , Mexican politician. *See* Politicians and Western Myth

FRÉMONT, JOHN CHARLES

1813–1890

John Charles Frémont, the "Pathfinder" of the West, occupies a significant place in the American historical imagination. As an officer in the U.S. Army Corps of Topographical Engineers and subsequently as a privately funded adventurer, Frémont led five well-publicized expeditions in the 1840s and 1850s that laid the groundwork for the development of his romantic myth.

Frémont and his parties explored an even larger portion of the West than did the **Lewis and Clark expedition.** The Pathfinder's expeditions covered substantial parts of modern-day Arizona, California, Colorado, Idaho, Kansas, Nebraska, Nevada, New Mexico, Oregon, Utah, and Wyoming. At the time, most of this territory was almost unknown to European Americans, with the exception of a few mountain men. Frémont made detailed topographical maps and carefully selected routes that would be suitable for future overland travel by both wagon and railroad. His reports skillfully combined careful descriptions of the region's animal and human inhabitants, geography, and plant life with an appealingly adventurous tone that caught the popular imagination and stimulated subsequent westward migration. Born with the family name of Fremon on 21 January 1813 in Savannah, Georgia, the explorer later added an accent and a final *t* to his name.

Historians have often idealized the explorer and his wife, whom he married in 1841. Jessie Benton Frémont (daughter of legendary Missouri Senator Thomas Hart Benton) and her dashing husband became a glamour couple of the Victorian era. Senator Benton's great enthusiasm for westward expansion plus his considerable influence and sponsorship greatly furthered his son-in-law's career. Jessie, beautiful, intelligent, and politically savvy, and her adventuresome husband were rich, attractive, and deeply in love, and both were strongly committed to bolstering his career. This idealized view of the Frémont marriage is a key aspect of his enduring myth.

Frémont's public persona still retains much of its luster. Some modern biographers continue to see the Pathfinder's explorations and reports as key contributions to the process of western expansion and the fulfillment of the nation's **Manifest Destiny.** These historians express little concern for the fact that American expansion involved massive dispossession of land from its original inhabitants, accompanied by organized violence. Jessie Benton Frémont anticipated this future hagiography with her many published books and articles glorifying her husband's career.

Frémont's supporters generally explain away or otherwise apologize for major negative aspects of his career. These historians attribute his court-martial and conviction on charges of mutiny following the Mexican War to the jealousy, vindictiveness, and perjury of his fellow officers. In similar fashion, they blame the overwhelming failure of his 1856 presidential campaign on a vicious smear campaign by the opposition and on the actions of his father-in-law, who short-sightedly refused to support him. President James K. Polk pardoned Frémont, who remained high in the public's regard despite the affair.

According to Frémont apologists, external factors also caused the disasters of his Civil War career. The forces under Frémont's command in Missouri in 1861 and Virginia in 1862 suffered an unbroken series of defeats. His admirers blame these fiascoes on his superiors, who gave him inadequate amounts of supplies and troops, and on orders that were either imprecise or impossible to execute. Furthermore, according to this view, the hostility and intrigue of rival politicians poisoned President Abraham Lincoln against Frémont and prematurely ended his military career a second time. Those who accept the myth of the noble Pathfinder blame a wide variety of villains for their hero's travails.

In reality, Frémont's personal shortcomings amply account for his troubles: He was intensely paranoid, undisciplined, and egotistical. When a member of his poorly planned, ill-fated fourth expedition froze to death, the self-absorbed, egotistical Frémont railed furiously against the dead man. He had let the Pathfinder down, betrayed him, by expiring. Frémont's blatant disregard of orders accounts for both his court-martial and his later removal from command. His inept speeches, poor campaign strategy, and strained relations even with his supporters doomed his presidential campaign. Not even the millions of dollars he made during the California gold rush lasted. He lost most of his fortune in the 1870s and ended his career as a political appointee: governor of Arizona Territory until 1883.

Similarly, Frémont's fairy-tale marriage to Jessie did not measure up to the dream union that myth would make it. In reality, the marriage fit a typical pattern in the old army. Ambitious but relatively low-paid officers tended to court and marry women based on their family wealth and political connections rather than on love or affection. John probably believed that Jessie would help advance his career, as indeed she did. However, long separations and John's recurrent infidelities suggest a less-than-perfect match.

Many historians have also failed to critically analyze the most central aspect of the Frémont myth: his achievements as an explorer. The talents and efforts of others mostly account for his successes. Skilled artists and cartographers Charles Preuss, Edward Kern, and F. W. von Egloffstein laboriously created the maps that the public credited to the Pathfinder. Jessie largely wrote the reports that bore her husband's name and won him so much acclaim. Mountain man Kit **Carson** guided Frémont's first three expeditions, and his considerable talents greatly contributed to their success. Frémont's first major attempt at exploration without Carson, a winter trek across the Rocky Mountains, was an utter failure. One-third of the party died, and some of the survivors resorted to cannibalism. Without Carson's survival skills, Jessie's literary ability, and the mapmaking talents of his subordinates, the Pathfinder's prodigious reputation could not have been built.

Frémont died on 13 July 1890 in New York. The acerbic Ambrose Bierce well understood the disparity between Frémont's public persona and his actual character and achievements: "[Frémont] has all the qualities of genius, except ability."

—*Michael Thomas Smith*

References

Egan, Ferol. *Frémont: Explorer for a Restless Nation.* Garden City, NY: Doubleday, 1977.

Nevins, Allan. *Frémont: The West's Greatest Adventurer.* 2 vols. New York: Harper, 1928.

Rolle, Andrew. *John Charles Frémont: Character as Destiny.* Norman: University of Oklahoma Press, 1991.

GALLATIN WRITERS, INC.

"Every culture has a creation myth," writes Christopher Reardon, "an account of how the world came to be. In the American West, the tale has long been told of pioneers who overcame drought, disease, and armed conflict to open a vast frontier. By venerating these settlers and their ability to live off the land, subsequent generations of Westerners have found not only fortitude but also a sense of purpose and pride" (Reardon 1997). Western writers continue to confront past myths as well as newly born ones. The Gallatin Writers, Inc., a group of Montana writers, is striving to cover the gamut of western history, life, and myth. William H. Honan linked the new initiative to older precedents: "Like the old Federal Writers' Project of the Great Depression, which provided jobs for unemployed authors, Gallatin Writers Inc. of Bozeman, Montana, puts writers in harness to help uplift a depressed area. Where the Writers' Project turned out still-useful guidebooks and local histories, the Gallatin writers examine local conflicts and try to come up with solutions" (Honan 1998).

The writers meet periodically at various locations in Bozeman and other sites in Gallatin County in southwestern Montana. The brainchild of a retired economist and sheep rancher, John Baden, the project began in 1991. Baden took stock of the area's declining economy as poor and intensive land use pushed local industries into decline. Echoing the long-standing American belief that knowledge is power, Baden organized meetings where writers and policy analysts discussed the problems of the West. "The goal," according to the group's founder, "is a West that is ecologically and economically sustainable, tolerant of diversity, and humane and locally based in its politics" (Reardon 1997). A document issued by the group elaborates on the seminar's goals: "deconstruct how the West has made decisions about its lands; cut the ties with centralist thinking and experiment with indigenous local solutions and new philosophical juxtapositions (e.g., the intersection between market liberal approaches and communitarian approaches); find the moral base behind market-driven economics; discover the honest communitarian truths that lie behind Western myths; discover how all of these might become ingredients for a new society."

Some of the seminar's conclusions then made their way into a newspaper column, "Range Writers," that appears in syndication in a number of newspapers throughout the West. According to Bill Wilke, editor of the *Bozeman Daily Chronicle,* "The Gallatin Writers can be counted on to address the key issues here—timber, mining, ranching, agriculture and the environment—and do so in such a way that causes people to soften their views or even adopt new ideas" (Honan 1998).

With strong financial support from the Ford Foundation, Baden's brainchild has grown into a powerful force molding western public opinion and pushing the region toward more progressive solutions. The group's mission statement, philosophy, and solution appear on its Web site:

Recognizing the critical role which writers and artists have sometimes played in influencing public policies, Gallatin intends to orchestrate a new "voice" to speak to the West. This will be the voice of the contemporary writer, skilled to speak to broad and large audiences and educated (partly through the programs of Gallatin) to bring to the public translations of the best available knowledge of ecology, conservation biology, econom-

ics, political economy, and other disciplines which bring truth to examinations of the West's future. [We seek to] construct a new paradigm to guide future development in the American West—a paradigm based not on outmoded thinking about centralized natural resource management and the subsidized exploitation of the environment, but on scientific and economic truth.

Today, most rural Westerners still believe that the only economy that matters is the natural resource economy, and that all other economic and social goods are tied to the continuing, largely unrestrained, use of timber, water, minerals and grass. That this rural folk wisdom no longer squares with reality (if it ever did) seems to be lost in the great public debates which national magazines have described as the "War for the West."

The West's economic destiny is tied increasingly not to exploiting natural resources, but to protecting them. Roadless public lands, wilderness areas, free-flowing rivers, national parks and forests, the open range and healthy wildlife habitat are now the true "engines" of much, perhaps most, new economic activity in the West, yet a substantial portion of the region's population still believes that unrestrained resource development is the key to a prosperous future. (Gallatin Writers, Inc., Web Site)

The writers are thus engaged in a massive public-education campaign. They use seminars, publications, radio, and other media to get out their message.

In today's West, Bermuda-shorts-clad tourists and yuppies far outnumber ranchers, miners, and loggers, so political and economic changes are bound to come, often accompanied by conflict. As Reardon notes,

> Like the Federal Writers Project of the 1930s, Gallatin Writers' programs are based on the idea that writers can add to our understanding of social and economic issues because they are skilled at observation and expression. Through the written word, Gallatin seeks to foster debate on change at the local level, to promote understanding and cooperation that can reconcile conflicting visions of the West, and to highlight initiatives that offer promise and hope for impoverished rural communities in the region. (Reardon 1997)

In their musings and policy initiatives, the Gallatin writers challenge many western shibboleths, especially the archaic notion that the region's resources are inexhaustible. According to Jill Belsky, a group member and professor of sociology at the University of Montana, that also means taking on western icons: "The challenge for the Gallatin Writers group is to update the old western myths in a way that accounts for the forces that are reshaping people's lives. There's a need for new cultural icons. We have to replace the cowboy with the image of the steward. Where does that come from? Writers. Use your writing to help communities tell their stories" (in Reardon 1997). Western writers of all stripes—journalists, poets, novelists—are lifting their voices to help save the region they love.

References

Gallatin Writers, Inc., Web Site: *http://www. gallatin.org.*

Honan, William H. "Montana Writers' Sessions Teach Language of the Land." *New York Times,* 25 March 1998.

Reardon, Christopher. "Range Writers of the New West: Telling Stories to Reconcile the West's Past and Present." *Ford Foundation Report,* Summer–Fall 1997.

GARRETT, PAT

1850–1908, lawman. *See* Billy the Kid; *Outlaw, The*

GENTLE TAMERS

In 1958 Dee Brown wrote one of the first important books about women in the West. He titled his book *The Gentle Tamers,* a description that makes many feminist scholars bristle. Brown, however, discussed a wide range of western women, not all of them meek and gentle. He writes of the formidable Ann Eliza Webb **Young** and the fiery Carry Nation. Indeed, Brown wrote to correct what he saw as Emerson Hough's earlier (1918) portrait of "the gaunt and sad-faced woman sitting on the front seat of the wagon, following her lord where he might lead, her face hidden in the same ragged sunbonnet which had crossed the Appalachians and the Missouri long before" (Hough 1918). This mild "Madonna of the Prairie" image also appeared in romantic western paintings.

Most romanticized stereotypes prevalent in pop fiction and movies portrayed women as weak, swooning, and always in need of saving by the gallant cowboy hero. The real frontier West, however, re-

Rodeo cowgirls (Library of Congress)

quired much more of women than gentility. Historical studies and memoirs document the gritty, dangerous lives they led. Like men, women needed courage, strength, and determination to survive on the frontier. Some women went to extraordinary lengths to escape the strict sex roles imposed by Victorian values, to the point of donning male clothing to live the life they wanted in the West.

In 1879 the *Caldwell Post* described "A Female Cattle Dealer in Male Attire":

She represents herself to be the nephew of August Belmont, and the son of one of the largest cattle dealers in Texas. She is said to be a good talker. . . . We learn

from a gentleman where she stayed all night, that she admitted herself to be a fraud, but denied that she was a woman. She has a traveling companion, a young man, who says that this great cattle dealer is a woman, and he knows it. California and Missouri have been giving their reports of females doing their state in male attire, and we are glad to see Kansas toe the mark while such things are all the go. (13 February 1879)

Charlotte Darkey Parkhurst similarly masqueraded as "Cockeyed Charlie" and became a famed stagecoach driver in 1850s California.

Just getting west took tremendous strength, courage, and effort. Catherine

Although some western women rode sidesaddle, in proper Victorian fashion, most women in the West did not fit the "Gentle Tamer" stereotype. (Library of Congress)

Sager Pringle kept a diary of crossing the Great Plains in 1844: "The motion of the wagon made us all sick, and it was weeks before we got used to the seasick motion. Rain came down and required us to tie down the wagon covers, and so increased our sickness by confining the air we breathed." As they became accustomed to their "prairie schooner," spirits improved, and "merry talk and laughter resounded from almost every camp-fire" (Sager Pringle).

On the long trek, however, disaster could strike without warning. "Soon after crossing South Platte the unwieldy oxen ran on a bank and overturned the wagon, greatly injuring our mother. She lay long insensible in the tent put up for the occasion." A little later, Catherine herself suffered an accident:

August 1st we nooned in a beautiful grove on the north side of the Platte. We had by this time got used to climbing in and out of the wagon when in motion. When performing this feat that afternoon my dress caught on an axle helve [handle] and I was thrown under the wagon wheel, which passed over and badly crushed my limb before father could stop the team. He picked me up and saw the extent of the injury when the injured limb hung dangling in the air. In a broken voice he exclaimed: "My dear child, your leg is broken all to pieces!" (Sager Pringle)

Julia Louisa Lovejoy, born in 1812, wrote letters back to a New Hampshire newspaper recounting her travels in Kansas. On 5 September 1856, she wrote:

MR. EDITOR—I am not able to sit up but a few moments, having had a severe attack of bilious intermittent fever, and my husband sick with bilious fever at the same time, and our nurse, who kindly proffered his aid, being an old gentleman upwards of 70, crippled with rheumatism. Altogether, in these "dark days" of crime, we have had a sorry time of it, as every hour almost, of our sickness, some startling intelligence of new murders and depredations saluted our acutely nervous senses. Thanks to an ever watchful Providence, we are both now convalescent. (Lovejoy)

Once they arrived in the West, most women on the ranching frontier lived as the wives, widows, or daughters of ranchers. Most did not spend their days at dainty "feminine" tasks; there was too much to do on the ranch. Take Helen Jane Wiser Stewart, for example. Born in Illinois in 1854, she moved with her husband Archibald and three children (ages three, six, and eight) to a remote southern Nevada ranch in April 1882. Five months later, she bore her fourth child, without benefit of neighbor, nurse, or midwife. She continued tending to all the cooking and ranch chores and to raising four children.

In July 1884 she received a terse note from a neighboring rancher: "Mrs. Stewart send a team and take Mr. Stewart away he is dead." She quickly traveled to the ranch. Finding her husband's body, "I knelt down beside him took his hands placed my hand upon his heart and looked upon his face and saw a bullet hole about two inches above the temple" (Lovejoy). Archibald Stewart had been ambushed; his murderers were never caught. Helen continued to run the ranch, educating her children along the way, until 1903. She remarried and lived in Las Vegas, Nevada, until her death from cancer in 1926.

Women on ranches did all the domestic chores plus many of the "men's" jobs, too. Right into the twentieth century, ranching remained hard work. As a teenager in the 1940s, June Cotton Martin Finn did ranch work with her father in the Osage country of Oklahoma:

Daddy had all girls. I mean, yeah, all girls, and—the baby was a boy, but he was a lot younger than the rest of us, so I was his boy. . . . I talked 'em into letting me have my own string of horses, and I worked on the ranch just like a cowboy. I did everything the cowboys did. Daddy and I took care of those [five pastures], all those, by ourself. And when we was workin' cattle on our side of the ranch, the first part of the week, on Monday, Tuesday and Wednesday, we rode fence and prowled, and looked for sick cattle, doctored sick cattle (screw-worms and things like that). Then on Thursday and Friday we'd start the roundups.

Daddy and I'd get up about three o'clock in the morning. . . . We didn't have any electricity over there, and Daddy and I'd get up about three, and he'd put the coffeepot on, and we'd go to the barn. And he'd milk, and I'd feed all them horses. Go in that barn, and it'd be dark as pitch. And fumble around in there until I got the feed, and feed all them horses. We'd go back and have breakfast, and then go back down to the corral, and we'd saddle up. And we'd ride. (Osage Transcripts)

Another Oklahoma ranch wife, Lenora Meeks, recalled cooking during the Great Depression of the 1930s:

Well, my daddy and I used to go fishin', and we'd cook Squirrel Mulligan. And you'd have corn, and potatoes, and tomatoes in it. And put it on and boil your squirrel, and then add your stuff to it, kinda like you would stew, only we called it Mulligan. And I've baked quail and I've fried quail, and I've cooked elk roast, elk steak, deer meat, and you know, just about anything like that. (Osage Transcripts)

Montana cowgirl, 1909 (Library of Congress)

Meeks cooked without benefit of electricity or refrigeration, of course.

During the 1930s, Rebecca Higgins survived under similarly austere circumstances on a Wyoming ranch.

The kitchen especially was anything but adequate to the demands made on it. The lean-to was dark, with only one small window, rather high in the wall opposite the stove. There wasn't a real sink, nothing but a bench for the dishpan with a faucet bobbling at the end of a pipe. . . . To reach supplies at the back of the storeroom, Rebecca had to get down on her hands and knees and crawl, or send one of the children in for whatever she needed. (Osage Transcripts)

Despite the hardships, privations, and dangers, many ranch women loved the life as dearly as they did their men. June Finn summed it up well:

One of my fondest memories, and if you don't, never live in Oklahoma you don't know it, but we'd get up like I said, and start out, and it's so quiet at that time of morning, the only sound would be the creakin' of the saddle and the horse snortin' once in awhile, and the soft breeze blowin'—it's a beautiful time. (Osage Transcripts)

The special magic of family, nature, and land kept many a woman cooking squirrel stew and doing whatever was necessary to keep the ranch going.

Attitude counted for a lot in surviving the West, whether in the 1840s or 1940s. As June Finn recalled, "My daddy was a cowboy all his life. I think he made $60 a month, or something like that. When you're raisin' eight kids on $60 a month, that's not much money. We was poor. But it was a good life" (Osage Transcripts). Gentle tamers? Hardly.

For more evidence refuting the meek and mild stereotype, *see also* Brown, Molly; Calamity Jane; Cattle Kate; Fields, "Stage Coach" Mary; Poker Alice Ivers

References

Brown, Dee. *The Gentle Tamers: Women of the Old Wild West.* New York: G. P. Putnam's Sons, 1958.

Hough, Emerson. *The Passing of the Frontier: A Chronicle of the Old West.* New Haven, CT: Yale University Press, 1918.

Lovejoy, Julia Louisa. "Selected Letters from Kansas, 1855–1863": *http://www.pbs.org/ weta/thewest/resources/archives/four/love joy1.htm.*

Osage Transcripts. Interviews with ranch people of Oklahoma's Osage Region, provided by Jeanne Ronda, author's collection. For further excerpts, see Richard W. Slatta and Jeanne Ronda. "Cowboying at the Chapman-Barnard Ranch." *Persimmon Hill* 21, no. 3 (Spring 1993): 36–41.

Sager Pringle, Catherine. "Across the Plains in 1844" (diary): *http://www.pbs.org/weta/the west/resources/archives/two/sager1.htm.*

Westermeier, Clifford P., ed. *Trailing the Cowboy: His Life and Lore As Told by Frontier Journalists.* Caldwell, ID: Caxton Printers, 1955.

GHOST TOWNS

When one envisions a ghost town, the image that usually comes to mind is that of a tumbleweed rolling through a desolate, abandoned, boarded-up western town whose former inhabitants have long since departed. This popular image is not too far from the truth. Ghost towns are located in most western states, with Colorado (700 plus) and Texas (350 plus) having especially large numbers. These dust-covered sites are lonely reminders of the impermanence and the very real possibility of failure that characterized frontier life.

Two central characteristics define a ghost town. First, the initial reason for a town's settlement, such as the establishment of a mine or a railroad, no longer exists. After resources were depleted, a competing railway was built, or the mines ran out, people rapidly abandoned the community, especially if the surrounding region offered little economic opportunity. Natural disasters, such as fire and flood, also played a part in the demise of western boomtowns. People departed when the economy died. This sudden departure of the townsfolk led to the second characteristic of a ghost town: a quick, drastic decrease in population.

A good example of this process is the demise of the mining town of Copper Hill, Arizona. In 1925 this small boomtown reached a population of 500. But when the mines petered out, the townsfolk quickly left. By 1930 only 40 people remained; by 1933 no trace of human life could be found. Another example of a boomtown gone bust is Bodie, California, a mining town where gold was discovered in 1859. By 1879 Bodie was thriving, with a population of 10,000 (some historians estimate up to 15,000) and with more than 2,000 buildings. The boom lasted only four years, however, and the gold mines quit producing.

Bodie slid into rapid decline, and its population dwindled. By 1920 only a few dozen inhabitants remained.

Most ghost towns began as boomtowns. Many adventuresome folks moved westward during the nineteenth century in the hope of striking it rich, perhaps by discovering minerals such as gold, silver, or copper. If the local economy boomed, saloon keepers, shopkeepers, prostitutes, clergymen, legislators, and others followed. The new settlers built an urban infrastructure, including a post office, a general store, churches, schools, hotels, saloons, and restaurants, as well as a variety of other businesses.

Ghost towns like those depicted in westerns—that is, with all of the original buildings intact but abandoned—are actually quite rare. Only a few remnants and artifacts generally survive from these nineteenth-century sites: a few dilapidated buildings, structural foundations, and evidence of mining or other economic activity. Time and the elements, of course, took a toll on the sometimes-fragile wooden structures. But departing settlers also stripped the town's buildings and took what they could with them when they moved on.

Not all ghost towns became completely deserted. A few residents sometimes remain, and in some cases a small community may even persist. Those who remained might rebuild their former communities. Many of these restored towns came back to life and became viable again in the twentieth century with the advent of tourism. Hordes of tourists from the East and from other countries visited to seek out the Old West. Tourists continue to make frequent visits to such western towns as Central City, Colorado, and Virginia City, Nevada. Today, folks can even thrill to gunfights staged to recall the gory, glory days of Tombstone, Arizona.

Many ghost towns in the western states—including Columbia, California; Elkhorn, Montana; Silver City, Idaho; and Tombstone, Arizona—are listed on the National Historic Register as historic sites. Fortunately, preservation laws protect these sites from both vandalism and looting. Local residents can even earn an income giving guided tours of the sites, which have become popular monuments to the American frontier. The myth of the West promised opportunity and success to all who worked hard. The ghost town reminds us that even good, hardworking people often failed. Today ghost towns, once the stark symbol of failure in the West, are enjoying a cultural and economic revival. Maybe the West remains a land of opportunity after all.

Endangered Ghost Town

A historic ghost town in Montana is in danger of disappearing altogether. Southern Cross started off as a boomtown during the gold rush of the 1860s, and mining continued there for the next 80 years. Following the decline of the mining industry, a small but loyal population remained. Many people who live in Southern Cross today have preserved and restored their homes, as well as other structures of historic significance, creating a tight-knit community in the process. The people of this ghost town, however, may have to vacate their homes against their will. In March 1998 the Southern Cross Company (SCC) bought the land on which their homes sit and served all residents with eviction notices. SCC plans to log timber from the mountainside and conduct exploratory drilling—activities that do not, however, require removing the local population. Residents of Southern Cross are not taking this lying down. They are taking action. On 6 May three town members filed a suit against SCC in order to safeguard their town from destruction.

On 4 November 1998, Judge Ted Mizner of Anaconda, a neighboring town, ruled that his court had jurisdiction to hear the Southern Cross case. He issued a preliminary injunction to keep residents in their homes, pending a future trial. There is no set date for a trial as of yet.

—*Jane Veronica Charles Smith*

References

Florin, Lambert. *Ghost Towns of the West.* New York: Promontory Press, 1973.

Ghost Towns: *http://ghosttowns.com/.*

Silverberg, Robert. *Ghost Towns of the American West.* Athens: Ohio University Press, 1968.

Varney, Philip. *Arizona Ghost Towns and Mining Camps.* Phoenix: Book Division of *Arizona Highways* Magazine, Arizona Department of Transportation, 1994.

GLASS, HUGH

?–1833

Left by his fellow mountain men for dead after being severely mauled by a bear, Hugh Glass survived to tell the tale. As part of an 1823 expedition financed by Gen. William H. Ashley and Maj. Andrew Henry, Glass worked with other western legends, including Jedediah S. Smith, Thomas "Broken Hand" Fitzpatrick, the Sublette brothers (William and Milton), Jim **Bridger,** James Clyman, Moses "Black"' Harris, and Jim **Beckwourth.** A fellow trapper, George C. Yount, said that Glass had been a pirate with Jean Laffite and had lived with the Pawnee, stories that cannot be corroborated.

The Ashley trading expedition up the Missouri opened the heart of the great American fur trade. French and British trappers to the north had long exploited the beaver and other fur-bearing animals of the Rocky Mountain West. At about age 40, Glass was already old compared to most mountain men. He and his companions endured unbelievable hardships, blazed new trails, fought with Indians, named rivers and peaks, and trapped for profitable furs. The annual **rendezvous** (meetings where trappers sold their wares) provided an occasion to celebrate, socialize, trade, and tell tall tales.

However, in August 1823, Glass had a different sort of encounter. Many of his group had already died in conflicts with Native Americans. Glass had suffered a gunshot wound in the thigh. A she-grizzly, protective of her two cubs, severely mauled "Old Glass," as he was called, on the back, neck, and limbs. His companions quickly concluded that his days, perhaps his hours, were numbered. Yet he survived, alone, and another western legend was born.

His story must be pieced together from various accounts of varying reliability. According to a trapper named Hiram Allen, his companions carried the grievously injured man on a litter for at least two days. Near the fork of the Grand River (in present-day South Dakota), the trappers faced the fact that all ten of them might perish trying to save one man. They decided to leave Glass behind to recover or die in peace. John S. Fitzgerald and 19-year-old Jim Bridger agreed to stay behind and bury Glass when he expired. Both would be paid a bonus.

Fitzgerald and Bridger gave Glass water, waved off flies, and warily watched for signs of Indians. Two days passed, and Glass still clung tenaciously to life. The trappers feared they might never catch up with their comrades, so they dug a grave to enable them to hasten their departure when Glass did die. Fitzgerald then convinced Bridger that they must move on. He gathered up Glass's rifle and other equipment; dead men needed no supplies.

According to Glass's own account, he survived on water, buffalo berries, and the meat of a slow-moving rattlesnake that happened nearby. Though somewhat revived, he had only one good arm and one good leg. Nevertheless, he began to crawl downstream toward a French fur post 250 miles away, Fort Kiowa on the Missouri River. He dug up breadroot, robbed eggs from nests, sucked the marrow from buffalo bones, and scavenged.

Some of his wounds healed, but those on his back became infested with maggots. In October he reached the Missouri, where a party of Sioux took pity on him, tended his wounds, and helped him downriver to Fort Kiowa. After only a couple days of rest, Glass, his mind filled with vengeance, joined a French expedition up the Missouri to Dakota. Arikara Indians attacked the seven men in their boat, and only Glass and one other escaped alive.

In late November, Glass continued his journey of revenge toward Fort Henry on the Yellowstone. He covered the last 250 miles in a month, walking in freezing weather. When he reached the fort, he found it deserted. He picked up the trail of Major Henry and the other trappers as they headed south down the Yellowstone River. About New Year's Day, 1824, the gaunt and frozen Glass staggered into a new stockade that Henry had built at the mouth of the Bighorn River.

Glass angrily spewed out the story of his betrayal. He forgave the youthful Bridger but demanded to know the whereabouts of John Fitzgerald. On 28 February 1824, Glass hit the trail again, with several comrades. Another Indian attack killed two in his party, and Glass became separated from the other survivors. "Although I had lost my rifle and all my plunder, I felt quite rich when I found my knife, flint and steel in my shot pouch," he said later (Peterson 2000). Alone again, he continued toward the Missouri River, 400 miles east. Arriving at Fort Atkinson, he learned that Fitzgerald had enlisted. The army refused to let a civilian, however well justified, execute one of its soldiers. Glass recovered his rifle, accepted a small purse collected by sympathetic troopers, but left without taking revenge on Fitzgerald. Glass spent nine more years trapping before Arikaras killed him and two other trappers on the Yellowstone River in early 1833.

Oral tradition and a handful of written sources preserved Glass's saga. In 1915 John G. Neihardt penned an epic poem titled "The Song of Hugh Glass." In 1954 Frederick Manfred published *Lord Grizzly,* a gripping, fictionalized account of his crawl for survival. More recently, John Myers Myers added a reconstruction of the historical record, as best it can be established, in *Pirate, Pawnee, and Mountain Man: The Saga of Hugh Glass* (1963). Glass's heroic tale of survival and revenge gave him some measure of immortality among the pioneers of western exploration.

References

Myers, John Myers. *Pirate, Pawnee, and Mountain Man: The Saga of Hugh Glass.* Boston: Little, Brown, 1963.

Peterson, Nancy M. "Hugh Glass' Crawl into Legend." *Wild West* 13, no. 1 (June 2000). Also available: *http://www.thehistorynet. com/WildWest/articles/2000/0600_text.htm.*

GREY, ZANE

1872–1939

One of the most prolific western novelists of all time, Zane Grey left a lasting impression of the romantic American West on each reader. He created characters of individualism and strength living in a West of grandeur. Generations of readers and film-goers have enjoyed the mythologized West portrayed in his novels.

Pearl Zane Gray was born 31 January 1872 in Zanesville, Ohio. His parents, Dr. Lewis and Mrs. (Josephine Alice) Gray, believed that children should be seen and not heard. His father used a stick to enforce this rule quickly and often. Dr. Gray, a dentist, tried to impose his strict principles on all aspects of Zane's life, including his after-school activities and above all on his passion for fishing. Zane's parents feared that fishing led to excessive laziness and alcoholism. To escape, young Zane became close friends with Old Muddy Miser, a ragged hermit who took him fishing. Old Muddy became the other most influential person in Zane's young life, instilling a respect for nature and a penchant for truancy.

The youngster also enjoyed baseball, read omnivorously, and wrote. Pearl and his grade school chums often met secretly in the woods to read, by the light of an oil lamp, the work of **pulp novelists,** such as Beadle's Dime Novels, as well as James Fenimore Cooper's books. He earned a baseball scholarship to the University of Pennsylvania, where, at his father's insistence, he studied dentistry. Upon graduation, however, he played semiprofessional baseball for several years, only taking up dentistry halfheartedly in the off season. Through it all, he kept to his chosen path of a writing career.

Gray chose New York City for his dental practice because of the large number of publishers located there. He vacationed frequently on the Delaware River near Lackawaxen, Pennsylvania. The trips provided material for his early writing, and he enjoyed his first success with a magazine article describing one of his fishing experiences ("A Day on the Delaware," *Recreation* magazine, May 1902).

In 1900 he met Lina Elise Roth, whom he called Dolly. She shared his fondness for literature and supported him with part of her inheritance. He wrote, illustrated, and published his first full-length novel, *Betty Zane,* in 1903, with Dolly's financial and editorial help. He changed his surname to "Grey" with this beginning of his novel-writing career. For the next 30 years, Zane had at least one novel in the top ten every year.

In 1905 the couple married. They moved to Lackawaxen, Pennsylvania, and took a honeymoon trip to the Grand Canyon in Arizona, Zane's first trip to the West. He immediately became infatuated with the vast country and its astounding beauty. Upon their return, he took up writing full-time.

In 1907 Grey met Charles Jesse "Buffalo" Jones at a Camp Fire Club dinner in New York City. A contemporary of William F. **Cody,** the old frontiersman recounted his adventures in the West at every opportunity. He hoped to develop retail markets for meat from crossbred buffalo and Black Galloway cattle. Jones's frontier tales thrilled the young Grey. At Dolly's urging, he used additional money from her inheritance to join Jones on a trip to the Grand Canyon. Jones captured live mountain lions for eastern zoos. While outfitting for the trip, Grey also met a Mormon rancher and outdoorsman named Al Doyle. He invited Doyle to join the expedition as a guide and helper. They became close friends, and Doyle strongly influenced Grey's writing.

Dolly's faith in her husband was well placed. On that 1907 trip, the first of nearly 70 to remote regions of the West, Grey became acquainted with many legendary figures. Hanging on their every word, he soaked up stories of the West and hired guides and packhorses to explore the backcountry. Grey photographed and took detailed notes of everything he saw and heard on the trail. Back home, he used these materials, as well as his growing knowledge of the West, in writing his manuscripts.

Similarities between the people and places Grey experienced on these trips and the characters and locations in his novels are obvious to the careful reader. Al Doyle served as the model for Logan Huett in *Thirty Thousand on the Hoof.* Kayenta trader John Wetherill, Grey's guide on a 1913 trip to Nonnezoshe (Rainbow Bridge, Utah), became trader Withers in *The Rainbow Trail.* Indian guide Nasja Begay became Nas Ta Bega in the same book. While traveling into the Segi Canyon from Kayenta, Arizona, the party camped at Bubbling Spring and explored the Keet Seel and Betatakin cliff dwellings, familiar sites to readers of *The Rainbow Trail.*

Other westerners inspired more of Grey's characters. Grey modeled August Naab, in *Heritage of the Desert,* perhaps his most memorable character, on Jim Emett, another of his Mormon guides. Emett's mischievous son, Snap, became the evil Snap Naab. The description of Naab's home matches Lee's Ferry, Emett's Colorado River ranch and ferry operation. Although Grey exaggerated many characters and plots to meet the literary requirements of the romance novel, some were inspired by real people and actual events.

Dolly supported his efforts and pushed his writing on publishers, until one finally accepted *The Last of the Plainsmen* in 1908. Grey's 1910 novel *Heritage of the Desert,* finally presented the breakthrough success that allowed Zane to become self-sufficient with his writing. Other popular works, including **Riders of the Purple Sage** (1912) and **Wildfire** (1917), followed.

In 1918 Doyle guided Grey to the Tonto Basin below the Mogollon Rim in central Arizona. Born in the late 1840s, Doyle had lived the life of a true pioneer, the kind who explored and opened the West. He was a treasure trove of memories of those early days, and he freely shared his experiences around the campfire. Honest, courageous, wiry, and muscular, the hard-working Doyle exhibited the traits Grey admired. The writer also learned the unwritten Code of the West from Doyle's tales night after night around the campfire.

Zane built a new home in Lackawaxen and another in California. He never lost his passion for fishing and owned two yachts. During his lifetime, he wrote nearly 90 books, including 60 westerns. Readers bought his books by the millions. By 1939, the year that he died of heart failure, he had an estimated 54 million readers, nearly half the U.S. population. By 1975, 50 million Grey books had been sold in the United States alone. In addition, 50 million more had been sold overseas. Add 50 book serializations, 145 Zane Grey Theater episodes, uncounted newspaper serializations, many short stories, and at least 131 films, and Grey's impact is staggering. Given the huge readership and continued popularity of Grey's books (his westerns still sell more than half a million copies annually), it is not surprising that his type of western hero became the standard.

The National Park Service preserves his home in Lackawaxen as the Zane Grey Museum. Zane Grey High School in Reseda, California, near another of his homes, likewise honors his memory. In Payson, Arizona, where he had yet another residence, an annual 50-mile endurance run is held on the Highline Trail, one of his favorite places. In Australia, fishermen can charter the *Zane Grey* boat for large gamefish expeditions. His granddaughter promotes video collections and T-shirts on the Internet at *www.zane-grey.com.*

Grey still has a huge following today. Many home libraries contain one or more of his novels or short stories in their famous cream, red, and blue book jackets. Book collectors seek out early editions of his novels. A quick flip through the television channels on any given Sunday afternoon will probably turn up a film based on one of his novels. His own personal brand of romanticism retains its appeal today because for many people, the mythical West continues to hold the same allure it held a century ago. His romantic vision of the West continues to enthrall reading and film audiences.

—*Julie J. Anders and Z. Ervin*

See also Grey, Zane, and the Code of the West

References

Gruber, Frank. *Zane Grey: A Biography.* New York: World Publishing, 1970.
Jackson, Carlton. *Zane Grey.* Rev. ed. New York: Twayne Publishers, Inc., 1973, 1989.

GREY, ZANE, AND THE CODE OF THE WEST

Themes from the old Code of the West are common in Zane Grey's writings. The virtues expected of old-time frontiersmen appear often in Grey's heroes. Concerning loyalty, he wrote, "Wal, loyalty means you'll stick by her in these bad times, fight to save her rancho, her herd, an' if necessary—die for her. . . . Miss Holly is boss of this outfit an' you're beholden to her. . . . She doesn't care what you do so long as you're loyal to her. . . . thet means not to steal from her—not to stand fer a pard double-crossin' her" (*Knights of the Range*). On generosity, he wrote, "He'll lend you anything but his guns. Give you his last smoke. Stand your watch and do your chores" (*Shadow on the Trail*).

Although there are exceptions, Grey's characters are more often western "types" than individuals. The western "type" is muscular, courageous, persistent, loyal, shrewd, and hardworking. He is resolute, quiet-spoken, and capable, he has a clear view of right and wrong, and his vengeance is swift and sure. He is imbued with duty and honor and lives by the Code of the West, a set of principles Grey believed in and also tried to live by.

Beginning with **Riders of the Purple Sage** and extending throughout many of his western books, Grey reprised this character type and set plots. A noble hero battled ruthless cattle thieves or land grabbers. Grey helped to make this kind of epic conflict the norm for romance westerns in popular literature and later in film, radio, and **television**. This view of the legendary American West is still held by millions around the world.

Grey believed that the natural environment shaped people more strongly than any other element. In the face of rapid industrialization and urbanization, Grey feared that the spiritual experience with nature enjoyed by earlier generations would be lost. He believed that traditional virtues, exemplified in the frontiersman, would be lost to the loose morals prevalent in eastern cities. His readers appreciated his strong morality and simple tastes, devotion to family, love of nature, codes of chivalry and sportsmanship, and honesty in admitting his own prejudices and shortcomings. His heroes, basically decent and capable of noble action, served as powerful, attractive role models.

Owen Wister has been called an armchair westerner, and his novel, *The Virginian,* a parlor western. In contrast, Grey avidly experienced and explored the wilderness about which he wrote. He was a rugged outdoorsman who knew every foot of the country in his stories from personal experience. Grey's myth of the American West elegantly blends imagination and fantasy with real people and places. He described things so accurately, said one critic, "that they only could have been described by one who lived and worked with these people." Even his professional rival, Louis **L'Amour,** praised Grey for "having been there" and for writing from life experience.

Grey believed that romance writing should tell the story within the framework of historical truth. In *To the Last Man,* he wrote, "Romance is only another name for idealism; and I contend that life without ideals is not worth living." Following this rule, Grey held his heroes to the ideals embodied in the Code of the West. His own life exhibited the hard work, devotion to family, and traditional American values that he espoused. He identified with his readers, and they with

him. Thus, his mythical cowboy figure was accepted and imitated by many who followed. Grey is largely responsible for much of America's western hero stereotype. Few others have exerted a greater influence on the mythical American cowboy than Zane Grey.

–Z. Ervin

See also Wister, Owen, and Winthrop, Washington

References

Grey, Zane. *The Rainbow Trail.* New York: Grosset and Dunlap, 1915.

_____. *Riders of the Purple Sage.* New York: Harper and Brothers, 1912

_____. *Tales of Lonely Trails.* New York: Harper and Brothers, 1922.

_____. *To the Last Man: A Novel.* New York: Harper and Brothers, 1922.

Lutman, Richard A. "Zane Grey's Women: Fiction and Family." *The Zane Grey Review* 12, no. 4 (June 1997): 1.

Wheeler, Joseph L. "Zane Grey's Impact on American Life and Letters: A Study in the Popular Novel." Ph.D. diss., George Peabody College for Teachers, 1975; UMI Dissertation Services, Ann Arbor, MI.

GROOM LAKE, NEVADA

See Area 51

GUN CONTROL

Thousands of shoot-outs in western movies have created the illusion that there were high levels of violence and

Anti–gun control ad on a bus bench sponsored by the John Birch Society

gunplay in the Old West. Judging by popular-culture sources, westerners walked about armed to the teeth and shot one another at the drop of a hat. Thus, for many anti–gun control groups, gun shows, and gun advertisers, cowboys and the Old West provide ideal icons for pushing their ideas and products. As historian Robert R. Dykstra notes, "The uniquely savage and homicide-ravaged Old West is a construct as phony as America's favorite 'invented tradition'— the quick-draw street duel reenacted every day in a score of tourist venues" (Dykstra 2000). The reality of gun use and prevalence differed sharply from the "gorified" images of movie and pop-culture mythology.

Western publications of more than a century ago clearly show that political leaders and ranchers of the time argued in favor of and took decisive action for gun control. Residents of the old cattle towns knew from bitter experience that armed men meant trouble. The *Baxter Springs Republican* (Kansas) complained that "scarcely a night passes but some villain recklessly shoots up or down the streets, endangering the lives of peaceable citizens" (14 July 1876). The newspaper urged that public authorities take ac-

tion. A few years later, the *Las Animas Leader* (Colorado) agreed: "The day of the Winchester rifle, ivory handled pistol and cartridge belt belongs to the past–it is gone never to return, and with it should go every many who cannot discharge his duties on the ranch without being thus accoutered" (24 February 1882).

Many western towns and organizations did take action. In 1878, infamous Dodge City, Kansas, posted a simple sign at the town's busiest intersection: "The carrying of Fire Arms Strictly Prohibited." At a cattlemen's convention in Caldwell, Kansas, in March 1882, E. M. Hewens offered a strong antihandgun resolution. The group "resolved unanimously that the six-shooter is not an absolute necessity adjunct to the outfit of the cowboy working on the range of the Cherokee Strip" (*Breeder's Gazette* [Chicago], 23 March 1882). A month later, stock growers of Las Animas County, Colorado, also "passed a resolution condemning the practice of carrying revolvers by cowboys on the range" (*Denver Daily Times* [Colorado], 12 April 1882). The *Caldwell Commercial* (Kansas) editorialized that "the six-shooter is a relic of barbarism, as it were, in the annals of stock raising;

Reenactors at WestFest play the roles of old-time western gunfighters

but, withal, so handy that some of the cowboys will cling to it with tenacity. But it must go" (2 March 1882).

In 1884 the *Black Hills Daily Times* of the Dakota Territory described carrying firearms into the city as a "dangerous practice," dangerous not only to others but to the person packing the gun. The story's title explained the antigun logic: "Perforated by His Own Pistol." Even the best of gunmen could have accidents. The *Wichita Beacon* reported that Wyatt Earp's revolver had slipped from his holster as he sat in a local saloon. The gun hit the floor and fired. "The ball passed through his coat, struck the north wall then glanced off and passed through the ceiling. It was a narrow escape and the occurrence got up a lively stampede from the room" (12 January 1876).

The *Caldwell Post* (Kansas) reported the accidental shooting of cowboy Hugh Calvert. While helping unload a wagon, "he picked up a blanket or something, and the revolver fell from it, the hammer striking upon a skillet and exploding the cartridge, the ball striking Mr. Calvert just above the eye and coming out at the base of the brain." The newspaper observed that "it is a well-known fact that five cowboys and cattlemen are killed by the accidental discharge of fire arms, and especially six-shooters, where one is killed by a murderer. The practice of carrying six-shooters on the range and leaving them around the camp and wagons should be condemned by the ranchmen" (20 July 1882).

Even the "Cowboy President," Theodore Roosevelt, recalled with approval that when he ranched in the Dakota Territory, his town allowed "no shooting in the streets." The town's newspaper, *The Bad Lands Cow Boy of Medora,* demanded that guns be banned entirely within the city limits. The *Daily Express* (Fort Collins, Colorado) summed up local sentiments well: "Strange as it may seem to the average eastern reader, and particularly the younger ones who have devoured any great quantity of yellow covered literature, several Wyoming ranchmen have disarmed their employees. A similar movement among Texas stockmen is now said to be making considerable headway" (9 January 1883).

Indeed, as early as 1882, Texas cattlemen had banned six-shooters from the cowboy's belt. "In almost every section of the West murders are on the increase, and cowmen are too often the principals in the encounters," declared the *Texas Live Stock Journal* (5 June 1884). "The six-shooter loaded with deadly cartridges is a dangerous companion for any man, especially if he should unfortunately be primed with whiskey. Cattlemen should unite in aiding the enforcement of the law against carrying of deadly weapons." In 1885 Pat Garrett took charge of the V. V. range in New Mexico. "Cowboys are not allowed to carry arms, and he will discharge any man in his employ who disobeys this rule. Every ranchman in the country should do likewise. The six-shooter must go" (*Cattlemen's Advertiser* [Trinidad, Colorado], 3 December 1885).

Only in the work of **pulp novelists,** in B-westerns, and in spaghetti westerns did men go about armed to the teeth. Leaders of the Old West recognized, as many fail to in the New West, that guns mean violent death. They took strong measures to reduce that risk. Robert Dykstra notes that "[what] none of us wants to see is western violence become a full-scale political myth, potentially as lethal as that 'Lost Cause' nonsense underlying resurgent neo-Confederate racism in this land. Because that's not comic" (Dykstra 2000).

References

Collins, Ross. "Gun Control and the Old West." History News Service (on-line), 14 July 1999: *http://www2.h-net.msu.edu/~hns/.*

_____. "Shot Full of Holes" (18 January 2000): *http://www.tompaine.com/history/2000/01/19.*

Dykstra, Robert R. "Imagining Dodge City: A Political Statement." *Western Historical Quarterly* 31, no. 3 (Autumn 2000): 278–284.

Westermeier, Clifford P., ed. *Trailing the Cowboy: His Life and Lore As Told by Frontier Journalists.* Caldwell, ID: Caxton Printers, 1955.

GUTHRIE, WOODROW WILSON "WOODY"

1912–1963

Born on 14 July 1912, in Okemah, Oklahoma, young Woodrow Wilson "Woody" Guthrie suffered a nearly unbearable string of family tragedies. Fire killed his older sister and badly injured his father; his mother fell victim to Huntington's chorea and mental illness. The family moved to Pampa, Texas, where they suffered through the Great Depression of the 1930s. Seeing few opportunities in

Oklahoma or Texas, in 1937 Woody headed west to Los Angeles, hoping to make a career as a cowboy singer. During the next few years he performed on radio programs and wrote some of his best-known tunes, including "Oklahoma Hills," "Philadelphia Lawyer," "Do, Re, Mi," "So Long, It's Been Good to Know Yuh," and "This Land Is Your Land." His western populism took on a harder edge in his writings for the Communist Party's *Daily Worker* and other leftist publications.

Guthrie, like many Depression-era Americans, benefited from government programs. In 1941 the Bonneville Power Administration (BPA) in Oregon hired him to write and sing songs praising the public ownership of electric power. Bonneville officials planned a film to sell the idea of public power to a skeptical public and to combat the negative propaganda of private power interests. The agency hired Guthrie to write songs for the soundtrack, paying him $266 for a month's work. Bonneville got its money's worth: The prolific songster turned out 26 tunes. War delayed the film's completion until 1948. In the early 1950s Red-baiting Republicans, unhappy with Guthrie's leftist politics, ordered all copies of the film and songs destroyed. Happily, the attempt failed.

During the 1980s the BPA began plans to celebrate its fiftieth anniversary. A diligent employee named Bill Murlin located lyrics to all 26 Guthrie songs as well as original recordings of 17. Included among them is "Roll On, Columbia":

Roll on, Columbia, roll on,

Roll on, Columbia, roll on.

Your power is turning our darkness to dawn,

So roll on, Columbia, roll on!

During the 1940s the westerner turned his sights eastward and traveled to New York City. With the collaboration of folklorist Alan Lomax, he recorded *Dust Bowl Ballads* for RCA Victor, an album that gained him national recognition. He performed with the best folk and blues musicians of the time, including Pete Seeger, Burl Ives, and Leadbelly. His best work, however, reflected his Oklahoma roots and the grit and optimism that carried him and many westerners through the terrible Depression.

Guthrie's health began to deteriorate in the early 1950s. The already unpredictable poet's actions became increasingly erratic, and in 1952 he learned the cause: He had Huntington's chorea. In 1954 he scribbled two sentences in a hand now nearly illegible: "I want you to pay a lot more attention to all my words longer and deeper and quieter and louder than I ever could. You'll get more out of them than I did around here." The cruel illness left the wandering minstrel unable to walk, speak, or care for himself. He died on 3 October 1967, confined to a hospital bed.

Guthrie left a considerable archive of works that display the full range of his genius. The collection includes more than 10,000 items, including personal papers, 300 letters, 700 photographs, 98 scrapbooks, 3,000 song lyrics, 700 works of art, and another 700 unpublished manuscripts. The archive also contains some 500 films, videos, and recordings. His wife, Marjorie Mazia Guthrie, worked to organize the materials and provide them with an appropriate home. It took 30 years before money could be raised to form the Woody Guthrie Archives in New York City. George Arevalo, an archivist and ethnomusicologist, signed on to preserve and organize the archive. Guthrie's daughter, Nora, and Harold Leventhal manage the collection. Artists, scholars, and other researchers may make appointments to view the materials.

As Arevalo observed,

Woody was not just some guy who played guitar and wrote songs. He was the consummate diarist. He was an illustrator, artist, painter. And more than anyone I can think of, he embodies so much of the American spirit, someone who could hang out with blues musicians in the Deep South, migrant workers in California, come to New York and hang out on the Bowery and move in intellectual circles at the same time.

Best known for his powerful folk ballads, Guthrie also wrote a song about flying saucers that he titled "Supersonic Boogie."

Woody's widow, Marjorie, had her own career as a dancer. Following her husband's death, however, she devoted herself to building an awareness of Huntington's chorea, the disease that killed her husband. She died of cancer at her home in Manhattan on 13 March 1983, at the age of 65. The Guthries' survivors include two sons, Joady and folk singer Arlo, and daughter Nora.

Some of the materials from the Woody Guthrie Archives have already been put to good use. In 1998 Billy Bragg and Wilco released a CD titled *Mermaid Avenue,* named for the street in Coney Island where Woody and Marjorie once lived. With the collaboration of daughter Nora, Bragg and Jeff Tweedy wrote new tunes for 15 of Guthrie's previously unrecorded songs from the archive. The collaboration brings Guthrie's wit and wisdom to a new, international genera-

tion of listeners. Some of the lyrics, such as those of "Christ for President," reflect the Oklahoman's social criticism:

Every year we waste enough
To feed the ones who starve.
We build our civilization up
And we shoot it down with wars.

In addition to his musical compositions, Guthrie left several books about his life and times: *Bound for Glory* (1943; a film version appeared in 1976), *Born to Win* (1965), and two works published posthumously, *Seeds of Man* (1976) and *Pastures of Plenty: A Self-Portrait* (1990). His true legacy, however, lies in the stimulus he provided for a powerful generation of folk artists. Singers from the 1960s (including his son Arlo, Bob Dylan, Phil Ochs, Joan Baez, and Judy Collins) through the 1980s (John Mellencamp, Bruce Springsteen) continue to draw inspiration from Guthrie.

References

Guthrie, Woody. *Born to Win.* Edited by Robert Shelton. New York: Macmillan, 1965.

_____. *Bound for Glory.* New York: New American Library, 1943, 1970.

_____. *Pastures of Plenty: A Self-Portrait.* Edited by Dave Marsh and Harold Leventhal. New York: HarperCollins, 1990.

_____. *Seeds of Man: An Experience Lived and Dreamed.* New York: E. P. Dutton, 1976.

Klein, Joe. *Woody Guthrie: A Life.* New York: A. A. Knopf; distributed by Random House, 1980.

Woody Guthrie Foundation: *http://www. woodyguthrie.org.*

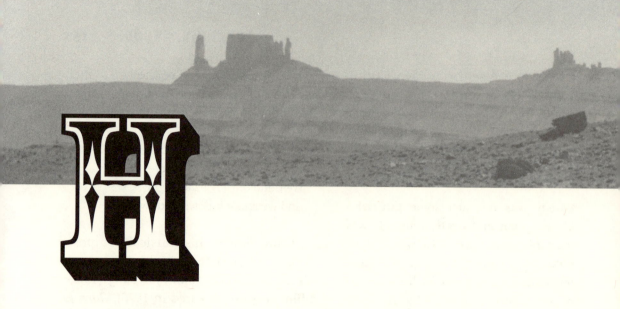

HAYDUKE

See Monkey Wrench Gang

HERDING CATS

The trail drive ranks among the most storied events in all of western American history. Tens of thousands of men drove hundreds of thousands of cattle north from Texas to Kansas cow towns for about 20 years beginning in 1865. Hollywood films from *Red River* to *City Slickers* have embellished the trail-drive motif. Not surprisingly, an inventive Texas company named EDS found yet another way to build on the legendary, quintessential western drama of the trail drive. A powerful image for doing the nearly impossible, "herding cats" is a vivid part of American vernacular. On 30 January 2000, in a memorable Super Bowl television ad, EDS brought the metaphor to life.

Formed in the early 1960s, EDS of Plano, Texas, a computer services company, describes itself as "a global leader in information technology and electronic business services" (EDS Web Site). Its memorable television ad—grizzled cowboys herding thousands of cats across the plains—"illustrate[d] the complexities of managing E-Business" (EDS Web Site). The ad continued to play through the year 2000 and is still available on the company's Web site.

EDS also created an on-line game, "The Good, the Bad, the Furry." Players test their herding skills by taking the role of old-timer Earl, greenhorn Dusty, or cowgirl Sal. Players must move several quick, uncooperative cats into a corral. "Bringing together information, ideas and technologies and making them all go where you want is no easy task," notes EDS official Don Uzzi. "As our online game players will find, herding cats is similarly complicated. Players will quickly understand why we in technology use 'herding cats' as a catchphrase when referring to something that's extraordinarily difficult" (EDS Web Site).

Minneapolis-based Fallon McElligott created the television ad. Visually, it wonderfully mimics an epic western trail drive, complete with cowboys' commentary on the rigors of the work. "Being a cat herder is probably about the toughest thing that I've ever done," says one cowhand. "Anybody can herd cattle," snorts another. "We've found an extremely visual way to illustrate what EDS does for its clients," said David Lubars, president and creative director at Fallon McElligott. "It's funny, unique and smart, and we think sure to be memorable to the world's largest viewing audiences on Super Bowl Sunday" (EDS Web Site). Others have taken up the phrase "herding cats" as a powerful marketing tool. Gaelic Storm, the steerage party band seen in the hit movie *Titanic,* released an album titled *Herding Cats,* filled with the rollicking Irish dance music the quintet is known for. In 1997, Warren Bennis published a book titled *Managing People Is Like Herding Cats.* In November 1999 Chester A. Crocker, Fen Osler Hampson, and Pamela Aall edited a book titled *Herding Cats: Multiparty Mediation in a Complex World.* It has become a workplace catchphrase that "dealing with [fill in the blank] is like herding cats."

Reference

EDS Web Site: *http://www.eds.com.*

HICKOK, JAMES BUTLER "WILD BILL"

1837–1876, gunfighter, gambler. *See* Dead Man's Hand

HILL, JOE

1879–1915

Joe Hill, songwriter, legend, and martyr of the Industrial Workers of the World, spent most of his life working and fighting on behalf of workers and against the capitalist system. As a young man, he went west to California, where he joined the Industrial Workers of the World (**Wobblies,** or IWW). The most important stage in his life took place in Utah, where he was executed on 19 November 1915. Hill's ideology both embraced and challenged the ideals of the West. He believed in freedom, opportunity, and equality. Because of his song writing, his martyrdom, and his ideals, he became an icon for unions everywhere. Debates over his trial, character, and place in history continue.

On 7 October 1879, Margareta Hagglund gave birth to Joel Emmanuel Hagglund in Gävle, Sweden. She and husband Olof, a railroad worker, had nine children. In 1902, after his mother's death, Joel left for America. He later became known as Joseph Hillstrom. He settled in New York City working at various odd jobs. He then moved to Chicago, where he worked in a machine shop for two months. After being blacklisted for trying to organize the workers, he again changed his name and became Joe Hill. From 1903 to 1910, Hill lived in Philadelphia, the Dakotas, Portland, Oregon, and San Francisco, where he worked odd jobs and retained his interest in organizing workers. In 1910, after moving to San Pedro, California, he joined the IWW, a radical labor union.

Hill also began to write labor songs that promoted the views of the Wobblies. His songs became popular and appeared in later editions of the *Little Red Songbook,* a collection of Wobbly music. After organizing and defending the IWW in the West, in 1913 Hill decided to head back to Chicago. He stopped in Salt Lake City, Utah, along the way to break up the trip and perhaps to visit a relative. He extended his stay and went to work in various mines in Utah.

On the night of 10 January 1914, two masked men shot a grocery store owner, J. G. Morrison, and his son, Arling, in Salt Lake City. After police investigation and confusion, the police placed Hill under arrest for the murders. The evidence against Hill did not appear to be strong. However, he did have a gunshot wound that could have connected him to the murders. Hill said he'd gotten shot in a fight with an angry husband over a supposed affair. He did not help his own case because of his pride and mistaken trust that justice would set him free. He might have also consciously decided to accept martyrdom to further the cause of "the One Big Union." He steadfastly maintained his innocence until he died. Under Utah law, Hill had the option of a firing squad or the gallows. "I'll take the shooting," Hill told the judge. "I've been shot a couple times before, and I think I can take it" ("Joe Hill: The Man behind the Martyr").

Despite mass support by workers, President Woodrow Wilson, young Helen Keller, and the Swedish government, the State of Utah executed Hill at sunrise on 19 November 1915. His death turned him into a martyr for the labor movement. He died for a cause he believed in.

He chose to be killed by a firing squad, rather than being hung. Irving Werstein, author of *Pie in the Sky* (also the title of a Joe Hill song), asserts that Hill faced the firing squad without a blindfold. This is false, another embellishment of the martyr's legend. Other discrepancies appeared in the *New York Times* and still appear on the Joe Hill Internet home page. According to the *Times,* from the day after his death, "Hillstrom declared . . . that he did not wish any of his friends to see the execution." In contrast, the Joe Hill home page states that "Hill's request to invite friends was denied based on their membership in the Industrial Workers of the World."

Hill possessed great pride, loyalty, and courage. He did shout "fire" to the squad to initiate his death. Did the State of Utah seize the opportunity to get rid of a labor agitator? Statements by Governor William Spry show that he wanted to use Hill as an example to those who defied the law. Media coverage urged people to defend against a mythical "IWW invasion." Some of Hill's last statements have become common labor slogans and symbols. "Don't mourn—organize!" and "I will die a true-blue rebel!" added to Wobbly folklore. Donald E. Winters Jr., author of *The Soul of the Wobblies,* states that his "martyrhood is sometimes paralleled with the crucifixion of Christ" (Winters 1985). As Irving Werstein observes, "Alive, Joe Hill was merely . . . a working-class poet and songsmith; dead, he became the symbol of revolution" (Werstein 1969).

Joe Hill's funeral took place in Chicago with an estimated 15,000–30,000 people in attendance. People sang Hill's songs and read aloud his last words. He requested in his will that his body be cremated and his ashes distributed by the wind. The Wobblies did not make it that simple. The IWW distributed envelopes of his ashes across the country, and on May Day, 1916, people disbursed his ashes in every state expect Utah. May Day only seemed fitting for a labor hero.

Not everyone scattered the ashes sent them. Ashes may have been distributed to South America, Europe, Asia, Australia, and South Africa. During a raid of an IWW headquarters in 1917, police discovered some of Hill's ashes behind a framed picture of him. Billy Bragg, a socialist musician of today, even swallowed some of Hill's ashes. He also recorded the song "Joe Hill" in the early 1990s. Canadian singer and songwriter Len Wallace received a locket containing some of Hill's ashes in 1991. An IWW local in Toronto presented it to him for keeping the tradition of Joe Hill alive.

Songs are a major reason why Joe Hill is remembered. His most popular works include "The Preacher and the Slave," "Rebel Girl," and "Casey Jones." Hill's songs attacked capitalism and religion. Timothy E. Scheurer, author of *Born in the U.S.A.,* says, "For Hill, . . . joining the union is the real **manifest destiny** of the nation" (Scheurer 1991). Hill recognized that music would be remembered over time, but he did not live to see the great impact of his songs in popular culture.

A number of Hill's songs have been performed and recorded by many musicians. A duo from New England called the Hobo Minstrels still plays Joe Hill songs today. A minstrel group called the Almanac Singers dedicated an album to Joe Hill. Utah Phillips, a folk singer, recorded "The Preacher and the Slave" in 1988.

Joe Hill also became the subject and inspiration of additional songs. In 1925 Alfred Hayes wrote a tribute poem, "Joe Hill," later set to music:

I dreamed I saw Joe Hill last night,
Alive as you and me.
Says I, "But Joe you're ten years dead,"
"I never died," says he

Earl Robinson recorded the song in 1936. Paul Robeson sang "Joe Hill" to a packed Carnegie Hall in 1958. Robeson is partially responsible for spreading Hill's popularity to England. In 1983 Utah Phillips also recorded the song.

Famed folk singer Woody **Guthrie** recorded a song called "Joe Hillstrom" in 1947. Phil Ochs also wrote a song called "Joe Hill." Joan Baez sang "Joe Hill" at Woodstock in 1969, thus introducing the legend of Hill to the rebellious youth there. In 1990 Si Kahn wrote a song, "Paper Heart," about Hill's execution. (The title refers to the paper target pinned on Hill's chest.) Kahn's publishing company is called Joe Hill Music. In 1989 Marc Levy sang a song at the Smithsonian Institution called "Joe Hill's Ashes." Joe Hill is remembered and revered by many people.

A Swedish movie called *Joe Hill* came out in 1971. It sympathetically depicts Hill and ignores his conviction for murder. In one fictitious scene, Wobblies are dancing around Hill's ashes. A famous painting by Mary Latham originally hung in the Joe Hill Hospitality House in Salt Lake City. It portrays his execution with the image of Jesus Christ on the cross hovering above the smoke rising from the guns of the firing squad.

Like composers, many writers have

paid homage to Hill. One of the most popular and controversial books is Wallace Stegner's novel *Joe Hill*. The novel does not treat Hill as a legend; rather, it presents him as fully capable of murder. The book sparked protest because of ethical issues and the negative treatment of Hill. In contrast, Ralph Chaplin's book, *Wobbly,* presents Hill as a hero. Chaplin, an ex-Wobbly, talks about how crushed he felt when Hill died. Although Chaplin never met Hill, he felt "a spiritual kinship." In 1951 Barrie Stavis published a play called *The Man Who Never Died,* which documented Hill's life. In 1980 another play about Hill's life, *Salt Lake City Skyline,* appeared on Broadway.

The labor hero Joe Hill remains a controversial western legend. Gatherings each 19 November commemorate his death. Protest signs and buttons repeat his sayings. An e-mail I received on 22 September 1999 from *Z Magazine* contained the phrase "don't mourn—organize." PBS television aired an excellent documentary of his life on Labor Day, 2000. Hill continues to inspire labor unions and popular movements everywhere. He will always be a martyr of the Wobbly cause.

—Michael L. Sileno

References

Hampton, Wayne. *Guerilla Minstrels.* Knoxville: University of Tennessee Press, 1986.

"Joe Hill: The Man behind the Martyr." PBS documentary site: *http://www.pbs.org/joehill.*

Scheurer, Timothy E. *Born in the U.S.A.: The Myth of America in Popular Music from Colonial Times to the Present.* Jackson: University Press of Mississippi, 1991.

Smith, Gibbs M. *Joe Hill.* Salt Lake City: University of Utah Press, 1969.

Stegner, Wallace. *Joe Hill: A Biographical Novel.* Lincoln: University of Nebraska Press, 1950.

Werstein, Irving. *Pie in the Sky.* New York: Delacorte Press, 1969.

Winters, Donald E., Jr. *The Soul of the Wobblies: The I.W.W., Religion, and American Culture in the Progressive Era, 1905–1917.* Westport, CT: Greenwood Press, 1985.

Sources of Further Information

Joe Hill's songs on-line: *http://206.220.140.75/radio.*

Phil Ochs's song "Joe Hill": *http://hillstrom.iww.org/joehill.html.*

HISPANICS IN WESTERN FILMS

Racial discrimination marred social relations in the Old West just as it did elsewhere in the nation. African Americans, Asians, members of many European immigrant groups (such as Basques), and Hispanics all felt the sting of Anglo-American racism. Many negative cultural stereotypes also carried over into popular culture, especially films. Furthermore, films generally stereotyped Hispanic characters, who spoke with thick accents and played stock roles, like the scar-faced *bandito* or the swarthy Mexican cantina dancer/temptress. Perhaps more so than any other ethnic group, Hispanics have suffered from a long history of negative stereotypes presented on the silver screen.

In 1977 historian Allen L. Woll published the first serious critical study of the portrayal of Hispanics on film in *The*

Latin Image in American Film. "Americans thus receive," he wrote, "a dominant picture of Latin society populated by murderous *banditos* and submissive, but sensual, peasant women. Unfortunately, there is little to balance this all-too-prevalent stereotype" (Woll 1977). Early silent movies demonized Hispanics, especially Mexicans, even more thoroughly than they did American Indians. In *Indian Scout's Revenge* (1910), a pioneer family helps a Mexican man. He falls in love with a daughter in the family, but she rejects his affections. Enraged, he ungratefully wreaks havoc on his hosts. *Captured by Mexicans* (1914) graphically depicts the horrible fate suggested in the title. The conflict of the Mexican Revolution probably inspired the thin plot of *The Challenge of Chance* (1919). A professional prizefighter, who also owns a ranch, defends his property against attacks by a dangerous band of Mexican insurgents. Countless films, such as *Arizona Cat Claw* and *Desert Gold,* both filmed in 1919, present villainous Mexican bandits whose actions reflect their barbarism and immorality.

Hollywood produced a string of "greaser" movies that were representative of racial attitudes of the time. The derogatory term "greaser" for Mexicans extends well back into the nineteenth century, and in the racially insensitive era of the early twentieth century, films perpetuated the negativity. *The Greaser's Gauntlet* (1908), *The Greaser's Revenge* (1914), *Bronco Billy and the Greaser* (1914), and *Guns and Greasers* (1928) represent just a few of many films perpetuating demeaning, villainous images of Mexicans. In *The Cowboy's Baby* (1910), the "greaser" throws a baby into a river.

"The greaser," noted Ramon Novarro, "was too popular to be successfully opposed by anyone in Hollywood. I, among several others, made strenuous objections to my studio and others. But we could not argue with financial success" (Hadley-Garcia 1993). "Greaser" for a time became the most common label for Mexicans, portrayed as violent, sadistic, untrustworthy, and immoral. After vehement protests by many parties, including the Mexican government, Hollywood finally abandoned the term in the 1920s.

Although such negative images predominated, occasional positive roles did appear for Hispanic actors. In 1960 Hispanic actor Ramon Novarro looked back wistfully at the silent era. "They say silence is golden," he noted, "and for actors of Hispanic origin, silent movies were wonderful. We were not limited by our voices or accents, so Hollywood welcomed us with open arms. It has never been the same, since" (Hadley-Garcia 1993).

The flamboyant cowboy hero Tom Mix presented one of the earliest sympathetic and positive screen portrayals of Mexicans. *The Mexican* (1914) presents a poor Mexican ranch hand who suffers the taunts and harassment of his white coworkers. The rancher fires him. However, he nobly saves the life of the rancher's baby, thereby earning the respect of whites in the film. The rancher rehires him in the film's happy ending. In *The Lone Wagon* (1923), a Mexican protects a family of pioneers from attacking Indians. *Fighting Fury* (1924) presents the common western theme of revenge for an injustice or assault against one's family. In this case, however, the avenger is a Mexican who tracks down three ranchers who unjustly killed his parents.

In many cases, skin color, not ethnicity per se, determined the roles an actor could play. Dark-complexioned Warren Baxter, for example, often portrayed Indians or Hispanics during the silent era. He played a Mexican, smartly dressed in a wide sombrero and embroidered charro jacket, alongside Dorothy Burgess, in the 1929 film *In Old Arizona*. Actress Dolores Del Rio recalled the era: "Skin tone was very important then, and Spanish-speaking actors in Hollywood fell into two categories. If light-skinned, they could play any nationality, including American. Dark-skinned actors were fated to play servants or appear as villains" (Hadley-Garcia 1993).

Furthermore, white actors often portrayed Hispanic heroes. Douglas Fairbanks Jr., for instance, played the Old California Spanish swordsman **Zorro.** Later, other white actors would again play the role, including Tyrone Power (1940), Frenchman Alain Delon (1974), and George Hamilton (1980). Not until 1998 would a Spanish-speaking actor, Antonio Banderas, don the famous mask and sword of one of Hollywood's most famous Hispanic heroes.

During the 1930s, talkies presented new language and cultural challenges for Spanish-speaking actors. Protests from throughout Latin America greeted the 1932 film *Girl of the Rio,* which perpetuated two long-time stereotypes. Leo Carrillo played a "greaser-like" villain, and Dolores Del Rio starred as a sexy cantina dancer named "the Dove." As in previous decades, most Hispanic roles portrayed illegal and often violent activities.

In 1933 president-elect Franklin Del-

ano Roosevelt announced his Good Neighbor Policy to improve relations with Latin American nations. However, Hollywood's version of reality generally had Anglo heroes again combating corrupt, lawless Mexicans. Examples include *Durango Valley Raiders* (1938) and *Border G-Man* (1938). During the late 1930s and into World War II, many cowboy heroes made films with Borderlands or Mexican settings, including singing cowboys Gene **Autry,** Tex Ritter, and Roy **Rogers,** as well as Hopalong Cassidy and the **Lone Ranger.**

Although Spanish-speaking actors found roles in the talkies, the old practice of white actors playing Hispanic heroes continued. Beginning in 1931, Warren Baxter made a series of films as the Cisco Kid. He also played a fictionalized version of the California bandit Joaquín Murieta in the 1936 film *Robin Hood of El Dorado.* In 1965 a blue-eyed Jeffrey Hunter would reprise the role of Murieta. In 1971 the role finally went to a Spanish-speaking actor when Ricardo Montalban played the hero in a made-for-television production, *The Desperate Mission.* Young Jane Russell played the fiery "mixed-blood" heroine Rio in *The Outlaw,* a 1943 Howard **Hughes** production.

Beginning in 1939, Hollywood belatedly embraced the Good Neighbor theme. Indeed, Latino themes and actors came into their own. As Allen Woll notes, "talent scouts brought planeloads of Latin American talent to Hollywood, as viewers discovered and delighted in Carmen Miranda, Desi Arnaz, and Cesar Romero" (Woll 1977). The Cisco Kid role finally went to a Hispanic actor, Duncan Renaldo, as did that of his comic sidekick Pancho, played by funnyman Leo Carrillo. Cesar Romero also starred in six Cisco Kid adventure films shot in 1940–1941. Although she did not star in westerns, Carmen Miranda enjoyed huge popular success as the "Brazilian Bombshell." Indeed, Latin rhythms and songs, along with incredibly silly costuming, poured out of Hollywood. Among westerns, romanticized portrayals of Old Spanish California, with white Castilian heroes, predominated. Examples include *The Mark of Zorro* (1940), with Tyrone Power, and *California* (1946), with Ray Milland, Anthony Quinn, and Barbara Stanwyck.

Hispanic actors enjoyed very limited benefits of the golden age of movie and **television** westerns during the 1950s. Katy Jurado left the Mexican film industry and gained critical acclaim as Helen Ramirez in Fred Zinneman's classic *High Noon* (1952). On a lighter note, Richard "Chito" Martin played Tim Holt's sidekick in 29 B-westerns. He provided both humor and stereotypical "Latin lover" charm. He also appeared with Robert Mitchum and James Warren. Among his films are *Brothers in the Saddle* (1949), *Dynamite Pass* (1950), and *Gunplay* (1951). Indeed, since the 1920s, dark-haired, irresistible "Latin lovers," like Ramon Novarro, have joined the pantheon of durable Hispanic stereotypes.

Old stereotypes die hard, however, and the evil Mexican bandit resurfaced with a vengeance in Anthony Quinn's portrayal of José Esqueda in *Ride Vaquero!* (1953). Similarly, Rodolfo Hoyo's version of Pancho Villa in *Villa* (1958) presents the hero of the Mexican Revolution as a cruel, selfish, low-life bandit. And another Mexican revolutionary hero, Emilio Zapata, would be portrayed by an Anglo actor, Marlon Brando, in *Viva Zapata* (1952). Yet another blue-eyed Anglo actor, Paul Newman, played a Mexican bandit in *The Outrage* (1964). In 1969, outraged Hispanic actors, led by Ricardo Montalban, formed the group Nosotros ("We" in Spanish) to lobby Hollywood for better roles and better, more believable images of Latinos.

The spaghetti western craze of the 1970s marked a new low point in the screen depiction of Mexicans. Beginning with *The Good, the Bad, and the Ugly* (released in 1967), leering, sweaty Mexican villains swarmed across the screen, led by Eli Wallach as Tuco. An avalanche of violent, demeaning sequels followed, as directors in Italy, Spain, Mexico, the United States, Israel, and a host of other countries tried their hand at "pasta oaters" (spaghetti westerns). Likewise *The Wild Bunch* (1969) presents the evil, vicious Mexican general Mapuche, played by Emilio Fernandez, and his forces in a climactic bloodbath.

The decline of westerns in general in the 1970s also meant a decline in Hispanic roles. However, a minor renaissance followed in the 1980s. In 1982 Edward James Olmos starred in *The Ballad of Gregorio **Cortez**.* In this film, based on historical events in Texas, the Mexican bandit is a popular hero, not a dastardly villain. Three Latino actors, Emilio Estevez, Lou Diamond Phillips, and Charlie Sheen, enjoyed popular and critical acclaim in a number of commercially successful films, including *Young Guns* (1988).

A new social and ethnic consciousness has infused some of the more recent films. Ruben Blades starred as the sheriff in a very different type of western, *The*

Milagro Beanfield War (1987). Based on John Nichols's popular and moving 1974 novel, Robert Redford's movie version unfortunately flopped at the box office. It did, however, illuminate ethnic, class, and environmental conflicts in New Mexico, with a lone Chicano (Joe Mondragon, played by Chick Vennera) trying to stave off developers who are using all the town's water. Likewise, *The Border* (1982) criticized corruption and abuses in the *migra,* the U.S. Border Patrol. In spite of its contemporary theme, the film ends with an old-fashioned, bloody shoot-out.

Signs of progress include annual American Latino Media Arts (ALMA) awards honoring outstanding Latino performers and positive portrayals in film and television. The National Council of La Raza (NCLR) sponsors the ALMA awards, now broadcast on national television. Likewise, recognizing the fast-increasing numbers of Spanish speakers, in March 2000 HBO television announced plans for a Latino Channel. This would compete with Univision, the current leader among Spanish-language television outlets.

Despite these hopeful signs, Hispanics have not fared well over the past century at the hands of those making western films. Despite some progress, stereotyping continues. Throughout the 1960s and '70s, "all major Latin roles [were] portrayed by North Americans," notes Allen Woll, "and the South American remains an object of scorn. Instead of progress, only a vicious circle emerges" (Woll 1977). However, most distressing is the fact that despite fast-growing numbers of Hispanics in the general population, they remain largely invisible in Hollywood productions.

References

Hadley-Garcia, George. *Hispanic Hollywood: The Latins in Motion Pictures.* New York: Citadel Press/Carol Publishing, 1990, 1993.

Halnon, Mary. "Indians and Mexicans: Alternative Cultures in the Silent Western": *http://xroads.virginia.edu/~HYPER/HNS/Westfilm/indian.htm.*

Woll, Allen L. *The Latin Image in American Film.* Los Angeles: UCLA Latin American Studies Center Publications, 1977.

HOLLYWOOD THE HARD WAY

See Van Meter, Jerry

HOOVER DAM

Abraham Lincoln said, "What people think is, is more important than what actually is so." Lincoln should know. A lot of people think he participated in the Lincoln-Douglas debates when he ran for president, that Ann Rutledge was his great lost love, and that he wrote the Gettysburg Address on the back of an envelope. None of which is true.

From Betsy Ross's mythical needlework to Ronald Reagan's supposedly never getting the girl in the movies, our history is filled with "facts" that everyone knows are true—except they aren't. Such folklore seems to grab the public imagination more tenaciously than the usually more interesting reality. Year after year, stories with no substance are repeated and retold while the facts remain buried.

In Nevada a number of tall tales have become accepted as truth and have in some cases resisted all efforts at correction. Here is one of the best known: Workers are buried in Hoover Dam. This myth is the despair of Hoover Dam tour guides. Someone in every group taking the tour is sure to ask how many men are buried in the concrete of the gigantic dam. According to the story, on several occasions during the dam's construction in the 1930s, a worker slipped, fell, and was covered by concrete as it was being poured. Unable to stop the cascade of concrete before the worker suffocated, supervisors had no choice but to allow the concrete to continue flowing, covering the worker and sealing him in the dam. This happened seven times during construction, according to the tale's most popular version.

In 1986 Tom King, director of the University of Nevada Oral History Program, interviewed several men who had labored on the construction of Hoover Dam. They told him that a number of bodies lie buried in it. "These stories were made somewhat plausible by the authority of the tellers, themselves dam workers, and by our knowledge that building the dam was indeed an extremely hazardous enterprise," said King; "however, further questioning revealed that none of the storytellers had actually witnessed such a tragedy or knew the identity of any of the victims. This was not surprising: the tellers believed what they were saying, but their stories were folklore—there are no bodies in the dam."

"The idea of workers forever entombed in the giant structure that they had helped build was so irresistibly poetic, so deliciously macabre," wrote Joseph Stevens in his award-winning book *Hoover Dam: An American Adventure,* "that it became the basis for the most enduring legend of Hoover Dam, and article of faith for millions of visitors who down through the years would insist, despite the firm denials of tour guides, Bureau of Reclamation engineers, and historians, that the great arch was not only a dam but a sarcophagus" (Stevens 1988).

Actually, the dam was poured in relatively small sections, so about all a fallen worker would have had to do to get his face clear of the rising concrete was to stand up. Officially, 96 dam workers died of various causes (112 persons unofficially), but none was permanently buried in concrete.

The closest any worker came to being buried was on 8 November 1933, when the wall of a form collapsed, sending hundreds of tons of recently poured concrete tumbling down the face of the dam. One worker below narrowly escaped with his life; W. A. Jameson, however, was not so lucky and was covered by the rain of debris. Jameson was the only man ever buried in Hoover Dam, and he was interred for just 16 hours before his body was recovered.

A structural engineer interviewed for a Discovery Channel documentary on Hoover Dam pointed out that it would be sheer folly to leave a worker buried in the dam. A decomposing body would jeopardize the dam's structural integrity and risk the multimillion-dollar project and consequently the property and lives downstream of people on the Colorado River.

—*Guy Louis Rocha and Dennis Myers*

Reference

Stevens, Joseph E. *Hoover Dam: An American Adventure*. Norman: University of Oklahoma Press, 1988.

HORN, TOM

1860–1903

Legendary western scout, Pinkerton detective, and range detective, Horn hired out his gun to the highest bidder. Successful in getting his man, he eventually died at the gallows for a murder he may not have committed.

Born in Memphis, Missouri, on 21 November 1860, Horn grew up a farm boy. He reveled in outdoor life and hated school, which he often skipped. His very strict father whipped the 14-year-old so severely that the boy ran away from home and headed West. The youth worked at odd jobs, night-herding cattle, on the Santa Fe railroad, and for freight and stagecoach companies.

At age 16, Horn scouted for the army, serving for more than a decade. In 1886 he tracked Geronimo and his band to his hideout in the Sierra Gordo outside of Sonora, Mexico. He rode into the Indian camp alone and negotiated Geronimo's surrender. Geronimo, with Horn guiding him and his tribe, crossed the border, officially surrendered, and ended the last great Indian war in America. According to Horn's autobiography (not always a reliable guide), the Apache nicknamed him "Talking Boy" because of his translation skills in Apache and Spanish. After Horn's death, the army's chief scout, Al Sieber, recalled that "often-times I needed the help of a man I could rely on, and I always placed Horn in charge. For it required a man of bravery, judgment and skill, and I ever found Tom true to the last letter of the law to any and every trust confided in his care" (Cunningham 1996).

After quitting his post as chief army scout, Horn wandered through the Arizona gold fields and then became a ranch hand. He proved himself a capable rider and roper at a rodeo in Globe, Arizona, in 1888. He won the steer-roping competition. Three year later, he set a record in Phoenix, Arizona, by roping a steer in 45.5 seconds.

In 1890 Horn joined the Pinkerton Detective Agency, working out of the Denver office. He tracked down train and bank robbers and other criminals and showed himself to be fearless. In October 1891 Horn himself went on trial, mistaken for a train robber by a Reno, Nevada, sheriff. Horn reportedly rode into the famous Hole in the Wall outlaw hideout and single-handedly captured a notorious train robber named Peg-Leg Watson. This feat marked the beginning of Horn's legend in the West. He quit detecting after a reported 17 killings, saying "I have no stomach for it anymore." (Horn probably quit in 1892, although his own writings give the date as 1894.)

However, Horn's aversion to killing appears to have been short-lived. In 1892 the Wyoming Stock Growers Association hired him as a detective to gather evidence of rustling and to track and kill the culprits. Such a job had many names, including "regulator" and "range, stock, or livestock detective." In many cases, unwanted settlers and small ranchers, who infringed on the open range used by large ranchers, became the targets of a regulator. Horn also worked for the Swan Land and Cattle Company, officially as a horse breaker but unofficially as a killer. Horn earned $500 to $600 for every cattle thief he killed. He ruthlessly and successfully tracked down rustlers and gained a reputation as a killer. According to dubious legend, as a trademark and warning, he would place a stone or two under the head of each victim.

Utilizing his prodigious tracking skills, he carefully observed his victim over a period of days. After planning his ambush, he loaded his long-distance buffalo gun and generally killed his victim with a single, large-caliber bullet. "Killing men is my business," he proclaimed, and another dozen bodies attested to his skill.

Horn fought in Cuba during the War of 1898 (Spanish-American War), then returned to the West. In 1900 he probably shot and killed accused cattle rustlers Matt Rash and Isom **Dart** in Colorado. He then rode to the Wyoming ranges to kill for cattle baron John Coble. He also regaled wealthy ranchers at the Cheyenne Club with stories of his days stalking Apaches and driving herds up the **Chisholm Trail.** He was once again a hunter of rustlers, and his tactics had changed little since he had begun the bloody business a decade earlier.

In 1901 Horn investigated a rustling problem near Iron Mountain, north of Laramie, Wyoming. A feud brewed between neighboring cattle ranchers Jim Miller and Kels P. Nickell. The two fought in February, and Miller stabbed Nickell. That spring, Nickell committed a serious crime in cattle country: He brought in hated sheep. On the morning of 18 July, on the Powder River Road near Cheyenne, someone set an ambush for Nickell. Instead, two shots struck and killed Nickell's tall 14-year-old son. The gunman, several hundred yards from his target, possibly mistook the boy for his father. According to prosecutors, the unfortunate youth had worn his father's coat and hat, but his mother insisted that he had dressed in his own clothes.

Suspicion immediately turned to Horn, feared and generally hated in the Cheyenne area. Deputy Marshal Joe Lefors obtained a confession while Horn was drunk. The prosecution never established a reasonable motive for Horn to kill the boy, but on 23 October 1902 the jury found him guilty. Horn succeeded in escaping on his third attempted jail break, on 6 August 1903, but he was quickly recaptured. The Wyoming Supreme Court turned down his appeal in September 1903.

A wealthy cattleman, John Coble, and Horn's girlfriend, a schoolteacher named Glendolene Myrtle Kimmel, pushed unsuccessfully for a commuted sentence. According to the latter, Horn "was a man who embodied the characteristics, the experiences and code of the old frontiersman." Horn's biographer, Dean Krakel, has argued that officials framed the gunman for the Nickell shooting. Eugene Cunningham has likewise concluded that Horn was innocent of the shooting. Later, Jim Miller's son Victor, who had often fought with Willie Nickell, allegedly confessed to the murder.

Horn spent the last months of his life writing his memoirs and weaving the rope that would be used to hang him. On the day of his hanging, officials put Cheyenne under martial law, fearing that

Horn's "cowboy friends" might try to free him. Officials had reason to worry, given that they had found five sticks of dynamite outside the jail the previous December. According to witnesses, Horn told the executioner to "hurry it up. I got nothing more to say." He was hanged at 11:08 A.M. on 20 November 1903. His last words were reputed to have been "that's the sickest-looking lot of damned sheriffs I ever saw" (Cunningham 1996). Family members removed the body to Boulder, Colorado, for burial.

Horn's death did not end the controversy that surrounded his life. Novelists and filmmakers have found his violent, somewhat tragic life an appealing topic. McDonald Carey played him as a hired killer named Bus Crow in the 1953 film *Hannah Lee.* In 1975 Will Henry penned the novel *I, Tom Horn.* David Carradine starred in *Mr. Horn,* a 1979 **television** movie based on the stock detective's life. A year later, Steve McQueen presented Horn as a rather sympathetic but anachronistic figure in an exquisitely photographed but rambling film, *Tom Horn.* Critic Brian Garfield called the movie "an abysmal mess."

Despite his protestations of innocence, Horn lost the battle of history and is generally viewed as a bloodthirsty murderer, an anachronism who outlived his violent times. His girlfriend, loyal to the last, penned a fitting epitaph: "Riding hard, drinking hard, fighting hard—so passed his days, until he was crushed between the grindstones of two civilizations."

References

Cunningham, Eugene. *Triggernometry: A Gallery of Gunfighters.* Norman: University of Oklahoma Press, 1941, 1996.

Horan, James D. *The Gunfighters: The Authentic Wild West.* New York: Gramercy Books, 1976, 1994.

Nash, Jay Robert, ed. *Encyclopedia of Western Lawmen and Outlaws.* New York: Paragon House, 1992.

HORSES, MYTHICAL

See Wildfire

HORSES, WILD

See Wild Horses

HUGHES, HOWARD

1905–1976

As motion pictures became a dominant factor in American culture during the 1920s, California witnessed a new migration very similar to that of the 1840s. This time, people came to seek their fortune in movies, not gold. Among them was Howard Hughes Jr. This young millionaire's interests in film and aviation helped shape the future of California during the 1920s and '30s.

Hughes influenced the West tremendously during this period, yet he is rarely listed as an important regional figure. This is owing in large part to his eccentric lifestyle and to the wide range of his activities.

Hughes entered the world on Christmas Eve, 1905, outside of Houston,

Texas. Foreshadowing the mysteries surrounding his later life, he possessed no birth certificate, even though respected doctors attended. The lack of a certified date of birth posed a problem during World War II when he tried to prove his age. The only records of his birthday are two sworn affidavits by relatives

Howard's father, a lawyer, initially put the family in a precarious financial situation. After earning $50,000 by leasing Texas oil property, he took his new bride, Allene Gano, on a European honeymoon; he returned $50,000 in debt. After settling in Houston, he began one of the city's most influential companies, Hughes Tools, to serve the region's burgeoning oil industry. Howard Sr. leased his newly patented bit, the Sharp-Hughes rolling bit, to each well for $30,000. This bit, which had 166 cutting edges, quickly dug through the thick Texas soil. The cash flowed freely to Howard Sr. after his partner, Walter B. Sharp, died in 1915.

After oil discoveries in California, Hughes Tools expanded to Los Angeles. After Allene's death during the spring of 1922, Howard Jr. and his father moved to Hollywood. In January 1924, while Howard Jr. was studying at Rice University, his father died suddenly from a heart attack. The sudden deaths of both parents probably led to Hughes's obsession with germs and health, an obsession that would characterize his later years.

Howard Jr. was the primary beneficiary of his father's will, receiving three-quarters of the estate. A provision in the will required Howard to have a guardian and to finish college; however, he won a petition for full control of his inheritance.

Hughes's movie career began uneventfully. In 1925 he provided $80,000 to a friend for the production of *Swell Hogan,* a movie never released. Undismayed, he paid $150,000 for *Everybody's Acting,* which turned a modest profit. *Two Arabian Knights* (1927) proved a box office hit, and its director, Lewis Milestone, received an Oscar at the first Academy Awards ceremony. The positive trend continued over the next two years with *The Racket* and *The Mating Call.*

Howard's passion in life was undoubtedly aviation, which drove him to create a film with an aeronautical theme. He spent $4 million on *Hell's Angels* (1930). One million dollars paid for the creation of airfields throughout the Los Angeles area and for the purchase and reconditioning of 87 World War I biplanes. Initially, the movie received terrible reviews. However, as is often the case with bad reviews, the movie opened to pandemonium. The public loved the film and the new actress Hughes introduced, Jean Harlow. His next picture, *Jazz Singer,* revolutionized the motion picture business by adding sound. Hughes redid his movie, incorporating the new sound technology, allowing it to continue in theaters across the world for the next 20 years.

Following the success of *Hell's Angels* and *Scarface,* Hughes turned his attention back to his true passion. In 1932 he took a modest-paying job with American Airlines. He masqueraded as a baggage handler and even as a copilot. He spoke often with passengers and learned the ropes of the airline industry. This experience would serve him well several years later when he purchased a struggling airline, TWA.

During the early 1930s, Hughes flew in many airplane races. In 1935 he brought the speed record to the United States, hitting almost 353 miles per hour. He accomplished this feat in a custom-built plane, creating a legend and a mark for pilots everywhere.

With the onset of World War II, the Hughes Aircraft Corporation busily contracted with the government to produce warplanes and even a giant wooden transport (called the "Spruce Goose"). Hughes turned his attention back toward film, especially his most infamous movie, *The Outlaw.* This movie, although of extremely poor quality, set box office records because of the new lead actress, Jane Russell.

Following World War II, Congress conducted hearings into many companies that had contracted for war materials. Hughes testified about his involvement in the construction of the Spruce Goose. This wooden seaplane, the largest aircraft ever built, had still not flown by war's end. In fact, the first and only flight of the Spruce Goose came ten months after Japan surrendered. Although his assertions that this plane would fly eventually proved to be correct, Hughes left the public eye for several years, returning to test piloting.

During the 1950s, while piloting an experimental aircraft, Howard crashed and suffered severe head and neck injuries. The accident left him a tattered man. He became more paranoid and addicted to painkillers. By 1960 Hughes, severely emotionally disturbed, let his paranoia about germs begin to take over his life. He hired a former CIA agent and bodyguards, all Mormons because Hughes believed Mormons to be the purest Americans.

The bodyguards whisked him away to seclusion, and he eventually settled in Las Vegas. His hotel of choice was the Desert Inn. One day, the hotel management, upset because Hughes occupied an entire floor of the finest suites, asked him to leave immediately. Instead, Hughes purchased the hotel the following afternoon. He would also acquire the Sands, Frontier, Castaway, and the tiny Silver Slipper. He purchased the last because the hotel's marquee shined into his room. Although in seclusion, he still faced governmental pressure.

Hughes never seemed concerned with federal taxes, even claiming that he never paid them. When legal pressures became too great, he fled to the Bahamas. During this period, Clifford Irving concocted one of the greatest hoaxes of the twentieth century: He sold a manuscript, presumed to be the memoirs of Howard Hughes, for $1 million. Hughes telephoned a denial, thus revealing the fraud. Eighteen months after leaving for the Bahamas, Hughes died on an airplane over Mexico while returning for medical treatment.

Following his death on 5 April 1976, myths about his lifestyle continued. Many centered on a debate over the distribution of his estate, which had an estimated value of $600 million to $900 million. A host of relatives, including ex-wives, bickered over the fortune. The legal battles continued for years. Lawsuits were even filed accusing Hughes's physicians of negligence in his death.

Hughes has been portrayed in several films, many dealing with aviation. In Disney's *The Rocketeer,* Hughes is the inventor of the rocket pack. At the end of the movie, he presents the hero Clifford Secord with a new racing plane. Several of his own movies also still survive. Some critics now consider *Hell's Angels* one of the best movies ever made. Even *The Outlaw* ranks as the seventh most financially successful western, when receipts are adjusted for inflation.

The Spruce Goose, perhaps Hughes's greatest technological accomplishment, still survives. Shortly before the airplane was scheduled for destruction in the mid-1970s, the Wrather Corporation concluded a deal to buy the cruise ship *Queen Mary*. With this purchase, the corporation opened up a tourist attraction in Long Beach, California. The Spruce Goose, berthed next to the great cruise ship, remains the world's largest aircraft.

Hughes also left a philanthropic legacy, including the Hughes Medical Institute. Located in Chevy Chase, Maryland, this research facility is a leading medical center. The University of Illinois also has an undergraduate education program named after him. From medical research to aviation to the oil industry to film, Hughes left his eccentric, often egocentric mark on the West.

—*Thomas Edward Davis*

References

Barlett, Donald L., and James B. Steele. *Empire: The Life, Legend, and Madness of Howard Hughes*. New York: W. W. Norton, 1979.

Brown, Peter Harry, and Pat H. Broeske. *Howard Hughes: The Untold Story*. New York: Penguin, 1996

Drosnin, Michael. *Citizen Hughes*. New York: Holt, Rinehart, and Winston, 1985.

IVERS, ALICE

See "Poker Alice" Ivers

JACKALOPES

Douglas, Wyoming, claims to be the "home of the jackalope," a rare western animal that looks like a jackrabbit except that it has antlers like those of an antelope or deer sprouting from its head. According to legend, a much larger variety became extinct, leaving only today's smaller variety. Westerners have long enjoyed regaling tenderfeet with tall tales of mythical beasts, such as Montana's fur-bearing trout, which evolved to survive the region's icy waters. The jackalope, supposedly named by a little boy in Douglas, belongs to the same family of mythical animals.

Wyoming residents claim that retired welder and taxidermist Doug Herrick created the first jackalope, scientific name *Lopegigrus lepusalopus ineptus,* in Douglas in 1939. In 1985 Governor Ed Herschler issued a proclamation commemorating the feat. No western tourist trap is complete without postcards of the elusive little critter. Mounted jackalope heads often hang proudly on tavern walls. Hunters can order a special jackalope license from the Douglas Area Chamber of Commerce. The town hosts an annual Jackalope Days Celebration each June. The State of Wyoming also issues hunting licenses for the varmint, but for only one day each year, 31 June.

The Douglas Area Chamber of Commerce has also published a seven-chapter on-line "history" of the animal.

Historically, the first recorded observation occurred in 1829 when an occasionally sober trapper, named Roy Ball, observed one in what is now the area of Douglas, Wyoming. Even before this, the Indians knew them and referred to them as "Dust Devils" freely translated (the Ogallala phrase was "kick-upa-the-dust"). It is believed that this name evolved from the swirling winds that are caused when the jackalope quickly accelerates or stops on a still day. It is not true that the larger jackalopes cause tornadoes, but their speed and quickness is

Jackalope in Fort Worth, Texas

verified by the fact that they do mate during lightning flashes. (Douglas, Wyoming, Web Site)

The animals travel in groups of ten or so, called "committees."

Douglas is not the only western town to take advantage of the jackalope's notoriety. Mounted specimens may be viewed throughout the West. In Santa Fe, New Mexico, tourists may visit Charles H. "Darby" McQuade's shopping complex named "Jackalope." It stands on Cerrillos Road, southwest of the town's historic downtown plaza. The entrepreneur has a prairie dog village, a petting zoo, and "folk art by the truckload" from around the world. In addition, dozens of folk artists work and sell their creations on the grounds.

Back in Douglas, Herrick's nephew Jim has continued the family tradition of creating jackalopes at Herrick's Big Horn Taxidermy. He makes some 1,500 mounted heads a year, which sell for $45 to $60. For a price, outfitters will take tourists on a jackalope hunt. Alas, most hunters report only seeing jackalope does; unlike the bucks, they don't sprout antlers. As the Douglas Area Chamber of Commerce admits, "most sightings of the smaller animals have come from the intoxicated cowboys and U.F.O. groupies." When visiting Douglas, be sure to photograph the world's largest specimen, standing more than eight feet head-to-tail in Jackalope Square at Third and Center Streets downtown.

References

Barrier, Michael. "Prairie Dogs, Pottery, and More." *Nation's Business,* October 1994.

Davis, Elizabeth A. "Only 35 Days Left Till You Can Bag a Crafty Jackalope." *Salt Lake Tribune,* 27 May 1998.

Douglas, Wyoming, Web Site: *http://www. jackalope.org.*

JACKSON, HELEN HUNT

See Ramona

JAMES, JESSE

1847–1882

Jesse James earned his place in the history of the American West as head of the

James-Younger Gang. Among the most famous of outlaws, he made a name for himself by robbing banks, trains, and stagecoaches after the Civil War. In that turbulent era, James became a symbol of a South unwilling to surrender, a sentiment widely shared by southerners. He frustrated and infuriated government officials and pursuers but generated a great deal of loyalty and support from the American public. A good-hearted man, he loved his family. Religious, fiery, and intense, he was unafraid of committing theft or murder. As a result, estimations of his character range from wanton killer to Robin Hood.

Jesse Woodson James was born in Kearney, Missouri, on 5 September 1847 to Robert and Zerelda James. His father, a quiet Baptist preacher, had an ardent desire to spread the Gospel. Jesse read the Bible during his outlaw years and probably got his religious zeal from his father. His spunk probably came from his mother, who was known as a spitfire who openly voiced her opinions. The family worked a farm, and Robert also worked hard at his ministry at New Hope Baptist Church. Well respected in the community, he helped establish William Jewell College and served on its initial board of trustees. In the spring of 1850, Robert planned to take his ministry to the California goldfields, but he died later that year of cholera. Zerelda remarried twice and had four more children with her third husband.

Jesse's elder brother Frank joined the Confederate Army at the beginning of the Civil War, but Jesse was too young. In the fall of 1862, Frank joined the guerrilla band led by William Quantrill, who used brutal raiding tactics to counter the more numerous northern foe. Union militia came to the James house looking for Frank. They reportedly hanged Jesse's stepfather, nearly killing him, and they beat Jesse and his mother. In retaliation, Jesse, age 16, joined the ranks of Bloody Bill Anderson's troops and practiced raiding tactics similar to Quantrill's. These raids and guerrilla tactics taught the James boys the tools they needed later as outlaws. Jesse suffered wounds twice during the war; the second time, he was shot through the lung while trying to surrender. His first cousin Zerelda, named for his mother, slowly nursed him back to health. The two fell in love and later married.

When the war ended, Frank and Jesse returned to their farm and tried to make a straight living. Some say carpetbagger retaliation against raiders turned Jesse and Frank back to their wartime ways. However, according to historian William A. Settle Jr., boredom and an inability to adjust to postwar life provided more likely motives. This time, they practiced raiding as outlaws. The brothers committed what some consider the first daylight bank robbery in peacetime, killing one man and stealing $60,000 from a Liberty, Missouri, bank.

With the addition of Jim and Cole Younger and others, Jesse and Frank formed the James–Younger gang. Jesse led the gang on a run from the law that lasted 16 years. They gained notoriety for robbing banks, trains, and stagecoaches, targeting the rich and especially the railroads. Robbing the rich helped create their Robin Hood image. Banks and railroads hired the Pinkerton Detective Agency to stop the gang, but Jesse had already become a regional and national folk hero. By the end of their spree, they had committed at least 15 successful robberies and killed as many as 25 people in the process. Then, in 1876, the gang decided to rob the First National Bank in Northfield, Minnesota. Townsmen ambushed them and killed or captured all but Frank and Jesse.

With the rest of the gang dead or in prison, Frank and Jesse went into hiding. Jesse moved back to St. Joseph, Missouri, to hide out. He lived there with his wife and family under the alias Tom Howard. The next year, he tried to buy a small farm in Nebraska but didn't have enough money. He planned to rob the Platte City Bank in Nebraska, and he recruited Bob and Charlie Ford to help him. The Ford brothers had been offered $10,000 and full pardons to kill Jesse, an offer that proved too appealing to resist. While Jesse dusted and straightened a picture at his home in St. Joseph, Bob Ford drew his gun and shot the outlaw in the back of the head.

Mythmaking accelerated rapidly after Jesse's death, enhancing his Robin Hood image. In the gang's heyday, Frank and Jesse supposedly used this image to their advantage, publishing letters in newspapers to move public opinion in their favor. The brothers, both literate, may well have written these letters. However, John Newton Edwards, a Confederate veteran and newspaperman of the day, may have written or at least aided in publishing them. Edwards remained their staunch supporter. He arranged for Frank to surrender and prepared a legal defense that saw him successfully acquitted of all charges. Whether Edwards was involved or not, the newspaper letters helped create an image of the James

brothers as folk heroes rather than common thieves.

A whole series of dime novels chronicled the Jameses' exploits and reinforced their "chivalrous" reputation in the eyes of the public. In these fanciful stories, the James boys stole from the rich and respected the poor. They would check a person's hands for calluses. If he appeared to be a working man, he kept his money. Pinkerton detective John Whicher experienced this policy firsthand. He planned to disguise himself as a laborer and get work on the James farm. Sheriff George Patton warned him of the danger, explaining that his soft hands would tip the James boys off. Whicher proceeded anyway. Officials found his body the next morning, bound, gagged, and shot in the head, heart, and stomach.

The Pinkerton Detective Agency's attacks further added to the popularity of the outlaws. Robert Pinkerton wrote a letter to the *New York Star* claiming that Sheriff Patton had betrayed Whicher. Patton responded by calling Pinkerton a "villainous slanderer and falsiter [*sic*]." Once while Jesse and Frank were away, someone threw a bomb in the James house, setting it on fire. Metal shards from the explosion killed Jesse's youngest half-brother, Archie. The boys' mother, Zerelda, had to have her arm amputated because of her wounds. The local press immediately blamed the Pinkerton Detective Agency because several agency men had departed town on a train that night. In later years, Zerelda gave tours of the house with her stump of an arm, continuing to remind visitors of the evil forces pitted against her sons.

As in the case of **Billy the Kid,** debate continues over the number of people

Jesse killed. According to the heroic view, he caused only a single death. Engineer John Rafferty died when the James gang forced his train to derail and turn over. The historical record, however, shows James responsible either directly or indirectly for at least 18 deaths.

And as was also true for Billy the Kid, many people denied Jesse's death and contended that the man Bob Ford killed really wasn't him. Some argued that Jesse had conspired with Ford in order to get his pursuers off his trail. According to this theory, they staged the death and killed someone else in Jesse's place. Another tale reports a mysterious sixth pallbearer at Jesse's funeral, a man whom no one knew; yet he ran the affair. This mystery man was supposedly none other than Jesse James himself.

Between 1901 and 1903, one publisher alone put out 121 dime novels about Jesse James. He appeared in books and articles that depicted him saving a damsel in distress or fighting Mexican or Chinese villains. Although a variety of historical books have been published about James, the myths remain firmly entrenched in the minds of the American people.

In 1921 Jesse James Jr. starred in the first film about his father, *Jesse James under the Black Flag.* Later that year, he returned in *Jesse James as the Outlaw.* The real emergence of the famous outlaw on the silver screen came in Tyrone Power's successful 1939 film, *Jesse James.* This movie inspired many sequels, and the Hollywood legacy of Jesse James has flourished ever since. Between 1921 and 1994, when Rob Lowe produced *Frank and Jesse,* more than 30 movies about the outlaw hero were made. The films run the

gamut from drama, horror, and pornography to comedy and absurdity. For example, Bob Hope put out a 1959 comedy entitled *Alias Jesse James,* which some rank among his best works. It features cameos by James Garner, Gene **Autry,** and Roy **Rogers.** The Three Stooges starred in a movie about Jesse in 1965 called *The Outlaws Is Coming.* A real cross-genre gem appeared the next year, as John Lupton starred in *Jesse James Meets Frankenstein's Daughter,* an absurd companion piece to *Billy the Kid versus Dracula.* Both films have acquired a cult following.

The legend of Jesse James even inspired a variety of musical performances. Minstrel Billy Gashade created "The Ballade of Jesse James," which spread across the country, sung by lumberjacks, cowboys, and rogues. In the 1930s Woody **Guthrie** rewrote the song to fit the mood of the Depression. Some years later, he told the story of Jesus set to the Jesse James tune. A 1979 album entitled *The Legend of Jesse James* featured the musical talents of Johnny Cash, Levon Helm, Emmylou Harris, and Charlie Daniels. Michael Martin Murphey sings Gashade's ballad on his *Rhymes of the Renegades* album. "Just Like Jesse James" became one of Cher's top-ten hits. Lyrics by artists ranging from country music star Toby Keith to Geto Boyz rap artist Scarface take up the James legend.

Retailers use the James name to attract attention and sales. For motivation and corporate sales training, one can hire Jesse James, an internationally recognized speaker who is "Wanted." Jesse James Real Estate in Buchanan Dam, Texas, proclaims "Jesse James is just as famous for selling Real Estate as the Old West Jesse James was for robbing trains!"

For outdoor lovers, Sierra Designs makes a Jesse James model sleeping bag.

During Jesse and Frank's narrow escape from Northfield, Minnesota, they made a daring jump over Split Rock Creek. Today visitors can take Jesse James River Run pontoon rides at the spot. In Logan, Utah, the Inn on Center Street houses the Jesse James Hideout, a "backwoods retreat complete with a pool table, rustic furniture, queen-size log bed with down pillows and comforter, large-screen TV, kitchenette, and covered 900-gallon outdoor hot tub." Jesse James Woodcrafters of Laramie, Wyoming, fashions hardwood furniture. Every year, Jesse's hometown hosts the Jesse James Barbeque cookout, which attracted 47 teams of competitors in 1996.

Jesse James Snider, a death row inmate convicted of forgery in James's home state of Missouri, sits where officials of years ago wished they could have put the original outlaw. The Bannister Foundation is campaigning on Snider's behalf. Road Dogg Jesse James preserves the fiery visage of Jesse James in the World Wrestling Federation.

Over the years, a host of people have claimed to be the real Jesse James, often seeking to make money from his legend. In 1933 an Illinois man named John James announced that he was Jesse James. He toured with fairs and carnivals until his sister finally signed an affidavit contradicting his claim. A store in Kentucky displayed Jesse's purported skeleton in its front window. In 1951 J. Frank Dalton announced on his one hundredth birthday that he was the real Jesse James.

Modern science seemingly put all these claims to rest. Twenty years after his death in 1882, Jesse's body was re-buried beside that of his wife. In 1996 a team of forensic scientists exhumed the body in Kearney, Missouri, and conducted tests attempting to determine its true identity. Speculation arose even here, however, because 1902 reports state that Jesse had been buried in a metal casket. Investigators found no metal casket, and James's bones lay face down rather than up.

Regardless of these circumstances, the scientists proved almost undeniably that the buried individual was James. They located a single bullet wound behind the right ear and a .36-caliber bullet lodged in the ribs, no doubt from his Civil War injuries. Scientists compared mtDNA from the body's teeth to the mtDNA of two known descendants of his sister. The resulting match affirmed kinship. Tests on the hair showed it had been dyed, probably as a disguise.

Tests also revealed that James had not used any drugs, such as opium or cocaine, for three months prior to his death. Some people had speculated that his many wounds had driven him to addiction to these painkillers. An examination of his jawbone revealed a missing tooth, which would have given him a gap-toothed smile. This could explain why he never smiled in pictures. Stains on the teeth indicated regular tobacco use. Jesse had reportedly killed a companion over chewing tobacco. Scientists concluded that the man killed in 1882 had a 99.7 percent chance of being Jesse James.

Even this evidence, however, fails to convince dissenters, who argue that the tested remains were those of Jesse's cousin Wood Hite. Bud Hardcastle, an Oklahoma used-car salesman, has tirelessly championed the theory that James faked his death and lived out his life in Texas. He claims that a man named J. Frank Dalton was really Jesse James. Dalton, late in his life, did claim to be the legendary train robber. He sometimes charged admission for curious tourists to view him. He died in Granbury, Texas in 1951.

However, in the spring of 2000, Hardcastle and an exhumation team learned that "Jesse Woodson James" did not lie under the headstone marking Jesse's supposed grave in Granbury, Texas. They found a steel vault instead of the wooden casket that most believe holds Dalton. According to Hardcastle, the remains they found belonged to Henry Holland, a one-armed man who may have married into the Rash family. The Rashes cared for Dalton in the last days of his life. For some doubters, the search continues.

The pride and honor that typified the James family still lives on today. One can join and support the James-Younger Gang, which holds annual conferences and conventions. Jesse James historical sites appear throughout the nation, including the Patee House, where Jesse's family went during the investigation into his death; the Jesse James House, where he died; the Jesse James Farm, where he grew up; and Meramec Caves, where he purportedly hid out. Northfield, Minnesota, celebrates the Defeat of Jesse James Days every year. Clearly, the legend of Jesse James lives on.

—*Kaleb J. Redden*

References

Ross, James R. *I, Jesse James*. Los Angeles: Dragon Publishing, 1988.

Settle, William A., Jr. *Jesse James Was His Name*. Columbia: University of Missouri Press, 1966.

JOHNNY KAW

In 1955 the centennial committee of Manhattan, Kansas, searched for ways to generate interest and excitement in the city's history. They asked a professor of horticulture at Kansas State University named George Filinger (1897–1978) to help. He obliged by creating a Great Plains farmer version of lumberjack Paul Bunyan and cowboy **Pecos Bill.** He called his creation Johnny Kaw, the Pioneer Kansas Wheat Farmer. Filinger spun tall tales about Kaw for the *Manhattan Mercury* and later gathered them into a self-published booklet.

According to Filinger, Kaw shaped the Kansas landscape. He dug the river valley that bears his name. He grew the first wheat and laid pioneer trails, all of which appear on the Kansas state seal. He invented sunflowers and raised gigantic potatoes. After Paul Bunyan tromped through his wheat fields, Kaw used the big lumberjack's nose to plow the bed of the Mississippi River. Ever helpful, he went west and helped Finn McCool, the prodigiously strong Irish warrior, dig the Grand Canyon. The two of them then stacked up the rubble to form the Rocky Mountains. Like his counterparts, Kaw could control the weather, taming tornadoes and ending droughts. The Dust Bowl came about because of a fight between Kaw's pets, a wildcat and a jayhawk.

Filinger's creation charmed Kansans, who erected a 30-foot-tall statue of Kaw in 1966. It stands in the Manhattan City Park.

Reference

Garretson, Jerri. "Johnny Kaw: The Pioneer

Kansas Wheat Farmer": *http://www.manhattan.lib.ks.us/johnny.htm.*

JOHNSON, JEREMIAH

1824–1900, mountain man. *See* Liver-Eating Johnson

JOHNSON, LYNDON BAYNES

1908–1973, politician. See Politicians and Western Myth

KANSAS

See Johnny Kaw; *Wizard of Oz, The Wonderful*

KELTON, ELMER

1926–

Elmer Kelton was born to and grew up in a ranch family in Andrews County, Texas. "With all that heritage," he says, "I should have become a good cowboy myself, but somehow I never did, so I decided if I could not do it I would write about it. . . . My mother was a teacher," he says, "so she taught me how to read when I was 5. I just loved to read, so after enjoying other peoples' stories, I just started making up my own. I didn't get to the point where I was trying to get something published 'til I was grown, but I was always writing something when I was a kid, drawing pictures, then writing

stories to go with the pictures" (Boggs 1998).

Kelton attended Crane High School, and after earning a BA at the University of Texas at Austin, he pursued a career in journalism and wrote fiction on the side. Service in Europe for two years during World War II interrupted his college career. However, thanks to the war, he met and married his Austrian wife, Ann. They celebrated their fiftieth wedding anniversary in 1998. He wrote for a number of agricultural publications, most notably spending 22 years with the *Livestock Weekly*. He began selling a few stories to *Ranch Romances. Hot Iron,* his first novel, appeared in 1955. He sums up his writing philosophy simply: "A good novel of the West is just as valid as a novel set anywhere as long as it is honest and reflects reality. My real subject is the human condition, and this is universal" (Walker).

By the 1970s, Kelton's fiction had begun to receive well-deserved praise. He writes historical fiction, often based on events in Texas. His books are far more believable than the work of **pulp novelists,** in part because he steeps himself in western history. Nonetheless, earlier western writers exerted a strong influence on Kelton:

> When I was trying to get started as a writer, I studied the works of Luke Short and Ernest Haycox in particular. I always considered Short a master at characterization as well as of sharp, crisp narrative. And I admired the way Haycox could bring a literary flavor to what was often essentially a formula story. I read Zane Grey as a boy growing up, though I can't say that I studied his style as I did Short, Haycox, Will James, S. Omar Barker, Wayne D. Overholser, Walt Coburn, Norman A. Fox, Thomas Thompson, Harry Sinclair Drago and W. C. Tuttle when I was trying to learn the craft. (Walker)

Kelton is a four-time winner of the Spur Award, presented by the **Western Writers of America, Inc.,** as well as other literary prizes. Three novels by Elmer Kelton that are excellent in catching the real cowboy spirit and reflecting their culture and thought process are *The Time It Never Rained, The Good Old Boys,* and *The Man Who Rode Midnight.* The National Cowboy Hall of Fame awarded Kelton its prestigious Western Heritage Wrangler Award for all three novels.

After more than 40 years in journalism, in 1990 Kelton turned his full energies to writing novels and historical nonfiction. This focus has led to a prodigious string of novels: *Cloudy in the West* (1997), *The Wolf and the Buffalo* (1997), *Traildust* (1997), *A Thousand Miles of Mustangin'* (1998), *Smiling Country* (1998), *Legend* (1999), and *The Buckskin*

Line (1999). The last treats the lives of **Texas Rangers.** By 2000, he had penned 35 novels and more than 50 short stories. Time, however, has extracted a few concessions. Today he rarely wears cowboy boots. "I've got two glass ankles and flat feet, and they don't respond to high heels too well. I will wear 'em if I'm walking through grass or in a feedlot or, though I haven't done it in years, getting on a horse" (Boggs 1998).

Kelton's concern with preserving historical authenticity in his novels has paid off handsomely. "The traditional Western hero," he notes, "was 7 feet tall and invincible. I write about people who are 5-feet-8 and nervous" (Boggs 1998). His historical novel *The Day the Cowboys Quit* is an excellent example. Based on a failed Canadian River cowboy strike in 1883, it does what good historical fiction should: It remains true to the facts as we know them and pushes along a strong, engaging story line. "I think if you don't understand your history," he writes, "you can't really understand yourself. If we don't know our history, we have no basis for understanding the present or predicting the future" (Boggs 1998)

Kelton has strong links to the western past:

> In my viewpoint toward Western history and tradition, I was strongly influenced during my formative years by Texas folklorist J. Frank Dobie. Incidentally, like other critics, Dobie regarded Owen Wister's *The Virginian* as a watershed work in Western fiction, but he pointed out that the Virginian was a cowboy who never seemed to work with cows. He was always busy doing something else. So I have made it a point when I write about

cowboys to show them out there with the cattle. (Walker)

This talented, gentle, self-effacing writer looms among the great talents produced by the West in the twentieth century.

References

Boggs, Johnny D. "Elmer Kelton." *Cowboys & Indians* 22 (January 1998): 162–168.

Kelton, Elmer. *The Day the Cowboys Quit.* New York: Bantam, 1971, 1992.

Tuska, Jon, and Vicki Piekarski, eds. *Encyclopedia of Frontier and Western Fiction.* New York: McGraw-Hill, 1983.

Walker, Dale L. "A Good Talk with Elmer Kelton": *http://readwest.com/elmerkelton.htm.*

KISKADDON, BRUCE

See Cowboy Poetry

L'AMOUR, LOUIS

1908–1988

Probably America's best-selling author, the novelist Louis L'Amour created a pantheon of western heroes, mostly cut from the same cloth. Like B-western movies, his tales are filled with larger-than-life heroes, black-hatted villains, right that trumps wrong, vivid western scenery, and no sex. L'Amour trumpeted his own social values and views through a long procession of fictional, mythical western heroes.

The prolific writer, born Louis Dearborn LaMoore, the youngest of seven children, began his eventful life in Jamestown, North Dakota. He characterized himself and the basis of his success well: "I think of myself in the oral tradition—as a troubadour, a village tale-teller, the man in the shadows of the campfire. That's the way I'd like to be remembered—as a storyteller. A good storyteller" (Weinberg 1992). His first book, a collection of poems, appeared from a small Ok-lahoma publisher in 1939. It would be western novels, however, that brought his name to readers around the world.

His mythical western heroes, virtually all large, strong, white men, often looked like the author, who at six foot, two inches tall and more than 200 pounds, won 51 of 59 fights as a professional boxer. His heroes play key roles as agents of **Manifest Destiny** in the "civilizing of the West," bringing law and order to the savage frontier. In a 1980 interview, critic Jon Tuska asked L'Amour to comment on the near-extermination of the buffalo. The writer replied with a Darwinian clarity and simplicity that echo earlier ideas expressed by Zane **Grey:**

They had outlived their usefulness. It was necessary that they be killed. Now there are farms throughout that whole area, farms that grow food to feed one third of the world. It's a matter of progress. The Indians didn't own the lands they occupied. Many of the tribes, in fact, had only recently occupied certain regions before the white man arrived. The Indians took the land from others, the cliff dwellers, for example. And the white man took the land from the Indians. It wasn't the Indians' to claim or to sell. It went to the strongest. The white men were stronger. (Weinberg 1992).

Also like the author, his heroes are often self-educated, self-made men. They proudly rely on pluck, spunk, determination, and native intelligence. "One major thread in my books is that people are always trying to improve themselves," he said. "Boys who come out of the Tennessee mountains can barely read and write, but they study at night by campfire." They often carry Blackstone's law books in their saddlebags and sometimes read Latin.

Family loyalties are another key virtue of L'Amour's heroes. He created multigenerational family sagas of the Sacketts and others. His heroes operate with an absolute black-and-white moral code. They hold an unquestioning faith in the inevitable and righteous conquest of the West by white American civilization. To accomplish this end, the heroes must act upon and spread their frontier cultural values of loyalty, hard work, tenacity, and cunning survival skills. Like true heroes, they persevere, fighting on to victory, sometimes against overwhelming odds. Although his heroes never die in action, it's clear that they are always ready to face death—nobly, honorably, and bravely—for what they believe is right.

In his 1989 autobiography, *Education of a Wandering Man,* L'Amour explained the lack of sex in his works: "I am not writing about sex, which is a leisure ac-

tivity. I am writing about men and women who were settling a new country, finding their way through a maze of difficulties and learning to survive despite them." Like his heroes, L'Amour worked hard, at an amazing variety of jobs, before devoting himself full-time to writing.

L'Amour wrote more than 100 novels, and all remain in print. Total sales topped 225 million, with 40 million books sold since his death. Early in his career, he established himself as a **pulp novelist**, spewing out ranch romances, other formula westerns, and, under the pseudonym Tex Burns, four brief Hopalong Cassidy books. His fast-paced formula demanded a new twist or dramatic action every 800 words or so.

More than 45 of his novels and short stories have been adapted for films and **television.** The movie *Hondo* (1953), based on his original story "The Gift of Cochise," gave his career a huge boost. The popular film starred John Wayne (not surprisingly, a big L'Amour fan), Ward Bond, and James Arness, later of *Gunsmoke* fame. James Edward Garnt wrote the movie screenplay based on the L'Amour short story. The film's popularity boosted sales of L'Amour's novel titled *Hondo.* He used Garnt's screenplay to pen his first best-selling novel, without acknowledging his reliance on the other writer's work. Later popular films included *The Sacketts* (1982), with Glenn Ford, Tom Selleck, and Slim Pickens; *The Shadow Riders* (1982), with Tom Selleck and Sam Elliott; and *Conagher* (1991), with Sam Elliott and Katharine Ross.

L'Amour's work is an odd mix of minute attention to detail and indifference to many other elements of careful writing. He bragged of the historical grounding of his fiction. "Every incident in any story I write is authentic and usually based either on something I personally experienced or something that happened in history" (Weinberg 1992). Well, yes, and no.

He described natural landscapes with almost photographic accuracy. As he said, "I walked the land my characters walk" (Weinberg 1992). Indeed, his widow, Kathy, whom he met in 1952 and married four years later, still lives on their 1,800-acre ranch in southwest Colorado. She described the rugged land, mostly purchased in 1983, as "a research place for Louis. There are three Indian tribes—the Utes, the Navajos and the Apaches—in the area. It's cattle country, sheep country, horse country, mining country." She and their children, Beau and Angelique, continue to oversee the Bantam Books publication of reprints and new L'Amour materials.

On the other hand, his rather wooden, stereotypical characters are straight from pulp fiction. His heroes often deliver weighty soliloquies, pontificating on various moral lessons. They serve as spokesmen for the author's own brand of white hegemony and social Darwinism. Little wonder that ultraconservatives like John Wayne and Ronald Reagan praised his novels. Likewise, a character might be shot dead, only to reappear later in the story.

When critic Jon Tuska pointed out to L'Amour a discrepancy in one of his books, the brash writer took it in stride. "You know, I don't think the people who read my books would really care" (Weinberg 1992). He wrote and dictated his novels at tremendous speed, so his haste and aversion to revising probably produced these inconsistencies. His son Beau explained his father's writing process: "He didn't worry about the process—he didn't re-write at all. He didn't outline. So, he was anticipating the story just as you are. I think that is what gives the stories a certain immediacy." It also accounts for the contradictions and lapses.

Although critics tended to overlook his work as too pulpy, he earned several awards for his labors. In 1981 the appreciative Western Writers of America gave him a Golden Saddleman Award. The following year he received the Congressional (National) Gold Medal, and in 1982 President Ronald Reagan awarded him the Medal of Freedom. His novels remain immensely popular, well after his death of lung cancer (he did not smoke) in Glendale, California, in 1988.

References

Tuska, Jon, and Vicki Piekarski, eds. *Encyclopedia of Frontier and Western Fiction.* New York: McGraw-Hill, 1983.

Weinberg, Robert. *The Louis L'Amour Companion.* Kansas City, MO: Andrews and McMeel, 1992.

Sources of Further Information

L'Amour Fans: *http://www.veinotte.com/lamour/intro.htm.*

Official Louis L'Amour Web Site: *http://www.louislamour.com.*

Random House: *http://www.randomhouse.com/features/louislamour/.*

LATINOS

See Baca, Elfego; Cortez Lira, Gregorio;

Cortina, Juan Nepomuceno; Selena; Zorro

LEE, JOHN DOYLE

1812–1877

John Doyle Lee, the reputed mastermind of the Mountain Meadows massacre, stands as one of the most controversial figures in Mormon history. Born in 1812 in Kaskaskia, Illinois Territory, he suffered a difficult childhood. When he was 3 years old, his mother died after a long illness. After a few years with his alcoholic father, the boy lived from age 7 to 16 with an uncle's family. After a succession of jobs, he moved to Vandalia, Illinois, where in 1833 he married for the first time.

Lee converted to the new religion of Mormonism (Church of Jesus Christ of Latter-Day Saints) on 17 June 1838, at Ambrosia, Missouri. A zealot, Lee spent the remainder of his life driven by religious passion. Lee became a member of the Danite Band, a militia organized to protect Mormons from attack by "gentiles" (i.e., non-Mormons). His devotion and zeal led to his selection in 1843 as a guardian for the church's founder and prophet, Joseph Smith.

In June the following year, a mob dragged Smith and his brother from their jail cell in Carthage, Illinois, and killed them. Lee transferred his loyalty to the new leader, Brigham Young, and traveled with him on the Mormon flight, first to winter quarters near the confluence of the Platte and Missouri Rivers and then on to Utah.

Lee also accepted the doctrine of plural marriage. This is his own account of his marriages, given in his postmortem confession, published in 1877 as *Mormonism Unveiled:*

I took my wives in the following order: first, Agathe Ann Woolsey; second, Nancy Berry; third, Louisa Free (now one of the wives of Daniel H. Wells); fourth, Sarah C. Williams; fifth, old Mrs. Woolsey (she was the mother of Agathe Ann and Rachel A. I married her for her soul's sake, for her salvation in the eternal state); sixth, Rachel A. Woolsey (I was sealed to her at the same time that I was to her mother); seventh, Andora Woolsey (a sister to Rachel); eighth, Polly Ann Workman; ninth, Martha Berry; tenth, Delithea Morris. In 1847, while at Council Bluffs, Brigham Young sealed me to three women in one night, viz., eleventh, Nancy Armstrong (she was what we called a widow. She left her first husband in Tennessee, in order to be with the Mormon people); twelfth, Polly V. Young; thirteenth, Louisa Young (these two were sisters). Next, I was sealed to my fourteenth wife, Emeline Vaughn. In 1851, I was sealed to my fifteenth wife, Mary Lear Groves. In 1856, I was sealed to my sixteenth wife, Mary Ann Williams. In 1858, Brigham Young gave me my seventeenth wife, Emma Batchelder. I was sealed to her while a member of the Territorial Legislature. Brigham Young said that Isaac C. Haight, who was also in the Legislature, and I, needed some young women to renew our vitality, so he gave us both a dashing young bride. In 1859, I was sealed to my eighteenth wife, Teressa Morse. I was sealed to her by order of Brigham Young.

Amasa Lyman officiated at the ceremony. The last wife I got was Ann Gordge. Brigham Young gave her to me, and I was sealed to her in Salt Lake by Heber C. Kimball. This was my nineteenth, but, as I was married to old Mrs. Woolsey for her soul's sake, and she was near sixty years old when I married her, I never considered her really as a wife. True, I treated her well and gave her all the rights of marriage. Still I never count her as one of my wives. That is the reason that I claim only eighteen true wives. After 1861, I never asked Brigham Young for another wife. By my eighteen real wives I have been the father of sixty-four children. Ten of my children are dead and fifty-four are still living. (Lee 1877)

In southern Utah, Lee prospered as a farmer and businessman. He also held various public offices, including that of Indian agent. However, after a decade, gentiles complained bitterly about the power of the Mormon Church and expressed horror at the practice of polygamy. In response, the U.S. government dispatched soldiers to Utah in 1857, generating fears among Mormons of a major violent attack on them and their beliefs.

At this volatile point, on 11 September, Mormon militia and Paiute Indians attacked the immigrant wagon train, led by John T. Baker and Alexander Fancher, of 120 people passing through southwestern Utah. This so-called Mountain Meadows massacre transformed Lee into one of the most infamous, murderous figures in western history. The Mormons' motivations remain unclear. Greed? Did they covet the wagon train's herd of 1,000 cattle and other valuables? Blackmail? Did the Paiutes, who had unsuccessfully attacked the emigrants before, demand that Mormons assist them or face attacks themselves? Mass hysteria? Paranoia?

Lee's exact involvement in the massacre is still vigorously disputed. In a letter to Brigham Young written just after the massacre, Lee blamed the Paiute Indians. However, even his Mormon neighbors whispered rumors of his deadly role. In 1858 Lee went into hiding when a federal judge appeared to investigate the massacre. Young and other Mormons refused to cooperate with officials.

Young stood by his Danite loyalist, and in 1861 the Mormons of Harmony, Utah, elected Lee their presiding elder. However, most gentiles and some Mormons considered him guilty of leading the bloody massacre. He received threatening letters, and his children were ostracized. In early 1870 a Utah paper condemned leader Brigham Young for whitewashing Lee and the massacre. In February Young ordered Lee to "make yourself scarce and keep out of the way," exiled him to northern Arizona, and excommunicated him from the church. Whether Young actually considered Lee guilty or whether he simply used him as a scapegoat to provide closure to criticism of the massacre remains unclear.

In the wild canyon lands of northern Arizona, Lee established a cabin at what became known as Lee's Ferry (Lonely Dell) on the Colorado River. In 1872 he hosted the expedition led by John Wesley Powell; however, his economic fortunes declined sharply. He suffered severe illness. Drought alternating with torrential rains destroyed his buildings and crops. Faced with such adversity, several of his wives deserted him. Finally, in November 1874, a sheriff arrested him at Panguitch, Utah.

Lee's first trial for murder ended with a hung jury. In a second trial, however, a jury found him guilty. Anti-Mormon sentiments, especially fear of their growing political and economic power, probably influenced the decision as much as evidence from Mountain Meadows. Lee steadfastly professed his innocence, but he was shot at Mountain Meadows on 23 March 1877. Young himself would die a few months later, on 29 August, from complications of appendicitis. Lee felt betrayed by Young's treatment, but he remained true to his faith to the end: "I have but little to say this morning. Of course I feel that I am at the brink of eternity, and the solemnities of eternity should rest upon my mind at the present. . . . I am ready to die. I trust in God. I have no fear. Death has no terror" (Lee 1877).

Along with his confusing legacy, he left a controversial confession, *Mormonism Unveiled, or The Life and Confessions of the Late Mormon Bishop, John D. Lee; (Written by Himself) Embracing a History of Mormonism from Its Inception down to the Present Time, with an Exposition of the Secret History, Signs, Symbols, and Crimes of the Mormon Church. Also the True History of the Horrible Butcher Known as the Mountain Meadows Massacre.* In his book, published the year of his death by his lawyer, William W. Bishop, Lee charges that 58 Mormons, acting under "orders of the Mormon Priesthood," carried out the attack:

I did not act alone; I had many to assist me at the Mountain Meadows. I believe that most of those who were connected with the Massacre, and took part in the lamentable transaction that has blackened the character of all who were aiders or abettors in the same, were acting under the impression that they were performing a religious duty. I know all were acting under the orders and by the command of their Church leaders; and I firmly believe that most of those who took part in the proceedings, considered it a religious duty to unquestioningly obey the orders which they had received. (Lee 1877, 213)

Lee named people who he claims met to plan the attack:

Amongst those that I remember to have met there, were Samuel Knight, Oscar Hamblin, William Young, Carl Shirts, Harrison Pearce, James Pearce, John W. Clark, William Slade Sr., James Matthews, Dudley Leavitt, William Hawley, (now a resident of Fillmore, Utah Territory), William Slade Jr., and two others whose names I have forgotten. I think they were George W. Adair and John Hawley. I know they were at the Meadows at the time of the massacre, and I think I met them that night south of the Meadows, with Samuel Knight and the others.

Sidney Littlefield, of Panguitch, has told me that he was knowing to the fact of Colonel Wm. H. Dame sending orders from Parowan to Maj. Haight, at Cedar City, to exterminate the Francher [*sic*] outfit, and to kill every emigrant without fail. Littlefield then lived at Parowan, and Dame was the Presiding Bishop. Dame still has all the wives he wants, and is a great friend of Brigham Young.

Lee also alleged a cover-up after the attack:

> I will here state again that on the field, before and after the massacre, and again at the council at the emigrant camp, the day after the massacre, orders were given to keep everything secret, and if any man told the secret to any human being, he was to be killed, and I assert as a fact that if any man had told it then, or for many years afterwards, he would have died, for some "Destroying Angel" would have followed his trail and sent him over the "rim of the basin."

A Web site called "Response to the Mormon Critics," run by Russell Y. Anderson, explains the events this way:

> Although this is an abhorrent chapter in Utah history, Indians had some braves die because of meat that was poisoned by the members of the wagon train. The indians [*sic*] threatened to come against the Saints if they didn't help. The Missourians threatened to return from California with armed troops. The Saints were currently at war with the United States. All these things together led the Saints to throw better judgement to the wind and assist the indians [*sic*] in setting up a trap to kill the members of the wagon train. When Brigham Young was notified of the situation he sent word that the members of the wagon train were to be left alone. However his counsel arrived too late. (Anderson)

On 20 April 1961, the Mormon Church repented of its treatment of Lee. The Council ordered that "authorization be given for the re-instatement to membership and former blessings to John D. Lee."

References

Anderson, Russell. "Response to the Mormon Critics": *http://www.lightplanet.com/response/ brigham.htm#Mountain-Meadows.*

Lamar, Howard R., ed. *The New Encyclopedia of the American West.* New Haven, CT: Yale University Press, 1998.

Lee, John Doyle. *Mormonism Unveiled* (1877): *http://www.xmission.com/~country/reason/ lee_pref.htm.*

"Mountain Meadows Massacre": *http://asms. k12.ar.us/armen/brondel/index.htm.*

PBS. *The West: http://www.pbs.org/weta/the west/wpages/wpgs400/w4lee.htm.*

Thrapp, Dan L., ed. *Encyclopedia of Frontier Biography.* 4 vols. Lincoln: University of Nebraska Press, 1988; CD-ROM ed., 1994.

LEGENDS OF THE WEST STAMPS

See Stamps

LEVIS AND RIVETS

An Associated Press (AP) story—datelined San Francisco, 11 January 1999—noted that the president of Levi Strauss & Co. had just stepped down. The news article also gave Levi Strauss, the founder of the company, credit for inventing the prototype for 501 jeans. "San Francisco–based Levi's, founded in 1853 by a Bavarian entrepreneur who designed the riveted work jeans for Gold Rush miners," the news report stated, "increasingly has been looking outside the company to fill its management positions."

The reporter failed to do his history homework. Although Levi Strauss did sell work jeans, it was an obscure Jewish tailor working in Reno, Nevada, who added the rivets. A federal patent-infringement case filed in February 1874 in the U.S. Circuit Court of California (whose records are housed in the National Archives regional branch in San Bruno, south of San Francisco) contains the facts.

Born in 1831, Jacob Youphes was a native of Riga (now the capital of Latvia) on the Baltic Sea. The German Jew changed his name to Jacob W. Davis after immigrating to the United States in 1854, and he operated a tailor shop in New York City and Augusta, Maine. In 1856 he arrived in San Francisco, and shortly thereafter he moved north to Weaverville to work as a tailor. With the gold rush to the Fraser River in 1858, he left California for western Canada, where he lived for nine years, married, and started a family.

Davis returned to San Francisco by ship from Victoria, British Columbia, in January 1867. He soon traveled to Virginia City, Nevada, where he first opened a cigar store, but within three months he again turned to his trade as a tailor. In June 1868 he relocated once again, this time to the fledgling railroad town of Reno. Investing in a brewery, he lost virtually everything. By 1869 he had opened a tailor shop on the town's main thoroughfare, Virginia Street. He began fabricating wagon covers and tents from a rugged, off-white duck cloth sold by San Francisco's Levi Strauss & Co.

Events in January 1871 changed Jacob

Davis's life forever and made him a wealthy man. His trial testimony told of a woman who needed a sturdy pair of pants for a husband too big to wear ready-made clothes. "She, his wife, said she wanted to send him to chop some wood," Davis testified, "but he had no pants to put on." The wife, claiming her enormous husband was too ill to visit the shop to be measured, tied knots in a piece of string provided by Davis and took the requisite waist and inseam measurements and brought them to the tailor.

Davis went on to testify that he was paid three dollars in advance for the pants, which he made of white duck purchased from Levi Strauss & Co. The woman wanted the trousers made as strong as possible. In the tailor's shop were copper rivets, used to attach straps to horse blankets made for local teamsters. "So when the pants were done—the rivets were lying on the table—the thought struck me to fasten the pockets with rivets," Davis recounted. "I had never thought of it before."

As word of the new pants began to spread, orders trickled in at first, but soon Davis was deluged with requests. In the following 18 months, he made and sold 200 pairs to persons in need of heavy work clothing. Concerned that his idea might be pirated, Davis asked Levi Strauss to help him with a patent application. A preliminary application was approved in July 1872, and the full patent was granted on 20 May 1873. By then, Davis had been named the San Francisco production manager. (The Davis family still lives in the Bay Area and owns the Ben Davis Clothing Company.)

The truth in this story lay undiscovered for 100 years until Ann Morgan Campbell, chief of the San Bruno branch of the National Archives, brought it to light in an article in the *Nevada Historical Society Quarterly* in 1974. For 25 years now, the story has received considerable attention in Nevada, appearing in newspapers, books, and other historical journals. Davis is also mentioned in a brief biography of Levi Strauss in the World Book encyclopedia. Actually, all the AP reporter in San Francisco needed to do was call the corporate headquarters of Levi Strauss & Co. Historian Lynn Downey would have set the record straight. Anyway, the next time you look at your Levi 501 jeans, think of Jacob Davis and Reno, Nevada, where it all began in 1871.

—*Guy Louis Rocha*

Source of Further Information

Campbell, Ann Morgan. "In Nineteenth Century Nevada: Federal Records as Sources for Local History." *Nevada Historical Society Quarterly,* Fall 1974.

LEWIS AND CLARK EXPEDITION

On a muggy afternoon in the spring of 1804, 30 men loaded sturdy boats with supplies for a momentous journey. Supplies, costing almost $38,000, included compasses, quadrants, telescopes, cloth, fishing lines and hooks, trail food, clothing, bullets, and gifts for the Indians they would surely meet. Despite all the preparations, these men faced grave uncertainties in the wilderness known simply as "the West." The Corps of Discovery, as they called themselves, prepared to embark under the leadership of two spirited and courageous adventurers, Meriwether Lewis and William Clark.

Appointed by President Thomas Jefferson, their mission presaged the nation's prodigious nineteenth-century expansion. Lewis and Clark hoped to establish an accessible river-trading route to open commerce between this new West and the eastern regions of the United States. The mission not only discovered a trading route but also expanded the frontiers of imagination for Americans in the East.

At President Jefferson's inauguration at the turn of the nineteenth century, two out of every three Americans lived within 50 miles of the Atlantic coast. England controlled Canada, and their traders were slowly drifting southward into the valuable lands of Minnesota and Dakota. Russia controlled Alaska and northwestern California, and Napoleon Bonaparte maintained a firm grip on the territory of Louisiana. Several countries aspired to control the West, but no one had actually explored this vast wilderness. Jefferson hoped to change this and to capitalize on the unknown treasure lying undiscovered. This venture would not only explore the unknown; it would also demonstrate the feasibility of living in the western regions.

Lewis and Clark, schooled in the many aspects of science and nature, carefully documented their experiences down to the very last detail. Lewis seemed naturally gifted at observing his new surroundings. He recorded the daily temperature and wind conditions and even took celestial readings. They recorded plants and animals new to science in the

East, carefully preserving and shipping them back for examination. Some animals were dissected or preserved; the travelers brought others home with them, alive and well. The expedition recorded for science some 178 plants and 122 animals that had not previously been described. Many of their new discoveries remain vital symbols of the West: the prairie dog, ponderosa pine, grizzly bear, and coyote.

The Corps of Discovery had their hands full trying to survive while documenting their surroundings. They also assumed the task of being the first U.S. ambassadors to the dozens of Indian tribes they met along the way. Jefferson wanted them to befriend as many as possible, knowing that future encounters would be inevitable. They met cautiously and displayed the wealth and intelligence of Americans by passing out magnets, compasses, and spyglasses. The explorers also distributed other useful items—including cloth, needles, and tobacco—in the hopes of spawning friendships as they passed.

Without the Indians, the mission might not have survived. Several times, Indians provided invaluable food and survival tips to the beleaguered explorers. During a grueling 12-day journey through the Bitterroot Mountains, a tribe of Indians kept them from complete starvation. Many of the explorers quickly became infatuated with Indian culture and made many recordings and observations about Native American life. These records serve as an ethnological benchmark between the two cultures and provide a window on tribal life before white expansion altered or destroyed traditional lifestyles.

Eastern Americans quickly learned more and more about their new western neighbors. At Jefferson's request, the expedition sent crate after crate of Indian artifacts back East to be viewed by eager crowds. Lewis and Clark served as both pioneers and gatekeepers to an eagerly awaiting audience. Their documents became the authoritative word on the West for decades, and their observations helped shape America's initial vision of the frontier.

Lewis and Clark explored lands that had already been inhabited, but they were not the first whites to venture into this wilderness. Alexander Mackenzie, for example, had traveled through the northwest and through Canada in search of a route for trade several years earlier. The importance of their adventure lies on a grander scale. Lewis and Clark became the archetypal pioneers and explorers, rugged men who sought out the treasures of the West with an insatiable thirst for discovery and knowledge. They demonstrated the traits believed essential to America's success: courage, team spirit, the desire to see new ideas and cultures, the ability to observe, the will to persevere under horrible conditions, and the ability to make one's own path in life. They survived the wilderness and brought images of it home safely. They documented their travels so thoroughly that one can relive their adventures. They left Indian cultures with a favorable image of white society.

The importance of the Lewis and Clark expedition does not end there. In mid-November 1805, almost a year and a half after the expedition began, the Corps of Discovery reached the Pacific Ocean. They stood proudly on the western edge of the continent, but they also faced the peril of surviving the upcoming winter. They considered climate, availability of food and trade, and proximity to fresh water. After evaluating several suggestions, Lewis and Clark made an extraordinary decision. They waived their position as military commanders and brought the decision up for a vote.

This move in itself is a remarkable example of American frontier democracy, exhibiting a powerful collective bond and sense of mutual trust and interdependence. The explorers faced the decision together, just as they had faced all the other obstacles that stood before them. In this vote, every man and woman had his or her say. York, Clark's slave, cast his vote almost 60 years before another black man would do the same. Sacagawea, an Indian woman, voted as well—more than a century before women across the country would enjoy the same right. Here the roots of expansion, opportunity and success through struggle, and democracy become evident.

Now, some two centuries later, Lewis and Clark continue to influence popular culture and the mass media. They are hailed as adventurers, artists, historians, patriots, and fine statesmen. Two colleges (one in Portland, Oregon, and one in Lewiston, Idaho) bear their names, as do countless historical features and documentaries. In 1993 the Lewis and Clark Art Exposition at the Native American Art Exhibit displayed some of the artwork collected during their journey. Tourists can purchase a Lewis and Clark vacation tour package, on which they can travel the famous preserved trail along the original route, fishing and camping along the same waters the Corps of Discovery did. Of course, in the age of mass consumerism and tourism, a theme park represents the crowning glory. In 1998 a $40 million theme park was proposed for construction in Montana; it would bear the adventurers' names and feature such realistic attractions as a canoe ride.

Much like Christopher Columbus, Lewis and Clark remain convenient historical heroes. These two legendary figures are not only historically significant, but they have also created a positive image of frontiersmen, rugged and strong, that lives on today. Synonymous with exploration and discovery, they modeled the characteristics of the rugged, intrepid explorer who braved the unexplored wilderness for the benefit of all Americans.

—William F. Zweigart

References

Duncan, Dayton, and Ken Burns. *Lewis and Clark: An Illustrated History.* New York: Knopf, 1997.

Holloway, David, and A. K. Wilkinson. *Lewis and Clark and the Crossing of North America.* New York: Saturday Review Press, 1974.

Rawling, Gerald. *The Pathfinders: The History of America's First Westerners.* New York: Macmillan, 1964.

Sources of Further Information

Discovering Lewis and Clark: *http://www.lewis-clark.org.*

Lewis and Clark Home Page: *http://www.lewisandclark.org.*

PBS. "The Journey of the Corps of Discovery": *http://www.pbs.org/lewisandclark/.*

Planning the Expedition: *http://www.lib.virginia.edu/exhibits/lewis_clark/ch4.html.*

LINCOLN COUNTY WAR

FEBRUARY–JULY 1878

In 1878 New Mexico witnessed months of political and economic conflict commonly known as the Lincoln County War. Young William H. Bonney, alias **Billy the Kid,** began the creation of his mythical reputation during this so-called war. The fact that the conflict began the Kid's rise to fame is interesting in itself, because he played only a minor role. Rich, ambitious, powerful, and corrupt men played the lead in the bloody war. Lawrence Murphy and later James J. Dolan represented the Murphy-Dolan faction, a group that dominated business in Lincoln County. These men fixed prices and used intimidation to control the economy of the entire area. Along with his economic domination of the area, Murphy also gained political power in the territory through the Democratic Party.

In 1877 Alexander McSween and Englishman John Tunstall opened a mercantile business in Lincoln, competing directly with Murphy and Dolan. McSween also represented the growing strength of the Republican Party in Lincoln County, adding another layer to the clash. Murphy and Dolan saw their control challenged for the first time.

The competition turned bloody on 18 February 1878, when men representing Dolan gunned down Tunstall in cold blood. McSween created a posse called the Regulators, which included Billy the Kid. On 1 April 1878 Billy and a small group of men stole into the town of Lincoln and assassinated Sheriff William Brady, a Dolan partisan, and one of his deputies. In July 1878 the Kid made one of his most daring moves, one that cemented his place in the legends of the Old West. McSween and several Regulators found themselves trapped in the McSween house on the outskirts of Lincoln, surrounded by some 40 Dolan supporters and soldiers from Fort Stanton. Realizing, after a five-day siege, that they would not be able to storm the house, Dolan and his men took drastic action. They set aflame a barrel of highly flammable tar and launched it into the house, setting the wooden structure on fire. In an incredible escape, Billy burst from the house, ran across 30 yards of open terrain, rolled under a fence, and escaped unharmed. Soldiers and Murphy-Dolan supporters shot and killed the remaining Regulators as they attempted to escape. Soldiers also gunned down McSween as he tried to make his escape, effectively ending the conflict.

The fact that the Lincoln County War initiated the legend of Billy the Kid is not in dispute. The true controversy surrounds the role he played in the conflict. He did not fit the picture of the gunslinging, killing machine that legend portrays. Many accounts of the time suggest that the Kid created the Regulators. In reality, Alex McSween created the group immediately after the murder of Tunstall. Nor did leadership of the group fall on the shoulders of the Kid. Richard Brewer, Tunstall's former foreman, led the group on its rampage through New Mexico. He put together a group of men who each vowed vengeance for the slain Tunstall and swore loyalty to McSween. Accounts vary on this point as well. Some stories claim that Billy stood over the grave of the slain Tunstall and swore that he would not stop killing until he himself had killed every man involved in the death of his friend.

Many accounts of the events surrounding the Lincoln County War erroneously attempt to reduce the conflict to one between law and outlaw. Although the Murphy-Dolan faction did have the sheriff of Lincoln County as an ally, the Regulators also represented the law. Justice of the Peace John B. Wilson had deputized Billy and many of the group early in the conflict. They rode under the authority of Justice Wilson and Lincoln Constable Atanacio Martinez. Thus, much of the bloodshed that took place during the conflict occurred under the guise of legality on both sides.

Most of the Regulators died violent deaths during the war. Somehow, Billy survived the many gun battles and bullets. In fact, the Kid survived until July 1881, when Sheriff Pat Garrett gunned him down in cold blood at Fort Sumner. The fact that he continued to ride and fight after most of his companions had died further enhanced his reputation.

Like so many myths and legends concerning the Old West, this one began as merely an interesting, exciting tale. Those responsible for the newspaper accounts of the time greatly exaggerated and dramatized the exploits of the Kid. The editors of these papers concerned themselves more with titillation than fact. Most of the stories consisted of word-of-mouth accounts and tales told by those who fancied themselves as having witnessed the events. Very few of the stories told in the newspapers of the time can be confirmed.

Tales of the conflict and its protago-nists continue to enthrall the public. Popular movies, such as *Young Guns* and *Young Guns II,* chronicle the events surrounding the war. These films perpetuate a mythical picture of the character of Billy the Kid. He is portrayed as an almost godlike figure because of his gunfighting ability and fame. Clearly, the Lincoln County War and Billy the Kid will continue to fascinate generations to come.

The consummate work on the subject of the Lincoln County War is Robert M. Utley's *High Noon in Lincoln.* Utley demonstrates that although Billy the Kid became the most famous participant in the war, neither he nor anyone else involved could be considered a hero. Many works concerning Lincoln County paint the war as a morality play, replete with legendary heroes and villains. In reality, the conflict involved rich and corrupt politicians and their henchmen, all trying to augment their power. Like the equally famous gunfight at the OK Corral, the Lincoln County War comes down to us as stylized myth, not as a historical event.

—Daniel C. Gunter III

References

Nolan, Frederick. *The Lincoln County War: A Documentary History.* Norman: University of Oklahoma Press, 1992.

Utley, Robert M. *High Noon in Lincoln: Violence on the Western Frontier.* Albuquerque: University of New Mexico Press, 1987.

LITTLE BIGHORN

The Battle of the Little Bighorn, long known as the "Custer Massacre," remains the central iconic event of western plains history. The full-blown military disaster left a powerful, mixed legacy for the cavalry commander George Armstrong Custer and his command. Bumbling, incompetent egomaniac? Brave, loyal, tragic martyr? Custer's legacy remains hotly debated, and the Little Bighorn remains a powerfully contested political and historical site.

James Welch well expressed the cultural significance of this event:

The Battle of the Little Bighorn may be the most depicted event in our nation's history. Hundreds of books, from Custer biographies to as-told-to Indian accounts, have been written; thousands of illustrations from the famous Anheuser-Busch lithograph of Custer's Last Fight (which hung in saloons and tobacco stores all across America) to Sioux and Cheyenne ledger drawings, have been displayed; and at least forty films, from *They Died with Their Boots On* to *Little Big Man,* have played in theaters around the world. Clearly, from the number of books still being published, there is a fascination with this tiny event that just won't die. (Welch 1994)

Following service in the Civil War, in July 1866 Custer was appointed lieutenant-colonel of the Seventh Cavalry. The next year he led a muddled cavalry campaign against the southern Cheyenne. For his efforts, Custer suffered a court-martial and suspension from rank and command for one year. He also forfeited his pay for the period. Specifically, the court found him guilty of "Absence without leave from his command and conduct to the prejudice of good order and military discipline." Serious character flaws, including recklessness and a propensity for throwing tantrums, marked Custer's life.

Custer steadfastly maintained that he had been made a scapegoat for a failed campaign. His old friend Gen. Philip Sheridan agreed, calling Custer back to duty in 1868. In the eyes of the army, Custer quickly redeemed himself by his November attack on Black Kettle's band on the banks of the Washita River. However, even this victory was tainted. Maj. Joel Elliott and his 19 men died after holding off attacking Indians for a day because Custer did not bother to look for them after the battle. Custer's standing among enlisted men and officers dropped sharply.

Deployed to the northern plains in 1873, Custer participated in a few small skirmishes with the Lakota in the Yellowstone area. The following year, he led a 1,200-person expedition to the Black Hills, whose possession the United States had guaranteed the Lakota just six years before. The expedition discovered gold, however, and the ensuing gold fever made the Lakota treaty and land rights a moot point. The Sioux retaliated for the broken treaties, led by Chief Sitting Bull, Chief Crazy Horse, and Chief Gall, attacking the swarms of prospectors invading their territory.

In 1876 Custer was scheduled to lead part of the anti-Lakota expedition. Military politics again struck the brash general. In March he had testified about corruption in the Indian Service. An embarrassed and angry President Ulysses S. Grant relieved Custer of his command and replaced him with Gen. Alfred Howe Terry. Popular outcry among Custer's supporters forced Grant to relent, and Custer rode off, leading the Seventh Cavalry, to meet his destiny.

Custer, astride his sorrel gelding Vic, advanced impetuously and neared what he thought was a large Indian village on the morning of 25 June 1876. Perhaps he should have studied harder at West Point, where he finished at the bottom of his class. His rapid advance put him far ahead of John Gibbon's slower-moving infantry brigades.

Furthermore, Crazy Horse had rebuffed Gen. George Crook's forces at Rosebud Creek, and Maj. Marcus Reno, seeing his first action, had perhaps panicked in the face of a strong Sioux attack.

Without understanding the weakness of his support, Custer impulsively ordered an immediate attack on the Indian village. Contemptuous of Indian military abilities, he split his forces into three parts to prevent Indians from escaping. Based on past experience, he expected the enemy to break and run in the face of his attack. Instead, thousands of Lakota, Cheyenne, and Arapaho warriors besieged the unsuspecting Custer and forced his unit to retreat to a long, dusty ridge above the Little Bighorn River. There, the Native American forces surrounded the cavalrymen and killed all 210 of them. Custer's famous luck had run out. Initially interred at the spot, Custer's remains were later removed to West Point.

Custer's appalling blunders cost him his life but gained him everlasting fame. The Battle of the Little Bighorn became an American icon, memorialized in paintings, songs, books, and films. His widow, Elizabeth Bacon Custer, did what she could to repair his reputation. She

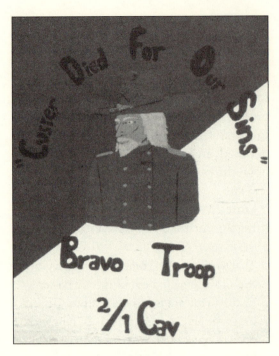

Custer's legacy still influences the U. S. Army, Fort Hood, Texas

portrayed her husband not only as a military genius but also as a refined and cultivated man, a patron of the arts, and a budding statesman. Popular artists created innumerable paintings of "Custer's Last Stand." These paintings, along with the misnomer "Custer Massacre," depicted Custer as a gallant victim, surrounded by savages.

The battlefield, established as a national monument in 1886, carried the name Custer Battlefield National Monument until 1991. Then changing political sensibilities led to its renaming as the Little Bighorn Battlefield National Monument.

The drama and tragedy of this epic battle, in the year of the nation's centennial, has kept its appeal and controversy over the years. Early depictions, such as the Tom Mix silent movie of 1909, *On* the *Little Big Horn, or Custer's Last Stand,* perpetuated Custer's heroic image. The movie *Little Big Horn,* issued in 1951, carried on in the same tradition. *Custer,* a **television** program starring Wayne Maunder, aired briefly during the fall of 1967. The battle and Custer have also infiltrated popular culture, as in the title of Gerry Mulligan's jazz album *Little Big Horn.*

Whispered and then printed charges of betrayal arose among Custer's supporters. They argue that the indecision and possibly panic of Major Reno denied Custer the backup forces that could have saved his command. Reno suffered a court-martial and dismissal from the military after the fiasco. Some historians have also questioned the actions of Capt. Frederick W. Benteen, a staunch Custer foe, who failed to reinforce Custer's command. The 1996 film *Betrayal at Little Big Horn* makes this case. Forensic scientists have scoured the site with metal detectors to determine more about the actual troop deployments of that fateful day.

However, Custer's critics have moved the imagery of besieged, tragic heroes in an entirely new direction. Most famously, the 1970 film *Little Big Man,* based on Thomas Berger's novel of the same name, portrays Custer as a vainglorious madman. Post-Vietnam revisionism took a much darker, more critical view of white expansion across the plains. Indian accounts of the battle have received scholarly attention and have proved to be credible and enlightening. In 1992 Peter Stekler issued an hour-long documentary titled *Last Stand at Little Big Horn.* This film drew upon journals, oral accounts, Indian ledger drawings, and other materials. For the first time, it presented the battle from the perspective of the Sioux, Cheyenne, and Crow. In 1999 Herman J. Viola issued *Little Big Horn Remembered: The Untold Indian Story of Custer's Last Stand.* The motto outside the First Cavalry barracks at Fort Hood, Texas, captures well the irony and pathos of Custer's last stand: "Custer died for our sins."

References

Custer Battlefield: *http://www.intuitive.com/ sites/cbhma/.*

General George A. Custer: *http://www.garry owen.com/.*

Little Bighorn Cover-up: *http://www.thehistory net.com/WildWest/articles/0696_text.htm.*

PBS. *The West: http://www.pbs.org/weta/the west/wpages/wpgs400/w4custer.htm.*

Welch, James, with Paul Stekler. *Killing Custer: The Battle of the Little Bighorn and the Fate of the Plains Indians.* New York: W. W. Norton, 1994.

LITTLE HOUSE ON THE PRAIRIE

See Television

"LITTLE JO" JOSEPHINE MONAGHAN 1850?–1903

The 1993 postfeminist film *The Ballad of Little Jo* brought the tale of an unusual nineteenth-century woman to the movie screen. Director Maggie Greenwald filmed her low-budget independent production in Montana and attracted a cult audience for this quirky feminist western starring Suzy Amis. The film's title also echoes images from the famous traditional cowboy song, "Little Joe the Wrangler."

Based on the life of a real woman, the film traces the tragedy of a young, upper-class eastern woman who disgraces her family by bearing a child out of wedlock. To support her infant son, Laddie, and spare him the shame of bastardy, she leaves him with her sister Helen and strikes out west in 1866.

Her misadventures begin early as she barely escapes being raped and must don men's clothes to replace her torn dress. She decides to adopt a male persona, cutting her hair and even slashing her face with a razor to leave a decidedly masculine scar. For a woman to pass as a man was certainly not unheard of in the Old West.

Jo secures employment in Ruby City, a mining boomtown. She suffers more turmoil and another attempted rape by a man who learns her real sex. More violence, however, drives her from town to work as a sheep herder in the employ of crusty, racist Frank Badger (played by Bo Hopkins).

Years later, Jo buys a ranch and returns to raising sheep. She hires a Chinese railroad worker Tinman Wong (David Chung) to help her. He knows she is a woman, and they fall in love. In a classic example of cattle rancher–sheep herder violence, she is ambushed but shoots two of her attackers. After she dies, Badger discovers her body and takes it back to town. There, the townsfolk learn her secret when the undertaker prepares the corpse for burial.

Film critic Stephen Hunter calls *The Ballad of Little Jo* a "snowy weather Western": "The great snowy weather Western," he writes,

> was Robert Altman's *McCabe and Mrs. Miller,* and I doubt this one would exist if that one didn't. Still, Greenwald, like Altman, has a real feel for the austere beauty of the muddy, frozen tundra of the prairie and the landscapes a-glisten with white stuff and just vibrating with the chill of the cold. It's far from *Shane* country and it's far from heroic myth. But it's real and affecting, just like the movie. (Hunter)

In addition to the better-known film, playwright Barbara Lebow has written a drama, *Little Jo Monaghan,* for four actors.

The actual historical record is as compelling as the fictionalized versions. A cowboy named Jo did indeed work in the Ruby, Idaho, area from 1868 until 1880. His small stature and penchant for privacy, although a bit odd, did not work against him. He dutifully sent money back east and also left part of his wages with a mining superintendent to hold for him. However, in 1880, the superintendent disappeared, along with Jo's savings.

After losing his savings, Jo left Idaho for a homestead on Succor Creek in Malheur County, Oregon. He built a shack and accumulated a small herd of cattle marked with his JM brand, living quietly, alone for more than 20 years. One day in 1903, a neighbor named Fred Palmer noticed a lack of smoke from the chimney on Jo's cabin. He found the little cowboy, mortally ill, inside. As in the fictionalized versions, the undertaker did indeed make the discovery that Jo was in fact a woman. Letters found in her shack revealed her family ties in Buffalo, New York. She had dutifully sent money to support her son throughout her life. Friends laid her to rest beside the creek that ran through her property.

See also Gentle Tamers; Women in Western Films

References

Hunter, Stephen. "Little Joe" (film review): *http://www.sunspot.net/our_town/film/data/mov_839386291_113.html.*

Kaufman, Seth. *TV Guide,* film review: *http://www.tvguide.com/movies/database/ShowMovie.asp?MI=35618.*

Lebow Drama Site: *http://www.dramatists.com/text/littlejo.htm.*

Seagraves, Anne. *Daughters of the West.* Hayden, ID: Wesanne Publications, 1996.

Teegarden, John. "Joe on Her Toes" (film review): *http://www.film.com/film-review/1993/8275/26/default-review.html.*

LIVER-EATING JOHNSON

The legend of Liver-Eating Johnson is based on the story of real-life mountain man John Johnson (1824–1900). His exploits, real and imagined, have been recounted directly from the fantastic stories of fellow mountain men and indirectly through written histories and journals by various authors. Like many larger-than-life characters of western

lore, a few sparse, factual dates and events form the skeleton for a huge array of entertaining tales and happenings, embellished through the years. Even his exact name remains in dispute, sometimes rendered Johnson and at other times Johnson. Unlike many legendary westerners, however, Johnson never sought fame nor expected that his life would someday become the stuff of legend.

Two very different books provide the basis for much of the mountain man's life and mythology. Carbon County Historical Society compiled one account, *Red Lodge: Saga of a Western Area.* Johnson served the last few years of his life as constable of the town of Red Lodge, in Carbon County, Montana. The pertinent chapter of this book, written by Gawn West (aka Harry Owens), claims to recount the true and full life of Liver-Eating Johnson. The second book, *Crow Killer: The Saga of Liver-Eating Johnson,* written by Raymond W. Thorp and Robert Bunker, tells a much different tale, a tale that folklorist Richard Dorson calls "the Heroic Age version of Liver-Eater." This version represents the finished product of the oral legend of Johnson, transcribed from the accounts of J. F. "White-Eye" Anderson, a fellow mountain man, at the age of 90.

Legend has it that on a May morning in 1847, Crow Indians killed and scalped Johnson's wife, and with her killed their unborn son. That tragedy transformed Johnson into an avenger, and for years afterward he waged a vendetta against the Crow. He supposedly killed and scalped more than 300 Crow Indians and then devoured their livers. As his reputation and collection of scalps grew, Johnson became an object of fear among the

Indians and respect among his fellow mountain men.

Known as Dapiek Absaroka, "Killer of Crows," Johnson is remembered by most accounts as a stern, taciturn fellow who would not respond to questions about his personal life. However, mountain men in general made most of their own entertainment by telling tales during their annual **rendezvous.** These frontiersmen admired the feared Indian fighter.

The formidable Johnson stood six feet, two inches tall and weighed around 220 pounds. In his prime, Johnson is credited with Herculean strength, physique, and endurance. Stories claim that with the power of his feet and hands he could twist off an Indian's neck or kick him airborne. Like other western heroes, he is associated with trusty weapons, a rosewood-handled Walker Colt, a Bowie knife, and a richly crafted stone tomahawk given to him as a tribal antique. His faithful horse, Big Black, could smell out Indians and never left his side.

His most heroic quality, as depicted in the stories of his fellow mountain men, lay in combat etiquette and morality. He always gave a disadvantaged opponent more equal terms by lending him a weapon or allowing first draw, only to crush him with a kick or a blow. Amid all the savagery associated with the nickname "Liver-Eating," Johnson stuck to the code of the mountain man. He only killed to avenge the loss of his wife and son. He ended his vendetta with the Crow when they showed respect for the grave of Crazy Woman, the deranged widow of a murdered husband and family, also killed by Indians.

One famous tale tells of 20 Crow warriors sent individually to pursue and de-stroy their enemy, Johnson. One by one, Johnson killed them in single combat, each time taking the scalp and eating the liver. Another fantastic story tells of Liver-Eating Johnson simultaneously fighting off a grizzly bear and a mountain lion in a cave, wielding the frozen leg of a dead Blackfoot Indian. Still another anecdote highlights his amazing stamina: He supposedly escaped, half-naked, from a Blackfoot camp and traveled 200 miles in a snowstorm to safety. Johnson is also credited with killing Sam Grant, a famous African-American cowboy, in a gunfight.

Johnson shares many of the heroic attributes of Buffalo Bill **Cody** and Davy Crockett, but he is much more the product of oral tradition. As Thorp and Bunker admit in the acknowledgments to their book, most of their information came from White-Eye Anderson in 1940. Anderson heard most of the stories from Del Gue between 1885 and 1900. Although Gue had actually trapped with Johnson in the 1850s and '60s, almost 30 years passed before he told his stories, and another 40 went by before Anderson recounted his. Seventy years is a long time for exact oral history to survive, which helps account for the embellishment of the adventures.

According to research conducted by the Carbon County Historical Society and by other historians, Johnson was actually born John Garrison in Little York, New Jersey, in July 1824. While serving in the U.S. Navy, he struck a lieutenant and deserted. Because desertion was a capital offense, Garrison took up a new name, Johnson, and a new life. His career as a mountain man began around 1843, and many of his legendary adventures began thereafter. Crow Indians did kill his wife in 1847, and Johnson probably went on to kill a few during his lifetime, although not to the extent asserted in myth. Johnson earned his famous nickname, Liver-Eating Johnson, during an exchange with Indians while working as a sharpshooter with the Colorado cavalry. After killing one of the Indians, Johnson decided to play a prank on a younger cavalryman. Carving out the liver of his fallen enemy, he walked over to the boy, and proceeded to ask him if he wanted a bite while it was still warm.

Later in life, Johnson served as sheriff of Red Lodge, Montana, where he recounted many tall tales to the townspeople. While there, he turned down an offer to appear in Buffalo Bill's Wild West Show. Townspeople remember him saying dismissively, "The only Indian Bill Cody ever touched was a squaw."

In 1899, at the age of 72, Johnson left Red Lodge and entered a veterans hospital in Los Angeles. On 21 January 1900, the wearied mountain man passed away. In 1965 Vardis Fisher published a novel, *Mountain Man,* based on Johnson's life as a trapper in the Rockies. Fisher's book inspired the making of *Jeremiah Johnson,* the 1972 movie directed by Sydney Pollack and starring Robert Redford.

John Garrison was originally buried in the hospital cemetery in Los Angeles. After requests from friends and historians, officials agreed to move the body to Old Trail Town in Cody, Wyoming. Robert Redford served as one of the pallbearers.

—*Andrew Mebane Southerland*

References

Fisher, Vardis. *Mountain Man.* New York: Morrow, 1965.

Thorp, Raymond W., and Robert Bunker. *Crow Killer: The Saga of Liver-Eating Johnson.* Foreword by Richard M. Dorson. Bloomington: Indiana University Press, 1969.

Source of Further Information

Old West Grave Sites, John Garrison: *www. dimensional.com/~sgrimm/jjohn.htm*

LONE RANGER

One evening several years ago, a conductor led the Detroit Symphony through a stirring rendition of *The William Tell Overture.* One listener, struck with inspiration and pride at the sound of his favorite childhood television show's theme song, blared a rousing "Hi-ho Silver!" at the top of his lungs. No doubt others in the audience found themselves struck with a mixture of alarm and nostalgia. The Lone Ranger ranks among the most famous and revered popular culture heroes of all time. His name and likeness have trickled through almost every form of mass media: novels, comic strips, movies, merchandising, and successful radio and **television** series. Together with his trusty white horse, Silver, and his Indian companion Tonto (with horse Scout), the Lone Ranger has become an American cultural and commercial icon.

The Lone Ranger came to life at the hands of John King and George W. Trendle in 1932. Harold True came up with the name. The radio drama series on WXYZ radio became an immediate hit. Fran Striker joined the staff and wrote many of the early scripts. Striker described the mysterious character in an early script: "a masked rider, a picturesque figure that performed deeds of the greatest daring. A modern Robin Hood . . . seen by few, known by none. Whence he came and where he went, no one ever knew" (Van Hise 1990). According to Texas folklore, the Lone Ranger is based on the **Texas Rangers.** Supposedly, only one of six Rangers survived a vicious attack by a gang of outlaws. That one survivor became the Lone Ranger.

The radio show first aired in January 1933, with George Seaton as the hero. At least ten different men would later portray the Lone Ranger in various media, including Earle W. Graser, Brace Beemer, Lee Powell, Robert Livingston, and the legendary Clayton Moore, who died in 1999. John Todd played Tonto on the radio show through its last airings in 1954. The radio series lasted for hundreds of episodes and is remembered as the era's most popular action drama. As technology changed, Clayton Moore and John Hart got their respective chances to become one of the first television series heroes. Moore played the Lone Ranger from 1949 through 1957, except from 1952 to 1954, when Hart filled the role. Clayton Moore gained fame as the *true* Lone Ranger, starring also in the movies *The Lone Ranger* (1956) and *The Lone Ranger and the Lost City of Gold* (1958).

Several aspects of the Lone Ranger's character (or lack thereof) may explain his phenomenal popularity. The Lone Ranger became a convenient, straightforward, one-dimensional hero for anyone and everyone. This atypical, clean-cut Ranger frowned upon drinking, smoking, and using bad language. The masked rider brought virtue and integrity to living rooms across America. Parents praised him for his high ideals: brotherhood, fair play, and seeking justice with honor. His mask and mysterious identity added flavor and intrigue. Kids adored the Lone Ranger as an adventurous hero and role model, full of good spirit and with a flawless character. He wasn't afraid to use his pistol, but only to shoot the gun from a criminal's hand.

His Indian sidekick proved the hero's good will toward Native Americans, even though the word *tonto* is Spanish for "fool." The producers claimed that it meant "wild one," a label used by the Potowatomie Indians of western Michigan. This tribe is also allegedly the source of the affectionate term "Kemosabe," which is interpreted to mean "faithful friend" or "trusty scout." In actuality, the word probably came from the name of producer James Jewell's father-in-law's summer camp, Camp Kee Mo Sah Bee, at Lake Mullet, Michigan.

Silver, the famous solid white horse, became a costar, able to save the day at any given moment. Originally, Tonto, who first appeared in the fourth radio episode or thereabouts, also rode a white steed. To keep attention focused on the hero, the producers took away the Indian's powerful white stallion and gave him a blandly colored horse. The Lone Ranger's grammar, like the rest of his character, was flawless. He spoke profoundly and avoided the use of slang, setting a higher standard for the cowboy image in general.

Sponsors climbed over each other to back such a popular, positive hero, and merchandise with his wholesome logo flew off the shelves. In 1935 radio voice Earle W. Graser offered a chance for kids to join the Lone Ranger Safety Club, if they would agree in writing to tell the truth and look carefully before crossing streets. General Mills, one of 66 different licensed manufacturers of Lone Ranger products, handled the demand for more than 2 million Safety Club badges. At one point, the factory had to run 24 hours a day, sending out more than 500,000 Lone Ranger masks and 2 million Lone Ranger photographs to demanding children across the nation. The Lone Ranger Atom Bomb Ring remains the most popular prize ever offered. Its 1945 release drew well over 2 million requests.

In July 1933 the Detroit Department of Recreation promised children a live appearance of their favorite hero on Belle Isle. The Lone Ranger appeared astride Silver. Police blockaded the area, prepared for an estimated 20,000 spectators. More than 70,000 arrived, causing such a dangerous commotion that Trendle never dared this type of promotional event again.

Pulp novelists' stories about the Lone Ranger sold very well. Street and Smith, a major publisher of Lone Ranger material, kept millions of children hanging in suspense with *Street and Smith's Wild West Weekly*. Gaylord Du Bois released juvenile literature about the hero, such as *The Lone Ranger and the Secret Killer* (1937). At the Lone Ranger's peak popularity, some 120 newspapers carried his comic strip. The Lone Ranger Rock, located in Chatsworth, California, remains a popular tourist attraction for nostalgic fans.

Some analysts attribute the Lone Ranger's undying popularity to shrewd marketing of a well-written radio and television series. Others point to the hero's ability to transcend time and age, appealing to youngsters and adults alike. The Lone Ranger stands out as a monolith of virtue, an ageless cowboy who represents the best ideals of America. All told, the Lone Ranger yielded some 3,000 radio episodes, two movie serials, two feature films, 18 novels, 221 television episodes, and a host of comic strips, comic books, and animated television cartoons.

The character has permeated every aspect of society and popular culture through seven decades. He has never uttered a mean word, yet he has also never smiled. His mask hides any true personality, yet he somehow manages to distinguish himself from scores of other heroes as a memorable icon of the chivalrous and heroic West.

—*William F. Zweigart*

References

Clayton Moore, the Lone Ranger: *http://members.tripod.com/~ClaytonMoore*.

Largent's Lone Ranger Page: *http://users.ticnet.com/mlargent/LR1.html*.

Van Hise, James. *Who Was That Masked Man? The Story of the Lone Ranger*. Las Vegas, NV: Pioneer Books, 1990.

LOS ALMAGRES MINE

See San Saba Mine

LOST DUTCHMAN'S MINE

For more than a century, the myth of the Lost Dutchman's Mine has inspired controversy among treasure hunters. A mixture of storytelling, scattered facts, and personal accounts present a difficult question. The fabled mine allegedly contains hundreds of thousands of dollars' worth of pure gold. Does the mine actually exist in the Superstition Mountains of Arizona, or is it simply a myth? Many sources offer conflicting theories and discoveries.

The story begins with a prospector named Jacob Waltz (spellings vary), born in 1810. The "Dutchman" (who actually hailed from Würtemberg, Germany) arrived in America about 1839 hoping to make a decent living prospecting. After failed attempts in North Carolina and Georgia, he made his way west into heavily mined areas of Arizona. Waltz reportedly worked with a man named Jacob Wiser. Some reports indicate that Wiser, who does not appear in any records after his work with Waltz, was murdered either by Waltz or by Apache Indians. The accounts surrounding Wiser's death and other events differ greatly, although we do know that he became a citizen of the United States on 19 July 1861.

Jacob Waltz first appeared in Arizona documents by filing for a gold vein, the Gross Claim, on 21 September 1863, in the Pioneer District of Yavapai County. He drew attention to himself by returning to town, after long expeditions, flaunting the gold in his pockets and bragging about his treasure. As a result, several myths arose in an attempt to explain his sudden wealth.

Myth 1: Jacob Waltz gained access to a hidden mine when he and Wiser stumbled upon two Mexicans working the area in the Superstition Mountains. After killing them, Waltz and Wiser took over the profitable venture, keeping its location a secret.

Myth 2: The Peraltas, a wealthy Mexican prospecting family from Sonora, Mexico, discovered and mined the area during an Arizona expedition. One of the sons, Miguel Peralta, found himself in a troublesome position at a cantina late one night. Two other Mexicans threatened his life, but the virtuous Waltz and Wiser saved his life at the last minute. Filled with gratitude, Miguel rewarded Waltz with a map of the Superstition Mountains, showing where gold could be found. Waltz found the mine, killed Wiser, and kept the riches for himself.

Myth 3: Waltz, a mean and psychopathic killer, rampaged around town, flaunting his wealth and threatening those around him. As an eccentric old man, he mentioned nothing of his mine or where gold might be hidden. Later, one of his servants found gold underneath his bed.

Myth 4: No such mine ever existed. The Dutchman had bought or stolen his gold from the nearby Vulture Mining Company. Lying on his deathbed, Waltz created an elaborate story of his secret mine and where it could be found. He dropped clever, vague hints to whoever would listen. Statements such as "No miner will ever find my mine" have been interpreted to mean that the gold is located where a normal prospector would not look. He also left geographical clues: "From my mine you can see the military trail but you can't see my mine from the military trail."

Little or no factual information supports the first three myths. Waltz did not appear in any newspapers or publications during his alleged period of wealth, and he lived modestly. With such riches hiding away in the nearby mountains, why would Waltz live until his death without cashing in on his discovery?

From a factual standpoint, the Peralta family did discover and mine profitable amounts of gold from the area in the midnineteenth century. Their last known expedition (1847–1852) ended in tragedy. Apache Indians living in the area attacked and massacred the family as they returned south with their gold. The area south of the Superstition Mountains is now known as the "massacre grounds," and researchers have confirmed this event with evidence from the group's caravan. The massacre has been tied to a 400-year-old Apache curse, which supposedly protects Waltz's mythical mine and sacred Apache Indian burial grounds.

Almost 100 years later (in either 1952 or 1954), a man named Travis Tumlinson discovered the items known now as the Peralta Maps while vacationing with his family. The four elaborate maps each featured symbolic images pointing to the whereabouts of treasure. No location has yielded any discovery of gold, but interest in the area has remained active ever since.

On 31 December 1983, the U.S. Department of Agriculture closed the area to mineral prospecting of any kind, thereby making it harder to track down any facts on the elusive Lost Dutchman's Mine. Enthusiasts still search the area, and the Superstition Mountains draw tourists every year to learn more about the mining folklore. More than three dozen books explore the subject, ranging from legendary accounts to archaeological research studies. The Lost Dutchman Museum includes a Jacob Waltz exhibit. Located at the base of the Superstition Mountains, Lost Dutchman State Park is a 292-acre recreational facility, where visitors can camp, picnic, and search for the legendary hiding place of Waltz's gold.

—*William F. Zweigart*

References

Superstition Mountain–Lost Dutchman Museum: *http://ajnet.ci.apache-jct.az.us/museum1.htm.*

"Tale of the Lost Dutchman": *http://www.lost-dutchman.com.*

LOVE, NAT

See Deadwood Dick

LUCKENBACH, TEXAS

Let's go to Luckenbach Texas with Waylon
  and Willie and the boys
This successful life we're livin' has got us
  feuding like the Hatfields and McCoys.
Between Hank Williams pain songs,
  Newberry's train songs,
And blue eyes cryin' in the rain.
Out in Luckenbach Texas, ain't nobody
  feelin' no pain

Until "western outlaw" singers Waylon Jennings and Willie Nelson recorded the hit song "Luckenbach, Texas (Back to the Basics of Love)" in 1977, not many people outside the Texas hill country had heard of this tiny hamlet. Immediately, signs bearing the town's name became hot collectibles and quickly disappeared. No

Danelle Crowley and the author at the Luckenbach post office

other town in modern memory has rocketed into the national consciousness with such verve and speed.

Luckenbach had indeed existed as a real place long before it became a metaphoric retreat from life's squabbles, pressures, headaches, and travails. Nostalgia for a simpler time in the past, "the good old days," is a powerful force in American culture. Like another popular song, "Hero," the Jennings/Nelson tune shows the continuing allure of that mythical past in American life.

The Luckenbach of reality is located in the scenic central Texas hills, along both sides of Ranch Road 1376, 13.5 miles from Fredericksburg in southeastern Gillespie County. The setting is a mix of caliche hills, creek bottoms (notably Grape Creek, a tributary of the Pedernales River), century-old live-oak trees, and rolling farmlands.

The town got its start in the mid-nineteenth century. German-speaking families, including those of Jacob Luckenbach and August Luckenbach, settled in the Fredericksburg area in 1846. Six years later, the Luckenbach family naturalized and moved to the site that later became the town of Luckenbach. Jacob received a deed to 640 acres of land from the Texas immigration program.

The Reverend Albert Engel and his wife Mrs. August (Minnie) Engel get official credit for establishing the town. In about 1860, Minnie Engel established the town's first store, where local residents and Indians traded. The town did not get its name until 1886, when Minna Engel, August's sister, applied to postal authorities in Washington, D.C., to create a post office. Minna decided to honor her fiancé, Albert Luckenbach, and placed his name on the post office form.

By the late nineteenth century, Luckenbach also boasted a dance hall, a cotton gin, a blacksmith shop, and several cemetery plots. The community became more heterogeneous, with Methodists, Lutherans, and Roman Catholics the predominant religious groups. The population remained small, however, numbering 150 in 1896 and reaching its peak of 492 in 1904. Thereafter, numbers dropped sharply, with only about 20 full-time residents from the 1920s through the 1950s.

Even before its recent musical notoriety, Luckenbach had made a name for itself in Texas mythology. Supposedly, a German-born schoolteacher named Jacob Brodbeck built an airplane in the 1860s. Local legend insists that he flew his machine successfully in 1863, some four decades before the Wright brothers made their famous flight. A large coiled spring supposedly powered the propeller that flew his ship-shaped airplane. According to one account, he successfully flew his craft from a field some three miles east of Luckenbach on 20 September 1865. He reportedly flew at an altitude of 12 feet for a distance of about 100 feet before crashing. Alas, only stories, no artifacts or drawings, remain to confirm the tale. Brodbeck is buried on his farm near Luckenbach.

School consolidations and better economic opportunities elsewhere kept the town a tiny hamlet. In 1971 John Russell "Hondo" Crouch purchased the town from Benno Engel. Kathy Morgan and Guich Koock joined Crouch as partners. The white-haired, white-bearded Crouch, self-proclaimed "Clown Prince of Luckenbach," declared his town to be "a free state . . . of mind," a kind of counterculture counterpoint to Lyndon Baines Johnson's nearby ranch on the Pedernales River. A great fan of the Austin music scene, Crouch sponsored a wondrous range of festivals, such as Mud Daubers' Day, a Hug-In, a women's chili cook-off, and the Luckenbach Great World's Fair.

The irrepressible Crouch died in 1976, a year before Jennings and Nelson put his town on the world's cultural map. The hamlet continues to host a variety of reunions and celebrations, including the 1995 Willie Nelson Fourth of July picnic. Today only a blacksmith shop; a combination post office, bar, and general store; a dance hall; and a cotton gin remain on the ten-acre "downtown" site. However, Luckenbach is still a great place to sip a beer and listen to guitar strumming under the shade by tall, stately live-oak trees. Thanks to local guide and fellow Peace Corps alum Danelle Crowley, I made the pilgrimage to Luckenbach on 14 October 2000. On that picture-perfect Texas autumn day, the few dozen people in Luckenbach were indeed "feelin' no pain."

References

Baker, T. Lindsay. *Ghost Towns of Texas*. Norman: University of Oklahoma Press, 1986.

Luckenbach, Texas, Web Site: *http://www.luckenbachtexas.com*.

Source of Further Information

Handbook of Texas Online: *http://www.tsha.utexas.edu/handbook/online/articles/view/LL/hnl48.html*.

MAGAZINES

Since the earliest forays into the western frontier by the **Lewis and Clark expedition** and other explorers, most people have gotten their images of the region from print publications. The federal government subsidized and printed many of the important early exploration reports, along with drawings and later photographs. As the region opened to white settlement, however, boosters and promoters of every stripe joined in the avalanche of printed materials about the West.

Government-funded exploration had as its goal a scientific, accurate recording of the places, resources, and potential of the West; not so for later, private-sector boosters. They had as their goal to hype the region uncritically in order to attract settlers, sell land, and make money. Posters, pamphlets, books, guides for emigrants, and newspaper ads provide a vast corpus of evidence on visions of the mythical West. During the nineteenth century, emigrant societies, railroad builders, dude ranch operators, and a host of others promoted the virtues and wonders of the West. Foreign-language ads attracted European immigrants to the Golden West. One colorful lithograph promised 43,795,000 acres of land in "California, the Cornucopia of the World, Room for Millions of Immigrants, a Climate for Heath and Wealth, without Cyclones or Blizzards." An 1885 Northern Pacific Railroad ad drew inspiration from Lewis Carroll's *Alice in Wonderland.* It urged customers to explore, with Alice, "Adventures in the New Wonderland" of Yellowstone National Park.

Boosterism continues in the twentieth century, with a variety of current magazines offering their own compelling visions of the region's charms. Special-interest groups have every reason to communicate both with their members and with the public at large. In 1914 the Texas and Southwestern Cattle Raisers Association began publishing *The Cattleman.* Texas, with 14 million head of cattle, and Oklahoma, with 5.4 million, together comprise 19.3 percent of the U.S.

total of 101.2 million head. The magazine is aimed at the ranchers who own and raise those animals. It seeks to help them "make sound, informed business decisions. It has kept readers up-to-date and helped them anticipate trends, legislation and technology that could significantly impact their profits."

However, the publication, which has some 17,000 subscribers, is not all work. It also includes profiles, historical articles, and humor. Recognizing new markets and clients, *The Cattleman* has published since 1990 an annual issue on the Mexican cattle industry, with articles and ads in both Spanish and English.

Whereas *The Cattleman* promotes the interests of western ranchers, other publications have promoted state tourism and travel. In 1925, just 13 years after achieving statehood, Arizona began the publication of *Arizona Highways* magazine. The publication had one simple, straightforward goal: to promote tourism to the state. Over its 75-year-history, the glossy publication has succeeded magnificently. Stunning, colorful, landscape photography has long served as the magazine's signature. In fact, the magazine's Web site features pictures of vintage *Arizona Highways* covers going back to 1941.

Great color photography remains an *Arizona Highways* mainstay, but in recent years, it has livened up its content and format. Recognizing the appeal of western culture as well as landscape, the magazine now includes much more than simply photo essays and destination pieces. It now contains profiles, recipes, humor, bits of folklore, and much more.

The magazine's Web site likewise has a very modern feel. It includes "QuickTime VR" (virtual reality) views of Sedona, the Grand Canyon, and other scenic Arizona spots. The technology allows one to (virtually) stand on a mesa in Sedona and rotate around for a 360-degree view. One can peer over the dramatic edge of the Grand Canyon and examine stunning formations all around.

Not to be outdone, the Travel Division of the Texas Department of Transportation publishes *Texas Highways.* The state established the Texas Highway Department in 1917 to administer federal funds for the construction and maintenance of highways across its vast open spaces. *Texas Highways* grew out of an in-house newsletter, the *Construction and Maintenance Bulletin,* first published in July 1950. In November 1953 the newsletter's name was changed to *Texas Highways.* The first issue as a statewide public travel publication appeared in May 1974.

As the magazine's Web site explains, the publication "encourages recreational travel to and within Texas and tells the Texas story to readers around the world." As of the year 2000, the publication reached 300,000 subscribers and newsstand buyers throughout the United States and in more than 100 other countries. Unlike most western glossies, *Texas Highways* carries no advertising, relying on sales of the magazine itself and related products to cover production expenses.

Other western states also publish travel magazines designed to make their locales as tempting to potential visitors as possible.

Special-interest magazines have focused not on destinations, as *Arizona Highways* does, but rather on specific activities. Westerners certainly did not invent humankind's love affair with the horse, but they may have perfected it. In 1936 Paul and Wirth Albert founded *Western Horseman* in Lafayette, California, as a regional publication with a mere 12 pages. After Paul's death from cancer in 1942, Wirth sold the magazine to John Ben Snow of Speidel Newspapers, Inc. Snow upgraded and moved the magazine, first to Reno, Nevada, and then to Colorado Springs, Colorado, in 1949.

Don Flint, owner of Flying North Ranch north of Colorado Springs, nurtured the magazine as general manager and then publisher until his retirement in 1969. Texan Dick Spencer took over as editor in 1951 and nurtured the magazine's expansion until his death in 1989. Randy Witte succeeded Spencer as editor and then became publisher, with Pat Close as editor.

The editorial content targets horse owners, riders, and admirers of the western breeds. It includes many "nuts-and-bolts" and "how-to" service articles on horse training, riding, and care. Articles also cover reining and quarter horse competitions and ranch life. Given its editorial location—the Pro-Rodeo Hall of Fame is also located in Colorado Springs—the magazine naturally extends coverage to rodeos. It also features articles of interest to anyone who owns or likes horses, regardless of breed. One advertisement invited westerners to "read all about cowboys and cowgirls, rodeos and horse shows, trail rides and pack trips, hard work and great fun, cattle ranches and dude ranches, fantastic vacations, fashions and tack, and much, much more." Like all publications, *Western Horseman* has its editorial strengths and weaknesses, but today it enjoys a worldwide readership and reaches more horse lovers than any other horse magazine.

Western Horseman has achieved a predictable, long-lasting, and substantial readership. Other special-interest magazines have targeted smaller audiences; many have been ephemeral. *American Cowboy Poet,* for example, arose in response to the revival of **cowboy poetry** performances in the 1980s. *Boots* magazine advertised itself "for the cowboy artisan; it matters not the medium—words, leather, paint, song, or carving materials." *Song of the West* focused on contemporary western music. *Southwest Art* covers the historical and contemporary art scene for that region of the West.

Like western states, western organizations and institutions have recognized the importance of printed advertising. In 1964 the new Western History Association, founded just three years earlier, began sponsoring a glossy magazine, *The American West,* in addition to its flagship scholarly journal, the *Western Historical Quarterly.* (The former publication should not be confused with *American West,* the in-flight magazine of American Airlines.) Intended as a western version of *American Heritage* magazine, *The American West* had as its mission to bring authoritative but popular and entertaining western history to a general reading audience. The magazine succeeded wonderfully for some two decades. The January 1970 issue, for example, included articles by leading western writers Helena Huntington Smith, Kent Steckmesser, Canada's Hugh Dempsey, and Odie B. Falk. The November 1977 issue focused on "The Cowboy's West" and included essays by art experts Peter H. Hassrick, Owen Ulph, and C. L. Sonnichsen.

The American West shifted its focus during the late 1980s. It went commercial, dropping serious historical topics in favor of lighter fare of interest to buffs and collectors of western art and memorabilia. In response to the new focus, the Western History Association dropped its sponsorship and instead backed *Montana: The Magazine of Western History. Montana* had been published since 1951 by the Montana Historical Society in Helena. Chuck Rankin served as magazine editor during the 1980s and '90s, ably attracting quality historians and nicely balancing readability and authority. *Montana* continues the tradition of popular scholarship, presenting readable, well-illustrated, footnoted articles on a wide range of historical and cultural topics.

Montana: The Magazine of Western History initially focused only on its namesake state. However, with support from the Western History Association, it broadened its coverage considerably to include a wide range of serious but highly readable western history topics. The magazine still engages the concerns of Montana residents, however, with such regular features as The Montana Traveler and Montana Reflections. Like *The American West* in its early years, *Montana* publishes works by outstanding western scholars. The winter 1999 issue includes essays by Carlos A. Schwantes and Robert M. Utley and a commentary by Stewart L. Udall. A "Special Gold Rush Issue" (autumn 1999) included two pieces by Martin Ridge and an article, "Golden Dreams," by Elliott West. Incidentally, all states now publish a host of magazines, of varying quality, with the state name in the title—for example, *Montana Living Magazine, Montana Land Magazine,* and *Montana Magazine.*

Like the Western History Association, the National Cowboy Hall of Fame in Oklahoma City saw a need to reach out to its membership in printed form. Since 1970, five years after the museum's official opening, *Persimmon Hill* magazine has kept patrons abreast of museum activities, including featured exhibits, expansion projects, and special events. The publication takes its name from the museum's hilltop location. It entertains and educates readers on many themes of western Americana. The magazine discontinued publication in 1985/1986. Then, energetic M. J. Van Deventer took over as editor, raising the editorial and artistic content to new highs. The quarterly publication, which runs about 10,000 copies, often features themed issues. The autumn 2000 issue, for example, celebrated "First Americans: Ancient Legends." The spring 2000 issue focused on cowboy "Matinee Idols." Each issue includes features on western history, art, literature, folklore, popular culture, and more. Other major western museums, such as the Buffalo Bill Historical Center in Cody, Wyoming, also publish informative promotional newsletters and magazines.

The cowboy renaissance of the late 1980s prompted a western publishing boom. Many of those boom magazines, such as *Western Styles,* survived only briefly. However, others prospered. *Cowboy Magazine* premiered in the summer of 1990, with a hearty welcome from veteran cowboy actor Richard Farnsworth. In a brief essay, the actor acknowledged the declining economic fortunes of ranching and cowboy life in the West. He pointed out, however, the continuing mystique of the cowboy. "Still," noted Farnsworth, "much of the West is unsettled, and the land is best suited for cattle grazing. The cowboy is still out there turning grass into beef. With America now in the age of space technology, and only ten years away from the 21st century, the cowboy still endures. *Cowboy Magazine* is being published because the world still loves to cowboy." As the magazine's Web site proclaims, "We know the real working cowboy better than anyone."

Cowboys & Indians appeared in 1993. Its publisher, Robert Hartman, sought to interest fans both of cowboy culture and history and of Native American culture and history. Hartman and skilled editor Charlotte Berney created a publication both lively and diverse. Splendid color photography and paintings adorned each issue.

Texas entrepreneur Reid Slaughter purchased the magazine and took over as publisher in 1996. He added more coverage of western and Native American art, handicrafts, and collectibles and devoted more attention to architecture and celebrities. In early 2000 Eric O'-Keefe replaced Charlotte Berney as editor and the editorial offices shifted from Santa Fe to Dallas. Circulation has topped the 100,000 mark, making it one of the larger "western lifestyle" publications in print.

A glance through the ads in *Cowboys & Indians* reflects the upscale consumer frontier that appeals to a host of westerners and wanna-bes. The November 2000 issue includes lush pages of ads for Double D Ranch women's wear, western artifacts from Christie's, Ariat and J. B. Hill boots—some 40 advertisers, all told.

Readers are tempted with everything western from barbecue sauce to belt buckles to bronze statues, items that cost from a few dollars to tens of thousands. Vendors run the historical and cultural gamut from Navajos selling traditional silver and turquoise to a Web site for the American Paint Horse Association. The magazine has also developed a colorful Web site, with an monthly trivia contest, bonus book and music reviews, and other features. The magazine's Web site proclaims itself "the ultimate western lifestyle site. Authoritative guides to art, fashion, home interiors, fine food, and much more."

In sum, old-time promoters tried to lure people to a place called the West. Today's entrepreneurs still sell real estate, but they also market the West as a lifestyle, as a state of mind, as a dream. Thus, the power and magnetism of a region now extends, through a host of publications, to people around the world who still wish to share in the wonders of the mythical West.

References

American Paint Horse Association: *http://www.apha.com.*

Arizona Highways: *http://www.arizonahighways.com.*

The Cattleman Magazine: *http://www.thecattlemanmagazine.com/.*

Cowboy Magazine: *http://www.datasys.net/edpak/cowb.html.*

Cowboys & Indians: *http://www.cowboysandindians.com.*

Montana: *http://www.his.state.mt.us/departments/magazine/mag.html.*

National Cowboy Hall of Fame: *http://www.cowboyhalloffame.org/persim.html.*

Texas Highways: *http://www.texashighways.com/.*

Western Horseman: http://www.westernhorse man.com.

Wheeler, Keith. *The Railroaders.* New York: Time-Life Books, 1973.

MAGNIFICENT SEVEN, THE

Director John Sturges adapted *The Magnificent Seven* from Akira Kurosawa's 1952 *The Seven Samurai*. It starred Charles Lang Jr., Yul Brynner (Chris Adams), Eli Wallach (Calvera), Steve McQueen (Vin), Horst Buchholz (Harry Luck), James Coburn (Britt), Charles Bronson (Bernardo O'Reilly), and Robert Vaughn (Lee). The evil bandit Eli Wallach and his 40 thugs repeatedly despoil a hapless Mexican village. The desperate villagers hire down-on-their-luck gunmen, unemployed because of civilization's encroachment on the West. With lots of shooting and heroics, the film achieved great popular and respectable critical success. Charles Bronson, James Coburn, Steve McQueen (see also Tom **Horn**), and Robert Vaughn all enjoyed great career boosts because of the film.

The successful film has spawned several movie spin-offs, notably *Return of the Magnificent Seven, Guns of the Magnificent Seven,* and *The Magnificent Seven Ride.* In 1998 a CBS **television** series reprised the popular film. John Watson was the executive producer of the series, which starred Michael Biehn, Eric Close, Andrew Kavovit, Dale Midkiff, Ron Perlman, Anthony Starke, and Rick Worthy.

The story line of the TV series involves several uniquely talented, multicultural heroes who band together to fight a common foe. Each character has his own special weapon and ability in the fight against the classic Western bad guys: armies of bandits, evil landowners, oppressive cattle ranchers, corrupt lawmen. In this case, they defend a Seminole rather than a Mexican village. The music for the film and series is as classically western as the story lines and characters. Composed for the film by Elmer Bernstein, it was rerecorded in 1993. Bernstein loved the new version for the television series, which utilizes more than 90 percent of his original score. That original music, highly recognizable even today, accompanied the Marlboro Man cigarette commercials of the 1960s.

Although the original film was highly successful, the CBS series has not been. Several TV episodes have gone unaired, despite an immense fan-base and intense popularity among some groups. TNN picked up 21 episodes of the program for syndication after CBS lost interest in the spring of 1999. But the archetypal characters and immortal setting of the American West make this particular story appealing on many levels, and it is likely that the series and the movie will continue to enjoy the support of die-hard fans who enjoy action, adventure, and friendship in the sweeping scope of the West.

The Magnificent Seven deftly echoes several voices of earlier western films. Like *Shane,* the seven heroes defend the weak against the strong and abusive. Like the multiple-hero serials of B-western days (such as *The Three Mesquiteers*), the seven heroes show that the effort of the whole is greater than the sum of the parts. In short, the twin themes of western individualism (the seven differ substantially from one another) and group cooperation intertwine in an entertaining, mythical package.

—P. S. Crane and Richard W. Slatta

References

Hardy, Phil. *The Overlook Film Encyclopedia: The Western.* Woodstock, NY: Overlook Press, 1991.

Hollywood.com: *http://Hollywood.com.*

MANIFEST DESTINY

Manifest Destiny is a concept of imperialism that has existed in the United States since its foundation. It holds that God ordained the expansion of America and that the nation's history reflects this divine plan. John O'Sullivan, an influential editor and Democratic activist, coined the phrase in 1845:

the right of our manifest destiny to over spread and to possess the whole of the continent which Providence has given us for the development of the great experiment of liberty and federative development of self government entrusted to us. It is a right such as that of the tree to the space of air and the earth suitable for the full expansion of its principle and destiny of growth.

Many scholars hold that the ideals of Manifest Destiny existed long before O'Sullivan wrote the phrase. Ironically, even O'Sullivan himself did not realize that he had created an American slogan until his political opponents called attention to it. However, once the phrase existed, U.S. territorial expansion into the

unsettled West preserved it as a rallying cry justifying American growth.

Many Americans saw the freedom and liberty that flourished in America as a gift that they should spread across the continent. This conviction stemmed from their faith that Divine Providence mandated the glory and growth of America. Since God so decreed it, the American people saw no limit to the extension and enlargement that the nation not only could but inevitably would achieve.

The phrase "Manifest Destiny" elegantly and simply justified a large variety of notable political and historical occurrences. Both the Santa Fe Trail to New Mexico and the Oregon Trail to the Pacific Northwest became popular routes. More than 30,000 pioneer grave sites testified to the hardships that these settlers faced. Many urged northward expansion to latitude 54.40. America's occupation of the Oregon Territory became an important national goal and political issue. As William Gilpin said in 1846, "The *untransacted destiny* of the American people is to subdue the continent—to rush over this fast field to the Pacific Ocean—to animate the many hundred millions of its people, and to cheer them upward—to establish a new order in human affairs—to set free the enslaved—to change darkness into light" (Goetzmann 1986).

James K. Polk's expansionist platform helped him to edge out Henry Clay in the campaign for the presidency in 1844. He began his presidency in 1845, the year the phrase "Manifest Destiny" first made its way into print. He stayed true to this agenda, which led to conflicts with Mexico over what are now the southwest regions of the United States. With success in the Mexican-American War, the nation added more than a million square miles of territory in the Southwest and Far West. For the first time, America stretched from the Atlantic to the Pacific, rendering it more powerful and far safer from foreign invasion.

As the concept of Manifest Destiny took hold in the thoughts and minds of the American people, it also appeared as a theme in American artwork. The most obvious incarnation is a work by John Gast, variously titled *American Progress* or *Westward Ho.* In it, the goddess of Liberty moves over the American frontier, stringing telegraph wire with one hand and carrying a school book in the other. With her comes the light of day and civilization out of the East, spilling over the plains and ridding the West of its dark and backward ways. Covered wagons, farmers, and fences come with her, and trains rush westward not far behind. Buffalo and Indians flee before her, and only a few bones remain behind as a reminder of the West before its enlightenment. This painting ably captured the prevailing outlook of the times, and it was distributed by the thousands on lithograph.

Westward the Star of Empire Takes Its Way–Near Council Bluffs, by Andrew Melrose, and *The Old House of Representatives,* by Samuel Morse, also depict the inevitability of America's westward conquest. In Melrose's work, train tracks and an ominously advancing train interrupt a peaceful scene of deer in the forest. The bright light of the train, the force of "progress," breaks nature's serenity and startles and scatters the deer and everything else in its path. Morse's painting shows the House of Representatives in session. An apprehensive Indian watches quietly from a balcony while the white men below determine the fate of his people and of the West.

White Americans of the time felt little remorse for displacing Indians from the land and stripping them of their culture. People believed that God had destined them to civilize and enlighten others, to conquer and Christianize the land. This belief often led to the death of Indians, to their relegation to reservations, and to the eventual destruction of their culture and identity.

In more recent times, the belief in Manifest Destiny has still rung true to Americans. The concept played a vital role in the nation's struggle against the Communist Soviet Union. Cold War policy makers in the United States viewed the Soviet Union as a force bent on global conquest, a force that only the United States could contain. Many Americans viewed their nation as "the leader of the free world," a bulwark against a totalitarian Soviet regime. Turning the American people and leaders toward this outlook encouraged expansion, not unlike the movement westward in the 1840s. In order to contain Soviet influence, the United States worked to extend its global influence and dominance over the capitalist world. Any area at risk of falling to Communist influence–Korea, Vietnam, Central America–created a venue for U.S. intervention. This global extension was an enormous commitment by the American people, one that echoed the ideals of divinely ordained actions that are the very essence of Manifest Destiny.

Ronald Reagan heightened the struggle against what he dubbed the "Evil Empire." Coming from the West, he frequently employed western imagery and ideas in appealing to the American people. He spoke of America as "a beacon of hope to the rest of the world." He used these Cold War themes to initiate enormous military increases and to establish a "rollback" policy to push back the Soviet Union. This vision of good versus evil and the role of America in upholding the values of freedom undergirded the Reagan administration's foreign policy. Reagan made emotional appeals to the American people, not unlike Manifest Destiny in its original context.

Beyond the political arena, the phrase "Manifest Destiny" has entered the vocabulary of the American people and revealed itself in a variety of modern forms. In the music industry, several bands use the phrase to explain their motivations and music. One band, actually named Manifest Destiny, explains the motivation for its name: "This band as a whole truly believes that through hard work and commitment, success in the heavy metal music industry is their MANIFEST DESTINY." Other rock groups, including Local H and Brand X, employ the phrase as either a record or single song title.

In addition to musical references, the phrase appears in other media. For example, there is a book titled *Your Manifest Destiny: Nine Spirited Principles for Getting Everything You Want.* "Manifest Destiny" is the name of a film production company that makes "low budget, high quality, dramatic feature films." It is also the name of a job-matching company whose slogan is "Where opportunity takes flight." In the minds of the American people, the phrase implies progressive thinking, greater gains, destined stardom, and inevitable success.

Not surprisingly, then, it appears often in the vocabulary of employers and marketers. By using the phrase, individuals and companies hope to convey a message of predestined validity, growth, and success that will reassure their customers and followers. The use of "Manifest Destiny" in promoting conquest or colonization of new frontiers has not yet ended. A new video game, "Manifest Destiny," allows for conquest of an imaginary world. The First Millennial Foundation, a group concerned with the concept of spreading the existence of humankind beyond earth and colonizing the universe, also makes frequent use of the term in its literature.

The concept of Manifest Destiny provided a strong underlying impetus to American nationalism and historical expansionism. Beyond the conceptual vision of a colonized western frontier, the phrase has survived its original context to come to mean a variety of things to the American people. Presidents have employed its ideals to unify and motivate the American people. In doing so, they transformed it into a widely accepted tenet of both domestic and foreign policy.

–*Kaleb J. Redden*

References

Goetzmann, William H., and William N. Goetzmann. *The West of the Imagination.* New York: W. W. Norton, 1986.

Lubragge, Michael T. "Manifest Destiny": *http://grid.let.rug.nl/~usa/E/manifest/manifxx.htm.*

Stephanson, Anders. *Manifest Destiny: American Expansionism and the Empire of Right.* New York: Hill and Wang, 1995.

MARYSVILLE, CALIFORNIA

See Beckwourth, Jim

MASK OF ZORRO, THE

See Zorro

MCCARTY, HENRY

1859–1881, outlaw. *See* Billy the Kid

MCJUNKIN, GEORGE

1851–1922

In the 1920s, the discovery in New Mexico of human bones and spear points more than 11,000 years old, first near Folsom and later near Clovis, electrified the world of archaeology. However, proper credit for the discovery would have to wait until the 1960s. Today we know that George McJunkin, ex-slave, cowboy, and ranch foreman, made this monumental find.

McJunkin, a slave born in Texas, joined the large number of cowboys trailing cattle north after the Civil War. As a teenager, he rode with a drive to Dodge City, Kansas, and then worked on a number of ranches in New Mexico. His considerable skills elevated him to foreman on the Crowfoot Ranch, a rare achievement for a freed slave. The intellectually curious McJunkin had gotten a couple of boys to teach him to read in exchange for teaching them about horses. He read works of science and always rode with a telescope strapped to his saddle.

In August 1908 McJunkin was at work, mending fences in Dead Horse Arroyo near Folsom in northeastern New Mexico. Using his telescope, he spotted bones, probably exposed by a rainstorm. He contacted several people, including Carl Schwachheim, a blacksmith and collector of fossil bones. However, no one took any action until after McJunkin's death in 1922. Thereafter, the relics, bones, and spear points identified the remains known as Folsom man. That finding would spur the further, competing searches by Jesse Figgins and Aless Hrdlicka that turned up Clovis man. They, not McJunkin, would receive credit for the find until decades later.

Regional folklore, however, kept alive the tale that an ex-slave had actually made the Folsom discovery. George A. Agogino of Eastern New Mexico University had tape-recorded interviews with people who had known McJunkin. Writer Franklin Folsom began following up scattered pieces of the old story of "McJunkin's Bone Pit." He gathered his evidence into a children's book, *The Life and Legend of George McJunkin,* published in 1992. Jaxon Hewett and Mary Edmonston have also done biographical work on McJunkin.

The cowboy scientist got more acclaim during the 1990s. In January 1999 Lamb's Players Theatre's educational outreach included him in its production of *Real American Heroes.* The SWAT (Slightly Wild, Accessible Theatre) Team includes Paul Maley, Kerry Meads, and Vanda Eggington. The presentation is billed as "a fast-paced blend of multicultural storytelling, music, and history following the lives of American men and women of Hispanic, Asian, European, and African American ancestry whose heroic lives have shaped and enriched our country."

References

Folsom, Franklin. *Black Cowboy: The Life and Legend of George McJunkin.* Niwot, CO: Roberts Rinehart Publishers, 1992.

Large, Jerry. "Clovis Man—Giving Credit Where It's Due." *Seattle Times,* Sunday, 23 February 1997: *http://archives.seattletimes. nwsource.com/cgi-bin/texis/web/vortex/dis play?slug=jdl&date=19970223.html.*

Locke, Robert. "A Bitter Tale of Old Bones." *Scientific American: Discovering Archaeology* 6 (November 1999): *http://www.discov eringarchaeology.com/0699toc/6cover4 -bones.shtml.*

MCMURTRY, JAMES

1962–

Born in Fort Worth, Texas, in 1962, James Lawrence McMurtry faced a daunting life growing up in the shadow of his father, literary legend Larry McMurtry. He found his own path, however, and his own voice. "I learned to play the guitar when I was seven years old," he remembered. "My mother (a professor of English) taught me three chords, and the rest I just stole as I went along. I learned everything by ear or by watching people" ("James McMurtry"). His parents divorced shortly after his birth, and James grew up in Houston with his father. "I can hardly remember back to a time when James didn't play the guitar," the elder McMurtry recalled. "The irony of James being such a fine musician is that I am no musician in any sense [and] there wasn't any great amount of music around the house" ("James McMurtry").

What did abound around the house was literature. But James did not pursue literature in the form of books, as his father did. "I hate books," he says.

I'm not much of a reader. I like someone like Walker Percy, but anyone I've read goes into my head and never comes out in any kind of tangible way in my own writing. I had to deal with a lot of books when I was a kid. My dad had a rare book store, and he was always bringing home another pile of books. I ended up having to stack 'em. I never read any of 'em. Reading was my dad's thing. ("James McMurtry")

Although he had no love of books, James did love stories, and he enjoyed hearing them from both of his parents: "I guess I might have picked up something from them in that way." He grew to become a very gifted musical storyteller and word painter. His portraits are as bare and arresting as a southwestern desert landscape. He populates his music with exquisitely wrought portraits of people overwhelmed with conflicting, often destructive emotions. McMurtry creates compelling characters and can turn a phrase with the best of them, including his famous father. In "Fast as I Can," he wrote:

He was a drinking man with a guitar
   problem
Didn't have a dollar to his name
He didn't seem to mind it all that often
He mostly took whatever came
If it came too late or if it came to nothing
Sometimes he'd swear beneath his breath.

McMurtry's musical people exist in a place both surreal and very real, a space that historian William Goetzmann called "The West of the Imagination." A good example of the emotive power of his descriptions is "Levelland" from his *Where'd You Hide the Body?* album:

Flatter than a table top
makes you wonder why they stopped here
wagon must've lost a wheel
or they lacked ambition, one.

As a teenager, James loved bluegrass music, but his tastes later expanded. Asked to identify his most important influence, he straightforwardly names Johnny Cash: "He was the first singer I ever listened to when I was a kid. I spun his records backwards, forwards, and sideways on an old mono record player" ("James McMurtry"). "The celebrated singer/songwriter's voice has been labeled everything from 'deadpan' to 'plain' to 'Lou-Reed-gone-Texas,'" says Frank Rabey, "and, as with other Texas songwriting giants like Townes Van Zant and Guy Clark, what McMurtry's singing lacks in overall vocal dynamism and range, it makes up for in uncanny emotional resonance. It's a voice you can trust" (Rabey 1996). McMurtry's low-key

delivery and striking poetic lines remind some listeners of a young Bob Dylan. "James writes like he's lived a lifetime," observed rock-and-roll singer John Mellencamp, who produced *Too Long in the Wasteland,* McMurtry's 1989 debut album.

I hadn't intended
to bend the rules
but whiskey don't make liars
it just makes fools
so I didn't mean to say it
but I meant what I said
too long in the wasteland
too long in the wasteland
must've gone to my head.

McMurtry attended high school at what he called "an esteemed Southern boarding school, real small, kind of rag-tag, way out in the Virginia woods." Then he returned west to Tucson and studied English and Spanish at the University of Arizona, his guitar still at his side. He performed at the Saw Mill Cafe. "I could sort of sing, but I decided I would really play. In those days, I wanted to be a major flat-picker like David Bromberg and Doc Watson. That was before I figured out I didn't really have the speed," he says with typical modesty. "I'm more of an endurance guitarist." Later he would reflect unfavorably on this self-description. "That's one of the stupider things [I've said]. I was selling myself a little short there. Of course, that was '89 when I said that, and I wasn't doing as much: I played pretty good acoustic guitar, but I hadn't really learned how to mess with it" ("James McMurtry").

McMurtry's desire to perform even took him briefly to Talkeetna, Alaska, in the shadow of mighty Mt. McKinley. He then returned to the family homestead outside of Wichita Falls, Texas, and began to refine the songs that would appear on his first album.

During the mid-1980s, James lived in San Antonio, doing odd jobs and performing in the St. Mary's entertainment district. He befriended other musicians there, including talented singer/songwriter Tish Hinojosa, who said of him, "I knew his thing was going to be his own music. . . . He's a private kind of self-motivated person" ("James McMurtry").

"Then in 1987, a friend in San Antonio suggested I get into the New Folk songwriting contest that Rod Kennedy runs in Kerrville." Previous winners at the competition included Nanci Griffith and Lyle Lovett. McMurtry emerged as one of the year's six winners. "I lucked out. I had Ian Tyson [producer], Jim Rooney and the previous year's winner as judges" ("James McMurtry"). That modesty and brevity again.

In 1989 McMurtry headed to Austin and began performing there. At the same time, his father, Larry, was collaborating on a screenplay with John Mellencamp. Larry gave Mellencamp an audiotape of his son's work. The rocker's good ear told him this kid could sing, and with Mellencamp's help James cut his first album.

McMurtry's follow-up album, *Candyland,* appeared from Columbia Records in May 1992. That same year, he received a Country Music Association nomination for Vocal Event of the Year as a part of Buzzin' Cousins. *Where'd You Hide the Body?* followed on Columbia in 1995. Then Columbia rather unceremoniously dumped McMurtry. "The term for the option expired," McMurtry noted laconically, "and they didn't ask for an extension" ("James McMurtry"). He moved to Sugar Hill Records for his next albums, *It Had to Happen* (1997) and *Walk between the Raindrops* (1998).

Some of the places and people James describes evoke images akin to those created by his father in *The Last Picture Show* and other novels. A good example is "Talkin' at the Texaco":

> well, if you're lookin' for a good time
> you're a bit late
> we rolled up the sidewalks
> at a quarter to eight
> it's a small town
> we can't sell you no beer
> it's a small town, so
> may I ask what you're doin' here?

McMurtry works hard at his trade. With characteristic self-deprecation, he says, "There's no real process. There's really nothing I can do to make it happen. There's no technique involved in getting those words out of the air." His gripping stories are not born easily. "Writing is hard and tedious," he says. "It's not the fun part. It's what you do so you can do the other. The fun part is turning up the amp real loud and playin'. Movin' molecules" ("James McMurtry").

References

"James McMurtry." *Artist Direct: http://imusic. artistdirect.com/showcase/contemporary/ jamesmcmurtry.html.*

Ouellette, Dan. "The Rocking Story-Songs of James McMurtry." *Acoustic Guitar,* February 1996.

Rabey, Frank. "A Voice You Can Trust: Texan James McMurtry Hones Honesty in Song." *Asheville Mountain Xpress,* 12 June 1996.

MILLER, ALFRED JACOB

1810–1874

Born to the family of a Baltimore grocer, the artist Alfred Jacob Miller created stunning, visual documentation of the Rocky Mountain West. On an expedition in the summer of 1837, along what would become the Oregon Trail, he made hundreds of sketches that he later painted in with a myriad of watercolors. Miller brilliantly captured what makes the Old West both mythical and alluring. He was the first painter to capture on canvas the horse races, ball games, wrestling, singing, dancing, drinking, and feasting of the annual **rendezvous** (meetings where trappers sold their wares) between Indians and fur traders. He witnessed the thirteenth such annual gathering along the Green River in Wyoming. He was also the first painter to both see and depict the people and landscapes of the Wind River Range and the Rocky Mountains.

Miller showed an avid interest and talent for drawing in his youth. In 1833 he studied painting in both Italy and France. The following year, he rented a studio in Baltimore, where he painted mostly portraits for about two years. Not doing very well, he then moved to New Orleans, where he again set up shop. There, in 1837, William Drummond Stewart, a retired captain of the British army, chanced to see a Miller painting. The adventuresome Scot, taken with Miller's skills, asked the young artist to join him on an expedition to the Rocky Mountains of Wyoming to sketch both the lands and inhabitants. The adventure of Miller's life was about to begin.

During his brief trip along the Oregon Trail, Miller made some 300 sketches of western life. He took a romantic approach to his subject matter, which included genre scenes of Indian men and women. Several Indians even posed for portraits. Miller identified the Indian physique with classical body types and thus depicted them in neoclassicist form. He considered the Indian way of life as one of curiosity, free-spiritedness, and frequent ferociousness—a viewpoint typical of the "noble savage" mythology of the time. Although Miller generally depicted Indians with ennobling grace, he felt considerable ambivalence toward them. He believed in white superiority and thus felt whites were justified in their domination of an "inferior race."

Relying on sketches and memory, Miller painted most of his Indian portraits in his studio after the expedition. He presented the individual in bust format. He only rarely completely filled in the sitter's headdress or costume, which reduces the documentary value of his work. Instead, Miller focused on his subject's facial features and expression, which he powerfully portrayed using a variety of water media and bold orange-red pastel colors. The artist frequently chose who would sit for him based on the beauty of the sitter's face and the perceived goodness of his or her character. Indeed, Miller romanticized his portraits of the American Indian with a soft touch: His subjects serenely and dreamily gaze beyond the viewer as if in reverie. Miller's Indian portraits that exemplify these traits include *Kaw Man; Kansas; Shim-a-co-che, Crow Chief; Kaw Indian;* and *A Young Woman of the Flat Head Tribe.*

Miller's Indian genre scenes also depict the interaction between whites and Indians. *The Trapper's Bride* portrays the coming together of "civilization" and wilderness. An Indian woman at the center of the painting demurely extends her hand to a seated fur trapper, her betrothed. This hazy, romantic painting underscores the popular Indian princess myth, most famously personified in the person of Pocahontas. Another painting that brings together Indian and Anglo is *Laramie's Fort*. The work depicts the fort, with an American flag looming authoritatively high above, teepees, Indians, and frontiersmen. *Advent of the Locomotive in Oregon* also presents the inevitable white encroachment on Indian culture. Miller has a tiny "iron horse" in the distance causing mass panic among Indian people in the foreground.

Miller also sketched and painted native American recreation, interaction with trappers, domestic life, hunting, and warring. He painted many images of Indian women, whose exoticism fascinated him. "Some of the dresses worn were magnificent," he observed, "and although vermilion was worth four dollars per ounce, a lavish use of that article was exhibited on their bodies and faces." He painted women frolicking about, riding horses, reclining, and swimming, either partially clothed or entirely nude. Such works include *Indian Girls Making Toilet, Scene on the River,* and *Indian Girls Swinging.*

Miller's portrayals of Indians during the hunt and at war are highly theatrical and idealistic. He brings his central figure to the forefront by creating a misty atmosphere and by placing the action close to the picture's plane. Although Miller never witnessed Indians at war, he painted several works based on hearsay. Paintings of war and hunting include *Blackfeet on the Warpath* and *Indians Tantalizing a Wounded Buffalo.*

Miller also painted fur trappers, the famous mountain men of western lore. He met western legends, including Kit **Carson** and Jim **Bridger.** His romantic pictures of trappers portray simple lives of men who depended on nature for their livelihood. Miller represented these men in repose, as in *Trappers,* and participating in the rendezvous with Captain Drummond and local Indians, as in *Cavalcade.* The latter work captures the pageantry of the rendezvous, a very important event.

Two final categories of Miller's work are his animal paintings and his landscapes. Deeply interested in the relationship between animals and humans, he often showed men on the hunt *(Buffalo Hunt)* as well as at rest with animals *(Pierre, a Rocky Mountain Trapper).* Miller also painted animal portraits, such as *Buffalo Head,* in which he seemingly lent human characteristics to his renderings of animals. The artist took a picturesque and even playful approach to his landscapes, such as *Lake in Wind River Mountain.* He employed shading and scumbling (a technique in which a painter softens the colors of a painting by rubbing) to create an atmospheric effect. The spontaneous appearance and soft lines that define his landscapes in fact characterize all of Miller's works.

Miller exhibited his first western landscapes in Baltimore in July 1838. The sketches and paintings that he made while exploring the western frontier continued to influence his subsequent works. Over the next 30 years, he painted western scenes almost exclusively. His work failed to attract widespread notice until historian Bernard De Voto utilized several of his works in his 1947 book *Across the Wide Missouri.* Since then, however, Miller's powerful images have become well known. The ethereal quality of his work further romanticized the central characters in a key period in western history: the American Indian and the mountain men during the height of the fur trade, just before its rapid decline. Indeed, Miller effectively captured on canvas the mythical "noble savage" through his nostalgic depictions of a people who would soon vanish and a pristine western landscape that would soon become "civilized."

Today Miller's paintings may be viewed in many collections, including those of the Gilcrease Museum in Tulsa, Oklahoma, or the Joslyn Art Museum in Omaha, Nebraska.

—Jane Veronica Charles Smith

References

Ross, Marvin C. *The West of Alfred Jacob Miller.* Norman: University of Oklahoma Press, 1968.

Troccoli, Joan Carpenter. *Alfred Jacob Miller: Watercolors of the American West.* Tulsa, OK: Thomas Gilcrease Museum Association, 1990.

Tyler, Ronnie C. *Alfred Jacob Miller: Artist on the Oregon Trail.* Fort Worth, TX: Amon Carter Museum of Western Art, 1982.

Source of Further Information

Joslyn Art Museum Web Site: *http://www. joslyn.org.*

MONKEY WRENCH GANG

The Monkey Wrench Gang, the most famous environmental activists of western fiction, sprang from the fertile imagination of writer Edward Abbey (1927–1989). His 1975 novel, *The Monkey Wrench Gang,* recounts the escapades of a diverse band of eco-guerrillas in Utah and Arizona. They use vandalism and an "end justifies the means" morality to attack government and corporate targets ranging from heavy equipment to the Glen Canyon Dam.

The book inspired a host of real-life activists—such as Earth First and the Earth Liberation Front—to move "monkey wrenching" from fiction to action. Earth First introduced itself in 1981 by unfurling a 100-yard-long black plastic streamer that mimicked a deep crack down the face of Glen Canyon Dam, an image from the book's opening pages. The book also inspired other writers, such as Claire Wolfe, author of *101 Things to Do 'til the Revolution: Ideas and Resources for Self-Liberation, Monkey Wrenching, and Preparedness.*

Abbey, born 29 January 1927 in Home, Pennsylvania, left his farm roots as a youngster and hitchhiked west. He found the deserts and canyon lands of the Southwest irresistible. He remained and studied, earning a BA (1951) and an MA (1956) at the University of New Mexico. His master's thesis, "Anarchism and the Morality of Violence," provided an early insight into his philosophy. Abbey worked as a National Park Service ranger and fire lookout, often in solitary locations of the Southwest. His deep, introspective, telluric connection with the desert Southwest emerged powerfully and vividly in his writings, both fiction and nonfiction.

Abbey saw and feared the destruction of natural beauty and of ancient Indian cultures by encroaching industrialization and urbanization. His pro-wilderness, antimodernity viewpoint emerged early in *The Brave Cowboy* (1958), *Desert Solitaire* (1968), *Abbey's Road* (1979), and other books—a total of 17. His hilarious antiheroes of the Monkey Wrench Gang, however, reached the broadest audience with his "save the wilderness" message. And its adroit tone, part Henry David Thoreau, part Hunter Thompson, appeals to a broad readership.

Abbey's alter ego in the novel is George Washington Hayduke, ex–Green Beret medic, anarchist, "wilderness avenger, industrial development saboteur, night-time trouble-maker, barroom brawler, free-time lover." He is passionate and extreme in his likes (bombs, beer, and nature) and in his dislikes (real estate developers, their stakes, bulldozers, and dams). And he is always vulgar. Seldom Seen Smith adds local color as a Mormon riverboat guide, watermelon rancher, and polygamist who woefully neglects his three wives. The most unlikely ecoguerrilla is A. K. (Doc) Sarvis, a wealthy heart specialist with a penchant for burning billboards. "God Bless America: Let's Save Some of It" reads his bumper sticker. Bonnie Abzug rounds out the gang. Sexy, smart, inquisitive, mouthy, the stereotypical Jewish exile from the Bronx, she teams up with Doc. She points out, however, that "she was half WASP (white anglo sexy Protestant); her mother's maiden name was McComb."

The unconventionality and chaos of his character's lives somewhat reflect Abbey's personal life. He married and divorced four times, marrying his final wife, Clarke Cartwright, in 1982, and fathered five children. Humor, often irreverent and sometimes tasteless, abounds. Bonnie keeps her marijuana stash in a tampon tube. Tucson to Flagstaff is a three-six-pack drive.

In addition to the slapstick and raucous humor, however, the book also delivered yet another version of Abbey's unswerving environmental ethic: As he says in the novel, "We can have wilderness without freedom. We can have wilderness without human life at all; but we cannot have freedom without wilderness." The gang also practices nonviolence, at least when it comes to people. Violence is directed against machines and other objects; not against people.

The book was reissued in a 1985 edition and reprinted five years later. HarperPerennial released a twenty-fifth anniversary edition in the spring of 2000. In 1987 a Monkey Wrench Gang Calendar appeared, illustrated by cartoonist Robert Crumb. In 2000 Deric Washburn (author of the screenplays of *The Deerhunter* and *Silent Running*) completed a screenplay based on the novel. Gary Burden is the coproducer and partner on the planned film.

The year after the author's death, *Hayduke Lives!* appeared, a sequel to *The Monkey Wrench Gang*. The old gang teams with Earth First to battle a giant, walking earth mover called Goliath. Abbey also resurrects an anti-Mormon theme, somewhat akin to that in Zane **Grey's *Riders of the Purple Sage.*** Mormon Bishop Dudley Love reprises his role from *The Monkey Wrench Gang*, still aligned with uranium strip miners and other industrial developers. He accepts environmental destruction as necessary to create jobs and thus keep youth from venturing to "California or Salt Lake City (one near as wicked and Godless a place as the other)." Abbey's happy, sometimes crazed band of eco-guerrillas continues to warn of the imminent loss of the West's precious natural heritage.

The gang's influence shows little sign of waning. Judging by the spirited reader comments on Christer Lindh's Internet site, Abbey's Web, the Monkey Wrench Gang continues to inspire the ecologically minded around the globe. One Web site features "An Introduction to Monkey Wrenching: Code of the Eco-Warrior":

Nobody gets hurt. Nobody. Not even yourself.
Don't get caught.
If you get caught you're on your own.
Pass on the cost to the enemy.
Work alone or in a small circle of trusted friends.
Expect no reward.
Keep fit.
No domestic responsibilities.
If married, do not breed.

—Inspired by Ed Abbey's "The Monkey Wrench Gang" (Code of the Eco-Warrior)

Many continue to practice Hayduke's mantra: "Always pull up survey stakes anywhere you find them."

References

Abbey's Web: *http://www.utsidan.se/abbey/*.
Brinkley, Douglas. "Edward Abbey: Critic and Crusader": *http://www.calendarlive.com/calendarlive/books/lat_0123brinkley.htm*.
Code of the Eco-Warrior: *http://www.geocities.com:0080/RainForest/4544/mwinfo.htm*.

MONUMENT VALLEY

This remarkable landscape is located in the Four Corners area of the Southwest, about 175 miles northeast of Flagstaff, Arizona. Straddling the northeast border of Arizona and the southeast border of Utah, Monument Valley sits about a mile above sea level in the southeast portion of the Great Basin Desert. Ancestral home to the Navajos, the heart of the area is preserved as the nearly 30,000-acre Monument Valley Tribal Park.

Some 25 million years ago, a bulge in the earth's crust, called the Monument Valley Uplift, pushed upward, cracking open huge fissures everywhere. Through these openings flowed molten lava from many volcanoes. Thereafter, the forces of wind and water slowly eroded several layers of buildup to reveal the remarkable, otherworldly monoliths, channels, buttes, and spires that now dot the landscape.

As writer Gerald Knowles observed, "Monument Valley is a land of 'room enough and time enough' for all mysteries and theories" (Knowles). Native legends of the place abound. However, shortly after Kit **Carson**'s removal of the Navajos from the valley in the 1860s, a new legend arose: that of the lost silver mine of Monument Valley. Two of Carson's men, Ernest Mitchell and James Merrick, observed the beautiful, bountiful silver jewelry worn by the Navajos. They decided to locate the rich mine where the ore originated. According to

Monument Valley (Photo by Z. Irvin)

legend, they did so. However, wary investors demanded additional ore samples. Thus, acting against the warnings of the Navajo Chief Hoskinnini, they secretly returned to the mine site.

According to legend, Hoskinnini exacted a high price from the trespassers. Merrick died at night below the butte that now carries his name, felled by a Navajo bullet. Mitchell suffered a bullet wound in his side as he ran away from the campfire into the safety of the night. However, morning's light revealed him, hidden in a small crevice. Once he had spent all his ammunition, the Navajos finished him off as well.

To ward off further conflict with whites, the Navajos blamed the men's disappearances on a renegade band of Paiutes. By the early 1880s, lawmen had abandoned the search for the missing men and their rich silver mine. However, other would-be silver miners scoured the region, so that the Navajo *natannis* (chiefs) decided to cover the mine entrance with sand and rock. Thus, the location remains hidden to this day.

It was not silver mines but the silver screen that gave Monument Valley its greatest fame. In 1925 director George B. Seitz filmed the first movie in the valley, *The Vanishing American* (Paramount Productions), starring Richard Dix, Lois Wilson, and Noah Beery Sr. It was director John Ford, however, who brought the valley to the world's attention.

Valley inhabitants Harry Goulding and his wife "Mike" suffered through the Great Depression of the 1930s, as did the Navajo people there. One evening the Gouldings heard over the radio that United Artists was searching for a movie location for a western. The Gouldings gathered a few essentials and drove west along Route 66 to Hollywood.

Ignoring rebuffs from United Artists staff, Harry unfurled two bundles of photographs taken in the valley. One shot in particular, of the magnificent Mittens, caught the eye of the location manager for the movie *Stagecoach*. The next day, director John Ford and the location manager flew out to see Monument Valley for themselves. The site and the director were a perfect match. As actress Maureen O'Hara later observed, "Ford painted a picture every time that camera was turned on." Monument Valley provided a magnificent landscape for him.

Ford then asked Goulding whether he could arrange logistics for the hundred people who would take part in the filming, which was to begin in only three days. Goulding sprang into action, aided by a check from Ford for $5,000. Along with Goulding, Hosteen Tso, a Navajo medicine man, played an important role in the filming of *Stagecoach*. Affectionately called "Fatso" by Ford, he became a living legend on the set. During the first week of shooting, Ford requested that billowing clouds follow the fast-moving stagecoach. Seemingly at the medicine man's bidding, a large cluster of fast-moving clouds appeared for the next day's shooting. Each afternoon, Hosteen Tso and Ford would consult in a room above Goulding's Trading Post on the weather that Ford needed for the next day's shooting.

Another time, Ford needed a sandstorm to heighten the drama of the stagecoach journey. Goulding interrupted lunch the next day to announce an upcoming sandstorm and quickly led the crew to a ridge where they could film it. But Tso's greatest feat came in early October, when Ford wistfully inquired about snow. It generally did not snow in the valley for another two months. However, when the director awoke the following morning, he looked eastward over a valley blanketed in snow. "My goodness, Harry, I owe you an apology!" said Ford. "I thought you were just kidding me about that old medicine man!" *Stagecoach*, released in 1939, made John Wayne, as the Ringo Kid, a star.

Ford returned repeatedly to the landscape he came to love. In 1946 he shot *My Darling Clementine* there. Two years later, he opened his **cavalry trilogy** with *Fort Apache*, and in 1949 he shot *She Wore a Yellow Ribbon*. In 1956 he made one of his finest films, *The Searchers*, followed four years later by *Sergeant Rutledge*. He shot his final feature film, *Cheyenne Autumn*, at Monument Valley in 1964. His final visit came in 1971, when he filmed a documentary about the place that had figured so prominently in his career.

Navajos appeared in Ford's films, but another Monument Valley legend arose during World War II. The U.S. military enlisted the help of some 450 Navajo "code talkers" to transmit messages in the Pacific theater. The Japanese never broke the "code," which was the Navajo language. The project remained classified until 1968, when the world finally learned of the secret Navajo contribution to the war effort.

Inspired by the grandeur of Ford's films, other directors flocked to the valley to shoot an amazing range of movies. In 1962 George Marshall filmed the epic *How the West Was Won* (Metro-Goldwyn-

Mayer). In 1968 Stanley Kubrik brought the area's incredible scenery into *2001: A Space Odyssey.* The following year brought a very different script and cast to the valley as Dennis Hopper and Peter Fonda worked on the cult classic *Easy Rider.* That same year brought Peter's father Henry Fonda and a new type of western to Monument Valley as Sergio Leone made his dark, menacing *Once upon a Time in the West.*

An amazing range of stars and films followed: *Electra Glide in Blue* (1973), Clint Eastwood's *The Eiger Sanction* (1975), *National Lampoon's Vacation* (1983), and Robert Zemeckis with *Back to the Future II* and *III* (1989, 1990) as well as the blockbuster *Forrest Gump* (1993).

Today Monument Valley retains its mythical hold on Navajos and whites. The Moab to Monument Valley Film Commission promotes filming in the region from southern Utah to northern New Mexico. Actor John Wayne, who contributed so much to the place's legendary status, perhaps best explained its power. In 1961 someone asked Wayne why *The Comancheros* was being filmed in the Moab area. "TV you can make on the back lot," said the Duke, "but for the big screen, for the real outdoor dramas, you have to do it where God put the West . . . and there is no better example of this than around Moab" (Moab to Monument Valley Film Commission).

References

Knowles, Gerald. Essays: *http://www.unink. com/passages/Monument-Valley/.*

Moab to Monument Valley Film Commission: *http://www.moab.net/moabfilm/.*

MORMONISM UNVEILED

See Lee, John Doyle

MORMONS

See Grey, Zane; Lee, John Doyle; Monkey Wrench Gang; Rockwell, Orrin Porter; Young, Ann Eliza Webb

MOUNT SAINT HELENS

See Truman, Harry R.

MOUNTAIN MEADOWS MASSACRE

See Lee, John Doyle

MOUNTAIN OYSTERS

At roundup, cowboys enjoyed a delicacy variously called "calf fries," "mountain oysters," or "prairie oysters." Whatever the term, these fried or roasted calves' testicles made gourmet eating for ranch folk. Obviously, a large number of these prize delicacies could be gathered when hands castrated calves during roundup. Cowboys attributed to calf fries an amazing number of benefits. Some considered them a wonderful elixir or aphrodisiac.

As with many unusual foods, mountain oysters generated considerable folklore.

Carol Taylor of the Harrison Public Library in Greenville, Texas, recalls the clear gender lines that divided life on the traditional ranch. These gendered divides even governed choices of food, in particular calf fries:

I cannot cite any documentation as to the effects of ingesting calf fries, but I can relate a true story. My grandfather (b. 1892 in Indian Territory) was a rancher in north Texas for over 50 years. The ranch had been in the same family for three generations. When it was time to work cattle in the summer, my female cousin and I were occupied in the house by our grandmother (b. 1896). My brother, however, was put on a horse and helped with roundup and the requisite chores associated with this yearly event. At lunch, my grandmother would fry the calf fries, which look like fried oysters. Only men were allowed to eat them. My cousin and I were told that they were not acceptable for young ladies. This was in the late 1950s. Recently I located a short memoir that my grandfather's sister had written. She, too, indicated that women were never around when cattle were worked. In fact, her memory of the corral was in the wrong place on the ranch. I am sure the mention of calf fries was unheard of in her day and age.

The preparation of calf fries at branding time might consist of nothing more than tossing the testicles into the branding fire and waiting for them to pop open, ready to eat. Stella Hughes, in *Chuck Wagon Cookin',* offers a slightly more elaborate recipe. She suggests soaking the oysters in salt water for an hour and then drying them. The oysters are then seasoned, rolled in flour or cornmeal, and fried in hot grease until crisp—a great end to a long day of branding. Another variant suggests soaking the harvest in buttermilk instead of salt water.

Garry's Home Cookin' Web site offers an even more complete recipe for "Rocky Mountain Oysters on the Half Shell."

Ingredients:
  2 pounds bull testicles*
  1 cup flour
  1/4 cup cornmeal
  1 cup red wine
  salt
  black pepper
  garlic powder
  Louisiana Hot Sauce
  cooking oil**

*aka: calf fries, Rocky Mountain Oysters (sheep or turkey testicles may be used also)

**pure hog lard is the best, but a mixture of 60% peanut oil and 40% vegetable oil will do

With a very sharp knife, split the tough skin-like muscle that surrounds each "oyster." Remove the skin. Set "oysters" into a pan with enough salt water to cover them for one hour (this takes out some of the blood). Drain. Transfer "oysters" to large pot. Add enough water to float "oysters" and a generous tablespoon of vinegar. Parboil, drain and rinse. Let cool and slice each "oyster" into 1/4 inch thick ovals. Sprinkle salt and pepper on both sides of sliced "oyster" to taste.

Mix flour, cornmeal and some garlic powder to taste in a bowl. Roll each "oyster" slice into this dry mixture. Dip into milk. Dip into dry mixture. Dip into wine quickly (you may repeat the procedure if a thicker crust is desired). Place each "oyster" into hot cooking oil.

Add Louisiana Hot Sauce to cooking oil (go wild with it, but watch out for repercussions—hot splashes). Cook until golden brown or tender, and remove with a wire mesh strainer (the longer they cook, the tougher they get).

Serve in one of those cardboard beer cartons that four six packs come in, layered with paper towels. Eat 'em, don't wait for nothin'! Chase with beer. Variations include serving cooked "oysters" on a real oyster half shell with a sprig of parsley and a few drops of lemon juice. (Garry's Home Cookin' Web Site)

Maria Elena Raymond reports on the popularity of this delicacy in Missouri several decades ago and on a new California variation:

It was a great treat when deep-fried testicles were offered on restaurant menus. I remember going to a weekend blowout in the Ozarks in the early 1970s. Big oil drums full of hot grease were used and fried testicles were the main reason everyone was there (aside from the beer and a lake). Now here in the 1990s in Northern California the big deal is always turkey testicles. The turkey farms take orders months ahead of time (true) for the testicles long before anyone orders their turkeys for holidays. Locally the testicles are sold right at the farms . . . never

make it to the stores. I can say they taste great, but now a low-fat person, I just sauté them in olive oil w/a little garlic and mushrooms. Good stuff!

Calgary, Alberta, Canada restaurateur Stuart Allan serves several varieties at his Bottlescrew Bill's English Pub and Buzzard's Cowboy Cuisine. In 1996 he hosted the third annual Testicle Festival there. Dishes include Au Naturel (pan-fried in beer, herbs, and garlic butter), Mixed Nuts (coated in crushed nuts and smothered in a rum-butter sauce), and Buckaroo Balls (served with three kinds of beans and bacon). "People expect them to be very powerfully flavoured and pungent," says Allen, "but they're very mild and easily overpowered by the sauces."

Allan admits that the delicacy does not appear very appetizing in its natural state. "You wouldn't want to look at it before it's skinned," he says, but "most people, once they get their mind past what it is, actually enjoy it" ("Going Nuts over Prairie Oysters").

Photographer Lynn Donaldson enjoyed an oyster feed at the Jersey Lilly Saloon in Ingnomar, Montana. She recorded the event in photographs as the "Rocky Mountain Oyster Feed." As one ranch wife told her, "Honey, you won't hear the word 'testicle' come out of one of these guys' mouths. They call em 'nuts' or 'fries'" (Donaldson 2000). Not all Montanans shy away from the *t* word. Rock Creek Lodge outside of Clinton hosts an annual Testicle Festival the third week of September. Rod Lincoln created the event in the mid-1980s. It has grown from 300 people to more than 8,200. Lincoln serves his guests some

4,500 pounds of beer-marinated, breaded, deep-fried bull testicles (Rod Lincoln's Web Site).

Mountain oysters have made their way into western popular culture. One Colorado band calls itself the Rocky Mountain Oysters. Surely the most famous and humorous cultural depiction of this western delicacy is the poem "The Oyster," written by cowboy humorist and one-time large-animal veterinarian Baxter Black (*see also* **cowboy poetry**):

The sign upon the cafe wall said OYSTERS:
    FIFTY CENTS.
"How quaint," the blue-eyed sweetheart
    said, with some bewilderance.
"I didn't know they served such fare out
    here upon the plain?"
"Oh, sure," her cowboy date replied,
    "We're really quite urbane."
"I would guess they're Chesapeake or
    Blue Point, don't you think?"
"No ma'am, they're mostly Hereford
    cross . . . and usually they're pink.
But I've been cold, so cold myself,
    what you say could be true
And if a man looked close enough,
    their points could sure be blue!"
She said, "I gather them myself out on the
    bay alone.
I pluck them from the murky depths and
    smash them with a stone!"
The cowboy winced imagining a calf with
    her beneath.
"Me, I use a pocket knife and yank 'em
    with my teeth."
"Oh, my," she said, "you animal!
    How crude and unrefined!
Your masculine assertiveness sends shivers
    up my spine!
But I prefer a butcher knife too dull to
    really cut.

I wedge it in on either side and crack it
    like a nut.
I pry them out. If they resist, sometimes I
    use the pliers
Or even Grandpa's pruning shears if that's
    what it requires!"
The hair stood on the cowboy's neck.
    His stomach did a whirl.
He'd never heard such grizzly talk,
    especially from a girl!
"I like them fresh," the sweetheart said and
    laid her menu down,
Then ordered oysters for them both when
    the waiter came around.
The cowboy smiled gamely, though her
    words stuck in his craw
But he finally fainted dead away when she
    said "I'll have mine raw!"

References

Donaldson, Lynn. "Rocky Mountain Oyster Feed." *Cowboys & Indians,* November 2000, 58–66.
Garry's Home Cookin' Web Site: *http://texascooking.netrelief.com/recipes/oysters.htm.*
Hughes, Stella. *Chuck Wagon Cookin'.* Tucson: University of Arizona Press, 1974.
"Going Nuts over Prairie Oysters." *Alberta Report/Western Report,* August 5, 1996, 23–26.
Rod Lincoln's Web Site: *http://www.testyfesty.com/.* (Parental alert: The site includes photos of nude party-goers.)

MOVIE SETS

The West's incredible natural beauty combined with the rise of Hollywood as the world's film capital meant that many movies, western and otherwise, would be shot in the region. Over time, natural settings, like **Monument Valley,** have become movie icons. However, many movie sets have also been constructed in various places and thus become familiar to generations of viewers.

Old Tucson came to life in 1939 when Columbia Pictures built a replica of the town as it had looked during the 1860s. The film *Tucson,* starring William Holden and Jean Arthur, moved westerns to a much greater level of realism than had been achieved on earlier indoor studio sets.

However, the movie set quickly became a ghost town, with only occasional filming done there. In 1945 Bing Crosby and Ingrid Bergman came to town in *The Bells of St. Mary's,* followed five years later by Jimmy Stewart in *Winchester 73.* Ironically, the classic *Gunfight at the OK Corral,* the film that made Tombstone famous, was filmed at Old Tucson in 1956.

In 1960 Old Tucson reopened, adding a family fun park to its movie set. From 1959 to 1970, John Wayne filmed four movies there, *Rio Bravo, McClintock, El Dorado,* and *Rio Lobo.* He added more buildings for each film, including a saloon, bank, hotel, cantina, and jail. Many other famous film presentations of the mythical West would follow, more than 300 total. Films shot at Old Tucson include Disney's *Hawmps!* (1975), based on the army's **camel corps;** *The Outlaw Josey Wales* (1976), with Clint **Eastwood;** *Tom Horn* (1979), with Steve McQueen; and ***Calamity Jane*** (1983), with Jane Alexander. The popular TV series *The Young Riders* (1989–1991), based on the **Pony Express,** was also filmed there. In 1993 Old Tucson again hosted the gunfights of the OK Corral for the filming of *Tombstone.*

In 1995 disaster struck when an arsonist's flames destroyed nearly half of Old Tucson. Restoration required 18 months and $13 million. Today, the town features historic storytelling, rock concerts, and other activities in addition to filmmaking.

Tombstone, Arizona, "the town too tough to die," served as the site for the West's most famous gunfight. In October 1881, the **Earp brothers** and Doc Holliday shot it out with the Clantons and McLaurys at the OK Corral. Although Tombstone did not become a major site for filming movies, the gunfight is reenacted daily on the streets of Tombstone, to the thrill of tourists filming with their video cameras. The Boot Hill Museum and shoot-outs on Front Street also entertain visitors to another famous Old West town, Dodge City, Kansas.

Several western film pioneers joined together in 1946 to create Pioneertown, located in a scenic desert spot about 130 miles east of Hollywood. Actor Dick Curtis discovered the spot and convinced 17 other investors to back the creation of a movie ranch, along with homes, resorts, and dude ranches. Roy **Rogers,** the Sons of the Pioneers, Russell Hayden, Frank McDonald, Tommy Carr, Terry Frost, and Bud Abbott each invested $500 to purchase 32,000 acres, the entire valley surrounding Pioneertown. After dropping the original name (Rogersville), the movie town became Pioneertown, honoring the famous singing group.

During the 1940s and '50s, leading western stars filmed TV and movie productions at Pioneertown. The town hosted programs featuring Gene **Autry,** the Cisco Kid, Annie **Oakley,** Buffalo Bill Jr., Judge Roy **Bean,** and many more.

In 1927 Paramount Pictures purchased 2,400 acres of Rancho Las Virgenes at Agoura Hills, California, some 35 miles north of Los Angeles. From the 1920s through the early 1950s, the studio shot hundreds of westerns there, framed by the rugged Santa Monica Mountains.

William Hertz, a western movie buff, bought the site in 1953 and built a permanent set using original Paramount props. He sold the ranch in 1955, and it was seldom again used for filming. In 1970 the location became known as Paramount Ranch. In 1980 the National Park Service paid $6 million for the property and again restored the Old West town for the benefit of filmmakers and tourists.

Despite having plastic windows, fiberglass log cabins, and hard-shelled foam "stone" fireplaces, the location looks authentic on film. In the early 1990s Paramount Ranch enjoyed a revival when it became a nineteenth-century Colorado mining town, home to the popular CBS-TV series *Dr. Quinn, Medicine Woman,* starring Jane Seymour.

Other photogenic western locations have also enticed film directors. The rugged desert and mountain scenery of Paria Canyon, which lies between Kanab, Utah, and Page, Arizona, provided a backdrop for many B-westerns of the 1940s. The town of Kanab is trying to revive the movie and tourist industries. Buildings and sites include the usual: a mining camp with an authentic mine, saloon, hotel, jail, and assay and blacksmith shops. Likewise Gammons Gulch in Pomerene, Arizona, seeks to lure a new generation of filmmakers to its sets. The Old West may be gone, but the public's thirst for mythical sites reflecting life there seems insatiable.

References

Old Tucson Web Site: *http://www.oldtucson. com.*
Tombstone, Arizona, Web Site: *http://www. cityoftombstone.com.*

MUFFLER MEN

See Stone, Glenn

MURIETA, JOAQUÍN

Ca. 1830–1853, California social bandit. *See* Zorro

MUSTANG RANCH, NEVADA

One of the most notorious locales in the West, the Mustang Ranch stood as a fixture in the Nevada desert for more than 30 years. The ranch, a legal brothel, and its owner and founder, Joe Conforte, a one-time cab driver, became living legends. Customers from all corners of the United States and other countries frequented the establishment. At any one time, Conforte employed from 40 to 100 "working girls." Even long after its closing, the fame and myths surrounding the fabled ranch continue to permeate popular culture.

The Mustang Ranch first opened its

doors in 1955, occupying some 440 acres outside of Reno. In its earliest days, a tangle of tacked-together trailers housed all the activities. Arsonists twice burned Conforte's business to the ground. However, the ranch at this time generated more than 25 percent of the county's budget, giving its owner considerable political clout. He established enemies who would have loved to see him go under.

In 1971 Conforte won a court case against the State of Nevada that legalized prostitution. During the 1970s he spent more than a million dollars on the Mustang Ranch, aiming to create an establishment with class. He used the House of All Nations, a brothel in Paris, France, as his model. In one room, he created a replica of the legendary Le Train Bleu to Monte Carlo, complete with full sound effects. Another room boasted stained-glass windows, organ music, and "working girls" dressed in nun's habits.

The new Mustang Ranch opened its doors in 1979; its main feature was the Orgy Room, for less-sophisticated fantasies. Soon after, the ranch became a household name all over the Southwest. Despite his millions of dollars in earnings, however, Conforte refused to pay taxes. In March 1981 he posted a $200,000 bail after his arrest for bribing a district attorney in Lyon County. Soon after, he paid another $40,000 bond for tax evasion. While appealing his conviction for tax evasion and its 20-year prison sentence, he fled to Brazil, breaking his bond and bail.

Several months later, Hank Greenspun, an attorney for Conforte, contacted the FBI and agreed to have Conforte testify in a trial against Judge Harry Claiborne of Reno. Judge Claiborne hated the FBI's sting tactics and often ruled against the Bureau. Consequently, FBI agents, with the help of Conforte, concocted a case against the judge, alleging he had accepted a bribe from Conforte. However, because the FBI gave Conforte faulty information concerning the fake bribe, the frame failed, and the court dropped all charges against Claiborne.

In 1990, after Conforte had accumulated some $13 million in debt for back taxes, the federal government seized the Mustang Ranch. After a brief attempt to maintain the ranch and to send all its profits to the government to pay Conforte's debt, the establishment and all of its property went on the auction block. When all was said and done, the government made a little more than $2 million from the sale of items ranging from nude paintings to cartons of condoms to toilet seats. The ranch itself went to a lawyer named Victor Perry, who represented an anonymous client. The attorney would not disclose the name of his client, but Perry happens to be the brother of Conforte's lawyer, opening many intriguing possibilities for the future of the Mustang Ranch.

Perhaps the most controversial event involving the Mustang Ranch is the murder of Oscar Bonavena, a heavyweight boxer from South America. The talented fighter had taken on such greats as Joe Frazier and Muhammad Ali. Conforte liked Bonavena and believed he could help the fighter. In the late 1960s Conforte brought Bonavena to the ranch, where Conforte's wife, Sally, and the fighter immediately fell in love. Sally doted on the South American, which suited Conforte perfectly, as he now had more time to sample the wares of his business.

In 1979, at the grand opening of the new Mustang Ranch, Conforte heard that Bonavena had said casually to a visitor, "How do you like my new joint?" Conforte had no problem with the sexual relationship between the boxer and Sally, but he would not stand for his control being threatened. He ordered both of them off the ranch. After several days, Sally returned to the ranch to pick up a few things, and despite her protests, Bonavena accompanied her. After they had arrived, a rifle shot rang out, and a high-velocity bullet shattered the fighter's heart. Conflicting stories abound, although one thing is certain: Ross Brymer, Conforte's number-two bodyguard, pulled the trigger.

Conforte claimed that Bonavena had come to the ranch to kill him, and indeed, authorities discovered a pistol under the fighter's body. Later, however, Lloyd McNulty, chief of security for the Mustang Ranch, confessed that the gun had accidentally slipped out of his belt when he bent over. Throughout the investigation, witnesses disappeared, and others were too afraid to testify. Brymer received a two-year sentence for voluntary manslaughter, and Conforte got off completely unscathed.

Stories of the fabled Mustang Ranch have spread across the nation. Hundreds of adult entertainment clubs now go by the name "Mustang Ranch." Automobile repair shops specializing in the repair of the Ford Mustang car use the same name. The classic song "Mustang Sally" by Wilson Pickett contains many thinly veiled references to the notorious ranch.

Currently in Nevada, a new brothel is open for business in the smaller of the two buildings that once comprised the Mustang Ranch. Tales from those who once did business at the ranch help keep the memory and myth alive. Conforte had hoped to return to the brothel, but as of late 1999 he remained in hiding, reportedly in South America. The lawyer who represented him, Peter A. Perry, was slapped with a $20,000 fine, six months of community confinement, an equal amount of home confinement, and 100 hours of community service. The ranch's checkered history continues.

–Daniel C. Gunter III

References

Conrad, H., and N. Mauskopf. "Sex and Taxes." *Rolling Stone,* 18 April 1991, 85.

Cruickshank, Douglas. "Last Roundup at the Mustang Ranch." *Salon.com,* 12 August 1999.

NEWTON BOYS

Between 1919 and 1924, Willis, Dock, Jess, and Joe Newton robbed more than 60 banks and six trains, making them the most successful bank and train robbers in American history. Growing up under trying conditions in the impoverished town of Uvalde, Texas, these self-acclaimed "cowboys" initially earned mediocre livings as bronco busters and cotton farmers. The fraternal band did not conform to the stereotype of the traditional western bad man. Most witnesses to their crimes remembered their very "mannerly and congenial" attitude. In the crime-ridden setting of the 1920s, the Newton brothers meshed the chivalry of the cowboy with the thrill of the Texas outlaw, thus creating their own original brand of western antihero.

Before forming the gang in 1919, both Dock and Willis had served time behind bars. Dock spent ten years in the state penitentiary for stealing cotton and then trying to escape several times. Willis served a short stint for robbing his first train with a fellow cotton picker. He received a pardon by forging a petition with signatures from a sheriff, a judge, and 60 other inmates. While serving his short prison term, Willis began thinking about robbing banks. In his mind, stealing from banks served a noble social purpose, which involved "hurtin'" the banks and insurance companies that had "stole" the money from the "poor farmer." Willis did not see a right or wrong side of the law, because government and police officials comprised a corrupt, bribe-taking justice system.

Willis tried to organize partnerships with former inmates, but he soon realized that their habits, which included excessive drinking and "blabbering," did not suit the line of work. In considering what candidates might make reliable accomplices, Willis thought of his own brothers. He soon set up headquarters at a hotel in Tulsa, Oklahoma, and wrote to his brothers Jess and Joe. Realizing the two younger brothers would be reluctant to join a crime operation, Willis simply sent them two $20 bills and said he had a job for them. The two brothers arrived in Tulsa with saddles and spurs, expecting jobs busting broncos, their true love. Willis laughed and said, "Yeah, I got a job for you, but it ain't that kind of a job" (Newton and Newton 1994). He soon convinced Jess, Joe, and Dock, fresh out of the penitentiary, to join him. Finally assembled, the partners embarked on a robbing spree that racked up numbers unprecedented in the history of crime.

The brothers' efficiency greatly contributed to their success. They hit the banks in the fall and winter to catch freshly deposited autumn harvest revenues. They always used the fastest, most durable cars they could find in case a quick getaway was required or a car chase ensued. They struck at night during subfreezing temperatures to ensure that no one would be roaming the streets. In between hits, Willis spent most of his time studying bank security, searching for the next susceptible target. Finally, and most important, the Newton brothers mastered the art of breaking into bank safes.

Brentwood Glasscock, an early accomplice of Willis's, had taught him to use nitroglycerin detonated by a dynamite cap that would literally "peel off" the door to the safe. This quick nitro-method, however, worked on safes with square doors, most common to small-town banks. Most big-city banks had upgraded to safes with more-secure, round doors by the 1920s. Denied the richer, bigger targets, the Newtons hit banks in small towns throughout the Midwest, from west Texas all the way to Canada.

Many of the stories surrounding the Newton robberies have been mythologized and exaggerated to suit the glamour associated with the archetypal "cowboy outlaw" or social bandit. For instance, the gang is credited with twice having blown safes in two banks the same night: once in Hondo, Texas, and again in Spencer, Indiana. Another story says the Newtons robbed couriers in Toronto, Canada, as they carried big satchels of cash from the bank to the clearinghouse at midday. When the "crazy Canucks" refused to release the satchels, the gang had to shoot several of them. According to legend, however, the Newtons never fatally shot anyone.

The biggest heist in their career turned out to be their last. On 12 June 1924, in the tiny crossroads of Rondout, Illinois, 30 miles north of Chicago, they pulled off the largest train holdup in American history. An insider in the U.S. Postal Service tipped off the boys on the time the secret mail train would reach Rondout. As a result, the gang made off with more than $3 million in negotiable bonds and diamonds.

In the confusion of the robbery, however, an accomplice who was not a Newton mistook Dock for an officer and shot him six times with a .45-caliber handgun. The brothers had to take Dock to town, where an underground Mafia doctor treated him. Supposedly, the Mafia tipped off the police because the Texas cowboys had infringed on their turf. Miraculously, Dock survived, only to be apprehended along with Willis and Joe. Jess escaped to Mexico, but a wily undercover **Texas Ranger** later caught him. The savvy lawman lured Jess back into Texas by betting him he couldn't break one of the Rangers' broncs—a bet Jess couldn't resist.

The Newton boys' luck held. The postal inspector who tipped them off took the major rap, and none of the brothers received a major sentence. The judge treated them leniently because of their gracious apology and because they told several humorous and entertaining stories about their crimes. Jess, for example, stated that while holding the train engineer at Rondout at gunpoint, he had asked him, "Ain't this a helluva way to make a livin'?"

If the Newton brothers were indeed so successful, why have they not been immortalized with the likes of **Billy the Kid** and Bonnie and Clyde? One reason is that the criminal history of the 1920s is already filled with larger-than-life characters, such as Al Capone, and with the many bootlegging rings active during Prohibition. Perhaps there is not enough room for the exploits of "mannerly cowboy" bank robbers from Texas. However, **Pretty Boy Floyd** managed to establish a reputation for being well-mannered and a friend of the poor. Another reason may be that the Newton boys killed no one. Asked later in his life about Bonnie and Clyde, Willis Newton snorted in disgust and said, "Silly kids. Didn't rob nothin' except fillin' stations and small places like that . . . spoilin' for a fight with the law, sooner or later they was bound to get themselves killed." The Newton brothers didn't want to be remembered as bank robbers. According to Willis, "We was just businessmen like doctors and lawyers and storekeepers. Robbin' banks and trains was our business, maximizing profit and minimizing risk" (Newton and Newton 1994).

In 1968, at the age of 77, Dock Newton was arrested trying to rob one last bank in Rowena, Texas. The police believed that Willis was driving the getaway car, but he called an hour later from Mexico with an alibi. In 1973 a Texas author named Claude Stanush met Willis and Joe and began transcribing their stories, which he published in 1994 as *The Newton Boys: Portrait of an Outlaw Gang*. In 1980, at the age of 79, Joe Newton appeared on Johnny Carson's *Tonight Show,* where his exuberance and storytelling enthralled the host and audience. Joe, the last surviving brother, died in 1989.

In 1994 a motion picture, *The Newton Boys,* based on Stanush's book, hit the box office and enjoyed major Hollywood success. With a dramatic flavor and humorous tone, the movie brought long-overdue attention to the Newton brothers. The movie's slogan said it best: "History's about to catch up with America's most successful Outlaws."

—Andrew Mebane Southerland

References

Newton, Joe, and Willis Newton (as told to Claude Stanush and David Middleton). *The Newton Boys: A Portrait of an Outlaw Gang.* Austin, TX: State House Press, 1994.

Stanush, Claude. "Every Time a Bank Was Robbed, They Thought It Was Us." *Smithsonian* 24, no. 10 (1994): 74–83.

OAKLEY, ANNIE

1860–1926

Born into poverty as Phoebe Ann Moses (or Mosey), Annie grew up on a poor farm in Darke County, Ohio. By age seven, she had learned to trap birds and small game for food. Forced to work for unscrupulous employers while still a child, Annie suffered privation and abuse. But she developed strength of character and many survival skills, including the ability to shoot accurately. At 15 she bested marksman Frank E. Butler in a shooting competition. He held no grudge; they married the following year and began performing together.

In 1885 Butler and Oakley joined Buffalo Bill **Cody**'s Wild West Show. Oakley, five feet tall and weighing about 100 pounds, would spend the next 17 years as a star performer in Cody's show. She shot an estimated 40,000 rounds per year practicing and performing. Another famous cast member, Chief Sitting Bull,

adopted her and gave her the nickname "Little Sure Shot."

A serious injury from a 1901 train wreck and several operations slowed but did not stop her. She continued to perform until the early 1920s, when ill health finally defeated her. Oakley and her husband died within three weeks of each other, and both are buried in the Brock Cemetery in Darke County.

Like many legendary westerners, Oakley played a prominent role in creating her own legend. In her autobiography, she gives her birth date as 1866, thereby shaving six years from her age. She gives her legal name as Phoebe Ann Oakley Mozee. The mythmaking would continue well after her justifiably legendary shooting exhibitions had ended. Only one year after her death, the first biography of her appeared: *Annie Oakley: Woman at Arms,* by Courtney Ryley Cooper. The first film version of her life, *Annie Oakley* (1935), starring Barbara Stanwyck, drew heavily on the Cooper biography.

In 1946 Oakley's niece, Fern Campbell Swartwout, published *Missie: An Historical Biography of Annie Oakley.* In May of the same year, the irrepressible Ethel Merman opened in the Rogers and Hammerstein musical production *Annie Get Your Gun.* Merman's Annie, like the woman portrayed by Swartwout, was a more feminine than western figure, dressed in a fringed, sequined suit with matching boots, hat, and gloves. Fans and reviewers loved the production, which ran on Broadway for three years. In 1947 Mary Martin took the show on the road and later to **television.**

In 1948 Oakley rode even further into American popular culture, appearing in a comic book. In this incarnation, a blow on the head turned the singing cowgirl Dale Evans into Annie Oakley. As the "Two-Gun Terror of the West," she cleaned up a gang of outlaws and the town of "Boom City" to boot. In 1950 Betty Hutton and Howard Keel starred in the MGM film version of *Annie Get Your Gun.* This treatment continued to portray Oakley as feminine and cuddly, not as the strong, independent, athletic person she was in reality. Many similarly romanticized portrayals would follow in fictional literature, film, and television.

The historical Oakley, as opposed to the romanticized image, reappeared in the 1980s. Several writers, including Isabelle Sayer and R. Douglas Hurt, presented versions of her life and character more in line with historical evidence. Actress Jamie Lee Curtis brought an accurate depiction to television in a 1985 portrayal for *Tall Tales and Legends.* Once again, Oakley's independence, strength, and western persona emerged.

Oakley remains an important cultural

Annie Oakley (Library of Congress)

icon. In 1992 actor Keith Carradine starred in a 30-minute Rabbit Ears Production as Will Rogers. As part of the performance, he accurately retells the story of Oakley's life. Los Lobos added a rollicking musical score. Perhaps the true benchmark of making it as a cultural icon: Oakley has her own line of namesake fragrances for men and women, fragrances "true to the spirit that brought romance to the West." Oakley memorabilia continue to command high prices. Teri Dellapina, a woman from Cary, North Carolina, inherited an old photo album from her grandmother. It included autographed pictures of Buffalo Bill Cody and Annie Oakley. In 1996 the former was appraised at $2,000; the latter, at $11,500. Oakley still commands respect.

Historian Glenda Riley has crafted the most complete and accurate account yet of Oakley's life: her 1994 book *The Life and Legacy of Annie Oakley.* "In truth," concludes Riley, "Annie Oakley became a westerner by affinity rather than by birth, and she created a model western woman. As a result, she has become a western heroine for all time—she has proven as enduring as the West itself."

References

Havinghurst, Walter. *Annie Oakley of the Wild West.* Lincoln: University of Nebraska Press, 1954, 1992.

Kasper, Shirl. *Annie Oakley.* Norman: University of Oklahoma Press, 1992.

Riley, Glenda. *The Life and Legacy of Annie Oakley.* Norman: University of Oklahoma Press, 1994.

Vonada, Damaine. "Annie Oakley Was More than 'a Crack Shot in Petticoats.'" *Smithsonian* 21, no. 6 (1990): 131–148.

OK CORRAL

See Earp Brothers

OLD TUCSON

See Movie Sets

OUTLAW, THE

Motion picture makers have long viewed westerns as an important category. In the 1930s and '40s, Westerns, mostly B-rate films, played at theaters across the country. *The Outlaw,* a 1943 western produced and directed by Howard **Hughes**, enjoyed widespread acclaim from the public. Its appeal, however, came not from a superior plot or acting but rather from the bustline of its star, young Jane Russell.

The plot centers on the relationship between Doc Holliday (veteran actor Walter Huston) and **Billy the Kid** (newcomer Jack Beutel) after Holliday discovers that Billy possesses Doc's stolen horse. This relationship grows as the two share several adventures together. Their friendship creates turmoil and conflict, which provides the thin foundation for the film's plot. A variety of forces that attempt to pull these would-be companions apart manifest themselves in the supporting characters, famed lawman Pat Garrett (Thomas Mitchell) and Rio (portrayed by Jane Russell).

Pat Garrett, at the opening of the movie, considers himself a close friend of Doc Holliday. Consequently, he tries to reclaim the stolen horse for his friend. Once it appears that Holliday and Billy respect each other, Garrett flies into a rage. The rumors regarding the exploits of Billy the Kid, including all the sheriffs he has murdered, have reached Garrett. Under a combination of pressures, the famed lawman eventually snaps.

One of the most memorable moments of the film occurs in a little cantina. A trap for Billy is set; however, the wily outlaw discovers it and kills his assailant. Garrett storms in to arrest the Kid, but Doc prevents it. An angry Garrett opens fire on Billy, severely wounding him. After finding refuge at his girlfriend Rio's home, Doc leaves Billy to heal and leads

Garrett and the posse on a wild goose chase through the wilderness. He further alienates Garrett by firing on the posse at several different points.

Eventually, a second confrontation arises between Garrett, Holliday, and Billy. In a fit of rage, the officer kills his old friend. At the conclusion of the film, Garrett attempts to trick Billy one last time, but he is foiled and left tied to a fence post. Although Garrett's role is central to the plot, Rio provides the real turbulence in the film.

Russell's character Rio generated most of the attention garnered by the film. Although the sexual overtones provided by Rio increased public interest in the movie, these same events destroy what little plot the movie originally contained. In her first appearance, Billy rapes her in a barn, after her unsuccessful attempt to shoot him for allegedly killing her father. Despite the rape, she accepts the responsibility to nurse Billy after he has been shot in the cantina. She undresses and climbs into bed with him to "warm him up."

In another memorable scene, Doc and Billy argue over which is more valuable, a woman or a horse. They agree, to nobody's surprise, that a horse represents a man's true wealth. Finally, after the viewer has been tortured enough, there is a brief romantic, nonsexual scene in which Rio climbs onto a horse with Billy and rides into the desert. Russell's "character" contributes nothing more than sex appeal to the film.

For Howard Hughes, the sexuality and in particular Russell's breasts proved to be the key ingredients to his story. Hughes developed a type of cantilevered bra to push up Russell's breasts. Both in the film and in its publicity campaign, Russell's fulsome figure looms large. One movie poster asked, "What are the two reasons for Jane Russell's rise to stardom?" At an event in Los Angeles, a sky plane advertised the film by spraying two circles side by side with a dot inside each.

This picture's many production problems generated a host of stories and myths. Problems began almost immediately. Keenly aware of the intense competition in westerns, the budgetary allotment increased to $1.5 million. This large sum of money, in those days, excited public attention. One week after shooting began, director Howard Hawks quit. The director of many classics, including *Sergeant York,* could not work with the eccentric Hughes. None other than Hughes himself soon filled the role of director, albeit not very ably.

Continuous delays prompted rumors that Hughes withheld the movie to edit and reshoot many parts. The censorship board, which exercised tight moral standards in the 1940s, further complicated the release of the film. The so-called Hays Commission finally approved a film for general distribution. Approval proved hard to obtain because of the film's sexual content. Only after Hughes removed two scenes showing Russell dressed in a loosely fitting blouse did the Hays Commission accept the film.

This acceptance did not guarantee a viewing everywhere, however. The state censorship board of New York, one of the prime viewing locations, would not approve the Hays version. Instead, the State of New York forced Hughes to do yet a third version. The Catholic Legion of Decency condemned the film. Hughes and his lawyers fought many court battles with censorship agencies, winning some and losing some. All the litigation delayed the film's release by a full two years.

In total, of 18,000 dates signed to project the film during the first two releases, only 5,000 were met. Critics rightly hated the film. Yet after the first week, the film set box office records, earning $30,000. Over its six-week run in 1943, it earned $158,000. Then the ever-unpredictable Hughes removed his work from theaters. In 1946 the second release of the film earned more than $3 million. Hughes released the film twice more during the 1950s, after most of the opposition to the movie had dissipated. Following the fourth release, Hughes, through his attorneys, prevented the screening of the movie for 25 years. Shortly before Hughes died, however, a lost lawsuit permitted the film to be shown again.

The legacy of *The Outlaw* certainly continues to this day. Television stations, such as Turner Classic Movies, still air the western, which seems rather tame by today's standards. Retailers, such as Suncoast, sell the film at reduced rates. Critics uniformly agree that this is one of the worst westerns of all time. Nevertheless, it is also one of the most successful. *The Overlook Film Encyclopedia* claims that when adjusted for inflation, *The Outlaw* ranks seventh among all westerns in money earned.

—Thomas Edward Davis

Reference

Barlett, Donald L., and James B. Steele. *Empire: The Life, Legend, and Madness of Howard Hughes.* New York: W. W. Norton and Company, 1979.

PACKER, ALFRED

1842–1907

It was not valor, outlawry, or misfortune that distinguished Alfred Packer but rather his survival during a harsh Colorado winter by eating his comrades. Although members of the Donner Party also resorted to cannibalism, Packer appears to be the only American ever convicted of a crime related to cannibalism. Speculation surrounds many of the details of his life. Even though the complete details of his story may never be known, the uniqueness and morbidity of his crimes have magnified his presence in western myth and popular culture.

Alfred Packer was born on 21 November 1842 in Pennsylvania. In April 1862 he enlisted in the Sixteenth U.S. Infantry of Minnesota to fight in the Civil War. The army discharged him only eight months later because he suffered an attack of epilepsy. The determined young man enlisted again in July 1863 with the Eighth Regiment of the Iowa Cavalry,

only to be discharged again for the same reason. Following the war, he headed west, where he attempted to earn a living as a guide for gold prospectors in Colorado and Utah. Packer's fateful descent into cannibalism came as he guided a group of prospectors near Breckenridge, Colorado, in the fall of 1873.

Discrepancies abound about what happened on this trip into the Colorado wilderness. The most widespread version (which Packer swore to in his confession) is as follows: He and his party of 21 left Provo, Utah, in November 1873. They lacked sufficient supplies from the very beginning. After facing extended cold and hunger, in January 1874 they came upon the camp of Chief Ouray near what is now Montrose, Colorado. The chief explained that winter snows made the mountains impassable. He allowed the company to camp nearby and sold them supplies. Against Chief Ouray's advice, Packer and five others departed on 6 February, determined to reach their mining destination. They exhausted their provisions after only nine days of travel. After three or four days, hunger compelled them to cook and eat their moccasins and to stew and eat rose hips to survive.

As the story goes, the group camped one night near the Gunnison River. Hunger so afflicted a man named Bell that he became mentally deranged. The next morning, Packer ascended a nearby mountain to look for signs of civilization. When he returned, he found only Bell. In Packer's own words,

> I spoke to him, and then, with the look of a terrible maniac, his eyes glaring and burning fearfully, he grabbed a hatchet and started for me, whereupon I raised my Winchester and shot him. The report from the rifle did not arouse the camp, so I hastened to the campfire and found my comrades dead. . . . In looking about I saw a piece of flesh on the fire, which Bell had cut from Miller's leg. I took this flesh from the fire and lay it to one side, after which I covered the bodies of my dead comrades. I remained there with them during the night. In the morning I moved about 1,000 yards below, where there was a grove of pine trees. I distinctly remember of taking a piece of the flesh and boiling it in a tin cup. I also know that I became sick and suffered most terribly. My mind at this period failed me. (Alfred Packer Collection)

According to another confession, Packer tried to go for help every day thereafter, but the deep snows prevented him: "I camped that night at the fire, sat up all night, the next morning I followed my tracks up the mountain but I could not make it, the snow was too deep and I came back. . . . I tried to get away every day but could not so I lived off the flesh of these men, the bigger part of the 60 days I was out" (Alfred Packer Collection).

Packer finally emerged at Los Pinos Indian Agency on 6 April. According to some stories, he arrived looking well fed and seemingly more concerned about purchasing whiskey than food. He claimed that he had become separated from his companions, but suspicion mounted when he exhibited some of their personal possessions. He claimed that four of the men had died from the harsh conditions on the journey and that the others had eaten them. He also insisted that he had only killed Bell in self-defense. When the bodies were all found around a single campsite, this story too became suspect. Packer supposedly then reverted to the confession recounted above.

Packer signed a confession of his actions on 8 May 1874. The local authorities at the agency sent him to the jail at Saguache. Three months later, he escaped when someone gave him "a key made out of a pen knife blade with which I could unlock the irons" (Alfred Packer Collection). He lived nine years under the name John Schwartze before Frenchy Carbazon found him in Cheyenne, Wyoming. He then signed a second confession and went to trial for murder. On 13 April 1883 the jury found him guilty, and the judge sentenced him to hang. The Colorado Supreme Court reversed his sentence because of a grandfather clause: Colorado had become the nation's thirty-eighth state in 1876, and Packer had been charged under territorial law but tried under state law. Packer then faced a second trial, in which he was charged with five accounts of manslaughter. The court sentenced him to 40 years in the Colorado State Prison (eight years per death).

Polly Pry, a reporter, and the editors of the *Denver Post* worked for Packer's parole. One story says that the owners of the *Post* also owned the Sell-Floto Circus and wanted Packer for their show. Owing to these efforts and to Packer's failing health, Governor Charles Thomas granted him a conditional parole in January 1901. He moved to Deer Creek Canyon, near Littleton, Colorado.

Some sources say that Packer went to work as a guard for the *Post*. Others argue that he even became a vegetarian after his release from prison. He died in Littleton on 23 April 1907. Local residents recalled that Packer was very kind to children during his later years. He generously gave them candy and told them stories. In return, they followed him around—"like a Pied Piper"—and mourned his death. As one resident said, "He was an awful nice man. I was a kid, and he used to talk to my dad. He did what he did to protect himself. He never was the kind of man they say he was" (Alfred Packer Collection).

Controversy even surrounds Packer's name. His first name is sometime spelled "Alferd" instead of "Alfred." This discrepancy might have arisen because Packer, only semiliterate, used both spellings. Some authorities insist that his family misspelled the name just after his birth. Another explanation holds that a tattoo artist misspelled his name. From then on, he supposedly went by Alferd, except on official documents.

One of the most popular myths about his trial adds a political twist. When Judge Gerry passed down his sentence, he said, "There was siven Dimmycrats in Hinsdale County! But you, yah voracious, main-eatin son of a bitch, yah et five of them, therefor I sentence ye t' be hanged by the neck until y're dead, dead, dead!" (Hinsdale County Web Site). This story is probably a journalist's fabrication. The judge was a well-educated man, and there is no record of such a comment in the transcript of the death sentence in the Colorado State Archives.

What the judge does say in the transcript is that "what society cannot forgive it will forget. As the days come and go, the story of your crimes will fade from the memory of men" (Alfred Packer Collection). This, however, has not been the case. Reminders of Packer and his deeds have proliferated over time. In fact, four men popularized the judge's supposed political bias when they started the Packer Club, whose $1.50 membership fee included an official membership card with the judge's biased statement against "Dimmycrats" printed on it. The bottom of the club's official charter form reads: "I agrees to eliminat five Nu Deal Dimmycrats witch makes me a member of th' Packer Club of Colorado."

In 1964 Phil Ochs wrote "The Ballad of Alfred Packer." The chorus runs:

> They called him a murderer, a cannibal, a thief;
> It just doesn't pay to eat anything but Government-inspected beef. (Ballad of Alferd Packer Web Site)

Ochs published the song in *Broadside* magazine, which also featured a cartoon with Republican politicians celebrating the fact that Alfred had eaten five Democrats.

The Legend of Alfred Packer, produced in 1980, is a dramatic film that attempts to portray his life as accurately as possible. *Cannibal! The Musical,* a film released in 1994, took a very different approach. It is the work of Trey Parker, creator of the offbeat, hit television cartoon series *South Park.* Described as "'Cannibal Apocalypse' meets 'Oklahoma,'" the quirky film features an Indian population that is Japanese. The musical's songs borrow from George Gershwin and Rogers and Hammerstein.

Packer's eating habits are a part of daily life at the University of Colorado in Boulder. The Alferd Packer Grill is the main dining hall at the University Memorial Center. It serves such meals as the El Canibal, touted as "Boulder's BIGGEST burrito, tacos, nachos, enchiladas and the best green chile in town." The university also hosts an Alferd Packer Day each year. Attendance has declined in recent years, so the festival has been renamed the Alferd Packer Day Music Celebration. The traditional raw meat–eating contest is no longer part of the celebration. It has been replaced by other activities, including concerts, a hot food–eating contest, an Al Packer look-alike contest, a belching contest, and a chubby-bunny contest. Some wags in Colorado are campaigning to have Packer named the State Cannibal.

One Internet site lists Alfred Packer first on a list of ten people not to invite to dinner. Not surprisingly, his name is associated with a variety of food-related items and events. Windy and Kimberly Spurred published *Alferd Packer's High Protein Cookbook,* and James Banks produced *Alferd Packer's Wilderness Cookbook.* Lake City, Colorado, sponsors an Alfred Packer Jeep Tour and Barbeque each September. Gunnison, Colorado, holds an annual Alfred Packer Barbeque each May. There is supposedly a brand of trail mix called Alfred Packer Gorp.

According to one source, a bishop named Frank Hamilton Rice took the time to lead a goat and six followers to Alfred Packer's grave site in 1940. There, they performed a ceremony to transfer the sins of Alfred Packer and his victims onto the goat. The goat was reportedly not impressed. In 1989 Scientific Sleuthing, Inc., exhumed Packer's victims to re-examine the evidence. After examining historical and forensic evidence, the scientific team concluded that "Alfred Packer was as guilty as sin and his sins were all mortal ones. . . . It remained for this scientific investigation to prove with overwhelming conviction that Alfred Packer was not only the Colorado man-eater, not merely America's most celebrated anthropophagist but also the Caliban of Colorado who butchered his five fellow prospectors to death and then skinned them for all their bones were worth as he feasted and feted on their flesh" (Taylor 1993). Thus, the weight of science adds further evidence securing Packer's place in the "western hall of infamy."

–Kaleb J. Redden

References

Alferd Packer Cannibal Treats, Roadside America: *http://www.roadsideamerica.com/set/MEATpacker.html.*

The Alfred Packer Collection at the Colorado State Archives: *http://www.archives.state.co.us/packer.html.*

Alfred Packer for State Cannibal: *http://mem bers.aol.com/saluteths1/packer/packer.html.*

The Ballad of Alferd Packer: *http://www.cs. pdx.edu/~trent/ochs/lyrics/ballad-alferd -packer.html.*

Brief History of Colorado: *http://hometown. aol.com/vikkigray/3rd.htm.*

CANNIBAL: The Musical. A Film by Trey Parker: *http://www.screenedge.com/edge34. htm.*

Centennial Publications: *http://www.gorp. com/cl_angle/bookindx.htm#b19.*

COG Ride the Divide "Color": *http://www.con cours.org/rtd-color.html.*

Colorado Food Service: *http://umc.colorado. edu/food/grill_pages/index.html.*

Good Reading: Ten People NOT to Invite to Dinner: *http://emhain.wit.ie/~jmcdonal/ scruff/cuisine.htm.*

Hinsdale County Web Site: *http://campus press.colorado.edu/cpa/Book/hinsdale.html.*

Lake City: *http://www.onroute.com/destina tions/colorado/lakecity.html.*

The Legend of Alfred Packer: http://www.jps. net/mwmovies/packer/.

The Legend of Alfred Packer: Review: *http:// www.coastnet.com/~greywizard/rev4.htm.*

Littleton, Colorado, History, Alfred Packer: *http://www.littletongov.org/history/packer_a. htm.*

San Juan Cannibal: *http://www.ellensplace. net/hcg_fac5.html.*

State 51 on Alfred Packer: The Musical: *http: //www.state51.co.uk/reviews/packer.html.*

Taylor, Gary. "The Dead Rise Again in the Courtroom." *National Law Journal,* 21 June 1993: *http://www.hal-pc.org/~gtaylor/dead. html.*

This Rogue: *http://www.gorp.com/gorp/con tests/packer.htm.*

Waters, Helen E. "The Other Side of the Coin": *http://www.du.edu/~kmurcray/packer.html.*

PARKER, ISAAC CHARLES

1838–1896

Isaac Charles Parker, "the hanging judge," secured his place in history by his service during the late 1800s. Under Parker's court, 168 or 172 people received a sentence to die by hanging during his 21 years as judge. Although only 79 or 88 men actually died by hanging, Parker became a potent symbol of law and order in the Indian Territory, where he presided. Yet many questions about his life remain in dispute. Fort Smith, on the border of Arkansas and Oklahoma, became a place both praised and feared because of his court. Many people revere Parker as a hero who helped tame the Wild West. Others, however, criticize his lethal brand of justice as an example of frontier barbarism, not civilization.

Parker, born on 15 October 1838 in Ohio, grew up in a family with strong Methodist beliefs and a background of service in public office. At the age of 17, Parker decided he wanted to be a lawyer. His admission to the Ohio bar in 1859 started his lifelong involvement in law. That same year, the attraction of the West drew him to St. Joseph, Missouri. Parker held two public positions there, from April 1861 to April 1864. He served as a corporal in the state militia and as a city attorney. In 1864 he became the state attorney of the Twelfth Judicial Circuit of Missouri, and his reputation began to grow. Elected in 1870, Parker became a representative in Congress from the Sixth Missouri District.

In 1875 President Ulysses S. Grant appointed Parker chief justice of the Territory of Utah. Parker asked Grant if he could fill the position at Fort Smith, Arkansas, instead. He feared that the position in Utah would be temporary because Utah would soon become a state. He also wanted to stay closer to Missouri. Others supported his case, arguing that he could control the lawlessness in the Indian Territory. Grant, after hearing these pleas, changed the appointment and sent Parker to Fort Smith.

The judge began his 21-year career over the Western District of Arkansas in May 1875. Curiosity greeted him. Many wondered how effective he would be. Only eight days after his arrival, he presided over his first day of court. He sentenced eight people to be hanged for murder, quickly establishing his reputation as the hanging judge.

Supporters praised Parker's strict interpretation of the law. During this time, a person convicted of murder or rape faced death by hanging. Parker steadfastly followed the law. He oversaw the hiring of about 200 marshals to help capture fugitives. Many looked at Fort Smith as a model of law enforcement for the rest of the country. A just and caring man, Parker often expressed the sympathy he felt for the victims of crime. He wanted to rid the Indian Territory of the sizable criminal population that infested it. Native Americans in the region correctly believed that Parker protected them against outlaws. Parker showed his concern for Native American rights throughout his career.

Critics claimed that Parker's court could be tyrannical and unjust. Those who opposed him called him "Hanging Parker," "Bloody Parker," and "Butcher Parker." Until 1889 he possessed full and final jurisdiction over all federal criminal cases. Convicted felons had no right to appeal a sentence during this period. At least 25 people attempted to escape from Fort Smith under Parker's court. Many agreed with the sign near the Canadian River that read "500 miles to Fort Smith—and Hell" (the latter phrase added by one of the judge's critics).

During Judge Parker's reign over the Indian Territory, 79 people died on the gallows. He dealt with famous outlaws, including Belle **Starr**, Cherokee Bill, the Dalton Gang, the Rufus Buck Gang, and Henry Starr. Parker presided over more than 600 cases annually, totaling 13,940 cases in his career. He rarely missed a day in court and worked long hours. This zeal took a toll on his health, and he died on 17 November 1896 at the age of 58. A large crowd attended his funeral, and many mourned his death. Many prisoners in the jail, however, cheered loudly when they heard of Parker's death.

Various aspects of the judge's life remain in dispute. Estimates of the number of men he hanged range from 79 to as many as 300. *Hell on the Border* (1898, reprinted 1992), by S. W. Harman, is generally critical of Parker as being overzealous and even enjoying the hangings at Fort Smith. However, Harman also claims that Parker actually believed in abolishing the death penalty. The few known quotations from Parker on the subject leave his position unclear.

In 1995 the House of Representatives passed a bill to honor Parker by renaming a building in Washington, D.C., after him. This proposal sparked heated debate between those who viewed Parker as a hero and those who viewed him as a villain. Opponents painted Parker as a racist. Fred Patton, a Parker supporter and historian of Fort Smith, disputes the charge. He claims that Parker appointed the first black U.S. marshal west of the Mississippi and employed other blacks as well. Patton also points to Parker's sympathy for Native American rights.

Judge Parker has made his way into popular culture in a number of ways. Some biographies treat Parker as a hero and someone who should be praised: Fred Harrington's *Hanging Judge* and Glenn Shirley's *Law West of Fort Smith*. Several western films incorporated Judge Parker into the story line. *Lonesome Dove* and *True Grit* included him as a character. In these two movies, he is depicted as a bloodthirsty judge.

In 1996 Coca-Cola issued a commemorative eight-ounce bottle in honor of Judge Parker. The bottle features his picture and reads "celebrating one hundred years of law and order." The Fort Smith National Historical Site, especially Parker's reconstructed courtroom and gallows, remains a popular tourist destination.

The phrase "hanging judge" is still used today. Many judges after Parker have proudly adopted the term. Albert F. Sabo, a former judge in Pennsylvania, adopted the term for his support and advocacy of the death penalty, especially in the case of Mumia Abu-Jamal. Isaac Parker's character is still debated, but his importance and impact on American judicial history is unquestionable.

—*Michael L. Sileno*

References

Harman, S. W. *Hell on the Border: He Hanged 88 Men*. 1898. Reprint, Lincoln: University of Nebraska Press, 1992.

Harrington, Fred Harvey. *Hanging Judge*. Caldwell, ID: Caxton Printers, 1951.

Shirley, Glenn. *Law West of Fort Smith: A History of Frontier Justice in the Indian Territory, 1834–1896*. Lincoln: University of Nebraska Press, 1957.

PARKER, ROBERT LEROY

1866–1911, outlaw. *See* Butch Cassidy and the Sundance Kid

PECOS BILL

The mythical cowboy hero of the Pecos River region of Texas, Bill provides a typically exaggerated version of bedrock western characteristics: bravery, ingenuity, loyalty, and love of adventure.

Edward O'Reilly, writing in *Century* magazine in 1923, created the figure, and subsequent writers added new tall twists and tales. Unlike some legendary heroes, we find no preexisting historical model or oral tradition about such a figure. Drawing on his knowledge of the West, O'Reilly created him out of thin air.

According to the stories, Bill was born in Texas about 1832 but suffered the trauma of being lost by his parents. Unnoticed, he fell out of the family wagon into the Pecos River, but friendly coyotes found and raised him. Thus, like previous heroes raised by animals, he learned nature's ways. He could howl with the coyotes and sometimes played with bighorn sheep. As an adult he could ride a mountain lion and twirl a live rattlesnake like a lariat. He wrestled a monster, part grizzly, puma, gorilla, and tarantula, until the dazed beast had to quit.

Bill's adventures multiplied. After a long hot, dry spell, Bill carried water from the Gulf of Mexico to water the parched Texas soil. When he tired of the arduous journey, he dug a little ditch to carry the water, thus creating the Rio Grande. And he did even more digging while looking for gold in Arizona. As a result, he created the Grand Canyon.

Of course, a cowboy needs a mount, so he headed up into the mountains to catch a wild horse named Lightning. In another version, he names the "unridable" horse Widow Maker. Shortly after catching and taming Lightning, he met Slewfoot Sue, who rode by on the back of a giant catfish the size of a whale. It was love at first sight for Bill. Sue agreed to marry him but set two conditions: He had to buy her a wedding gown, complete with bustle, and he had to let her ride Lightning.

Unfortunately, when Sue's bustle hit the saddle, Lightning bucked and tossed her all the way around the moon. When gravity brought her back to earth, she would bounce on her bustle and roar off into space again. Finally, the ever-inventive Bill lassoed a tornado to catch up with his bouncing bride. They rode the storm all the way to California, where they landed on top of a wagon. It turned out to hold Bill's parents, searching for a new home. After listening to Bill extol the virtues of west Texas, they all returned to live there on Bill's ranch. According to one version, Bill died after washing down a meal of barbed wire with a draught of nitroglycerin. According to another story, he took one look at a city slicker from the East and laughed himself to death.

Pecos Bill's adventures have passed into many different media. James Cloyd Bowman published another version of the tales in 1937. More recently, in 1995 Patrick Swayze starred in *Tall Tales: The Unbelievable Adventures of Pecos Bill,* an animated film. Bill teams up with Paul Bunyan and John Henry to help save a family's farm. One reviewer summed up the movie's message as upholding a simple "code of the West: 'Respect the land; defend the defenseless; never spit in front of women and children'" (Film Values.com).

Robin Williams used his distinctive expressive voice to narrate the adventures for a "Pecos Bill" audiocassette later ported to the computer as a reading program for young children. Ry Cooder added musical accompaniment. Disney has been the biggest purveyor of Pecos Bill programs. No trip to any Disney theme park would be complete without a quick lunch at the Pecos Bill Tall Tale Inn and Café.

See also Disney Frontierland

References

FilmValues.com. "Tall Tale (1995)" (film review): *http://www.filmvalues.com/Review. cfm?RecordID=570.*

Pecos Bill Web Site: *http://wwlegends.9ug. com/pecos.html.*

PETRIFIED-HUMAN HOAXES

See Solid Muldoon

PHOTOGRAPHY

See Adams, Ansel

PICKETT, WILLIE M. "BILL"

1870?–1932

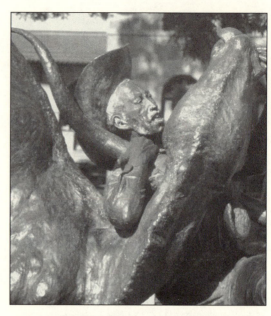

Statue of Bill Pickett, Forth Worth Stock Yards

Born in Travis County, Texas, 30 miles northwest of Austin, Will Pickett grew up with a dozen siblings. His mixed ancestry included whites, blacks, and Cherokees. As a youngster in rural Texas, he learned to read brands and toss a rope. One day, he said, he had watched a small bulldog bite a cow's lip and thus control the large animal. He decided that a person could do likewise. He first demonstrated his technique to a group of cowboys in 1881. According to legend, because a bulldog inspired the feat, it became known as "bulldogging." Later rodeo competitors would drop the lip biting but continue the dangerous practice of steer wrestling.

Will worked on central Texas ranches during the late 1880s and 1890s. He married Maggie Turner in 1890. They had nine children. With his brothers, he started the Pickett Brothers Broncho Busters and Rough Riders Association in Taylor, Texas. "We ride and break all wild horses with much care," read their ad. "Catching and taming wild cattle a specialty."

By the early twentieth century, Pickett was bulldogging steers with his teeth at county fairs and other gatherings in many western states. He performed at the 1904 Cheyenne Frontier Days celebration. The *Wyoming Tribune* reported breathlessly that Pickett could

attack a fiery, wild-eyed and powerful steer, dash under the broad breast of the great brute, turn and sink his strong ivory teeth into the upper lip of the animal, and throwing his shoulder against the neck of the steer, strain and twist until the animal, with its head drawn one way under the controlling influence of those merciless teeth and its body forced another, until the brute, under the strain of slowly bending neck, quivered, trembled and then sank to the ground. (1 September 1904)

Rodeo announcer Frederick Melton "Foghorn" Clancey reported seeing Pickett bulldog a steer in Dublin, Texas, in 1905. Some white cowboys, including Lon Seeley and Milt Hinkle, began using

Pickett's technique as well. The same year, Pickett tied in with the Miller Brothers' 101 Ranch Wild West Show. He performed with Tom Mix, Guy Weadick, Milt Hinkle, and other cowboy stars.

While with the 101, Pickett became known as Bill rather than Will. Strong, athletic, compact (five feet, seven inches; 145 pounds), and mustachioed, he dressed like a Spanish bullfighter. He performed his brand of bulldogging in Calgary, Alberta, Canada; Sonora, Mexico; and throughout the United States. The 101's program listed him as "the Dusky Demon who throws steers with his teeth." In late 1908 he accepted a challenge to take on a Mexican fighting bull. The bull gored both Pickett and his prized mount Spradley, one of several times the athlete suffered injury. In late 1913–1914 the troop toured South America and Europe.

In the 1920s Pickett retired from competitive bulldogging but continued to give exhibitions. He also starred in a few black western movies that highlighted his rodeo skills. *The Crimson Skull* opened in 1921, and *The Bull-Dogger* opened a year later. Pickett returned to work for Zack Miller and continued to break horses. His wife, Maggie, died in 1929, a devastating loss to Pickett.

Pickett died on the 101 Ranch on 2 April 1932 after having been kicked by a horse several days before. Miller eulogized Pickett as the "greatest sweat and dirt cowhand that ever lived—bar none." Miller also wrote a commemorative poem titled "Old Bill Is Dead." The concluding lines read:

> He left a blank that's hard to fill
> For there'll never be another Bill.

> Both White and Black will mourn the day
> That the "Biggest Boss" took Bill away.
> (Hanes 1989)

Pickett had been the only black member of the Cherokee Strip Cowpunchers Association. In 1936 the group erected a sandstone marker at his grave site. A highway marker along U.S. Highway 77, some three-fourths of a mile south of the grave site, points visitors to his final resting place. In 1972 he became the first black cowboy admitted to the select company of the National Cowboy Hall of Fame.

In 1994 another attempt at honoring the rodeo pioneer went awry. The U.S. Postal Service planned to commemorate Pickett, along with 19 other famous western figures, with a series of **stamps** called Legends of the West. Unfortunately, stamp designers picked an erroneously labeled picture as the basis for the stamp. The notoriety of the mistake, however, actually brought Pickett to the attention of far more people.

In 1998 poet Paul Harwitz honored the legendary performer with "The Ballad of Bill Pickett":

> Bill Pickett's father started life in
> servitude.
> Of thirteen children, Bill was the eldest of
> the brood.
> How could anyone beforehand ever know
> That Bill would teach the world how a
> steer to throw?
> A Texas Longhorn steer, somehow
> different from the rest,
> Thought it would instead of entering a
> corral, digress.
> Now, in a cattle operation, that can cause
> quite a mess,

When one mean-spirited steer decides to make itself a pest.
"Someone ought to teach that cantankerous steer who's boss,"
Said Bill, "And make it savvy that to make trouble is a loss."
That stubborn steer kept snorting, and running, and pawing the ground,
Challenging the cowboys, who saw the other cows looking around.
It doesn't take much to get cattle to balk and act spoiled.
Now, Bill Pickett's disposition was starting to get roiled.
"Someone ought to teach that cantankerous steer who's boss,"
Said Bill, "And make it savvy that to make trouble is a loss."
Now that renegade steer was starting to interfere,
To try to keep all the other cows from cooperating.
It kept deliberately scattering the herd there and here,
And tried to get them to act ornery and full of fear.
"Somebody's got to teach that bum steer who's boss,"
Said Bill, "And make it savvy that to make trouble is a loss."
Finally, Bill's patience wore plumb out,
And he rode full speed alongside that rampaging ruminant,
Leaned over and grabbed its head and horns all about,
And leaped off his horse in an instant descent.
"I'm gonna teach you," he yelled, "you stupid steer,
Just who the heck is boss around here!"
Bill dug in his heels to slow down and stop the beeve,

And then he did something the other cowpokes could scarcely believe.
He started to wrassle that bovine to the dirt!
It still resisted, so Bill bit its lower lip till it hurt!
The stunned steer went kind of limp from the sudden surprise,
And a cunning gleam shone out of Bill Pickett's eyes.
He quickly wrestled that steer flat onto the ground,
And that was the beginning of his bulldoggin' renown.
"I've shown you," he bragged, "you uncooperative steer,
Just who the heck's in charge around here!"
All the people from miles and miles around,
Said they'd pay cash money to see Bill Pickett "bulldog" steers.
And each time he did, they'd applaud and give wild cheers.
And that's the way, people say, that Bill did bulldoggin' found.
"I've shown you," he bragged, "you uncooperative steer,
Just who the heck's in charge around here!" (Harwitz)

Today, a large bronze statue by Lisa Perry, *The First Bulldogger,* honors Pickett. The impressive piece, depicting him biting the lower lip of a steer as he brings it down, stands outside the Cowtown Coliseum in Fort Worth, Texas. The nation's only touring black rodeo is named in his honor: the Bill Pickett Invitational Rodeo. In 1998 artist Burl Washington offered a 27-by-37-inch watercolor, *Bill Pickett, Bulldogger,* for sale at a price of

$6,850. He also offered limited edition prints for $100. The honor of inventing bulldogging has been attributed to others, including the Alberta, Canada, black cowboy John Ware. Whether inventor or not, Pickett certainly sensationalized the event and made it a hit with large numbers of people. He is thus justifiably commemorated in many media and in many places for this contribution to western folklore and rodeo.

References

Hanes, Bailey C. *Bill Pickett, Bulldogger: The Biography of a Black Cowboy.* Norman: University of Oklahoma Press, 1977, 1989.

Harwitz, Paul. "The Ballad of Bill Pickett": *http://www.isis-intl.com/paul/poems/billp.html.*

Johnson, Cecil. *Guts: Legendary Black Rodeo Cowboy Bill Pickett.* Fort Worth, TX: Summit Group, 1994.

Russell, Don. *The Wild West: A History of the Wild West Shows.* Fort Worth, TX: Amon Carter Museum, 1970.

PIKES PEAK GOLD RUSH

Soaring to 14,100 feet, Pikes Peak shines as a bright jewel in the central Colorado Rockies. In 1893 the view from the summit inspired Katharine Lee Bates to write her most famous poem, "America the Beautiful." Long before whites explored the area, Ute Indians skirted the foot of the mountain as they migrated from summer campgrounds to winter hunting grounds. Spanish explorers, notably Juan de Anza, who traversed the side of the mountain in 1779, remarked its presence.

Fur trappers harvested the area's rich bounty of beaver, deer, elk, bear, buffalo, bighorn sheep, and mountain lions.

Lt. Zebulon Montgomery Pike viewed the peak in 1806. He called the mountain "Grand Peak," but later cartographers labeled it "Pikes Peak" on their maps. A cold November storm kept Pike from climbing the mountain, and he predicted that "no one would ever reach the summit." Edwin James proved Pike wrong in 1820, making the first recorded ascent to the top. In 1858 Julia Archibald Holmes became the first woman to reach the summit.

In that same year, prospectors located gold on Cherry Creek near present-day Denver. The following spring brought hordes of miners to the "Pikes Peak diggings." In 1859 prospectors unearthed a rich lode of gold-bearing quartz near Central City. Most miners, however, got nothing more than blisters as they wielded pick and pan, placer or gulch mining in the region's waterways. By the mid-1860s, the gold boom had gone bust.

The Pikes Peak economy began a revival in 1873, however, when the Samuel Womack family purchased a homestead in the crater of an extinct volcano on the mountain's western slope. They built a log ranch house and pole corral on the banks of Cripple Creek. The grassy, rolling hills of the basin made ideal rangeland. Bob Womack, Sam's youngest son, took up residence in a log shack he built several hundred feet northeast of the main house. During the next several decades, he would keep up a tantalizing but fruitless search for gold. Countless others, however, would strike it rich on the elusive Pikes Peak gold.

Each day, while herding the family's cattle, Womack searched the ground for indications of gold. In May 1878 the cowboy-prospector spotted a piece of "float," a type of rock from which centuries of rain and wind have washed much of the sediment. This washing process leaves a lightweight, gray rock, often rich in gold. A Denver assay valued the fragment at $200 per ton.

Womack continued searching and found other chips of the material during his rides throughout the basin. The tales of gold that he told during frequent visits to the bars of Colorado City heightened expectations. Lured by promising indications found by Womack and others, more prospectors moved into the region, but in spite of the increased activity, no one struck it rich.

The Womacks sold their claim in 1884, but Bob got permission to continue his quest. Late in 1889 he persuaded his Colorado Springs dentist, John Grannis, to grubstake him with $500. Bob made the dentist a 50–50 partner in any gold he might find. Following a trail of float fragments in the fall of 1890, Womack sank a shallow shaft about one-third of a mile northeast of his shack. At ten feet down, he tunneled north. Thirty feet into the tunnel, Womack struck a dome of rock that he recognized as a volcanic upthrust. After clearing the earth above, he blasted into the top of the dome, uncovering a vein of sylvanite. He took samples, and the next morning, 20 October 1890, he posted his claim to the El Paso Lode. The samples assayed at $250 to the ton, the richest strike in the region to date.

Unlike placer mining, where the gold is taken from on top of the ground, hard-rock mining requires digging and blasting to get to the ore. The raw ore must then be milled to extract the gold, but neither Bob nor Grannis could afford mill costs. They failed in their attempts to attract other investors, so even though others struck rich lodes nearby, Bob Womack remained penniless.

By that time, 18 years after the Womacks began their homestead, exploratory shafts dotted the surrounding hillsides. The region's population had grown to 3,000, including prospectors, miners, saloon keepers, merchants, bankers, mining engineers, assayers, prostitutes, and assorted camp followers. On 5 April 1891, camp leaders formed the Cripple Creek Mining District. The group declared Bob Womack's El Paso Lode the "discovery shaft" and formally recognized him as the discoverer of Cripple Creek gold.

With some fame but no fortune, Womack still could not develop the mine. He sold his interest in the El Paso Lode to his partner for a mere $300. Although the mine eventually produced more than $3 million in gold, Bob never enjoyed the wealth. Instead, he prospected, sold a bit of ore now and then, and lived from hand to mouth. More rich strikes in the area followed in 1892. Production grew from $50,000 per month to $200,000 and kept rising through 1893.

Living a disappointed, whiskey-sodden existence, Womack also faced failing health. He contracted pneumonia two weeks before Christmas 1893. Recovering slightly, he sold his last mining interest, the Womack Placer, for $500 the day before Christmas. Changing his payoff to one-dollar bills, he stood at the corner of Third and Bennett Avenues and gave passersby a single dollar each for Christmas. The next day, at his sister Lida's insistence, Bob left Cripple Creek for Colorado Springs, where they bought and operated a rooming house.

In 1891 a Colorado Springs carpenter named Winfield Scott Stratton arrived in Cripple Creek to search for precious metal. After studying the topography, Stratton staked his claim on a rocky ledge on the south slope of Battle Mountain. Stratton dug several tunnels off the main shaft, but ore samples remained poor. Discouraged, he sold a six-month option on the mine. As he gathered his tools in a previously unpromising tunnel, just hours before the new owner would arrive, Stratton discovered a rich vein that later assayed at $580 to the ton. Carefully concealing his discovery, Stratton held his breath during the option period. The evening before the option came due, Stratton persuaded the option holder to give it up. Reclaiming his mine, Stratton took $3 million out of that first vein alone.

The discoveries of 1892 and '93 attracted miners from other camps. By early 1894 the population had soared to 12,000. Many of the newcomers had experience as hard-rock miners in the silver camps of Georgetown, Leadville, and Silverton. Many belonged to the Western Federation of Miners (WFM). Cripple Creek mine owners paid $3 per day for eight hours' work. When they added an hour to the workday without an increase in pay, the miners revolted. Led by experienced WFM members, miners struck the offending mines, and production plummeted.

The ensuing battles between union miners, owners, and free miners drew statewide attention. The governor sided with the unions and ordered the state militia into the district. Free miners faced down the well-armed troops but stood down in defeat when the militia threatened to use their Gatling guns. In April 1894, WFM members constructed a log fort atop Bull Hill and pointed fake cannons at their adversaries. Mine owners raised an army of 1,200 Colorado Springs "deputies," and the battle was on. As the deputies approached the district by train, the Bull Hill gang dynamited the shaft house and buildings of the Strong Mine, raining down chunks of iron, timber, and rock on the deputies. When the deputies retreated, Bull Hillers roared their approval, and a tumultuous celebration followed. Celebrants broke into whiskey warehouses, and drunken miners attacked people and property.

State Adjutant General Thomas J. Tarsney openly sided with the WFM. Although he represented the law, he was "conveniently absent from" Cripple Creek when the strikers illegally took Bull Hill. He later led the militia personally against the deputies when they returned after their first disastrous trip. Eventually, the strikers and militia won because of sheer numbers. But the 130-day strike cost some $3 million in lost wages and the destruction of buildings and equipment.

While the victorious WFM miners returned to work for $3 per eight-hour day, Tarsney relaxed in a Colorado Springs hotel room before returning to Denver. Disgruntled deputies lured him from his room one night and took him to a farm east of the city. After coating his body with hot tar and chicken feathers, the deputies took Tarsney to the railroad tracks and ordered him to walk the 70 miles to Denver.

With the end of the Bull Hill war, Cripple Creek entered a period of unprecedented prosperity. Production doubled and redoubled. Stratton took $1 million a year from his Independence Mine, and his other interests paid off almost as well. Never enamored with wealth, he became a philanthropist and gave generously to the Salvation Army, Colorado College, and the Colorado School of Mines. He loaned money freely to down-and-out miners, tearing up their IOUs. He also gave money to a variety of ministers to build churches in Cripple Creek, Colorado Springs, and Denver.

As peace returned to Cripple Creek, the district's social life flourished. Socialites flocked to town and sponsored dances, concerts, and operas. In 1895 the city hosted the only Spanish-style bullfight ever held in the United States. By the end of 1896, the population reached its zenith at 40,000. That same year, disaster struck when a fast-moving fire destroyed the center of the board-and-log city. Almost before the embers had died, a second blaze consumed still more of the city, putting 12,000 residents out of their homes. Citizens replaced the burned buildings with brick structures, and the ramshackle look of bare-board and tarpaper shacks disappeared. Cripple Creek became a neat, clean metropolis.

Stratton moved to Colorado Springs late in 1895. He watched in dismay as his friends fought one another in court over money. With people continually badgering him, he became disillusioned and concluded that wealth brought nothing but heartache. Discouraged and in failing health, he sold the Independence Mine to a European corporation in 1899, adding $10 million to his already considerable fortune. He gave away even more of his wealth and planned to rid himself of all of it as quickly as possible. He died on 14 September 1902 of a liver disease he had suffered from for years. Although he had given millions away, nearly $7 million remained. Disappointing the money-hungry crowd of Colorado Springs, he bequeathed $6 million to establish a home, to be named for his father, for poor children and old people. The rest went to his nieces and nephews and to his estranged son, Zeurah, born of an unhappy early marriage.

Stratton's death marked the end of the great Cripple Creek gold rush. In 1902 the mines produced $19 million in ore. But the next year, production plummeted to $13 million, and it never rose again. During the next several years, the rich hard-rock ore ran out. Mines closed, miners, merchants, and businessmen left the district, and the beehive of activity fell silent.

Meanwhile Bob Womack and his sister continued to operate their Colorado Springs rooming house. Lida managed the place and did the cooking and cleaning. Bob did the maintenance and ran errands for the guests. Although he had visited Cripple Creek only once in the intervening years, he kept informed of the camp's activities from newspaper accounts and friends who occasionally came to call. Long years of alcohol abuse caused his health to decline rapidly. On 10 August 1909, the discoverer of Cripple Creek gold died without a cent to his name.

From 1890, the year of Womack's first discovery, until the year after his death, miners took more than $213 million in gold from Cripple Creek. That would equal more than $4.25 billion today. Through 1962, output totaled $421 million, about $8.5 billion at current prices.

Today gamblers in Cripple Creek casinos have replaced the gambling miners of a century ago. This new gold rush of casino gambling has revitalized the old mining town. Visitors can place limited-stakes bets of up to $5 each at slot machines, video and live poker, and black-jack tables in some twenty casinos. The town's Web site features Bob Womack as a guide to the area's activities and entertainment. Visitors can glimpse past glories at the Cripple Creek District Museum, at the Lowell Thomas Museum in Victor, and on the popular Cripple Creek Ghost Walk Tours.

The summit of Pike's Peak, climbed by Edwin James long ago, remains another popular destination, accessible by cog railway, by car, or on foot. The Pikes Peak Cog Railroad, built in 1891, remains in operation. The Pikes Peak Toll Road, second highest highway in the world, was completed in 1916 at a cost of $350,000. Each Fourth of July, automobile and motorcycle racers from all over the world converge for the Pikes Peak Hill Climb. Competitors negotiate the 12 miles, with 156 hair-raising turns, in a little more than ten minutes.

Mining also continues. Cripple Creek and Victor Gold Mining Co., a subsidiary of Anglo Gold, operates the largest open-pit and heap-leach gold mine in the state at its operation located between Cripple Creek and neighboring Victor. With new chemical processes to extract gold, low-grade ore and tailings from old mines, once left as worthless, are now being processed. The saga of Pikes Peak gold continues.

—Z. Ervin

References

Cripple Creek Web Site: *http://www.cripple creek.co.us/.*

Cunningham, Chet. *Cripple Creek Bonanza.* Plano: Republic of Texas Press, 1996.

Lee, Mabel Barbee. *Cripple Creek Days.* Garden City, NY: Doubleday, 1958.

Sprague, Marshall. *Money Mountain.* New York: Ballantine Books, 1953, 1971.

PIONEERTOWN

See Movie Sets

PLEASANT, MARY ELLEN
1814?–1904

Mary Ellen Pleasant is best remembered for her financial genius and as the mother of the civil rights struggle in California. However, owing to conflicting stories and political slander, many questions remain unanswered about her eventful life. She claimed to have been born in Philadelphia on 19 August 1814. However, what happened thereafter remains a mass of conflicting accounts. During the gold rush, she did go to California, where she became highly influential and very wealthy.

Legends, both noble and base, swirl around Pleasant. She is depicted negatively as a blackmailer and procurer for San Francisco's high and mighty men.

However, she is also heralded as a champion of civil rights who provided important financial support to noted abolitionist John Brown.

In one version of her early life, she lived as a slave girl in Philadelphia. A Mr. Price bought her her freedom and sent her to Boston to be educated. There, the bright young woman met William Lloyd Garrison and other prominent abolitionists. She married one Alexander Smith, vaguely described as a Cuban planter. His death left her with an inheritance of $45,000, money she deployed on behalf of abolitionism.

In 1849 or 1852—accounts vary—she journeyed westward to San Francisco with her second husband, John Pleasant. Referred to as "Mammy Pleasant" behind her back, she opened and ran several fashionable boardinghouses and restaurants. She worked with the help of her secret partner, a Scot named Thomas Bell. By some accounts, she provided sage financial advice to many clients who reaped considerable profits.

Along with her business acumen, Pleasant remained passionately committed to the black struggle. "I'd rather be a corpse than a coward" was her motto. She aided and hid fugitive slaves. She bravely traveled to rural areas to rescue slaves being held illegally by their masters. She challenged California's Jim Crow laws. She played a key role in getting state legislation passed in 1863 that gave blacks the right to testify in court. She filed a suit against two trolley lines whose conductors had refused her passage. According to her positive folk legend, she went north to Canada in 1858 and donated $30,000 to John Brown to help fund his historic raid.

Despite her accomplishments, or per-haps because of them, Pleasant lost the battle for her own good name. In the later years of her life, political enemies "scandalized" her name. For example, as early as 1883, she unsuccessfully challenged a powerful senator, William Sharon, charging him with human rights abuses. By the early twentieth century, the yellow press had labeled "Mammy Pleasant" a fiend, madam, and murderess. The realities of her life disappeared amid a welter of misinformation and gossip, accounts that became the accepted version of her life.

What is clear is that this celebrated philanthropist and businesswoman amassed a sizable fortune. She died, with hateful gossip swirling around her, in 1904 at the home of friends in San Francisco. She was buried in Napa's Tulocay Cemetery. Some say she left an estate in excess of $300,000 to those who cared for her in her declining years.

Thanks to excellent recent research by Susheel Bibbs, we now have lost writings and accounts by Pleasant and her contemporaries. These documents have helped disentangle fact from fiction in her colorful life. In 1997 Bibbs also curated an exhibit, titled Mary Ellen Pleasant: Mother of Civil Rights in California, at the San Francisco Art Commission Gallery. Thus, Pleasant's rehabilitation is well under way. Her eventful life illustrates many truths about the West. Racism tainted the region as it did other sections of the country. A strong, capable woman, especially a black woman, often would be greeted with suspicion and hostility.

References

Mary Ellen Pleasant: *http://www.toptags.com/ aama/bio/women/pleas.htm.*

Mother of Civil Rights: *http://www.kn.pac bell.com/wired/BHM/mepleasant.html.*

PLUMMER, HENRY

1837–1864

In 1864 vigilantes in Idaho Territory (now Montana) lynched 21 suspected criminals, including (William) Henry Plummer, sheriff of Bannack. His character and fate are still debated today. In 1993 Montanans held a posthumous mock trial to try to evaluate the evidence against the sheriff.

Born near Addison, in Washington County, Maine, on 6 July 1837, Plumer (the original spelling of his name, which he used) came from a prosperous seafaring family. A slight, sickly child, Henry did not take up seafaring but instead studied and worked on the family farm. At age 20, he joined the throngs heading west to California, arriving in San Francisco on 21 May 1852 (some sources say 1851). He spent the next decade seeking his fortune in California and Nevada.

While serving as town marshal of Nevada City, California, he killed a man named John Vetter in September 1857. He received a ten-year sentence. His detractors insist he was having an affair with the man's wife. His defenders insist he acted in self-defense, and the governor pardoned him after only six months in prison.

Plummer then traveled to the booming mining area of Idaho Territory, arriving in Bannack during the fall of 1862. Townspeople elected him sheriff the following May. He married Electa Bryan on 20 June 1863, and they settled in Bannack. His supporters say that thanks to his mining skills, he did well and owned portions of several rich claims. His enemies claim that Plummer supported himself by theft, not mining.

Like Mary Ellen **Pleasant** and other famous westerners, Plummer has been demonized—in this case, as a bloodthirsty killer, thief, and adulterer—by political enemies. Contemporary diaries and journals describe him as a "genteel-mannered" peace officer. He dressed formally, even fastidiously, wearing a long frock coat.

Others in the area decided to take action against what they perceived as a wave of lawlessness, including 100 robberies and murders. Sidney Edgerton, former congressman and chief judge of the new Idaho Territory, and his nephew Wilbur Sanders organized a secret vigilante committee. The vigilantes began secretly trying and lynching suspected criminals. Political disagreements also figured in this volatile time, Edgerton and Sanders being leading Republicans, Plummer a Democrat. Thus, both partisanship and suspicions about his criminal activities conspired against Plummer.

In early 1864, Plummer, ill after a long trip, was recuperating at the home of his sister-in-law, Martha Vail. On the evening of 10 January, a well-armed mob lured Plummer from his sickbed by threatening to lynch a robbery suspect in his custody. The unarmed Plummer stepped outside, where the vigilantes grabbed him and hauled him to a pine tree up the gulch. They bound his hands, put a noose around his neck, and slowly hoisted him off the ground. He probably died slowly, of strangulation rather than of a broken neck.

Early writings, notably *Vigilantes of*

Montana (1866), by Thomas J. Dimsdale, and *Vigilante Days and Ways* (1890), by Nathaniel Pitt Langford, painted righteous vigilantes ridding the territory of criminals, including Plummer. Scholars remain split on the sheriff's guilt and character. Recent revisionist writings, such as *Hanging the Sheriff: A Biography of Henry Plummer* and *Vigilante Victims: Montana's 1864 Hanging Spree,* by R. E. Mather and F. E. Boswell, respectively, challenge the conventional wisdom about Plummer's guilt. Richard Maxwell Brown (1998), a leading authority on frontier violence, accepts the early Dimsdale/Langford charges. Bill O'Neal (1979) agrees, arguing that Plummer's "huge band of desperadoes continually preyed upon stagecoaches, payrolls, and unwary travelers" (O'Neal 1979).

On 7 May 1993, schoolteacher Mark Webber arranged for a posthumous trial at the Madison (Montana) County Courthouse. The trial participants included Judge Barbara Brook presiding, adult jury members, and members of Webber's class playing historical roles, complete with period clothing. Attorney Doug Smith instructed the students on legal issues

After hearing testimony, based on the historical sources, the jury rendered their verdict and Judge Brook addressed the defendant: "Sheriff Plummer, the jury is unable to render a unanimous decision as required by law. You are free to go." The jury's split 6–6 decision resulted in a mistrial, thus granting Plummer his freedom.

Two months after the trial, Montana's Board of Pardons received an unusual document, an application for pardon submitted on behalf of Henry Plummer. Support for the measure came from au-thor R. E. Mather; Frederick Morgan, a publisher of western history books; and Jack Burrows, an author and professor of western history. In August, the board ruled that since a court had never convicted Plummer, they could not review the request for clemency. The debate continues in print and on the Internet, with no conclusive verdict in sight.

References
Brown, Richard Maxwell. "Plummer, Henry." In *The New Encyclopedia of the American West,* ed. Howard R. Lamar. New Haven, CT: Yale University Press, 1998.
Henry Plummer Revisited: *http://www.thehistorynet.com/WildWest/articles/1998/08982_cover.htm.*
O'Neal, Bill. *Encyclopedia of Western Gunfighters.* Norman: University of Oklahoma Press, 1979.
Vigilantes of Montana: *http://www.montana-vigilantes.org/.*

POETRY

See Cowboy Poetry

POKER ALICE IVERS

1853–1930

Born on 17 February 1853 in Devonshire, England, Poker Alice Ivers has become a western legend. A gambler, bootlegger, and madam, she is still represented in Deadwood, South Dakota's, Days of '76 parade. Her luck, skill as a dealer, and spending sprees in New York

City won her admiration and renown. As she said, "I would rather play poker with five or six experts than to eat" (El Buscaderos Web Site).

During her life, Alice married three men—all of them gamblers—and was widowed three times. Her first husband and love, Frank Duffield, taught her poker. Refusing to stay at home when he ventured out for a game, she showed great skill and cunning at poker. Duffield, a mining engineer, died in a dynamite blast at a mine in Leadville, Colorado. To support herself, Alice turned to gambling, counting on the good luck she had enjoyed in occasional games with her husband and others.

She met her longtime husband, Warren G. Tubbs, while gambling in Deadwood. Tubbs and Alice often faced each other as adversaries at the gaming table. Alice usually beat him, but he supplemented his income by painting. Supposedly, a drunken miner pulled a knife on Tubbs one night. Alice quickly drew her trusty .38 and put a slug into the miner's arm.

Alice's beauty and bravery won the gambler's heart, and they married in 1907. On a good night, she might win as much as $6,000. Drawing on a cigar, she sometimes gloated and challenged all comers. Her poker face aided her in bluffing and keeping opponents in the dark about her cards.

Tubbs suffered from tuberculosis, and Alice cared for him on their remote homestead during his last years. In 1910 he died in Alice's arms, of pneumonia, amid a raging Black Hills blizzard. She drove his frozen corpse in a sled 48 miles to Sturgis, where she pawned her wedding ring to pay for the burial.

After Tubbs's death, Alice returned to the gambling tables, this time in Rapid City, South Dakota, and then Sturgis, South Dakota. In Sturgis Alice engaged George Huckert to tend her sheep while she gambled. He proposed repeatedly, and she finally succumbed, saying, "It would be cheaper to marry him than pay him" (El Buscaderos Web Site). She owed him more than $1,000 in back wages. Alice's bad luck with husbands continued, and Huckert died soon thereafter, leaving her widowed for the third time.

As the boom times waned, Poker Alice faced tough times during her later years, which she spent in Sturgis. She took to wearing a khaki skirt, a man's shirt, and a frayed hat. She bootlegged alcohol to support herself and occasionally returned to the tables, such as for the Diamond Jubilee in Omaha, Nebraska. As a local madam, she obliged soldiers stationed at Fort Meade by running a house of ill repute in Sturgis.

Alice died at age 77 on 27 February 1930 in a Rapid City hospital following gall bladder surgery. She is buried at St. Aloysius Cemetery in Sturgis. Her home in Sturgis, moved to a new location by businessman Ted Walker, is now a tourist attraction.

Poker Alice retains her notoriety, having influenced people around the world. A Salt Lake City, Utah, restaurant bears her name. On 22 May 1987, Elizabeth Taylor played her in a made-for-TV film, *Poker Alice,* still available on videotape. George Hamilton played Alice's slick partner Cousin John. Susan Tyrrell engages Taylor in a memorable down-and-dirty fight. True to life, Alice finds true love with a bounty hunter, played by Tom Skeritt.

Two musical groups honor the memory of the gambling woman. The five-piece Poker Alice Band, hailing from South Dakota, performs a variety of acoustic and electronic music on fiddle, guitar, and other instruments. They seek to replicate the music that would have been heard during Alice's time at country gatherings and barn dances.

Across the globe, the alternative band Poker Alice, founded in 1995, bills itself as having "the songs for the next millennium." Although based in Switzerland, they list Duncanville, Texas, as their second address. They write their own lively songs, a sound they describe as "somewhere between folk, country, and rock." Appropriately, they've recorded a tune titled "Boy from Montana." Their recordings include two singles in 1997, "Half Past Midnite" and "Children in the Rain"; the 1998 album *Louisiana;* the single "Don't Call Me after 10" (1999); and several more singles in 2000, "The Plane," "Freedom," and "Blue Sky in Carolina."

The group originally included Rudy Birchler, Christof Hochuli, Daniel Schwarz, Mr. Blaze, and lead singer Monika Schär as Alice. Rene Hunziker later replaced Hochuli, and Dieter Senn joined as bass player. According to Birchler, "Originally the name came from a movie with Elizabeth Taylor. We liked the lady and the name. It reminds us to be 'free and easy.' That's what our music should be." To the group, Alice "stands for to be yourself as you are" (Birchler e-mail to author 2000).

The film in question, *Poker Alice,* appeared on television in 1987, with Elizabeth Taylor playing the lead as Alice Moffit (a Hollywood-created name with no basis in history). Alice's Boston Brah-

min family disowns her because of her incurable urge to gamble. She heads (where else?) to the West, winning a house along the way in a poker game on a train. Her acquisition turns out to be a bordello, which she decides to run until she finds a buyer. Meanwhile, she falls in love with bounty hunter Jeremy Collins (Tom Skeritt). Thus, from restaurants to movies to rock music, the legend of Poker Alice lives on.

References

El Buscaderos: Cowboy Action Shooting. "Feature: Poker Alice, 1851–1930." September 1998: *http://www.netw.com/~cowboy/_fea ture/feature0998.html.*

Poker Alice: *http://www.pokeralice.ch.*

Quinn, John W. "Poker Alice": *http://www. blackhills-info.com/Quinn/Pokeralis.html.*

POLITICIANS AND WESTERN MYTH

Politicians from Chester A. Arthur and Theodore Roosevelt to Lyndon Johnson and Ronald Reagan have manipulated cowboy and western imagery for political purposes. Even such obviously noncowboy figures as Henry Kissinger and Richard Nixon used cowboy rhetoric and imagery. Kissinger told an interviewer that he liked to act alone, like a cowboy riding into town: "He acts, that's all: aiming at the right spot at the right time, a Wild West tale, if you like." Nixon once argued that Americans should only leave Vietnam "as a cowboy, with guns blazing, backing out of a saloon."

In his first annual message to Congress

on 6 December 1881, President Chester Alan Arthur presented an unflattering appraisal of the wild and woolly Southwest:

> The Acting Attorney-General also calls attention to the disturbance of the public tranquility during the past year in the Territory of Arizona. A band of armed desperadoes known as "Cowboys," probably numbering from fifty to one hundred men, have been engaged for months in committing acts of lawlessness and brutality which the local authorities have been unable to repress. The depredations of these "Cowboys" have also extended into Mexico, which the marauders reach from the Arizona frontier. With every disposition to meet the exigencies of the case, I am embarrassed by lack of authority to deal with them effectually. The punishment of crimes committed within Arizona should ordinarily, of course, be left to the Territorial authorities; but it is worth consideration whether acts which necessarily tend to embroil the United States with neighboring governments should not be declared crimes against the United States.

In contrast, several later presidents depicted the West in much more positive terms. Theodore Roosevelt romanticized and internalized the experiences gained during his brief Dakota ranching career in the 1880s. He directly stated, "I never would have been President if it had not been for my experiences in North Dakota" (Theodore Roosevelt National Park Web Site). His failure as a rancher in Dakota Territory gave him a deep appreciation for those who could succeed. In *Ranch Life and the Hunting Trail* (1888), Roosevelt noted:

> There are very few businesses so absolutely legitimate as stock-raising and so beneficial to the nation at large; and the successful stock-grower must not only be shrewd, thrifty, patient, and enterprising, but he must also possess qualities of personal bravery, hardihood, and self-reliance to a degree not demanded in the least by any mercantile occupation in a community long settled. Stockmen are in the West the pioneers of civilization, and their daring and adventurousness make the after settlement of the region possible. The whole country owes them a great debt.

More-recent presidents, including John F. Kennedy, Lyndon Baines Johnson, and Ronald Reagan, also mobilized western imagery. Delivering his acceptance speech on 15 July 1960 in Los Angeles, Kennedy expressed a familiar frontier theme in American political rhetoric: "From the lands that stretch three thousand miles behind me, the pioneers of old gave up their safety, their comfort, and sometimes their lives to build a new world here in the West. . . . They were determined to make that new world strong and free, to overcome its hazards and its hardships." After recalling the Old Frontier, Kennedy shifted his focus to the future. He invited Americans to turn their energies toward "the uncharted areas of science and space, unsolved problems of peace and war, unconquered pockets of ignorance and prejudice, unanswered questions of poverty and surplus. It would be easier to shrink back from that frontier. . . . But I believe that the times demand invention, innovation, imagination, decision. I am asking you to be new pioneers on that New Frontier."

Kennedy's vice president and successor, Johnson, had much better roots in the frontier West than did his Boston Brahmin predecessor. Historian Melody Webb has called Johnson "the last frontier president." Johnson dressed the part, often wearing western-cut suits, boots, and a gray Stetson hat. The eldest of five children, Johnson was born in a three-room house in the Texas hill country. The family ranch, bordering the Pedernales River, did not provide much income, and Johnson grew up knowing poverty. However, he loved Texas and the family ranch, located near Stonewall, Texas (between Johnson City and Fredericksburg). The ranch would remain a vital part of his life, a refuge from Washington pressures, as well as his final resting place.

In November 1964, vice president–elect Hubert Humphrey joined Johnson at the ranch to celebrate their landslide victory. Humphrey joked that Johnson was to blame for the Minnesotan's "droopy" western clothes: "After all, the president was the man that dressed me." Humphrey had even braved a horseback ride with Johnson, who reveled in his role as First Horseman. The president-elect retorted, "Did you hear what Hubert announced in his speech here? By God, he said he'd resign if there was any more horseback riding."

Johnson had real roots in Texas ranching. Illinois-born Ronald Reagan, in contrast, drew more of his western inspiration and ideas from the movies. Reagan professed that as a child he had had a "yen to be like Tom Mix" (Slatta 1996). *Santa Fe Trail,* a 1940 western starring Errol Flynn, gave Reagan his first major film role. He badly wanted to star in big-budget westerns, but the studios offered him only B movies and other light fare. Four of the ten films he made during the 1950s were westerns. In 1953 he played a thinly disguised Wyatt Earp in a B-western called *Law and Order.* Movie posters announced that "his guns were the only law." The closest Reagan came to western stardom was as host of the popular **television** series **Death Valley** Days.

In 1981 Reagan became the nation's fortieth president, at age 69 the oldest man to ever take the oath of office. Like presidents before him, he spoke in frontier metaphors: "The conquest of new frontiers," he said in July 1982, "for the betterment of our homes and families is a crucial part of our national character." With characteristic optimism, he rejected the notion that the United States had no more frontiers and thus no more opportunities or challenges. "There are those who thought the closing of the Western frontier marked an end to America's greatest period of vitality. Yet we're crossing new frontiers every day."

During his frequent breaks from Washington, Reagan often retreated to his California ranch, where he rode horses, chopped wood, and enjoyed respite from the pressures inside the beltway. He donned jeans and cowboy boots for leisure-time activities, cultivating a western image as Johnson had done before him. He often repeated the adage, "There is nothing better for the inside of a man than the outside of a horse" (*New York Times,* 2 October 1981).

Reagan helped fuel the "Sagebrush rebellion" by naming avowedly anti-environmentalist James G. Watt as secretary of the interior. The abrasive Watt resigned in disgrace after just two years.

He had supported opening western lands and resources to corporate exploitation. To use B-western terminology, Reagan worked on behalf of the cattle and mining barons, not the working cowboy or the family ranch. Wallace Stegner termed Reagan an "ersatz Westerner" who affected the style but had little regard for protecting the region's special qualities and treasures.

Reagan's rhetorical imagery resounded with cowboy clichés. Long before assuming the presidency, he had skillfully painted political issues in simple black-and-white terms, not unlike old B-western plot lines. He played on the public's desire for simple, easy answers to frustratingly complex problems. Speaking on 27 October 1964, he observed that "they say the world has become too complex for simple answers. They are wrong. There are no easy answers, but there are simple answers." His political soul mate, John Wayne, shared this sentiment. "They tell me everything isn't black and white," said Wayne. "Well, I say why the hell not?"

Reagan looked and acted like a cowboy hero, with straight talk and seemingly decisive action. Appropriately, **Louis L'Amour,** who created similar one-dimensional heroes, ranked as Reagan's favorite author. Reagan enjoyed strong support across the nation but particularly in the western states. As Michael E. Welsh noted, "not since Theodore Roosevelt had a chief executive of the United States attached himself so closely to the myths of the American West" (Welsh 1987). Janet R. Fireman added, "that presidential policy actions were based on the mass-culture myth of the American frontier is absolutely astonish-

ing" (Fireman 1995). It's perhaps fitting that Reagan's major biographer, Edmund Morris, blithely chose a fictionalized format for his bizarre portrait, *Dutch: A Memoir of Ronald Reagan* (1999).

Like wily advertisers, American politicians have long recognized and played upon the power of western myth. In his 1988 bid for the Democratic presidential nomination, Governor Michael Dukakis of Massachusetts asked Americans to join him in facing "the next American frontier." The phrase, of course, recalled John Kennedy, but it also reminded Americans of the rich, comforting mythology associated with facing and overcoming frontiers past. Like Johnson before him, President George W. Bush often refers with pride to his Texas roots. Unlike Johnson, however, Bush was born not in Texas but in New Haven, Connecticut, where he also attended college at Yale. As a Tennessean, Al Gore does not claim to be a westerner. Nonetheless, both, as candidates during the 2000 presidential contest, often donned cowboy boots. Nor is the appeal of western imagery limited to U.S. politicians: Vicente Fox, elected president of Mexico in 2000, sports some of the gaudiest cowboy boots ever seen outside Nashville.

References

Fireman, Janet R. "Ronald Reagan and the Mythic West." *Journal of the West* 34, no. 2 (April 1995): 96.

Roosevelt, Theodore. *Ranch Life and the Hunting Trail.* 1888. Facsimile ed., Ann Arbor, MI: University Microfilms, 1966.

Slatta, Richard W. *The Cowboy Encyclopedia.* Santa Barbara, CA: ABC-CLIO Press, 1994; paperback ed., New York: W. W. Norton, 1996.

Theodore Roosevelt National Park Web Site: *http://www.nps.gov/thro/*.

Welsh, Michael E. "Western Film, Ronald Reagan, and the Western Metaphor." In *Shooting Stars: Heroes and Heroines of Western Film,* ed. Archie P. McDonald. Bloomington: Indiana University Press, 1987.

POLYGAMY

See Young, Ann Eliza Webb

PONDEROSA

See Bonanza

PONY EXPRESS

APRIL 1860–OCTOBER 1861

The Pony Express has attracted popular attention and generated mythology out of all proportion to its brief existence. During its short life of some 19 months, beginning on 3 April 1860, the young riders of the Pony Express made a place for themselves in western history and legend.

Then as now, businessmen and bankers wanted the speediest communication possible. Wells Fargo coaches took 20 days to cover the 1,966 miles between St. Joseph, Missouri, and Sacramento, California. West Coast entrepreneurs wanted quicker connections with the financial and political powers of the East. In response, Senator W. M. Gwin, Daniel E. Phelps, and Alexander Majors hatched a plan for a faster service to cut the transit time in half. Majors convinced his reluctant freight company partners, William H. Russell and William B. Waddell, to provide some of the capital and expertise to create the new venture.

Majors, Russell, and Waddell purchased 600 fast, tough broncos. They put out a call for "young, skinny, wiry fellows, not over 20. Must be expert riders, and willing to risk their lives for the job. Orphans preferred. Wages twenty five dollars a week." Adventure-seeking youths, including Buffalo Bill **Cody** and Wild Bill Hickok, poured in. The company hired 75 young men, tough and wiry, none weighing more than 110 pounds. They sought additional virtues in these young horsemen: exhibited bravery, ability to survive difficult frontier conditions, skill with firearms, and an understanding of how to deal with possible Indian attacks.

On 3 April 1860, Henry Wallace had the honor of instituting the service. In his *mochilla* (leather Mexican saddlebags that could be moved quickly from horse to horse), he carried a congratulatory message from President James Buchanan to the governor of California. Riders wrapped the mail in oiled silk for protection from the elements. Organizers broke their operation into sixes: Each man rode six hours on six different ponies over a 60-mile segment of the trip. The first mail reached Sacramento ten days later. Eventually, the Pony Express included 80 riders, 400–500 mounts, and 100 stations.

Like many western ventures, the Pony Express suffered from technological obsolescence. The completion of the transcontinental telegraph on 24 October 1861 rendered the young riders dispensable. The company suffered losses estimated at $100,000–$200,000. The new "talking wires" carried information instantly and cheaply across the country. But the Pony Express stirred the hearts and imagination of the nation. In less than 19 months, the youths had ridden 650,000 miles, delivering 34,753 pieces of mail. Only one mail sack was ever lost.

The drama of the short-lived experiment translated readily to popular culture. Harry Castlemon's book *The Pony Express Rider* appeared in 1898, followed ten years later by William Lightfoot Visscher's *The Pony Express: A Thrilling and Truthful History.* The topic was simply irresistible for **pulp novelists.** In the early twentieth century, Edward S. Ellis published two pulps: *The Pony Express Rider* and *Alden among the Indians: Search for the Missing Pony Express Rider.* Much of the literature and film about the Pony Express targeted a young audience. In 1949 Anne Hawkins wrote *To the Swift,* an adult novel about the Pony Express.

Filmmakers, beginning in the silent era, also seized upon the action and drama of fast-riding youth. Henry James Forman published a book, illustrated with movie stills, in 1925. Promotional copy described it as "A Mighty Romance of the Gallant Post Riders of the Western Frontier, a true RIP-ROARING tale of the west that never was. Several photos taken from the movie illustrate the narrative."

More films followed the pioneering silent treatments. Republic produced *Frontier Pony Express* in 1939, and Warner Brothers followed with *Pony Express Days* a year later. Four more films appeared during the decade: *Pony Post* (Universal, 1940), *The Pinto Bandit* (Producers Releasing Corp., 1944), *The Plainsman and the Lady* (Republic, 1946), and *Riders of the Pony Express* (Kayson/Screencraft, 1949). As the B-western era drew to a close, three more treatments appeared: *Stagecoach Driver* (Monogram, 1951), *Last of the Pony Riders* (Columbia, 1953), and *Pony Express* (Paramount, 1953). Charlton Heston and Forrest Tucker starred in the last, which was overblown and juvenile in spite of its sizable budget and big-name stars.

Movie serials included *Overland Mail* (Universal, 1942), *Cody of the Pony Express* (Columbia, 1950), and *Blazing the Overland Trail* (Columbia, 1956). The feature film *Pony Express Rider* (Doty-Dayton, 1976) featured a host of western character actors. A year later came *The Medicine Hat Stallion,* in which a young boy runs away to join the Pony Express after his father sells his horse. In happy-ending western fashion, the Pony Express had purchased the animal, so boy and horse are reunited.

On **television,** Flying "A" Productions issued *Range Rider* in 1951, and NBC later tried *Ride the Wind* in 1966. In 1972 Ed Speilman created *The Young Riders,* originally titling it *The Kid.* The program did not air on television, however, until September 1989. It ran for three seasons and featured veteran actor Anthony Zerbe, along with youngsters Stephen Baldwin, Josh Brolin, Travis Fine, and Gregg Rainwater. A little later, McGraw Hill Home Interactive produced a computer game, also named "The Young Riders." Today, the Pony Express Museum in St. Joseph, Missouri, honors the memory of the brave young riders in a more dignified fashion.

References

History of the Pony Express: *http://members. tripod.com/~pnyxpress/history.html.*

Home Station: *http://www.xphomestation.com/.*

National Historic Trail: *http://www.nps.gov/ poex/.*

When the Pony Express Was in Vogue: *http:// www.sfmuseum.org/hist1/pxpress.html.*

PRETTY BOY FLOYD

1904?–1934

During the 1920s and '30s, harsh times befell most people living on the Great Plains, particularly those residing in Oklahoma. The Wall Street crash of 1929 along with dust bowls and poor crops reduced the small farmers of this largely agrarian region to poverty. These factors coupled with the Volstead Act of 1919, which prohibited the sale and consumption of alcohol, led to the rise of roving bands of gangsters. The names Barrow, Nelson, Barker, and Dillinger are as much a part of American culture today as they were when these individuals terrorized the countryside. One gangster, Pretty Boy Floyd, created a niche for himself in American folklore that remains to this day.

Disagreement surrounds the actual birthday of Charles Arthur Floyd. Some sources say he was born in 1901 in Akins, Oklahoma. Others suggest that he was born in 1904 in Bartow County, Georgia. Before he was a year old, his family moved to a small farming community in Oklahoma. Charles grew up on a small, dirt-poor farm with six siblings. Bank foreclosure always loomed. In 1921

Floyd married a neighbor farmer's daughter, 16-year-old Ruby Hargrove, who soon bore a son, Jack Dempsey.

Charles found work hard to come by and soon turned to a life of crime. His first violent act came when he discovered that his father had been shot to death in a feud. Taking his father's rifle into the hills, Floyd went hunting for his father's killer, J. Mills, who was never seen again. In the mid-1920s Floyd moved to East Liverpool, Ohio, where he worked as a gunman for bootleggers. The move to Ohio foreshadowed his death a decade later in the same area.

Floyd also received his nickname "Pretty Boy" during this time. Dissent surrounds the origin of his nickname. Beulah Baird Ash, the madam of a brothel Floyd frequented, took a personal liking to him and called him her "pretty boy." She later became the leader of the gang he would work with.

In 1925, after arriving in St. Louis by train, Floyd and three accomplices robbed a Kroger's grocery store. They made off with more than $12,000, possibly as much as $16,000. He had previously only robbed small stores. Police soon apprehended the inexperienced thief and sentenced him to five years. Three years later Floyd left the penitentiary, having learned two important lessons. First, he vowed he would never be incarcerated again, a promise he kept. Second and more important, he learned the tricks to being a successful criminal from his fellow inmates. His wife had filed for divorce during his stay in the penitentiary, although they would remain close, even to the point of living together again.

Following his release, Floyd began a

crime spree through the Midwest and in particular Oklahoma. During this time, the bank insurance rates in Oklahoma doubled. The state formed posses totaling 500 men to track down and capture Floyd. Eventually, officers captured him in Ohio. However, while being transported via train to the penitentiary, he broke a window and leaped to freedom. In June 1933, however, a murder in a neighboring state focused the FBI's attention on Floyd.

On 17 June 1933, hired gunmen botched a mob rescue in Kansas City, Missouri, a gunfight that became known as the "Union Station massacre." Four law enforcement officials escorting Frank Nash, a noted underworld kingpin, walked into an ambush. The rescue attempt went badly awry; Nash and his escorts died in a salvo of gunfire. The FBI charged Floyd in the attack. He maintained until his death that he had not participated. The incident in no way resembled Floyd's modus operandi. He preferred hit-and-run attacks and rarely worked with a partner. The botched rescue attempt also undoubtedly angered the bosses who ordered the operation and resulted in the hitmen's punishments. The questionable notion that Floyd participated in the Union Station massacre nevertheless brought down the wrath of the FBI.

On 22 July 1934, FBI agents fatally shot John Dillinger in Chicago. It is rumored that Pretty Boy Floyd was at one point a member of his gang. With Dillinger's death, the FBI elevated Floyd to Public Enemy Number One. J. Edgar Hoover placed famed special agent Melvin Purvis in charge of his case. Floyd proved to be a difficult criminal to apprehend.

Many poverty-stricken midwesterners regarded Floyd as a hero. During his bank robberies, he never wore a mask and always showed courtesy to his captives. During one robbery in his hometown, he conversed with the local patrons while waiting for his money. During these robberies, Floyd also destroyed the banks' records of mortgages on small farms. Regional folklore holds that he distributed a portion of his gains to the poor. In exchange for his generosity, the poor provided the fugitive with safe havens and supplies. Despite the support of the local populace, Floyd would die less than six months after being labeled Public Enemy Number One.

On 19 October 1934, Floyd robbed the Tiltonsville, Ohio, Peoples' Bank. The following day, during a shoot-out in Wellsville, Ohio, he barely escaped by kidnapping a florist. On 22 October local officers and FBI agents spotted the criminal at the Conkle farm, where they shot him as he ran into a cornfield. When the officers reached his body, they discovered that Pretty Boy was not yet dead. They carried him to an apple tree, where he died. A rumor quickly arose that Agent Purvis had executed Floyd when the criminal refused to admit to the Union Station massacre. However, no evidence supports this claim. At the funeral home that evening, 10,000 people passed by the body in a three-hour period. A crowd of twice that number attended the funeral as supporters mourned their hero, their Robin Hood.

The farmers of the Midwest in large part generated the myths and folklore surrounding Charles "Pretty Boy" Floyd. People living in the East viewed him simply as another hoodlum whose reign of terror had to be stopped. To the locals, Floyd beat the capitalists who oppressed the poor farmers. They held no sympathy with the losses suffered by bankers. The mythology about Floyd involved some degree of fact and truth. During his heyday, he never robbed small, local merchants, only big capitalistic banks.

Just five years after Floyd's rampage ended, folksinger Woody **Guthrie** put his exploits to song. Guthrie portrayed Floyd as a decent, caring person. In one stanza, Floyd says, "You say I am an outlaw, you say I am a thief, Here's a Christmas dinner for the children on relief." Guthrie implied that Floyd committed crimes to feed needy families.

John Steinbeck presented this same idea in his literary masterpiece *The Grapes of Wrath*. At one point, Ma Joad claims that "I knowed Purty Boy Floyd. I knowed his Ma. They was good folks. He was full of hell, sure, like a good boy oughta be." Steinbeck would not be the last person to portray Floyd as a hero.

In 1960 Hollywood released the motion picture *Pretty Boy Floyd*, which portrays Floyd as the "sagebrush Robin Hood." A young, handsome actor, John Ericson, played the lead. Throughout the film, he continuously combs his hair and maintains the image of a courteous criminal.

In 1993 Larry McMurtry and Diana Ossana wrote another screenplay about Floyd. Although a film has yet to emerge, the authors turned their work into a novel entitled *Pretty Boy Floyd*. In the epilogue, family members and participants in Floyd's capture reminisce about the outlaw. Mamie Floyd, the criminal's mother, speaks out against the government. She says, "I sent a telegram to the U.S. Department of Justice. I forbade any

pictures of him. . . . They took the pictures anyway; I despise them for it."

During the 1980s and '90s, two rock-and-roll bands called themselves Pretty Boy Floyd. One group even received a recording contract from an independent studio. The folklore surrounding Charles "Pretty Boy" Floyd survives to this day. Along with the many references to him in the entertainment business, his myth can be seen at his final resting place. Throughout the decades, souvenir seekers have desecrated pieces of his grave site. In 1985 the marker to his grave disappeared and has never been recovered. In 1993 the East Liverpool Historical Society erected a marker on the site of the former Conkle farm where Floyd died. In August 1995 someone stole this marker too. It was eventually recovered and re-erected on the same site. These facts all suggest that the heroic image and the public's fascination with this former Public Enemy Number One continue today.

—Thomas Edward Davis

References

Bruns, Roger A. *The Bandit Kings*. New York: Crown Publishers, 1995.

King, Jeffrey S. *The Life and Death of Pretty Boy Floyd*. Kent, OH: Kent State University Press, 1998.

PULP NOVELISTS

The pulp novels (also known as dime novels) are given credit for satisfying the American public's craving for the action and adventure of the American western frontier during the late nineteenth century. These short literary works (printed on cheap paper, hence the term "pulp") gained popularity as early as 1860 and sold well for almost 100 years. The stories mostly consisted of predictable plots and heroes. Repetitive adventures containing romance, gunfights, cowboys, Indians, lawmen, and bandits predominated.

Most dime novels fell far short of the standards for great works of literature; instead, they served as a leisurely and affordable form of mass entertainment. As they gained in popularity and grew in numbers, the pulps became an important medium for expressing and solidifying mythical elements of the frontier. Famous westerners, both real and fictional, became powerful figures and archetypal heroes of the frontier fantasies that many authors (mostly easterners) created.

Pulp novels, particularly those involving the West, thrived on simple and entertaining story lines, low production costs and prices, and a working-class readership. The demand for western folklore and legendary tales of cowboys and outlaws encouraged hundreds of authors to produce thousands of titles, featured in either a paperback series or pulp magazines. Zane **Grey,** whom many consider the greatest storyteller of the American West, became one of several pulp novelists to create a large number of dime novels in his career. His 1912 *Riders of the Purple Sage* is a classic. His novels, although full of western lore and imagination, also remained valuable as credible insights into a culture that was often misinterpreted.

Western historian Ramon Adams wrote, "In my research, I found that Grey strayed from the truth on only a few issues. 'High Noon' style gun fights on Main Street were rare. Those who lived by the gun usually died young." Pulp novelists often carried the responsibility of the cultural brokers for easterners. Their tales of the wild and ruthless West shaped the impressions of readers of all ages. Years after his death in 1939, after several posthumous works were finally published, Zane left his fans with almost 90 books, at least 60 of which are westerns.

Max Brand is the best-known pen name for Frederick Faust, a writer who produced an impressive 30 million words—the equivalent of 530 books—during his lifetime. Brand is well known for the Dr. Kildaire series, which later spawned its own **television** series. Reluctant cowboy hero Destry, played by James Stewart in the 1939 Hollywood classic *Destry Rides Again,* also began as a character in one of Brand's novels. Brand wrote works in almost every genre, including crime, fantasy, historical romance, espionage, science fiction, adventure, animal stories, love, war, and fashionable society. Several radio and television programs were based on his writings, as well as more than 80 motion pictures. For 75 years, he averaged a book every four months. With such a large quantity of literature under his various pen names, this pulp novelist succeeded in reaching and influencing millions of readers over the years.

The name Buffalo Bill is familiar to most Americans, although most know little about his life or why he is so historically significant. One reason for this lack may be that although **Cody** is mentioned in some encyclopedias and reference books, he is most familiar from the legendary tales of author-adventurer Edward Zane Carroll Judson. Judson, better known as Ned **Buntline,** met frontier scout William F. Cody in 1869. His encounter with the outdoorsman inspired him to feature Cody as the hero in several dime novels. Buntline established Buffalo Bill as a frontier hero and a larger-than-life figure of the West. His 1869 *King of the Border Men* was a huge success. Cody became the archetypal heroic scout, freelance lawman, rescuer of maidens, and a living literary legend. Buntline wrote more than 400 pulp novels during his career, creating fanciful tales of Wild Bill Hickok and Texas Jack.

Pulp novelists also immortalized real-life criminals. Romantic outlaws **Jesse James, Butch Cassidy,** and the Sundance Kid are all featured in their own dime novels, strengthening their name recognition and heroic stature. Edward Wheeler popularized the "heroic" criminal **Deadwood Dick,** and the 64 novels in this series are now considered collector's items. A dedicated fan of the sharpshooter can visit Deadwood Dick's Saloon in Deadwood, South Dakota, to purchase anything from T-shirts featuring the saloon's logo to official Deadwood Dick condoms.

Pulp stories featuring women or minorities were few and far between. The readership for pulp novels and cheap paperback reading in the early 1900s was 90 percent male; the heroes reflected the reading audience. Some exceptions to this male-exclusive genre include Wheeler's Hurricane Nell, Rowdy Kate, and the legendary **Calamity Jane.** Typically, women as portrayed in the pulps were powerless and fragile, heroines in distress or up to mischief. Calamity Jane expanded the roles of women in western literature, fighting with outlaws and wearing a holster over her dresses. Pulp novels also played a role in forming the images of minorities in popular culture. Mexicans appeared as lustful degenerates, Native Americans as threatening savages, and terms such as "spic" and "greaser" flowed freely from pulp novelists' pens.

Pulp novels and their authors do not play as critical a role in the proliferation of mythical western culture into modern society, but they helped originate many of the myths. Dime novels also played a key role in opening literature to western influence. The men who created story after story did so with the intention of entertaining the reader, and little else. However, they opened an important market for the working-class literary audience. In doing so, they managed to keep many western folk tales and stories alive for generations, converting mythical people and events into part of western literature and history. Grey, Brand, Buntline, and hundreds of other pulp novelists helped capture and preserve the adventurous, often exaggerated, aspects of western life. Without such an easily accessible form of literature bridging the gap between folk tales of the 1860s and cinema of the 1930s, the myths, legends, and lore of the American West might not have survived through those fast-changing times.

—*William F. Zweigart*

References

Aquila, Richard, ed. *Wanted Dead or Alive: The American West in Popular Culture.* Urbana: University of Illinois Press, 1996.

Bold, Christine. *Selling the Wild West: Popular Western Fiction, 1860–1960.* Bloomington: Indiana University Press, 1987.

RAMONA

Helen Maria Hunt Jackson (née Fiske, 1830–1885) served on a federal commission investigating the plight of Indians on southwestern missions during the early 1880s. She used the knowledge she gained to write a novel, *Ramona* (1884), that aroused public opinion on the issue of mistreatment of Indians. However, her fiction also had another major impact: It created a nostalgic, romantic portrait of Old California just after the end of Mexican rule.

Born in Amherst, Massachusetts, Helen Maria Fiske married an army captain, Edward Bissell Hunt, and they had two sons. By the mid-1860s, however, her husband and young sons had died. Distraught, she turned her energies to writing, initially poetry and later prose. Like so many before her, in November 1873 she traveled west to improve her mental health and fortunes. She chose the mineral waters of Colorado Springs to help her recovery. Here she met a banker and railroad official named William Sharpless Jackson. They courted and were married on 22 October 1875.

Four years later, on a family visit to Boston, she listened to Standing Bear, a Ponca chief, describe the tragedies and mistreatment of his people. Jackson seized the moment as an opportunity to redirect her own life: She vowed to devote her time and talents to correcting wrongs against Native Americans. She made good on the promise by immediately spending three months researching the issues at the Astor Library in New York City. The resulting book, *A Century of Dishonor* (1881), powerfully detailed a litany of the white government's mistreatment, broken treaties and promises, and slaughters.

Many westerners, including her husband, did not take the criticism of white American policy well. Some vociferously demanded that the federal government deny the charges and silence the critic. Undeterred, Jackson returned east and delivered a copy of her book to every congressman and senator. In each copy, she wrote pointedly "Look upon your hands. They are stained with the blood of your relations." Given her celebrity, the publisher Charles Scribner's commissioned her to write a series of articles about the condition of the old Spanish missions in California. In July 1882 the administration of President Chester A. Arthur, eager to get her out of Washington, D.C., appointed her a special commissioner for the Bureau of Indian Affairs. She agreed to investigate conditions of Indians living in southern California, working with a friend named Abbott Kinney.

Jackson continued her research into 1883, examining records and visiting ranches and other sites in southern California. Rancho Camulos, located in Ventura County's Santa Clara Valley east of Piru, would become a southern California icon as the fictionalized home of Jackson's heroine *Ramona*. In San Bernardino County, she learned that a white man named Temple had recently gunned down a Cahuilla Indian named Juan Diego for stealing his horse. Understanding that a straightforward government report could be easily ignored, Jackson plotted another strategy. She decided to use the novel form to bring her criticisms to a broader reading public. "If I could write a story that would do for the Indian," she noted, "a thousandth part of what *Uncle Tom's Cabin* did for the Negro, I would be thankful the rest of my life" (Greenstein).

True to her word, she revealed her intentions to California friend de Colonel in a letter of 28 November 1883: "I am going to write a novel in which to set forth some Indian experiences in a way that will move peoples' hearts. I am going to New York and shall be busy there all winter on my book" (Greenstein). Working diligently and quickly, she finished her manuscript in late March 1884. *Ramona* appeared first in the *Christian Union* magazine as a serial and a month later as a book. Sales soared, and the author, vindicated but exhausted and ill, returned to her Colorado home.

Ramona recounts the story of a wealthy Spanish girl who is in reality an orphan and a *mestiza* (of mixed Spanish and Indian ancestry). She falls in love with Alessandro, an Indian sheepherder, and they elope and are married by Father Gaspara in San Diego. (Even though the work is fiction, local officials later got a site, called Casa Estudillo/Ramona's Marriage Place, designated as a National Historical Landmark.) The star-crossed lovers suffer social ostracism that ultimately ends in tragedy. Living among Indians, Ramona for the first time sees their desperate plight. The couple's first child dies for lack of proper medical care.

The novel had some real consequences. In the book, a white man murders Ramona's beloved Alessandro before her eyes. In the real-life incident, however, Juan Diego's killing had been ruled self-defense. Nonetheless, Temple, the killer, left the state to escape his unsavory notoriety. Since 1923 the people of Hemet, California, have staged an annual play that tells the story of Juan Diego's killing. Although criticized as overly romantic, even trite and saccharine, *Ramona* moved and continues to move readers to tears. Racial myth also appears in the novel, for both Ramona and Alessandro are described as olive- or light-skinned, not swarthy. Despite his humble origins, Alessandro reads and plays the violin.

Besides highlighting discrimination against Indians, *Ramona* somewhat inadvertently glamorized the lifestyle and landscape of southern California. The railroad pushed into southern California just as the novel appeared. With this new transportation link came a surge in tourism and immigration to the region. Instead of a condemnation of Indian policy, the novel became part of booster rhetoric. The book's engaging local color and romance reinforced the types of imagery that tourists love. Market-savvy photographers shot thousands of images supposedly depicting "Ramona's marriage place," "Ramona's home," and other locales from the book. These photographs, printed on postcards mailed throughout the world, further spread mythical visions of Old California.

Also capitalizing on the novel's popularity, public officials throughout southern California bestowed the name "Ramona" on a plethora of sites. From San Diego inland, one finds streets, major highways, and a small city carrying the name. In Palo Alto, Ramona Circle and Ramona Street honor the writer and her novel.

Jackson did not have long to savor the popular success of her novel. First she suffered a broken leg that healed very slowly. Then, in the spring of 1885, as she underwent treatment in San Francisco, she learned that she suffered from cancer. In June she wrote to a friend: "My *Century of Dishonor* and *Ramona* are the only things I have done of which I am glad now. The rest is of no moment. They will live, and they will bear fruit" (Green-

stein). In a final letter, written in August 1885, she addressed President Grover Cleveland: "From my deathbed I send you a message of heartfelt thanks for what you have already done for the Indians," she wrote. "I ask that you read my *Century of Dishonor.*" She added that every word of *Ramona* was true. "My heart and soul are in Ramona," she proclaimed. Her husband Will arrived, and they spent her last days together. She died on 12 August 1885. Her novel had already sold 15,000 copies.

Originally buried in San Francisco, where she died, Jackson was later moved to a private grave near the summit of Cheyenne Peak some four miles from Colorado Springs, Colorado. However, owing to the threat of vandalism at the remote site, her body was exhumed again and reburied in Evergreen Cemetery in the city.

Ramona remains in print and has inspired an opera and three motion pictures, the foremost starring Don Ameche and Loretta Young in a 1936 film directed by Henry King. In the fall of 1998, the California Historical Society published a special "Ramona" issue of *California History* exploring mythology as well as present-day controversies and their financial implications. In 2000 the Department of the Interior declared Rancho Camulos a National Historical Landmark. In addition, Ventura County received a $250,000 grant to boost tourism. The money will rebuild rail lines between Piru and Rancho Camulos and add bicycle paths and walkways. The historic complex includes 16 structures spread over 40 acres. The 11,000-square-foot main ranch house, or *casa grande,* is constructed of adobe dating from 1853. The ranch was part of the first Mexican land grant bestowed in California, in 1839. Visitors today can view Ramona's bedroom and the setting for the first half of the book. Performer Suzanne Lawrence appears at area functions portraying Helen Hunt Jackson. The myth of Old California with its lazy rancho days remains alive and well in Ramona country.

References

Evans, Rosemary. "Helen Hunt Jackson's Sympathetic Attitude toward Indians Was Reflected in Her Popular *Ramona*." *Wild West* 12, no. 1 (June 1999): 18–20.

Greenstein, Albert. "Helen Hunt Jackson": *http://www.socalhistory.org/Biographies/hhjackson.htm*.

Helen Hunt Jackson: *http://www.cateweb.org/CA_Authors/Jackson.html*.

Rancho Camulos: *http://www.ventura.org/heritage/Rancho_Camulos/rancho_camulos.html*.

RAMSEY, BUCK

1939–1998, singing cowboy and cowboy poet. *See* Cowboy Poetry

REAGAN, RONALD

1911–   , politician. *See* Adams, Ansel; Politicians and Western Myth

RED GHOST

See Camel Corps

REMINGTON, FREDERIC S.
1861–1909

"The name of Frederic Remington," writes his biographer Harold McCracken,

> has become synonymous with the realistic portrayal of our Old West. His impressive paintings, drawings and works of sculpture of the early day frontiersmen, cowboys and Indians are today well established as pictorial documentations of the most colorful and virile, as well as the most popular chapter in American history. Remington's subject was the length and breadth of the Old West, both geographically and historically—from Mexico to Canada and from the early Spanish explorers to the last of the Indian wars. (McCracken 1960)

Born in the small town of Canton, New York, Remington showed an early talent for sketching and painting. Sent to military school, he initially ran away, but eventually he accepted the regimen and made a few drawings of life there. At age 17, he entered Yale University, but in 1880, after less than two years of study, he packed up and headed west to seek adventure and his fortune. His father's death in February left him with a small inheritance and the freedom to escape school. Actually, he had devoted most of his energies at Yale to boxing, football, and sketching what he wished rather than what his art instructors required. The 19-year-old quickly learned that quick riches do not come easily, even in the magical West. He made repeated brief trips to the West, trying a bit of cowboying in Montana and sheep ranching in Kansas. *Harper's Weekly* published one of his Montana sketches on 25 February 1882, his first appearance in a major outlet. However, since a staff artist redrew the work, artistically it is not truly a Remington. The first painting to carry his full name graced the cover of the same magazine on 9 January 1886. In the fall of 1884 he married Eva Adele Caten, whom he had known for five years. In 1885 he sketched Apaches on the San Carlos Reservation. In 1888 *Century* magazine commissioned him to sketch and write about conditions on Indian reservations in the Southwest (a concern shared at the time by Helen Hunt Jackson, author of **Ramona**). His solid documentary style coupled with his ability to write as well as paint impressed eastern magazine editors.

The youthful artist's commissions grew quickly, and his circle of admirers grew to include Theodore Roosevelt. The future president commissioned the artist to draw sketches for his book *Ranch Life and the Hunting Trail* (1888). Remington fancied himself a writer as much as an artist, perhaps influenced by his father's career as a journalist. He published sketches of western life as *Pony Tracks* (1895) and *Crooked Trails* (1898). He also illustrated books for his friend Owen Wister. In 1902 Macmillan published his first novel, the successful *John Ermine of the Yellowstone.*

During the 1890s, Remington filled his studio in New Rochelle, New York, with western artifacts, notes, and other materials that provided the detail for his vivid paintings. In 1895 he began to work in a new medium: bronze sculpture. His action-packed bronzes, such as *Bronco Buster* (1895) and *Comin' through the Rye* (1902), became as popular as his paintings. Despite public acclaim, however, the eastern artistic establishment never accorded him any respect.

Although attentive to detail, Remington sentimentalized the Old West. The prejudices of his age and class show through. "Jews, Injuns, Chinamen, Italians, Huns—the rubbish of the Earth I hate—I've got some Winchesters and when the massacring begins, I can get my share of 'em and what's more, I will," he wrote in *Pony Tracks.* As historian Richard White has observed, "The West of Remington, Roosevelt, and Wister was an unabashedly masculine and nasty place, the domain of Anglo-Saxon men

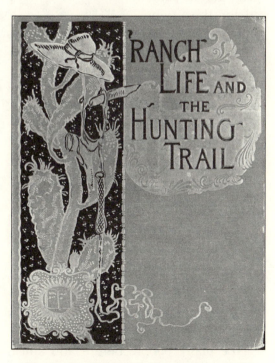

Remington illustrated Theodore Roosevelt's book, Ranch Life and the Hunting Trail *(Library of Congress)*

bent on keeping all they regarded as lesser breeds in their place" (White 1994). Remington's racial attitudes simply reflected the prevailing views of his time.

Remington's social attitudes have not stood the test of time, but his art has. Although he had far more talent, he targeted much the same audience as did the **pulp novelists** of his day. "I paint for boys, boys from ten to seventy." "He really meant, in effect," observes critic Matthew, Baigell, "that he painted for those who still wanted to believe in make-believe and for those who preferred strongly masculine, physical activities." Baigell explained Remington's magic well, his ability to have viewers identify vicariously with his subjects. "This quality of fantasy must ultimately lie as the center of Remington's general appeal. In the works of other painters of the West we look at figures performing specific actions. We keep a certain distance from them. In Remington's paintings we can slip easily into the roles played by the figures" (Baigell 1976).

Like many people before and since, Remington deeply lamented the passing of the Old West, even though his social philosophy deemed that passing proper

Cover of book Pony Tracks, *by Remington (Library of Congress)*

and inevitable. Most of his works are action-packed. However, a few works reflect a sadness and nostalgia for the good old frontier days. His 1895 painting *The Fall of the Cowboy* demonizes fencing as the end of the open range and thus of the cowboy's freedom. *The Last March* (1906) shows a tired, riderless horse, besieged by three snarling wolves.

Remington's powerful images remain among the most recognizable icons of the Old West. During his abbreviated life, he created some 2,750 paintings and drawings, 25 bronzes, eight books, and a host of magazine articles. Death came the day after Christmas 1909, of acute appendicitis. As death approached, he reportedly cried "Cowboys! There are no cowboys anymore!" Thanks to his marvelous outpouring of creativity, viewers can still appreciate his vision of hard-riding cowboys, grizzled trappers, fierce Indians, and brave soldiers.

References

Baigell, Matthew. *The Western Art of Frederic Remington.* New York: Ballantine Books, 1976.

McCracken, Harold, ed. *Frederic Remington's Own West.* New York: Dial Press, 1960.

Remington, Frederic. *The Collected Writings of Frederic Remington.* Edited by Peggy and Harold Samuels. N.p.: Castle, 1986.

White, Richard. "Frederick Jackson Turner and Buffalo Bill." In *The Frontier in American Culture,* ed. James R. Grossman. Berkeley and Los Angeles: University of California Press, 1994.

RENDEZVOUS

From the mid-1820s through 1840, western trappers and Indians met annually with merchants at a prearranged spot each summer to trade their beaver pelts for traps, tobacco, ammunition, and other supplies. The annual rendezvous involved not only trade and business but also celebration and feasting for days on end. The term originated in the late sixteenth century from the Middle French phrase *rendez vous,* "present yourselves." Mountain men, who often worked alone or in pairs, enjoyed the sociability that the annual gathering provided.

Jedediah Smith brought about the first such event on Henry's Fork on the Green River in July 1825. He talked merchant William Ashley into bringing supplies there from St. Louis to exchange with the trappers. With business completed, the trappers turned to a wonderful range of competitions. They gambled, exchanged tall tales, shot at targets, threw tomahawks and knives, raced horses, and generally tried to best one another. Ashley neglected to bring liquor to the first gathering, an oversight he did not repeat. Thus, drunken revelry also became a part of the rendezvous. Painter Alfred Jacob **Miller** captured the pageantry and fun of the rendezvous in some of his paintings. His work *Pipe of Peace at the Rendezvous* (1837) presents an idyllic moment of sharing and camaraderie between Native Americans and white trappers.

Each year thereafter, the men selected the location for the next rendezvous. Locations included Cache Valley, Bear Lake, Pierre's Hole, and several sites along the Green River. During the 1840s, permanent trading posts replaced the rendezvous system. Thanks to the storytelling prowess of many mountain men, such as Jim **Beckwourth,** Jim **Bridger,** and John **Colter,** the rendezvous became a highly mythologized part of western history. Today reenactors, such as the American Mountain Men, replete in long beards and animal skins, perpetuate the old-time tradition.

References

"American Mountain Men": *http://www.xmission.com/~drudy/amm/moreamm.html.*

"Mountain Rendezvous": *http://www.linecamp.com/museums/americanwest/western_places/mountain_rendezvous/mountain_rendezvous.html.*

RIDERS OF THE PURPLE SAGE

Riders of the Purple Sage is Zane **Grey's** most famous western novel. Since its publication in 1912, the immensely popular book has inspired several movies, musical groups, and other books. Its romanticism reflects simplistic frontier dualism and conflict, illustrated well through the characters and plot of the story. However, in his famous tale, Grey used not Native Americans but Mormons (communicants of the Church of Jesus Christ of Latter-Day Saints) to represent savagery and evil.

A lone Utah cowboy, Lassiter, is on a quest. His late sister, Milly Erne, had been wooed by Mormons to abandon her family, and during his search to find and revenge her, he meets Jane Withersteen. Jane is a Mormon whose loose adherence to the Mormon laws keeps her in constant conflict with the heads of the church. These church leaders use harsh pressure to force obedience to church doctrine, such as whipping her non-Mormon servants and kidnapping her adopted daughter. Lassiter agrees to protect Jane from Mormon violence, and together they fight to keep her land and her self-respect as a woman.

Meanwhile, Jane's servant Venters gets into a brawl with two outlaws, wounds one, and discovers that the outlaw happens to be a beautiful woman. He nurses her back to health in a lovely and secluded Eden, where, naturally, they fall in love. Back in town, Lassiter has killed a Mormon bishop. He also learns that it was Jane's father who had charmed Milly Erne away to Mormonism. Jane and Lassiter flee the town and encounter Venters and Bess, the outlaw. In the dramatic final scene, church elders surround Jane and Lassiter at their hiding place.

Lassiter claims to be too weak to move the boulder that would seal the cave entrance and that will kill Elder Tull, Jane's enemy. "He arose, tottering, but with a set face, and again he placed his bloody hand on the Balancing Rock. . . . *'Roll the stone! . . . Lassiter, I love you!'* Under all his deathly pallor, and the blood, and the iron of seared cheek and lined brow,

worked a great change. He placed both hands on the rock and then leaned his shoulder there and braced his powerful body." Jane's declaration of love gives the tough cowboy the strength to do her bidding, and he kills Elder Tull.

Throughout the book, Grey portrays the conflict between rugged individualism, an admirable Western characteristic, and the collectivism of the Mormons, abhorrent to Grey. As a woman in the Mormon Church without a husband or a father to protect her, Jane is vulnerable to attacks and schemes from the church leaders, who use her faith as justification for their demands. This conflict is perfectly manifested in a passage from chapter 1. Lassiter and Elder Tull meet when Lassiter rescues Jane's servant Venters from being whipped:

> "Where I was raised a woman's word was law. I ain't quite outgrowed that yet."
>
> Tull fumed between amaze and anger.
>
> "Meddler, we have a law here something different from a woman's whim—Mormon law! . . . Take care you don't transgress it."

Grey attacks Mormonism by depicting corrupt autocratic leaders of the church who try to harm the heroine of the novel.

At least five movies have been based on the novel. In 1918 Fox produced a silent film, starring William Farnum, Mary Mersch, William Scott, and Buck Jones. In 1925 another version featured Tom Mix, Beatrice Burnham, George Kohler Sr., and Arthur Morrison. The years 1931 and 1941 each produced another romanticized version of the story. In Hamilton McFadden's movie (1931), George O'Brien played Lassiter and Marguerite Churchill played Jane, and Noah Beery Sr. and James Todd also starred. William Farnum returned in the 1941 version, along with George Montgomery as Lassiter and Mary Howard as Jane.

The story retains its appeal. In 1995 Ed Harris portrayed Lassiter opposite Amy Madigan's Jane. Grey's hostile characterization of Mormon leaders as corrupt and sinister and of the church itself as manipulative do not play well in today's more-tolerant atmosphere. Thus, the 1995 version plays down the religious conflict in the story and simply shows that Jane's townsfolk have turned against her, without specifying why. In the novel, the leader of the church, Tull, plays the enemy and is portrayed as an evil man with "a dark relentless face": "He loomed up now in a different guise, not as a jealous suitor, but embodying the mysterious despotism she had known from childhood—the power of her creed."

Turning from film to music, a very successful western band took the name Riders of the Purple Sage in 1936. Buck Page started the band as a teenager, and soon the band's members became radio stars. A leading western-music nightclub in New York, The Village Barn, kept the band as regular performers. Because of their western sound, Page had specifically named the band after Zane Grey's popular novel, which remained famous through the 1930s and long thereafter. The name reflects the band's musical genre and creates a powerful, positive image through the public's immediate recognition of the name. The band's success mirrored the popularity of the original western novel.

In the 1970s Page reorganized the band, and the members began playing again. Today, Buck Page, Mike Ley, Dart Zubis, and Cody Bryant still tour on the West Coast, wearing cowboy hats and other western garb, playing guitars decorated with branding symbols and other western icons.

Another band that started in the late 1960s called itself New Riders of the Purple Sage. They exemplified a growing western and bluegrass belief that people will not confuse two bands if one group puts the word "New" at the beginning of their name. This *new* band included John Dawson, Jerry Garcia, Phil Lesh, Mickey Hart, Dave Nelson, and Bob Matthews. Their music also stayed within the stream of western tradition, leaning more toward the country side of western and the rock side of country. Their music reflected bluegrass, country, and rock influences. Jerry Garcia, Phil Lesh, and Mickey Hart were also members of the legendary Grateful Dead, which generated a huge cult following. Thus, a classic western novel becomes linked to "Deadheads," again showing the interconnectedness of American popular culture.

Recognizing the stature of *Riders of the Purple Sage,* many critics and authors use the phrase "writers of the purple sage" as a label for western authors in general. In Santa Fe, a store called Purple Sage sells handmade clothes, blown glass, and other collectibles from around the world. The store owners love the book *Riders of the Purple Sage* and chose the name to distinguish themselves from other art galleries and fashion stores in Santa Fe while retaining a western flavor.

The name *Riders of the Purple Sage,* or just *Purple Sage,* is used to title all kinds of companies and organizations wanting to create a western image. In Idaho, a golf course uses the name Purple Sage to beckon players. An Internet-based parody, Religion of the Purple Sage, simply plays on the romantic ring of the phrase and unknowingly reflects the strict, exclusive religious beliefs that Grey criticized.

The town of Purple Sage, Texas, population 4,500, is the seat of Wilmot County. The town ignores the fact that Zane Grey's novel takes place in Utah. Author Barbara Burnett Smith bases her Purple Sage mystery novels in this town in Texas. Myth begets myth.

If parody and imitation are the sincerest forms of flattery, then *Riders of the Purple Sage* is truly blessed. Grey used the romantic scenes and situations of the West as a basis for his work, and his work is now used as a model for many more western books and movies. Because of its huge success, other authors tried to create works like *Riders of the Purple Sage*. The dramatic rescues, daring duels, fierce romances, rough riding, and sharpshooting of later works often imitate Grey's story. *Riders of the Purple Sage* created an aura and images of the Old West that have penetrated deeply and widely through American culture.

—*Ellen J. Oettinger*

References

Jackson, Carlton. *Zane Grey*. Rev. ed. New York: Twayne Publishers, 1973, 1989.

Kimball, Arthur G. *Ace of Hearts: The Westerns of Zane Grey*. Fort Worth: Texas Christian University Press, 1993.

RINCHES

Tejano term for Texas Rangers. *See* Cortez Lira, Gregorio; Texas Rangers

ROBBINS, MARTY

1925–1982

Born Martin David Robinson, few men can claim to have had as much impact in their chosen lines of work as has the singer and composer Marty Robbins. He's best remembered for his distinctive, haunting, romantic "gunfighter ballads" and cowboy songs. Songs such as "El Paso," "Big Iron," **"Billy the Kid,"** and "Utah Carol" ring with his clear, evocative voice and vivid lyrics. Robbins added heartache to the mystique of the gunfighter and cowboy myths. His heroes were passionate men, driven by love and ambition. A true westerner, who briefly lived the life of a drifter, Robbins's voice in country music was authoritative. His songs bring to life the drama of the Old West, a place of strong men, beautiful women, and decisive, often deadly, actions.

Born to an impoverished family near the desert town of Glendale, Arizona, Robbins grew up making trouble in school and walking miles to see Gene **Autry** movies. As the youth's hero, Autry inspired him to take up the tradition of the Singing Cowboy. After serving in the South Pacific for three years in the navy, Robbins worked several odd jobs and eventually landed a singing job at a radio station in Phoenix. Working both radio and **television,** he slowly gained popularity and exposure. In 1951 Grand Ole Opry star Little Jimmy Dickens led Robbins to a contract with Columbia Records, and by 1953 he was a rising star. His first top-ten hit, "I'll Go On Alone," debuted that year, and he joined the roster of the Opry soon after. Robbins became an Opry mainstay for some 30 years, his popularity never flagging. He had a top-ten hit in all but three years of his career.

In addition to his considerable musical talents, Robbins projected a dynamic, likable, accessible image. Everyone in the Opry family respected him. His passion and drive carried over into other areas. He loved driving race cars and competed on the NASCAR Grand National circuit. Surviving two heart attacks and several car crashes, Robbins proved to be the kind of tough, resilient man about whom he sang. His racing schedule determined his Opry schedule, and the late 11:30 show with Marty Robbins became an institution. He continued full-tilt in both music and racing until his death from a third heart attack in 1982. Less than two months before he died, he was inducted into the Country Music Hall of Fame.

Robbins performed a wide range of music, but his enduring image is that of the Singing Cowboy. His talent and appeal crossed many musical boundaries, from country to pop to western to folk and even to Hawaiian. His pop song "A White Sport Coat (And a Pink Carnation)" virtually created the poignant image of the jilted teenaged prom date. He had many films to his credit, including *Badge of Marshall Brennan* (1957), *Ballad of a Gunfighter* (1963), *Guns of a Stranger* (1972), and *Honkytonk Man* (1982). Robbins's versatility revitalized country music, and he became one of the first performers to succeed simultaneously on the country and pop charts. He pioneered in such musical areas as multitrack recording and the now-common distortion effect known as "fuzztone."

Gunfighter Ballads and Trail Songs is a defining collection of both classic and original songs of the Old West. Perhaps the most famous of these is "El Paso," a tragic tale of romance he produced in 1959. Robbins wrote it himself, as well as its follow-ups "Feleena" and "El Paso City." "Big Iron" is another Robbins original, a dramatic description of the classic showdown between lawman and outlaw. In all of the ballads and trail songs, Robbins painted beautiful, dramatic pictures of the romance of the Wild West.

Robbins the innovator recorded a whopping 4-minute, 37-second version of "El Paso," which broke the conventional limit of approximately three minutes. A lovesick cowboy falls under the spell of the bewitching, beautiful "Mexican maiden" Feleena. Jealous of her flirting with another man, the cowboy challenges the intruder, "a wild young cowboy . . . / Wild as the West Texas wind." The lover kills his rival "in less than a heartbeat." He runs out the back door of the cantina and rides away from El Paso but soon returns: "It's been so long since I've seen the young maiden / My love is stronger than my fear of death." Shot almost immediately upon his return, the cowboy has just enough time to make it to the cantina and die in Feleena's arms.

The story is bittersweet and dramatic, the consummate western romance. Full of action and passion, it is a study of the human side of the gunfighter. After he kills the stranger,

Just for a moment I stood there in silence
Shocked by the foul, evil deed I had done.
Many thoughts raced through my mind as
   I stood there

I had but one chance, and that was to run.
(Mariposa Music, Inc.)

This cowboy is a hero, despite his hasty act of murder, and the intruder is a perfect image of a western challenger. The cowboy kills him in a passion and runs from the law, the classic profile of a western gunfighter. Consider his feelings as put forth in the lyrics:

I saddle up and away I did go
riding alone in the dark.
Maybe tomorrow a bullet will find me
tonight nothing's worse than this pain in
my heart. (Mariposa Music, Inc.)

Robbins's gunfighter/cowboy is a classic figure of mythology, a Lancelot or Romeo driven to desperate measures by the love of a woman.

Whereas "El Paso" is the cowboy's song, told from his point of view and ending with his death, "Feleena" relates the girl's story. Describing her early life and travels, it adds depth to the relationship between the girl and the cowboy. It also explains why Feleena acts the way she does:

In just a little while, she learned that with
a smile
She could have pretty clothes, she could
be any man's wife. . . .
She understood men and she treated them
all just the same. . . .
That was her nature and that was the way
that she lived. (Lyrics—Marty Robbins)

"Feleena" describes the same incident as does "El Paso," with the gunfight and the cowboy's desperate run out the back door. However, it reveals that the cowboy returns the very next day, and what happens after he dies in Feleena's arms:

Quickly she grabbed for the six-gun that
he wore
And screaming in anger and placing the
gun to her breast
"Bury us both deep and maybe we'll find
peace!"
And pulling the trigger, she fell 'cross the
dead cowboy's chest. (Lyrics—Marty
Robbins)

According to the end of the song, the lovers can be heard in the winds around El Paso.

The story of Feleena and her cowboy is a romance on a large, heightened scale—a true western. The cowboy rides away over a vast land and is driven back to die in the dust, seconds away from achieving his goal. The woman cannot bear to live without him and kills herself—with the gun that caused the trouble in the first place. There is no more tragic story in the world, and Marty Robbins's version is especially poignant because it takes place in "the West Texas town of El Paso." The image of a lonely cowboy riding over the windswept horizon is one of the most romantic settings America has to offer. Using Spanish guitar and the image of a Mexican woman whose eyes were "blacker than night" blended the traditional American perception of the West with the actual presence and influence of Hispanic culture. Although he deviated from the custom of his day, Robbins's acknowledgment of Hispanic influence added to the authority and authenticity of these songs.

The mystique of the songs extended beyond music; the U.S. Navy vessel USS

El Paso used Robbins's song as a theme, and it was an integral part of life on that ship. Robbins himself visited the *El Paso* and officially donated the song. Continuing the series, "El Paso City" is a later reflection on the mystery of the lovers; a man wonders whether his fascination with the story means he could have been that cowboy. Robbins's traveler asks:

> Could it be that I could be the cowboy in
> the mystery
> That died there in that desert sand so long
> ago?
> El Paso City
> By the Rio Grande. (Lyrics—Marty Robbins)

This man's fascination with the legend speaks for everyone. Who has not at one time wished to live a heroic past in another time?

In these three songs, Robbins created a legend and described the real reason it is so captivating. He added one more myth to the vast collection in the Old West. For many people, Feleena and her cowboy still walk in the winds of El Paso. Songs such as "The Ballad of the Alamo," "They're Hanging Me Tonight," "Cool Water," "Old Red," and "Running Gun" recalled other aspects of the Old West. Robbins described gunfights, stampedes, rodeos, love, and the brotherhood of cowboys on the trail. With his honest face and clear voice, Robbins represented the romantic idea of the singing cowboy. His songs are rich narrative poems whose lyrics force listeners to pay attention. The tunes are both original and traditional, recalling the easy melodies of early American folk songs. Marty Robbins's gunfighter ballads are easy to sing along with, and they can move listeners to tears. Nothing more is required for a Singing Cowboy to join the myth of the Old West. Robbins will forever be a part of the image of his native West. Almost a man out of his time, he represented well a bygone era and served as a powerful, enduring link between the twentieth century and the romantic Old West.

—*P. S. Crane*

References

Hagan, Chet. *Grand Ole Opry*. New York: Henry Holt, 1989.

Lyrics—Marty Robbins: *http://musik.freepage. de/slapers/lyrics-MartyRobbins.htm*.

Mariposa Music Inc.

Rogers, Jimmie N. *The Country Music Message: All about Lovin' and Livin'*. Englewood Cliffs, NJ: Prentice-Hall, 1983.

Source of Further Information

Kristy's Marty Robbins Web Page: *http://mem bers.aol.com/kkcowgirl/mrobbins.htm*.

ROCKWELL, ORRIN PORTER

1813–1878

The Mormon bodyguard and pioneer Orrin Porter Rockwell, called "the Destroying Angel," was born in Belchertown, Massachusetts. As a youth, he eagerly listened to religious discussions among his parents and other members of the Church of Jesus Christ of Latter-Day Saints (LDS), including the church's founder, Joseph Smith. He even did extra chores to help earn money to print *The*

Book of Mormon. He was received into the Mormon Church on 6 April 1830.

As a young man, Porter served as Smith's personal bodyguard and gun bearer. In 1843 officials charged Porter with the shooting death of Lilburn Boggs, ex-governor of Missouri. However, a grand jury failed to indict him. The following year, an anti-Mormon mob killed Smith in Carthage, Illinois, and Porter began protecting his successor, Brigham Young.

Porter personally led Mormons on their heroic journey west to the Great Salt Lake Valley in 1847. Porter worked as a scout, rancher, and deputy marshal, accumulating a handsome estate. The census of 1870 lists him as a farmer, with eight persons in his household, real estate wealth of $8,000, personal wealth of $5,000. According to his family, he never practiced polygamy, but he did father 19 children by his three wives.

He died on 9 June 1878, of natural causes, in Salt Lake City. He lies buried in the municipal cemetery, which includes more than 110,000 plots with the remains of many Mormon presidents and pioneers.

Porter has gained the status of folk hero among many Mormons. For example, his pair of 1851 Colt Navy Revolvers are proudly displayed in an exhibit called "The History of the Church Told through Guns" at the LDS Church Museum of History and Art. The same exhibit also includes the .36-caliber Allen Pepperbox used by Joseph Smith on the day of his assassination. Porter's Rock stands some seven miles west of Guernsey, Wyoming, north of Cottonwood Creek. He supposedly scouted from it on the journey west in 1847.

Porter's Place Restaurant, in Lehi, Utah, is owned by Bob Trepanier, who is also a partner in the 24-acre Porter Rockwell Business Park. A nine-foot-high statue of Porter is located at the park near Point of the Mountain. Clutching his long rifle, he guards the first of nine buildings in the business park.

Porter has been the subject of many books and films, not all faithful to the historical record. His major biographers include Nicholas Van Alfen (in 1964), Harold Schindler (in 1966), and Richard Lloyd Dewey (in 1986). Schindler incorporated non-Mormon references; the other two writers utilize predominantly Mormon sources. Dewey also published a novelized account of Porter's life in 1987 and a more recent, longer chronicle (1999).

Rockwell: A Legend of Life in the West, a very strange video biography, appeared in 1994. The amateurish production, only released on videotape, was written and directed by Richard Lloyd Dewey. Karl Malone of the Utah Jazz National Basketball Association team starred. Anachronisms mar the production—or perhaps it's meant to be a science-fiction spoof. The supporting cast is comprised mostly of local Utah actors, both professional and amateur. Far more successful and intelligible is *The Life and Times of Porter Rockwell,* 30 minutes of interviews with leading authorities, including Dewey, Schindler, Lee Nelson, and John Rockwell (a descendant).

In any case, the drama of Rockwell's life and the prominence of his family name will keep his memory part of the legends of the West. Like Bill Hickman, he is reviled as a "Danite chief," a hit man for the Mormon Church. However, the faithful revere both men for their steadfast willingness to fight for their faith and for their Prophets.

References

"It's a Bad, Bad, Bad, Bad Movie": *http://www.rinkworks.com/badmovie/reader/212.shtml.*

Rockwell Articles: *http://www.rockwell-fam ily.org/articles/article00002p1.htm.*

RODEO BALLET

See Copland, Aaron

RODEO BULLS

Weighing from 1,300 pounds to a ton, bucking bulls are quick, agile, strong, and sometimes deadly. Bred to buck, the best throw rodeo riders year after year. The greatest and toughest gain recognition by the Pro-Rodeo Hall of Fame and Museum of the American Cowboy in Colorado Springs, Colorado.

As of late 2000, the hall had honored just six bulls of the hundreds that have competed in rodeos. The distinguished list includes Tornado, Oscar, and Old Spec, inducted in 1979; Red Rock and Crooked Nose (a fighting bull), both inducted in 1990; and the most recent, Bodacious, inducted in 1999.

Good bucking bulls come in all breeds, sizes, and shapes. The best, however, usually include some Brahma blood. Riders find spinning bulls the most dangerous because of the risk of falling under the whirling animal's sharp hooves. Bulls that buck straight tend to throw their riders out of harm's way.

California stock contractors John Growney and Don Kish may be credited with building the modern rodeo bull dynasty. Growney's bull Red Rock (who died in 1994) went undefeated until its retirement in 1987. Kish and Growney bred Red Rock with offspring of Hall of Famer Oscar. Wolfman is one of the results. Although not yet a Hall of Famer, Wolfman holds the distinction of being the only bull to score a perfect ride of 100 points each for bull and rider. Retired to Red Bluff, California, the bull now extends his legacy to his offspring.

All riders have their list of the worst bulls (or best, depending on one's perspective). Eight-time National Finals Rodeo bull rider Cody Lambert puts Skat Kat Skoal (Sammy Andrews's bull no. 81) at the top of his list. The animal ranked as the 1995 PBR (Professional Bull Riders) Bull of the Year.

Tornado is probably the most-storied of these famous animals. The stock company owned by 16-time world champion Jim Shoulders handled the 1,850-pound Tornado, who tossed the first 200-some riders who climbed on his back. At the 1967 National Finals Rodeo, however, Tornado faced 1962 world champ Freckles Brown of Soper, Oklahoma. As Tornado burst from the chute, the 46-year-old bull rider stuck to the raging bull like glue, ending the giant's seven-year undefeated streak. "It was the greatest experience of my life," Brown recalled. "He came out of the chute and started kicking and bucking. I couldn't hear nothing. I just held on. When I got off I heard the crowd hollering and they wouldn't let up. They just kept on and I knew I'd done it." Brown rode the famous bull again later the same year. Tornado retired, having been ridden only five times total. Cancer took Brown's life on 20 March 1987.

People unfamiliar with rodeo often point a damning finger at the sheepskin-covered flank strap that encircles the bull near the hips. They mistakenly believe that the strap squeezes the animal's genitals, causing it to buck. The flank strap does not restrain sensitive areas and causes no more discomfort than a too-tight belt might to his rider. Instinct, training, and breeding make for world-class buckers. The flank strap, an unwanted encumbrance just like the rider, only makes the bull buck higher.

The latest Hall of Fame honoree, Bodacious (J31), earned a reputation as "the world's most dangerous bull." The 1,800-pound cross-bred Charbray threw 129 of 135 riders during his illustrious career. Strong and tricky, his signature head-snapping move gravely injured Terry Don West in 1994. The following year, Tuff Hedeman, one of the few to ride Bodacious for a full eight seconds, suffered major face injuries after another encounter with the brute. Hedeman later refused to face the animal, calling him "the baddest bull there has ever been" (Janet Ratzloff's Guide to Rodeo). In the bull's last rodeo appearance, he seriously injured then–world champion Scott Breding. Owners Sammy and Carolyn Andrews retired the bull "in the interest of cowboy safety."

The retired Bodacious remained a rodeo celebrity, earning press coverage in *GQ, Penthouse,* and the Fox TV Network program *Guinness World Records Prime Time.* Bodacious died of kidney failure on 16 May 2000. Fittingly, a memorial fund aids cowboys injured in rodeo competitions.

References

Elements of Professional Rodeo: *http://home. san.rr.com/tomtl/elements.htm.*

Janet Ratzloff's Guide to Rodeo: *http://rodeo. about.com/sports/rodeo/library/weekly/ aa052400.htm.*

Pro-Rodeo Hall of Fame: *http://www.prorodeo .com/.*

ROGERS, ROY

1911–1998

Happy trails to you, until we meet again.
Happy trails to you, keep smilin' until then.
Who cares about the clouds when we're together?
Just sing a song and bring the sunny weather.
Happy trails to you, 'till we meet again.
(Lyrics to "Happy Trails," by Dale Evans)

This theme song for singing cowboy star Roy Rogers, "King of the Cowboys," and his wife, Dale Evans, "Queen of the West," is among the most recognized in American musical history. It also captures the bubbling, joyous spirit and optimism of the pair, who entertained several generations of Americans with their songs, films, and **television** show.

Born Leonard Slye, the future cowboy star was born in Cincinnati and raised in Portsmouth and Duck Run, Ohio. In 1929 he purchased his first guitar, second-hand, for $20. A letter from an older sister in California beckoned the family west in the spring of 1930. Rogers came to adulthood during the Great Depression. He survived by taking on a variety of jobs, including truck driver, greens keeper, and peach picker. He learned a bit about cowboy work on a ranch in New Mexico.

By age 18, young Slye was performing as an amateur on radio programs. His talent led to an offer to join The Rocky Mountaineers in August 1931. He performed with many western bands during the early 1930s, playing live for dances and on the radio. His initially performed under the name "Dick Weston," which he used as a member of the legendary Sons of the Pioneers.

Turning to Hollywood, he acted in several films, beginning in 1935, when he appeared with the Sons of the Pioneers in the Liberty picture *The Old Homestead*. As a singer, he earned $75 a week from Hollywood's Republic Studios. From then on, his career took off. He left the Sons of the Pioneers (replaced by Pat Brady) in 1937, and the following year he starred in the film *Under Western Stars,* when he became Roy Rogers. He also made another Republic picture in 1938, **Billy the Kid** *Returns*. After signing with Republic, he spent some time at a Montana ranch to hone his on-screen skills, riding, roping, shooting, and boxing.

Rogers and Dale Evans first performed together in the 1944 film *Cowboy and the Senorita*. The two married in 1947, a year after the death of Rogers's first wife, Arlene Wilkens, whom he had married in 1936. Their warm, cheery personalities and lovely harmonies charmed movie audiences. Among their first films after marriage were two that evoked the romance and charm of Old Spanish California: *On the Old Spanish Trail* (1947) and *The Gay Ranchero* (1948). Sidekick Gabby Hayes joined them in several pictures. Rogers became the leading western star at the box office from 1943 to 1954.

His television program ran from 1951 to 1957. Roy and Dale shared their musical, often zany adventures at the Double R Bar Ranch, with his German shepherd, Bullet, and comic sidekick, Pat Brady (with his Jeep Nellybelle). Roy's famous palomino horse, Trigger, and Dale's horse, Buttermilk, costarred. Originally named Golden Cloud, Trigger enjoyed prominent billing as "The Smartest Horse in the Movies." He served Rogers from 1938 until 1957. After the horse died in 1965, Rogers had him stuffed and mounted.

Like many cowboy stars, Rogers and Evans took their jobs as role models seriously. During the 1950s, members of the Roy Rogers Riders Club agreed to obey a set of rules very similar to Gene **Autry**'s earlier Ten Commandments of the Cowboy:

1. Be neat and clean.
2. Be courteous and polite.
3. Always obey your parents.
4. Protect the weak and help them.
5. Be brave but never take chances.
6. Study hard and learn all you can.
7. Be kind to animals and care for them.
8. Eat all your food and never waste any.
9. Love God and go to Sunday school regularly.
10. Always respect our flag and our country.

In 1990 Rogers survived both heart surgery and a dangerous bout of pneumonia. The following year he recorded yet another album, *Tribute*. His son Dusty wrote a tune for the album titled "King of the Cowboys." K. T. Oslin, Randy Travis, Kathy Mattea, and other country-and-western stars performed with Roy. Roy and Dale also continued to make public appearances at fairs and rodeos. In 1999 Rhino Records produced a handsome, collectible four-CD box set of Rogers's performances from 1937 through 1990.

After retiring from show business, Rogers and Evans devoted much of their time and energy to televangelism. They appeared often on television, witnessing to the importance of Jesus Christ in their lives. Rogers died at age 86 of congestive heart failure in his home some 90 miles northeast of Los Angeles, where he and Dale Evans had lived for 33 years. The Queen of the West died on 7 February 2001. A crowd of 1,800 paid their last respects at a public memorial service held at the Church of the Valley in Apple Valley. Family and friends then braved the 106-degree heat to make the 13-mile trek to the Roy Rogers and Dale Evans Museum in Victorville, established in 1965. There, thanks to the skills of taxidermists, fans can still view the couple's faithful companions Trigger, Buttermilk, and Bullet the Wonder Dog.

Although the museum houses a collection of some 300 firearms, the gift shop does not sell toy guns for children. Rogers always minimized the violence in his films, shooting the gun from the bad guy's hand rather than killing him. Rogers supported the right to own guns, but he wanted children to understand that firearms are serious, dangerous business. "The shows you see now," Rogers criticized, "with all that killing and everything, I just don't know. Now you hear about all these guns at school, and it makes you sick."

References

The Official Roy Rogers, Dale Evans Web Site: *http://www.royrogers.com*.

"A Tribute to Roy Rogers": *http://classicfilm. about.com/movies/classicfilm/library/weekly /aa070698.htm*.

ROSWELL, NEW MEXICO

In early July 1947, an unidentified flying object (UFO) crashed just outside of Roswell, New Mexico, after radar screens at the Roswell Army Air Field (RAAF) Base in Alamogordo, New Mexico, had tracked the object for several days. Several witnesses, including two Catholic nuns, Mother Superior Mary Bernadette and Sister Capistrano; residents of Roswell, such as Mr. and Mrs. Dan Wilmot; and local ranchers, namely, William "Mac" Brazel, attested to seeing a bright light plunge from the sky and hearing odd, explosive noises. The next day, Mac Brazel discovered strange debris scattered across a pasture near the ranch he operated, the Foster Ranch. The unidentified materials consisted of metallic foil and wooden pieces that looked malleable yet would not bend, break, or burn. Mysterious markings or hieroglyphics appeared on some of the debris. That same day, W. Curry Holden and a team of archaeologists stumbled upon the crash site and a saucer-like ship about 35 miles north of Roswell. One of the archaeologists telephoned Sheriff George Wilcox of Chaves County, who in turn dispatched the Roswell Fire Department to the scene. Two campers, Jim Ragsdale and Trudy Truelove, also encountered the crash site. They spied something more than just a saucer-like ship, however; they saw bodies lying beside the craft.

While residents and visitors to Roswell reeled from the strange experiences associated with the unexplainable phenomena relating to the crash, the U.S. military swooped in, and within six hours they had sealed off and cleaned up the crash site. Military personnel interrogated and intimidated civilians found at the scene, forcing them with threats to maintain secrecy regarding the events. The military cleanup crew removed both the debris and the alien bodies to the nearby base. Sgt. Melvin E. Brown, who accompanied the truck that carried the bodies, disregarded orders and looked at the covered bodies of the alien flight crew. He subsequently described them as small beings with large heads and yellowish skin.

At the same time, several residents of Socorro, New Mexico, discovered another crashed saucer, along with its flight crew. The military again immediately sealed off the site and swore all observers to secrecy. The cleanup crew uncovered four alien bodies at this second site, located only two miles from the field where Brazel had discovered debris from the first crash. Government officials transported the bodies to a military hospital at Roswell Army Air Field, where, according to mortician Glenn Dennis of the Ballard Funeral Home in Roswell,

doctors performed a series of alien autopsies.

A nurse, Eileen M. Fanton, also known as Naomi Maria Selff, who worked at the military hospital and assisted the autopsy, informed Glenn Dennis about the top-secret procedure the following day. Although in a state of extreme anxiety, the nurse clandestinely met with Dennis and described her gruesome encounter with two small, mangled alien bodies. She explained how the presiding doctors forced her to record their findings during the autopsy. She described the aliens as small beings with disproportionately large heads, tiny mouths, large, sunken eyes, and concave noses. She even drew pictures of them on a prescription pad. When Dennis attempted to reach the nurse a few days after they had met, however, military personnel informed him that she had transferred to another base. The nurse had vanished without a trace.

Meanwhile, Mac Brazel notified Sheriff Wilcox about his discovery of unidentifiable debris strewn across the fields of the Foster Ranch. Wilcox in turn informed a reporter, Frank Joyce, affiliated with KSWS, a local radio station in Roswell, about Brazel's story. Wilcox also notified Maj. Jesse Marcel, an intelligence officer with the 509th Bomb Group stationed at Roswell, who decided to interview Brazel. Marcel reported his findings to his superior, Col. William H. Blanchard, the commanding officer at RAAF. Blanchard granted Marcel permission to examine both the mysterious debris scattered over an area about one mile long and 250 feet wide at the Foster Ranch and the black, circular gouge, approximately 500 feet long, located on the property (apparently the alien ship touched down on the property prior to the crash). Marcel, along with Counter Intelligence Corps (CIC) agent Capt. Sheridan Cavitt, discovered, like Brazel, that they could not cut, bend, or tear the mysterious material. They repeatedly beat the thin material with a 16-pound sledgehammer, yet they failed to even dent it.

Within a few days of the incident, Lydia Sleppy, a teletypewriter operator for a radio station in Albuquerque, received a phone call from Johnny McBoyle, one of the owners of KSWS radio station in Roswell. McBoyle informed Sleppy about the strange goings-on in Roswell and requested that she immediately transfer a story about the UFO crash on her teletypewriter to reach the ABC wire. Shortly after she commenced typing, however, the FBI office in Dallas cut off her transmission. Next, she received a message ordering her to stop communication at once. She instantly contacted McBoyle and told him what happened. McBoyle promptly instructed her to forget and say nothing of what he had told her. Apparently, in the interim, the FBI had gotten to him, too.

The next day Colonel Blanchard ordered a public information officer, Second Lt. Walter Haut, to release a statement to the media regarding the recovery of an unidentified flying disc in New Mexico. Haut distributed several copies of the press announcement to local radio stations and newspapers, including the *Roswell Daily Record*. The announcement confirmed that a UFO had landed near Roswell and that the intelligence office of the 509th Bomb Group of the Eighth Air Force at RAAF had both

removed and inspected it. Not only did local media feature the breaking news, but newspapers worldwide, such as the *New York Times* and the London *Times,* carried the story as well. Several military officers, however, including Brig. Gen. Roger M. Ramsey, the commanding officer of the Eighth Air Force at Carswell Air Force Base in Fort Worth, Texas, did not approve of Blanchard's actions. Ramsey ordered Blanchard to send the saucer debris to his office at once. Blanchard complied, and conveniently went on leave shortly thereafter.

Major Marcel accompanied the B-29 bomber that transported the wreckage to Ramsey's office. When the debris arrived, Ramsey had it examined and subsequently invited the press not only to examine it themselves but also to photograph it. Yet he also instructed them not to touch it. Shortly after, without members of the press realizing it, military personnel exchanged the wreckage of the Roswell saucer with the mangled remains of a weather balloon. Ramsey then announced that the identification of the object as a UFO of extraterrestrial origin represented a gross misunderstanding. He then stated that the debris before them was actually the remnants of an ordinary weather balloon. The Fort Worth base weather officer, Warrant Officer Irving Newton, confirmed Ramsey's claims. The media immediately corrected their assertion that a flying disk had crashed in the New Mexico desert and publicized Ramsey's version of the story. Meanwhile, military personnel covertly transferred the real UFO debris to Wright-Patterson Air Force Base in Ohio.

The story does not end there. Although the Roswell incident remained largely closed for nearly 30 years, renewed interest in the series of events that took place in New Mexico in early July 1947 emerged during the late 1970s and early 1980s. A number of self-proclaimed "UFOlogists," researchers who examine reports of alleged UFO encounters, have sprung up over the past 20 years. They have written countless books and articles, which have appeared in both scholarly and popular-culture magazines, about the Roswell incident. The media has also played a large role in bringing Roswell and the UFO phenomenon into the forefront of American consciousness. Movies, including *Roswell* (1994) and a recent documentary called *Six Days in Roswell,* propagate the idea that alien beings undoubtedly have had contact with earth. **Television** shows, such as *Unsolved Mysteries, X-Files,* and the recent *Roswell,* continue to deal with the idea that other life forms are out there, as exemplified by events at Roswell. Museums dedicated to the Roswell incident, namely, the UFO Enigma Museum and the International UFO Museum and Research Center, both in Roswell, have not only increased interest in Roswell and UFOs but have also generated a good deal of tourist dollars in the area.

UFO organizations, such as MUFON (Mutual UFO Network), CUFOS (Center for UFO Studies), and CAUS (Citizens against UFO Secrecy), have also cropped up over the past two decades. Numerous magazines and journals, including the *Journal of UFO Studies, Saucer Smear, UFO Magazine,* and the *Flying Saucer Review,* have also appeared recently on the scene. *Time* magazine has even featured articles about the Roswell incident.

Countless Web sites related to UFOs, Roswell, and **Area 51,** the site where the government supposedly stored the wreckage of the Roswell UFO crash, proliferate on the Internet. One can read contentious debates among the leading UFO experts, purchase T-shirts that sport images of the aliens that fell to earth in 1947, and visit sites that explain how the Roswell affair has drifted into American folklore. UFOlogists and other interested folk have held a number of conferences and conventions pertaining to the Roswell crash. Residents of Roswell celebrate their infamous UFO crash every Fourth of July.

Yet does the fact that scores of people commemorate, celebrate, heatedly discuss, and write about the Roswell incident give any validity to the whole affair? Many people, including scholars, skeptics, and nongovernment officials alike, decry the events and claim that people who believe a flying saucer filled with little green men crashed and burned on Earth more than 50 years ago are deluded. Furthermore, many scholars argue that increased antigovernment sentiment—resulting from Watergate, the Iran-Contra affair, and even the Monica Lewinsky scandal—has fomented a strong, widely held belief that the government blatantly hides the truth about extraterrestrials from the American people. This heightened cynicism prompted the U.S. General Accounting Office and the U.S. Air Force to investigate the government's role in the Roswell affair. Their probe resulted in a 1994 report that not only debunked the idea that alien beings had landed in New Mexico but also announced that the U.S. government had indeed participated in a cover-up. This cover-up, however, had nothing to do with flying saucers or little alien beings with enormous heads. It had to do with attempts to develop Cold War surveillance methods.

Since the end of World War II and the onset of the Cold War, military intelligence leaders had experimented with various methods of technical surveillance in order to learn about Soviet weapons capabilities. One method involved a mechanism that could detect high-altitude sound waves, which an atomic explosion would create. This mechanism took the form of a balloon containing sonic detectors. According to scientists, the balloon had to reach heights of 66,000 feet in order to detect sound from far away. In 1946 government officials awarded the contract to develop the balloons to scientists at New York University. The top-secret project became known as Project Mogul. According to members of the government, some scholars, and even some self-proclaimed UFOlogists, the "alien spacecraft" that went down in July 1947 was actually one of Project Mogul's weather balloons. Officials understandably shrouded the events in secrecy during the Cold War years in order to safeguard the American people from the alleged Communist menace.

Yet how does this explanation account for the testimony of the scores of eyewitnesses, and the alien bodies they observed, not to mention the alien autopsy film that surfaced in 1995? First, according to UFO researcher Kal K. Korff, only a handful of the eyewitness accounts represent firsthand encounters. In addition, many of the eyewitnesses have embellished and changed their stories over time. Moreover, several UFO researchers

have accused a key player, Maj. Jesse Marcel, of lacking credibility. Second, regarding the supposed sighting of extraterrestrials near the crash sites, the U.S. Air Force has issued an additional report asserting that people in Roswell probably mistook anthropomorphic dummies that the balloons carried during research launchings for alien corpses. Finally, in 1995 television stations aired a film that supposedly contained footage of an alien autopsy that doctors had conducted in 1947. Considerable evidence indicates that the film is a hoax. The cameraman who owns the film refuses to submit it to scientific tests and dating. What's more, jump cutting, conveniently unfocused shots, and lack of hot flashes, telltale visual imperfections often associated with the type of camera purportedly used to shoot the film (a Bell and Howell Filmo 70 model), all indicate deception. Furthermore, the "doctors" who perform the autopsy do not follow standard medical procedures: They do not place the severed alien organs into glass jars; they do not properly hold the surgical scissors; and they do not use a block to prop up the chests of the bodies. And the aliens themselves do not seem real: The bodies flexibly snap back after manipulation, much like latex.

The Roswell incident represents a multifaceted and complex narrative filled with heated debates. The story, which people have built upon and altered over the years, has permeated our culture and taken on mythic, even legendary proportions. Yet regardless of one's unwavering cynicism or zealous belief regarding the existence of alien beings, UFOs, and a government conspiracy linked to Roswell, we cannot ignore one crucial element of the story. The Roswell incident represents the first time in history that the U.S. government officially admitted to having captured an unidentified flying object. This reality has penetrated our psyches, thanks in large part to the media, on both conscious and unconscious levels. Otherwise, why would alien-seeking tourists pump millions of dollars into New Mexico's economy each year, and why would thinking Americans hold conventions and smugly wear T-shirts that read "I want to believe"?

—*Jane Veronica Charles Smith*

References

Korff, Kal K. *The Roswell UFO Crash: What They Don't Want You to Know.* New York: Prometheus Books, 1997.

Peebles, Curtis. *Watch the Skies! A Chronicle of the Flying Saucer Myth.* Washington, DC: Smithsonian Institution Press, 1994.

Saler, Benson, Charles A. Ziegler, and Charles B. Moore. *UFO Crash at Roswell: The Genesis of a Modern Myth.* Washington, DC: Smithsonian Institution Press, 1997.

Sources of Further Information

Clark, Jerome. *Extraordinary Encounters.* Denver, CO: ABC-CLIO, 2000.

Lewis, James R. *UFOs and Popular Culture.* Denver, CO: ABC-CLIO, 2000.

ROUGH RIDERS

The First United States Volunteer Cavalry, the "Rough Riders," are probably the most famous fighting unit in the history of the armed forces of the United States. Many myths surround this body of soldiers. Theodore Roosevelt and Col. Leonard Wood commanded the soldiers. Many of the stories deal with Roosevelt, who resigned his post as assistant secretary of the navy in May 1898 to join the volunteer cavalry. Their charge up San Juan Hill near Santiago de Cuba, catapulted the Rough Riders to mythical status. Books, movies, and reenactments have not only maintained but added to the legend that surrounds the First United States Volunteer Cavalry.

On 15 February 1898, a massive explosion rocked the battleship USS *Maine* in the Havana harbor. This disaster set off a wave of anti-Spanish sentiment in the United States. Many suspected that a Spanish mine killed the 250 sailors aboard the *Maine*. Cries of "Remember the *Maine*" rang across the country, and on 25 April 1898, Congress declared war on Spain, beginning the Spanish-American War. The wealthy and prominent Theodore Roosevelt immediately enlisted and became second-in-command, behind Colonel Wood, of the volunteer cavalry unit. Together, these two men began the task of gathering and then training the Rough Riders.

Of the 20,000 men who volunteered for duty, Roosevelt selected only "born adventurers," those who demonstrated great stamina and riding and shooting skills. The unit became one of the most diverse in the history of the U.S. military. From the West came cowboys, small-town sheriffs, Indians, and frontiersmen. These westerners faced the Cuban jungle and Spanish troops with the same courage and grit they had displayed back home. Policemen, high-society gentlemen, and college athletes flocked in from the East. The troops trained in San Antonio, Texas. Thanks to Roosevelt's

Colonel Theodore Roosevelt, 1899 (Library of Congress)

political connections, the Rough Riders received the best training, supplies, and weapons available, including the new, smokeless rifles. Given these advantages, how would they perform in battle?

In June 1898 the unit set sail for Cuba. Roosevelt became unit commander after Wood was reassigned. The troops fought at the Battle of Las Guasimas on 24 June 1898. In July the Rough Riders received their assignment: to drive the Spanish soldiers from the San Juan Heights overlooking the city of Santiago de Cuba. On 1 July, under heavy Spanish fire, the Rough Riders began their historic charge. The two sides exchanged withering fire. The Rough Riders staggered up the hill, but at a high cost as bullets tore through many of them. The charge left 15 dead and 76 wounded, yet still they struggled on.

Upon reaching the crest of Kettle Hill, Roosevelt set his sights on San Juan Hill, a short distance away. Yelling at his men to follow, he charged toward San Juan Hill. The din in the area was such that only five Rough Riders heard their commander. Roosevelt found himself seriously outnumbered. Undeterred, he regrouped his men and charged the hill in force. They drove back the Spanish and punctuated the victory by planting their yellow cavalry flag atop the hill. Two days later, on 17 July 1898, the final Spanish ship fled the Santiago de Cuba harbor, and Cuba was free. The *Tucson Arizona Star* came up with the name "Rough Riders" for the unit after Roosevelt had vetoed several other names, such as "Teddy's Terrors" and "Teddy's Texas Tarantulas."

One source of controversy is the question of which unit actually made it to the top of San Juan Hill first. Because of the incredible media coverage given to the Rough Riders, the obvious assumption would have been that Roosevelt and his men had crested the hill first. However, African-American **Buffalo Soldiers** may have actually preceded the Rough Riders.

Many stories and paintings have the Rough Riders charging uphill on horseback, in good cavalry fashion. However, owing to logistical foul-ups, their mounts had remained behind in Tampa. They fought on foot. Furthermore, the rough ground would have been very hard going for horses.

Many accounts from men actually present at the battle still exist. The most famous is the account by Theodore Roosevelt himself, called *The Rough Riders* (1899). This collection of writings, part diary and part letters, has been widely read and analyzed. Apparently, Roosevelt began to believe the legendary status he had achieved; he wrote, "This [the charge up San Juan Hill] hardly seemed a tribute to my military skill," he states at one point, "but it delighted the crowd, and as far as I could tell did me nothing but good."

Although many works have been written concerning the unit and its commander, *The Boys of '98,* by Dale L. Walker, is among the most widely acclaimed. He conveys well the politics and attitudes of the times as well as the personalities and thoughts of newspaper correspondents such as Stephen Crane and Richard Harding Davis.

In 1997 TNT aired a **television** miniseries, *The Rough Riders.* The series vividly captured the American military spirit and bravery of the times. Tom Berenger ably starred as Theodore Roosevelt, with Sam Elliott as Capt. William

O. "Bucky" O'Neill. The film is widely regarded as one of the most accurate military films of all time, with some of the most riveting battle scenes in cinema history.

The Rough Riders remain a shining, vivid example of U.S. military glory and bravery under fire. The images associated with Theodore Roosevelt and his volunteer cavalry abound. Because the media of the time worked so hard to cover every move the unit made and to glorify its efforts, the myths surrounding the unit began to grow almost instantly. These myths have continued to grow and to place the Rough Riders on a pedestal above all other military units in the history of the U.S. armed forces. Roosevelt, of course, became a war hero, candidate for vice president, and, following President William McKinley's assassination in 1901, president of the United States.

–*Daniel C. Gunter III*

References

Jeffers, H. Paul. *Colonel Roosevelt: Theodore Roosevelt Goes to War, 1897–1898.* New York: John Wiley and Sons, 1996.

Morelock, Jerry D. "'Colonel Teddy': Historians Examine the Spanish-American War's Most Famous 'Rough Rider.'" *Military Review* 78, no. 3 (May/June 1998): 94.

Pierson, David S. "What the Rough Riders Lacked in Military Discipline, They Made Up for with Patriotic Fervor and Courage." *Military History* 15, no. 2 (June 1998): 10.

Samuels, Peggy, and Harold Samuels. *Teddy Roosevelt at San Juan: The Making of a President.* College Station: Texas A & M University Press, 1997.

Walker, Dale L. *The Boys of '98: Theodore Roosevelt and the Rough Riders.* New York: Forge, 1998.

ROUND ROCK, TEXAS

See Bass, Sam

ROUTE 66

What the Oregon Trail was to the nineteenth century, Route 66 became for the twentieth. Like its predecessor, Route 66 carried vast numbers of people westward. It also become a cultural icon memorialized in song, fiction, **television,** and pop culture.

During the early 1920s, Cyrus Avery of Tulsa, Oklahoma, and John Woodruff of Springfield, Missouri, provided an early impetus for creating a highway link between the Midwest and California. They understood that such a route would provide an economic boost to their home states along the route. Spurred by the burgeoning automotive industry, Congress initiated legislation for a comprehensive plan of public highways in 1916, with revisions in 1921, and a finalized plan in 1925.

Following extended wrangling, Avery's proposed road became Route 66 on 26 November 1925. The road would run from Jackson and Michigan Avenues in Chicago southwest through St. Louis, Missouri, on to Tulsa and Oklahoma City, then straight west though the Texas Panhandle, northern New Mexico, and Arizona, ending in Pacific Palisades Park, California, where Santa Monica Boulevard meets Ocean Boulevard. However, the trauma of the Great Depression held up completion. The entire road would not be paved until 1930.

During the early 1930s, an estimated 210,000 desperate people headed west on Route 66 to escape the Dust Bowl. John Steinbeck re-created this epic migration in 1939 in *The Grapes of Wrath*. Like countless other families, the Joads joined the migrant stream on Route 66, "the Mother Road." The novel, together with the film the following year, made Route 66 a living legend as the path to opportunity.

Among the host of travelers during the 1930s and 1940s was Robert William "Bobby" Troup, of Harrisburg, Pennsylvania, and his wife. He wrote a song about the route, "Get Your Kicks on Route 66." Crooner Nat King Cole recorded the song in 1946, and it became a huge, long-lasting hit. Countless other singers have recorded the song as well, including cowboy song master Michael Martin Murphey, who gave it a Texas swing flavor:

If you ever plan to motor west;
travel my way, take the highway that's the
    best.
Get your kicks on Route 66!
It winds from Chicago to L.A.,
more than 2,000 miles all the way.
Get your kicks on Route 66!
Now you go thru Saint Looey, Joplin,
    Missouri
and Oklahoma City is mighty pretty.
You'll see Amarillo, Gallup, New Mexico;
Flagstaff, Arizona; don't forget Winona,
Kingman, Barstow, San Bernardino.
Won't you get hip to this timely tip:
When you make that California trip.
Get your kicks on Route 66!
Get your kicks on Route 66!

Motivated by Cold War concerns for moving military personnel and equipment, Congress passed the Interstate Highway Act in 1956, which began construction of new multilane interstates. Modeled on the German autobahns observed during World War II, they heralded the death knell for smaller two-lane roads, like Route 66, and for many small towns. As interstates bypassed small communities in the West, a new generation of **ghost towns** emerged.

During the 1960s, however, CBS television would immortalize the road in the popular series *Route 66*. The program first aired on 7 October 1960 and ran for 116 episodes, until 18 September 1964. The real star of the show was a flashy Chevrolet Corvette convertible. Martin Milner costarred as the car's owner, rich boy Tod Stiles. George Maharis as sidekick Buz Murdock and Glen Corbett as Linc Case costarred. The thin, contrived plot led the boys on various implausible adventures along the fabled route. Henry Mancini provided a wonderfully lyrical and soaring theme song. However, producers shot much of the show on other highways that they believed better represented the true spirit (if not the reality) of Route 66.

Television could not save the road. By 1970 modern four-lane interstate highways had replaced most of the route. In October 1984 the last, poorly maintained stretch of U.S. Highway 66 gave way to Interstate 40 at Williams, Arizona. It took five interstates to replace the Mother Road: I-55, I-44, I-40, I-15 and I-10.

The death of the real road, however, spawned a legion of legendary supporters. Writer Michael Wallis, born near the road, published *Route 66: The Mother Road* in 1990 and issued a video documentary, *Route 66 Revisited,* four years later. In 1993 NBC launched another TV series in which two new heroes inherited a Corvette and drove off in further search of adventure. Since the mid-1990s, the Annual Mother Road Ride/Rally has drawn hordes of motorcyclists to tour down the historic route. The Albuquerque Convention and Visitors Bureau and the New Mexico Route 66 Association developed a number of events to celebrate the route's seventy-fifth anniversary on 20–22 July 2001. PBS television produced an hour-long documentary.

Museums and associations keep the road's memory alive. The National Route 66 Museum in Elk City, Oklahoma, uses a road motif to carry visitors through all eight states along the original road. Murals and vignettes depict various eras and places of the road. Another museum, the California Route 66 Museum in Victorville, also honors the route. The road has been designated a Historic Monument administered by the National Park Service. As author Michael Wallis observes, many who search out the route today still "find the time holy."

Reference

Wallis, Michael. *Route 66: The Mother Road.* New York: St. Martin's Press, 1990, 1992.

Sources of Further Information

Adventure Series: *http://timvp.com/route66. html.*

California Historic Route 66 Association: 2127A Foothill Blvd., Suite 66, La Verne, CA 91750.

California Route 66 Museum: Address: P.O. Box 2151, Victorville, CA 92393; Web Site: *http://www.national66.com/victorville/in dex.html.*

Events Calendar: *http://wemweb.com/events/ evt.html.*

Explore Route 66: *http://www.national66.com.*

Historic Route 66 Association of Arizona: P.O. Box 66, Kingman, AZ 86402.

Kansas Historic Route 66 Association: P.O. Box 169, Riverton, KS 66770.

National Historic Route 66 Federation: P.O. Box 423, Tujunga, CA 91043–0423.

National Route 66 Fan Club: P.O. Box 66, Manchester, MI 48158.

National Route 66 Museum: Address: P.O. Box 5, Elk City, OK 73648; Web Site: *http:// www.national66.com/elk_city/index.html.*

New Mexico Route 66 Association: 1415 Central NE, Albuquerque, NM 87106.

Oklahoma Route 66 Association: 6434 NW 39th Expressway, Suite D, Bethany, OK 73008.

Old Route 66 Association of Texas: P.O. Box 66, McLean, TX 79057.

Route 66 Association of Illinois: P.O. Box 8262, Rolling Meadows, IL 60008.

Route 66 Association of Missouri: P.O. Box 8117, St. Louis, MO 63156.

66 Chronology: *http://route66.exmachina.net/ main/frameset_chronology.htm.*

Song of the Road: *http://route66.exmachina. net/main/frameset_song.htm.*

RUSSELL, CHARLES MARION

1864–1926

Born in St. Louis, Missouri, Charles Marion Russell grew up wanting to go west. His family tried to dissuade him by sending him first to military school and later to art school, but to no avail. He realized his dream and headed west to Montana, arriving in early March 1880. (Coincidentally, another western artist, Frederic **Remington,** made his first journey west that same year.) Russell worked at a variety of jobs, including hunting, trapping, and herding cattle. His spent his formative seventeenth and eighteenth years with old-time mountain man Jake Hoover in Pie-Eye Basin on the South Fork of the Judith River. Along the way, he worked at his art, sometimes modeling small clay and wax figures, which presaged his later impressive sculptures in bronze. While cowboying, he sketched the scenes around him, usually in watercolor. In 1882 he worked the Judith Basin roundup. During winter layoffs, he sometimes exchanged a painting for food or lodging in town.

Russell sometimes drew sketches on letters, some of which have been preserved. In 1886 a Helena cattleman asked him for a spring stock report. The horrendous winter had decimated herds on the northern ranges. Russell replied with a watercolor sketch he titled *Waiting for a Chinook.* The picture (also called *Last of the 5,000*) shows a single, gaunt steer with coyotes circling ominously in the background. Upon seeing the drawing, the ranch manager concluded that he didn't have to write anything to the cattle's owner. "Hell, he don't need a letter, this will be enough." Russell had earned his nickname "the Word Painter." In 1929 his wife, Nancy Russell, published a delightful collection of Russell's illustrated letters under the title *Good Medicine.* Reproductions of more than 400 of his fascinating letters

appeared in the 1993 book *Charles M. Russell, Word Painter,* edited by Brian W. Dippie and published by Abrams.

By his late 20s, Russell was concentrating on committing scenes of Montana range life to canvas. By the late 1880s, major eastern magazines were publishing his illustrations. In 1896 Russell met and married 17-year-old Nancy Cooper. He was 39. Thanks to her encouragement, he established a studio in Great Falls, Montana. Nancy's prodding gradually persuaded Russell to spend more time painting and less time hanging out at Bill Rance's Silver Dollar Saloon. Thanks to the growing eastern fascination with the Old West, Russell successfully sold paintings and illustrations. With Nancy handling the finances, his work began fetching higher prices.

Russell's first important national exhibit, The West That Has Passed, included six bronze statues. His work, especially the bronzes, got rave reviews from New Yorkers in the spring of 1911. There, the Montana artist took on the eastern favorite, Frederic Remington, head to head. He even created a new bronze piece, *A Bronc Twister,* for critics to compare with Remington's famous *Bronco Buster.*

Russell traveled a bit but always returned to his Great Falls studio. Except for his three-day stint at an art school as a teenager, Russell had no formal training. His flair for the dramatic and the fundamental honesty and realism of his work overshadowed their technical shortcomings. His heartfelt love of the Old West comes through clearly, as does a whimsical sense of humor. Russell, like Remington, lamented the changes that threatened the West's beauty and its inhabitants, including cowboys and Indians. He spent the summer of 1888 visiting often with the Blood Indians in neighboring Alberta, Canada. His painting *The First Furrow* foreshadows the negative impact of farming on traditional western life. He wrote a brief poem in 1917 indicating his sense of preserving a vanishing legacy:

> The west
> is dead my Friend
> But writers hold the seed
> And what they saw
> Will live and grow
> Again to those who read. (Range Writers Web Site)

Russell wrote this bit of philosophy and self-assessment, which concludes *Charlie Russell Roundup:* "To have talent is no credit to its owner; what man can't help he should get neither credit nor blame for—it's not his fault. I am an illustrator. There are lots better ones, but some worse. Any man that can make a living doing what he likes is lucky, and I'm that. Any time I cash in now, I win" (Dippie 1999).

In 1925 the Russells traveled to the Mayo Clinic in Rochester, Minnesota, where the artist had surgery on a goiter (enlargement of the thyroid) on 3 July. Tests, however, revealed other health problems. He suffered from a hernia on his right side, which might explain his fondness for wearing a wide sash that served as a truss. Probably due in part to a lifetime of smoking, he suffered from emphysema and an enlarged, seriously debilitated heart. The following year, on the evening of 24 October, Russell's heart gave out and he died at his home in Great Falls. Nancy died on 14 May 1940, having spent the remainder of her life zealously promoting and protecting her husband's work and legacy.

All major museums featuring western art include some works by Russell. However, the C. M. Russell Museum in Great Falls and the MacKay Gallery of Charles M. Russell Art at the Montana Historical Society in Helena boast the largest collections. Art collector Larry Len Peterson presents an excellent look at the artist's work in his book *Charles M. Russell, Legacy.* All told, Russell created some 4,000 works of art. The only major cowboy artist to live most of his life in the West, Russell knew, lived, and loved cowboy life and greatly respected Indian cultures. He rendered both with drama, liveliness, humor, and authenticity, making him the most beloved of western artists.

References

Dippie, Brian W., ed. *Charlie Russell Roundup: Essays on America's Favorite Cowboy Artist.* Helena: Montana Historical Society Press, 1999.

McCracken, Harold. *The Charles M. Russell Book.* Garden City, NY: Doubleday, 1957.

The Range Writers Web Site: *http://therange writers.com.*

Russell, Charles Marion. *Good Medicine: The Illustrated Letters of Charles M. Russell.* Garden City, NY: Doubleday, 1929.

_____. *Trails Plowed Under.* 1927. Reprint, introduction by Brian W. Dippie, Lincoln: University of Nebraska Press, 1996.

Taliaferro, John. *Charles M. Russell: The Life and Legend of America's Cowboy Artist.* Boston: Little, Brown, 1996.

SAN JUAN CAPISTRANO

See Swallows of San Juan Capistrano

SAN SABA MINE

ALSO LOS ALMAGRES MINE

In 1753 a Spanish expedition in Texas set out to locate a suitable site for an Apache mission. While traveling in what is now Llano County, they heard from Indians of a *cerro de almagre,* a hill of red ocher, often an indicator of mineral-bearing ore. Although they never found valuable ore, the legend of the rich Los Almagres Mine had begun.

In February 1756 the Spanish sent another small expedition commanded by Bernardo de Miranda y Flores. They located the hill (now known as the Riley Mountains, near Honey Creek) and dropped a shaft. Miranda reported find-ing "a tremendous stratum of ore" and proclaimed the mine San José del Alcazar, although assays did not show such richness.

Mining continued in the region until hostile Indians overran the local mission and presidio in March 1758. Apache attacks continued to thwart Spanish mining and other efforts in the area through the early nineteenth century. Miranda's optimistic report and a slag heap that the Spaniards left on the bank of the San Saba River, however, fueled an enduring tale of bountiful silver and fired the hopes of later generations of treasure hunters.

Anglo settlers in Texas heard about the tales of silver on the San Saba River and gold on the Llano River. Stephen F. Austin sent a force to investigate, but they found nothing. In 1829, however, the mythical "lost silver mine of San Saba" began appearing on Austin's maps. Cartographer Henry S. Tanner and others would also designate an area of silver mines on their maps of central Texas.

The entrepreneurial Austin understood that lost treasure would be a powerful magnet to draw immigrants to his Texas colony. He repeated the myth in an 1831 promotional pamphlet, and the lost mines became accepted fact in most subsequent publications about Texas.

In the 1830s James and Rezin Bowie made forays into the Texas hill country. Their trips added to the legend. They explored the San Saba River valley in what is now Menard County, about 250 miles inland from the Gulf of Mexico. (Today the county is bordered by Concho, Kimble, McCulloch, Mason, Schleicher, Sutton, and Tom Green Counties.)

In Anglo-Texan renderings, the old Los Almagres became the "lost San Saba Mine." In the late-nineteenth century, someone added "Bowie Mine" to the presidio's stone gatepost at Menard, which is located some 130 miles northwest of San Antonio. Today, the town celebrates an annual Jim Bowie Days, even though the actual site that inspired the legendary mine is more than 70 miles away.

Even accumulating factual evidence has not deterred the faithful. A U.S. Geological Survey listed the mine, described as unproductive, on a geologic map of Llano County in 1909. Historian Herbert E. Bolton also claimed to have found documents pinpointing the location. To many treasure hunters, however, the mine remains lost, and thus, its riches still await the right person.

Reference

Weddle, Robert S. "Los Almagres Mine": *http://www.tsha.utexas.edu/handbook/online/articles/view/LL/dkl5.html*.

SAND CREEK, COLORADO

See Battles or Massacres

SASQUATCH

See Bigfoot or Sasquatch

SELENA

1971–1995

The murder of Tejano vocalist Selena Quintanilla Pérez on 31 March 1995 shocked and saddened the singer's many fans. However, her tragic death moved both her and her music from a regional to an international audience. It also created a posthumous Selena industry.

The roots of Selena's Tejano sound reach back to Spanish and central-European songs of the nineteenth century. Her music's origins include lyrical Spanish songs *(canciones),* pointed political musical commentaries *(corridos),* and a mixture of instruments, including violin, guitar, and accordion. The popularity of fandangos, or rollicking dances, attest to the vibrancy of music in Texas before and after its independence from Mexico.

By the 1920s and '30s, so-called *conjunto* music had jelled, with traveling bands blending Mexican mariachi music with the "oom-pah-pah" accordion sounds of music from German, Polish, and Czech immigrant communities. Selena would draw upon these Tejano roots and extend them into new forms.

Born in Freeport, Texas, Selena, encouraged by her father when she was a preteen, began performing with her brother and sister under the name Selena y Los Dinos. By the late 1980s, the youngsters had attracted major-label backing from EMI, and in 1987 the Tejano Music Awards (TMA) honored Selena as Female Entertainer of the Year. She would go on to win many honors from the TMA.

Her sizzling sexual charisma and the powerful, adaptable voice issuing from her wide, expressive mouth made for memorable concerts and a fast-growing fan club. Musicologist Manuel Peña described his reaction to her live performance in 1992: "I found the sensuous power of Selena's stage presence intoxicating. Her lusty voice and lissome movements mesmerized the pulsating mass of five thousand bodies in attendance. More than that, this was a tejano audience adulating one of their own" (Peña 1999, 203).

Then, in the spring of 1995, Yolanda Saldivar shot and killed the singer at a Corpus Christi motel. Saldivar had founded Selena's fan club and then managed her boutiques. The tragedy and senselessness of the murder and the reality of another singer's life cut very short turned Selena into a martyr. Fans in the United States, Mexico, and elsewhere held spontaneous wakes, and 30,000 people filed past her coffin before her burial at Seaside Memorial Cemetery. The city constructed a kiosk, bronze statue, and memorial to her along the bay front. Unfortunately, unthinking fans defaced the statue with scratched initials and graffiti, forcing the city to enclose it behind a four-foot-high metal fence. A museum in Corpus Christi, built by Q Productions, also honors her memory.

A month after her death, five of her CDs graced the Billboard 200 chart, an accomplishment reached by only a tiny number of musicians. Within two years of her death, "Selenamania" had generated eight books, five videos, and two CDs. A feature motion picture appeared about her. Jennifer Lopez starred and Edward James Olmos played Selena's father in the critically acclaimed film. Jerell, Inc., of Dallas manufactures a line of children's clothing under the Selena label; the line is carried by Sears, JC Penney, and other national retailers.

Dreaming of You, her first crossover album, unfinished at her death, sold more than 3 million copies. Many Web sites provide venues for fans to communicate and commiserate over the loss of the charismatic young star. A musical based on her life, *Selena Forever,* premiered in San Antonio on 21 March 2000. The Selena Foundation raises money for musical scholarships and to found a Tejano music museum to honor her greatest love.

References

Burr, Ramiro. *The Billboard Guide to Tejano and Regional Mexican Music.* New York: Billboard Books, 1999.

Caller Radio Selena Page: *http://www.caller. com/selena/selena.htm.*

Peña, Manuel. *Música Tejana: The Cultural Economy of Artistic Transformation.* College Station: Texas A & M University Press, 1999.

Q Productions: Official Selena Home Page: *http://www.q-productions.com/.*

Selena, the Movie: *http://selena-themovie.warnerbros.com/main.html*.

Selena Foundation: *http://www.neosoft.com/selena/*.

SEVEN CITIES OF GOLD

The seven cities of gold entered recorded history upon the return of Spanish explorer Álvar Núñez Cabeza de Vaca to Mexico City in the summer of 1536. Initially on an expedition to explore Florida, Cabeza de Vaca and five other men became separated from their party in a storm. They trekked across Florida and floated over the Gulf of Mexico on horsehide rafts. Eventually crossing Texas, New Mexico, Arizona, and Mexico, Cabeza de Vaca and his men became the first white people to cross the North American continent. They brought stories from Indian tribes telling of land to the north "abounding in gold and silver, with [seven] great cities whose houses were many stories high, whose streets were lined with silversmiths' shops, and whose doors were inlaid with turquoise."

The residents of Mexico City seized on these tales of "riches beyond the wildest dreams of man" and rapidly formed a new expedition into the north to find the alleged cities. They returned with similar stories of "a big city . . . that in some sections . . . there are some very large houses ten stories high . . . of stone and lime . . . [and] the portals and fronts of the chief houses are of turquoise" (quotations from Hammond 1940).

Excited by the prospect of riches, the Spanish mounted another expedition in 1539 led by the Spanish priest Marcos de Niza. He ordered a black guide named Estevanico ahead to reconnoiter. Indians repeated tales to Estevanico about seven rich cities that lay to the north. Estevanico traveled as far north as Hawikuh, the largest of six Zuni villages near today's Gallup, New Mexico. Zunis killed him outside the town.

Hearsay and lust for gold continued to fuel Spanish ardor to discover these mysterious cities. Niza's exaggerated reports prompted the viceroy, in 1540, to amass an army, led by Francisco Vásquez de Coronado, to find and conquer the kingdom. After several months in the wilderness, they reached the so-called cities of gold in the land that Coronado named Cibola. The Spaniards met well-dressed citizens and admired large buildings covered in art that resembled cave paintings, but they found no hoards of gold or silver. They did see exceptionally beautiful turquoise, but only in small amounts. One of Coronado's men described Cibola as "a small, rocky pueblo, all crumpled up." Disillusioned, the army continued northward but never discovered any truly golden cities.

Despite Coronado's disappointment, the seven cities of gold have retained their powerful hold on our imagination. Located in Pojoaque, New Mexico, the Cities of Gold Casino lets gamblers continue the search for the illusive golden fortune. A more tangible souvenir may be purchased from the Lost Cities of Gold Wholesale Jewelry Outlet. Its catalog guarantees "no imports . . . all fine Navajo, Zuni, Hopi craftsmanship."

The media world abounds with allusions to the seven cities as well. Several pulp novels and western films, such as *The Lone Ranger and the Lost City of*

Gold (1958), perpetuated the tall tales of fortune. A popular 1980s computer game bore the title "Seven Cities of Gold." Along similar lines, an early 1980s cartoon called *The Mysterious Cities of Gold* generated a large cult following on the Internet. Douglas J. Preston wrote a popular historical novel (*Cities of Gold: A Journey across the American Southwest,* 1999) using local interviews and stories as its basis.

Myth has surrounded the seven cities of gold for more than 500 years. People continue to add new facets to the legend every day, as it seems to revitalize itself with each new generation of adventure seekers.

–Julie J. Anders

See also Comparative Frontier Mythology

References

Day, A. Grove. *Coronado's Quest: The Discovery of the Southwestern States.* Berkeley and Los Angeles: University of California Press, 1964

Hammond, George P. *Coronado's Seven Cities.* Albuquerque, NM: U.S. Coronado Exposition Commission, 1940.

SHE WORE A YELLOW RIBBON

See Cavalry Trilogy

SIERRA CLUB

See Adams, Ansel

SILVERADO

A lifelong love of Western films motivated brothers Lawrence and Mark Kasdan to create *Silverado*–starring Scott Glenn, Kevin Kline, Danny Glover, Kevin Costner, Brian Dennehy, Linda Hunt, Rosanna Arquette, Jeff Goldblum, and John Cleese–in the 1980s. They wrote, directed, and produced it in a decade in which the genre was not particularly popular. Devotedly inspired, they filmed through a frigid New Mexico winter to create a movie that would "remind people of the pleasures" of the western. Although not very successful at the box office, many critics and audiences laud *Silverado* as a high-quality film. The town-sized set created specifically for the movie in the desert outside Santa Fe is the largest western set ever built; it has been used many times since.

This well-made movie is full of flawlessly performed stunts and thrilling action scenes. Much of its appeal lies in the authenticity created by the talents of stunt coordinator Jerry Gatlin and especially gun trainer Arvo Ojala. Ojala trained all of the principal actors in gun handling, and the ease with which the Hollywood men use their weapons attests to his talent.

The musical score also creates the feel of a grand old western. It has two main themes, one for the family scenes and one for the dramatic scenes among friends. Composer Bruce Broughton describes the music as "in some ways a typical old movie score" but with a few modern twists. That statement well describes the entire film. The movie does not follow the introspective, brooding trend of most late-twentieth-century westerns; it is a great action adventure story in the old style. But it also has a few new angles, resulting in a refreshing addition to the grand tradition of western movies.

The plot is classic: A small group of good-hearted frontiersmen band together through circumstance and defend helpless townsfolk against a corrupt sheriff and a ruthless cattle rancher. Along the way, the heroes display amazing talent with firearms, while the bad guys have the traditional bad aim of all classic western villains. The heroes, of course, shoot accurately from incredible distances, shoot through walls, and hit two men at once. The main hero, Emmett, rides a white horse and overcomes nearly mortal wounds to save his family: his sister and her husband and child. Heroes do not have wives and children, and as one character notes in classic loner style, "A grown man can't have a little boy with him everywhere he goes."

The characters themselves are very traditional. Each of the four heroes represents a different classic type: gun-slinging loner, gentleman gambler, freeman farmer, and hotheaded youth. Scott Glenn is Emmett, the loner who loves his family; Kevin Kline is Paden, a firm believer in luck, with a soft spot for the helpless; Danny Glover plays Malachi, the wandering son of former slave; and Kevin Costner is Jake, Emmett's younger brother toting a "fancy two-gun rig."

Emmett and Paden are the center of much of the action facing the two main villains, their archenemies. Emmett has a history of bad blood with the McKendrick family, corrupt landowners outside the town of Silverado. Before the movie begins, Emmett has been in jail for killing the McKendrick patriarch. Paden once rode with the sheriff of Silverado, a man named Cobb, who keeps the peace on his own corrupt terms. Both McKendrick and Cobb are classic villains; the landowning rancher is appropriately sissified, and the corrupt sheriff is heartless but still charismatic and even likable.

The supporting characters and themes are likewise drawn from a pool of stock western types. *Silverado* features a smart horse, hookers with hearts of gold, a strong and beautiful pioneer woman, and a law-abiding family. Themes of the film include the conflicts between moral law and official-but-corrupt law and between cattle ranchers and homesteaders. Both the good guys and the bad guys are on quests to revenge murdered family members.

The characters are always moving westward. The ultimate goal for Emmett and Jake is California, a mythical land full of gold and promise. In their journeys, the heroes meet and part ways at forks in the road, having formed the kind of transient friendships that can only exist between independent frontiersmen in the Old West.

However, for all of its stock themes and classic images and characters, *Silverado* has a few modern twists that set it apart. It seems to be completely conscious of its genre; the Kasdans are very much aware of what they are making and of what they are modeling it on. *Silverado* often pokes gentle fun at some of the western's more dramatic conventions. In one of the opening scenes, Kline's Paden is in a gunfight to take back his horse. He fumbles with a decrepit gun while the man on his horse fires shot after shot, always barely missing him. Paden, of course, gains control of his weapon and shoots the rider dead in the street, taking back his horse. The twist is that Kline is in pinkish-red long underwear at the time, having been robbed of all of his possessions before the movie action begins. Emmett had found him in the desert, a stranger waiting to die in the sun. While taking care of him, Emmett relates the four-on-one attack that he endured in the movie's opening scene. He was puzzled by the sudden attack and had been asleep when the would-be assassins opened fire on him. Paden asks, "They just jumped you outta the blue?" Emmett replies, smiling slightly, "I had to get up anyway." The stoic, serious hero has his humorous moments in this film, as if the Kasdans knew they could poke fun at the excessive dramatics to which the Western is prone.

Emmett makes another tongue-in-cheek stab at the genre's drama later in the film. In the small town of Turley, John Cleese's Sheriff Langston informs Emmett and Paden that there will be a hanging at 10:00 A.M. the next morning. In the jail, Emmett and Paden learn that it is Jake who is to be hanged. Jake begs Emmett to do something, but Emmett remains stone-faced and resigned. Looking at his condemned brother, Emmett says, "Lying Pete always said you'd hang. I guess tomorrow at dawn he'll be proved right." Langston breaks in and says, "Ten A.M.," to which Emmett replies, "Oh, right. Always thought they did it at dawn."

The humor is subtle but effective. Who are the "they" who hang people at dawn? Obviously, "they" are all the average sheriffs in all the average old westerns. In a classic western, the condemned man would die at dawn, because it is more dramatic that way—but not in this film. In Turley, the man is scheduled to die at exactly 10:00 A.M. This is the kind of subtle, quirky twist that makes *Silverado* an interesting and entertaining film. Its mixture of old and new, of classic and modern, make it a valuable addition to the western genre. It seamlessly blends the grand scenery, music, plot, and characters of the older westerns with the modern humor and self-awareness that could only come after decades of western filmmaking. It succeeds in making fun of itself without ever becoming ridiculous, and it does so with an affection born of the Kasdan brothers' lifelong love of classic westerns.

—*P. S. Crane*

Reference

Hardy, Phil. *The Overlook Film Encyclopedia: The Western*. Woodstock, NY: Overlook Press, 1991.

SINGING COWBOYS

See Autry, Gene; Rogers, Roy; Steagall, Red

SMITH, HENRY NASH

1906–1986

Born in Dallas, Texas, on 29 September 1906, Henry Nash Smith made the study of American culture his life's work. He earned a bachelor's degree at Southern Methodist University in 1925 and completed a master's degree at Harvard four years later. Smith married Elinor Lucas on 10 April 1936. They had three children, Lloyd Mayne, Janet Carol, and Harriet Elinor. He continued his studies at Harvard, finishing his doctorate in American studies in 1940.

Smith's distinguished career took him back to faculty positions in Texas at Southern Methodist University (1927–1941) and the University of Texas at Austin (1941–1947). He later taught at the University of Minnesota at Minneapolis (1947–1953) and completed the last two decades of his career at the University of California at Berkeley. Smith died tragically on 6 June 1986, at the age of 79, after an automobile accident.

Smith published widely on American literature, concentrating his considerable energies on the works and life of Mark Twain. He broadened his focus with a 1978 book titled *Democracy and the Novel: Popular Resistance to Classic American Writers.* However, it was an earlier book, *Virgin Land: The American West as Symbol and Myth* (1950), that would establish his position as the leading investigator of myth and the West. That book (now available as an on-line hypertext document) brought him fame and prestigious awards: the John H. Dunning Prize and the Bancroft Prize.

Smith explored the growth and propagation of the West as myth and symbol by examining a wide range of literature—fiction, biography, periodicals and newspapers, and political speeches and government documents—as well as the role of boosters, such as press agents. Because he ended his study with the late nineteenth century, Smith did not contemplate the role of the electronic media.

Smith summarized his intention in *Virgin Land* in his introduction to the book.

The present study traces the impact of the West, the vacant continent beyond the frontier, on the consciousness of Americans and follows the principal consequences of this impact in literature and social thought down to Turner's formulation of it. Whatever the merits of the Turner thesis, the doctrine that the United States is a continental nation rather than a member with Europe of an Atlantic community has had a formative influence on the American mind and deserves historical treatment in its own right. (*Virgin Land,* on-line hypertext version)

Smith identified three major conceptual clashes at work in the mythological depictions of the West. We find proponents of a "Cult of Nature" promoting preservation and wildness versus a "Cult of Progress," a variant of **Manifest Destiny,** urging the taming and utilization of frontier resources. Likewise, we find images of bounty and opportunity in the "Garden of the World" myth in contrast to the bleak, arid visions of the "Great American Desert." Finally, the same "Garden of the World" myth can be juxtaposed with the "moonlight and magnolias" attributes of the "Southern Plantation" myth. Smith not only traced the proliferation of mythical visions of the West but also helped us understand them in wider national and international contexts.

In his preface to the on-line hypertext version of *Virgin Land,* University of Virginia scholar Ian Finseth offers some stimulating insights. He invites readers to look for evidence of the many important themes in the book. According to Finseth, Smith identifies as the primary motivations for Western mythology "economic ambition in settling or portraying the West and the political considerations in accomplishing that settlement" (Finseth, Preface). Finseth's on-line document includes specific references to the text of *Virgin Land* that support his interpretation of Smith's work.

"There are at least four principal mechanisms of mythologization at work in *Virgin Land*," Finseth continues.

The first is the active role of individual psychology in interpreting and describing the world, from which myth directly takes its form and color. Equally important is the simple repetition of a phrase or idea; its increasing currency; its gradual evolution from individual to social existence. After a certain threshold of self-consciousness has been crossed, myths, or the seeds of myth, can undergo deliberate manufacture. Another important mechanism, although not as critical as the first three, is the physical and public embodiment of an idea, as in art. (Finseth, Preface)

Finseth makes a good case that Western myth derived its power by tapping into a wide range of social, cultural, and psychological forces:

The myth constructs that Smith describes appeal almost universally to the imagination or to deeply held emotions, including personal well-being and national identity. Myths tend to resonate with a preexisting ethos in society. Perhaps most importantly, myths of the West tap into powerful and often ambivalent emotions regarding nature, ranging from a love of nature either for its own right or as a romantic ideal, to a fear of nature as an untamed and immoral place. (Finseth, Preface)

Smith showed, in Finseth's words, that

there are uniquely American qualities to the character of the myths of the West, or, to put it more precisely, ways in which the uniqueness of the United States imparted to its myths a distinctive coloring. The dominant hues involve liberty, the physical geography of the United States, and the images of an American empire and an American utopia. . . . Yet there still abided and thrived a longing to escape the past and tradition. (Finseth, Preface)

Myth, of course, undergoes change over time—a major theme of this book—and so Smith devoted considerable attention to such changes as well as to the interaction between historical reality and myth. As Finseth observes,

The most dramatic examples of how myth adapts or succumbs to history occur when reality flatly contradicts the assumptions or implications of a myth, often with wrenching effect. Yet even in such cases, myths can display a remarkable resilience and slowness in changing. Another dramatic reformulation can take place through the perversion of myth for purposes unrelated to its original motivating ideas. (Finseth, Preface)

In sum, Smith influenced an entire generation of cultural scholars. His work served as a noteworthy model for the then-new field of American studies. Subsequent scholars have gone beyond but continue to profit from his pioneering inquiry. Smith recognized and ably demonstrated the power and complexity of the Mythical West.

See also Comparative Frontier Mythology

References

Finseth, Ian. Preface to the on-line hypertext version of *Virgin Land: http://xroads.virginia.edu/~HYPER/HNS/preface.html.*

Lamar, Howard R., ed. *The New Encyclopedia of the American West.* New Haven, CT: Yale University Press, 1998.

SOLID MULDOON

In 1877, near Beulah, Colorado, William Conant and his son spotted an odd-looking stone. Upon examination, it turned out to be a foot, part of a seven-and-a-half-foot-tall stone body. A stone man, apparently lying in a grave, had features that suggested a "missing link" between apes and humans. The sensational story quickly spread to Pueblo, Denver, and then out across the nation. The *Denver Daily Times* emphatically declared: "There can be no question about the genuineness of this piece of statuary" (20 September 1877). According to writer Louis **L'Amour,** the rock man gained his name "Solid Muldoon" from William Muldoon, a wrestler and strongman of the day. A popular song called the powerful wrestler a "solid man."

Local press reports excitedly heralded the scientific importance of the find,

avowing solemnly that this Colorado fossil was not "anything like a repetition of the clumsy Cardiff Giant fraud" ("Go West, Stone Man!"). Unfortunately for the good citizens of Colorado, George Hull, creator of the fraudulent ten-foot-tall Cardiff Giant, had struck again. Hull, a New York cigar maker, had created his earlier petrified man, discovered near Cardiff, New York, in October 1869. Hull made thousands of dollars on his earlier hoax, until forced in court in February 1870 to reveal the truth. For his second effort, he spent three years crafting a more elaborate "petrified man." He skillfully blended mortar, rock dust, clay, plaster, ground bones, blood, and meat. He dried his long-armed creature in a kiln for several days.

At that point, he received assistance from the fossil's discoverer, William Conant. A former employee of circus legend P. T. Barnum, Conant helped Hull bury the giant figure, ready to be found as Colorado's first anniversary as a state approached. Solid Muldoon went on display in New York City in early 1878. Alas, one of Hull's business associates revealed the hoax to the *New York Tribune.*

Unlike the massive statue of the Cardiff Giant, the body of Solid Muldoon disappeared. However, the name lives on in history and contemporary life. A newspaper, edited by Daniel Day and published briefly in Ouray, Colorado, carried the name in the late 1880s. Rudyard Kipling wrote a short essay called "The Solid Muldoon," which appeared in a collection of short stories titled *The Soldiers Three* (1890). During the 2002 Winter Olympics, viewers from around the world will see events held at Utah's Deer Valley Resort. Some aerial competitions will be staged on a run called "Solid Muldoon." A publishing company in Durango, Colorado, also carries the name, as does an Austin, Texas, musical group and a Virginia City, Nevada, restaurant. Consummate pranksters Hull and Conant would doubtless be very pleased with the afterlife of their petrified creature.

References

"Go West, Stone Man!": *http://www.cardiff giant.com/muldoon.html.*

Shackle, Eric. "Letter to Walt Whitman: Jimplecute, Tombstone Epitaph, Flume, and the Solid Muldoon": *http://www.twenj.com/ouraymuldoon.htm.*

SOUTHERN CROSS, MONTANA

See Ghost Towns

SOUTHFORK RANCH

See Dallas

SPAGHETTI WESTERNS

See Eastwood, Clint

STAGE COACH MARY

See Fields, "Stage Coach" Mary

STAMPS

In September 1994 the U.S. Postal Service invited Americans to "put on your ten-gallon hat, pull up your boots and get ready for a showdown." This invitation announced the 18 October issue of Legends of the West stamps. These stamps became instant hits and collectibles with "westophiles."

Special events marked the official first day of issue. The University of Wyoming in Laramie held a special ceremony on its campus. Fort Sill in Lawton, Oklahoma, also hosted first-day ceremonies. Chiricahua Apache Chief Geronimo, one of the 16 figures honored by the stamps, is buried at Fort Sill. Old Tucson, Arizona, the setting for many beloved western movies, also hosted a first-day celebration.

The Legends 29-cent issue consisted of four themes: Native American Culture, Western Wildlife, the Overland Mail, and, of course, the American Cowboy. In addition to the themes, the stamps featured 16 legendary westerners. Honorees included Wild West showman Buffalo Bill **Cody;** explorers Jim **Bridger,** John **Frémont,** and Kit **Carson;** rancher Charles Goodnight; gambler and lawman Wild Bill Hickok; and lawmen Bat Masterson, Wyatt **Earp,** and Bill Tilghman. Nellie Cashman, Annie **Oakley,** and Sacagawea represented women of the Old West. Nellie Cashman, the least-known of the three, had earned the nickname "the Angel of Tombstone." She raised orphans, ran a boarding house, and campaigned against violence, including public hangings. Bill **Pickett,** cowboy and inventor of the rodeo sport of bulldogging, and mountain man Jim **Beckwourth** represented African Americans. Geronimo (Goyahkla, "One who yawns"), and Nez Percé Chief Joseph (Hin-mah-too-yah-lat-kekht, "Thunder traveling to loftier heights") represented Native American culture.

Sensing the marketability of the series, the Postal Service also offered for sale a *Legends of the West Commemorative Album,* an 80-page hardcover book, and two full sheets of stamps for $24.95. The Legends Postal Card Set reproduced the Legends' images on 20 postcards ($7.95). For the first time in history, the Postal Service sold a limited edition of 15,000 uncut, "six-up" panes containing 120 stamps each at the face value of the stamps, $34.80. The true philatelist could purchase an extremely limited edition of only 5,000 uncut panes, individually numbered and signed by stamp artist Mark Hess of Katonah, New York ($119.95).

The Postal Service basked in the warm reception accorded its innovative and attractive stamp offering, until someone closely examined the portrait of Willie M. "Bill" Pickett. Pickett, born near Taylor, Texas, worked along with his brothers as cowboys and is credited with inventing a trademark method of subduing cattle. Unfortunately, the Postal Service did not do its historical homework. Someone had erroneously selected a picture of Ben, one of Bill's three brothers, to be the model for Mark Hess's portrait. The entire run of stamps had already been printed before the error came to light. For the first time in history, the Postal Service recalled an entire stamp series. A chagrined Azeezaly Jaffer, manager of stamp services, explained that "the whole concept of the 'Legends of the West' stamps was to rec-

ognize the contributions of people. Unfortunately, history did not serve the African-American very well." A few of the erroneous stamps did make it to market, instantly becoming highly prized collectibles. The Postal Service destroyed 20 million sheets of about 250 million stamps. The error reminds us that recapturing the lives of history's missing African American and other peoples remains a challenging task.

It is perhaps appropriate that error should taint a major public attempt to honor western heroes. As this book makes clear, myth and mistake continue to cling to most of these and other "legends of the West."

Reference

"It's 'Westward Ho!' As Legends Stamps Hit the Trail," U.S. Postal Service Stamp News Release 94–050. Washington, DC: GPO, 12 September 1994.

STARR, BELLE

1848–1889

For more than a century, writers, movie producers, and musicians have romanticized the life of Belle Starr (also Bella or Star, "Bandit Queen"). Her legend as an outlaw and a lover of outlaws created an ambivalent fascination with this vivacious, rough frontierswoman. Criminals, shoot-outs, and danger filled her life. Almost all of her many husbands met a violent end; so did she. Belle Starr's criminal record was in fact short, but her association with many outlaws and the help she gave them extended her reputation. She seemingly relished her role as a promiscuous frontierswoman, using men to get her way with the law and to keep her company in a lonely land.

Myra Belle Shirley enjoyed a luxurious childhood in southwest Missouri. She grew up part tomboy and part refined young lady. Her father, John Shirley, ran a prosperous farm, where she and her two brothers enjoyed playing outdoors. She helped her older brother Bud scout before the law killed him when Belle was 16. A classical education in Latin, Greek, music (especially piano), and basic subjects, including mathematics, reading, and writing, occupied her young life. Later, as a mother herself, she wanted her own daughter to have a life in proper society, and she attempted to educate her accordingly. Her upbringing as a lady remained with her; Belle always rode sidesaddle, often dressed in velvet riding habits, and played the piano in her frontier home. The refined education and lifestyle of her childhood contrasted sharply with her later penchant for dangerous men and a dangerous life in the wilderness of the Canadian District of the Cherokee Nation (Oklahoma).

To escape debt in Missouri, the Shirley family moved to Texas, termed uncharitably by some a "refuge for the dregs of society." In Texas, Myra Belle excelled in school, being both older and better-educated than her peers. She had always flaunted her money in Missouri; in Texas she flaunted her intelligence.

A few outlaws sought refuge with the Shirleys, and Belle took an active interest in the men. She married an outlaw named Jim Reed in 1868. She bore two children during her marriage, Rosie Lee "Pearl" in 1868 and James Edwin in 1871.

Both her children fell into the stereotypical lifestyles of the Wild West. Pearl eventually became a prostitute and drunkard. Ed lived a life of crime and was in and out of prison until he was killed.

Jim's crimes became worse, and thanks to the price on his head, a bounty hunter killed him in Paris, Texas, in 1874. His death left Myra Belle with two children and little else. She raised her children in Kansas and Oklahoma. In 1880 she married Sam Starr, son of Tom Starr, a Cherokee outlaw. The couple lived in the Canadian District of the Cherokee Nation. Countless outlaws and hunted men used their homestead as a hideout. Hanging Judge Isaac **Parker** twice tried Belle for the crime of horse stealing. She served time in Detroit's Morgan Prison with Sam, and then both returned to Younger's Bend in Oklahoma. After a Christmas party in 1886, Sam, also fatally wounded, killed Frank West in a duel. In order to remain on the territory, Belle soon married an adopted son of Tom Starr, Billy July, later known as Jim Starr. He was 19 years her junior, and like her other love interests, he also led a life of crime.

Belle Starr's long list of lovers grew to include Blue Duck, a criminal hanged for his murders and robberies, as well as Jim Middleton, Jack Spaniard, and Cole Younger. Most historians identify Pearl's father as Cole Younger instead of Jim Reed, although both Belle and Younger denied it. Rumor has Myra Belle married to both Cole Younger and Blue Duck. Other tales tell of her marrying Jim Reed on horseback, with another gang member administering the vows.

Uncertainty shrouds Belle's death even as it did her life. After leaving a party one night in 1889, an unidentified gunman shot her as she rode home. Suspects abounded. Some fingered an enemy named Edgar Watson, while others charged her son Eddie or her husband Jim Starr. She and Eddie had quarreled earlier in the week. Various observers believed that Jim Starr coveted her hidden stash of money, gifts from her previous lovers. Belle's death made the headlines of the *New York Times,* but no one was ever tried for her murder.

Starr's transformation from life to legend began the year of her death with Richard K. Fox's dime novel *Bella Starr, The Bandit Queen, or The Female Jesse James.* Editor and owner of the sensationalist *National Police Gazette,* Fox knew how to sell pulp. His 25-cent book took advantage of the public's unquenchable thirst for yet another Western legend. His fables and tall tales of her involvement in robberies and other outlandish adventures created much of the Belle Starr myth.

Other media picked up the tale. Randolph Scott played Sam Starr opposite Gene Tierney as Belle in the 1941 movie *Belle Starr.* Isabel Jewell portrayed Belle in the 1948 sequel, *Belle Starr's Daughter.* More recently, Elizabeth Montgomery took on the role of Belle in a 1980 depiction. In each, Belle appears as a beauty, which is not how photographs record her. Her vitality, however, strongly attracted men.

Myra Belle's legend is also perpetuated through a music group named after her. A photograph of Starr appears as the cover of the group's second album *Far as the Wind Blows.* Their style combines country and rock, reminiscent of their namesake's lifestyle in the open country of the West.

Belle Starr's name appears in several songs written in this century by prominent artists. Singer Bob Dylan referred to her on his album *Highway 61 Revisited.* Woody **Guthrie** wrote an entire song, "Belle Starr," questioning her decisions and inquiring about her life and legend. His lyrics evoke pity in listeners for this lonely, troubled woman:

> Eight men, they say combed your waving black hair;
> Eight men knew the feel of your dark velvet waist
> Eight men heard the sounds of your tan leather skirt
> Eight men heard the bark of the guns that you wore.

Guthrie highlighted Belle's reputation as a lover of outlaws. Her proper manners and stylish clothes inspired the "velvet waist" reference, and Starr is reputed never to have gone out without her guns.

Bobby Barnett's "Ballad of Belle Starr" concentrates on Belle's criminal history. She is often associated with robberies carried out by her husbands. Some incarnations raise her to the status of leading a gang. Michael Martin Murphey tells her entire story in his poignant song "Belle Starr." He states the facts of her life, creating a stark image of "the outlaw Belle Starr." Murphey describes her as a clean, cultured, and fashionable woman. He recounts her marriages, the loss of several husbands, and her own mysterious death.

Starr's influence extended well beyond the realm of music and film. A woman named Belle Starr owns the Silverado Ranch in Arizona. The ranch houses rare animals, provides camping sites, and has replicas of Old West cabins, including a replica of the legendary Belle Starr's cabin. The ranch owner claims many similarities to the original western woman: Cherokee connections, a free spirit, and a criminal record. In Virginia, a bar bearing her name features "western" food on the menu. The Belle Starr Marina in Oklahoma, a lake campsite for travelers and families, uses her name to lure tourists to their scenic outdoors.

Myra Belle Shirley's name will always be associated with bandits and crime, but to many that's a part of her fascination. Her relationships with the men on the frontier and her own activities place her among the American legends of the Old West. Even taking into account exaggeration, her strength and unique character set her apart from other women of her time. Since she never settled into a stable household with one husband and a predictable life, Belle's image remains that of a gunslinging outlaw. A tough but polished woman of the wilderness, Belle Starr remains a complex, contradictory icon of femininity, independence, and freedom of spirit.

—*Ellen J. Oettinger*

References

Fox, Richard K. *Bella Starr, or The Bandit Queen.* 1889. Facsimile ed., Austin, TX: Steck Company, 1960.

Murphey, Michael Martin, with Bill Miller. "Belle Star." On *Cowboy Songs III: Rhymes of the Renegades,* Warner Western 4–45423, 1993. Musical recording.

Shirley, Glenn. *Belle Starr and Her Times: The Literature, the Facts, and the Legends.* Norman: University of Oklahoma Press, 1982, 1990.

STEAGALL, RED

1938–

Cowboys and poetry go together like biscuits and barbecue. Since 1991 Russell "Red" Steagall has proudly served as the "Official Cowboy Poet of Texas." He has also been honored with Western Heritage Awards from the National Cowboy Hall of Fame, in 1993 for "Born to This Land" and in 1996 for "Faith and Values."

Cowboy life came naturally to Steagall. "I think Mother would tell you that I started reading about cowboys and Indians as soon as I learned to read," he says. "I don't know that there's been more than five days in my entire life that I didn't read something about them" (Chapman 1996).

Born in 1938 in Forestburg, Montague County, Texas, he grew up in Sanford in the Texas Panhandle. "All of us who grew up there thought we were cowboys," Steagall says. "There were always horses to ride" (Chapman 1996). "The people I knew in my childhood, who were cowboys or had cowboys, knew those songs," he says. "I learned my first full song when I was three—'When the Work's All Done This Fall'" (Red Steagall at Warner Western).

As a youth, Steagall began to learn the piano but switched to guitar. Then, when he was 15, polio struck, crippling his left arm and hand. There was no strength, no way to grip a ball or grasp a saddle horn. As therapy, his mother signed him up for mandolin lessons, and gradually his strength returned. The grit he had shown in beating polio stayed with Steagall throughout his life.

Returning to the guitar, Steagall played in local bands during high school and after. "It was Bob Wills, Hank Thompson and Spade Cooley," he says. "I was 25 years old before I knew there was anything other than mesquite trees, buffalo grass, Phillips gasoline, barbed wire and Bob Wills" (Chapman 1996).

In 1965 Steagall, like so many performers before him, set his sights on California. He co-wrote the song "Here We Go Again." "Ray Charles recorded it and my whole life changed," he says (Chapman 1996). After his first hit song in 1969, Steagall placed 26 records in a row on the national charts.

Steagall played and recorded for 20 years. Then, in the mid-1980s, he joined the cowboy poetry revival. "I've always loved poetry; I've read it since I was just

Red Steagall
(Courtesy Warner Western Records)

a child" says the cowboy poet laureate (make that "lariat"). Of writing and reciting poetry, he says, "It has been the most rewarding time of my life, I think. It is not an art form palatable to the masses, but its market is fairly substantial" (Chapman 1996). In 1991 he performed "A Cowboy's Prayer," by Badger Clark, before a host of dignitaries at a White House prayer breakfast in Washington, D.C.

Since then, Steagall has been a major force in bringing cowboy songs and poems, old and new, to a national audience. He and his wife, Gail, live on a ranch near Azle, Texas. He's also an actor and author (*Ride for the Brand,* 1991). He airs a weekly radio show, *Cowboy Corner,* still performs and records, and hosts Red Steagall's Cowboy Gathering and Western Swing Festival each October in Fort Worth's historic Stockyards. He even has his own line of coffee, Red Steagall's Cowboy Coffee.

Steagall also tries to dispel erroneous myths about the cowboy. "The cowboy is not the hard-drinking, hard-fighting, devil-may-care person that Hollywood makes him out to be. The cowboy is someone who makes his living on horseback," he says,

who makes his living with the land, and is very dedicated to his way of life. He is strongly convicted about his belief in God, is a dedicated family man, and is honest, hard-working, and believes a day's pay is worth a day's work. I spend a lot of time with those people, and they're exactly the same folks who've been working that land for generations. And they're just as fiercely protective of it today as they were 100 years ago. (Red Steagall at Warner Western)

References

Chapman, Art. "From Smoky Bars to Cowboy Bard." *Fort Worth Star-Telegram,* 24 March 1996, Virtual Texan: *http://www.virtual texan.com/writers/chapman/artred.htm.*

Jolene's Kitchen: *http://www.songtek.com/fea tures/jkitchen/print/red_steagall.htm.*

Red Steagall at Warner Western: *http://www. wbr.com/nashville/warnerwestern/cmp/red. html.*

Red Steagall's Ranch Headquarters: *http:// www.redsteagall.com/.*

STONE, GLENN

For no apparent reason, a large statue of Paul Bunyan stands outside of Don's Hot Rod Shop (2811 North Stone Avenue) at the corner of Stone and Glenn Streets in Tucson, Arizona. The figure, dressed in an appropriate red shirt, holds a double-bladed ax and is surrounded by a chain-link fence. Local wits have dubbed the statue "Glenn Stone, the ax murderer," and thus he appears listed among Road-sideamerica.com's "muffler men."

Muffler men are another western contribution to American popular culture. They proliferated in California during the 1960s. Bob Prewitt created the first such statue in about 1962 for the Paul Bunyan Cafe on **Route 66** in Flagstaff, Arizona. Most statues thereafter came from that one mold, which accounts for their similarities.

Steve Dashew purchased Prewitt's business and renamed it International Fiberglass. He continued to mold large (18–25 feet tall) fiberglass figures that beckoned customers into Texaco and other gas stations. According to Dashew, "Our main business was working with the large oil and tire companies and restaurant chains for nationwide programs. For example, we built a series of Phillips Petroleum cowboys, Texaco Big Friends, and U.S. Rubber Miss Uniroyals. We also did ENCO and Humble tigers, and Sinclair Dinosaurs" (Roadsideamer ica.com).

The hands of these statues could hold tires or mufflers, hence the term "muffler man." As gas stations closed, the lantern-jawed muffler men moved to other locations. Variations, such as Paul Bunyan, cowboys, and other figures, are legion.

Why a lumberjack statue in Tucson? Perhaps it is the work of an alumnus of Northern Arizona University in Flagstaff, home of the Lumberjacks. Perhaps someone got carried away at a garage sale. At Christmas, Glenn Stone also holds a large candy cane. According to Tucson urban legend, new police officers are often dispatched to the corner of Glenn and Stone to investigate reports of "a huge man with an axe." According to one observer, "his eyes follow you whenever you move" (Roadsideamerica.com).

Reference

Roadsideamerica.com: *http://www.Roadside america.com/muffler.*

SUNDANCE KID

See Butch Cassidy and the Sundance Kid

SWALLOWS OF SAN JUAN CAPISTRANO

Without question, the most famous swallows in the world return regularly to the Spanish mission of this city in Orange County, California. The town lies near the Pacific coast in southern California, about halfway between San Diego and Los Angeles. In November 1776 a Franciscan priest, Father Junípero Serra, founded the Mission San Juan Capistrano, the seventh in the chain of 21 along the California coast.

San Juan Capistrano, the "Jewel of the Missions," included the largest, most ornate stone church of the chain. An earthquake in 1812 wrecked the original cruciform church, completed only six years earlier, and killed 29 people. Thereafter, aside from restoration efforts, the church has remained a jumble of broken arches around a quadrangle and garden. The adobe Serra Chapel has been restored and remains in use.

According to long-standing tradition, flocks of cliff swallows (*P. pyrrhonota*) return annually to Capistrano on 19 March, St. Joseph's Day. They come from the Holy Land, says the legend, carrying a twig in their beaks, which they drop on the ocean when they need to rest. The story is captivating, but it is just a legend. In reality, the birds winter in Goya, Argentina, then return to Capistrano in the spring to hatch and raise their young.

The cliff swallows, with their very strong homing instinct, have probably been returning to the area for centuries. Another legend says the swallows sought sanctuary at the mission after an innkeeper destroyed their nests. The mission's location near two rivers offers the birds quick, easy access to the mud they use in nest building. They return to the same nests each year. If a nest has not survived the winter, the birds often rebuild in the same place.

In the 1930s songwriter Leon Rene heard a radio announcement that the swallows were about to arrive at the mission. The event stimulated an idea for a song. Rene wrote the lyrical ballad, "When the Swallows Come Back to Capistrano." First performed in 1939, the melodic, romantic ballad became a big hit. The scenic mission has also often served as a film setting, such as for the 1927 movie *Rose of the Golden West.*

California development, however, is threatening the age-old relationship between the mission and the birds. Insects, the mainstay of their diet, are dwindling because of development in the area. In another sign of the times, the birds have shown an increasing preference for a new shopping mall rather than the mission. They can build nests in the mall's high archway, where they will not be disturbed. A nearby riparian corridor offers a convenient mud supply near Saddleback College. However, mission fans are fighting back. When the swallows are due back, they bait the grounds with delectable treats, including ladybugs and lace-wing larvae.

The mission gained fame throughout the world for the flock of swallows, which reputedly fly off on St. John's Day (23 October) and return "miraculously" to their mission nests on St. Joseph's Day. The San Juan Capistrano Fiesta Association coordinates annual parades and other activities marking the departure and return of the birds. The festivities attract up to 25,000 visitors to the small town.

Reference

Swallows Day Parade: *http://www.capovalley. com/fiesta/parade.html.*

Where Are They?: *http://www.ocnow.com/ news/1999/03/10/swallows1.html.*

Source of Further Information

Snodgrass, Mary Ellen. *Religious Sites in America.* Denver, CO: ABC-CLIO, 2000.

TABOR, BABY DOE

1854–1935

Born into a prosperous family in Oshkosh, Wisconsin, Elizabeth Bonduel "Baby" McCourt would experience many ups and downs during her eventful life in the West. Like "the unsinkable Molly **Brown,**" she would become famous as a socialite of Colorado's mining boom. However, unlike Mrs. Brown, her life would end in tragedy.

Baby married Harvey Doe in 1877, and the pair settled in Central City, a Colorado mining boomtown, where Harvey's father owned mines. Harvey turned out to be an indifferent provider and dragged his young wife aimlessly from place to place. The disgusted woman divorced Harvey after only a year of marriage and moved to the nearby mining town of Leadville. There, the 25-year-old beauty met Horace Tabor, "the Silver King," who would serve as the town's first mayor and later as lieutenant governor of the state.

Tabor had come to the state during the **Pikes Peak gold rush** of 1859.

Although Tabor was nearly twice her age, they began a quiet affair, which by July 1880 had become very public. Horace moved out of his home and asked his wife, Augusta, for a divorce. She refused, but he pushed on and secretly married Baby on 30 September 1882. Owing to legal irregularities concerning Tabor's divorce, their marriage did not become official until 1 March 1883. They had two daughters, nicknamed Lillie and Silver.

Unfortunately, their wealth and happiness lasted only a decade. Tabor spent lavishly, building an opera house in Leadville as well as Denver's first skyscraper. He also made risky investments in Latin America. Mining output began to decline, and then the repeal of the Sherman Silver Purchase Act in November 1893 made mining unprofitable. The Crash of '93 quickly destroyed the Tabor fortune along with many others. The Silver King died in poverty, of appendicitis, on 10 April 1899.

Before his death, Horace urged his wife to "hang on to the Matchless Mine, if I die, Baby, it will make millions again when silver comes back" (Ellensplace). Alas, his bad luck held; the mine never produced ore again. Baby Doe and her children moved briefly to Chicago to live with relatives. Later she returned to her beloved Leadville with Silver (Lillie refused), where they lived in a mining shack at the Matchless and sold her remaining jewelry to survive. Her tenacity and loyalty to her husband's dying wish won for her a place in the hearts of her Leadville neighbors.

As her funds dwindled, Baby wrapped her feet in gunnysacks held on with twine. Only the charity of neighbors kept her alive. Silver descended into a haze of alcohol and other drugs and died—murdered—in 1925. Her mother's life would likewise end in tragedy.

"Went down to Leadville from Matchless—the snow so terrible, I had to go down on my hands and knees and creep from my cabin door to 7th Street," Baby Doe wrote in March 1935. "Mr. Zaitz driver drove me to our get off place and he helped pull me to the cabin. I kept falling deep down through the snow every minute. God bless him" (Leadville, Colorado, History). Baby froze to death during that terrible spring blizzard. According to legend, neighbors found her in the cabin floor, arms outstretched, in the shape of a cross. She was buried next to Horace at Mt. Olivet cemetery in Denver.

Fittingly, an opera titled *The Ballad of Baby Doe* premiered in Central City, Colorado, in 1956. Author John Burke added a biography, *The Legend of Baby Doe,* in 1974. Today, Leadville still honors the memory of the riches-to-rags couple, whose lives reflected the glory days of this western boomtown even as their deaths reflected the failures that also marked western history.

References

Baby Doe Tabor: *http://www.ionet.net/~jellenc/hcg_fac2.html.*

Ellensplace. "Baby Doe Tabor and the Matchless Mine": *http://ellensplace.net/hcg_fac2.html.*

Horace Tabor: *http://www.linecamp.com/museums/americanwest/western_names/tabor_horace/tabor_horace.html.*

Leadville, Colorado, History: *http://www.leadville.com/history/tabor.htm.*

TEJANO MUSIC

See Selena

TELEVISION

Along with feature films, television has played a powerful role in mythologizing the West. Indeed, many TV programs and actors transferred to the new medium as it gained visibility in the 1950s. The **Lone Ranger** (Clayton Moore), Hopalong Cassidy (William Boyd), Roy **Rogers**, and Gene **Autry** all made successful transitions to the small screen. What sort of western images and places has television created?

Like all TV genres, the popularity of westerns waxes and wanes. For the 1950/1951 season, only two westerns figured among the top-ten programs. During the late 1950s, however, westerns dominated prime-time television. In 1958/1959 westerns held 12 of the top-20 slots and maintained 9 of the top slots the following season. By the mid-1960s, however, the appeal of westerns had dropped, leaving only *Bonanza, The Virginian,* and *Gunsmoke* among top picks for the next decade. Westerns enjoyed a modest resurgence in the early 1990s but again slipped out of the top-running programs after a few years.

Many TV westerns featured the word "adventures" in the title, associating the vast region of the West with exciting escapades. At various times, one could watch and thrill vicariously to the adventures of Jim Bowie, Judge Roy **Bean**, Kit **Carson**, Rin Tin Tin (a dog in the cavalry), and Wild Bill Hickok.

Likewise, the word "legend" appears in many titles, overtly recognizing the unreality characteristic of most programs. *The Life and Legend of Wyatt Earp* (1955–1961) brought a very positive image of the famous lawman, played by Hugh O'Brien, to television. *The Legend of Jesse James* aired briefly in the mid-1960s, and a short-lived series titled *Legend of Custer* followed in 1968. *Houston: The Legend of Texas* aired in 1986 with Sam Elliott as the hero. Two other television movies likewise played upon the theme: *The Legend of the Golden Gun* (1979) and *The Legend of Walks Far Woman* (1982), starring Raquel Welch.

Like several of the aforementioned programs, many television series dramatized, and often radically altered, the life and times of real historical personalities. Gail Davis starred as "Annie **Oakley**" (1953–1958); however, the TV character

had no basis in historical reality. Instead of a Wild West show sharp shooter, the TV Annie was a law enforcer who helped her uncle, a sheriff. Gene Barry played a very dapper Bat in *Bat Masterson* (1959–1961). In 1976 *Bridger* brought mythical tales of the life of the famous mountain man Jim **Bridger** to the screen. Elizabeth Montgomery played the outlaw *Belle Starr* for one season in 1980. Thousands of children donned coonskin caps to look like Fess Parker as *Daniel Boone* (1964–1970). *The Tall Man* (1960–1962) added more layers of myth to the relationship between Pat Garrett and **Billy the Kid.** *The Young Riders* (1989–1991) spotlighted the adventures of the **Pony Express.**

Literary creations, like historical figures, also provided fodder for TV scripts. *Dick Powell's Zane **Grey** Theater* aired from 1956 to 1961. It consistently offered high-quality, absorbing scripts. Initially its programs followed the Grey stories, but the series later branched out in creative, dramatic ways. Excellent casts included the likes of Ernest Borgnine, Walter Brennan, Sterling Hayden, Jack Lemmon, Jack Palance, and Robert Ryan. Max Brand's 1930 novel *Destry,* already filmed three times, enjoyed a one-season encore on TV in 1964. **Death Valley** Days, with its 20-year run beginning in 1952, became one of the longest-lived westerns. The program drew upon the 1930s radio series for material. Ronald Reagan, Robert Taylor, and Dale Robertson, among others, hosted. *Little House on the Prairie* (1974–1982) brought Laura Ingalls Wilder's famous family to television.

In the true white-hat–versus–black-hat fashion inherited from B-westerns, television tended to produce one-dimensional, uniformly good heroes, often lawmen. *Tales of the* **Texas Rangers** (1955–1960) glorified their heroics. Likewise, frontier lawmen, such as Guy Madison's Wild Bill Hickok, are unrelentingly good. Even the rascally Roy Bean becomes lovable, as played by Edgar Buchanan. Steve McQueen played likable bounty hunter Josh Randall, wielding a sawed-off rifle, in *Wanted Dead or Alive* (1958–1961).

In hopes of attracting adult viewers, however, a few television programs took chances by creating antiheroes or somewhat tarnished heroes. Richard Boone's Paladin, as a black-clad avenging angel, is the paradigmatic antihero. *Have Gun, Will Travel* (1957–1963) brought viewers an unusual atmosphere, plots, and assumptions about western heroes. A decade later, Boone returned as the title character in *Hec Ramsey* (1972–1974), a disheveled, grizzled old gunfighter-turned-lawman, very unlike the elegant epicure he played as Paladin.

In a lighter vein, James Garner's *Maverick* (1957–1962) and later incarnations brought America a lazy, cowardly gambler as the "hero." However, he did manage to rise to the occasion when pushed. Likewise, *Alias Smith and Jones* (1971–1973) followed bumbling and likable robbers around the West. Will Hutchins starred as Tom Brewster in *Sugarfoot* (1957–1961), another humorous, hapless, and unlikely hero, haunted by his evil twin, the Canary Kid. Brewster, too inept to be considered a tenderfoot, only ranked as a "sugarfoot." Surely the oddest western, *Kung Fu* (1972–1975) brought a Shaolin monk (David Carradine) and his Chinese philosophy and martial arts to the Wild West.

Violence provided the key programmatic element for most programs dealing with the West. In 1961 Federal Communications Commission chairman Newton Minnow chastised the television industry for high levels of gratuitous violence. If TV scripts were to be believed, the West would have been depopulated in a single season, owing to Main Street shoot-outs, ambushes, and other gunplay. In 1993 the American Psychological Association reported that the average American child had seen "8,000 television murders and 100,000 acts of violence by the end of elementary school." Who knows how many people Sheriff Matt Dillon alone killed during the 20 years of *Gunsmoke* (1955–1975)? The white-hat–versus–black-hat mentality of the Cold War decades added political sanction to the glorification of violence.

The grandeur of the West begged for epic treatment, especially the grand family saga. *Wagon Train* (1957–1965) starred Ward Bond as the head of a virtual family en route to California and opportunity. **Bonanza** (1959–1973) reigned as one of the longest-running television westerns. Like *Bonanza, Rawhide* (1959–1966) featured a predominately male cast, appropriate to the trail-drive venue. That series, of course, brought young Clint **Eastwood** to a national viewing audience. *The Big Valley* (1965–1969) set a powerful ranching family in California and added strong female characters. *The High Chaparral* (1967–1971) performed a similar feat for frontier Arizona. Finally, *The Virginian* (1962–1970) brought Owen Wister's famous Shiloh Ranch to the small screen as television's first 90-minute color western series. **Dallas** (1978–1991) updated the ranch family epic and spiced it with soap-opera melodrama.

Television drew heavily upon earlier media, from pulp fiction to radio to movies. Its depictions of the West thus reprise rather than innovate. As in prior popular media, male characters and male perspectives dominate, *Annie Oakley* being the rare exception to the rule. Occasional strong female characters emerged, such as Barbara Stanwyck as the matriarch Victoria Barkley in *The Big Valley. Here Come the Brides* (1968–1970) pushed the mail-order bride theme to a ridiculous extreme. Not until the fall of 1992 did a successful, credible show with a female lead appear: *Dr. Quinn, Medicine Woman,* with Jane Seymour. The series broke new ground in abandoning tired stereotypes and embracing new themes of environmentalism, feminism (Quinn is a single parent and a professional woman), and ethnic harmony.

The 1990s witnessed other transformations of the western genre. Children could enjoy the zany antics of the singing group Riders in the Sky as they moved their *Riders Radio Theater* to television. Likewise, John Erickson's hilarious *Hank the Cow Dog* moved from print to television. To tickle adult funny bones, the whimsical and often magical *Adventures of Brisco County, Jr.* premiered on the Fox Network and later in syndication on TNT. On a more serious note, in 1998 CBS and TNN resurrected a multiethnic *Magnificent Seven,* featuring a leader (Michael Biehn), sharpshooter (Eric Close), "the Kid" (Andrew Kavovit), scoundrel (Dale Midkiff), preacher (Ron Perlman), gambler (Anthony Starke), and healer (Rick Worthy).

Of the major networks, TNT became *the* place for westerns during the 1990s. From adaptations of Louis **L'Amour** novels, such as *Conagher,* to docudramas, such as *Rough Riders,* TNT produced high-quality, enjoyable western fare. The films featured strong casts, with such stars as Sissy Spacek and Tommy Lee Jones in Elmer **Kelton**'s *The Good Old Boys* (1995), Danny Glover in *Buffalo Soldiers* (1997), Kris Kristofferson in *Two for Texas* (1998), Sam Elliott and Katharine Ross in *Conagher* (1991), and Sam Shepard in *Purgatory* (1999).

Although the 1990s showed a burst of creativity, over the past 50 years, television characters, characteristics, plots, and places have been mostly predictable and derivative. White male heroes dominated, with occasional exceptions like *The Cisco Kid* and **Zorro** featuring Hispanic leads. Small wonder that, with a few notable exceptions, television westerns died quick, unlamented deaths. Of the 50 longest-running TV series, only two westerns make the cut: *Gunsmoke* (third, at 20 years) and *Bonanza* (seventeenth at 14 years). Nonetheless, thanks to syndication and Internet-based fan clubs, many of these old warhorses continue to shape attitudes across the globe about the mythical American West.

See also Wister, Owen, and Winthrop, Washington

Reference

Vahimagi, Tise. "Television Westerns." In *The BFI Companion to the Western,* ed. Edward Buscombe. New York: Da Capo, 1988.

Source of Further Information

Lowe, Denise. *Women and American Television.* Denver, CO: ABC-CLIO, 1999.

TEXAS EMBASSY

As all good Texans are quick to remind their listeners, the Lone Star State was once—from 2 March 1836 until 29 December 1845—a republic. Like any self-respecting republic, Texas established embassies and sent out ambassadors. The upstart republic established diplomatic relations with a number of European nations, including France, Belgium, the Netherlands, and several German states. The ambassador to Great Britain resided at No. 3 St. James Street, where the Berry Brothers wine store is now located. When Texas became a state in 1845, the embassy closed.

Some 150 years later, Texas entrepreneurs decided to capitalize on this little-known piece of Texas/British history. Oilman Russell J. Ramsland Jr. and attorney A. Hardcastle Jr., both residents of Dallas, longed for savory Tex-Mex food and Texas hospitality on their trips to London. They joined with Dallas restaurateur Gene Street and former lord mayor of London Sir Alan Traill to create the Texas Embassy Cantina. The new incarnation is housed at No. 1 Cockspur Street, next to the Canadian embassy, just a few blocks from the original Texas embassy. Situated at the bottom of the Haymarket and one block west of Trafalgar Square, the restaurant faces the National Gallery on Pall Mall. Prior tenants of the 90-year-old Oceanic House building included Barclays Bank and a ticket office for the *Titanic*.

Upstairs patrons lounge in an 1880s saloon, replete with a 29-foot bar and ornate mirrors. Like its nineteenth-century predecessors, the bar includes the requisite nude, copied from an 1882 oil painting. A large wall mural features marauding Mexican bandits, old saddles from a **Texas Rangers** auction, rodeo bunting, a white longhorn-steer head, and authentic replicas of several of the flags of Texas. The Lone Star flag flies proudly outside this border cantina and bar. The mostly American staff adds to the restaurant's authenticity. From "high noon" until midnight daily, patrons enjoy the atmosphere and food of the old-time Texas border country.

Reference

Texas Embassy Cantina: *http://www.texasem bassy.com*.

TEXAS RANGERS

According to John Salmon "Rip" Ford (1846), a Texas Ranger could "ride like a Mexican, trail like an Indian, shoot like a Tennessean, and fight like the very devil" (Webb 1982). This characterization, a bit politically incorrect today, captures well the focus, mind-set, and political incorrectness of the Texas Rangers during their 175-year existence. One of the last major western organizations to admit Hispanics, blacks, or women, the Rangers nevertheless keep a powerful hold on the public imagination.

In 1823 Stephen F. Austin authorized the hiring of ten men "to act as rangers for the common defense" ("The Texas Rangers"). They fought Indians and tracked murderers, rustlers, smugglers, and other criminals across the vast, wide-open spaces of what would become the Lone Star State. The Rangers earned

$15 a month, paid not in cash but in land. A decade later, Rangers earned the competitive wage of $1.25 a day but had to furnish their own arms, mounts, rations, and equipment. They elected their own officers and formed intermittently as volunteer companies when the occasion demanded. The name "Texas Rangers" became official in 1835, with three companies of 56 men on patrol.

In late 1838 Mirabeau B. Lamar became president of the Republic of Texas and quickly increased the role of Rangers in frontier defense. He expanded the number of Ranger companies and charged them to wage all-out war on hostile Indians. Rangers fought the Cherokee War in east Texas in July 1839, battled Comanches in the Council House Fight at San Antonio in March 1840, and five months later reengaged some 1,000 Comanches at Plum Creek (near present-day Lockhart). Sam Houston succeeded Lamar in December 1841 and kept the Ranger presence strong. Capt. John Coffee "Jack" Hays commanded 150 Rangers, many of whom helped fight off Mexican invasions in 1842. Hays raised Ranger esprit de corps and built a more effective fighting unit.

Some Rangers, including Rip Ford, became legends in their own times. He earned his nickname "Rip" during the Mexican War when he labeled death notices "RIP" for "Rest in Peace." Owing to the Rangers' ferocity and tenacity in battle, Mexicans nicknamed them "Los Diablos Tejanos" (the Texas Devils). As a Ranger captain stationed between the Nueces and the Rio Grande, Ford fought both Indians and Mexicans. During the Civil War, he commanded the Second Texas Cavalry and took part in the Battle of Palmito Ranch, one of the last battles of the war. His long and active life also included stints as a doctor, journalist, and politician.

In 1842 William A. A. "Big Foot" Wallace and several other former Rangers invaded Mexico as part of the ill-fated Mier expedition. Mexican forces captured them and used a lottery to determine who lived and who died. Prisoners drew from a pot of beans; a white bean meant life; a black bean, death. Wallace and other lucky prisoners drew a white bean, and the "Black Bean Episode" entered Texas folklore.

Samuel H. Walker did not fare as well as Ford: He drew a black bean and died. Walker had served ably with Capt. Jack Hays's company of Rangers and engaged in many fights with Indians. His name comes down to us in history because Walker assisted gun maker Samuel Colt in developing a new sidearm, the Walker Colt.

The Rangers' exploits, real and imagined, provided fodder for **pulp novelists** and writers of popular poems and songs. For example, in 1859 Juan **Cortina** occupied the town of Brownsville, Texas. Capt. Rip Ford and other Rangers launched a bloody counteroffense that cost the lives of 151 Tejanos and at least 80 Anglo-Texans, including some Rangers. Ford described the typical Ranger:

A large proportion . . . were unmarried. A few of them drank intoxicating liquors. Still, it was a company of sober and brave men. They knew their duty and they did it. While in a town they made no braggadocio demonstration. They did not gallop through the streets, shoot, and yell. They had a specie of moral discipline which developed moral courage. They did right because it was right. ("Silver Stars and Sixguns")

During the 1870s the Frontier Battalion of six companies with 75 Rangers each continued battling hostile Indians. Working with the U.S. Cavalry, they ended the threat from Comanches and Kiowas by 1875. In 1878 Rangers stalked legendary train and bank robber Sam **Bass.** An informant told them of Bass's plan to rob the bank in Round Rock. Following a shoot-out with Rangers, Bass died. The Rangers also handled gunfighter John Wesley Hardin, restored law and order in rollicking Big Bend mining towns, hunted down train robbers, patrolled the border for rustlers and illegal immigrants, and even tried (unsuccessfully) to keep Judge Roy **Bean** from holding an illegal prizefight. By 1882 their successes had rendered their services unnecessary.

According to official records, in 1894–1895 stalwart Rangers scouted 173,381 miles, arrested 676 suspects, recovered 2,856 head of stolen livestock, and otherwise assisted other law enforcement officers. In 1901 the parsimonious state legislature cut the force to four companies, with a maximum of 20 men each. About the same time, conflict broke out in Cameron County. Ramón Cerda, his wife, and two sons, Ramón Jr., and Alfredo, owned El Rancho de San Francisco de Assis. Early in 1900 a Brownsville city policeman killed Ramón Cerda Sr. Less than two years later, Rangers killed Ramón Jr., suspected of cattle theft. Fearing for his life, Alfredo fled across the border and offered a $1,000 reward to whoever killed the offending *rinche* (the Tejano term for a Texas Ranger). On 9 September 1902, someone killed one Texas Ranger and wounded two others in an ambush. Officials charged Alfredo with the crime. Shortly thereafter, Rangers killed him at a Brownsville store while he was out on bail. These events stirred Tejano hatred against *los rinches.*

During the twentieth century, new law enforcement agencies arose, such as the Department of Public Safety and the State Highway Patrol. In many ways, Rangers found themselves marginalized as the State of Texas modernized and urbanized. In a 1932 election, the remaining 44 Rangers made a serious political error. They supported Governor Ross Sterling against Miriam A. "Ma" Ferguson in the Democratic primary. In retaliation, Ferguson fired every Ranger for partisanship when she took office in January 1933.

However, Rangers still found a way to leave their mark. In 1955, inmates at Rusk State Hospital for the Criminally Insane rioted and took hostages. Ranger Captain R. A. "Bob" Crowder had another chance to carry out the old Ranger motto, "One Riot, One Ranger." Armed with a pair of Colt .45s and backed by a century of Ranger tradition, he marched alone into the maximum-security unit. Following a brief conversation, the mob surrendered. The Ranger legend lives on. (A later Ranger revised the motto to "One Riot, Two Rangers," arguing that only a fool went into a conflict without backup.)

Many Texans remain sensitive to any slights to their heroes. In 1994 Robert

Draper pointed up a historical truism: Leander H. McNelly, a Texas legend, had not technically been a real Ranger. As Draper points out, "Muster rolls, vouchers, and state correspondences indicate that from 1874 until 1876, McNelly was the captain of the Washington County Volunteer Militia, and from 1876 until his departure in January 1877, captain of a brigade worded in state legislation as 'special state troops'" (Draper 1994). Outraged Rangerphiles upheld the spirit rather than the letter of law and asserted that McNelly most certainly belonged to the pantheon.

Draper clearly appreciates the power of Texas Ranger mythology.

Rangers are faithful keepers of Ranger mythology, and it all begins with McNelly, the youthful captain under whose command a pintsize brigade slaughtered countless criminals and Mexicans from 1874 until 1877. To the Rangers and their admiring historians, McNelly is an appealing composite of warlord and Christ figure: courageous and gentlemanly, utterly devoted to his men and his mission, a remorseless killer, and dead himself by the holy age of 33. From McNelly flows the rich blood of Ranger lore. (Draper 1994)

An extremely conservative organization, the Texas Rangers have been very slow to adapt to changing social realities. In 1969 Arturo Rodriguez became the first Hispanic officer to serve in some 50 years. Ray Martinez joined the force four years later. Women and African Americans did not gain fieldwork positions until the early 1990s. Toward the end of the twentieth century, the Rangers had diversified slightly, now including, among males, 5 African Americans, 14 Latinos, and 1 Asian, and 2 women, 1 white and 1 black.

Popular culture has generally lionized the organization. In 1946 Texan actor King Vidor and Fred MacMurray starred in *The Texas Rangers.* A remake in 1949 carried the title *Streets of Laredo.* It featured William Holden, MacDonald Carey, and a rather out-of-place William Bendix. *Texas Rangers Ride Again* (1940) and *The Texas Rangers* (1950) continued the tradition. Joseph Kane directed yet another version in which cowboy singing star Roy **Rogers** and sidekick George "Gabby" Hayes prevent an evil general from overthrowing the government of Texas. More recently, *A Perfect World* starred Clint **Eastwood** as a Ranger. Chuck Norris brought a martial arts approach to the role in the television series *Walker, Texas Ranger.* Yet another *Texas Rangers* appeared in the spring of 2001, staring James Van Der Beek, Dylan McDermott, and Rachael Leigh.

Countless novelists, including the estimable Elmer **Kelton** (*The Buckskin Line,* 1999), have provided fictionalized accounts of Ranger heroics. The Texas Ranger Hall of Fame in Waco celebrates the organization. Walter Prescott Webb wrote a more-or-less official history in 1935, *The Texas Rangers: A Century of Frontier Defense.* The University of Texas Press issued a second edition in 1965, with a foreword by President Lyndon Baines Johnson. In 2000 Charles M. Robinson III published *The Men Who Wear the Star: The Story of the Texas Rangers.*

However, the Rangers are not heroes to all Texans. Disc jockey and songwriter

Willie López composed a *corrido* (border-lands folk song) titled "Los Rinches de Texas" in 1967. It criticized Rangers for the violent suppression of a legal melon strike in Starr County. To many Tejanos, *los rinches* worked to protect the power of rich Anglo ranchers against the poor. Capt. A. Y. Allee was sued and investigated countless times for his reckless, violent conduct in south Texas. He explained his conduct during a 1968 U.S. Commission on Civil Rights hearing: "We are not instructed in any way [about the use of force]. We use what force we deem necessary to make any kind of arrest" ("The Twilight of the Texas Rangers"). In 1979 Julian Somora, Joe Bernal, and Albert Peña formalized much of the criticism in *Gunpowder Justice: A Reassessment of the Texas Rangers*.

Rangers continue their law enforcement mission today. The arsenal of the modern Rangers includes a semiautomatic pistol, 12-gauge shotgun, and a Ruger Mini-14 or a Colt AR-15 semiautomatic rifle. Like the **Alamo,** the Texas Rangers remain a powerful icon in the Lone Star State.

References
Draper, Robert. "The Myth of the Rangers." *Texas Monthly,* February 1994.
Procter, Ben H. "Texas Rangers." Handbook of Texas Online: *http://www.tsha.utexas.edu/handbook/online/articles/view/TT/met4.html.*
Samora, Julian, Joe Bernal, and Albert Peña. *Gunpowder Justice: A Reassessment of the Texas Rangers*. Notre Dame, IN: University of Notre Dame Press, 1979.
"Silver Stars and Sixguns: The Texas Rangers." Texas Department of Public Safety: *http://www.txdps.state.tx.us/director_staff/texas_rangers/history.htm.*
Texas Ranger Hall of Fame: *http://www.texasrangers.org.*
"The Texas Rangers": *http://www.lsjunction.com/facts/rangers.htm.*
"The Twilight of the Texas Rangers": *http://www.tdi.swt.edu/hmh3/twilight.htm.*
Webb, Walter Prescott. *The Texas Rangers: A Century of Frontier Defense*. Boston: Houghton Mifflin, 1935; reprint, Austin: University of Texas Press, 1982.

TEXODUSTERS

See Exodusters

THOUSAND PIECES OF GOLD

See Bemis, Polly

TITANIC

See Brown, Molly

TOMBSTONE

See Earp Brothers

TONTO

See Lone Ranger

TORNADO

See Rodeo Bulls

TRAIL DRIVES

The trail drive or cattle drive is the most storied event of cowboy history. The dust, drama, stampedes, attacks by Indians and rustlers, and dangerous river crossings served as the backdrop for the golden age of the cowboy. Cowhands drove millions of longhorns north from Texas to railheads from the mid-1860s through the 1880s. This short period of history, punctuated by those epic journeys of cattle and men, did much to create the grand mythology of the American cowboy. The difficulties and travails of driving cattle is one of the lasting, powerful images of the Old West. Like all icons, it is subject to parody, as in the modern metaphor of **herding cats.**

Real-life trail drives were not quite as dashing, although they were perhaps as dangerous, as the cattle drives of film and television. In 1846 Edward Piper made what may have been the first great northern drive when he moved a herd from Texas to Ohio. The heyday of the great drives, however, began after the Civil War. During the war, most Texas men left to fight for the Confederacy. Their untended cattle multiplied in their absence, and Union blockades and troops cut Texas off from outside markets. Following the war, Texas ranchers faced problems: overstocked ranges and low cattle prices. They resolved to move the animals out of Texas to Kansas railheads and northern ranges.

Charlie Siringo published what is generally considered to be the first cowboy memoir, *A Texas Cowboy,* in 1885. His graphic descriptions of trail drives set the tone for many later writers and filmmakers. With wry humor, he described an average drive. "Everything went on lovely with the exception of swimming swollen streams, fighting now and then among ourselves and a stampede every stormy night, until we arrived on the Canadian river in the Indian territory; there we had a little indian [*sic*] scare." If that weren't enough, a hand might even lose his boots! As one old-timer recalled, "Your boots must be tucked away safely to keep them dry, and beyond the reach of coyotes, who will steal into camp at night and carry off anything made of leather" (Slatta 1996).

In 1924 a silent film titled *North of '36* featured an action-packed cattle drive. The film, starring Jack Holt, was based on a realistic novel penned by Emerson Hough. Without question, however, Howard Hawks directed the greatest film version of a trail drive, his 1948 epic *Red River.* The taut script pitted aging, inflexible, steel-willed cattle baron Tom Dunson (John Wayne) against his more humane, young, tender-hearted protégé Matthew Garth (Montgomery Clift). A host of stock western actors filled out the stellar cast, including Joanne Dru, Walter Brennan, John Ireland, Harry Carey (Sr. and Jr.), Noah Beery Jr., Colleen Gray, Shelley Winters, Hal Taliaferro, and Tom Tyler.

The script is rather like "the Old West meets *Mutiny on the Bounty."* Young Clift, faced with Wayne's increasingly tyrannical, violent, and reckless behavior on the trail, leads a mutiny and takes over the herd. Wayne then hunts down his "stolen herd" and Clift, and the two confront one another in the climactic ending. Stunning black-and-white photography by Russell Harlan adds to the film's grandeur. However, as is usual in western films, not even the setting is authentic. The mythic film, representing a Texas-to-Kansas trail drive, was shot in Arizona.

Decades later, *City Slickers* (1991) would pay homage to the classic film and its trail drive. In this comic update of the trail drive theme, eastern yuppie tourists must move a cattle herd after Curly, the tough trail boss, dies en route. As with cowboys of old, their first loyalty is to the herd. As they begin their drive, they mimic the famous scene of cowboy yells, waving hats, and twirling lassos that kicks off the trail drive in *Red River.*

Probably the best evocation of the rigors and dangers of a trail drive came in the television drama *Lonesome Dove.* The film series grew out of the Larry McMurtry novel published in 1985. In one scene, a rider falls into a swollen Texas stream and is attacked by a host of water moccasins. One purist critic pointed out that moccasins were not supposed to infest rivers in that part of Texas. However, overall the film delivers a powerful sense of the day-to-day problems and drudgery of moving thousands of head of cattle down the trail.

With or without snakes, rivers posed a severe hazard because most cowboys could not swim. Cattle might panic and begin milling about in midstream. In such cases, riders had to try to drive them across. Spring runoffs could swell streams and sweep men and animals downstream. Cattle buyer Joseph G. McCoy judged the lack of sizable river crossings on the Chisholm Trail to be a

major advantage of that route. Following one drive over many flooded rivers, Texas rancher Shanghai Pierce took to calling his longhorns "sea lions."

The 800-mile Chisholm Trail became the main cattle route, carrying about half the animals herded out of Texas. It ran north from San Antonio, Texas, through Fort Worth, on to Indian Country (Oklahoma), and ended at Abilene, Kansas. The appropriately named Eastern Trail and Shawnee Trail ran to the east of the Chisholm, en route to other cattle towns. The Western Trail crossed the Oklahoma Panhandle into western Kansas and on to Dodge City, Kansas. Drovers moved cattle even further northward into the Dakotas, Montana, and Wyoming on other trails, including the Bozeman, Northern, and Jones and Plummer.

Although movies may have exaggerated the frequency of trail-drive disasters, they often depicted real tragedies. Cowboys faced a frightening number of dangers: lightning, range fires, blinding rain and floods, hail, blizzards, tornadoes, and rustlers. "Blue northers" (aptly named for the dark, threatening color of the northern sky) quickly dropped temperatures below freezing. The harsh north wind drove the windchill even lower. Such conditions could blind cows and cowboys. As cattle drifted before such storms, riders had to try to turn them away from fences, ravines, and other obstacles. Otherwise herds would stack up and perish in the cold.

The St. Louis, Missouri, *Republic* reported the tragic outcome of a blizzard that struck near Folsom, New Mexico:

The snow was so blinding that it made it impossible to see 50 feet ahead. [Henry]

Miller called his men together and they started to follow the herd and made an attempt to keep them bunched so far as possible. The men became separated. . . . At noon the frozen bodies of Henry Miller, Joe Martin and Charlie Jolly were found on the open plains not far from Folsom. The other men succeeded in finding their way into camp before being overcome with cold. (7 November 1889)

Mounts could step into holes and throw their riders. A foot tangled in a stirrup meant death or serious injury if a bolting horse dragged a cowboy across the plains. Exhausted riders might take extreme and unwise measures to stay in the saddle. The *Denver Daily Times* recorded the unhappy end of one tired cowboy: "A herder near Pueblo, named Albert Jones, a few nights ago, became sleepy and tied himself on his horse with his lariat. He was found dead, having been dragged and jumped over the prairie for a long distance" (7 October 1872).

One trail driver, however, survived the attack of a wild longhorn, thanks to the animal's long horns: "Not long since a herder was knocked down by a wild steer and his face disfigured for life. His nose was torn completely from his face. That he was not killed was owing to the fact that the long horns, wide apart, touched the ground on either side of the poor fellow's head as he lay prostrate" (*Cheyenne Daily Leader,* 2 August 1882).

Stampedes posed a grave threat to both the herd and the riders. Night riders especially feared stampedes because of the poor nighttime visibility. A coyote's call, a lurking mountain lion, or a flash of lightning could startle a herd to its feet. Cowboys had to dash to the head of the herd and turn or stop the leaders. One of Teddy Blue Abbott's pardners fell victim to a stampeding herd: "Horse and man was mashed into the ground as flat as a pancake. The only thing you could recognize was the handle of his six-shooter" (Abbott and Smith 1955).

One of the most famous cowboy songs of all time memorializes the death by stampede of Little Jo the Wrangler. N. Howard "Jack" Thorp wrote the song in 1898 while trailing cattle from Chimney Lake, New Mexico, to Higgins, Texas. It recounts the tragedy of the young horse wrangler who, with his horse Rocket, dies trying to turn a stampede. At daylight, the other hands discover the boy's sacrifice, as the song's final verse explains:

Next morning just at day break, we found
  where Rocket fell,
Down in a washout twenty feet below;
And beneath his horse, mashed to a pulp,
  his spur had rung his knell,
Was our little Texas stray, poor Wranglin'
  Joe. (Thorp 1984)

Again, films have exaggerated the frequency of attacks on trail drives, but human conflict also posed risks. Some Kansans, fearful of the fever-bearing ticks carried by Texas longhorns, used violence to halt herds. Indians in "The Nations" (Indian Territory, now Oklahoma) might demand a few head as a transit fee. Rustlers could also strike a herd. Teddy Blue Abbott described one nighttime rustler tactic: "They would watch you as you rode around the herd on night guard—always two men, and you rode to meet—and then when the two of you come together they would slip up to the far other side of the herd and pop a blanket. And the whole herd would get up like one animal and light out" (Abbott and Smith 1955).

Novelist Ralph Compton turned trail drives into a book-publishing industry. Beginning in 1992, he penned a series of titles commemorating the great trails of the West. In *The Goodnight Trail,* the first of the series, Benton McCaleb and several former **Texas Rangers** ride for legendary cattleman Charles Goodnight to move his herd from the Trinity River brakes (marshes) of Texas to Denver. In the process, they meet up with Judge Roy **Bean** and gunfighter Clay Alison and encounter a host of misadventures. Compton then turned his attention to *The Western Trail* (1992), where hero Mc-Caleb and other cowboys push 2,400 head of cattle into Wyoming's Sweetwater Valley. Buffalo Bill **Cody** makes an appearance in this novel. Compton continued his series through the 1990s, covering other famous trails, including the Chisholm, Bandera, California, Shawnee, Virginia City, Dodge City, and Oregon Trails. All the novels feature strong heroes, plenty of adversity on the trail, and strong local color.

Novels are one thing, but real trail drives are quite another. Why did men try to move herds of recalcitrant cattle such distances? Profits! Texas rancher George Webb Slaughter and his six sons drove herds to Kansas from 1868 until 1875. During that period, they sold more than 12,000 cattle for a total of about half a million dollars. Alas, cattlemen could not depend on consistent markets or prices, nor could they count on getting all their animals through alive.

Despite the many dangers, cowhands tried to move a herd 12 to 16 miles a day. A slower pace allowed cattle to graze and gain some weight on the trail. But a drive might cost the owner of the herd $500 per month, so there was no dawdling. Most cowboys took the hazards of the trail in stride and took pride in overcoming them without complaint. Those characteristics of faithfulness and fearlessness, of "riding for the brand," regardless of dangers, appears to be part of western fact, not fiction.

See also Chisholm, Jesse, and Chisum, John

References

Abbott, Edward Charles "Teddy Blue," and Helena Huntington Smith. *We Pointed Them North: Recollections of a Cowpuncher.* 1939. Reprint, Norman: University of Oklahoma Press, 1955.

Garfield, Brian. *Western Films: A Complete Guide.* New York: Da Capo, 1982.

Slatta, Richard W. "Life and Death on the Great Trail Drives." *Cowboys & Indians* 4, no. 3 (Fall 1996): 42–47.

Thorp, N. Howard "Jack." *Songs of the Cowboys.* 1921. Reprint, Lincoln: University of Nebraska Press, 1984.

TRUMAN, HARRY R.

1896–1980

Not to be confused with the president Harry S., Harry R. Truman's primary claim to fame was as the most famous and flamboyant casualty of the Mount St. Helens eruption of 1980. He is one of the few figures of the West whose fame comes far more from circumstance and fate than from personal feats. His notoriety is the product not of any legendary skill or gallantry but of his unbendable character and response to the forces of nature. He spent the better part of his life in his lodge on the shores of Spirit Lake, located on the northern slope of Mount St. Helens. In the face of numerous earthquakes and the ominous possibility of volcanic eruption, Truman steadfastly refused to leave his lodge. Because of this stubborn and hardheaded behavior, he eventually became a folk hero and the focus of national media attention.

When reporters came to cover events at Mount St. Helens, an interview with Truman became a necessity to add color and flare to their stories. Before long, he became the only person at Mount St. Helens known nationwide. Though the mountain cost him his life, it also immortalized him as a figure with many of the embellished qualities of the western hero. Consequently, the Harry R. Truman preserved by the national spotlight exists in a romanticized western form and is in some ways quite different from his true character.

Harry R. Truman was born in West Virginia into a family of foresters in October 1896. Mystery shrouds his earliest history. To this day, no one knows what the *R* in his name stood for, and although he settled on 30 October, Truman himself did not know his actual birth date. Like so many others before them, the Truman family headed west, lured by tales of beautiful, affordable land and a flourishing timber industry in Washington. Although he was not a native of the West, once there, Harry's tenacious character

easily molded into a rugged Western persona. Other observers, however, saw Truman in a different light. To some, he was nothing more than a crusty codger.

In some ways, Truman embodied the qualities of a typical westerner. Fiercely patriotic, he enlisted in World War I. He thrived on taking risks and did well in crises. Tough as nails, he loved the ruggedness of the outdoors and worked tirelessly at the chores nature provided him. Because of his risk-taking and independent attitude, he often suffered injuries, yet he refused medical attention and never stayed a night in a hospital.

Because the mediocrity of a normal, humdrum life did not appeal to him, he decided to go to Nevada to try his luck at prospecting. Failing to strike it rich, Truman next turned to a much easier and more suitable profession: bootlegging. The thought that he had fought for his country but could not have a drink because of Prohibition offended him deeply. He smuggled liquor from San Francisco to Washington State. Before long, however, bootlegging came under the control of gangsters, and Truman had to go into hiding. He fatefully settled where no one would find him, in the wilderness surrounding Mount St. Helens.

There Truman began to gain local notoriety for his antics and attitude. He rekindled his love of the great outdoors, building a lodge on Spirit Lake that he successfully ran for a living. However, he did so with typical belligerence. He did whatever he wanted whenever he wanted, regardless of the restrictions of authority. When a local forest ranger prohibited him from burning a large pile of brush, Truman simply got the ranger drunk and then went ahead as planned.

He routinely stole gravel from the National Park Service and often poached, although the law strictly forbid it. When he wanted to fish illegally on Indian lands, he would show a phony game-warden badge and then do as he pleased. Although rangers knew of his activities and tried to catch him in the act, not once were they successful.

The opinionated Truman cussed incessantly, and at times treated people poorly. He loved discussing political issues and hated Republicans. He even went so far as to create a "shit list" that, along with Republicans, included hippies, young children, and old people. Despite the fact that he himself was around 80 years old, he despised the elderly: "All they've got is their aches and complaints. They need somebody to push them around in a goddamn wheelchair" (Rosen 1981). When the state passed a ruling that changed the sales tax, Truman continued to charge the old rate anyway. When an employee of a Vancouver, Washington, tax office rented a boat but refused to pay the tax, Truman pushed him into the lake. On one occasion, Supreme Court Justice William O. Douglas arrived inconspicuously at the lodge. In his usual form, Truman told his niece to "go out in the lobby and tell that old coot that if he wants a cabin we don't have any. Tell him we're full up" (Rosen 1981). When told whom he had just rejected, Truman chased Douglas a mile down the road and convinced him to come back and stay.

Truman's cantankerous character brought him fame. In 1980 modest volcanic activity brought the media to what scientists called an unlikely but possible "small eruptive event." The Forest Service often sent the journalists to Truman to add color to their stories. True to form, he did not disappoint. "I'm the only one up here. . . . If the son-of-a-bitch blows, all they've got to do is find me. I'm not going to leave" (Rosen 1981).

As earthquakes and volcanic activity increased, authorities ordered the evacuation of the area, and news coverage increased. Truman steadfastly refused any attempts to remove him. He thrived on the media attention. His presence even caused a problem for law enforcement officials, who had difficulty keeping the media out of the restricted zone as they all tried to get to Truman. He richly rewarded them with choice comments and salty language. He offered his own simple solution to the problem, saying that "if I had anything to do with it, I'd have dropped a bomb right down in the middle of it. . . . ice would have filled the hole and it would have been over all at once" (Rosen 1981).

While scientists spoke of foreboding danger, Truman countered with such statements as "The mountain has shot its wad and it hasn't hurt my place a bit, but those goddamn geologists with their hair down to their butts wouldn't pay no attention to ol' Truman." Best of all, Truman continued to feed the media's frenzy with defiant statements about leaving: "You couldn't pull me out with a mule team. That mountain's part of Truman and Truman's part of that mountain" (Rosen 1981).

With these colorful statements, Truman's fame grew exponentially. Before long, he appeared on the front page of the *San Francisco Examiner* and the *New York Times*. He soon drew the interest of United Press International and *National*

Geographic. His family watched his television appearances, although the ever-increasing danger dampened their excitement. Mail poured in from around the United States. One woman sent a letter saying that she was a good housekeeper and an outdoors person and would make him a good wife. Truman, with typical tact, replied, "I wrote that old biddy fast and told her to stay put" (Rosen 1981). NBC-TV's *Today* show even flew a team in for an interview.

Truman's celebrity status grew as the nation's interest continued to increase. *National Geographic* provided him with a helicopter to visit an elementary school. A fifth-grade class in Grand Blanc, Michigan, wrote letters that made even the hardened Truman cry. He sent back a can of volcanic ash with a letter as a present. The class later sold the ash and made $50 at the science fair. They planned to send the money to Truman so that he could paint his lodge. Unfortunately, they never got the chance. On Sunday morning, 18 May 1980, Mount St. Helens erupted. The children used the money to buy flowers instead of paint.

A close look at Harry Truman reveals traits that few people would describe as heroic. His fiery attitude, brash speech, love of the outdoors, and fierce independence, however, made him a folk hero the media could adore. As Truman himself understood, "The press is all powerful." Reporters took his rough charac-teristics and stubborn defiance and transformed them into the colorful, rugged individualism long associated with the West. People came to identify with Truman and to see him as a representation of the western spirit. Major magazines, including *Time, Life, Newsweek, National Geographic, Field and Stream,* and *Reader's Digest,* profiled him. In his words, "I've made up with every newspaper, every television, every radio in the United States of America" (Rosen 1981).

Even today, the legacy of Harry Truman lives on. Posters, books, songs, and a movie memorialize him. Although his lodge now lies beneath hundreds of feet of volcanic ash and debris from the eruption, a marker stands next to the raised waters of Spirit Lake. It serves as a tribute to Truman and a reminder of his story for all who visit.

–*Kaleb J. Redden*

References

Findley, Rowe. "The Mountain That Was—and Will Be." *National Geographic* 160 (1981): 713–719.

Rosen, Shirley. *Truman of St. Helens: The Man and His Mountain.* Bothell, WA: Rosebud Publishing, 1981.

TWENTY-FIFTH INFANTRY

See Bicycle Corps

UFOS

See Area 51; Roswell, New Mexico

VAN METER, JERRY

1923–

Born in Guthrie, Oklahoma, Jerry Van Meter is the second of five sons born to Vearl and Edna Goodnight Van Meter. After graduating from Guthrie High School in 1944, he joined the navy and shipped off for preflight training in Missouri. A serious back injury sustained in an inter-squadron baseball game not long after his arrival ended his training and his military service, with an honorable discharge. After recuperating at his grandfather's Bar R Ranch near Marshall, Oklahoma, Van Meter undertook his famous Oklahoma-to-Hollywood horseback ride in May 1946. He returned to the Bar R as foreman for the next five years, then worked in a number of gold, silver, copper, uranium, and zinc mines throughout the West. He retired in Kalispell, Montana, in 1983.

Oklahoma in 1946, like the rest of the nation, was in the throes of a new awakening: the promise of good times to come. Although World War II had ended, life for most Americans still meant victory gardens, meat and grocery shortages, and gasoline rationing. Unsure about his future, Van Meter returned to Oklahoma in the winter of 1945, grateful that he could still walk.

Fourteen months later, he was riding a frisky Osage Indian mare, intent on winning a bet his grandfather Rolla Goodnight had made. (The 75-year-old cattle rancher refused to disclose the amount of the bet.) To prove that cowboyin' (as Goodnight called it) was an honorable way of life and that cowboys worth their salt still existed, Rolla bet that Van Meter could ride from Oklahoma to Hollywood, California, in 50 days. Jimmy **Wakely,** a singing cowboy and star of Monogram Pictures, took the bet. He felt certain that one man on one horse could not possibly cover 1,500 miles, let alone in 50 days. Rolla's lifelong cowboy friend Frank "Pistol Pete" Eaton also got into the act. He backed his faith in Van Meter by giving him one of his notched Colt .45s and his Osage mare Fan to make the ride.

Van Meter rode out of Guthrie, Oklahoma, on 4 May 1946. On his third night out he made camp beside famous **Route 66.** Staring westward, he realized that between him and the palm-lined boulevards of Hollywood lay some of the West's toughest terrain. He and his pony faced the Texas Panhandle, the *Llano Estacado* (the high plains of New Mexico), the Rockies, and the Continental Divide, not to mention a stretch of Arizona and California desert mean enough to kill any fool trying to cross it. The vision struck a reservoir of fear in Van Meter.

Yet he remained determined to win the bet. Why? Because that's what a cowboy did: He kept his word and did his best. When asked what motivated him to ignore his injured back and light out for California on a horse, Van Meter simply said, "In those days, you did it because your granddad told you to, to prove something to people like Jimmy [Wakely], and I guess to prove it to yourself" (interview with author).

To comprehend the *why* of this particular journey is to understand the times, values, and mind-set of a 20-year-old westerner representative of a generation we have lately come to fully appreciate. To understand Van Meter's decision to honor a wager his grandfather would not disclose, risk reinjuring his back, and give no thought of reward for himself is to grasp the essence of a cowboy, the essence of the true western hero.

Rolla Goodnight, Van Meter's maternal grandfather, came from solid western stock. Cousin of legendary cattle baron Charlie Goodnight, at age 15 he rode from his Kansas home to the JA Ranch in the Texas Panhandle so that Goodnight could teach him cowboying. He learned well and devoted the next 60 years of his life to tending cattle. He initiated the bet with Wakely by saying, "I'm willing to put my money where my mouth is. Are you?" (Dickinson 1999).

Following Route 66 across the Texas Panhandle as far as Amarillo, Van Meter then turned south and camped for a night in Palo Duro Canyon, site of the former Goodnight JA Ranch. He realized full well that Rolla's bet had also put the Goodnight tradition on the line. Its honor and integrity would remain intact if he made it to Hollywood on time; it would be forever tarnished if he failed.

Problems mounted. Two days' ride from the Palo Duro, Fan came down with distemper. Near the top of the Continental Divide, three bandits tried to rob Van Meter in the dark of a New Mexico night. The next night he and Fan found themselves caught in the middle of a mustang stampede. A run-in with a mountain lion, nearly drowning in a runaway river, and a host of other challenges on the rest of the ride tested not only Van Meter's strength and resolve but everything he stood for.

With ten days to go, he arrived at the Arizona/California border, where an officious border guard enforced an interdiction against horses entering California. Not to be foiled, Van Meter and Fan sneaked across the Colorado River 15 miles upriver. Recalling the guard's threat that he could lose Fan if he got caught, the young cowboy had to make another fateful decision. Should he turn around and head home or go on? Earlier in the trip he had written to his family, "This is not a journey for quitters" (Dickinson 1999). Those seven words answered his quandary.

Fearful of being caught but determined to win, Van Meter decided to steer clear of the highway. Considering Fan's exhaustion and the blistering heat, he knew his horse would not survive carrying his weight. The pair headed straight across the Mojave Desert on foot, the youth leading his horse. That fateful crossing would almost cost them their lives.

Of his 100-mile walk from the Colorado River to Indio, California, Van Meter recalls, "It was the first time I thought I was going to die. I couldn't bring myself to put Fan out of her misery and, after the heart she had shown, I sure wasn't going to leave her out there to die by herself. So we just kept walking." When asked what he wrote to his family about such a terrible experience, he answered with typical cowboy understatement, "There weren't any words to describe it, so I just wrote that I didn't like it much" (interview with author).

Three days later, he and Fan stumbled out of their desert hell into Indio. Kevin Lamb, a rodeo rider, befriended them. Lamb and his horse were on their way to a Gene **Autry** rodeo in Los Angeles—exactly where Van Meter and Fan were going. Lamb offered them a ride. "Who would know?" he asked. Van Meter remembers the offer to this day. When asked why he didn't accept, he replied, "Kevin said nobody would know, but I would know. I could no more cheat than I could give up" (interview with author).

After a much-needed two-day rest, Van Meter left Indio on 17 June 1946, still leading Fan. He had just five days to get to Hollywood. At Banning, California, weary to the bone, he climbed back in the saddle for the first time since leaving the Colorado River. At San Bernardino he and Fan encountered the last 50 miles of Route 66, the palm-lined boulevard he had dreamed about. What he also discovered was the future: freeways, cars, and people as thick as ants, men and women flocking to the city like moths to a flame, and all around a building boom unlike anything he could imagine.

Van Meter and Fan arrived at the North Hollywood ranch that was their destination on 21 June 1946—the forty-ninth day. Of his journey, Van Meter states that he encountered breathtaking vistas so vast and so silent that they swamped him with loneliness and made him feel as insignificant as a grain of sand. Not only did Van Meter conquer loneliness, but he also triumphed over fear, danger, weather, exhaustion, and hunger. "I saw this country in a way that most people would never get to see," he recalled.

When asked if he ever found out what the bet was and what he earned from the trip, he smiled.

Grandpa would never tell me what the bet was, Frank either. The best thing? I had my first horse at age six. In high school I rode in rodeos all around Guthrie and Enid. When I left I was foreman of the Bar R so I thought of myself as a man and a pretty good cowboy. I found out somewhere out there that it takes more than riding and roping. By the time I got to Hollywood, I figured I had earned both. But the best thing was seeing the respect on my granddad's and Frank's face when I got home. (Interview with author)

As a new century begins, this epic journey on horseback to win a bet, to prove a point, and to honor family tradition takes on a deeper, greater meaning. Reminiscent of the deeds of nineteenth-century cowboys whose exploits fuel our legends of the Great American Cowboy, Van Meter's 49-day odyssey, depicted in Dickinson's *Hollywood the Hard Way: A Cowboy's Journey* (1999), places him in the lofty company of legendary western heroes and epic deeds.

Asked if he would do it again if he could, he quickly answered, "You bet I would." When asked if he thought it could be repeated today, he shook his head wistfully. "Times are different now, youngsters too. I don't think I'd bet money on it today" (interview with author).

From the epilogue of *Hollywood the Hard Way:* "[From our vantage point] Jerry's journey speaks not just of courage, determination and integrity, but of a national innocence lost, of new values and definitions. Still after over fifty years of unparalleled progress, we continue to search for those unselfish men upon whom an indefinable light shines—men we like to call *heroes.*"

—Patti Dickinson

References

Dickinson, Patti. *Hollywood the Hard Way: A Cowboy's Journey.* Lincoln: University of Nebraska Press, 1999.

VIGILANTES

See Plummer, Henry

VIRGINIAN, THE

See Wister, Owen, and Winthrop, Washington

WAKELY, JIMMY

1914–1982

Ever the creative individualist, singer and actor Jimmy Wakely left his mark on cowboy and country music, radio, film, and television. During his prime he ranked fourth among cowboy film stars and third among male singers on jukeboxes (his discography runs to 11 pages)—not a bad showing for a lad who grew up dirt poor in Depression Oklahoma.

Not everyone applauded his creativity. "Thirty years ago, I was accused of prostituting country music by helping to take it out of its own narrow boundaries by crossing over. Nowadays, of course, we know country music is a hybrid sound. . . . We know it represents input from jazz, blues, gospel, cowboy, rock and pop music" (Jimmy Wakely in 1976, six years before his death; quoted in Wakely 1992). Nonetheless, the music business caught up with his innovations,

and today the lines between various genres are more blurred than ever. Wakely would be happy to see the change.

Born James Clarence in a log cabin in Mineola, Arkansas, on 16 February 1914, Wakely's ambition, energy, and talent would take him far beyond his humble roots. His family moved to Oklahoma when Jimmy was still a youngster. He took to strumming a cheap guitar and pestered adults to help him. He recalled how he learned his first chords: "My sister Effie started to receive visits from a gentleman caller, Lee Weeks. In order to get rid of me while they were courting, Lee taught me to play three basic chords on that guitar. The first song I ever learned was 'Nearer My God to Thee'" (Wakely 1992).

His professional career began in 1937 when WKY radio in Oklahoma City hired him to sing as part of the trio The Bell Boys (later The **Rough Riders**). But his big break came in 1940 as he drove along through the night. As Wakely told the story,

In 1940, a flash of lightning changed my life. . . . The clouds opened up and a sudden flash of lightning lit up the sky. I caught a glimpse of a face that caused me to stop. I backed up so the car lights would shine on the tree. Tacked there was a placard photo of my favorite star—Gene **Autry**—announcing his appearance in Okemah (Oklahoma). Instead of going home, I drove to Okemah. . . . When the parade started, we climbed to the top of an old store building hoping Gene would recognize us. As he approached on his horse, Champion, we waved our cowboy hats. He spotted us and waved his white Stetson, "Come on over to the hotel!" he shouted. . . . The long shot paid off in more ways than one. Gene hired my trio to come to Hollywood and join him on his CBS radio show, the Melody Ranch. I will always be grateful for that flash of lightning and for the kindness of Gene Autry. (Wakely 1992)

Wakely's sonorous voice and strong song writing gave flight to his career. In 1942 he spread his wings and soared with "I'm Sending You Red Roses," which climbed to the number-two spot on the country charts. "Slipping Around," his 1949 duet with Margaret Whiting, hit country music's number-one spot and crossed over to the pop market as well. At the peak of his career, he won back-to-back Cash Box Awards as the nation's most popular country singer.

Throughout his life, Wakely insisted on doing things his way. "Country singers must have the courage," he said in 1976, "to do their own sound rather than to follow somebody else. Waylon, Willie, Asleep at the Wheel, Alabama, they are a few examples that I admire. They do their own thing" (Wakely 1992). Jimmy would continue to write and sing a wide range of ballads, western swing, jazz, pop, and other songs until the late 1970s.

Like other singing western stars, Wakely also moved to films. He debuted in 1939 in the Republic production *Saga of **Death Valley**,* starring Roy **Rogers.** The film also featured Gabby Hayes, Donald Barry, and Doris Day. Jimmy continued to appear with many other cowboy stars, including Charles Starrett, Tex Ritter, Hopalong Cassidy, and Johnny Mack Brown. He continued to make films through 1954, when he playing along with Sterling Hayden and Colleen Gray in *Arrow in the Dust.* "I guess I am the only person" he recalled, "who became a star in the forties type shoot-em-up Westerns who supported every other star prior to my own stardom" (Wakely 1992). His lead roles began with *Song of the Range,* a Monogram production released in 1944. During his 15-year movie career, he made some 56 films, as both a singing cowboy and an action cowboy.

From 1952 to 1958, he starred in his own CBS radio program, returning to the medium that had first brought him fame. His program aired Sunday nights just before *The Jack Benny Show.* Tex Williams, Bonnie Guitar, Eddie Dean, Tex Ritter, and many other western stars appeared on the show. His wife, Inez, sometimes sang duets with him. "I married Inez on Friday, December 13, 1935. That was the best thing I ever did. Our marriage was the beginning of my dream coming true. With the help of God and Inez, and some good friends, my dreams did come true" (Wakely 1992).

Wakely continued to perform on television, in concert, and at clubs in Nevada through the 1970s. Jimmy and Inez had four children: Deanna, Carol, Johnny, and Linda Lee. Linda Lee sang with him from 1960 until his death in 1982. She also wrote a delightful biography of her father, *See Ya' up There, Baby: The Jimmy Wakely Story* (1992). Inez died on 2 July 1997. Jimmy's talent, strong moral compass, and buoyant optimism carried him through the many ups and downs of his long career. He summed up his philosophy this way:

Don't worry about tomorrow. When my movie career ended, I wondered: what next? A record career happened. And when the records stopped selling, there was radio and television. When that ended, I wondered what next? And the Nevada circuit fell into my lap. Just remember, God never closes a door that He doesn't open another one. (Wakely 1992)

[An earlier version of this essay appeared in *Persimmon Hill* magazine.]

References

Wakely, Linda Lee. *See Ya' Up There, Baby: The Jimmy Wakely Story*. Canoga Park, CA: Shasta Records, 1992.
Wakely Web Site: *http://home.att.net/~llscribe/*.

WESTERN WRITERS OF AMERICA, INC.

The geographical vastness and consequent need for cooperation in the West has long spurred a spirit of community and mutual assistance. Following this tradition, a group of writers in early 1953 founded the Western Writers of America, Inc. (WWA), "an organization of professionals dedicated to the spirit and reality of the West, past and present." As the official statement indicates, the group includes both mythmakers and myth breakers. The group "provides a unique fellowship for those using the written word or film to examine or celebrate the heritage of the West and its future." Membership is open to any published writer, of fiction or nonfiction, who treats the American West. The organization has various membership levels: One book or several magazine articles qualifies a writer for associate membership; at least three books and numerous articles are required for active membership. Over the past several decades, the WWA has grown into the most important and diverse organization promoting western writing today.

Like most Western associations, the WWA has diversified from its original, rather homogeneous membership. Founded largely by white males who wrote traditional "shoot-'em-up" fiction, the early WWA represented "Writers of the Purple Sage." The founding fathers included Harry Sinclair Drago, Norman A. Fox, D. B. Newton, Nelson C. Nye, Wayne D. Overholser, and Thomas Thompson. Today these purveyors of the mythical West have been joined by an expanded membership of more than 500 historians, journalists, and other nonfiction writers, young adult and romance writers, poets, scriptwriters, and others. Past presidents include S. Omar Barker, Elmer **Kelton**, Brian Garfield, Don

Worcester, Leon C. Metz, David Dary, Dale L. Walker, and W. C. Jameson. Tensions and debates arise between partisans of fiction versus non-fiction and between academic and popular writers. But the organization tries hard to promote dialogue not confrontation among its varied and individualistic constituency.

Women now play prominent roles in the group. As of 1999, women served as membership chair (Rita M. Cleary), magazine editor (Candy Moulton), elections chair (Kay L. McDonald), and books editor (Doris Meredith). The June 1996 issue of the group's bimonthly *Roundup* magazine included the articles "Women Rewriting the West" and "Women Captives." The magazine includes helpful research tips for utilizing historic archives, museums, and the Internet. It also publishes book reviews, market analyses, writer profiles, reports from annual conventions, lively, informative articles, and more. The April 1998 issue focused on the book industry. The December 1998 issue treated **Billy the Kid**'s height, the **Alamo,** and the Buffalo Bill Historical Center.

The WWA also recognizes that changing technology strongly affects writers and how they work. From early 1999 through late 2000, Richard W. Slatta wrote and edited a column, Riding the Cyber Range, for *Roundup* magazine. Each column pointed out ways in which western (and other) writers could take advantage of the Internet and new electronic tools to work more efficiently and profitably.

Members hold an annual convention in the last week of June in a western city. The gathering brings together members, guests, editors, and agents to socialize, network, attend spirited panels, and enjoy field trips. The WWA convention concludes with the Spur Awards banquet, honoring the best publications of the past year. The group awards prizes in many categories: fiction, short story, non-fiction, biography, history, and juvenile literature as well as **television** or motion-picture drama and documentary. Past Spur Award winners include Larry McMurtry for *Lonesome Dove,* Michael Blake for *Dances with Wolves,* Glendon Swarthout for *The Shootist,* and Tony Hillerman for *Skinwalker.* The WWA also rewards lifelong contributions to the field of western literature with the annual Owen Wister Award. Recent winners include Douglas C. Jones, David Lavender, Max Evans, and artist José Cisneros. The vibrancy and diversity of the WWA serves as a clear reminder that, far from being moribund, western writing in all its varieties is very much alive and well.

References

Membership information: Rita Cleary, Cove Woods Road, Oyster Bay, NY 11771.

Secretary-treasurer: James Crutchfield, 1012 Fair Street, Franklin, TN 37064.

Western Writers of America, Inc., Web Site: *http://www.westernwriters.org.*

WHITE BUFFALO

Many Native Americans have long esteemed the white buffalo as a special, even magical animal that plays a central role in their spiritual belief system. Over the years, people have debated the existence of the white buffalo. Does the celebrated beast merely represent the stuff of

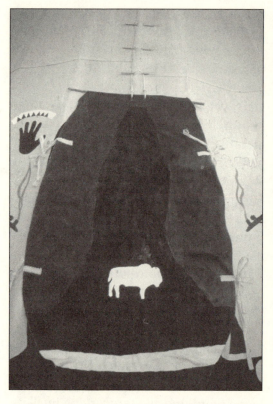 

The white buffalo is revered among many Native Americans today. White buffalo decorations on Native American tipi

Native American mythmaking, or did the animal really exist during the glory days of the American frontier? Stories of such beasts, which Native American peoples have passed down from generation to generation, do in fact represent more than just legend or folklore. A buffalo cow's chance of birthing an albino is slim. Even during their nineteenth-century heyday, only one white buffalo occurred out of every 10 million regularly colored ones. The white buffalo exists, as many credible witnesses have attested. During the 1990s, for example, two normally pigmented buffalo cows gave birth to two purely white calves.

Before Europeans arrived in the Americas, millions of buffaloes roamed the lands that now comprise the United States. Europeans incorrectly categorized the beast as a buffalo, although scientists now have properly labeled the animal a bison, since the American buffalo is directly related to the European bison. (True buffaloes, which have no humps on their shoulders, live only in Asia and Africa.) During the 1870s, the white man's rapid slaughter drastically reduced the animal's population to only a few hundred. Today, buffaloes live in either zoos or supervised sanctuaries. The nearly complete decimation of the species did not, however, prevent further incarnations of the sacred white buffalo.

On 20 August 1994, Dave Heider searched for one of his pregnant buffalo cows on his 48-acre farm in Janesville, Wisconsin. When he finally found her, he saw next to the new mother a white calf. The birth of this albino calf represented both a historic and scientific rarity. Even before the nineteenth century, when buffaloes freely roamed the American plains, there was little chance of finding a white buffalo. To produce a white calf, both cow and bull must possess the recessive gene for the trait. Even this rare combination, however, yields only a one-in-four chance that the cow will give birth to a white calf. What does all this indicate? That the likelihood of a white calf's being born is roughly one in a billion. Yet in the present century, several white buffaloes have been born. In the 1930s a brown buffalo gave birth to a white calf named Big Medicine, which lived for 36 years. This buffalo, however, did not wear a purely white coat: It had a tuft of brown hair on its head. A second white buffalo was born in the 1960s, but the animal did not survive. But Heider's white calf, now universally known as Miracle, did.

Once word of the "miraculous" birth of the white calf got out, visitors from all over the world besieged Heider's farm. Curious sightseers traveled great distances to the exotic-animal farm. Representatives from major news organizations came as well. Nearly 100,000 people made pilgrimages to see the calf in its first year alone. Celebrity visitors included Shirley MacLaine and Billy Ray Cyrus. Native Americans have visited the Heider farm more frequently than any other group. Because the white calf is central to their folklore and belief system, Heider has welcomed several Native American leaders. Over the past few

years, elders from several tribes have performed religious ceremonies there. They believe that Miracle represents the fulfillment of a nineteenth-century prophecy indicating the dawning of a new age when people will learn to live peacefully side by side. This prophecy is rooted in a sacred story: the legend of the white buffalo woman.

According to Lakota myth, many years ago, during a great famine, two young warriors went out in search of buffalo. Along the way they came upon a comely woman who floated as she walked. The first warrior, who coveted the mysterious woman, attempted to touch her. She turned him into a pile of bones. She then told the remaining hunter to return to his people to tell them of her coming. Upon her arrival, she gave them a sacred pipe with which to pray. She advised them to value not only the buffalo but their women and children as well. As the holy woman walked away, she changed into a white buffalo calf. According to legend, from that day forward the Lakota honored their pipe, and buffaloes again became plentiful, at least for a while.

Floyd Hand, a prominent Sioux medicine man, claims that the arrival of Miracle is synonymous with the second coming of Christ. After the massacre at Wounded Knee in 1892, which marked the climax of Native American conflict with the ever-encroaching Anglos, tribal elders began praying for the return of the white buffalo. Lakota Chief Crazy Horse predicted that the sacred white buffalo would return to restore harmony. According to the prophecy, the birth of the white buffalo would occur in the seventh generation. The first Lakota of the seventh generation, the grandson of

Lakota Chief Joseph Chasing Horse, was born two days after Miracle.

Many Native Americans still believe that this animal, with its great healing powers, will bring about a new purity in mind, body, and spirit and will unify people of every color and creed all over the world. The second coming of the white buffalo thus marks an end to discord and to evils such as racism and pollution, as long as people renew their spirituality. The fact that Miracle has changed colors over the years, from yellowish gray to nearly all black to auburn, signifies the fulfillment of the prophecy, since these color transformations represent the four major "races" of the world: red, white, yellow, and black. The four colors also represent the earth's life forces: land, air, water, and fire, respectively. According to Hand, when the earth's people become unified, the sacred animal, now blond, will turn white again.

Miracle, however, is no longer the only white buffalo. In 1996 a buffalo cow gave birth to an albino at the Shirek Buffalo Farm, just north of Michigan, North Dakota. This calf, White Cloud, lives at the National Buffalo Museum in Jamestown, North Dakota. White Cloud also attracts many visitors from all over the country. Miracle returned to the headlines with the birth of her first calf in May 1998. The new calf, named Millennium, sports a reddish coat, unlike her famous, highly celebrated mother.

We can also see the influence of the legendary white buffalo in many aspects of our culture. For instance, in 1993, Ted Nugent wrote the song "Great White Buffalo," which bemoans the loss of all buffaloes. He also tried unsuccessfully to purchase Miracle. An episode of the tele-vision show *Unsolved Mysteries* reviewed the legend of the white-buffalo-calf woman. A Native American on the popular show *The X-Files* compared the lead character's spiritual journey to that of the white buffalo. Authors have written scores of poems and novels about the sacred white buffalo and white-buffalo-calf woman. One can purchase Miracle T-shirts and hats at the Heider farm museum gift shop. Retailer FAO Schwartz sells a lifelike white buffalo toy. Many Internet sites commemorate the white buffalo. Each 27 August, people in New Orleans celebrate White Buffalo Day. Buffalo associations and foundations, such as the White Buffalo Day Foundation, the American Bison Association, and the National Buffalo Association, have also contributed to the story of the white buffalo. The American Bison Association, for example, has tested the animals' pedigrees, and the White Buffalo Foundation oversees the celebration of its namesake.

Will either Miracle or White Cloud fulfill the prophecy that Native Americans believe will someday become reality? Only time will tell. Clearly, if peace and understanding reign on Mother Earth any time soon, we will all have to take an active step in the right direction. Yet even if neither white buffalo represents the widely touted "second coming," their rare beauty has certainly brought at least part of the prophecy to pass. Thousands of people from all over the globe have come together in peace to appreciate their otherworldly majesty.

—*Jane Veronica Charles Smith*

References

Bly, Robert, ed. *The Soul Is Here for Its Own*

Joy: Sacred Poem for Many Cultures. Hopewell, NJ: Ecco Press, 1995.

McCracken, Harold. *The Great White Buffalo.* New York: J. B. Lippencott, 1946.

WILD BUNCH AND WINNEMUCCA, NEVADA

The story of the Wild Bunch is the best-known instance of fantasy overtaking reality in Nevada. The story goes that **Butch Cassidy,** the Sundance Kid, and several companions robbed the First National Bank in Winnemucca, in northern Nevada, on 19 September 1900. The story became so popular the town began holding an annual Butch Cassidy Days celebration.

Then, in the fall of 1982, the myth was challenged by the *Humboldt Historian,* which published a carefully researched article by Lee Berk. Berk, who had unearthed papers of banker George Nixon that contained new evidence, had replowed all the old ground—bank records, investigative files, newspaper accounts—and discovered that although Wild Bunch members pulled the heist, Butch was not among them.

For instance, Nixon had "negatively identified" Cassidy. That is, after viewing photographs of the Wild Bunch outlaws, Nixon had said positively that Cassidy was not among the robbers. A web of additional evidence also supports Berk's thesis, such as evidence that Cassidy was robbing a passenger train in Tipton, Wyoming—600 miles from Winnemucca—on 29 August 1900, only 21 days before the Winnemucca holdup. The bank robbers were known to have camped in a field north of Winnemucca 10 days before the holdup. If Cassidy had committed both crimes, he would have had to make the 600-mile ride from Tipton to Winnemucca in 11 days. "I figured that Cassidy couldn't have gotten there," said Berk. "He had to go on horseback."

No one knows for sure where the story originated, but it may have been the work of the Pinkerton Detective Agency, which, after the robbery, issued two wanted posters crediting the robbery, among others, to Butch and Sundance.

The myth includes a photograph of the Wild Bunch sent from Fort Worth, Texas, to the First National Bank a few months after the robbery. An unsigned note thanked the bank for the cash. The photo of five men included Harry Longabaugh (the Sundance Kid) and Leroy Parker (Butch Cassidy). The presumption was that everyone in the photo was associated with the robbery. Only three of the gang entered the bank and robbed it (of $32,640), giving birth to a legend. In fact, it was the Pinkertons who sent George Nixon the photograph more than five months after the robbery. A Wells Fargo detective in Fort Worth found the photo at the Swartz Photography Studio and recognized the Wild Bunch gang. Wells Fargo sent a copy of the photo to the Pinkertons, who were investigating the robbery on behalf of the American Bankers Association.

—Guy Louis Rocha

See also Butch Cassidy and the Sundance Kid

Source of Further Information

Toll, David. "Great Winnemucca Bank Robbery." *Nevada Magazine,* May/June 1983.

WILD HORSES

Wild horses, often called "mustangs," are the quintessential symbol of the mythic American West. No other animal, not even the bison, is so closely associated with the frontier West, evokes such popular sentiment, or is given such imaginative play in popular culture. This may seem paradoxical, since from a biological perspective, North American wild horses are not an indigenous species, as are bison, wolves, or coyotes. Although horses began an evolutionary development in North America, biologists believe they became extinct here some 10,000 years ago. Spanish explorers and other European colonists reintroduced horses in the sixteenth century. Furthermore, some argue that the ensuing herds of horses were not truly "wild" but simply feral; that is, they were domestic animals that had escaped from human control.

And therein lies the ideological potency and allure of wild horses. They are domesticates that have repudiated civilization and thoroughly reverted to a natural life of independence and self-determination, thus realizing the dreams of the Romantic philosophers and the aspirations of pioneer settlers. Ever since the first Spanish horses escaped and bolted across the vast grasslands of the American plains, cowboys and vaqueros have been trying to recapture them. Cowboy culture depended upon having wild horses to tame. So wild-horse roundups became a staple of countless western works by **pulp novelists** and of films, **television** shows, and campfire legends. But because wild horses seem to embody the loftiest values and most cherished

promises of the mythic West, and because they are themselves an integral byproduct of the frontier experience, a deep ambivalence colors their capture. Each roundup reenacts the "taming" of the frontier, highlighting myriad tensions and contradictions peculiar to the western experience. These powerful associations have been felt by movie moguls, schoolchildren, and working cowboys. Frank Dobie, the mustang's greatest historian, noted that "the aesthetic value of the mustang topped all other values. The sight of wild horses streaming across the prairies made even the most hardened of professional mustangers regret putting an end to their liberty" (Dobie 1934, 111).

The wild-horse chase is an enduring leitmotif of the mythic West, and its hero is the freedom-loving, uncatchable mustang stallion. Often the stallion assumes the role of an antihero, whose masculine vigor and determination is challenged by his human counterpart. Successful "mustangers" (wild-horse catchers), such as the famous black cowboy Bob Lemmons, sometimes themselves became western legends. But cowboys on every western range have told of chasing a stallion that eluded every trap, ducked every rope, and outran his pursuers for days, only to thwart their ambitions by leaping off a precipice to his death when finally cornered. Dobie and others have memorialized many unconquerable mustang stallions, whose names—Blue Streak, Black Devil, Starface—still strike awe around campfires.

During the nineteenth century, the most famous of these legendary horses may have been the white Ghost Horse of the Plains, also known as the Pacing

White Stallion. Anthropologist Elizabeth Atwood Lawrence, who collected and analyzed versions of his legend (1991), notes that sightings of this indomitable horse were reported from Mexico to Canada over a span of more than 50 years. Western travelers, like Washington Irving (who popularized the story) and Josiah Gregg, wrote of his marvelous exploits, which became so well known that P. T. Barnum put a bounty on his head. Paying homage to revered white creatures, Herman Melville rhapsodized that the evasive white stallion was "a most imperial and archangelical apparition of that unfallen, western world" (quoted in Price 1999).

Wild horses have been viewed as the antithesis of civilization and, by some, even as a direct and unwelcome threat to it. Wild stallions became notorious for "stealing" domestic ranch mares, a behavior seen as reflecting their ungovernable instincts. Since wild horses select their mates without the guiding hand of rational human selection, ranchers dedicated to "improving" the West and its livestock through controlled breeding reviled such thefts. Many ranchers regarded "randomly bred" wild horses with disdain and shot them when possible. Wild stallions that "poached" mares were considered "rogues" and "renegades"; their perceived "polluting" effect echoed the boundary-trespass theme of captivity narratives. Likewise, wild horses that refused to submit to being handled and ridden became known as "outlaws" and "broncos." This aspect of "wildness" has been perpetuated and institutionalized in the rodeo bronco, essentially a performing wild horse. Nevada, home of the "Sagebrush Rebellion," recently issued a commemorative state coin featuring wild stallions engaged in battle, while Wyoming imprints the silhouette of a bucking bronco on state license plates.

Wild horses have been a favorite

theme of pictorial artists and a visual symbol of the West since George Catlin sketched them in the 1830s. B. Byron Price, director of the Buffalo Bill Historical Center (1999), has summarized the paean that nineteenth- and early-twentieth-century western artists paid to the wild horse, from Catlin to Frederic **Remington** and Charles M. **Russell.** As the frontier experience receded into the twentieth century, novels, films, and television amplified the romantic appeal of wild horses.

The best-known wild horse hero of American letters is probably *Smoky, the Cowhorse* (1926), the creation of Will James, a Nevada cowboy, writer, and artist. Smoky's life story, told in the horse's voice, is punctuated by transitions between freedom and captivity, thus recapitulating the historical experience of wild horses. Born wild, Smoky is captured and befriended by a sympathetic cowboy. But when he falls into bad hands, he vows to fight confinement to the death and becomes a notorious saddle bronc. James's poignant tale won the Newberry Medal for (children's) Literature in 1927. The subject of several films, Smoky inspired several generations of equine heroes in a variety of media. Between the two world wars, horses such as Rex (in *Rex, King of the Wild Horses*) and **Wildfire** helped to construct the mythic "Wild West" on the silver screen. Writers such as Thomas C. Hinkle enthralled young readers with books featuring the adventures of wild horse protagonists such as *Hurricane Pinto: The Story of an Outlaw Horse* (1935).

Smoky's most direct descendant in the age of television was probably Fury, the star of an immensely popular children's show of the same name that ran from 1955 to 1960. That program helped to cultivate young baby boomers' imaginative understanding of wild horses. Fury, a wild black stallion, follows Smoky in befriending a single human being, Joey, "the only person on earth that could ride him." Fury became one of the biggest commodities of 1950s popular culture. The television show spawned a comic-book series, trading cards, toys, lunch boxes, and a board game. Today, Fury continues to roam the mythical West on the Internet, where a Web site memorializes the series.

The reality of wild horses being literally turned into commodities was explored in *The Misfits* (1961). The film starred Marilyn Monroe, Montgomery Clift, and Clark Gable. Set in the contemporary West, this elegiac yet gritty film positions wild horses in a liminal zone, trapped between an expansive but ordered past and a shrinking, despoiled present. American's deep identification with wild horses is fully exploited in the moral conflicts of the world-weary cowboy protagonists, who set out to capture wild horses, not for glory or for use, but to sell as dog food. Their tools are no longer simply horses and ropes; now they include trucks and airplanes. Like the miner's canary, this treatment of wild horses registers the health of the American West, which is revealed to be dominated by an increasingly visible national and global economy.

Gender and color are important semiotic devices in the popular representation of wild horses. Stallions epitomize the indomitable spirit of wild horses. Many famous cowboy stars billed their mounts (Roy **Rogers'**s Trigger, the **Lone**

Ranger's Silver, and Gene **Autry**'s Champion) as (sometimes formerly wild) stallions, thus emphasizing the power, mastery, and masculinity of their riders. Manufacturers of so-called muscle cars, sports utility vehicles, motorcycles, and wines have named their products "mustangs," "broncos," and "wild horses" to suggest strength, speed, power, and autonomy. Sports teams throughout America have adopted similar monikers. A recent Internet search for "wild horses" yielded more than 640,000 hits on one search engine.

Dozens of songs mentioning wild horses have been written in the past century, from cowboy ballads to rock anthems. Many refer to stallions or, more metaphorically, to stallion-like qualities, and many (such as "The Strawberry Roan") indicate a specific color. Horses are integral to Native American cultures of the Great Plains. Many Native Americans have expressed the view that the historical experience of wild horses, constantly forced to elude agents of the dominant society, parallels their own colonial past. Contemporary Native American singer-songwriters, such as John Trudell ("Tina Smiled") and Cherokee Rose ("To All the Wild Horses"), have recorded songs in which wild horses symbolize resistance and survival, both emotional loss and a people's spirit.

Like the Pacing White Stallion, most wild horses are popularly depicted as being of an unusual color, a feature that helps to differentiate them from domesticated animals. Roan, buckskin, dun, gruella, paint (pinto), and appaloosa are rare colors and coat patterns that have historically been discouraged or disallowed by the horse-breed registries or-ganized in western Europe and its colonies. Paint, or pinto, horses, which are solid colored with an overlay of splotched white markings, have historically been associated with wild horses and with "Indian ponies," their symbolic brethren. As such, paint horses often appear as visual symbols of "Indian-ness." Buckskin and dun coat colors are considered to be a mark of atavism, since the most-primitive horses are thought to have been that color. In the early twentieth century, such colors were denigrated as akin to the "savagery" ascribed to Native Americans. In recent decades, nostalgia and a longing for the "authentic primitive" have made them desirable again.

With the publication of *Misty of Chincoteague* in 1947, Marguerite Henry may have introduced the first female into the literary pantheon of wild horse heroes. Captured in the annual roundup of wild ponies on Assateague Island, off the coast of Virginia, Misty became not only a superstar of children's literature but a living icon of wild horses and an ambassador for their welfare. Henry claimed that Misty, a paint mare, had a marking in the shape of a United States map over her withers, and another in the shape of a plow on her side. Henry wrote a celebrated series of books chronicling the lives of Misty's family and that of a wild burro (*Brighty of the Grand Canyon*, 1935). She further popularized the view that wild horses were "live mementos of frontier days," symbols of liberty, and iconic of America itself.

The romantic view of wild horses has an unrelenting hold on the national imagination. Its expansion through emerging venues of popular culture helped to foster one of the most successful grassroots campaigns in U.S. history. In the 1950s it became apparent that the number of wild horse was rapidly declining. Nevada ranch wife Velma "Wild Horse Annie" Johnson mounted a national crusade to expose the cruelty of mechanized roundups and to win support for the protection of wild herds. Fueled by the letter-writing campaigns of schoolchildren, thousands of Americans responded to Johnson's appeals and deluged Congress with pleas to save the mustangs. New York journalist Hope Ryden published an impassioned expose titled *America's Last Wild Horses* in 1970. Marguerite Henry chronicled Wild Horse Annie's mission in *Mustang: Wild Symbol of the West* (1966). Legislators listened and responded. In 1959 Congress passed the so-called Wild Horse Annie Act, prohibiting the use of motorized vehicles to hunt wild horses and burros. In 1971 Congress voted unanimously to pass a much broader law, providing protection for free-roaming horses and burros on federal lands and establishing guidelines for their management. The Wild and Free-Roaming Horse and Burro Act legalized the obvious in declaring wild horses "living symbols of the historic and pioneer spirit of the West."

Thirty years later, this interpretation of the place of wild horses has only gained ground in the popular-culture arena. As the mythic West becomes increasingly cannibalized by the expanding "heritage industry," images of wild horses have proliferated in consumer-products catalogues (L. L. Bean, Coldwater Creek), travel brochures, and popular song lyrics (Kenny Rogers, "She Rides Wild Horses"). Western states that once tried to eradicate wild horses now entice travelers by broadcasting images of local herds on postcards, sweatshirts, and state Web sites. A wide array of environmental and animal-rights groups circulate images of wild horses in photographic calendars, with stereotypical images of running herds and fighting stallions.

But this celebratory view of wild horses has always been contested by their opponents, including some ranchers, biologists, and federal land managers. The federal protection of wild horses has placed them at center stage in the "range wars" over federal land use in the rapidly changing West. In Nevada, which hosts roughly half of the nation's estimated 43,000 wild horses, they have been the targets of episodic mass shootings for the past two decades. A half-dozen wild horse advocacy groups draw on common symbolic currency to debate their management, both with the federal government and with each other. Spreading suburbia is encroaching on wild-horse ranges in some states. The tension of these threats, coupled with their own paradoxical nature, only regenerates the symbolic power of wild horses. They not only represent the mythical West, but they also interrogate the New West. Their stubborn quest for freedom still represents the rugged individualism long cherished by many Americans. To paraphrase rocker Neil Young, long may they run.

—*Castle McLaughlin*

References

Dobie, J. Frank. *The Mustangs*. New York: Bramhall House, 1934.

Lawrence, Elizabeth Atwood. "The White Mustang of the Prairies." *Great Plains Quarterly* 1 (Spring 1991): 81–94.

Wild horses remain a powerful western icon. Photo taken at WestFest

Price, B. Byron. "Wild Horses in Popular Culture." In *Unbroken Spirit: The Wild Horse in the American West,* ed. Frances B. Clymer and Charles R. Preston. Cody, WY: Buffalo Bill Historical Center, 1999.

WILD WEST SHOWS

See Cody, William Frederick "Buffalo Bill"

WILDFIRE

The idea of Wildfire, a mythical horse (perhaps a ghost horse?), shows up many times in the modern American West. Western singer Michael Martin Murphey created the myth with the 1975 release of the song "Wildfire" (coauthored with Larry Cansler) on his album *Blue Sky–Night Thunder.* It tells the story of a young woman and her cherished pony, Wildfire, both of whom are lost in a blizzard in Nebraska.

She comes down from Yellow Mountain;
On a dark flat land she rides
On a pony she named Wildfire,
A whirlwind by her side,
On a cold Nebraska night.
Oh they say she died one winter
When there came a killin' frost,
And the pony she named Wildfire
Busted down his stall.
In a blizzard, she was lost.
She ran callin' Wildfire . . .
Callin' Wildfire . . .

Callin' Wildfire . . .
So by the dark of the moon I planted,
But there came an early snow.
Been a hoot-owl howlin' outside my
  window now
'Bout six nights in a row.
She's comin' for me, I know,
And on Wildfire, we're both gonna go.
We'll be riding Wildfire . . .
Ridin' Wildfire . . .
Ridin' Wildfire . . .
On Wildfire we're gonna ride.
Gonna leave sodbustin' behind;
Get the hard times right on outta our
  minds,
Ridin' Wildfire . . . (Murphey 1975)

Murphey says the many old ghost-horse legends of the West inspired the idea of Wildfire and that he came up

Cowboy singer Michael Martin Murphey

with the story in his sleep one night: "I woke from a dream with the name Wildfire and all these images in my head. The song came from that. A girl and her pony were both lost one winter, but they reappear occasionally to help westerners. It's all about the dream of freedom and escape" (Murphey 1975).

In March 1917 western author Zane **Grey** published a paperback novel titled *Wildfire.* It tells the story of Lin Sloan, a "horse hunter," who chases a wild stallion named Wildfire. He is injured while attempting to rope the horse, and a woman named Lucy saves both of them. The plot includes all manner of intrigue and competition between Sloan and a rival for both horse and woman. In April 2001, Murphey stated, "Zane Grey did not inspire me. I was not aware of the plot of the book, though the title of the book might have been stuck in my subconscious mind." Whether Grey inspired Murphey or whether it was the ghostly legends that inspired him, the horses reflect similarly mysterious, unattainable, unearthly qualities.

A 1989 novel by Nancy Springer, *They're All Named Wildfire,* is a story of two young girls of different races who form a friendship based on their mutual love of horses. Beginning in September 1986, Hanna-Barbera produced an animated series, *Wildfire,* about a kingdom of magical horses. Although it only ran for 13 episodes, it retains quite a following on the Internet. The story lines centered around a young girl called Sarah and a very noble horse named Wildfire. Wildfire and Sarah frequently crossed the borders between their worlds for their adventures. She wore an amulet that glowed when Wildfire was coming for her. She climbed on his back and rode to the magical horse kingdom of Dar-Shan.

Although the idea of magical ghost horses already existed, Michael Martin Murphey created the modern myth with his memorable song. All of the Wildfires since then have been dashing, strong, romantic images of horses. The animated Wildfire was black with a fiery red mane and tail, the epitome of the romantic dark horse. Wildfire is an icon, the perfect mustang, the perfect name for a ghostly prairie pony or a wild canyon stallion. It's the perfect name for a western horse, real or apparition, because it embodies the spirit of the ideas of the West: freedom and strength.

—*P. S. Crane*

See also Wild Horses

References

Michael Martin Murphey Home Page: *http:// www.michaelmartinmurphey.com.*

Murphey, Michael Martin. *Blue Sky–Night Thunder.* Epic Records/CBS, 1975. Record album.

Wildfire Animated Series: *http://wildfirecartoon.tvheaven.com.*

WISTER, OWEN, AND WINTHROP, WASHINGTON

1860–1938

Born to an intellectual family in Germantown, Pennsylvania, Wister enjoyed a good education in Europe and the United States. Early in life, he exhibited considerable musical talent and considered following a musical career. He majored in music at Harvard and graduated in 1882. Teddy Roosevelt figured among Wister's undergraduate acquaintances, and the former's enthusiasm for the West doubtless influenced Wister. The future novelist would make some 15 trips west, beginning in 1885 with a journey to Wyoming. The West captivated him, and subsequently he spent many summers in Wyoming; the notes he jotted there provided inspiration and material for future writings. He would make the area around Medicine Bow famous.

A lesser-known part of his life came during time spent in the mountain village of Winthrop, nestled in the Methow Valley of the Cascade Mountains in Washington. He traveled there in early October 1892 to visit another college chum, Guy Waring. A year earlier, Waring had established the first store in Winthrop, which later became the Methow Trading Company. Wister endured a long, arduous journey via train, stage, and buckboard. He reported a sign at one place in dry eastern Washington that read, "Forty-five miles to water. Seventy-five miles to wood. Two and one-half miles to hell."

Wister finally arrived at Winthrop, where he welcomed "moderate pulls at the bottle." He spent some six weeks hunting mountain goats and exploring the region. The day after Thanksgiving, with snow already drifting high, Wister made a hasty departure with a freight wagon to avoid spending all winter in the Cascade Mountains.

In 1898 Wister married his cousin Mary Channing, and the newlyweds decided to brave the trip to the Northwest again. This time, the couple faced a hair-raising trip on a Columbia River stern-wheeler.

Methow Valley residents believe that some of its sights and citizens may have made their way into Wister's only western novel, *The Virginian: A Horseman of the Plains* (1902). Many residents there believe that New York–born Milton S. Storey, who died in 1920, provided the model for Wister's Virginian. Storey—tall, thin, fair-haired, and blue-eyed—had a reputation as a crack shot. He also rode a white horse. According to Anna Green Stevens, Guy Waring's step-daughter, "When I asked Owen Wister who was the Virginian, he said it was a composite picture of three men, Milton S. Storey being the principle, my daddy, and Pete Bryan." Mary Carry, who taught at Fairview school, could have been the model for the Virginian's sweetheart Molly Wood. Pete Bryan supposedly contributed various quaint northwestern phrases, such as "foggin' down the trail."

Methow Valley residents also claim that Wister wrote his novel there during the summer of 1901. According to Stevens, "Mr. Wister wrote part of *The Virginian* at our place [in Winthrop] and part of it in Wyoming" (Wilson and Duffy 1965). However, the author's daughter, Fanny Kemble Wister, insisted that he did the writing in Charleston, South Carolina, and Philadelphia, with possibly some written in San Francisco. "He never speaks of *The Virginian* as a novel until he is in Charleston the winter of 1902," she reported. "It is a myth that he wrote *The Virginian* in the State of Washington" (Wilson and Duffy 1965).

Wister's famous novel made the western cowboy a subject acceptable to the eastern cultural establishment. However, the book has rightly been criticized for its romanticized, stylized, inaccurate portrayal of cowboy life. The author dedicated the book to the nation's new president, Theodore Roosevelt, who had criticized the manuscript rather harshly. The book's cowboys never herd cattle! Wister viewed the cowboy as a modern medieval knight. He appealed to eastern readers by layering artificial, proper, eastern "civilized" values on his western subjects. Like many easterners, Wister saw what he wanted to see in the West, not what really existed.

No one would confuse Wister's cowboy hero, chivalrous and bold as a medieval knight, with the real working cowhand. Wister's cowboy combined eastern civility and western roughness and virility. According to scholar David Mogen, the Virginian represented "that last pioneer nobleman, roaming a frontier beyond the dominion of a mother culture in the East, representing both its rebellious runaway sons and its most poignant dream of manhood and freedom" (Mogen 1979).

Wister skillfully assembled the essential ingredients and imagery emulated by countless later writers and filmmakers. He combined a larger-than-life hero, a love story, a stirring western landscape (albeit one without cows), and occasional violence, but he did so with more literary skill than the pulp practitioners. Historian Richard Etulain (1991) summarized well the importance of Wister and Frederic **Remington** in reshaping the cowboy's image:

> While some of the earliest literary and artistic depictions of the cowpuncher treated him as unruly and in need of a

dose of refinement, by the time novelist Owen Wister and artist Frederic Remington became his champions in the 1890s they pictured him as a buoyant, romantic hero stripped of the excessive heroics of earlier Wild West characters but sufficiently vivacious and charming to gain large audiences for theirs and similar works dealing with the cowboy. (Etulain 1991)

Like many of his generation, Wister lamented the passing of his romanticized Old West. Soon after publishing *The Virginian,* he became disillusioned with the West and quit going there. Changing western realities failed to live up to his highly romanticized notions. He continued to write but seldom turned back to the West for subject matter. When he did take on a western theme, his stories exhibited cynicism and nostalgia. He died in North Kingston, Rhode Island, in 1938.

In 1903 Dustin Farnum starred in a play in Boston based on the novel. The musical Wister composed a song, "Ten Thousand Cattle," for the play. Farnum also starred in the first (in 1914) of several movies of *The Virginian.* Another film version appeared in 1923, starring silent-film actor Kenneth Harlan. The novel made the cowboy into a folk hero, spawned countless imitators, and gave us the famous phrase, "If you want to call me that, smile." The best-known film version appeared in 1929, with Gary Cooper in the lead, supported by Richard Arlen (Steve) and Walter Huston, in his first film role, as Trampas. Director Victor Fleming ably retained the tension and drama of the novel, including the climactic final shoot-out.

Grosset and Dunlap publishers took advantage of the excitement generated by the new medium of film. They reprinted the original Macmillan novel, "illustrated with scenes from the all talking photoplay, a Paramount Picture." Another film version, this time in color, appeared in 1946. In September 1962 the story, starring James Drury, moved to **television,** airing on NBC as the first 90-minute western. After a rather weak start, the program ran for eight years. Doug McClure played Trampas, Lee J. Cobb played Judge Henry Garth, and Charles Bickford appeared as John Grainger.

Many western places commemorate the famous author. A mountain in the Teton Range of Wyoming is named for him. *The Virginian* brought fame to Goose Egg Ranch, located in a beautiful Wyoming valley. The two-level house commands an impressive view of the North Platte River and the surrounding red cliffs. The Owen Wister Western Writers Reading Room houses the University of Wyoming's Hebard Collection of materials on state history. The university also publishes the *Owen Wister Review.* Likewise, residents of Winthrop, Washington, remain proud of the author who visited their fair valley a century ago.

References

Etulain, Richard, ed. *Writing Western History: Essays on Major Western Historians.* Albuquerque: University of New Mexico Press, 1991.

Mogen, David. "Owen Wister's Cowboy Heroes." In *The Western: A Collection of Critical Essays,* ed. James K. Folsom. Englewood Cliffs, NJ: Prentice-Hall, 1979.

Payne, Darwin. *Owen Wister: Chronicler of the West, Gentleman of the East.* Dallas: Southern Methodist University Press, 1985.

Slatta, Richard W. *The Cowboy Encyclopedia.* Santa Barbara, CA: ABC-CLIO Press, 1994; paperback ed., New York: W. W. Norton, 1996.

Wilson, Bruce A., and Barbara Duffy. "When You Call Me That, Smile." *Okanogan County Heritage,* June 1965, 3–16. Mimeographed.

Wister, Owen. *Owen Wister's West: Selected Articles.* Ed. Robert Murray Davis. Albuquerque: University of New Mexico Press, 1987.

Source of Further Information

Owen Wister Review: P.O. Box 4238 University Station, Laramie, WY 82071.

WIZARD OF OZ, THE WONDERFUL

The Wonderful Wizard of Oz, written by L. Frank Baum and first published in 1900, is one of America's best-known fairy tales. The 1939 MGM movie version, *The Wizard of Oz,* has become a classic. Baum's story continues to affect children and adults today. Although most view the story as simple fantasy, some claim the story symbolizes real life issues. One of the most popular interpretations connects *The Wonderful Wizard of Oz* with the Populist movement. Despite L. Frank Baum's claim that he wrote the story "solely to pleasure children," some scholars suggest he intentionally wrote the story as Populist allegory. Regardless of Baum's intentions, new interpretations of his story are constantly being created and reinforced.

The late 1800s saw the formation of the Populist Party. The party included western farmers and workers who challenged private banks, railroad companies, and the eastern elites. Populists fought to end the gold standard, to enact an income tax, to eliminate life terms for federal judges, and to end the printing of paper money by private banks.

Their main concern dealt with the gold standard. During the mid- to late-1800s, the United States moved toward using only gold to support its monetary system. The scarcity of gold in the early 1890s helped cause a major economic depression in 1893. Farmers faced low crop prices, unemployment, and deflation in general. They wanted the United States to move away from the gold standard and adopt a policy that would allow the free coinage of silver, which they believed would solve their economic problems. Pro-silver sentiment concentrated mostly in the West. William Jennings Bryan ran for president in 1896 as a Populist on a platform of free silver coinage.

In 1887 L. Frank Baum moved to Aberdeen, South Dakota, where he wrote for a newspaper, the *Aberdeen Saturday Pioneer.* The people of South Dakota suffered greatly during the time Baum lived there, and in his editorials, he often wrote of the farmers' hardships. In 1891 Baum moved to Chicago. At this time, mainly because of hard economic times, Chicago was the home of progressive social reformers. Baum marched in at least one of candidate William Jennings Bryan's torchlight parades in 1896. William Harvey, from Illinois, published *Coin's Financial School,* a popular pro-silver story. It seems evident that Baum knew of the Populists and of the social activity taking place around him. He witnessed the struggles of the Populists and the effects of the depression before writing his fantasy in 1900. Although Baum never called himself a Populist, he did sympathize with groups who participated in the movement.

The first interpretation of the story as Populist allegory appeared in 1964. Henry Littleton, with the help of his students, first developed this theory in his essay "The Wizard of Oz: Parable on Populism." Of all the interpretations, this one is the most popular. Littleton admits that "the allegory always remains in minor key, subordinated to the major theme and readily abandoned whenever it threatens to distort the appeal of fantasy" (Littleton 1964). Most interpreters agree that Baum focused on the children's fantasy first and the allegory second. Even if Baum did not intentionally mean to symbolize the Populist movement, there are many connections that support Littleton's theory.

"Oz," an abbreviation for ounce (a measure associated with gold), appears in the story's title. According to family tradition, the Land of Oz obtained its name on 7 May 1898. On this day, news of Adm. George Dewey's victory in Manila reached Chicago. The taking of Manila in the Spanish-American War may be seen as an act of imperialism. Baum may have viewed it as an act driven by the desire for gold and power. Thus, the name "Land of Oz" may be a reference to the United States and its interest in money.

The Wonderful Wizard of Oz begins in Kansas around the time of the depression of the 1890s. Kansas, an agricultural state, held Populist Party interests. Aunt Em and Uncle Henry are introduced as poor, unhappy farmers. Dorothy Gale, the main character, is said to represent the people of America. She is honest, kind, and naive, which are characteristics of America, particularly the West. A cyclone, the Populist movement, carries Dorothy and her house into the Land of Oz. The house falls on and kills the Wicked Witch of the East, representing eastern business and financial interests. The Munchkins, the little people, are freed from slavery after the witch is killed. Dorothy obtains the witch's silver shoes from the Witch of the North. She is advised to take the yellow brick road, representing the gold standard, to the Emerald City, Washington, D.C., where the Wizard of Oz lives. Emerald is a greenish color that can be associated with paper money. Dorothy's silver shoes walk on the yellow brick road that represents the battle for bimetallism, a central Populist concern (indeed, a fixation).

Along the way, Dorothy meets the Scarecrow, the Tin Woodman, and the Cowardly Lion. The Scarecrow represents the American farmer. His lack of a brain is how many perceived farmers during this period. Journalist William Allen White wrote a famous editorial in 1896 called "What's the Matter with Kansas?" He claimed the farmers created their own problems through their ignorance and inability to adapt to the modern world. The Scarecrow wants to join Dorothy to ask the Wizard for a brain.

Next, Dorothy and the Scarecrow find the Tin Woodman, who represents the industrial worker. He is rusted when they meet him, symbolizing the worker's inability to work during the depression. After being oiled, the Tin Woodman explains how he came to be made of tin. The Wicked Witch of the East cursed his ax. Every time he used it, he would cut off a part of his body. Tin (silver) replaced these missing parts and solved his problem. The curse also made the Tin Woodman work faster and harder. The bankers and elites of the East controlled the worker much as the witch did the Tin Woodman. He wanted to join the group to ask the Wizard for a heart, which symbolizes how eastern power dehumanized the industrial worker.

The final member to join the group is the Cowardly Lion, William Jennings Bryan himself. Some critics accused Bryan of having more bark than bite. His enemies called him a coward for being a pacifist and an anti-imperialist. Some supporters did not like the fact that he took time off from his presidential campaign to help free Cuba. He is also remembered for his great oratory skills, which could represent the roar of a lion. When the group encounters the Lion, he strikes the Tin Woodman with his claws. Surprisingly, "he could make no impression on the tin" (Baum 1910). Although Bryan's "Cross of Gold" speech attracted many followers, he did not successfully recruit industrial workers.

The order in which Dorothy meets the group is significant. First, the farmers in America formed the base of the Populist movement. Then, to a small extent, the workers joined the movement. Finally, William Jennings Bryan became the party leader for the movement. The group's journey to the Emerald City is reminiscent of the trip made by Coxey's Army, unemployed workers who traveled to Washington to make demands of President Grover Cleveland in 1894.

When Dorothy and her companions finally arrive at the Emerald City, the Guardian of the Gates confronts them. They are ordered to wear green glasses with gold bands so they will not be blinded by the green light. They are forced to see the land through the perspective of money. The group is allowed to stay in the Palace, the White House, until they meet the Wizard. Dorothy is led "through seven passages and up three flights of steps" (Baum 1910) to her room. This number, 73, recalls the so-called Crime of '73, when the United States stopped the coinage of the silver dollar. This "crime" became a pivotal event in Populist ideology. On the way through the hall to meet the Wizard, they see "many ladies and gentlemen of the court, all dressed in rich costumes" (Baum 1910), representing the bureaucrats of Washington. When they meet the Wizard, he seems both powerful and fearful. He asks them to go back to the West and kill the Wicked Witch of the West. If they kill the witch, he promises to give them what they came for.

The group then travels west, where they finally encounter the witch. She wears a golden cap that gives her special powers, such as calling for the Winged Monkeys. The Winged Monkeys, whom the witch has enslaved and displaced, represent Native Americans. These actions against Native Americans coincide with the Populist's anti-imperialist view. The witch makes Dorothy angry by playing a trick on her. Dorothy throws a bucket of water on the witch who then melts away. Water, a valuable resource to the drought-ridden farms of the depression, helped eliminate evil.

Dorothy and company head back to

tell the Wizard that they killed the Wicked Witch of the West. The group finally sees the real Wizard, who turns out to be a weak, common man. He admits he has been fooling everyone all along as a ventriloquist and mimic. Here Baum is criticizing the presidents of the late 1800s. The Wizard gives the Scarecrow, the Tin Woodman, and the Cowardly Lion items that make them think they got what they came for. Then the Wizard departs in his balloon before he can take Dorothy back to Kansas. The Wizard can solve "problems" that do not really exist, but he cannot solve Dorothy's real problem. He took advantage of their ignorance, which is how Populists viewed the presidents during their time.

Glenda, the Good Witch of the South, represents the region sympathetic to the Populist movement. She tells Dorothy that her silver shoes can get her back home; the silver shoes hold the power to solve Dorothy's, thus America's, problems. Dorothy uses the shoes to return home, but when she lands back in Kansas, she is missing them. The shoes are "lost forever in the desert" (Baum 1910), just as the issue of free silver lost in the political arena. The Gold Standard Act, passed in 1900, recommitted the United States to a gold standard. That same year, Bryan lost in his second bid for the presidency.

Baum uses the colors silver, gold, and green throughout the story. Silver and gold are sometimes seen in pairs, as in the new ax given to the Tin Woodman after the Wicked Witch of the West dies. This pairing represents the issue of bimetallism. Silver is usually associated with positive images, such as the Tin Woodman. Gold is associated with the power and evil of the East, a view held by Populists.

This allegory of the Populist Party is still taught today in some middle school, high school, and college classrooms. People continue to build upon and adapt Henry Littleton's theory. Some form their own theories on how L. Frank Baum intended the story to be read. People have connected the story to feminism, Marxism, secularism, and teaching health to children.

The MGM movie keeps *The Wonderful Wizard of Oz* fresh in the minds of people today. However, the movie lost some of the allegory by making Dorothy's shoes ruby instead of silver and by making other changes in the story line. Nevertheless, the book remains the central focus of everything associated with *The Wizard of Oz*.

Even though Henry Littleton admits that his essay is just a theory, he affirms that the allegory "is too consistent to be coincidental" (Littleton 1964). The issue may never be resolved, but *The Wonderful Wizard of Oz* adds yet another entertaining chapter to Western mythology.
  —*Michael L. Sileno*

References

Baum, L. Frank. "The Wonderful Wizard of Oz." 1910 ed. Project Gutenberg: *http://www.cs.cmu.edu/People/rgs/wizoz10.html*.

Littleton, Henry M. "The Wizard of Oz: Parable on Populism." *American Quarterly* 16, no. 1 (1964): 47–59.

Parker, David B. "Oz: L. Frank Baum's Theosophical Utopia." Paper delivered at the Kennesaw Academic Forum, April 1996: *http://ksumail.kennesaw.edu/~dparker/history/oz/oztheos.html*.

Ritter, Gretchen. "Silver Slippers and a Golden

Cap: L. Frank Baum's *The Wonderful Wizard of Oz* and Historical Memory in American Politics." *Journal of American Studies* 31 (1997): 171–202.

Rockoff, Hugh. "The 'Wizard of Oz' as a Monetary Allegory." *Journal of Political Economy* 98, no. 4 (1990): 739–760.

WOBBLIES

The Wobblies, members of the Industrial Workers of the World (IWW), created a legacy that gives the IWW a permanent place in history and myth. Although the IWW recruited in most of the United States, it was in the West that their membership was highest and their most important events occurred. The union's ideals of freedom and equality resonate with the myths associated with the West. Their collectivism, syndicalism, and anticapitalism challenged the myths of the West. Their vision of creating "one big union" and their rebellious spirit scared the capitalist class. Strikes and public meetings made the Wobblies highly visible and thus vulnerable to criticism. By being so visible, they remained in constant strife with those who relied on the working class. Between the Wobblies, who romanticized their union, and authorities, who tried to discredit them, numerous myths have been created. To this day, the true history of the IWW remains in question owing to this battle between the Wobblies and those they threatened.

The Industrial Workers of the World formed on 27 June 1905 in Brand's Hall in Chicago. William "Big Bill" Haywood, a miner and ex-cowboy, oversaw the meeting. Throughout the union's struggle, Big Bill always stood by the Wobblies and made critical decisions. Socialist leaders Eugene Debs, Mother Mary Jones, and Daniel DeLeon also attended the meeting.

The delegates at the meeting rejected craft unions in favor of "one big union." The IWW could be joined by anyone who wanted to organize against the unfair labor practices of capitalist industry, regardless of skill, trade, race, color, or creed. The union embraced socialist thought. Although some members claimed to be anarchists, radicals, revolutionaries, or Communists, the union as a whole did not embrace these ideologies. Its members became known as "Wobblies," a term of uncertain origin. The union preached nonviolence and self-defense. Through their newspaper, *Solidarity,* and other publications, the Wobblies attacked capitalism and continued to organize workers.

The union split in 1924 for a number of reasons, including World War I, repression by the government, and the infiltration of the Communist Party. Although the IWW has been out of the public eye for a long time, the union still exists and continues to organize in cities across the United States.

Both the Wobblies and their opponents used propaganda to justify their positions on labor. The Wobblies distributed pamphlets to promote the union's position on certain issues. Wobblies also used songs to organize. Joe **Hill** wrote many songs, such as "The Preacher and the Slave," that criticized the Wobblies' opponents. This song is a part of folk tradition in America. Songs such as "Solidarity Forever," by Ralph Chaplin, also glorified the union. *The Little Red Songbook* is a collection of some of these songs. Wobblies also used cartoons, posters, and stickers as propaganda to promote their views.

Their opponents' propaganda usually involved spreading falsehoods about them, such as the idea that they were bomb-throwing anarchists. The *San Diego Tribune* published articles that used such extreme language as, "Hanging a Wobbly is too good," "A Wobbly is much better dead," and "They should be left to rot." According to opponents, the initials "IWW" stood for "I Won't Work" and "I Want Whiskey." Disney contributed to anti-Wobbly mythology with a cartoon called "The Little Red Henski." The cartoon portrayed labor and unions as tough, annoying, and unnecessary. Opponents called the Wobblies un-American and alien, but this claim was not totally true. A large majority of the Wobblies and their leaders have been American citizens. During World War I, "about 95 percent of all union members registered with draft boards" (Kornbluh 1964). A former Arizona senator named Harry Ashurst called the IWW "Imperial Wilhelm's Warriors," implying that the Wobblies supported Germany in the war. Ashurst tried to discredit them, but the draft board registration of the Wobblies disproves this statement. Many foreign-born Wobblies who tried to become citizens of the United States had a hard time doing so. Even those who entered the country legally and qualified for citizenship were commonly turned down because of the stereotypes associated with the Wobblies and because of the capitalists' need to suppress the union.

The Wobblies became known for being violent, antisocial, and antipolitical. The IWW was blamed for bombings and other crimes and thus acquired the reputation of being violent. Most of these accusations were false. For example, the American Federation of Labor (AFL) actually had a greater tendency toward violence than did the IWW. The Wobblies used direct action—strikes, picketing, and sabotage—to oppose capitalism. Sabotage meant causing a work slowdown. Many Americans, however, took the term to mean violent action. The union did practice self-defense when in danger; however, during the Colorado strike of 1927, the IWW told workers not to abuse or strike anyone. Big Bill Haywood openly rejected violence, but many Americans viewed him as the symbol of violence.

Although the Wobblies preached nonviolence, their actions did not always reflect this. On rare occasions, some Wobblies participated in arson and destruction of labor machines. Joe Hill was executed after being convicted of murder, even though evidence points to his innocence.

However, the Wobblies gained a reputation for supporting women and inviting them into the union. Ann Schofield, in the article "Rebel Girls and Union Maids," is very critical of the role of Wobbly women. The term "Rebel Girl" came from the title of a romanticized song about Wobbly women by Joe Hill. Schofield claims that women did not become free of their domesticity by being in the union. The IWW focused on women inside the union but rarely recognized their position outside the workplace. They recognized only capitalism as the cause for the women's oppression, a limited vision of the oppression of women.

The Wobblies included minorities in the union. The IWW organized different races to strike with each other for the first time. In "Radicalism and Race," Leland Bell depicts the Wobblies as attacking racial prejudice. Bell also points out that Wobblies promoted racial harmony. As with the issue of women, the fight against racism outside the workplace was in question.

The Wobblies have been associated with the qualities of the West. Joseph Conlin has suggested that Wobblies believed they were "the last frontiersmen." They possessed the lawless, independent spirit, working-class roots, and lack of respect by society characteristic of western heroes.

Wobblies also countered myths of the West. They attacked capitalism, which they associated with the exploitation of workers in the West. Individualism prevails over collectivism in this part of the United States. The idea of unionization has never been popular in the West. These myths are so strong that it prevented the IWW from achieving its goals.

Recent decades have brought about a revitalization of the Wobblies. Books such as Joseph Conlin's *At the Point of Production,* Dione Miles's *Something in Common,* and Joyce Kornbluh's *Rebel Voices* spurred this revitalization. With *We Shall Be All,* historian Melvyn Dubofsky surfaced as a latter-day supporter of the IWW. A documentary film entitled *The Wobblies* came out in 1979; it included interviews of living Wobblies, photographs, and old footage. It is only appropriate that the Wobblies would resurface during this rebellious era.

The locations of Wobblies' activities are now tourist attractions. In Park City, Utah, an old mining town, the Wobblies left their mark. In the basement of a museum stands the former Utah Territorial Jail. People can see where the Wobblies burned their insignia into a cell wall with candle smoke after a labor demonstration in 1916.

Wobblies also appear on the Internet. Someone who calls himself "Wobbly" has a home page. There is a Web page for a softball team at Rutgers University called the Wobblies. These people chose these names to refer to the results of too much alcohol, not because of the labor union. But the name still permeates our culture. The Wobblies have continued to influence popular culture.

Today the visibility of the union is far less, but over time the Wobbly spirit has influenced many labor unions and social movements. Both the Wobblies and their opposition created many myths. The Wobblies themselves glorified and romanticized their existence. Those who opposed them created myths to discredit them. For this reason, it is hard to make out what is truth and what is myth. The Wobblies will always be remembered for their struggle and their attempt to organize against what they saw as evil.

—*Michael L. Sileno*

References

Conlin, Joseph R. *At the Point of Production: The Local History of the I.W.W.* Westport, CT: Greenwood Press, 1981.

Kornbluh, Joyce L. *Rebel Voices: An I.W.W. Anthology.* Ann Arbor: University of Michigan Press, 1964.

Miles, Dione. *Something in Common: An IWW Bibliography.* Detroit: Wayne State Press, 1986.

Source of Further Information

Industrial Workers of the World Home Page: *http://www.iww.org.*

WOMEN

See Bemis, Polly; Bulette, Julia; Calamity Jane; Cattle Kate; Fields, "Stage Coach" Mary; Gentle Tamers; "Little Jo" Josephine Monaghan; Oakley, Annie; *Outlaw, The;* Pleasant, Mary Ellen; "Poker Alice" Ivers; *Ramona;* Selena; Starr, Belle; Tabor, Baby Doe; Young, Ann Eliza Webb

WOMEN, WILD

Women who broke with conventional gender roles in the Old West became either infamous or famous, and sometimes both. Like the rest of Victorian America, the West carefully and clearly segregated men and women into appropriate roles and duties. However, a handful of women ignored sexist barriers and pursued their own western dreams. Sometimes admired, sometimes chastised, these "wild women" served notice that the **"gentle tamer"** stereotype of western women did not apply to all.

Lynch law brought an abrupt end to many lives on the frontier. Hangings, legal and vigilante, claimed many men and also a few women. In 1863 Benjamin F. Neal of the Fourteenth District Court in Texas tried Chipita Rodríguez (birth date unknown) for murder. Neal found Rodríguez guilty of killing a stock dealer named John Savage for his money and sentenced her to hang. The rope carried Rodríguez to eternity on 13 November 1863 in San Patricio, Texas. Rodríguez is the only woman known to have been hanged in the state of Texas.

Two other women met their ends at the hands of lynch mobs. Elizabeth Taylor (born Elizabeth Jones in Wales about 1854) was lynched on 15 March 1885 alongside her twin brother, Thomas Jones. Elizabeth, Thomas, and Elizabeth's three children farmed in Clay County, Nebraska, during the 1870s and 1880s. Several suspicious incidents aroused the neighborhood's suspicion against Elizabeth: When her husband died in May 1882, neighbors charged that Elizabeth had poisoned him. Her father also died, and a hired hand disappeared—both mysteriously. Neighbors also suspected Elizabeth and Thomas of cattle rustling but never produced any evidence.

The last straw came when one of Elizabeth's sons apparently shot a neighbor during a dispute. The besieged Taylor-Jones clan moved to a sod hut on the Blue River. About midnight on 15 March 1885, a vigilante mob grabbed Elizabeth and Thomas and dragged them out of the house. The vigilantes took the pair about half a mile away to a bridge over the Blue River and hanged them. They were then buried at Spring Ranche Cemetery.

Elizabeth Taylor's guilt in the various incidents remains unproven. Described as a "domineering woman," she may have suffered vilification for not behaving in proper Victorian, ladylike fashion. She had conflicts with neighbors over fences and wandering cattle. She had also spurned the advances of Rees T. Rees, a member of the gang that hanged her. The five vigilantes came to trial, and the *Omaha Daily Bee* recorded the outcome: "The applause in the courtroom was deafening when Judge Burnett declared the evidence against the five prisoners insufficient and ordered their release." Vigilantes hanged another

Rodeo cowgirl, 1919 (Library of Congress)

woman in the 1880s, "**Cattle Kate**" Ella Watson.

Woman performing what society considered "men's work" often attracted commentary in the Old West. Cowboying, stagecoach driving, and stagecoach robbing were prime examples of men's work. To perform such labor, a few women decided to pass as men. Charlotte Darkey "Cockeyed Charlie" Parkhurst's parents abandoned her shortly after her birth in 1812 in New Hampshire. Independent even when young, she dressed in boys' clothing and ran away from the orphanage where she had been placed. Charlotte, now "Charlie," continued to pass as a man as she made her way West. She learned to handle a coach and horses and in 1851 became one of California's most competent stagecoach drivers. Her use of cigars, chewing tobacco, and an eye patch added to her masculine image.

Still in disguise, she may have been the first woman to vote. On 3 November 1868 she cast her ballot (as Charlie) in Santa Cruz County. Charlotte lived a long life, which also included work as a logger and rancher, until her death from cancer on 29 December 1879. An autopsy finally revealed her lifelong secret.

Herding cattle on **trail drives** was also men's work. We have a record of only one woman ever making such a drive (although there may have been more Charlie Parkhursts passing as men out West).

Mary Taylor Bunton made the long trek from Texas to Kansas in 1866. As the young bride of J. Howard Bunton, she is thought to be the only woman to make her way with a herd up the Chisholm Trail.

In 1939 she published a book about her adventures, *A Bride on the Old Chisholm Trail in 1866*. "I was the first woman to ride astride in our part of the State," she recalled, "and you may be sure it caused a stampede among the cowboys and cattle." Bunton began her journey "afraid to go to sleep as I remembered the harrowing tales I had heard of snakes, bugs and crawling and stinging things." It didn't take her long to adjust to trail life. Spotting a large rattlesnake, she "gathered some stones that were near. . . . With much squeamishness I managed to kill the snake and cut off his rattles which I proudly displayed to the cheering cowboys." She also shot a deer but "was entirely too 'chicken-hearted' to shoot at the antelope with their great big human eyes." She lived out her long life in Texas and died in Austin in 1952.

Whereas Parkhurst made a name for herself driving stagecoaches, Pearl Taylor Hart became a legend as the only woman known to rob them. In 1899 Hart, not yet 30 years old, committed the nation's last stagecoach robbery outside of Globe, Arizona. Unfortunately, she and her male partner got lost, and a posse quickly hunted them down.

Hart was an unlikely outlaw. Raised in a middle-class family in Ontario, Canada, she attended finishing school. Alas, a rakish gambler named Frederick Hart charmed the 17-year-old into eloping and marrying him. The two survived by working at odd jobs. Excited by Wild West shows she had seen in the East, Pearl left her husband and headed west in 1893. After several years of hard-scrabble work and wandering, Pearl learned that the glittering promises of the romanticized West often went unfulfilled. While she was living in Arizona in 1899, her mother, back in Ontario, desperately needed money owing to serious illness. The distraught young woman, aided by a man named Joe Boot, plotted to get the money by robbing the Florence-Globe stage.

Wielding a .44 Colt, Hart clipped her hair short and dressed as a man for the holdup. The act netted the amateur desperadoes $450. Unfortunately for them, they knew as little about the Arizona countryside as they did about robbery. A posse found them exhausted and asleep next to their campfire. Tried and convicted, Hart served about three years of her five-year sentence at the Yuma Territorial Prison. Following appeals by her family, Governor Alexander O. Brodie paroled her in December 1902. Neighbors described her in her declining years as "soft-spoken, kind, and a good citizen in all respects" (Slatta 1996).

Laura Bullion (aka Della Rose, Clara Hays) had a more successful life of crime. Born in either Kentucky or Texas, she grew up on her mother's sheep ranch in Concho County, Texas. In her early teens, she became a prostitute and befriended many an outlaw. Her buddies outside the law included Sam and Tom Ketchum, and Wild Bunch train thieves Will (or Bill) Carver and Benjamin Kilpatrick.

Beginning in 1895, she road with the Wild Bunch on some of their escapades.

Described as slender, with hazel eyes and close-cropped black hair, Bullion was not a great beauty. In fact, she passed for a man during holdups. Her courage, loyalty, and riding ability, however, more than compensated for her plainness. Bullion and Kilpatrick passed the winter of 1900/1901 on an Arizona ranch in Cochise County. They probably took part in robbing the Great Northern train in Wagner, Montana, on 3 July 1901. Lawmen arrested the pair in St. Louis in November 1901. Incriminating cash and notes from the Wild Bunch robbery the previous July convicted them both. Bullion served either a two-and-a-half or a five-year prison sentence at the Jefferson County, Montana, penitentiary. After serving her time, she faithfully awaited Kilpatrick's release. He died in 1912 attempting to rob yet another train. Thereafter, Bullion disappeared from the historical record. Her date of death remains unknown.

Women also took up another activity usually associated with men: gambling. **Poker Alice Ivers,** for example, gambled successfully for four decades. "I've never seen anyone grow humpbacked carrying away the money they won from me," she proclaimed proudly. She retired on her winnings and died in 1930 at the age of 79.

Belle Siddons, also known as Madame Vestal, was probably the best-known female gambler of the Old West. She operated her own gambling dens in Wichita, Kansas; Deadwood, South Dakota; and Denver, Colorado. She fell in love with a stagecoach robber and accidentally gave him away, so that lawmen shot him to pieces in an attempted robbery. The grief- and guilt-stricken Siddons turned

to drugs. In 1881 she was found dead at the age of 40 in a Chinese opium den in San Francisco.

Taos-born Gertrudes "La Tules" Barcelos found fame and fortune in Santa Fe, New Mexico. Her contemporary Susan Magoffin described Barcelos in 1846 as "a stately dame of a certain age, the possessor of a portion of that shrewd sense and fascinating manner necessary to allure the wayward, inexperienced youth to the hall of final ruin" (that is, into a life of gambling and whoring). "She was considered the most expert monte dealer of her time. Of fascinating manners and distinctly Spanish type of beauty, she became a great favorite in official circles." Thanks to her gambling and her income as a madam, she even opened her own bank. After the Mexican-American War, Barcelos became "a great favorite among American officers," who replaced the Mexican officers as her best customers. She reportedly even loaned the U.S. government $1,000 to help finance a military mission. She died about 1851, age unknown.

Like their male counterparts, many wild women ended their lives tragically and violently. Kitty LeRoy lived a very full if short life. The actress entertained cowboys, miners, and others and gambled in saloons from Dallas, Texas, to Deadwood, South Dakota. Along the way, she had married five men by the time she turned 27. Unfortunately, not everyone took the institution of marriage as lightly as she. A faro dealer in Deadwood named Sam Curley numbered among her husbands. Enraged upon learning of his wife's bigamy, he shot her dead in a room above the Lone Star Saloon and then turned the gun on himself. Thus ended LeRoy's short, eventful life.

"Normal" hardworking men and women, of course, far outnumbered criminals and characters in the West. Some people in frontier regions like the Old West, however, took advantage of the great distances, low population, and general lack of legal and governmental resources to break the law or to flout social conventions. Until recently, conventional popular-culture media have mostly ignored such gender-breaking women. However, a new generation of feminist writers and filmmakers are bringing some of these fascinating, independent, and, yes, wild women to public attention. The film *The Ballad of Little Jo* is an excellent case in point.

References

Nash, Jay Robert, ed. *Encyclopedia of Western Lawmen and Outlaws.* New York: Paragon House, 1992.

Slatta, Richard W. "Wild Women of the Old West." *Cowboys & Indians* 15 (Holiday 1996): 48–53.

WOMEN IN WESTERN FILMS

Male characters and perspectives have long dominated the western scene in popular culture. Male heroes graced the pages of the works of countless **pulp novelists,** B-western movies, and **television** programs. Women are often absent or relegated to scenery, much like the mountain and desert vistas. When women did appear, they played the role of the faint-hearted, fainting heroine, ever in need of rescue by the relentlessly masculine hero. Recent scholarship on women in the West has revealed real western women to be far more varied, interesting, and proactive people than the caricatures created by dime novelists and hack screenwriters. Nevertheless, the old gender stereotypes die hard.

Almost invisible on-screen, women pioneered in the early film industry. Film historians credit France's Alice Guy Blaché with shooting the first "cowboy" short films as well as military films. In 1906–1907, she directed about 100 sound films, each a minute or two long. Thus, she earned the honor of being the first person to bring a narrative film to the screen. A secretary for Gaumont, a French photographic equipment company, she shot a short film called *La Fée aux choux* in 1906. The film promoted sales of Gaumont's equipment. The company's owner recognized the power of her creation and put her in charge of a new production department. She went on to experiment with a variety of techniques and technologies. Some of her off-beat, innovative work included westerns featuring lasso-twirling heroines.

Alas, early westerns in the United States showed little of Blaché's creativity. Male heroes and their horses have long dominated film credits. At most, a woman might serve as the prize that the cowboy hero covets. In the most common scenario, a hapless woman is about to be cheated in some way, most likely by losing the family ranch. In *Bar Nothin'* (1921), for example, the hero saves the ranch and marries one of the ranch women. In *Back Trail* (1924), the hero helps a women save her estate from scoundrels and wins her love as a result. *Shane* (1952) is the most famous example of the cowboy hero (Alan Ladd) saving the day and winning the love of the heroine (Jean Arthur). In this case, however, he does not get the girl, because she is already married.

If they exhibit any agency at all, women serve as agents of reform and civilization. In *Hell's Hinges* (1916) the outlaw hero reforms after falling in love with the new minister's sister, Faith Henley. In *Angel Citizens* (1922), a drifter stops to rid a town of criminals in order to win the love of a local woman. He then abandons his drifting ways. In *High Noon* (1952), Amy Kane (Grace Kelly) is a devout, pacific Quaker, wedded to Sheriff Will Kane (Gary Cooper). She fails in her efforts to dissuade him from violence and from defending a town that does not deserve it. However, in the end, her love overrides her religion, and she shoots one of the villains to save her husband.

In the movies, women who challenged their ascribed social roles often faced disappointment. In *Maiden and Men* (1912), an eastern woman reads romance novels that stir her desire for love and adventure. She goes west to a ranch. However, her presence disrupts life on the ranch as men vie for her affections. She is dispatched back home to her father, where she furiously rips up the novel that inspired her journey.

Jane Russell as Rio in **The Outlaw** (1943) provided the most notorious example of a woman disrupting male bonding, in this case between **Billy the Kid,** Doc Holliday, and Pat Garrett. Likewise, Pearl Chavez (Jennifer Jones) brings conflict and tragedy to the McCaneles ranch in *Duel in the Sun* (1947). These "dis-

rupters" are strong characters, but most women in westerns occupy clearly defined, constricted social roles, such as the schoolmarm, dance hall entertainers, the preacher's daughter, or, in racier films, the proverbial prostitute with the heart of gold.

Schoolteachers, agents of civilization and often easterners, reaffirm many of the stereotypes associated with the **"gentle tamer"** image. A teacher is the love interest of *The Virginian* (1929, starring Gary Cooper and Mary Brian). In John Ford's *My Darling Clementine* (1946), a schoolmarm (Cathy Downs) faced the formidable task of taming frontier marshal **Wyatt Earp** (Henry Fonda). Based on a real character, another teacher works hard to save *Tom **Horn*** from hanging (1980, starring Steve McQueen and Linda Evans).

Juxtaposed with the civilizers and gentle tamers were the stereotypical bad women. We find such a pairing in John Ford's *Stagecoach* (1939), where Claire Trevor plays the good-hearted prostitute, shunned by the proper eastern society woman (Louise Platt). Likewise, in *High Noon,* Katy Jurado plays a saloon girl from Will Kane's past. She provides a vivid counterpoint to Grace Kelly's prim and proper character. In these and many cases, however, the "bad" women show courage, compassion, and humanity that transform them into engaging and noble figures.

Occasionally, women rose above the victim role to appear as a strong heroine. *The Bad Man* (1907) is among the first silent westerns to feature a strong female character. In the eight-minute film, a female railroad agent falls in love with a tenderfoot. However, in a reversal of the usual plot, the heroine frees both of them from an outlaw who has tied them to the railroad tracks. *The Perils of Pauline* presented a much more proactive, capable heroine. These episodes appeared among 60 serial melodramas starring women between 1912 and 1920. In 1912–1913, Louise Lester starred in a series of *Calamity Anne* films. Other silent serials that presented strong female characters include *Tempest Cody, Adventures of Dorothy Dare,* and *Ruth of the Rockies. Galloping Gallagher* presents a crusading female minister, and *Arizona Cat Claw* (1919) features an Arizona rancher's daughter who defeats a Mexican bandit. Barbara Stanwyck portrayed many feisty heroines, including *The Great Man's Lady* (1942) and *The Cattle Queen of Montana* (1954).

Maureen O'Hara is another instantly recognizable strong woman in western film. O'Hara worked with many leading western actors, but some of her most memorable performances came when she paired with John Wayne, working under John Ford's direction. The 80-year-old O'Hara reminisced about those days in a National Public Radio interview with Scott Simon on 28 October 2000. Her self-description could apply equally well to the characters she played: "I'm tough, I'm strong, I'm quick-tempered." In *McClintock* (1963) and *Big Jake* (1971), she says, she stood, "toe-to-toe with Duke," green eyes flashing. In the former film, she wields a long hat pin and joins in a brawl that takes place at a mining mud pit. (The crew had to add chocolate filler to the mud so the actors would slide, not stick.) In the latter film, she bravely conspires with John Wayne to trick kidnappers who have taken their grandson.

Until recently, only a handful of westerns revolved around truly feminist plots with women portrayed as human, autonomous agents rather than scenery, foils, or stereotypes. *Johnny Guitar* (1954) pioneered feminist themes even before the birth of the modern women's movement. Critic Ed Buscombe describes Vienna (Joan Crawford), the film's heroine, as "one of the most compelling female images the Western has produced." She is "feminine in her white dress, masculine in black shooting gear, she moves between tomboy and mother figure with ease, demonstrating and maintaining a level of control allowed to very few women" in the movies (Buscombe 1988).

On a much lighter, comic note, Doris Day starred as a widow forced to make her own way in *The Ballad of Josie* (1967). She became a widow by accidentally shooting her worthless drunken husband. In trying to make a living, she provokes a range war by bringing sheep into Wyoming cattle country.

Female avengers also appear in a few films. In the spoof on the western genre, *Cat Ballou* (1964), Jane Fonda avenges her father's death. In a much grimmer treatment, *Hannie Calder* (1971), Raquel Welch becomes a Clint **Eastwood**–type avenger, even affecting the dress of the "Man with No Name." However, a male mentor (Robert Culp) must teach her to shoot. She then dons poncho, boots, and hat to track down the trio of bank robbers who raped her and murdered her husband. Ed Buscombe points out the limits of this feminist western. At the end, Calder "comes face to face with a mysterious man in black who has haunted her progress, and whose presence is a reminder of a final boundary

Hannie can never cross. For women can never really be heroes in the Western: that would mean the end of the genre" (Buscombe 1988).

During the 1990s, several filmmakers played with feminist themes in westerns. Film critic Stephen Hunter has called *The Ballad of Little Jo* (1993), based on a real-life character, the "first post-feminist Western." Little Jo, a woman, successfully passes as a man on the rugged Montana frontier. In 1995 Sam Raimi delivered a smart parody, with feminist and post-modernist elements, titled *The Quick and the Dead*. The film is set in 1870s Arizona. With Sharon Stone as Ellen, Gene Hackman as the evil Herod (right down to the name), and Leonardo DiCaprio as Kid, the film deftly and humorously bends the western genre to its own quirky needs. Stone (who also coproduced the film) stars as a skilled gunfighter who uses her brain rather than her fast draw to defeat evil.

Like history and mythology, films have rendered an overwhelmingly masculine version of the Old West. That the film industry has been dominated by men, as directors, producers, and actors, has further marginalized women from Hollywood treatments. However, as with other western genres, film has shown itself to be infinitely adaptable and creative. New types of women in westerns will undoubtedly continue to appear.

References

Buscombe, Edward, ed. *The BFI Companion to the Western*. New York: Da Capo, 1988.

Garfield, Brian. *Western Films: A Complete Guide*. New York: Da Capo, 1982.

Sources of Further Information

Kokkola, Sari. "The Nature and Significance of Hollywood Genres: The Genre of the Western as an Example." 1998. United States Popular Culture Paper: *http://www.uta.fi/FAST/US7/PAPS/sk-genre.html*.

Western Heroines: *http://xroads.virginia.edu/~HYPER/HNS/Westfilm/heroine.htm*.

WONDERFUL WIZARD OF OZ

See Wizard of Oz, The Wonderful

YOUNG, ANN ELIZA WEBB

1844–?

Like Fanny Stenhouse's book *Tell It All* (1874), Ann Eliza Webb Young's *Wife No. 19, or The Story of a Life in Bondage* (1875) shocked and titillated the public with its sensational insider stories of Mormonism and polygamy. The nineteenth wife of Mormon leader Brigham Young, Ann Eliza filed for divorce, publicly lectured about her ill treatment by the Mormon church, and then published her powerfully anti-Mormon book.

In her book, she gives a quick sketch of her life before her marriage to Brigham Young:

> On the 28th of July, 1873, I commenced an action for divorce against Brigham Young in the District Court of the Third Judicial District of Utah. It began by stating who and what I was; that I was born at Nauvoo, Illinois, but had, since the year 1848, been resident in Utah; that I

was the wife of Brigham Young; and that I was married to him on the 6th of April, 1868, when I was in my twenty-fifth year, and was the mother of two children by a former marriage, one four and the other three years of age; that neither I nor my children had anything to depend upon,—a fact of which Brigham was well aware,—and also that my children were boys, still living. (Young 1875)

The Mormon leader first spotted Ann Eliza when she was 17; he was 61. Before she married him, however, she endured an abusive three-year marriage to a young actor, James Dee. They had two sons. She obtained a divorce with Brigham Young's help, and he immediately courted her vigorously. Despite her reservations, the 25-year-old married the 68-year-old religious leader in 1869.

According to her, they initially had a happy marriage, with the Prophet "treating me with some degree of kindness, and providing, though inadequately, for my support; and that I had always fulfilled my duties as a wife toward him." However, she reported that in late 1872, "Brigham removed me to a house in Salt Lake City, where, however, he seldom visited me; that when I called upon him to ask a supply of the necessaries of life, he used the most opprobrious language toward me, and gave me so little that I had to work constantly to support myself and children" (Young 1875).

The leader of the Latter-Day Saints contested his own divorce, arguing that they had not actually been married. A compromise in April 1877 awarded Ann Eliza a token payment of $3,600 but ruled that the marriage, in the eyes of the government, had indeed not been legal. Regardless of the facts of the case, many gentiles (that is, non-Mormons) readily accepted Ann Eliza's charges. The woman's riveting narrative became a mainstay of anti-Mormonism. Indeed, the full text of the book is available online at an anti-Mormon Web site (see Young 1875). Not surprisingly, pro-Mormons dismiss the book as sensationalism. Ann Eliza continued her crusade against the church until her death. She widened her criticism from the ills of polygamy to broader, feminist concerns. However, her animosity toward her ex-husband remained strong, as evident in her conclusion to *Wife No. 19:*

> But one thing is certain. If one voice, or one pen, can exert any influence, the pen will never be laid aside, the voice never be silenced. I have given myself to this work, and I have promised before God never to withdraw from it. It is my life-mission; and I have faith to believe that my work will not be in vain, and that I shall live to see the foul curse removed, and Utah—my beloved Utah—free from the unholy rule of the religious tyrant, Brigham Young. (Young 1875)

Truth remains elusive, even about the exact number of Brigham Young's wives. Critic Fanny Stenhouse counted 19 wives, with Ann Eliza the fifteenth. Irving Wallace counted a total of 27, while Ann Eliza numbered herself nineteenth. Regardless of the exact number, the young woman clearly did not enjoy sharing her husband with other wives.

Her lecturing helped gain a federal ban on polygamy in 1882, five years after the Prophet's death. Ann Eliza married and divorced once more, but after 1908, she disappears from the historical record. Thus, even the date and place of her death remains a mystery.

References

Church of Jesus Christ of Latter-Day Saints: *http://www.lds.org.*

Seagraves, Anne. *High-Spirited Women of the West.* Hayden, ID: Wesanne Publications, 1992.

Wallace, Irving. *Twenty-Seventh Wife: The Story of Ann Eliza Young, Last Wife of the Mormon Prophet, Brigham Young, Who Divorced Her Husband to Lead in the Fight against the American Harem.* New York: Simon and Schuster, 1961.

Young, Eliza Ann. *Wife No. 19, or The Story of a Life in Bondage, Being a Complete Exposé of Mormonism, and Revealing the Sorrows, Sacrifices, and Sufferings of Women in Polygamy.* Hartford, CT: Dustin, Gilman, and Co., 1875: *http://antimormon.8m.com/young intro.html.*

YOUNG, BRIGHAM

See Lee, John Doyle; Rockwell, Orrin
Porter; Young, Ann Eliza Webb

ZORRO

The legend of Zorro began on 9 August 1919, when Johnston McCulley, a 36-year-old former police reporter, wrote "The Curse of Capistrano." His story first appeared as a serial in the 9 August issue of the pulp magazine *All-Story Weekly*. Set in early nineteenth-century California, the story focuses on Don Diego de la Vega, the son of a rich landowning family. To the chagrin of his father, the dainty Diego prefers reading poetry to more manly, violent pursuits. (McCulley's ruse anticipates a later hero's disguise when Superman masquerades as "mild-mannered reporter" Clark Kent.) Diego's false demeanor, however, literally masked his nighttime activities as Zorro ("fox" in Spanish), a noble, avenging crime fighter. Like Robin Hood, Zorro defended the weak, poor, and oppressed.

The precise inspiration for the figure remains uncertain. McCulley may have drawn upon the legendary California bandit Joaquín Murieta. Murieta, a miner, struck back at the avalanche of greedy Anglo gold seekers who overran California and abused its Spanish-speaking residents. The atmosphere of Zorro's time and place is reminiscent of that created by Helen Hunt Jackson in her 1884 novel **Ramona.** The reading public devoured successive installments, and a new Hispanic hero was born.

The story moved quickly to the silver screen. In 1920 Douglas Fairbanks donned the hero's mask and sword in *The Mark of Zorro.* He reprised the role five years later in *Don Q., Son of Zorro.* In 1936 Robert Livingstone created a new incarnation of Zorro in a film titled *The Bold Caballero.* Another dashing Hollywood figure, Tyrone Power, updated the Fairbanks *Mark of Zorro* with sound in 1940. Republic and other studios also released Zorro serials. Clayton Moore, later famous as the **Lone Ranger,** appeared in twelve episodes of *Ghost of Zorro* in 1949. Picking up on the Hispanic appeal, filmmakers in Mexico, Spain, and Italy also made a host of Zorro films during the 1960s. A French actor, Alain Delon, even played Zorro in a 1974 film. Like most western heroes, Zorro also fell victim to parody. In 1980 George Hamilton gave a swishing as well as slashing depiction in *Zorro, the Gay Blade.*

Disney acquired the TV rights to the California avenger in 1952. Guy Williams starred in 78 episodes of the popular *Zorro* ABC television series (1957–1959). He also made two feature films in 1958, *Zorro the Avenger* and *The Sign of Zorro.* The catchy theme song opened each Thursday evening show.

Out of the night,
when the full moon is bright,
comes the horseman known as Zorro.
This bold renegade
carves a Z with his blade,
a Z that stands for Zorro.
Zorro, Zorro, the fox so cunning and free,
Zorro, Zorro, who makes the sign of the Z.
Zorro, Zorro, Zorro, Zorro, Zorro.
    (Cotter 1999)

After a hiatus, Zorro made yet another comeback in July 1998, when Spanish-born actor Antonio Banderas starred in a new incarnation of *The Mask of Zorro.* This version drew consciously on the possible historical roots of the hero. An aging Don Diego (Anthony Hopkins) trains his young successor Alejandro Murieta to use whip and sword. The apprentice's name recalls the real Californio outlaw Joaquín Murieta. Martin Campbell directed the action-packed film, shot at various locations in Mexico. Like the hero he portrayed, Banderas had to hone his fencing and riding skills to make the movie. Catherine Zeta Jones, as Elena Montero, added a love interest to the new version. Like other Old West legends, Zorro seems to be immortal.

See also Hispanics in Western Films

References

Cotter, Bill. "Zorro: A History of the Series." 1999: *http://www.billcotter.com/zorro/history-of-series.htm.*

McCall, Elizabeth Kaye. "Z Is for Zorro." *Cowboys & Indians* 25 (July 1998): 76–84.

Zorro Official Web Site: *http://www.zorro.com.*

MYTHICAL WEST WEB SITES

These sites were in existence and researched for this book from 1998 through 2 November 2000. I have removed links that did not function, but Web sites are very ephemeral, so some of the following may have disappeared.

Abbey, Edward

Abbey's Web: *http://www.utsidan.se/abbey/*.

Brinkley, Douglas. "Edward Abbey: Critic and Crusader": *http://www.calendarlive.com/cal endarlive/books/lat_0123brinkley.htm*.

Code of the Eco-Warrior: *http://www.geoci ties.com:0080/RainForest/4544/mwinfo.htm*.

Action Shooting

The Gunfighter Zone: *http://www.gunfighter. com*.

How to Be a Pistolero: *http://www.sptddog. com/sotp/persona.html*.

The Single Action Shooting Society: *http:// www.sassnet.com/*.

Western Action Shooting Society, New Zealand: *http://www.wass.org.nz/*.

Adams, Ansel

Ansel Adams Gallery: *http://www.adamsgal lery.com/*.

Friends of Photography: *http://www.friendsof photography.org/*.

Kennerly, David Hume. "Ansel Adams: An American Icon": *http://www.enn.com/fea tures/1999/11/110299/ansel_5302.asp*.

Masters of Photography Biography: *http:// www.masters-of-photography.com/A/ adams/adams.html*.

Alamo

Alamo Official Web Site: *http://www.thealamo. org*.

CNN News Report 19 November 1998: *http:// www.cnn.com/US/9811/19/alamo.auction/ #4*.

Daughters of the Republic of Texas Library at the Alamo, select bibliography: *http://www. drtl.org/alamorev.html*.

Donald Burger's List of Films and TV Shows about the Alamo: *http://www.burger.com/ alafilms.htm*.

Lind, Michael. "The Death of David Crockett." *Wilson Quarterly*, Winter 1998: *http:// wwics.si.edu/organiza/affil/WWICS/OUT REACH/WQ/WQSELECT/CROCK.HTM*.

The Nitkpickers Site: *http://www.nitpickers. com/movies/titles/1219.html*.

Texas Military Forces Museum Web Site, maintained by Gary Butler: *http://www. kwanah.com/txmilmus/tnghist3.htm*.

Appleseed, Johnny

Johnny Appleseed Home Page, by Bill Wedemeyer: *www.msc.cornell.edu/~weeds/School Pages/Appleseed/welcome.html.*

Barbecue

Barbecuen on the Internet: *www.barbecuen. com.*

BBQ.COM Home Page: *www.bbq.com.*

Hale, Smoky. "Origins of Barbecue." *Gourmet Connection Magazine: http://gourmetconnection.com/ezine/articles/697bbori.shtml.*

Origin of Barbecue: *http://www.barbacoa. com.br/ingles/churrasc.htm.*

Battles or Massacres

Meyers, J. Jay. "The Notorious Fight at Sand Creek." *Wild West* 11, no. 4 (December 1998): *http://www.thehistorynet.com/Wild West/articles/1998/1298_cover.htm.*

Bean, Judge Roy

Judge Roy Bean's Visitor Center: *http://texas outside.com/roybeanp2.htm.*

Katz, Bob. "Judge Roy Bean: Law West of the Pecos." *Desert USA Magazine: http://www. desertusa.com/mag98/aug/papr/du_roy bean.html*

Bonanza

Bonanza History: *http://bonanza1.com/history/.*

Classic TV: *http://classictv.about.com/tvradio/ classictv/msub27.htm*

Ponderosa Ranch: *http://www.ponderosa ranch.com/.*

Bridger, Jim

Jim Bridger: *http://www.wtp.net/bridger/trap pers.html.*

Brown, Molly

Molly Brown House Museum: *http://www. mollybrown.org.*

Titanic's Molly Brown Birthplace and Museum Web Site: *http://www.mollybrownmu seum.com.*

Buffalo Soldiers

ABSRA (America's Buffalo Soldiers Re-Enactors Association): *http://www.thebuffalosol diers.com.*

Buffalo Soldier History: *http://www.desertusa. com/mccain/oct_buffalo.html.*

Buffalo Soldiers: *http://www.buffalosoldiers.net.*

Buffalo Soldiers Club: *http://www.clubs.ya hoo.com/clubs/buffalosoldiers.*

Buffalo Soldiers Law Enforcement Club: *http://www.gainweb.com/buffalo.*

Camel Corps

Jacobs, Ellen, The Camel Corps Page: *http:// artemis.simmons.edu/~jacobs/camel.html.*

Woodbury, Chuck. "U.S. Camel Corps Remembered in Quartzsite, Arizona." *Out West* 18 (April 1992): *http://www.outwest newspaper.com/camels.html.*

Cattle Kate

Cattle Kate, Inc.: *http://www.cattlekate.com/in troduction.html.*

Cattle Kate Page: *http://w3.trib.com/~leebo/ kate.htm.*

Cattle Kate's Lodge: *http://www.wmonline. com/cattlekates/.*

Colter, John

Sheldon, Addison Erwin. "John Colter's Escape." In *Histories and Stories of Nebraska: http://www.ukans.edu/~kansite/hvn/books/ nbstory/story9.html.*

Comparative Frontier Mythology

Australia: Beyond the Fatal Shore: *http:// www.pbs.org/wnet/australia/episode1and2. html.*

Comparative Frontiers Bibliography: *http:// courses.ncsu.edu/classes/hi300001/compare bib.htm.*

The Magic of Myth: *http://www.starwars.com/ smithsonian/.*

Cooper, D. B.

Bates, Jim. "Skulduggery by Parachute."

Aero.com Parachutes: *http://aero.aero.com/ publications/parachutes/9602/pc0296.htm.*

Cooper, D. B. Definitive Site: *members.conk. com/world/dbcooper.*

"Today's Top Stories: D. B. Cooper." *Seattle Times,* 17 November 1966: *www.seattletimes. com/extra/brose/html/coop-111796.html.*

Cortez Lira, Gregorio

Orozco, Cynthia E. "Cortez Lira, Gregorio." Handbook of Texas Online: *http://www. tsha.utexas.edu/handbook/online/articles/ view/CC/fco94.html.*

Sonnichsen, Philip. "More about the Corrido Gregorio Cortez": *http://www.sp.utexas.edu/ jrn/gcortez3.html.*

Cortina, Juan Nepomuceno

PBS, "Documents of the Brownsville Uprising of Juan Cortina": *http://www.pbs.org/weta/ thewest/resources/archives/four/cortinas.htm.*

Dallas

Classic TV: *http://classictv.about.com/.*

Dallas: http://www.dallas.ndirect.co.uk.

Southfork Ranch: *http://www.southforkranch. com.*

Dead Man's Hand

Aces and Eights: Winning Hand in Country Music: *http://members.mint.net/acesn8s/in dex.html.*

Dead Man's Hand—Aces and Eights: *http:// rat.whirl-i-gig.com/deadmans.htm.*

Ecker, Ronald. "Dead Man's Hand." *Screenplay,* 1990: *http://www.hobrad.com/deadmans. htm.*

Hobo Minstrels Home Page: *http://www.msc group.com/hobo/minstrel.html.*

Deadwood Dick

Saloon and Gaming Hall: *www.deadwood dicks.com.*

Death Valley

"Despair in Death Valley." 1996: *http://www. nativenet.uthscsa.edu/archive/nl/9603/0149. html.*

Geology of Death Valley: *http://geology.wr. usgs.gov/docs/usgsnps/deva/deva1.html.*

Historical Myth a Month: *http://dmla.clan.lib. nv.us/docs/nsla/archives/myth/.*

Movie Making Exterior Locations: *http:// www.oxy.edu/~jerry/homeloc.htm.*

Denver, John

CNN Interactive: *http://www.cnn.com/US/ 9710/13/denver.update/.*

Rocky Mountain High Fan Club with Emily Parris: *http://www.sky.net/~emily/.*

Disney Frontierland

The Disney Source: Frontierland: *http://dis neylandsource.com/frontier/index.html.*

Doug's Disneyland Trivia: *http://www.pacific sites.com/~drhoades/trivia.htm.*

Donner Party

Donner Party: *www.tahoenet.com/tdhs/tpdon ner.html.*

Donner Party on PBS: *www.pbs.org/wgbh/ pages/amex/donner/donnerts.html.*

Donner Party Roster: *www.metrogourmet. com/crossroads/Kjroster.htm.*

Donner Party Transcript: *www.pbs.org/wgbh/ pages/amex/donner/donnerts.html.*

Survivors and Casualties: *member.aol.com/ DanMRosen/donner/survivor.htm.*

Exodusters

American Memory, Library of Congress. Nicodemus, Kansas: *http://www.loc.gov/ex hibits/african/nico.html.*

Blankenship, Bill. "Exodusting Off History." Electric Café: *http://cjonline.com/stories/ 011599/ele_flyinwest.shtml.*

Digital History, Exodusters: *http://www.digi talhistory.com/schools/NortheastMiddle School/afram.htm.*

Lawrence, Dennis. "African-American's Migra- tion to Wyandotte County, 1860–1900":

http://KcK.Kancrn.org/immigration/disserta tion97.htm.

PBS. *The West* Web Site: *http://www.pbs.org/ weta/thewest/program/episodes/seven/the exodust.htm.*

Fields, "Stage Coach" Mary

Mary Fields: *http://www.lkwdpl.org/wihohio/ fiel-mar.htm.*

Westerners: *http://www.thehistorynet.com/Wild West/articles/02963_text.htm.*

Films

Goldstein, Richard. "A Lot of Woman, but Still Not a Lady." *The Examiner,* August 1997: *http://www.examiner.net/stories/082097/wes tern.html.*

Haggart, Stan. "Early History of Yellowstone National Park." Western Treasures: *http:// www.nezperce.com/yelpark9.html.*

Kokkola, Sari. "The Nature and Significance of Hollywood Genres: The Genre of the Western as an Example." 1998. United States Popular Culture Paper: *http://www.uta.fi/ FAST/US7/PAPS/sk-genre.html.*

Western Heroines: *http://xroads.virginia.edu/ ~HYPER/HNS/Westfilm/heroine.htm.*

Grey, Zane

Zane Grey Boat Charters: *http://www.boat charters.com.au/.*

Zane Grey High School: *http://www.lausd. k12.ca.us/Reseda_HS/ZaneGrey/zane.html.*

Zane Grey Museum: *http://www.nps.gov/up de/zgmuseum.htm.*

Zane Grey Web Site: *http://www.zanegreysws. org/zgwsmenu.htm.*

Zane Grey's New West: *http://zane-grey. com/index2.html.*

Zane Grey's West Society: *http://www.zane greysws.org/zgbio.htm.*

Hill, Joe

Joe Hill, Biography: *http://hillstrom.iww.org/ joehill.html.*

Joe Hill, PBS: *http://www.kued.org/joehill/ index.html.*

"Joe Hill Songs (and Tributes)." Fortune City Home Page: *http://www.fortunecity.com/tin pan/parton/2/hill.html.*

Hughes, Howard

The Howard Hughes Entrepreneur Site (maintained by Doug Barrese): *http://users. erols.com/dbarrese/.*

L'Amour, Louis

Lamour Fans: *http://www.veinotte.com/la mour/intro.htm.*

Random House: *http://www.randomhouse. com/features/louislamour/.*

Lee, John Doyle

Anderson, Russell. "Response to the Mormon Critics": *http://www.lightplanet.com/response /brigham.htm#Mountain-Meadows.*

Lee, John Doyle. *Mormonism Unveiled* (1877): *http://www.xmission.com/~country/reason/ lee_pref.htm.*

PBS. *The West: http://www.pbs.org/weta/the west/wpages/wpgs400/w4lee.htm.*

Lewis and Clark Expedition

Discovering Lewis and Clark: *http://www. lewis-clark.org.*

Lewis and Clark Home Page: *http://www.| lewisandclark.org/pages.*

PBS. "The Journey of the Corps of Discovery": *http://www.pbs.org/lewisandclark/.*

Planning the Expedition: *http://www.lib.vir ginia.edu/exhibits/lewis_clark/ch4.html.*

Little Bighorn

Custer Battlefield: *http://www.intuitive.com/ sites/cbhma/.*

General George A. Custer: *http://www.garry owen.com/.*

Little Bighorn Coverup: *http://www.thehisto rynet.com/WildWest/articles/0696_text.htm.*

PBS. *The West: http://www.pbs.org/weta/the west/wpages/wpgs400/w4custer.htm.*

"Little Jo" Josephine Monaghan

Kaufman, Seth. *TV Guide,* film review:

http://www.tvguide.com/movies/database/Sh owMovie.asp?MI=35618.

Lebow Drama Site: *http://www.dramatists. com/text/littlejo.htm.*

Teegarden, John. "Joe on Her Toes" (film review): *http://www.film.com/film-review/1993 /8275/26/default-review.html.*

Liver-Eating Johnson

Old West Gravesites, John Garrison: *www.di mensional.com/~sgrimm/jjohn.htm.*

Lone Ranger

Clayton Moore, the Lone Ranger: *http://mem bers.tripod.com/~ClaytonMoore.*

Largent's Lone Ranger Page: *http://users.tic net.com/mlargent/LR1.html.*

Magnificent Seven, The

Anthony Starke: *http://www.fortunecity.com/ lavendar/tomatoes/77/.*

Guns: *http://www.geocities.com/~colt45/.*

Magnificent Seven Web-Ring List: *http:// www.webring.org/cgi-bin/webring?ring =m7&list.*

Movie: *http://sites.hollywood.com/movietunes/ soundtracks/notes/1,1480,magnificent7,00. html.*

TV Series: *http://www.themagnificent7.com/in dex.html.*

Manifest Destiny

Manifest Destiny Productions, Inc.: *http:// www.manifest-destiny.com.*

Official Manifest Destiny Home Page, by Makk Short: *http://www.stormloader.com/ manifest/bio.html.*

McJunkin, George

Large, Jerry. "Clovis Man—Giving Credit Where It's Due." *Seattle Times,* Sunday, 23 February 1997: *http://seattletimes.nwsource. com/extra/browse/html97/altjdl_022397. html.*

Locke, Robert. "A Bitter Tale of Old Bones." *Scientific American: Discovering Archaeology* 6 (November 1999): *http://www.discov eringarchaeology.com/0699toc/6cover4 -bones.shtml.*

Monument Valley

Knowles, Gerald. Essays: *http://www.unink. com/passages/Monument-Valley/.*

Moab to Monument Valley Film Commission: *http://www.moab.net/moabfilm/.*

Packer, Alfred

Alferd Packer Cannibal Treats, Roadside America: *http://www.roadsideamerica.com/ set/MEATpacker.html.*

The Alfred Packer Collection at the Colorado State Archives: *http://www.archives.state.co. us/packer.html.*

Alfred Packer for State Cannibal: *http://mem bers.aol.com/saluteths1/packer/packer.html.*

The Ballad of Alferd Packer: *http://www. cs.pdx.edu/~trent/ochs/lyrics/ballad-alferd -packer.html.*

Brief History of Colorado: *http://hometown. aol.com/vikkigray/3rd.htm.*

CANNIBAL: The Musical. A Film by Trey Parker: *http://www.screenedge.com/edge34.htm.*

Centennial Publications: *http://www.gorp. com/cl_angle/bookindx.htm#b19.*

COG Ride the Divide "Color": *http://www.con cours.org/rtd-color.html.*

Colorado Food Service: *http://umc.colorado. edu/food/grill_pages/index.html.*

Good Reading: Ten People NOT to Invite to Dinner: *http://emhain.wit.ie/~jmcdonal/ scruff/cuisine.htm.*

Lake City: *http://www.onroute.com/destina tions/colorado/lakecity.html.*

The Legend of Alfred Packer: http://www. jps.net/mwmovies/packer/.

The Legend of Alfred Packer. Review: *http:// www.coastnet.com/~greywizard/rev4.htm.*

Littleton, Colorado, History, Alfred Packer: *http://www.littleton.org/LCN/governme/MU SEUM/lhistory/PM16.htm.*

San Juan Cannibal: *http://www.ionet.net/~jel lenc/hcg_fac5.html.*

State 51 on Alfred Packer: The Musical: *http://www.state51.co.uk/reviews/packer.html.*

Taylor, Gary. "The Dead Rise Again in the Courtroom." *National Law Journal,* 21 June 1993: *http://www.hal-pc.org/~gtaylor/dead.html.*

This Rogue: *http://www.gorp.com/gorp/contests/packer.htm.*

Waters, Helen E. "The Other Side of the Coin": *http://www.du.edu/~kmurcray/packer.html.*

Parker, Isaac Charles

Antique Treasures Home Page: *http://www.virtualhometown.com/attic/cocacola/bottles/misc/judgeparker.html.*

Eskridge, Ann. "T. J.'s Turn in Time: Urban Outlaws": *http://edcen.ehhs.cmich.edu/~annesk/home.htm.*

Fort Smith National Historic Site Home Page: *http://www.nps.gov/fosm/home.htm.*

Haines, Joe D., Jr. "Justice Judge Parker Style." *OKLAHOMBRES Journal* 7, no. 2 (Winter 1996): *http://209.35.75.65/parker.htm.*

Metheny, David. "Red, Black, and Deadly." *Metheny's Online Newsletter* 2, no. 1 (1998): *http://www.geocities.com/~methenyd/news-jan.html.*

Pleasant, Mary Ellen

Mary Ellen Pleasant: *http://www.toptags.com/aama/bio/women/pleas.htm.*

Mother of Civil Rights: *http://www.kn.pacbell.com/wired/BHM/mepleasant.html.*

Plummer, Henry

Henry Plummer Revisited: *http://www.thehistorynet.com/WildWest/articles/1998/08982_cover.htm.*

Vigilantes of Montana: *http://www.montana-vigilantes.org/.*

Poker Alice Ivers

El Buscaderos: Cowboy Action Shooting. "Feature: Poker Alice." September 1998: *http://www.netw.com/~cowboy/_feature/feature0998.html.*

Poker Alice: *http://www.pokeralice.ch/index_e.htm.*

Pony Express

History of the Pony Express: *http://members.tripod.com/~pnyxpress/history.html.*

Home Station: *http://www.xphomestation.com/.*

National Historic Trail: *http://www.nps.gov/poex/.*

When the Pony Express Was in Vogue: *http://www.sfmuseum.org/hist1/pxpress.html.*

Pretty Boy Floyd

Adkins, Wendy J. "Charles 'Pretty Boy' Floyd." Carnegie Public Library, East Liverpool, OH: *http://www.carnegie.lib.oh.us/personal.htm.*

Pulp Novelists

Kovalik, Thomas. "Ned Buntline, King of the Dime Novels": *http://www.story-house.com/op/ned/page1.html.*

Max Brand: *http://www.maxbrand-faust.com.*

Max Brand/Frederick Faust Web Site: *http://www.maxbrand-faust.com.*

Pulp History: *http:/www.adventurehouse.com/history.htm.*

Ramona

Helen Hunt Jackson: *http://www.cateweb.org/CA_Authors/Jackson.html.*

Helen Hunt Jackson on the Web: *http://www.amherstcommon.com/walking_tour/jackson.html.*

Rancho Camulos: *http://www.ventura.org/heritage/Rancho_Camulos/rancho_camulos.html.*

Riders of the Purple Sage

Coombs, Marian Kester. "Zane Grey's *Riders of the Purple Sage*." *Zane Grey's West Society:* *http://www.zanegreysws.org/specfea3.htm.*

New Riders of the Purple Sage: *http://www.skylineonline.com/sage.htm.*

Riders of the Purple Sage: *http://www.ridersofthepurplesage.com/.*

Robbins, Marty

Kristy's Marty Robbins Web Page: *http://members.aol.com/kkcowgirl/mrobbins.htm.*

The Mudcat Café: *http://www.mudcat.org.*

Rockwell, Orrin Porter

"It's a Bad, Bad, Bad, Bad Movie": *http://www.rinkworks.com/badmovie/reader/212.shtml*.

Rockwell Articles: *http://www.rockwell-family.org/articles/article00002p1.htm*.

Route 66

Adventure Series: *http://timvp.com/route66.html*.

California Route 66 Museum: *http://www.national66.com/victorville/index.html*.

Events Calendar: *http://wemweb.com/traveler/towns/00natl/evt.html*.

Explore Route 66: *http://www.national66.com*.

National Route 66 Museum: *http://www.national66.com/elk_city/index.html*.

66 Chronology: *http://route66.exmachina.net/main/frameset_chronology.htm*.

Song of the Road: *http://route66.exmachina.net/main/frameset_song.htm*.

Selena

Caller Radio Selena Page: *http://www.caller.com/selena/selena.htm*.

Q Productions: Official Selena Home Page: *http://www.q-productions.com/*.

Selena, the Movie: *http://selena-themovie.warnerbros.com/main.html*.

Selena Foundation: *http://www.neosoft.com/selena/*.

Seven Cities of Gold

Cartwright, Tyrone L. The Mysterious Cities of Gold: *http://www.whimsy.demon.co.uk/gold/index.html*.

PBS. *The West: www.pbs.org/weta/thewest/w pages/wpgs000/w010_001.htm*

Starr, Belle

Arnott, Richard D. "Bandit Queen Belle Starr." *Wild West,* August 1997: *http://www.thehistorynet.com/WildWest/articles/1997/08972_text.htm*.

Titchenal Cherokee Connection: *http://www.titchenal.com/Cherokee*.

Steagall, Red

Chapman, Art. "From Smoky Bars to Cowboy Bard." *Fort Worth Star-Telegram,* 24 March 1996, Virtual Texan: *http://www.virtualtexan.com/writers/chapman/artred.htm*.

Jolene's Kitchen: *http://www.songtek.com/features/jkitchen/print/red_steagall.htm*.

Red Steagall at Warner Western: *http://www.wbr.com/nashville/warnerwestern/cmp/red.html*.

Red Steagall's Ranch Headquarters: *http://www.redsteagall.com/*.

Swallows of San Juan Capistrano

Swallows Day Parade: *http://www.capovalley.com/fiesta/parade.html*.

Where Are They?: *http://www.ocnow.com/news/1999/03/10/swallows1.html*.

Tabor, Baby Doe

Baby Doe Tabor: *http://www.ionet.net/~jellenc/hcg_fac2.html*.

Horace Tabor: *http://www.linecamp.com/museums/americanwest/western_names/tabor_horace/tabor_horace.html*.

Leadville, Colorado, History: *http://www.leadville.com/history/tabor.htm*.

Texas Rangers

Corridos Related to Rangers: *http://www.utexas.edu/admin/opa/news/00newsreleases/nr_200006/nr_nicolopulos000629.html*.

Kolker, Claudia. "Mystique of Texas Rangers Is Enduring." *Seattle Times,* 15 July 1999: *http://seattletimes.nwsource.com/news/nation-world/html98/rang_19990715.html*.

Texas Journal: *http://www.public-humanities.org/tjfall97.html*.

Texas Rangers Hall of Fame: *http://www.texasranger.org/*.

Wildfire

Michael Martin Murphey Home Page: *http://www.michaelmartinmurphey.com*.

Wildfire Animated Series: *http://wildfirecartoon.webjump.com/index.html*.

Wizard of Oz, The Wonderful

Dreier, Peter. "Over the Rainbow: Once upon a Time, *The Wizard of Oz* Was a Populist Fable": *http://www.wccusd.k12.ca.us/elcer rito/history/oz.htm*.

Kolesinski, William. "Populism and *The Wizard of Oz*": *http://www.geocities.com/Bour bonStreet/Delta/6223/Wizard.htm*.

Miller, David K. "How Did Farmers Attempt to Solve Their Problems during the Industrial Revolution?": *http://www.socialstudieshelp. com/Lesson_51_Notes.htm*.

SNS Online. "Was *The Wizard* a Story for Kids or a Political Satire?" *Shawnee News-Star Online,* 18 September 1998: *http://www. news-star.com/stories/091898/new_oz.html*.

Tulloss, Janice K. "*The Wizard of Oz* as a Populist Tale": *http://www.uncg.edu/psc/courses/ jktullos/policy/oz.html*.

Wang, Grant, and Dan Jacobs. "*The Wonderful Wizard of Oz:* An Examination of the Underlying Political Allegory": *http://www.peo ple.cornell.edu/pages/dbj5/oz.html*.

Williamson, Rana K. "*The Wonderful Wizard of Oz:* A Populist Parable": *http://vrml.ced. tcu.edu/docw/wizoz.htm*.

Wobblies

Industrial Workers of the World Home Page: *http://www.iww.org*.

IWW International Radio Network Home Page: *http://206.220.140.75/radio*.

PBS. New Perspectives on the West: *http://www .pbs.org/weta/thewest/events/1900_1917.htm*.

BIBLIOGRAPHY

Abbott, Edward Charles "Teddy Blue," and Helena Huntington Smith. *We Pointed Them North: Recollections of a Cowpuncher.* 1939. Reprint, Norman: University of Oklahoma Press, 1955.

Adams, Andy. *The Log of a Cowboy: A Narrative of the Old Trail Days.* 1903. Reprint, Lincoln: University of Nebraska Press, 1964.

Adams, Ansel, with Mary Street Alinder. *Ansel Adams: An Autobiography.* Boston: Little, Brown, 1985, 1996.

Adams, Ramon Frederick. *Burs under the Saddle: A Second Look at Books and Histories of the West.* Norman: University of Oklahoma Press, 1964, 1989.

_____. *The Cowman and His Code of Ethics.* Austin, TX: Encino Press, 1969.

_____. *More Burs under the Saddle: Books and Histories of the West.* Norman: University of Oklahoma Press, 1979, 1989.

_____. *Western Words: A Dictionary of the Range, Cowcamp, and Trail.* 1945. Reprint, Norman: University of Oklahoma Press, 1968.

Alinder, Mary Street. *Ansel Adams: A Biography.* New York: Henry Holt, 1996.

Allard, William A. *Vanishing Breed: Photographs of the Cowboy and the West.* New York: Little, Brown, 1982.

Allen, Jules Verne. *Cowboy Lore.* San Antonio, TX: Naylor, 1933.

Alter, F. Cecil. *Jim Bridger.* Norman: University of Oklahoma Press, 1962.

Amaral, Anthony A. *Will James: The Last Cowboy Legend.* Reno: University of Nevada Press, 1980.

Ambrose, Stephen E., and S. Abell. *Lewis and Clark: Voyage of Discovery.* Washington, DC: National Geographic Society, 1998.

Ann, Melinda, Bobby Barnett, and James L. Hunter. "The Ballad of Belle Starr." On *American Heroes and Western Legends.* Bear Family Records. BCD 16-121-AH, 1997. Musical recording.

Applebome, Peter. "New Glimpses of Woody Guthrie's Imagination." *New York Times,* 27 April 1998.

Aquila, Richard, ed. *Wanted Dead or Alive: The American West in Popular Culture.* Urbana: University of Illinois Press, 1996.

Armitage, Susan. "Women and Men in Western History: A Stereoptical Vision." *Western Historical Quarterly* 16, no. 4 (October 1985): 381–396.

Armitage, Susan, and Elizabeth Jameson, eds. *The Women's West.* Norman: University of Oklahoma Press, 1987.

Armitage, Susan, et al., eds. *Women in the West: A Guide to Manuscript Sources.* New York: Garland, 1991.

Athearn, Robert G. *In Search of Canaan: Black Migration to Kansas, 1879–80.* Lawrence: Regents Press of Kansas, 1978.

_____. *The Mythic West in Twentieth-Century America*. Lawrence: University Press of Kansas, 1986.

Baigell, Matthew. *The Western Art of Frederic Remington*. New York: Ballantine Books, 1976, 1988.

Baker, Pearl. *The Wild Bunch at Robbers Roost*. 1965, 1971. Reprint, Lincoln: Bison Books, 1989.

Baker, T. Lindsay. *Ghost Towns of Texas*. Norman: University of Oklahoma Press, 1986.

Bakker, J. *The Role of the Mythic West in Some Representative Examples of Classic and Modern American Literature*. Lewiston, NY: Edwin Mellen Press, 1991.

Ball, Larry D. *Elfego Baca in Life and Legend*. El Paso: Texas Western Press, n.d.

Barlett, Donald L., and James B. Steele. *Empire: The Life, Legend, and Madness of Howard Hughes*. New York: W. W. Norton, 1979.

Barnett, Louise K. *The Ignoble Savage: American Literary Racism, 1790–1890*. Westport, CT: Greenwood Press, 1975.

Barr, Alwyn. *Black Texans: A History of African Americans in Texas, 1528–1995*. 2d ed. Norman: University of Oklahoma Press, 1973, 1996.

Barra, Allen. *Inventing Wyatt Earp: His Life and Many Legends*. New York: Carroll and Graf, 1998.

Barrier, Michael. "Prairie Dogs, Pottery, and More." *Nation's Business,* October 1994 (online).

Baum, L. Frank. *The Wonderful Wizard of Oz*. 1900. New York: Children's Classics, 1994.

Bayles, Fred. "Scoffers, Believers Abound in Mutilated-Cattle Mystery." *Washington Post,* 1 January 1986.

Beard, Tyler. *The Cowboy Boot Book*. Salt Lake City, UT: Peregrine Smith Books, 1992.

_____. *One Hundred Years of Western Wear*. Salt Lake City, UT: Peregrine Smith Books, 1993.

Beck, Warren A., and Ynez D. Haase. *Historical Atlas of the American West*. Norman: University of Oklahoma Press, 1989.

Bell, Leland V. "Radicalism and Race: The IWW and the Black Worker." *Journal of Human Relations* 19, no. 1 (1971): 48–56.

Bengston, Henry. *On the Left in America: Memoirs of the Scandinavian-American Labor Movement*. Carbondale: Southern Illinois University Press, 1999.

Benningfield, Damond. "The Boxing Championship That Wasn't." *American West* 23, no. 1 (1986): 63–65.

Benson, Jackson J. *Wallace Stegner: His Life and Work*. New York: Viking, 1996.

Berliner, Don, and Stanton T. Friedman. *Crash at Corona*. New York: Paragon Books, 1992.

Berlitz, Charles, and William L. Moore. *The Roswell Incident*. New York: Grosset and Dunlap, 1980.

Billington, Ray Allen. *Land of Savagery, Land of Promise: The European Image of the American Frontier in the Nineteenth Century*. Norman: University of Oklahoma Press, 1981.

Blackstone, Sarah J. *Buckskins, Bullets, and Business: A History of Buffalo Bill's Wild West*. Westport, CT: Greenwood Press, 1986.

Blevins, Winfred. *Dictionary of the American West*. New York: Facts on File, 1993.

Bloch, E. Maurice. *George Caleb Bingham: The Evolution of an Artist*. Berkeley and Los Angeles: University of California Press, 1967.

Bly, Robert, ed. *The Soul Is Here for Its Own Joy: Sacred Poems from Many Cultures*. Hopewell, NJ: Ecco Press, 1995.

Bogdanovich, Peter. *John Ford*. Berkeley and Los Angeles: University of California Press, 1968.

Boggs, Johnny D. "Elmer Kelton." *Cowboys & Indians* 22 (January 1998): 162–168.

Bold, Christine. *Selling the Wild West: Popular Western Fiction, 1860–1960*. Bloomington: Indiana University Press, 1987.

Bolton, Herbert E. *Coronado on the Turquoise Trail*. Edited by George P. Hammond. Albuquerque: University of New Mexico Press, 1949.

Bord, Colin, and Janet Bord. *The Evidence for*

Bigfoot and Other Man-Beasts. Whitstable, Kent: Whitstable Litho, 1984.

Bowden, Martyn J. "The Great American Desert and the American Frontier, 1800–1882: Popular Images of the Plains." In *Anonymous Americans: Explorations in Nineteenth-Century Social History,* ed. Tamara K. Hareven. Englewood Cliffs, NJ: Prentice-Hall, 1971.

Boyd, Eva Jolene. *Noble Brutes: Camels on the American Frontier.* Plano: Republic of Texas Press, 1995.

Bramlett, Jim. *Ride the High Points: The Real Story of Will James.* Missoula, MT: Mountain Press Publishing, 1987.

Brandon, William. *The Men and the Mountain: Frémont's Fourth Expedition.* Westport, CT: Greenwood Press, 1955.

Brown, Dee. *Bury My Heart at Wounded Knee: An Indian History of the American West.* New York: Henry Holt, 1970.

———. *The Gentle Tamers: Women of the Old Wild West.* New York: G. P. Putnam's Sons, 1958.

Brown, Peter Harry, and Pat H. Broeske. *Howard Hughes: The Untold Story.* New York: Penguin, 1996.

Brown, Richard Maxwell. *No Duty to Retreat: Violence and Values in American History and Society.* Norman: University of Oklahoma Press, 1991.

———. "Plummer, Henry." In *The New Encyclopedia of the American West,* ed. Howard R. Lamar. New Haven, CT: Yale University Press, 1998.

———. "Western Violence: Structure, Values, Myth." *Western Historical Quarterly* 24, no. 1 (February 1993): 5–20.

Bruns, Roger A. *The Bandit Kings.* New York: Crown Publishers, 1995.

Bryan, Howard. *Incredible Elfego Baca: Good Man, Bad Man of the Old West.* Santa Fe, NM: Clear Light Publishers, 1994.

Burr, Ramiro. *The Billboard Guide to Tejano and Regional Mexican Music.* New York: Billboard Books, 1999.

Buscombe, Edward, ed. *The BFI Companion to the Western.* New York: Da Capo, 1988.

Buskirk, Amy. *Charles Russell.* 1977. Reprint, London: Saturn Books, 1997.

Butler, Anne E. *Daughters of Joy, Sisters of Misery: Prostitutes in the American West, 1865–90.* Urbana: University of Illinois Press, 1985.

Butts, J. Lee. *Texas Bad Girls: Hussies, Harlots, and Horse Thieves.* Plano: Republic of Texas Press, 2001.

Caesar, Gene. *King of the Mountain Men: The Life of Jim Bridger.* New York: E. P. Dutton, 1961.

Caldwell, Wayne. *The Ghost Towns of Texas.* Richardson, TX: Caldwell Publishing, 1991.

Campbell, Joseph. *Creative Mythology.* New York: Penguin Books, 1968, 1976.

———. *Transformations of Myth through Time.* New York: Perennial Library, 1990.

Cannon, Hal, ed. *Cowboy Poetry: A Gathering.* Salt Lake City, UT: Peregrine Smith Books, 1985.

———, ed. *New Cowboy Poetry: A Contemporary Gathering.* Salt Lake City, UT: Peregrine Smith Books, 1990.

Cannon, Hal, and Thomas West, eds. *Buckaroo: Visions and Voices of the American Cowboy.* New York: Simon and Schuster, 1993.

Carnes, Mark C., ed. *Past Imperfect: History according to the Movies.* New York: Henry Holt, 1995.

Cary, Diana Serra. *The Hollywood Posse: The Story of the Gallant Band of Horsemen Who Made Movie History.* Norman: University of Oklahoma Press, 1975, 1996.

Catlin, George. *Episodes from Life among the Indians and Last Rambles.* 1868. Reprint, edited by Marvin C. Ross, Norman: University of Oklahoma Press, 1959.

Cawalti, John G. *The Six-Gun Mystique.* 2d ed. Bowling Green, OH: Bowling Green University Popular Press, 1984.

Chaplin, Ralph. *Wobbly.* Chicago: University of Chicago Press, 1948.

Cheung, King-Kok. "Self-fulfilling Visions in

The Woman Warrior and *Thousand Pieces of Gold."* *Biography* 3, no. 2 (1990).

Clark, Jerome. *Extraordinary Encounters.* Denver, CO: ABC-CLIO, 2000.

Clark, Jerome, and Nancy Pear, eds. *Strange and Unexplained Phenomena.* New York: Visible Ink Press, 1997.

Clark, Thomas L. *Western Lore and Language: A Dictionary for Enthusiasts of the American West.* Salt Lake City: University of Utah Press, 1996.

Coffman, Edward M. *The Old Army: A Portrait of the American Army in Peacetime, 1784–1898.* New York: Oxford University Press, 1986.

Colip, Lynn. *Colorado's Gold Cone.* Norton, KS: Published privately by author, 1996.

Collins, Michael L. *That Damned Cowboy: Theodore Roosevelt and the American West, 1883–1898.* New York: Peter Lang, 1989.

Collins, Ross. "Gun Control and the Old West." History News Service, 14 July 1999: *http://www2.h-net.msu.edu/~hns/.*

Conlin, Joseph R. *At the Point of Production: The Local History of the I.W.W.* Westport, CT: Greenwood Press, 1981.

_____. *Bread and Roses Too.* Westport, CT: Greenwood Press, 1969.

Conrad, H., and N. Mauskopf. "Sex and Taxes." *Rolling Stone,* 18 April 1991, 85.

Constant, Alberta Wilson. *Paintbox on the Frontier.* New York: Thomas Y. Crowell, 1974.

Corso, Philip J., with J. W. Birnes. *The Day after Roswell.* New York: Pocket Publications, 1997.

Cox, George W. *An Introduction to the Science of Comparative Mythology and Folklore.* Detroit: Singing Tree Press, 1968.

Cray, Ed. *Levi's.* Boston: Houghton Mifflin, 1978.

Crichton, Kyle S. *Law and Order, Ltd.: The Rousing Life of Elfego Baca.* Santa Fe: New Mexican Publishing, 1928.

Cruickshank, Douglas. "Last Roundup at the Mustang Ranch." Salon.com, 12 August 1999 (online).

Cunningham, Chet. *Cripple Creek Bonanza.* Plano: Republic of Texas Press, 1996.

Cunningham, Eugene. *Triggernometry: A Gallery of Gunfighters.* Norman: University of Oklahoma Press, 1941, 1996.

Cunningham, Keith, ed. *The Oral Tradition of the American West.* Little Rock, AR: August House Publishers, 1990.

Cusic, Don. *Cowboys and the Wild West: An A–Z Guide from the Chisholm Trail to the Silver Screen.* New York: Facts on File, 1994.

Daniels, Edwin. *Ghost Dancing: Sacred Medicine and the Art of JD Challenger.* New York: Stuart, Tabori, and Chang, 1998.

Daniels, George G., ed. *The Spanish West.* Alexandria, VA: Time-Life Books, 1976.

Darlington, David. *Area 51: The Dreamland Chronicles.* New York: Henry Holt, 1997.

Dary, David. *Cowboy Culture.* New York: Knopf, 1981.

Davis, Elizabeth A. "Only 35 Days Left Till You Can Bag a Crafty Jackalope." *Salt Lake Tribune,* 27 May 1998 (Utah On-Line).

Davis, Joe Tom. *Historic Towns of Texas.* Austin, TX: Eakin Press, 1992.

Davis, Robert Murray. *Playing Cowboys: Low Culture and High Art in the Western.* Norman: University of Oklahoma Press, 1992.

Davis, Ronald L. *Duke: The Life and Image of John Wayne.* Norman: University of Oklahoma Press, 1998.

Day, A. Grove. *Coronado's Quest: The Discovery of the Southwestern States.* Berkeley and Los Angeles: University of California Press, 1964

De Caux, Len. *The Living Spirit of the Wobblies.* New York: International Publishers, 1978.

Demeter, John. "Independent Film and Working Class History: A Review of 'Northern Lights' and 'The Wobblies!'" *Radical America* 14, no. 1 (1980): 17–26.

Deverell, William. "Fighting Words: The Significance of the American West in the History of the United States." *Western Historical Quarterly* 25, no. 2 (Summer 1994): 185–206.

Dippie, Brian W. *The Vanishing American: White Attitudes and U.S. Indian Policy.* Lawrence: University Press of Kansas, 1982.

———. *West-Fever.* Seattle: University of Washington Press, 1998.

———, ed. *Charlie Russell Roundup: Essays on America's Favorite Cowboy Artist.* Helena: Montana Historical Society Press, 1999.

Dobie, J. Frank. *The Mustangs.* New York: Bramhall House, 1934.

Donahue, Debra L. *The Western Range Revisited: Removing Livestock from Public Lands to Conserve Native Biodiversity.* Norman: University of Oklahoma Press, 2000.

Drago, Harry Sinclair. *Notorious Ladies of the Frontier.* New York: Dodd, Mead, 1969.

Dregni, Michael. "The Politics of Oz." *Utne Reader* 28 (1988): 32–33.

Drinnon, Richard. *Facing West: The Metaphysics of Indian-Hating and Empire-Building.* Minneapolis: University of Minnesota Press, 1980.

Drosnin, Michael. *Citizen Hughes.* New York: Holt, Rinehart, and Winston, 1985.

Duncan, Dayton, and Ken Burns. *Lewis and Clark: An Illustrated History.* New York: Knopf, 1997.

Durham, Michael S. *Desert between the Mountains: Mormons, Miners, Padres, Mountain Men, and the Opening of the Great Basin, 1772–1869.* New York: Henry Holt, 1997.

Durham, Philip, and Everett L. Jones. *The Negro Cowboys.* Lincoln: University of Nebraska Press, 1965, 1983.

Dusard, Jay. *The North American Cowboy: A Portrait.* Prescott, AZ: Consortium, 1983.

Earle, Neil. *The Wonderful Wizard of Oz in American Popular Culture: Uneasy in Eden.* Lewiston, NY: Edwin Mellen Press, 1993.

Earp, Josephine Sarah Marcus. *I Married Wyatt Earp: The Recollections of Josephine Sarah Marcus Earp.* Edited by Glenn G. Boyer. Tucson: University of Arizona Press, 1976.

Edmondson, J. R. *The Alamo Story: From Early History to Current Conflicts.* Plano: Republic of Texas Press, 2000.

Egan, Ferol. *Frémont: Explorer for a Restless Nation.* Garden City, NY: Doubleday, 1977.

Egan, Timothy. "For $266, Verse Low and Lofty by Guthrie." *New York Times,* 4 August 1991.

Eliade, Mircea. *Myth and Reality.* Translated by Willard R. Trask. New York: Harper and Row, 1963, 1975.

Eliot, Alexander. *The Timeless Myths: How Ancient Legends Influence the World around Us.* New York: Continuum, 1996.

Emmett, Chris. *Texas Camel Tales.* San Antonio, TX: Naylor, 1932.

Emmons, David M. "Constructed Province: History and the Making of the Last American West." *Western Historical Quarterly* 24, no. 4 (Winter 1994): 437–460.

———. *Garden in the Grasslands: Boomer Literature of the Central Great Plains.* Lincoln: University of Nebraska Press, 1971.

———. "Social Myth and Social Reality." *Montana: The Magazine of Western History* 39, no. 4 (Autumn 1989): 2–9.

Erdoes, Richard. *Saloons of the Old West.* New York: Random House, 1979.

Erickson, John R. *The Modern Cowboy.* Lincoln: University of Nebraska Press, 1981.

———. *Panhandle Cowboy.* Lincoln: University of Nebraska Press, 1980.

Erisman, Fred. "L. Frank Baum and the Progressive Dilemma." *American Quarterly* 20, no. 3 (1968): 616–623.

Ernst, Donna. *Sundance, My Uncle.* College Station, TX: The Early West, 1992.

Etulain, Richard W., ed. *The American Literary West.* Manhattan, KS: Sunflower University Press, 1980.

———, ed. *The American West in the Twentieth Century: A Bibliography.* Norman: University of Oklahoma Press, 1994.

———, ed. "Western Films: A Brief History."

Journal of the West 22, no. 4 (October 1983): 3–4.

_____, ed. *Writing Western History: Essays on Major Western Historians.* Albuquerque: University of New Mexico Press, 1991.

Etulain, Richard W., and Glenda Riley, eds. *With Badges and Bullets: Lawmen and Outlaws in the Old West.* Golden, CO: Fulcrum, 1999.

Evans, Rosemary. "Helen Hunt Jackson's Sympathetic Attitude toward Indians Was Reflected in Her Popular *Ramona.*" *Wild West* 12, no. 1 (June 1999): 18–20.

Faragher, John Mack. "Clint Eastwood's *Unforgiven:* The Western Is Back." *Montana: The Magazine of Western History* 43, no. 1 (Winter 1993): 74–78.

_____. "The Frontier Trail: Rethinking Turner and Reimagining the West." *American Historical Review* 98, no. 1 (February 1993): 109–117.

_____, ed. *The American Heritage Encyclopedia of American History.* New York: Holt, 1998.

Faulk, Odie B. *The U.S. Camel Corps: An Army Experiment.* New York: Oxford University Press, 1976.

Fielder, Mildred. *Wild Bill and Deadwood.* Seattle, WA: Superior Publishing Company, 1965.

Findley, Rowe. "The Mountain That Was—and Will Be." *National Geographic* 160 (1981): 713–719.

_____. "Mountain with a Death Wish." *National Geographic* 159 (1980): 17–33.

Fisher, Vardis. *Mountain Man.* New York: Morrow, 1965.

Fishwick, Marshall W. "The Cowboy: America's Contribution to the World's Mythology." *Western Folklore* 11, no. 2 (April 1952): 77–92.

Flood, Elizabeth Clair. "Dude Ranches: Where East Meets West." *Cowboys & Indians* 1, no. 3 (Winter 1993): 36–40.

Florin, Lambert. *Ghost Towns of the West.* New York: Promontory Press, 1973.

Flynn, Elizabeth Gurley. *Memories of the Industrial Workers of the World (IWW).* New York: American Institute for Marxist Studies, 1977.

Folsom, James K. *The American Western Novel.* New Haven, CT: Yale University Press, 1966.

_____, ed. *The Western: A Collection of Critical Essays.* Englewood Cliffs, NJ: Prentice-Hall, 1979.

Foner, Philip S. *The Case of Joe Hill.* New York: International Publishers, 1965.

Foote, Cheryl J. "Changing Images of Women in the Western Film." *Journal of the West* 22, no. 4 (1983): 64–71.

Forbis, William H. *The Cowboys.* Rev. ed. Alexandria, VA: Time-Life Books, 1978.

Foster-Harris, William. *The Look of the Old West.* New York: Bonanza Books, 1955.

Fowler, Arlen L. *The Black Infantry in the West, 1869–1891.* 1971. Reprint, Norman: University of Oklahoma Press, 1996.

Fowler, Harlan Davey. *Three Caravans to Yuma: The Untold Story of Bactrian Camels in Western America.* Glendale, CA: A. H. Clark Co., 1980.

Fox, Richard K. *Bella Starr, or The Bandit Queen.* 1889. Facsimile ed., Austin, TX: Steck Company, 1960.

Fox, William L, ed. *TumbleWords: Writers Reading the West.* Reno: University of Nevada Press, 1995.

Francaviglia, Richard. "Walt Disney's Frontierland as an Allegorical Map of the American West." *Western Historical Quarterly* 30, no. 2 (Summer 1999): 155–182.

Fredriksson, Kristine. *American Rodeo: From Buffalo Bill to Big Business.* College Station: Texas A & M University Press, 1984.

Gallagher, Tag. *John Ford: The Man and His Films.* Berkeley and Los Angeles: University of California Press, 1986.

Gard, Wayne. *The Chisholm Trail.* Norman: University of Oklahoma Press, 1954.

_____. *Frontier Justice.* Norman: University of Oklahoma Press, 1949.

Garfield, Brian. *Western Films: A Complete Guide.* New York: Da Capo, 1982.

Garry, Jim. *This Ol' Drought Ain't Broke Us Yet (But We're All Bent Pretty Bad): Stories of the American West.* New York: Orion Books, 1992.

Gavirati, Marcelo. *Buscados en la Patagonia: Butch, Sundance, Ethel, Evans y Wilson.* Buenos Aires: La Bitácora, 1999.

Genovese, Michael A. "The Wonderful Wizard Lives On: 'Oz' Maintains Its Appeal in Our Political Consciousness." *Los Angeles Times,* 19 March 1988.

Gibson, Elizabeth. "John Colter, Mountain Man." *The Old West,* 8 June 1999: *http://www.i5ive.com/article.cfm/old_west/2 0759.*

Gipson, Fred. *Fabulous Empire: Colonel Zack Miller's Story.* Boston: Houghton Mifflin, 1946.

Goetzmann, William H., and William N. Goetzmann. *The West of the Imagination.* New York: W. W. Norton, 1986.

Goldstein, Kenneth S. "Bowdlerization and Expurgation: Academic and Folk." *Journal of American Folklore* 80 (1967): 374–386.

Good, Timothy. *Alien Liaison: The Ultimate Secret.* London: Random Century, 1991.

Gordon, David George. *Field Guide to the Sasquatch.* Seattle, WA: Sasquatch Books, 1992.

Govenar, Alan B. *African American Frontiers.* Denver, CO: ABC-CLIO, 2000.

Gragg, Rod. *The Old West Quiz and Fact Book.* New York: Promontory Press, 1986, 1993.

Graham, Don. *Cowboys and Cadillacs: How Hollywood Looks at Texas.* Austin: Texas Monthly Press, 1983.

Grant, Bruce. *The Cowboy Encyclopedia: The Old and the New West from the Open Range to the Dude Ranch.* Chicago: Rand McNally, 1951.

Green, Archie. *Songs about Work: Essays in Occupational Culture for Richard A. Ruess.* Bloomington: Indiana University Press, 1993.

Green, Murray. "A Strange Encounter: Charles Lindbergh and Howard Hughes." *Aerospace Historian* 26, no. 2 (1979): 81–82.

Grey, Zane. *The Rainbow Trail.* New York: Grosset and Dunlap, 1915.

_____. *Riders of the Purple Sage.* New York: Harper and Brothers, 1912

_____. *Tales of Lonely Trails.* New York: Harper and Brothers, 1922.

Griffith, Tom. "Where Wild Bill Played His Last Hand." *Historic Traveler* 3, no. 1 (November 1996): *http://thehistorynet.com/His toricTraveler/articles/1196_text.htm.*

Gruber, Frank. *Zane Grey: A Biography.* New York: World Publishing, 1970.

Guild, Thelma S., and Harvey L. Carter. *Kit Carson: A Pattern for Heroes.* Lincoln: University of Nebraska Press, 1984, 1988.

Gunther, Max. *D. B. Cooper: What Really Happened.* Chicago: Contemporary Books, 1985.

Guthrie, Woody. "Belle Starr." 1947. On *Woody Guthrie and Songs of My Oklahoma,* James Talley. Cimarron Records, 2000. Audio CD.

_____. *Born to Win.* Edited by Robert Shelton. New York: Macmillan, 1965.

_____. *Bound for Glory.* New York: New American Library, 1943, 1970.

_____. *Pastures of Plenty: A Self-Portrait.* Edited by Dave Marsh and Harold Leventhal. New York: HarperCollins, 1990.

_____. "Pretty-Boy Floyd." 1939. On *Woody Guthrie and Songs of My Oklahoma,* James Talley. Cimarron Records, 2000. Audio CD.

_____. *Seeds of Man: An Experience Lived and Dreamed.* New York: E. P. Dutton, 1976.

Guttman, Jon. "Reviewed with 100 Years of Hindsight, Theodore Roosevelt's Account of War in Cuba Remains a Valuable Document." *Military History* 15, no. 2 (June 1998): 70.

Hadley-Garcia, George. *Hispanic Hollywood: The Latins in Motion Pictures.* New York: Citadel Press/Carol Publishing, 1990, 1993.

Hagan, Chet. *Grand Ole Opry.* New York: Henry Holt, 1989.

Hales, Peter B. *William Henry Jackson and the Transformation of the American Landscape.* Philadelphia: Temple University Press, 1988.

Hall, Shawn. *Old Heart of Nevada.* Reno: University of Nevada Press, 1998.

Hamilton, Edith. *Mythology.* Boston: Little, Brown, 1942.

Hammond, George P. *Coronado's Seven Cities.* Albuquerque, NM: U.S. Coronado Exposition Commission, 1940.

Hampton, Wayne. *Guerilla Minstrels.* Knoxville: University of Tennessee Press, 1986.

Hanes, Bailey C. *Bill Pickett, Bulldogger: The Biography of a Black Cowboy.* Norman: University of Oklahoma Press, 1977, 1989.

Hardy, Phil. *The Overlook Film Encyclopedia: The Western.* Woodstock, NY: Overlook Press, 1991.

Harman, S. W. *Hell on the Border: He Hanged 88 Men.* 1898. Reprint, Lincoln: University of Nebraska Press, 1992.

Harrigan, Stephen. "Davy Crockett and the Alamo: Thoughts on Truth, Fiction, and Smelling a Rat." *Montana: The Magazine of Western History* 50, no. 3 (Autumn 2000): 58–65.

Harrington, Fred Harvey. *Hanging Judge.* Caldwell, ID: Caxton Printers, 1951.

Harris, Charles W., and Buck Rainey, eds. *The Cowboy: Six-Shooters, Songs, and Sex.* Norman: University of Oklahoma Press, 1976.

Harris, Peggy. "Some Say Isaac Parker Was Racist: Jury Still Out on Effort to Honor 'Hanging Judge.'" *News and Observer,* 19 December 1995.

Harrison, Philip L., ed. *Seasons of the Coyote: The Legend and Lore of an American Southwestern Icon.* New York: HarperCollins, 1994.

Hassrick, Peter. *History of Western American Art.* New York: Exeter Press, 1987.

_____. *The Way West: Art of Frontier America.* New York: Abrams, 1977.

Havinghurst, Walter. *Annie Oakley of the Wild West.* Lincoln: University of Nebraska Press, 1954, 1992.

Hayano, David M. *Poker Faces: The Life and Work of Professional Card Players.* Berkeley and Los Angeles: University of California Press, 1982.

Hayes, M. Horace. *Points of the Horse: A Treatise on the Conformation, Movements, and Evolution of the Horse.* New York: Scribners, 1969.

Herr, Pamela. "Lillie on the Frontier." *American West* 18, no. 2 (1981): 40–48.

Herzberg, Max J. *Myths and Their Meaning.* Boston: Allyn and Bacon, 1984.

Hillis, Newell Dwight. *The Quest of John Chapman: The Story of a Forgotten Hero.* London: Macmillan, 1917.

"Hillstrom Is Shot, Denying His Guilt." *New York Times,* 20 November 1915.

Hirsch, E. D., Jr., Joseph F. Kett, and James Trefil. *The Dictionary of Cultural Literacy.* 2d ed. Rev. Boston: Houghton Mifflin, 1993.

Hogarth, Paul. *Artists on Horseback: The Old West in Illustrated Journalism, 1857–1900.* New York: Watson-Guptill, 1972.

Hoig, Stan. *The Humor of the American Cowboy.* Lincoln: University of Nebraska Press, 1958, 1970.

Hollman, Clide. *Five Artists of the Old West.* New York: Hastings House, 1965.

Hollon, William Eugene. *Frontier Violence: Another Look.* New York: Oxford University Press, 1974.

_____. *The Great American Desert Then and Now.* New York: Oxford University Press, 1966.

Holloway, David, and A. K. Wilkinson. *Lewis and Clark and the Crossing of North America.* New York: Saturday Review Press, 1974.

Honan, William H. "Montana Writers' Sessions Teach Language of the Land." *New York Times,* 25 March 1998.

Horan, James D. *The Authentic Wild West: The Outlaws.* New York: Crown, 1977.

_____. *The Gunfighters: The Authentic Wild*

West. New York: Gramercy Books, 1976, 1994.

"How the West Got Wild: American Media and Frontier Violence." Roundtable discussion. *Western Historical Quarterly* 31, no. 3 (Autumn 2000): 277–296.

Howe, Linda Moulton. *A Strange Harvest.* Cheyenne, WY: Pioneer Printing, 1989.

Howey, M. Oldfield. *The Horse in Magic and Myth.* London: Rider and Son, 1923.

Hoy, Jim. *Cowboys and Kansas: Stories from the Tallgrass Prairie.* Norman: University of Oklahoma Press, 1995.

Hughes, Stella. *Chuck Wagon Cookin'.* Tucson: University of Arizona Press, 1974.

_____. *Hashknife Cowboy: Recollections of Mack Hughes.* Tucson: University of Arizona Press, 1984.

Hunter, Don, with René Dahinden. *Sasquatch/Big Foot: The Search for North America's Incredible Creature.* Rev. ed. Buffalo, NY: Firefly Books, 1973, 1993.

Hutton, Paul Andrew. "Showdown at the Hollywood Corral: Wyatt Earp and the Movies." *Montana: The Magazine of Western History* 45, no. 3 (Summer 1995): 2–31.

Hyde, Anne Farrar. *An American Vision: Far Western Landscape and National Culture, 1820–1920.* New York: New York University Press, 1990.

Iversen, Kristen. *Molly Brown: Unraveling the Myth.* Boulder, CO: Johnson Books, 1999.

Iverson, Peter. *When Indians Became Cowboys: Native Peoples and Cattle Ranching in the American West.* Norman: University of Oklahoma Press, 1994.

Jackson, Carlton. *Zane Grey.* Rev. ed. New York: Twayne Publishers, Inc., 1973, 1989.

Jacobs, Wilbur R. *On Turner's Trail: One Hundred Years of Writing Western History.* Lawrence: University of Kansas Press, 1994.

Jeffers, H. Paul. *Colonel Roosevelt: Theodore Roosevelt Goes to War, 1897–1898.* New York: John Wiley and Sons, 1996.

Johnson, Cecil. *Guts: Legendary Black Rodeo Cowboy Bill Pickett.* Fort Worth, TX: Summit Group, 1994.

Johnson, Michael L. *The New Westers: The West in Contemporary American Culture.* Lawrence: University Press of Kansas, 1996.

Johnston, Moira. *Ranch: Portrait of a Surviving Dream.* Garden City, NY: Doubleday, 1983.

Johnstone, Iain. *Clint Eastwood: The Man with No Name.* New York: Quill/William Morrow, 1981, 1988.

Jones, Lois Stodieck. *The Ferris Wheel.* Carson City, NV: Grace Danberg Foundation, 1984.

Jordan, Roy A., and Tim R. Miller. "The Politics of a Cowboy Culture." *Annals of Wyoming* 52, no. 1 (Spring 1980): 40–45.

Jordan, Teresa. *Cowgirls: Women of the American West.* New York: Anchor Books, 1982.

_____, ed. *Graining the Mare: The Poetry of Ranch Women.* Salt Lake City, UT: Peregrine Smith Books, 1994.

Josephy, Alvin M., Jr. *The Civil War in the American West.* New York: Vintage Books, 1993.

Joyce, Davis D. *An Oklahoma I Had Never Seen Before.* Norman: University of Oklahoma Press, 1994.

Kadlec, Robert F., ed. *They "Knew" Billy the Kid: Interviews with Old-Time New Mexicans.* Santa Fe, NM: Ancient City Press, 1987.

Katz, William Loren. *Black People Who Made the Old West.* New York: Crowell, 1977.

Keller, Robert H. "'Joe Hill Ain't Never Died': Wallace Stegner's Act of Literary Imagination." *Montana: The Magazine of Western History* 46, no. 3 (Autumn 1996): 30–39.

Kelly, Charles. *The Outlaw Trail.* 1938, 1959. Reprint, Lincoln, NE: Bison Books, 1996.

Kelton, Elmer. *The Day the Cowboys Quit.* New York: Bantam, 1971, 1992.

Kesey, Ken. *Last Go Round.* New York: Viking, 1994.

Kimball, Arthur G. *Ace of Hearts: The Westerns of Zane Grey.* Fort Worth: Texas Christian University Press, 1993.

King, Jeffrey S. *The Life and Death of Pretty Boy Floyd.* Kent, OH: Kent State University Press, 1998.

Kiskaddon, Bruce. *Rhymes of the Ranges.* Edited by Hal Cannon. Salt Lake City, UT: Peregrine Smith Books, 1987.

Kistler, Ron. *I Caught Flies for Howard Hughes.* Chicago: Playboy Press, 1976.

Klein, Joe. *Woody Guthrie: A Life.* New York: A. A. Knopf; distributed by Random House, 1980.

Knowles, Thomas W., and Joe R. Lansdale, eds. *The West That Was.* New York: Wings Books, 1993.

Kohn, George C. *Encyclopedia of American Scandal.* New York: Facts on File, 1989.

Korff, Kal K. *The Roswell UFO Crash: What They Don't Want You to Know.* New York: Prometheus Books, 1997.

Kornbluh, Joyce L. *Rebel Voices: An I.W.W. Anthology.* Ann Arbor: University of Michigan Press, 1964.

Lake, Stuart. *Wyatt Earp, Frontier Marshall.* Boston: Houghton Mifflin, 1931.

Lamar, Howard R., ed. *The New Encyclopedia of the American West.* New Haven, CT: Yale University Press, 1998.

_____. *The Reader's Encyclopedia of the American West.* New York: Crowell, 1977.

Lamb, Gene. *Rodeo: Back of the Chutes.* Denver, CO: Bell Press, 1956.

L'Amour, Louis. "The Cowboy: Reflections of a Western Writer." *Colorado Heritage* 1 (1981): 1–6.

Larkin, Margaret. *Singing Cowboy: A Book of Western Songs.* 1931. Reprint, New York: Da Capo Press, 1979.

Larson, T. A., comp. *Bill Nye's Western Humor.* Lincoln: University of Nebraska Press, 1968.

Lawrence, Elizabeth Atwood. *Rodeo: An Anthropologist Looks at the Wild and the Tame.* Knoxville: University of Tennessee Press, 1982.

_____. "The White Mustang of the Prairies." *Great Plains Quarterly* 1 (Spring 1991): 81–94.

Lea, Tom. *The King Ranch.* Boston: Little, Brown, 1957.

Leckie, William H. *The Buffalo Soldiers: A Narrative of the Negro Cavalry in the West.* Norman: University of Oklahoma Press, 1967.

LeCompte, Mary Lou. *Cowgirls of the Rodeo: Pioneer Professional Athletes.* Bloomington: Indiana University Press, 1993.

_____. "The Hispanic Influence on the History of Rodeo, 1823–1922." *Journal of Sport History* 12, no. 1 (Spring 1985): 21–38.

LeCompte, Mary Lou, and William H. Beezley. "Any Sunday in April: The Rise of Sport in San Antonio and the Hispanic Borderlands." *Journal of Sport History* 13, no. 2 (Summer 1986): 128–146.

Lee, Katie. *Ten Thousand Goddam Cattle: A History of the American Cowboy in Song, Story, and Verse.* Rev. ed. Jerome, AZ: Katydid Books and Records, 1976, 1985.

Lee, Lawrence B. *Reclaiming the American West: A Historiography and Guide.* Santa Barbara, CA: ABC-CLIO, 1980.

Lee, Mabel Barbee. *Cripple Creek Days.* Garden City, NY: Doubleday, 1958.

Leeming, David Adams. *The World of Myth.* New York: Oxford University Press, 1990.

Lenihan, John H. *Showdown: Confronting Modern America in the Western Film.* Urbana: University of Illinois Press, 1980.

Lesiak, Christine. *Wild Horses: An American Romance.* South Dakota Public Television with Nebraska Educational Television, 1999. Video.

Lewis, James R. *UFOs and Popular Culture.* Denver, CO: ABC-CLIO, 2000.

Limerick, Patricia Nelson. "Turnerians All: The Dream of a Helpful History in an Intelligible World." *American Historical Review* 100, no. 3 (June 1995): 697–716.

Linderman, Frank Bird. *Recollections of Charley Russell.* Norman: University of Oklahoma Press, 1963, 1988.

Ling, Huping. *Surviving on the Gold Mountain: A History of Chinese American Women and Their Lives.* Albany: State University of New York, 1998.

Littleton, Henry M. "The Wizard of Oz: Parable on Populism." *American Quarterly* 16, no. 1 (1964): 47–59.

Logsdon, Guy. "Cowboy Poets." In *Hoein' the Short Rows,* ed. Francis Edward Abernethy. Fort Worth, TX: Southern Methodist University Press, 1988.

_____. *"The Whorehouse Bells Were Ringing" and Other Songs Cowboys Sing.* Urbana: University of Illinois Press, 1989.

Lomax, John Avery. *Songs of the Cattle Trail and Cow Camp.* London: T. F. Unwin, 1920.

Lomax, John Avery, and Alan Lomax, comps. *Cowboy Songs and Other Frontier Ballads.* New York: Macmillan, 1938.

Luccetti, Cathy, and Carol Olwell. *Women of the West.* New York: Orion Books, 1982.

Lutman, Richard A. "Zane Grey's Women: Fiction and Family." *The Zane Grey Review* 12, no. 4 (June 1997): 1.

Maguire, James H., Peter Wild, and Donald A. Barclay, eds. *A Rendezvous Reader: Tall, Tangled, and True Tales of the Mountain Men, 1805–1850.* Salt Lake City: University of Utah Press, 1997.

Manns, William, and Elizabeth Clair Flood. *Cowboys and Trappings of the Old West.* Santa Fe, NM: Zon International, 1997.

Marks, Paula Mitchell. *Turn Your Eyes toward Texas: Pioneers Sam and Mary Maverick.* College Station: Texas A & M University Press, 1989.

Markus, Kurt. *Buckaroo: Images from the Sagebrush Basin.* Boston: Little, Brown, 1987.

Marshall, Howard W., and Richard E. Ahlborn. *Buckaroos in Paradise: Cowboy Life in Northern Nevada.* Lincoln: University of Nebraska Press, 1981.

Martin, Phil, comp. *Coolin' Down: An Anthology of Contemporary Cowboy Poetry.* Tulsa, OK: Guy Logsdon Books, 1992.

Martin, Russell. *Cowboy: The Enduring Myth of the Wild West.* New York: Stewart, Tabori, and Chang, 1983.

Mathison, Richard. *His Weird and Wanton Ways: The Secret Life of Howard Hughes.* New York: William Morrow, 1977.

May, Stephen J. *Zane Grey: Romancing the West.* Athens: Ohio University Press, 1997.

Mayer, George H. *The Republican Party, 1854–1966.* 2d ed. London: Oxford University Press, 1967.

McAndrews, James. *The Roswell Report.* Washington, DC: U.S. Government Printing Office, 1997.

McCall, Elizabeth Kaye. "Z Is for Zorro." *Cowboys & Indians* 25 (July 1998): 76–84.

McClashan, C. F. *History of the Donner Party.* Stanford, CA: Stanford University Press, 1940.

McCracken, Harold. *The American Cowboy.* Garden City, NY: Doubleday, 1973.

_____. *The Charles M. Russell Book.* Garden City, NY: Doubleday, 1957.

_____. *Frederic Remington, Artist of the Old West.* Philadelphia: J. B. Lippincott, 1947.

_____. *The Frederic Remington Book: A Pictorial History of the West.* Garden City, NY: Doubleday, 1966.

_____. *Great Painters and Illustrators of the Old West.* 1952. Reprint, New York: Dover, 1988.

_____. *The Great White Buffalo.* New York: J. B. Lippencott, 1946.

McCunn, Ruthanne Lum. *Thousand Pieces of Gold: A Biographical Novel.* San Francisco: Design Enterprises of San Francisco, 1981.

McDonald, Archie P., ed. *Shooting Stars: Heroes and Heroines of Western Film.* Bloomington: Indiana University Press, 1987.

McDowell, Bart. *The American Cowboy in Life and Legend.* Washington, DC: National Geographic Society, 1972.

McDowell, R. Bruce. *Evolution of the Winchester.* Tacoma, WA: Armory Publications, 1985.

McGrath, Roger D. *Gunfighters, Highwaymen, and Vigilantes: Violence on the Frontier.* Berkeley and Los Angeles: University of California Press, 1984.

McLaird, James D. "Calamity Jane: The Life and the Legend." *South Dakota History* 24, no. 1 (Spring 1994).

_____. "Calamity Jane's Diary and Letters: Story of a Fraud." *Montana: The Magazine of Western History* 45, no. 4 (Autumn 1995): 20–35.

McLoughlin, Denis. *Wild and Woolly: An Encyclopedia of the Old West.* Garden City, NY: Doubleday, 1975.

McMurtry, Larry. *Anything for Billy.* New York: Simon and Schuster, 1988.

_____. *Buffalo Girls.* New York: Simon and Schuster, 1995.

_____. *Lonesome Dove.* New York: Simon and Schuster, 1985.

McMurtry, Larry, and Diana Ossana. *Pretty Boy Floyd.* New York: Simon and Schuster, 1994.

McNamee, G. *In the Presence of Wolves.* New York: Crown, 1995.

McRae, Wallace. *Cowboy Curmudgeon and Other Poems.* Salt Lake City, UT: Peregrine Smith Books, 1992.

Meadows, Anne. *Digging Up Butch and Sundance.* Rev. ed. New York: St. Martin's Press, 1994; Lincoln: Bison Books, 1996.

Meldrum, Barbara Howard, ed. *Old West–New West: Centennial Essays.* Moscow: University of Idaho Press, 1993.

_____, ed. *Under the Sun: Myth and Realism in Western American Literature.* Troy, NY: Whitson, 1985.

Mendenhall, Don. *The Truth about Cowboys and Indians and Other Myths about the West.* Bend, OR: Maverick Publications, 1980.

Meyer, Michael C., and William L. Sherman. *The Course of Mexican History.* New York: Oxford University Press. 1999.

Mickelson, Monty. "Disneyland Paris." *Cowboys & Indians* 4, no. 3 (Fall 1996): 48–53, 122.

Miles, Dione. *Something in Common: An IWW Bibliography.* Detroit: Wayne State Press, 1986.

Miller, Leo O. *The Great Cowboy Stars of Movies and Television.* Westport, CT: Arlington House, 1979.

Miller, Nathan. *TR: A Life.* New York: William Morrow, 1992.

Miller, Rick. *Sam Bass and Gang.* Austin, TX: State House Press, 1999.

Miller, Robert Henry. *Reflections of a Black Cowboy.* Englewood Cliffs, NJ: Silver Burdett Press, 1991.

_____. *The Story of Stagecoach Mary Fields.* Englewood Cliffs, NJ: Silver Burdett Press, 1995.

Milton, John R. *The Novel of the American West.* Lincoln: University of Nebraska Press, 1980.

Moench, Doug. *The Big Book of Conspiracies.* New York: Paradox Press, 1995.

Mogen, David. "Owen Wister's Cowboy Heroes." In *The Western: A Collection of Critical Essays,* ed. James K. Folsom. Englewood Cliffs, NJ: Prentice-Hall, 1979.

Montana, Gladiola. *Never Ask a Man the Size of His Spread: A Cowgirl's Guide to Life.* Salt Lake City, UT: Gibbs Smith Publisher, 1993.

Morelock, Jerry D. "'Colonel Teddy': Historians Examine the Spanish-American War's Most Famous 'Rough Rider.'" *Military Review* 78, no. 3 (May/June 1998): 94.

Morris, Michele. *The Cowboy Life: A Saddlebag Guide for Dudes, Tenderfeet, and Cowpunchers Everywhere.* New York: Simon and Schuster, 1993.

Moses, L. G. *Wild West Shows and the Images of American Indians, 1889–1933.* Albuquerque: University of New Mexico Press, 1996.

Moulton, Candy. "Many of the Boys of '98 Were Cowboys and Frontiersmen Who Wanted a Piece of the Action." *Wild West* 11, no. 1 (June 1998): 64.

Mueller, Ellen Crago. *Calamity Jane.* Laramie, WY: Jelm Mountain Press Publishing, 1981.

Murphey, Michael Martin. "How I Became a Singing Cowboy." *Cowboys & Indians* 2, no. 1 (Spring 1994): 77–78.

_____, comp. *Cowboy Songs.* Secaucus, NJ: Warner Brothers, 1991.

Murphey, Michael Martin, with Bill Miller. "Belle Star." On *Cowboy Songs III: Rhymes of the Renegades,* Warner Western 4-45423, 1993. Musical recording.

Myers, John Myers. *The Saga of Hugh Glass: Pirate, Pawnee, and Mountain Man.* Lincoln: University of Nebraska Press, 1976.

Nachman, Gerald. *Raised on Radio.* New York: Pantheon Books, 1998.

Napier, John. *Bigfoot: The Yeti and Sasquatch in Myth and Reality.* New York: E. P. Dutton, 1973.

Nash, Gerald D. *Creating the West: Historical Interpretations, 1890–1990.* Albuquerque: University of New Mexico Press, 1991.

_____. "The Great Adventure: Western History, 1890–1990." *Western Historical Quarterly* 22, no. 1 (February 1991): 5–18.

Nash, Jay Robert, ed. *Encyclopedia of Western Lawmen and Outlaws.* New York: Paragon House, 1992.

Nash, Roderick. *Wilderness and the American Mind.* 3d ed. New Haven, CT: Yale University Press, 1967, 1982.

National Cowboy Hall of Fame. *Frederic Remington: "An American Artist."* Exhibition catalog, Oklahoma City, 21 September 1996–1 June 1997.

Neel, Susan Rhoades. "A Place of Extremes: Nature, History, and the American West." *Western Historical Quarterly* 24, no. 4 (Winter 1994): 489–506.

Nevins, Allan. *Frémont: The West's Greatest Adventurer.* 2 vols. New York: Harper, 1928.

Newton, Joe, and Willis Newton (as told to Claude Stanush and David Middleton). *The Newton Boys: A Portrait of an Outlaw Gang.* Austin, TX: State House Press, 1994.

Nichols, David A. *Lincoln and the Indians: Civil War Policy and Politics.* Columbia: University of Missouri Press, 1978.

Nichols, Ronald W. *In Custer's Shadow: Major Marcus Reno.* Norman: University of Oklahoma Press, 2000.

Nissenson, Hugh. *The Tree of Life.* New York: Harper and Row, 1985.

Nix, Evett Dumas. *Oklahombres, Particularly the Wilder Ones.* 1929. Reprint, Lincoln: University of Nebraska Press, 1993.

Nixon, Stuart. "Big 'Spruce Goose' Will Settle Down Soon in a New Nest." *Smithsonian* 11, no. 9 (1980): 107–114.

Nolan, Frederick. *The Lincoln Country War: A Documentary History.* Norman: University of Oklahoma Press, 1992.

_____. *The West of Billy the Kid.* Norman: University of Oklahoma Press, 1999.

Null, Gary. *Black Hollywood: The Negro in Motion Pictures.* New York: Carol Publishing Group, 1975, 1990.

Nunis, Doyce B., Jr. *The Life of Tom Horn Revisited.* Arcadia, CA: The Westerners Los Angles Corral, 1992.

Oermann, Robert K., with Douglas B. Green. *The Listener's Guide to Country Music.* New York: Facts on File, 1983.

Ohrlin, Glenn. *The Hell-Bound Train: A Cowboy Songbook.* Urbana: University of Illinois Press, 1973, 1989.

O'Neal, Bill. *Encyclopedia of Western Gunfighters.* Norman: University of Oklahoma Press, 1979.

O'Neil, Paul. *The End and the Myth.* Alexandria, VA: Time-Life Books, 1979.

Ouellette, Dan. "The Rocking Story-Songs of James McMurtry." *Acoustic Guitar,* February 1996.

Painter, Nell Irvin. *Exodusters: Black Migration to Kansas after Reconstruction.* New York: Knopf, 1976.

Paredes, Américo. *A Texas-Mexican Cancionero: Folksongs of the Lower Border.* Forward by Manuel Peña. Austin: University of Texas Press, 1995.

_____. *"With His Pistol in His Hand": A Border Ballad and Its Hero.* Austin: University of Texas Press, 1958.

Parker, David B. "The Rise and Fall of the Wonderful Wizard of Oz as a 'Parable on Populism.'" *Journal of the Georgia Association of Historians,* 15 (1994): 49–63.

Patterson, Bruce, and Mary McGuire. *The Wild West: An Altitude SuperGuide.* Banff, Alberta, Canada: Altitude Publishing, 1993.

Patterson, Richard. *Butch Cassidy: A Biography.* Lincoln: Bison Books, 1998.

_____. *Historical Atlas of the Outlaw West.* Boulder, CO: Johnson Books, 1985.

Patton, Phil. *Dreamland: Travels inside the Secret World of Roswell and Area 51.* New York: Random House, 1998.

Pauly, Thomas H. "Howard Hughes and His Western: The Maverick and *The Outlaw.*" *Journal of Popular Film* 6, no. 4 (1978): 350–369.

Paxon, Frederic L. "A Generation of the Frontier Hypothesis: 1893–1932." *Pacific Historical Review* 2, no. 1 (March 1933): 34–51.

Payne, Darwin. *Owen Wister: Chronicler of the West, Gentleman of the East.* Dallas: Southern Methodist University Press, 1985.

Peebles, Curtis. *Watch the Skies! A Chronicle of the Flying Saucer Myth.* Washington, DC: Smithsonian Institution Press, 1994.

Peña, Manuel. "Folksong and Social Change: Two Corridos as Interpretative Sources." *Aztlán* 13 (1982): 13–42.

_____. *Música Tejana: The Cultural Economy of Artistic Transformation.* College Station: Texas A & M University Press, 1999.

Pendley, William Perry. *War on the West: Government Tyranny on America's Great Frontier.* Washington, DC: Regnery Publishing, 1995.

Perry, Kenneth D., and Luanne Cullen. "The Cowboy: Balancing Fact and Fantasy in a Museum Project." *Curator* 25, no. 3 (1982): 213–222.

Petersen, Gwen. "Git Along Li'l Doggerels: Cowboys and Poetry." *Persimmon Hill* 16, no. 1 (Spring 1988): 28–37.

Peterson, Nancy M. "Hugh Glass' Crawl into Legend." *Wild West* 13, no. 1 (June 2000): *http://www.thehistorynet.com/WildWest/articles/2000/0600_text.htm.*

Phelan, James. *Howard Hughes: The Hidden Years.* New York: Random House, 1976.

Phillips, David, and Robert Weinstein. *The Taming of the West: A Photographic Perspective.* Chicago: Henry Regnery, 1974.

Phillips, Robert W. *Singing Cowboy Stars: The Guys, the Gals, the Sidekicks.* Salt Lake City, UT: Gibbs Smith Publisher, 1994.

Pierson, David S. "What the Rough Riders Lacked in Military Discipline, They Made Up For with Patriotic Fervor and Courage." *Military History* 15, no. 2 (June 1998): 10.

Pitz, Henry C., ed. *Frederic Remington: 173 Drawings and Illustrations.* New York: Dover, 1972.

Pointer, Larry. *Rodeo Champions: Eight Memorable Moments of Riding, Wrestling, and Roping.* Albuquerque: University of New Mexico Press, 1985.

Preston, William, Jr. *Aliens and Dissenters: Federal Suppression of Radicals, 1903–1933.* 2d ed. Urbana: University of Illinois Press, 1994.

Price, B. Byron. "Wild Horses in Popular Culture." In *Unbroken Spirit: The Wild Horse in the American West,* ed. Frances B. Clymer and Charles R. Preston. Cody, WY: Buffalo Bill Historical Center, 1999.

Rabey, Frank. "A Voice You Can Trust: Texan James McMurtry Hones Honesty in Song." *Asheville Mountain Xpress,* 12 June 1996.

Rahn, Suzanne. *The Wizard of Oz: A Reader's Companion.* New York: Twayne Publishers, 1998.

Rainbolt, Jo. *The Last Cowboy: Twilight Era of the Horseback Cowhand, 1900–1940.* Helena, MT: American and World Geographic Publications, 1992.

Randle, Kevin D., and Donald R. Schmitt. *The Truth about the UFO Crash at Roswell.* New York: Avon Books, 1994.

_____. *UFO Crash at Roswell.* New York: Avon Books, 1991.

Rash, Nancy. *The Painting and Politics of George Caleb Bingham.* New Haven, CT: Yale University Press, 1991.

Rawling, Gerald. *The Pathfinders: The History of America's First Westerners.* New York: Macmillan, 1964.

Reardon, Christopher. "Range Writers of the New West: Telling Stories to Reconcile the West's Past and Present." *Ford Foundation Report,* Summer–Fall 1997: *http://www.gallatin.org/pub/971000ff.html.*

Rector, Ray. *Cowboy Life on the Texas Plains:*

The Photographs of Ray Rector. Edited by Margaret L. Rector. College Station: Texas A & M University Press, 1982.

Reed, Paula, and Grover Ted Tate. *The Tenderfoot Bandits: Sam Bass and Joel Collins, Their Lives and Hard Times.* Tucson, AZ: Westernlore Press, 1988.

Reiger, George, ed. *The Best of Zane Grey, Outdoorsman: Hunting and Fishing Tales.* Harrisburg, PA: Stackpole Books, 1992.

Reiter, Joan Swallow. *The Women.* Alexandria, VA: Time-Life Books, 1978.

Remington, Frederic. *The Collected Writings of Frederic Remington.* Edited by Peggy and Harold Samuels. N.p.: Castle, 1986.

_____. *Frederic Remington's Own West.* Edited by Harold McCracken. New York: Dial Press, 1960.

_____. *Pony Tracks.* Introduction by J. Frank Dobie. 1895. Reprint, Norman: University of Oklahoma Press, 1961.

Rhodes, Bernie. *D. B. Cooper: The Real McCoy.* Salt Lake City: University of Utah Press, 1991.

Riebsame, William, ed. *Atlas of the New West: Portrait of a Changing Region.* New York: W. W. Norton, 1997.

Rifkin, Jeremy. *Beyond Beef: The Rise and Fall of the Cattle Culture.* New York: E. P. Dutton, 1992.

Riley, Glenda. "Annie Oakley: Creating the Cowgirl." *Montana: The Magazine of Western History* 45, no. 3 (Summer 1995): 32–46.

_____. *The Life and Legacy of Annie Oakley.* Norman: University of Oklahoma Press, 1994.

_____. *A Place to Grow: Women in the American West.* Arlington Heights, IL: Harlan Davidson, 1992.

_____. "Women in the West." *Journal of American Culture* 3, no. 2 (Summer 1980): 311–329.

Riley, Michael O. *Oz and Beyond: The Fantasy World of L. Frank Baum.* Lawrence: University Press of Kansas, 1997.

Ritter, Gretchen. "Silver Slippers and a Golden Cap: L. Frank Baum's *The Wonderful Wizard of Oz* and Historical Memory in American Politics." *Journal of American Studies* 31 (1997): 171–202.

Roach, Joyce Gibson. *The Cowgirls.* 2d rev. ed. Denton: University of North Texas Press, 1990.

Robb, John Donald, ed. *Hispanic Folk Music of New Mexico and the Southwest.* Norman: University of Oklahoma, 1980.

Robbins, Peggy. "Law West of the Pecos." *American History Illustrated* 8, no. 4 (1973): 12–22.

Roberts, Monty. *The Man Who Listens to Horses.* Thorndike, ME: Thorndike Press, 1998.

Roberts, Randy, and James S. Olson. *John Wayne, American.* New York: Free Press, 1995.

Robinson, Charles M., III. *Bad Hand: A Biography of General Ranald S. Mackenzie.* Austin, TX: State House Press, 1993.

Robinson, Ray. *American Original: A Life of Will Rogers.* New York: Oxford University Press, 1996.

Rockoff, Hugh. "The 'Wizard of Oz' as a Monetary Allegory." *Journal of Political Economy* 98, no. 4 (1990): 739–760.

Rogers, Jimmie N. *The Country Music Message: All about Lovin' and Livin'.* Englewood Cliffs, NJ: Prentice-Hall, 1983.

Rogers, Meyric R., et al. *Four American Painters: Bingham, Homer, Ryder, and Eakins.* New York: Arno Press, 1969.

Rogin, Michael P. *Ronald Reagan, the Movie, and Other Episodes in Political Demonology.* Berkeley and Los Angeles: University of California Press, 1987.

Rolle, Andrew. *John Charles Frémont: Character as Destiny.* Norman: University of Oklahoma Press, 1991.

Rommel, Kenneth M., Jr. *Operation Animal Mutilation: Report of the District Attorney First Judicial District State of New Mexico.* Santa Fe, NM: Criminal Justice Department, 1980.

Roosevelt, Theodore. *Ranch Life and the*

Hunting-Trail, 1896, reprint. New York: St. Martin's Press, 1985.

Rosa, Joseph G. *The Gunfighter: Man or Myth?* Norman: University of Oklahoma Press, 1969.

———. *Wild Bill Hickok: The Man and His Myth.* Lawrence: University Press of Kansas. 1996.

Rosa, Joseph G., and Robin May. *Buffalo Bill and His Wild West: A Pictorial Biography.* Lawrence: University Press of Kansas, 1989.

Rosen, Shirley. *Truman of St. Helens: The Man and His Mountain.* Bothell, WA: Rosebud Publishing, 1981.

Rosenberg, Bruce A. *The Code of the West.* Bloomington: Indiana University Press, 1982.

Ross, James R. *I, Jesse James.* Los Angeles: Dragon Publishing, 1988.

Ross, Marvin C. *The West of Alfred Jacob Miller.* Norman: University of Oklahoma Press, 1968.

Russell, Charles Marion. *Good Medicine: The Illustrated Letters of Charles M. Russell.* Garden City, NY: Doubleday, 1929.

———. *Trails Plowed Under.* 1927. Reprint, introduction by Brian W. Dippie, Lincoln: University of Nebraska Press, 1996.

Russell, Don. *The Lives and Legends of Buffalo Bill.* Norman: University of Oklahoma Press, 1960.

———. *The Wild West: A History of the Wild West Shows.* Fort Worth, TX: Amon Carter Museum, 1970.

Russell, Sharman Apt. *Kill the Cowboy: A Battle of Mythology in the New West.* Reading, MA: Addison-Wesley, 1993.

Ruth, Kent. *Landmarks of the West: A Guide to Historic Sites.* 1963. Reprint, Lincoln: University of Nebraska Press, 1986.

———. *Touring the Old West.* Brattleboro, VT: Stephen Greene Press, 1971.

Rutherford, Michael. *The American Cowboy: Tribute to a Vanishing Breed.* New York: Gallery Books, 1990.

Sackett, Samuel John. *Cowboys and the Songs They Sang.* New York: William R. Scott, 1967.

Saler, Benson, Charles A. Ziegler, and Charles B. Moore. *UFO Crash at Roswell: The Genesis of a Modern Myth.* Washington, DC: Smithsonian Institution Press, 1997.

Samuels, Peggy, and Harold Samuels. *Frederic Remington: A Biography.* Garden City, NY: Doubleday, 1982.

———. *Teddy Roosevelt at San Juan: The Making of a President.* College Station: Texas A & M University Press, 1997.

Savage, William W., Jr. *The Cowboy Hero: His Image in American History and Culture.* Norman: University of Oklahoma Press, 1979.

———. *Singing Cowboys and All That Jazz: A Short History of Popular Music in Oklahoma.* Norman: University of Oklahoma Press, 1983.

———. "What You'd Like the World to Be: The West and the American Mind." *Journal of American Culture* 3, no. 2 (Summer 1980): 302–310.

———, ed. *Cowboy Life: Reconstructing an American Myth.* Norman: University of Oklahoma Press, 1975.

Savitt, Sam. *Rodeo: Cowboys, Bulls, and Broncs.* Garden City, NY: Doubleday, 1963.

Scheurer, Timothy E. *Born in the U.S.A.: The Myth of America in Popular Music from Colonial Times to the Present.* Jackson: University Press of Mississippi, 1991.

Schofield, Ann. "Rebel Girls and Union Maids: The Women Question in the Journals of the AFL and IWW, 1905–1920." *Feminist Studies* 9, no. 2 (1983): 335–358.

Scott, Douglas D., Richard A. Fox Jr., Melissa A. Connor, and Dick Harmon. *Archaeological Perspectives on the Battle of the Little Bighorn.* Norman: University of Oklahoma Press, 2000.

Sell, Henry Blackman, and Victory Weybright. *Buffalo Bill and the Wild West.* New York: Oxford University Press, 1955.

Sennett, Ted. *Great Hollywood Westerns.* New York: Abradale Press, 1990, 1992.

Settle, William A. *Jesse James Was His Name.* Columbia: University of Missouri Press, 1966.

Shackley, Myra. *Wildmen: Yeti, Sasquatch, and the Neanderthal Enigma.* Chichester, Sussex: Thames and Hudson, 1983.

Shirley, Glenn. *Belle Starr and Her Times: The Literature, the Facts, and the Legends.* Norman: University of Oklahoma Press, 1982, 1990.

_____. *Law West of Fort Smith: A History of Frontier Justice in the Indian Territory, 1834–1896.* Lincoln: University of Nebraska Press, 1957.

_____. *Pawnee Bill: A Biography of Major Gordon W. Lillie.* Albuquerque: University of New Mexico Press, 1958.

Shuker, Karl P. N. *In Search of Prehistoric Survivors.* London: Blandford, 1995.

Silliman, Lee, ed. *We Seized Our Rifles.* Missoula, MT: Mountain Press Publishing Company, 1982.

Silverberg, Robert. *Ghost Towns of the American West.* Athens: Ohio University Press, 1968.

Simons, Helen, and Cathryn A. Hoyt, eds. *Hispanic Texas: A Historical Guide.* Austin: University of Texas Press, 1992.

Sinclair, Andrew. *John Ford.* New York: Dial Press, 1979.

Sitchin, Zecharia. *The Lost Realms.* New York: Avon Books. 1990.

Slatta, Richard W. *Comparing Cowboys and Frontiers.* Norman: University of Oklahoma Press, 1997, 2001.

_____. *The Cowboy Encyclopedia.* Santa Barbara, CA: ABC-CLIO Press, 1994; paperback ed., New York: W. W. Norton, 1996.

_____. *Cowboys of the Americas.* New Haven, CT: Yale University Press, 1990; paperback ed., 1994.

_____. "Life and Death on the Great Trail Drives." *Cowboys & Indians* 4, no. 3 (Fall 1996): 42–47.

_____. "Regulators of the Old West." *Cowboys & Indians* 3, no. 1 (Spring 1995): 10–18.

_____. "Wild Women of the Old West." *Cowboys & Indians* 4, no. 4 (Holiday 1996): 48–53.

Slotkin, Richard. *The Fatal Environment: The Myth of the Frontier in the Age of Industrialization, 1800–1890.* New York: Atheneum, 1985.

_____. *Gunfighter Nation: The Myth of the West in Twentieth-Century America.* New York: Atheneum, 1992.

Smith, Gibbs M. *Joe Hill.* Salt Lake City: University of Utah Press, 1969.

Smith, Henry Nash. *Virgin Land.* Cambridge, MA: Harvard University Press, 1950.

Sollid, Roberta Beed. *Calamity Jane: A Study in Historical Criticism.* 1958. Reprint, Helena: Montana Historical Society Press, 1995.

Somora, Julian, Joe Bernal, and Albert Peña. *Gunpowder Justice: A Reassessment of the Texas Rangers.* Notre Dame, IN: University of Notre Dame Press, 1979.

Soule, Arthur. *The Tall Texan: The Story of Ben Kilpatrick.* Deer Lodge, MT: Trail Dust, 1995.

Sprague, Marshall. *The King of Cripple Creek: The Life and Times of Winfield Scott Stratton, First Millionaire from the Cripple Creek Gold Strike.* Colorado Springs, CO: Friends of the Pikes Peak Library District, 1994.

_____. *Money Mountain.* New York: Ballantine Books, 1953, 1971.

St. John, Bob. *On Down the Road: The World of the Rodeo Cowboy.* Englewood Cliffs, NJ: Prentice-Hall, 1977.

Stanush, Claude. "Every Time a Bank Was Robbed, They Thought It Was Us." *Smithsonian* 24, no. 10 (1994): 74–83.

Starrs, Paul F. *Let the Cowboy Ride: Cattle Ranching in the American West.* Baltimore: Johns Hopkins University Press, 1998.

Stegner, Wallace. *Joe Hill: A Biographical Novel.* Lincoln: University of Nebraska Press, 1950.

_____. *Wolf Willow: A History, a Story, and a Memory of the Last Plains Frontier.* 1955. Reprint, Toronto: Macmillan, 1977.

Stegner, Wallace, and Richard W. Etulain. *Conversations with Wallace Stegner on Western History and Literature.* Salt Lake City: University of Utah Press, 1990.

Stephanson, Anders. *Manifest Destiny: American Expansionism and the Empire of Right.* New York: Hill and Wang, 1995.

Stewart, George. *Ordeal by Hunger.* Lincoln: University of Nebraska Press, 1986.

Stuart, Granville. *Forty Years on the Frontier.* 2 vols. 1925. Reprint, Lincoln: University of Nebraska Press, 1977.

Swaim, Lawrence. "Plains Truth in a Fantasy Land." *In These Times* 19 (1987): 19–20.

Szasz, Ferenc Morton, ed. *Great Mysteries of the West.* Golden, CO: Fulcrum Publishing, 1993.

Taft, Robert. *Artists and Illustrators of the Old West, 1850–1900.* 1953. Reprint, Princeton, NJ: Princeton University Press, 1982.

Taliaferro, John. *Charles M. Russell: The Life and Legend of America's Cowboy Artist.* Boston: Little, Brown, 1996.

Tanner, Ogden. *The Ranchers.* Alexandria, VA: Time-Life Books, 1977.

Tatum, Steven. *Inventing Billy the Kid: Visions of the Outlaw in America, 1881–1981.* Albuquerque: University of New Mexico Press, 1982.

Taylor, Lonn, and Ingrid Maar. *The American Cowboy.* New York: Harper and Row, 1983.

Tefertiller, Casey. *Wyatt Earp: The Life behind the Legend.* New York: John Wiley, 1997.

Tessman, Norm. "Letters from a Rough Rider: Lieutenant Carter Writes Home from the Spanish-American War." *Humanities* 19, no. 3 (May/June 1998): 12.

Thomas, Tony. *The West That Never Was.* New York: Citadel Press, 1989.

Thompson, Peggy, and Saeko Usukawa. *Tall in the Saddle: Great Lines from Classic Westerns.* San Francisco: Chronicle Books, 1998.

Thorp, Daniel B. *Lewis and Clark: An American Journey.* New York: MetroBooks, 1998.

Thorp, N[athan] Howard "Jack," comp. *Songs of the Cowboys.* 1908. Reprint, Lincoln: University of Nebraska Press, 1984.

Thorp, N[athan] Howard "Jack," with Neil M. Clark. *Pardner of the Wind: Story of the Southwestern Cowboy.* 1945. Reprint, Lincoln: University of Nebraska Press, 1972.

Thorp, Raymond W., and Robert Bunker. *Crow Killer: The Saga of Liver-Eating Johnson.* Foreword by Richard M. Dorson. Bloomington: Indiana University Press, 1969.

Thrapp, Dan L., ed. *Encyclopedia of Frontier Biography.* 4 vols. Lincoln: University of Nebraska Press, 1988; CD-ROM ed., 1994.

Time-Life Books. *African Americans/Voices of Triumph: Perseverance.* Alexandria, VA: Time-Life Books, 1993.

Timmerman, Carolyn. "Zane Grey's Love Affair with the Grand Canyon." *The Zane Grey Review* 14, no. 2 (February 1999): 1.

Tinkelman, Murray. *Little Britches Rodeo.* New York: Greenwillow Books, 1985.

Tinsley, Jim Bob. *For a Cowboy Has to Sing.* Orlando: University of Central Florida Press, 1991.

_____. *He Was Singin' This Song.* Orlando: University Presses of Florida, 1981.

Tractman, Paul. *The Gunfighters.* New York: Time-Life Books, 1974.

Troccoli, Joan Carpenter. *Alfred Jacob Miller: Watercolors of the American West.* Tulsa, OK: Thomas Gilcrease Museum Association, 1990.

Tuska, Jon. *The American West in Film: Critical Approaches to the Western.* Westport, CT: Greenwood, 1985.

_____. *The Filming of the West.* Garden City, NY: Doubleday, 1976.

_____. *A Variable Harvest: Essays and Reviews of Film and Literature.* Jefferson, NC: McFarland, 1990.

_____, ed. *The Western Story: A Chronological Treasury.* Lincoln: University of Nebraska Press, 1982, 1995.

Tuska, Jon, and Vicki Piekarski. *The Frontier Experience: A Reader's Guide to the Life and Literature of the American West.* Jefferson, NC: McFarland, 1984, 1990.

_____, eds. *Encyclopedia of Frontier and*

Western Fiction. New York: McGraw-Hill, 1983.

Tyler, Ronnie C. *Alfred Jacob Miller: Artist on the Oregon Trail.* Fort Worth, TX: Amon Carter Museum, 1982.

_____. *American Frontier Life: Early Western Painting and Prints.* Fort Worth, TX: Amon Carter Museum, 1987.

_____. *Prints of the West.* Golden, CO: Fulcrum, 1994.

Utley, Robert M. *Encyclopedia of the American West.* New York: Wings, 1996.

_____. *Frontier Regulars: The United States Army and the Indian, 1866–1891.* New York: Macmillan, 1973.

_____. *High Noon in Lincoln: Violence on the Western Frontier.* Albuquerque: University of New Mexico Press, 1987.

_____. *The Indian Frontier of the American West, 1846–1890.* Albuquerque: University of New Mexico Press, 1984.

_____. *A Life Wild and Perilous: Mountain Men and the Paths to the Pacific.* New York: Henry Holt, 1997.

Van Dyk, Gregory. *The Alien Files.* Rockport, MA: Element Books, 1997.

Van Hise, James. *Who Was That Masked Man? The Story of the Lone Ranger.* Las Vegas, NV: Pioneer Books, 1990.

Varney, Philip. *Arizona Ghost Towns and Mining Camps.* Phoenix, AZ: Book Division of *Arizona Highways* Magazine, Arizona Department of Transportation, 1994.

Venturino, Mike. "Slingin' Lead." *Popular Mechanics* 175, no. 4 (April 1998): 76–80.

Viola, Herman J. *Exploring the West.* New York: Abrams, 1987.

Vonada, Damaine. "Annie Oakley Was More than "A Crack Shot in Petticoats." *Smithsonian* 21, no. 6 (1990): 131–148.

Wakely, Linda Lee. *See Ya' Up There, Baby: The Jimmy Wakely Story.* Canoga Park, CA: Shasta Records, 1992.

Wallechinsky, David. *The People's Almanac Presents the Twentieth Century.* Boston: Little, Brown, 1995.

Wallis, Michael. *The Real Wild West: The 101*

Ranch and the Creation of the American West. New York: St. Martin's Press, 1999.

_____. *Route 66: The Mother Road.* New York: St. Martin's Press, 1990, 1992.

Wallmann, Jeffrey. *The Western: Parables of the American Dream.* Lubbock: Texas Tech University Press, 1999.

War of the Rebellion: A Compilation of the Official Records of the Union and the Confederate Armies. Series I, vol. 41. Washington, DC: U.S. Government Printing Office, 1880–1901.

Ward, Geoffrey C. *The West: An Illustrated History.* Boston: Little, Brown, 1996.

Warner, Matt, as told to Murray E. King. *The Last of the Bandit Riders.* New York: Bonanza Books, 1940.

Watson, Bruce. "Hang 'Em Now, Try 'Em Later." *Smithsonian* 29, no. 3 (1998): 96–107.

Watts, Peter. *A Dictionary of the Old West, 1850–1900.* New York: Knopf, 1977.

Webb, Walter Prescott. *The Great Frontier.* Austin: University of Texas Press, 1951, 1979.

_____. *The Texas Rangers.* Austin: University of Texas Press, 1965.

Weber, David J. "The Spanish Legacy in North America and the Historical Imagination." *Western Historical Quarterly* 23, no. 1 (February 1992): 5–24.

Weinberg, Robert. *The Louis L'Amour Companion.* Kansas City, MO: Andrews and McMeel, 1992.

Welch, James, with Paul Stekler. *Killing Custer: The Battle of the Little Bighorn and the Fate of the Plains Indians.* New York: W. W. Norton and Company, 1994.

Welsch, Roger L., ed. *Mister, You Got Yourself a Horse: Tales of Old-Time Horse Trading.* Lincoln: University of Nebraska Press, 1981, 1987.

Werstein, Irving. *Pie in the Sky.* New York: Delacorte Press, 1969.

Westermeier, Clifford P., ed. *Trailing the Cowboy: His Life and Lore As Told by Frontier Journalists.* Caldwell, ID: Caxton Printers, 1955.

Weston, Jack. *The Real American Cowboy.* New York: Schocken, 1985.

Wheeler, Joseph L. "Zane Grey's Impact on American Life and Letters: A Study in the Popular Novel." Ph.D. diss., George Peabody College for Teachers, 1975; UMI Dissertation Services, Ann Arbor, MI.

Wheeler, Keith. *The Railroaders.* New York: Time-Life Books, 1973.

Whitacre, Christine. *Molly Brown, Denver's Unsinkable Lady.* Denver, CO: Historic Denver, 1984.

White, G. Edward. *The Eastern Establishment and the Western Experience: The West of Frederic Remington, Theodore Roosevelt, and Owen Wister.* New Haven, CT: Yale University Press, 1968.

White, John I. *Git Along, Little Dogies: Songs and Songmakers of the American West.* Urbana: University of Illinois Press, 1975, 1989.

_____. "A Montana Cowboy Poet." *Journal of American Folklore* 80 (July 1967): 113–129.

White, Richard. *"It's Your Misfortune and None of My Own": A New History of the American West.* Norman: University of Oklahoma Press, 1991.

Widmark, Ann Heath, ed. *Between Earth and Sky: Poets of the Cowboy West.* New York: W. W. Norton, 1995.

Williams, Brad, and Choral Pepper. *Lost Legends of the West.* New York: Promontory Press, 1970.

Wills, Garry. *John Wayne's America: The Politics of Celebrity.* New York: Simon and Schuster, 1997.

Wills, Kathy Lynn. "Herb Jeffries: The Bronze Buckaroo." *Cowboys & Indians* 3, no. 3 (Fall 1995): 72–74.

Wilson, Elinor. *Jim Beckwourth: Black Mountain Man and War Chief of the Crows.* Norman: University of Oklahoma Press, 1972.

Wilson, R. L., and Greg Martin. *Buffalo Bill's Wild West: An American Legend.* New York: Random House, 1998.

Winters, Donald E., Jr. *The Soul of the Wobblies: The I.W.W., Religion, and American Culture in the Progressive Era, 1905–1917.* Westport, CT: Greenwood Press, 1985.

Woll, Allen L. *The Latin Image in American Film.* Los Angeles: UCLA Latin American Studies Center Publications, 1977.

Wood-Clark, Sarah. *Women of the Wild West Shows: Beautiful, Daring Western Girls.* Cody, WY: Buffalo Bill Historical Center, 1991.

Wooden, Wayne S., and Cavin Ehringer. *Rodeo in America: Wranglers, Roughstock, and Paydirt.* Lawrence: University Press of Kansas, 1996.

Worcester, Don. *The Spanish Mustang: From the Plains of Andalusia to the Prairies of Texas.* El Paso: Texas Western Press, 1986.

Work, James C., ed. *Prose and Poetry of the American West.* Lincoln: University of Nebraska Press, 1990.

Yockleson, Mitchell. "Rough Riders and Buffalo Soldiers." *Cobblestone* 20, no. 5 (May 1999): 26.

Zaniello, Tom. *Working Stiffs, Union Maids, Reds, and Riffraff: An Organized Guide to Films about Labor.* Ithaca, NY: ILR Press, 1996.

Ziaukas, Tim. "Baum's *Wizard of Oz* as Gilded Age Public Relations." *Public Relations Quarterly* 43. no. 3 (1998): 7–11.

Zinn, Howard. "The Wobbly Spirit." In *The Zinn Reader: Writings on Disobedience and Democracy.* New York: Seven Stories Press, 1997.

Zupan, Shirley, and Harry J. Owens. *Red Lodge: Saga of a Western Area.* Red Lodge, MT: Carbon County Historical Society, 1979.

CONTRIBUTORS

Julie J. Anders is a student at North Carolina State University.

Daniel Buck is a contributing editor of *True West* and *South American Explorer.* He lives in Washington, D.C. For more information about his work on Butch Cassidy and the Sundance Kid, see the on-line bibliography at *http://our world.compuserve.com/homepages/danne/.*

P. S. Crane is a student at North Carolina State University.

Michael Crawford has built one of the largest collections of western-related action figures. He maintains an on-line archive for the interested collector at: *http://www.atom group.org/WAFA1.htm.* He also writes a number of other toy-related columns on various Web sites.

Thomas Edward Davis is a graduate of North Carolina State University.

Patti Dickinson is the author of *Hollywood the Hard Way, A Cowboy's Journey* (1999).

Z. Ervin is a writer living in western New York.

Daniel C. Gunter III is a graduate student at North Carolina State University.

Castle McLaughlin is a research associate at the Peabody Museum and a lecturer in the Department of Anthropology at Harvard University. She is a cultural anthropologist whose primary area of interest is the American West.

Anne Meadows is a contributing editor of *True West* and *South American Explorer.* She lives in Washington, D.C. For more information about her work on Butch Cassidy and the Sundance Kid, see the on-line bibliography at *http://ourworld.compuserve.com/home pages/danne/.*

Dennis Myers is a Nevada-based journalist.

Ellen J. Oettinger is a student at North Carolina State University.

Kaleb J. Redden is a student at North Carolina State University.

Guy Louis Rocha, is the Nevada state archivist.

Michael L. Sileno is a student at North Carolina State University.

Richard W. Slatta is professor of history at North Carolina State University and the author of *Comparing Cowboys and Frontiers,*

The Cowboy Encyclopedia, and *Cowboys of the Americas.* For further information, visit his home page at *http://social.chass.ncsu.edu/slatta.*

Jane Veronica Charles Smith is a graduate (M.A., history) of North Carolina State University.

Michael Thomas Smith is a graduate (M.A., history) of North Carolina State University.

Andrew Mebane Southerland is a student at North Carolina State University.

William F. Zweigart is a student at North Carolina State University.

INDEX

CREDITS

"Annie's Song" • Words and music by John Denver. Copyright © 1974 Cherry Lane Music Publishing Company, Inc. (ASCAP) and DreamWorks Songs (ASCAP). Worldwide rights for DreamWorks Songs administered by Cherry Lane Music Publishing Company, Inc. International copyright secured. All rights reserved.

"Belle Starr" • Words and music by Woody Guthrie. TRO—D copyright © 1963 (Renewed) Ludlow Music, Inc., New York, NY. Used by permission.

Theme from "Bonanza" • Words and music by Jay Livingston, Ray Evans. Copyright © 1959 St. Angelo Music administered by Universal–MCA Music Publishing, a division of Universal Studios, Inc. (ASCAP) 50.000%. International copyright secured. All rights reserved.

"Christ for President" • Words by Woody Guthrie. Copyright © 1998 by Woody Guthrie Publications, Inc. All rights reserved. Used by permission.

"El Paso" • by Marty Robbins. Copyright © 1959. Renewed 1987. Mariposa Music, Inc./BMI (administered by ICG). All rights outside U.S.A. administered by Unichappell Music, Inc. All rights reserved. Used by permission.

"El Paso City" • by Marty Robbins. Copyright © 1976. Mariposa Music, Inc./BMI (admin-istered by ICG). All rights reserved. Used by permission.

"Faleena (From El Paso)" • by Marty Robbins. Copyright © 1966. Renewed 1994. Mariposa Music, Inc./BMI (administered by ICG). All rights reserved. Used by permission.

"Fast As I Can" © 1998, "Levelland" © 1998, "Too Long in the Wasteland" © 1989, "Talkin' at the Texaco" © 1989 • Written by James McMurtry. Published by SHORT TRIP MUSIC (BMI)/ Administered by BUG. All rights reserved. Used by permission.

"Fly Away" • Words and music by John Denver. Copyright © 1975 Cherry Lane Music Publishing Company, Inc. (ASCAP) and DreamWorks Songs (ASCAP). Worldwide rights for DreamWorks Songs administered by Cherry Lane Music Publishing Company, Inc. International copyright secured. All rights reserved.

"Joe Hill" • Words and music by Alfred Hayes, Earl Robinson. Copyright © 1938 Universal–MCA Music Publishing, a division of Universal Studios, Inc. (ASCAP) 100.000%. International copyright secured. All rights reserved.

"Luckenbach, Texas (Back to the Basics of Love)" • Words and music by Bobby Emmons, Chips Moman. Copyright © Universal–Songs of Polygram International, Inc.

"The Oyster" • Reprinted with permission from *Croutons on a Cowpie,* Volume 2, by Baxter Black.

"Rocky Mountain High" • Words by John Denver. Music by John Denver and Mike Taylor. Copyright © 1972; Renewed 2000 Cherry Lane Music Publishing Company, Inc. (ASCAP), DreamWorks Songs (ASCAP), Anna Kate Deutschendorf, Zachary Deutschendorf, and Jesse Belle Denver for the U.S.A. All rights for DreamWorks Songs, Anna Kate Deutschendorf, and Zachary Deutschendorf administered by Cherry Lane Music Publishing Company, Inc. All rights for Jesse Belle Denver administered by WB Music Corp. All rights for the world excluding the U.S.A. controlled by Cherry Lane Music Publishing Company, Inc. and DreamWorks Songs. International copyright secured. All rights reserved.

"Roll On, Columbia" • Words by Woody Guthrie. Music based on Goodnight, Irene by Huddie Ledbetter and John A. Lomax. TRO−D copyright © 1936 (Renewed) 1957 (Renewed) and 1963 (Renewed) Ludlow Music, Inc., New York, NY. Used by permission.

"Route 66" • by Bobby Troup. Copyright © 1946, Renewed 1973, Assigned 1974 to Londontown Music. All rights outside the U.S.A. controlled by E. H. Morris & Company. International copyright secured. All rights reserved.

"Wildfire" • by Michael Martin Murphey and Larry Cansler. Copyright © Warner-Tamerlane Publishing Corp. All rights reserved. Used by permission. Warner Bros. Publications U.S. Inc., Miami, FL.